D1172251

Addison-Wesley

# Introduction to Physical Science

**Michael B. Leyden**
Eastern Illinois University
Charleston, Illinois

**Gordon P. Johnson**
Northern Arizona University
Flagstaff, Arizona

**Bonnie B. Barr**
State University of New York at Cortland
Cortland, New York

**Addison-Wesley Publishing Company**
Menlo Park, California    Reading, Massachusetts    Don Mills, Ontario
Wokingham, England    Amsterdam    Sydney    Singapore
Tokyo    Madrid    Bogotá    Santiago    San Juan

Consultants

**Elaine Barrett**
Highland Junior High School
Bellevue, Washington

**Brian Hartley**
Mount Pleasant High School
San Jose, California

**Marcile Hollingsworth**
Former Science Director
Houston, Texas

**Pat Obenauf**
College of Human Resources and Education
West Virginia University
Morgantown, West Virginia

**Marilyn Linner**
Fulton High School
Fulton, Illinois

**Daniel Peterson**
Gunn High School
Palo Alto, California

**Nathan Unterman**
**Lynne Zielinski**
Glenbrook North High School
Northbrook, Illinois

Cover Photo: Michael Melford/The Image Bank West

ISBN 0-201-22885-8

7 8 9 10 - VH - 95 94 93 92 91

# Contents

Good

Good

## Careers

Career titles are preceded by the chapter number.

## Our Science Heritage

Our Science Heritage titles are preceded by the chapter number.

## Activities

Activity titles are preceded by the activity numbers.

# Safety in the Classroom and Laboratory

The materials that you will be using for your Physical Science activities and labs are not normally dangerous. They have been very carefully selected from the standpoint of safety. However, accidents can happen with any materials if they are not handled carefully. For the sake of your own safety and that of your classmates, it is important that you always follow each of the safety precautions listed below.

## General Safety Precautions

1. Make sure that your teacher is present while you are working and knows what you are doing.
2. Read instructions carefully; follow them exactly.
3. Read all caution notices; follow them exactly.
4. Pay close attention to what you are doing. Do not use this as a time to chat with friends.
5. When working with chemicals and/or flames, always wear safety goggles and other protective clothing.
6. When you have finished your work, check that all water, gas, and electricity sources are turned off. Dispose of waste materials only as directed by your teacher.
7. Know the locations of safety equipment such as fire extinguishers, first aid kits, eye wash fountains, water faucets, etc. Be sure that you know how to use the equipment.

## Special Safety Precautions

**Glassware.** Heat substances only in heat-resistant glass containers. (Pyrex ® and Kimax ® are common trademarks for such products.) Never handle broken glass with bare hands; use heavy gloves or a dustpan and brush. Place glass objects in secure places where they are not likely to be knocked over. Never force glass tubing or a thermometer into a dry stopper. The hole in the stopper should always be lubricated with soapy water or glycerin.

**Chemicals.** This program does not recommend that you handle caustic or dangerous chemicals. However, all chemicals should be handled carefully. Read all caution labels on bottles and follow the directions strictly. Never taste a substance. Keep your hands away from your mouth when handling chemicals. Wear safety goggles. Do not breathe fumes. Wash your hands before leaving the lab.

**Heat and flames.** Never allow papers or other flammable substances anywhere near flames. Keep loose clothing and hair away from flames. Do not try to put out a fire from a leaking alcohol lamp with water; use sand or baking soda. Do not let water get onto hot-plate coils. Always wear safety goggles.

**Electricity.** Remember that **you should never experiment with house current.** This is the source of power for lamps and hot plates. Wires and plugs for these devices should be in good condition and should not be allowed to get wet. Electrical setups in the activities should never be plugged into house current.

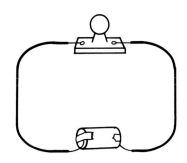

**Radioactive materials.** Do not handle radioactive materials unless they are supplied by your teacher. A few activities in this book call for the use of very weak, commonly found sources. These are usually sealed in plastic and should not be broken into. Always return these to your teacher so that they can be locked away in a safe place.

**Sunlight.** Some activities with light may be performed with direct sunlight. Always remember, **never look directly at the sun.** It could cause injury to your eyes.

**Weights, sharp objects.** Be careful not to swing weights so that they hit someone. Sharp knives should be used with care.

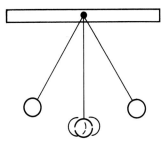

### Emergency Procedures

Report all injuries and accidents to your teacher immediately. Know the locations of fire extinguishers, the nearest exit, water sources, first aid equipment, and the school nurse's office.

| Emergency | What to do |
|---|---|
| Burns | Flush with cold water until the burning sensation subsides. |
| Cuts | If bleeding is severe, apply pressure directly to the cut. If cut is minor, allow to bleed briefly and wash with soap and water. |
| Electric Shock or Fainting | Provide fresh air. Adjust the person's position so the head is lower than the rest of the body. If breathing stops, use artificial resuscitation. |
| Eye Injury | Flush eye immediately with running water. Remove contact lenses. Do not allow the eye to be rubbed. |
| Fire | Turn off all gas outlets and disconnect all electric circuits. Use a fire blanket or fire extinguisher to smother the fire. *CAUTION:* Never aim a fire extinguisher at a person's face. |

# Chapter 1

# Properties of Matter

Section 1
**Classifying Matter**

Matter can be described in different ways. Different kinds of matter that are similar in some ways can be grouped together. If you know something about some members of the group, you can expect other members of the group to be similar.

Section 2
**Working with Data**

Many descriptions of matter are based on measurements. Scientists all over the world use the same system of measurement. One way of studying measurements is to graph them.

Section 3
**Changes in Matter**

Some changes in matter do not change the matter from one kind to another. Other changes can form a different kind of matter. During a change, certain clues indicate whether a different kind of matter has been formed.

In this chapter you will learn how matter can be described and compared to other matter. The photo at the left shows a potter creating a bowl from a lump of clay. Clay is a firm, fine-grained soil which can be molded when wet. The soft clay bowl will become hard when heated in a special oven called a kiln.

# Classifying Matter    Section 1

**Section 1 of Chapter 1 is divided into seven parts:**

Properties of all matter

Properties that identify substances

Classifying into groups

Classifying in order

Solids, liquids, and gases

Metals and nonmetals

Mixtures, compounds, and elements

*Practical Science: Candlemaking*

## Learning Objectives

1.  To distinguish between substances on the basis of their differences in properties.

2.  To group and to order substances using similarities and differences in the properties of the substances.

3.  To describe the properties of each of the phases of matter—solid, liquid, and gas.

4.  To differentiate among mixtures, solutions, compounds, and elements.

Figure 1-1. By which properties can you classify the sports equipment in this photo?

Figure 1-2. What different kinds of matter are pictured here?

In this course, you will be studying **physical science.** Physical science is the branch of science that is concerned with the study of matter and energy in the nonliving world. It is distinguished from life science, which focuses on matter and energy in the living world. In any physical science course, the first question that must be addressed is "What is matter?".

Many kinds of matter are shown in the photo above. The utensils are made of one kind of matter. The dishes are made of another kind. The glass is made of a different kind. The ice in the glass is floating in still another kind of matter.

The ice is floating in a clear, colorless liquid. You might guess that the liquid is water, because you know that water is clear and colorless. You recognize water by its **properties**— things that describe how it is different from other kinds of matter. Of what kind of matter are the forks made? What properties helped you decide?

Glass is a kind of matter. It has many properties that help you identify it. You can see through glass. Glass breaks easily, leaving sharp edges. Glass does not bend unless it is very hot. The surface of glass is hard. Glass has no odor.

Each kind of matter is called a **substance** (SUB′-stuns). Water, wood, and glass are examples of different substances. What properties make these three substances different from each other? What properties do some of them share?

## Properties of all matter

There are two properties that all kinds of matter share. First, matter takes up space. Suppose a drinking glass is filled to

### Main Idea

What is meant by properties of matter?

Safety
Handle broken glass very carefully. Dispose of it in a special container, not in the wastepaper basket.

the very top with water. An ice cube is gently lowered into the water. What will happen? Does the ice cube take up space? Does the water take up space? Can the ice cube and water take up the same space at the same time?

Look at Figure 1-3. Someone is trying to pour water into the flask. The water will not go in. Can you figure out why it won't?

Did you realize the flask was not really empty? If so, you were right. The flask contained air. Even air takes up space. There was no way for the air to get out of the flask. The water could not take up the same space as the air. How could you get the water into the flask?

The second property of all matter is that matter has mass. **Mass** is the property that makes the earth pull downward on matter. All matter has mass, but some has more mass than other matter. The more mass that something has, the stronger is the earth's pull on it. Two things have the same mass if they balance each other on an equal-arm balance. If one has more mass, on the other hand, its side of the balance will be pulled down.

Figure 1-3. What prevents the water from going from the funnel into the flask?

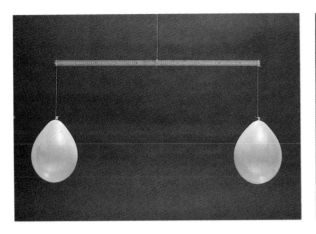

Figure 1-4 shows how the masses of an empty balloon and a balloon full of air can be compared. A meter stick is suspended from its center with a string. A balloon filled with air is attached to each end of the meter stick. The meter stick balances. It is an equal-arm balance with equal masses at each end. Then a pin is used to poke a hole in one of the balloons. The meter stick is no longer balanced. Which has more mass—the balloon filled with air or the empty balloon? Is it correct to say that air is matter? Explain.

All matter takes up space and has mass. These two properties define matter. That is, anything with both properties is matter. Anything without both properties is not matter. Do you think sunlight is matter? Explain.

The amount of space something takes up is called its **volume** (VOL′-yoom). Sometimes volume and mass are confused. Different kinds of matter may take up the same amount of space. They have the same volume. Yet, they may have different masses. For example, a baseball and a plastic foam ball can have the same volume. Which would you expect to have more mass? Suppose a steel ball had the volume of a baseball. Which would you expect to have more mass—the baseball or the steel ball?

A small shovel is used to move sand. A much larger shovel is used to move snow. A small shovel of sand may have the same mass as a large shovel of snow. Yet, the snow takes up much more space. Why wouldn't you use a snow shovel to move sand?

Figure 1-4. Does air have mass? How do you know?

### Check yourself

What two properties do all kinds of matter share?

## Properties that identify substances

Metal is a different substance from plastic. Yet, either one can be used to make things such as forks, rulers, or bowls. How do you know if a material is metal or plastic? What properties are different for the two substances?

For example, do metal and plastic make the same sound when you tap them? Is a plastic bowl as heavy as a metal bowl? Are metal and plastic both shiny? Do they both bend easily?

You probably recognize a metal by its shininess. It is usually silvery gray or golden yellow. Metals also make a ringing sound when they drop to the floor. Thin strips of metal bend easily. Metals are hard and are quite heavy for their size. Some metals rust. Some forms of plastic may have some of these properties. But plastics do not have all the properties of metals. You are able to distinguish metal from plastic because they have some properties that are different.

Other substances have different properties. Paper is quite different from plastic or metal. Most forms of paper bend easily. Paper burns quickly. It is not very heavy for its size. What properties do you use to identify paper?

Substances are identified by their different properties. Still, many different substances have similar properties. Both paper and plastic bend easily. Thin sheets of metal also bend easily. Plastic wrap, paper, and aluminum foil can all be used for packaging of foods. Before you can decide what a substance is, you need to know several of its properties.

**Safety**
Never try to identify an unlabeled substance just by its looks! Other properties must be used to identify a substance safely.

### Check yourself

1. Describe two ways in which paper and metal differ.
2. Describe two properties paper and metal have in common.

## Classifying into groups

Identifying every substance by its many properties is difficult. A lot of information about each substance must be remembered. It is much easier to group similar substances together. Then you can remember properties for the whole group.

## Activity 1–1A     Distinguishing Among Substances

### Materials

safety goggles
4 vials of white powder labeled "W," "X," "Y,"
  and "Z"
5 sheets of colored paper labeled "W," "X,"
  "Y," "Z," and "M"
magnifying glass
5 clear containers each holding 100 mL of
  warm water and labeled "W," "X," "Y," "Z,"
  and "M"
5 stirring rods
mystery vial of white powder

### Purpose

To determine the differences among
substances that look very much alike.

### Procedure

1. Put on safety goggles.
2. Pour a small amount of the substance from
   the vial marked "W" onto the sheet of colored paper labeled "W."
3. Examine the substance closely with a magnifying glass. Record the size and shape of
   the particles.
4. Rub a small amount of the substance
   between your fingers. Observe the texture.
   SAFETY NOTE: *Do not taste any of the substances. Unknown substances may be
   poisonous.*
5. Using the same procedure, test each of the
   other substances. Record all your observations about each substance.
6. Pour about half of the substance out of vial
   "W" into 100 mL of warm water. Stir with a
   *clean* stirring rod.
7. Record the color, odor, and clarity of the
   liquid.
8. Use the same procedure to test the other
   three substances. Be careful to match the
   labels on the paper, vials, and beakers with

each other. Use *clean* water each time for
each test. Record your observations.
9. Repeat the entire testing procedure with the
   mystery substance. Record the results of
   each test. Compare these results with the
   results for the other substances you tested.

### Questions

1. Describe what each substance looks like
   when it is magnified.
2. Which of the substances has a noticeable
   odor when dry? When mixed with water?
3. What other properties describe each of the
   substances?
4. Which of the substances dissolves when
   put in water and stirred?
5. Which of the substances causes the water
   to become cloudy? Why do you think this
   happens?
6. For which of the vials are the test results the
   same as in the mystery vial?

### Conclusion

What are some of the methods you can use to
determine the different properties of substances that look very much alike?

People organize all kinds of things into groups. Books are in groups in the library. Groceries are in groups in the supermarket. Businesses are in groups in the telephone directory.

The same things may be organized into different groups, based on different properties. For example, school children are put in grades based on age and educational background. People may be put into groups based on their occupation. Sales people may make up one group, teachers another, and so on. People may be put into groups based on where they live. What are some ways you could group your classmates?

You put familiar substances into groups, perhaps without thinking about it. You group foods by their taste. Some are sweet, others sour, and others bitter. You may group other substances by their texture. Substances can be smooth or rough. They can be shiny or dull. Some substances have a definite shape. Others change their shape. Substances can be organized into groups using any of these properties. Other properties might also be used to group substances.

The process of organizing information is called **classification** (klas-ih-fuh-KAY′-shun). Putting things into groups based on shared properties is one example of classification. This process is widely used in science.

## Main Idea

What is meant by the classification of things?

### Check yourself

What properties are used to group school children in grades?

### Classifying in order

Putting things into groups is not the only way of classifying them. For example, names in a telephone directory are put in alphabetical order. Singers in a choir may be put in order by height. Baseball players may be listed in order of batting average. In other words, things can be classified in order according to the order of one property.

Substances, also, are classified by putting them in order according to one property. For example, solid substances can be put in order by hardness. Diamond is the hardest natural substance known. It is placed at one end of the list. Talc, the white substance used in bath powder, is very soft. It would go at the other end of the list.

Another way to put solid substances in order is by how easily they change their shape. Some substances are very rigid.

## Library research

Find out about the Mohs scale of hardness of minerals. How are samples of minerals tested for hardness?

## Activity 1–1B        Classifying Objects

### Materials

random collection of 10–12 different objects

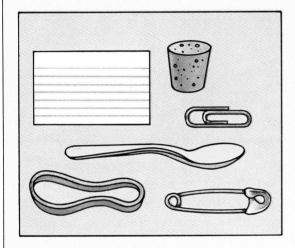

### Purpose

To learn the different ways objects can be classified.

### Procedure

1. After examining the collection of objects, select a property that some, but not all, of the objects share in common.
2. Separate the objects into two groups. One group will have the property you just selected, the other group will not have that property.
3. Have the other students in your group identify the property you selected to classify the objects.
4. Select a property that can be used to rank the objects in order. On a sheet of paper, list the objects in rank order according to the increasing degree to which the property applies.
5. Now ask the other students to identify the property you used and to rank order the objects.

### Questions

1. What property did you select to divide the objects into groups?
2. Were the other students able to identify the property you chose? If not, why not?
3. What was the first property you chose to arrange the objects in rank order?
4. How did the way you ranked the objects compare to the way the other students in your group ranked them?

### Conclusion

What can you conclude about the different ways substances can be classified into groups and ranked within a group?

Others bend easily. The most rigid would be at one end of a list, the least rigid at the other end.

Classification is widely used in all branches of science. For example, in astronomy stars are classified. In health science, diseases are classified. When things are put into groups, all the things in one group must have one property in common. When things are put in order, all the things have different amounts of one property. They are put in order of amount of that property.

Figure 1-5. What properties are used to classify clothing in a store? Which property is used to put clothing in order?

The classification skills you learn in science can be applied outside of science. These skills can help you organize any kind of information. The information may be about the physical world. It may be about how people behave. It may be about activities you enjoy doing. Organizing information by classifying often leads to understanding. Some examples from physical science will help demonstrate the importance of classifying.

### Check yourself

Give three examples of classifying things in order according to the order of one property they all share.

### Solids, liquids, and gases

Scientists use several classification systems for matter. One very useful system classifies matter as solid, liquid, or gas at ordinary temperatures. Solids, liquids, and gases are referred to as the three common **phases** (FAY'-zuz) of matter.

A **solid** has a definite shape. That is, a solid keeps its original shape when put in a container of another shape. It is difficult for other matter to penetrate, or pass into, a solid. You hear the phrase "solid as a rock." Rocks are good examples of solids. Some other common examples of solids include wood, plastic, iron, copper, and cardboard.

**Main Idea**

What are the properties of a solid?

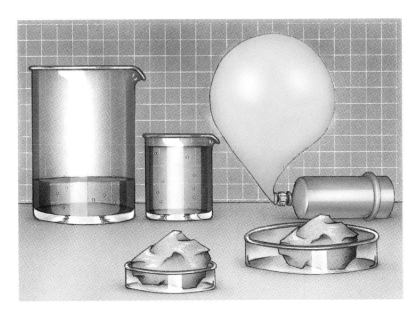

Figure 1-6. What property do solids and liquids have in common? Liquids and gases?

A **liquid**, on the other hand, does not have a definite shape. A liquid takes the shape of the container it is in. The shape of a liquid changes with the shape of the container. But even when its shape changes, a liquid still fills the same amount of space. Like a solid, a liquid has a definite volume.

Water is the most familiar liquid. The properties of liquids are illustrated well by the behavior of water. Vinegar, alcohol, cooking oil, gasoline, syrup, and mercury are some other familiar liquids.

Liquids can be poured from one container to another. Other matter can penetrate a liquid easily.

Like a liquid, a **gas** has no definite shape. It takes the shape of its container. Unlike a liquid, a gas has no definite volume, either. Instead, it tends to fill whatever space is available to it.

The air that we breathe includes several gases. Nitrogen and oxygen are the most abundant. Smaller amounts of carbon dioxide, water vapor, and other gases are also present. In addition to the gases in air, common gases include hydrogen, ammonia, helium, and natural gas. Some gases are becoming familiar because of the threat they pose to health. Sulfur dioxide, nitrogen dioxide, and carbon monoxide are some examples. Ozone, too, is a gas that currently attracts attention.

At very high temperatures, a fourth phase of matter can exist. This phase of matter is called **plasma** (PLAZ′-muh). Plasma exists inside stars, where temperatures reach several thousand degrees Celsius.

**Main Idea**

What are the properties of a liquid?

**Main Idea**

What are the properties of a gas?

**Library research**

The properties of matter change at very low temperatures. Cryogenics is the study of low temperature conditions. Read about some of the unusual properties of matter at low temperatures and write a report.

Examples of solids, liquids, and gases surround you. In most cases, you would have little trouble deciding the phase of a substance. But you have also seen substances change from one phase to another. For example, a solid ice cube will melt and become a liquid. Classifying substances as solid, liquid, or gas may not always be useful.

**Check yourself**

1. How do solids differ from liquids?
2. How do gases differ from liquids?

## Metals and nonmetals

Substances are often classified as metals or nonmetals. Copper, tin, iron, aluminum, silver, and gold are all familiar examples of metals. What do metals have in common?

Metals are shiny. They can be formed into thin wires or flattened into thin sheets of foil. Metals are good conductors, or carriers, of heat and electricity. Copper and silver are especially good conductors.

As a general rule, nonmetals are poor conductors of heat or electricity. Nonmetals vary in appearance. Glass, plastic, and polished wood are shiny. Most nonmetals, however, have a dull appearance.

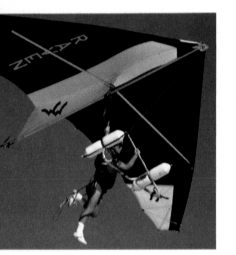

Figure 1-7. Which parts of a hang glider are made of metal? How can you tell?

**Check yourself**

List three properties metals have in common.

## Mixtures, compounds, and elements

In a third classification system, substances are grouped by whether they can be separated into other substances. A **mixture** contains two or more substances. Sometimes both substances remain visible. For example, if you drop sand into water, the sand and water both can be seen.

You can mix just a little sand with water. Or you can add a lot of sand to the water. The mixture can contain varying amounts of sand. The amounts of the substances in a mixture can be changed. This is a characteristic of all mixtures.

## Activity 1–1C          Electrical Conductors

### Materials

"D" cell
3 10-cm copper wires
flashlight bulb and holder
masking tape
aluminum foil
paper
iron nail
string
foil gum wrapper
wood
coins

### Purpose

To determine which materials are better conductors of electricity—metals or nonmetals.

### Procedure

1. Connect the wires, bulb, holder, and cell as shown. Make sure the wires are secure on the terminals.
2. Test the bulb by touching the unconnected ends of the two wires to each other. Make certain the bulb becomes lit.
3. Place both unconnected ends of the wires on the aluminum foil in different places. Observe the bulb.
4. Replace the aluminum foil with paper, and repeat Step 3.
5. Test as many other materials as are available. Classify the materials as conductors or nonconductors of electricity.

### Questions

1. Does the bulb become lit when the aluminum foil is touched with the wires? Why?
2. Is paper a conductor of electricity?
3. Which of the materials tested are conductors?
4. Which of the materials tested are nonconductors?
5. Do all the metals tested conduct electricity?

### Conclusion

What can you conclude about the ability of metals and nonmetals to conduct electricity?

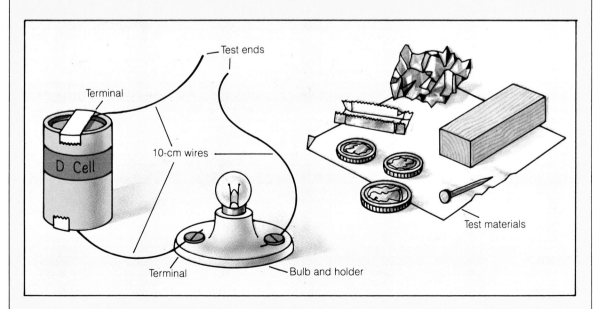

Figure 1-8. Both beakers contain mixtures. Which mixture is a solution? How can you tell?

**Main Idea**

What is a solution?

**Safety**
Never taste chemicals in the laboratory.

**Main Idea**

What is the difference between a solute and a solvent?

Air is a mixture of several invisible gases. It contains oxygen, nitrogen, carbon dioxide, and several other substances. The amounts of some of the substances in air change. When it is humid, there is a lot of water present in the air as a gas.

A **solution** (suh-LOO′-shun) is a special kind of mixture. The substances are spread evenly throughout each other in a solution. Samples taken from different parts of the solution will be completely identical.

The most common solutions are mixtures of water and something else. For example, suppose sugar is added to water in a beaker. The water is stirred. The grains of sugar are no longer visible. The solution of sugar in water is as clear as the water alone. Tasting samples of the solution from different parts of the solution confirm that the sugar is spread evenly through the water. The sugar remains spread evenly through the water even after a few days. It does not settle out. The sugar is said to have **dissolved** (duh-ZOLVD') in the water.

Food coloring dissolves in water. A drop of food coloring added to a beaker of water will spread evenly through the water. The solution is colored but clear. No particles can be seen in the solution. You could also mix more food coloring with the water. Solutions can vary in the amount of dissolved substance.

The substance that dissolves is the **solute** (SOL′-yoot). The substance in which the solute dissolves is the **solvent** (SOL′-vent). In a sugar water solution, sugar is the solute. Water is the solvent.

## Activity 1–1D     Preparing and Separating Solutions

### Materials

100-mL graduated cylinder
grease pencil
distilled water
tap water
magnifying glass
15 mL chemically pure (or kosher) table salt
4 beakers
4 glass slides
4 medicine droppers
stirring rod

### Purpose

To demonstrate the separation of a solid from a liquid by the evaporation method.

### Procedure

1. Number the beakers 1, 2, 3, and 4 with a grease pencil.
2. Number the glass slides 1, 2, 3, and 4 with a grease pencil.
3. Put the amount of water specified below into the four numbered beakers as follows:
     Beaker 1: 75 mL of tap water
     Beaker 2: 75 mL of distilled water
     Beaker 3: 100 mL of distilled water
     Beaker 4: 50 mL of distilled water
4. Add 15 mL of table salt to Beaker 3 and mix with a *clean* stirring rod until the salt has dissolved.
5. Measure 25 mL of the salt solution from Beaker 3 and add it to Beaker 4. Mix with a clean stirring rod.
6. Using a clean medicine dropper, put five drops of water from Beaker 1 onto Slide 1.
7. Use a medicine dropper to place five drops of solution from each of the other three beakers onto the slide labeled the same number as the beaker.
8. Place the slides where they will not be disturbed. Leave them overnight.

9. On the next day, examine the residue on each of the four slides under the magnifying glass. Record your observations on a table like the one shown.
10. Make a chart to record your observations. Use these headings: Beaker #, Contents of beaker, Slide #, Description of residue on slide.

### Questions

1. Which of the beakers has the saltiest solution?
2. How did the five drops of solution change on the slides when left overnight?
3. Describe the amount and the properties of the residue on each of the numbered slides.
4. Which of the slides has the most salt residue? Why?
5. How do the residues found on Slides 1, 3, and 4 differ from one another? How are these differences related to the solutions in the beakers with corresponding numbers? Explain your answer.
6. What does the presence of residue on Slides 1 and 2 tell you about the difference between tap water and distilled water?

### Conclusion

How does the evaporation method allow you to study a solid?

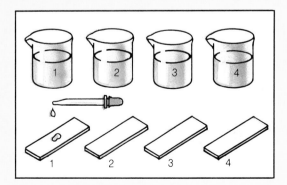

**Main Idea**

What is the most common solvent?

Water is the most common solvent. More substances dissolve in water than in anything else. Tap water contains many dissolved substances. Alcohol is another good solvent. Not all substances dissolve in water or alcohol. Special cleaning fluids must be used to dissolve substances such as tar and oil.

Solutions can be classified by the phases of the solute and solvent. Both solutes and solvents may be solids, liquids, or gases. For example, carbon dioxide (gas) dissolves readily in water (liquid). Carbonated beverages are solutions of carbon dioxide in water. A solid can be dissolved in another solid. Sterling silver is a solution of silver and copper.

The substances in a mixture can often be separated quite easily. For example, sand can be strained out of water. When water in a solution evaporates, it leaves the solute behind.

Water itself can be broken down into other substances. Yet it is not a mixture. The two substances into which water can be broken down are hydrogen and oxygen. They are both gases. A mixture made of two gases, on the other hand, will always be a gas.

There is another important difference between water and a mixture. When two substances are mixed together, the amount of each can be changed. There will still be a mixture. The chemical recipe, or **chemical formula** (KEM′-ih-kul FORM′-yoo-luh), for water is always the same, on the other hand. For a certain amount of hydrogen, there is only one amount of oxygen that will combine to form water. When water is broken down, the amounts of hydrogen and oxygen fit the same formula.

A third difference between water and a mixture is that it is harder to break down water. Boiling water or freezing it does not break it down.

**Data Search**

What is the melting point of sodium? What is its boiling point? Search page 559.

Table salt, too, is formed from two other totally different substances, sodium and chlorine. Sodium is a soft, silvery metallic solid. Chlorine is a greenish-yellow gas. Again, the amounts of chlorine and sodium are fixed. The formula never changes.

Substances such as water and table salt are called **compounds** (KOM′-powndz). All compounds are combinations of two or more substances. Unlike mixtures, compounds always have the same formula. It is normally hard to break them

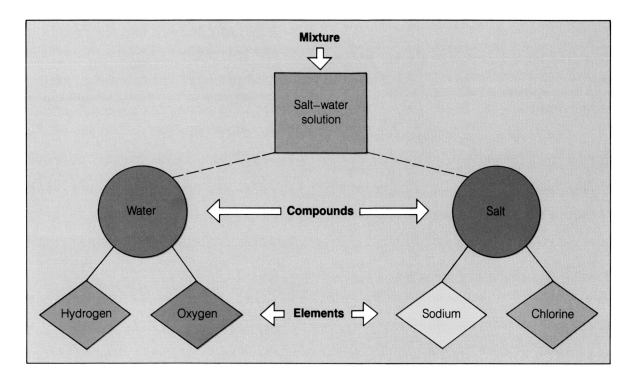

down. And compounds have very different properties from those of the substances that make them.

Hydrogen and oxygen, the substances that form water, cannot be broken down into other substances. They are examples of **elements** (EL′-uh-ments). Sodium and chlorine are also elements.

Only about one hundred substances have been identified as elements. All other substances can be thought of as different combinations of those elements. The elements are sometimes referred to as building blocks. They are rearranged in different ways to form many different substances.

Figure 1-9. How are mixtures, compounds, and elements different?

## Check yourself

1. How does a solution differ from a mixture that is not a solution? Give an example of each.

2. How does a solution differ from a compound? Give an example of each.

3. How does a compound differ from an element?

# Practical Science

## Candlemaking

Candles have been in use for thousands of years. The ancient Egyptians used candles. The ancient Romans also used candles. In France, a fragment of a candle 900 years old was found.

You already know that a candle is a solid, usually cylindrically-shaped mass of tallow, wax, or other fatty substance. It has a wick through its center that can be burned to provide light and heat.

**How a candle burns**  Wax is a fatty, heat-sensitive solid. As a candle burns, it passes through all three phases of matter—from solid to liquid to gas. When the wick is lit, the wax in it melts, becomes liquid, and then gas, or vapor. The vapor burns as it combines with oxygen. The burning gas vapor gives off light and heat.

The heat is important, for it melts wax in the candle body. The melted wax then passes upward through the wick. When it reaches the base of the flame, the melted wax ignites and burns. The process continues until the candle is extinguished or the wax is consumed.

Most candles have a cylindrical shape with a wick running down the middle. This form promotes even heating, melting, and burning of the wax in a candle.

**How candles are made**  During the Middle Ages, candles were made from animal fat, tallow, and beeswax. Tallow candles were made by dipping strands of yarn in melted animal fat and allowing them to cool. The process was repeated until the desired thickness was reached. Beeswax candles were made by repeatedly pouring melted wax over a wick suspended vertically. The process continued until the desired thickness was reached.

Early in the history of candles, people made their own candles. As time went on, some people became professional candlemakers. Professional candlemakers are called *chandlers*.

The 19th century brought many improvements in candlemaking. Among these was the development of *stearin*, a chemically purified fat superior to tallow, and paraffin, a wax made from petroleum. These developments, and the invention of production candle molds, made mass production of high-quality candles possible. The candles we use today are usually made of paraffin to which a small amount of stearin is added as a hardener. Modern wicks are *plaited*, or braided, by machine. Then they are chemically treated to form a curve as they burn. The curve promotes even burning of the vaporized wax.

**Something to try**  Light a candle. Let it burn for about one minute. Now strike a match and blow out the candle. Then slowly pass the burning match across the column of smoke flowing from the extinguished wick. The match should pass about 1/4 inch above the wick. Did the flame jump from the match to the wick? What does this tell you about the gases flowing off the wick?

## Section 1 Review   Chapter 1

### Check Your Vocabulary

| | |
|---|---|
| compound | plasma |
| element | solute |
| mass | volume |
| mixture | |

*Match each term above with the numbered phrase that best describes it.*

1. Can contain varying amounts of other substances

2. Phase of matter that exists at very high temperatures

3. The amount of space something takes up

4. Made of other substances according to a specific formula

5. Measured on a balance

6. Cannot be broken down into other substances

7. Dissolves when mixed with a solvent

### Check Your Knowledge

*Multiple Choice: Choose the answer that best completes each of the following sentences.*

1. All matter takes up space and ?.
   a) dissolves in water
   b) has mass
   c) has a definite shape
   d) is visible

2. The three common phases of matter used to group substances are ?.
   a) solids, liquids, and gases
   b) elements, compounds, and mixtures
   c) solvents, solutes, and solutions
   d) metals, plastics, and wood

3. The number of elements now known is about ?.
   a) 30           c) 1000
   b) 100          d) 100 000

4. Salty water is best classified as a(n) ?.
   a) element          c) mixture
   b) compound         d) plasma

5. A property metals have in common is that they ?.
   a) conduct electricity
   b) take the shape of their container
   c) dissolve in water
   d) can be broken down into other substances

### Check Your Understanding

1. Explain why a solution is classified as a mixture rather than as a compound.

2. In your own kitchen, find three examples of classification. Try to find at least one example of classification into groups and one in order.

3. Carbon dioxide is one of the invisible gases in air. It can be broken down into carbon, a black solid, and oxygen, another invisible gas. Is carbon dioxide an element, compound, or mixture? Explain your choice.

4. When salt is poured into a salt shaker, it takes the shape of the salt shaker. Explain why salt is classified as a solid rather than a liquid.

### Practical Science

1. Describe what happens to a candle when the wick is lit.

2. Of what materials are modern candles made?

3. Explain why the wicks of modern candles are chemically treated to form a curve as they burn.

# Working with Data    Section 2

**Section 2 of Chapter 1 is divided into nine parts:**

Length

Area

Volume

Mass

Density

Temperature and Time

Measurement errors

Graphing measured values

Estimating and indirect measurement

*Practical Science: Equal Arm Balances*

### Learning Objectives

1.  To use the common SI units for length, mass, temperature, time, and certain other derived units.

2.  To recognize the presence of some amount of error in every measurement that is made.

3.  To determine if a relationship exists between two variables using graphical analysis.

4.  To estimate the value of a large or small measurement using indirect procedures.

Figure 1-10. The mass of the apple is being measured by the scale.

Some properties are described with words alone. For example, chlorine is an element that is a yellowish-green gas. Three properties of chlorine have just been described in words.

Other properties are described with numbers. They include properties that answer "how" questions—"how much," "how hot," "how long," etc. When you observe a property that is described with numbers, you are making a **measurement**. Suppose you find that a certain amount of salt balances a 50-gram piece. You have measured the mass of the salt. Your measurement answers the question, How much salt is there?

Mass, length, and volume are three properties often measured in science. Another property often measured is temperature. Temperature describes the hotness or coldness of a substance. It doesn't depend on the amount of substance. A glass of water and a bathtub of water can be at the same temperature.

Something else is often measured in science, but it is not a property of matter. That something is time. In science, you may measure how long it takes for some event to happen.

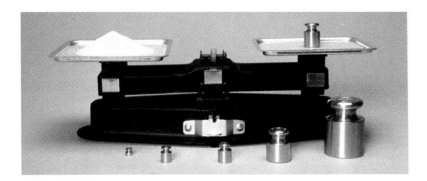

Figure 1-11. The mass of the salt is 50 grams. What unit has been used in the mass measurement?

Measurements have two parts. There is a number followed by a unit. A mass cannot be simply 50. Rather, it is 50 grams or 50 kilograms or perhaps 50 metric tons. The modern metric system, known as **SI**, contains all the units scientists have agreed to use for all their measurements. The letters *SI* come from the French name for *international system*. SI has units for measurements of all sizes—from very large to very small. In this course, you will be using SI units. You will also use a few older metric units convenient for everyday use.

**Main Idea**

What is the modern metric system called?

## Length

The basic SI unit of length is the **meter**. One meter is about the distance from the floor to the knob of a door. The short form, or symbol, for the name *meter* is m. Most doors are about 2 m in height. Try holding your hands a distance of 1 m apart. Now compare the distance between your hands to the length of a meter stick. How close were you?

Large distances are described and measured in **kilometers** (KIL'-uh-meet'-erz). The prefix *kilo-* means *one thousand*. One kilometer (symbol km) is one thousand meters. A fast runner can run a distance of 1 km in just under three minutes.

Smaller distances may be measured in **millimeters** (mm). The prefix *milli-* means *one thousandth*. A millimeter is 1/1000 of a meter. A dime is about 1 mm in thickness.

Another unit for measuring small distances is the **centimeter** (cm). The prefix *centi-* means *one hundredth*. A centimeter is 1/100 of a meter. A centimeter is equal to 10 mm. Your little finger is about 1 cm across.

Examine a meter stick. Identify the marks indicating the length of a centimeter and a millimeter. How many centimeters are in a meter? With a little practice it is easy to change from one unit to another.

Meter, kilometer, centimeter, and millimeter are the common units used to describe length. Other units of length are also used. They have different prefixes but all end in *-meter*. Even very large and very small distances can be described.

Figure 1-12. How well can you estimate a distance of 1 m?

**Check yourself**

1. Give the name and symbol for four SI length units.
2. State the meaning of each of the following prefixes.
   a. kilo-          b. centi-          c. milli-

## Area

The amount of space on a surface is called **area**. For example, a rug covers a certain area of a floor. The top of your desk has a certain area. A tennis court has a definite play area.

A square that is 1 m on each side has an area of one **square meter**. The basic SI unit of area is the square meter (symbol $m^2$). An open newspaper covers an area of about 1 $m^2$. The surface of an ordinary door is about 2 $m^2$.

Smaller areas can be described in square centimeters or square millimeters. A **square centimeter** ($cm^2$) is the area of a square 1 cm on each side. A **square millimeter** ($mm^2$) is the area of a square 1 mm on each side.

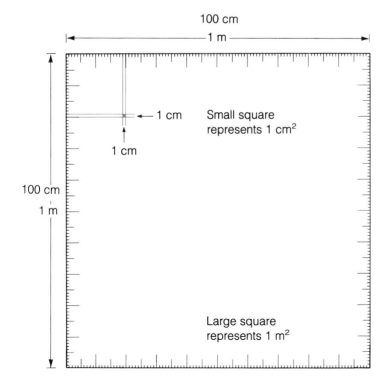

Figure 1-13. How many square centimeters are there in a square meter?

What units would you use to describe the area of the top of your desk? The area of a sheet of writing paper? The area of the floor in your classroom?

### Check yourself

Give the name and symbol for the basic SI unit of area.

### Volume

Figure 1-14. A crouching person can fit inside a space of a cubic meter.

The amount of space something fills up is its volume. A cube that is 1 m on each side has a volume of one **cubic meter**. The basic SI unit of volume is the cubic meter (symbol $m^3$). The volume of a refrigerator is a little over 1 $m^3$. The volume of a bedroom is about 40 $m^3$.

A cubic meter is quite a large volume. You often need to measure much smaller volumes. A **cubic centimeter** ($cm^3$) is the volume of a cube that is 1 cm on each side. A small die has a volume of about 1 $cm^3$.

For everyday use, a metric volume unit between a cubic centimeter and a cubic meter is convenient. A **liter** (LEE'-ter) is the volume of a cube 10 cm on each side.

How many cubic centimeters equal a liter? Ten small cubes 1 cm on a side fit along one side of a bigger cube 10 cm on a side. Ten rows of small cubes would cover the bottom of the bigger cube. And ten layers of small cubes would fill up the bigger cube. Altogether, it takes 10 × 10 × 10, or 1000, small cubes to fill the bigger cube. Each small cube has a volume of 1 $cm^3$. So a liter (L) equals 1000 $cm^3$.

The prefix *milli-* means *one thousandth*. A **milliliter** (mL) is equal to 1/1000 of a liter. One thousandth of a liter is also equal to 1 $cm^3$. So 1 mL equals 1 $cm^3$. The two volume units can be substituted for one another. Containers for measuring the volume of liquids are usually marked in milliliters.

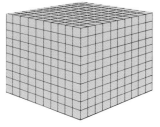

Figure 1-15. How many little cubes of volume 1 $cm^3$ fit inside a bigger cube of volume 1 L? (Note that the Figure is not full-scale.)

### Check yourself

1. How many cubic centimeters are there in one liter?

2. How many cubic centimeters are there in one milliliter?

3. List the following volume measurements in order from smallest to largest: 1 L, 1 mL, 1 $m^3$, 10 $cm^3$, 100 mL.

## Activity 1–2A          Comparing Units

### Materials

construction paper or tagboard
pencil
metric ruler
scissors
masking tape
plastic bag
100-mL graduated cylinder

### Purpose

To determine the volume and the mass of a cube that is 10 cm on a side.

### Procedure

1. Make a cube 10 cm on each side like the one shown in the diagram. Measuring exactly, draw a full-scale enlargement of the pattern on heavy construction paper or tagboard.
2. Cut on the solid lines, and fold on the dashed lines, as shown. Use masking tape to hold the sides of the cube in place.
3. Carefully line the cube with a small plastic bag.
4. Study the space inside the cube. Estimate how many cylinders of water will be needed to fill the cube.
5. Carefully fill the lined cube with water using the 100-mL cylinder. Measure the amount of water you use.
6. Lift the cube of water and estimate how much mass it has. Empty the water from the cube.

### Questions

1. How many full containers of water fit into the cube?
2. How does your estimate compare with the actual amount of water the cube holds?
3. After lifting the cube filled with water, how much mass do you estimate that it has?

4. Give some examples of objects that have about the same mass as the cube filled with water.
5. How much mass does the cube filled with water have?

### Conclusion

What is the volume and the mass of a cube 10 cm on a side when it is filled with water?

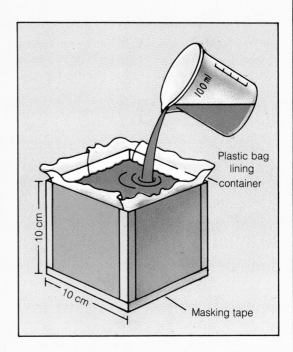

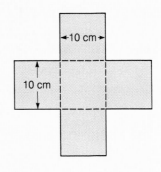

Automotive painters work indoors and wear masks to protect themselves from hazardous fumes.

## Automotive Painter

Production automotive painters spray brightly colored paint on new cars as the final step in automobile assembly lines. Other automotive painters refinish cars damaged by collisions, rust, or normal wear and tear.

Most automotive painters work in autobody repair shops. Painters remove rust and old paint with power sanding machines. Filling small scratches and dents with body putty gives the car a smooth surface ready for priming. Using a spray gun, the painter applies several coats of primer and finishes with a layer of enamel paint.

As painters gain experience, they complete more complex jobs. Many become skilled at extensive autobody repair.

Painters are exposed to dangerous fumes from paint and paint-thinning solutions. They wear protective masks which prevent the inhalation of hazardous vapors. Strength, good health, and a keen sense of color are necessary in automotive painting. High school graduates who have taken auto mechanics classes have the best chance of being hired as automotive painters.

Surveyors use instruments that help them to measure long distances accurately.

## Surveyor

Surveyors make measurements. They may prepare specialized surveys for government agencies, real estate developers, construction companies, or engineering and industrial firms.

Training for a career in surveying is usually obtained through special courses beyond high school, community college programs, or even on the job. High school courses in mathematics, science, and drafting are good background preparation.

Surveying requires work with tools and instruments, attention to detail, and physical stamina. Surveyors often work as members of a team. Much of the work is outdoors, in a variety of locations.

## Mass

The **kilogram** (kg) is the basic SI unit for mass. A liter of water has a mass of one kilogram, or 1 kg. One kilogram equals one thousand **grams** (g). A large paper clip has a mass of about 1 g.

You know that 1 L equal 1000 mL. So 1 mL of water has a mass of 1 g. If you know the volume of some water, you can calculate its mass. For example, the mass of 15 mL of water is 15 g. What is the mass of 175 mL of water?

For masses of less than 1 g, the **milligram** (mg) is used. From the prefix, can you tell how many milligrams are in a gram? A straight pin has a mass of about 120 gm.

### Check yourself

What is the mass of 1 L of water?

## Density

Suppose you have two cubes having the same volume, 1 cm$^3$ each. Suppose one cube was made of wood and the other of iron. Would the cubes have the same mass? Obviously not! The iron cube would have more mass. Iron has greater density than wood.

The mass of a substance per unit volume is its **density**. Density is really a measure of how much matter is packed into a given space. It is often expressed in units of grams per cubic centimeter or g/cm$^3$. This is the mass of one cubic centimeter of the substance.

One cubic centimeter of iron has a mass of 7.8 g. Therefore the density of iron is 7.8 g/cm$^3$. Densities of liquids are sometimes stated in g/mL. A mL of liquid has a volume of 1 cm$^3$, so the two units are equivalent. One mL of water has a mass of 1 g. Therefore the density of water can be stated as 1g/mL or as 1g/cm$^3$. See Table 1–1 for the densities of other substances.

Density does not depend on the amount of substance. A small iron cube has the same density as a large iron frying pan.

Figure 1–16. What is the mass of the water? The paper clips? The pins?

Table 1–1. Densities of a few common substances

| Substance | Density (in g/cm$^3$) |
|---|---|
| Gold | 19.3 |
| Lead | 11.3 |
| Steel | 7.8 |
| Aluminum | 2.7 |
| Pine wood | 0.50 |
| Balsa wood | 0.12 |
| Water at 4°C | 1.00 |
| Hydrogen gas | 0.00009 |
| Oxygen gas | 0.0013 |

**Data Search**

Which of the common elements has a density equal to that of gold? Search page 559.

## Activity 1-2B        Density of Liquids

### Materials

100 mL salad oil
100 mL dark corn syrup
equal-arm balance
two 250-mL graduated beakers
100-mL beaker

### Purpose

To compare the densities of water, oil, and corn syrup.

### Procedure

1. Measure and record the mass of the 100-mL beaker and each 250-mL beaker. Make a chart like the one shown.
2. Put 100 mL of water into one of the 250-mL graduated beakers and measure its mass. Subtract the mass of the beaker. Record the mass of 100 mL of water.
3. Put 100 mL of salad oil in the other 250-mL beaker. Put 100 mL of dark corn syrup into the 100-mL beaker. Measure the mass of 100 mL of corn syrup. Measure the mass of 100 mL of salad oil. Record each mass.
4. Calculate the density of each material.
5. Slowly pour about half of the salad oil (50 mL) into the beaker of water. Observe what happens. Slowly pour about half of the dark corn syrup (50 mL) into the same beaker. Observe what happens.

6. Predict what would happen if you poured corn syrup into the beaker containing the salad oil. Test your prediction.

### Questions

1. Which material has the least mass per 100 mL? Which material has the most?
2. What happened when you added the oil to the water? Why?
3. What happened when you poured the syrup into the water and oil? Why?
4. Which material in the beaker is the most dense? the least dense?
5. What did you predict would happen when you poured corn syrup into salad oil?

### Conclusion

How do the densities of water, oil, and corn syrup compare to each other?

| Material | Mass (grams) | Volume (mL) | Density (mass ÷ volume) |
|---|---|---|---|
| Water | g | 100 mL | g/mL |
| Oil | g | 100 mL | g/mL |
| Corn syrup | g | 100 mL | g/mL |

You can calculate the density of a substance if you know its mass and volume. Density equals mass divided by volume.

$$\text{density} = \frac{\text{mass}}{\text{volume}}$$

### Check yourself

1. A block of marble 3 cm$^3$ in volume has a mass of 7.8 g. What is the density of marble?
2. What would be the mass of 1 cm$^3$ of pine wood?

## Temperature and time

Figure 1–17 Some important Celsius temperatures.

The everyday temperature scale used with SI units is the **Celsius** scale. On the Celsius scale, the melting temperature of ice is 0°C. Liquid water boils at 100°C (at sea level). Room temperature is about 20°C. Normal body temperature is 37°C. On a very warm day the temperature may surpass 30°C.

The basic SI unit of time, the **second** (s), is very familiar to you. In scientific work, only the second and the appropriate prefixes are used. In everyday measurements, the minute (min) and hour (h) are also used. Table 1–2 lists units for length, area, volume, mass, temperature, and time.

### Check yourself

1. What changes take place at 0°C and 100°C?

2. What is the name and symbol of the basic SI unit of time?

Table 1–2. Some common SI units.

| Unit | Symbol | Unit | Symbol | Unit | Symbol |
|------|--------|------|--------|------|--------|
| Length<br>  meter<br>  kilometer<br>  centimeter<br>  millimeter | <br>m<br>km<br>cm<br>mm | Volume<br>  cubic meter<br>  cubic centimeter<br>  *liter<br>  *milliliter | <br>$m^3$<br>$cm^3$<br>L<br>mL | Temperature<br>*degree Celsius | <br>°C |
| Area<br>  square meter<br>  square centimeter<br>  square millimeter | <br>$m^2$<br>$cm^2$<br>$mm^2$ | Mass<br>  kilogram<br>  gram<br>  milligram | <br>kg<br>g<br>mg | Time<br>  second<br>  *minute<br>  *hour | <br>s<br>min<br>h |
| *Not an SI unit but may be used along with SI units. | | | | | |

## Activity 1–2C    Differences in Length Measurement

### Materials

meter stick
large desk or table
index card or small piece of paper (one per
student)

### Purpose

To discover how different measurements of the
same object can have different values.

### Procedure

In the following procedure, each student will
make the same measurement with the same
meter stick.

1. Measure the length of a large desk or table
   with a meter stick. Read the meter stick to
   the nearest tenth of a centimeter.

2. Record the measurement on the card or
   paper. Do not tell anyone the value of the
   measurement you made.
3. Give the card with your name and measurement on it to your teacher. When everyone has finished, your teacher will write each
   value on the board.
4. Calculate the sum of all the measurements.
   Find the average value of these measurements by dividing the sum by the number
   of measurements made.
5. Find the largest measurement made. Calculate the difference between the largest
   measurement and the average.
6. Find the smallest measurement made. Calculate the difference between the smallest
   measurement and the average. The larger
   of the two differences found here and in
   Step 5 is an estimate of the possible error.

### Questions

1. Were all the values the same?
2. Why do you think there were different values
   for the same measurement? List at least three
   different reasons.
3. What is the possible error in the measurement of the desk?
4. How could the error in the measurement be
   reduced?

### Conclusion

Why is the average value probably the best
value for the size of the desk?

## Measurement errors

Different observers using the same measuring device often
find different values. Also, different instruments used for
measurement give different values. For example, a student
using different meter sticks may report different values for

the same length. Measurements can never be exact. Some error in measured values is always present.

An average value can be calculated if the same measurement is repeated. The average is usually better than a single measurement. Values that are too large are cancelled out by values that are too small. Measurements in science are repeated to reduce the amount of possible error in the measurement.

### Check yourself

Why is it better to use the average of several measurements rather then a single measurement?

### Graphing measured values

Graphing is a way of looking for possible relationships between two measurements. For example, two different measurements of a circle can be made. The **diameter** (dī-AM′-uh-ter) of a circle is the straight-line distance across the circle through the center of the circle. The **circumference** (ser-KUM′-fer-ens) of a circle is the distance around the circle. The diameter and circumference of several different size circles can be measured. Suppose the results shown in Table 1-2 are obtained.

The measurements can be plotted on a graph. A simple graph is made as follows. On a piece of graph paper, draw a horizontal line along one of the printed lines near the bottom. Draw a vertical line along one of the printed lines near the left. The intersection, or meeting point, of the two lines is called the **origin.** The vertical line is the **vertical axis.** The horizontal line is the **horizontal axis.** The other lines on the graph paper divide the axes into equal-length sections.

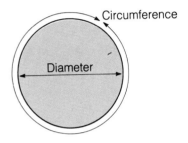

Figure 1-18. Is the circumference of a circle always larger than the diameter?

| Diameter | Circumference |
|----------|---------------|
| 5.0 cm   | 15.7 cm       |
| 4.0 cm   | 12.6 cm       |
| 3.0 cm   | 9.4 cm        |
| 2.0 cm   | 6.3 cm        |
| 1.0 cm   | 3.1 cm        |

Table 1-3. Measurements of five circles.

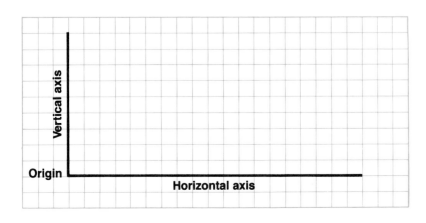

Figure 1-19. On a graph, what point is the origin?

Assign each of the two measured quantities to one of the two axes. Label each axis with the quantity and the units used to measure it.

Study Figure 1-20. Notice that the value of each quantity is represented by a certain distance from the origin. For each quantity, a scale was chosen that included all the values measured. For example, all the circumference values fall between 0.0 cm and 16.0 cm. Each small space along the vertical axis represents 1.0 cm. Values are marked every 2.0 cm to avoid cluttering the axis. What does each small space along the horizontal axis represent?

Notice the five points on the graph. Each point marks the intersection of the diameter and circumference values for one circle. For example, for the first circle, the dashed vertical line for diameter 5.0 cm intersects the dashed horizontal line for circumference 15.7 cm. The position of 15.7 cm is found by reading to the nearest tenth of a space.

Notice that the five points for the five circles happen to lie along a straight line. This line shows how the two measurements of a circle are related. The line can be used to predict the circumference of any other circle if the diameter is known.

Figure 1-20. Graph of the measurements in Table 1-3.

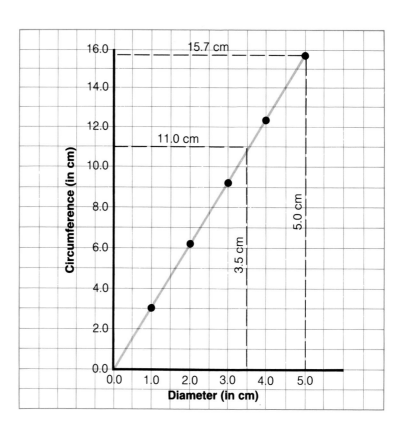

## Activity 1–2D         Graphing Measurements of Blocks

### Material

5 rectangular blocks of the same kind of
   wood but of differing sizes
graph paper
balance
meter stick

### Purpose

To determine how the mass and volume of different size blocks of the same wood are related.

### Procedure

1. Use a table like the one shown to record your data.
2. Measure and record the mass in grams of one wood block.
3. Measure and record the length, width, and thickness in centimeters of the same block.
4. Calculate and record the volume in cubic centimeters. (*Hint:* The volume is equal to the length times the width times the thickness.)
5. Make and record the same measurements (mass, length, width, and thickness) for three more blocks. Save the fifth block for Step 7.
6. Calculate the volume for each block. Record your results.
7. Measure *only* the length, width, and thickness of the fifth block. DO NOT measure the mass of this block at this time. Record your measurements and calculate the volume.
8. Prepare a graph with the vertical axis labeled *Mass (in grams).* Label the horizontal axis *Volume (in cubic centimeters).*
9. Plot your mass and volume values for each block of wood. Draw a straight line through your points.
10. Using your graph, predict the mass of the fifth block of wood. Record your prediction. Check your prediction by measuring the mass of the block on the balance.

### Questions

1. Do the points on your graph lie on a straight line?
2. What happens to the mass of a wood block as the volume is increased?
3. According to your graph, does doubling the volume double the mass?
4. What is the mass of a wood block having zero volume? Is this the answer you would expect?

### Conclusion

How is the mass of a wood block related to its volume?

| Block | Mass (in g) | Length (in cm) | Width (in cm) | Thickness (in cm) | Volume (in cm³) |
|-------|-------------|----------------|---------------|-------------------|-----------------|
| 1     |             |                |               |                   |                 |
| 2     |             |                |               |                   |                 |
| 3     |             |                |               |                   |                 |
| 4     |             |                |               |                   |                 |
| 5     |             |                |               |                   |                 |

### Check yourself

1. What is the name of the point on a graph where the horizontal axis and the vertical axis meet?

2. When two measured quantities are plotted on a graph, how should the axes be labeled?

### Estimating and indirect measurement

You measure the length of a table by comparing it to a meter stick. You measure the volume of a liquid by comparing it to the space in a marked container. You measure mass by comparing it to marked standard masses. Direct measurements are made by comparing something with marked objects.

How could you measure the height of a friend without a meter stick or measuring tape? If you knew your own height, you could **estimate** (ES´-tuh-mayt) your friend's height. That is, you could make a rough measurement by guessing how much taller or shorter your friend is than you. Similarly, you can use the known height of a door to estimate the height of a ceiling.

Direct measurement may often take too much time. It may not always be convenient or even possible. Estimating is a valuable skill that improves with practice.

Direct measurement of very small distances or very small amounts may not be possible. But the measurements may be made indirectly. Suppose you wanted to measure the thickness of a sheet of paper. A measuring instrument of the right size may not be available. You could, however, measure the thickness of a ream (500 sheets) of paper. Suppose the thickness of the ream is 5 cm. Then the thickness of each sheet is 5 cm ÷ 500, or 0.01 cm.

The mass of a light object such as a rubber band is hard to measure directly. You can count out 100 rubber bands. Then measure the total mass of the rubber bands. Divide the total mass by 100. Is the result really the mass of one rubber band? What do you have to assume about each of the rubber bands?

Small time intervals are also difficult to measure directly. Suppose you wanted to measure the time between pulse beats. You could measure the time for fifty pulse beats. The time between pulse beats would be the time for 50 beats divided by 50.

Figure 1-21. What is the approximate height of this ceiling?

Figure 1-22. What is the thickness of a single sheet of typing paper?

## Activity 1–2E      Estimating

### Materials

jar of beans
clock or watch that indicates seconds
nickel
5 pennies

### Purpose

To learn to make reasonable estimates.

### Procedure

**Part 1** Estimating the number of beans in a jar

1. Record the number of beans you think are in the jar.
2. Determine about how many beans touch the bottom of the jar. Record your answer.
3. Determine about how many beans fit in a straight line from top to bottom along the side of the jar. Record your answer.
4. Multiply the number of beans touching the bottom by the number that fit from top to bottom.
5. Find out from your teacher how many beans are actually in the jar.

**Part 2** Estimating how long it takes for one minute to pass

6. While a partner watches a clock or watch, estimate how long it takes for one minute to pass. Record how much time had actually passed when you thought one minute had passed.
7. Determine how many seconds away from one minute your estimate was. Record this.
8. Use the clock or watch to measure how many times your pulse beats in 30 seconds. To feel your pulse, press the fingers of one hand on the thumb side of the wrist of your other hand. Record your answer.
9. While your partner watches the clock, use your pulse count to estimate one minute. Record the length of time you estimated.
10. How many seconds were you off this time?

**Part 3** Estimating the mass of a penny

11. Guess the mass of a penny in grams. Record your guess.
12. The mass of a nickel is 5 grams. Decide how many pennies have about the same total mass as a nickel. Record your answer.
13. Using the information in Step 2, estimate the mass of one penny. Record your answer.

### Questions

1. Was there a difference between your first and second estimates in Part 1? in Part 2? in Part 3?
2. Which estimate was closest to the correct value, your first one, or the second one based on additional information?

### Conclusion

How can you improve the accuracy of your estimates?

Figure 1-23. How could you estimate the height of the building?

**Library research**

The distances to the stars cannot be measured directly. Find out how astronomers measure these large distances indirectly.

Large distances and large amounts can also be measured indirectly. You can compare the large distances to smaller distances that can be measured. For example, suppose you wanted to find the height of a 50-story building. You can use the height of one story. The floor-to-ceiling height in most buildings is close to 3 m. To get the building height, multiply the height of one story by 50. The height of the building is about 3 m × 50, or 150 m.

Suppose you want to measure the mass of a carton of textbooks. The carton is too big to fit on your balance. How can you measure the mass indirectly?

**Check yourself**

1. What is the difference between a direct measurement and an estimate?

2. What is the difference between a direct measurement and an indirect measurement?

# Practical Science

## Equal Arm Balances

The basic equal arm balance has been in existence for centuries. It is an application of the lever used to measure mass. An equal arm balance consists of uniform bar or beam supported at its midpoint by an edge called a *fulcrum*. Because it is supported at the midpoint, the beam has two equal arms which are balanced. Two pans of equal mass are supported by the beam, one on the end of each arm.

The object to be measured is placed in one pan. Known masses are added to the other pan until the beam is balanced. The sum of the masses equals the object's mass.

**Refining ways to measure mass**   To provide the accuracy needed for scientific work, refinements were added to the basic equal arm balance. This refined balance is often called a scientific, or analytical, balance. Some uses for the balance include doing quantitative chemical analyses and preparing pharmaceutical prescriptions.

To determine when the beam is exactly balanced, a pointer is fastened to the beam at the fulcrum. A graduated scale, with a zero point centered exactly below the fulcrum, is mounted near the bottom of the balance. The beam is balanced when the end of the pointer is on the zero mark. A small threaded mass at each end of the beam allows the beam to be balanced, or "zeroed," with the pans empty.

A set of precision masses ranging from 100 g to 0.01 g is used to measure mass. For more precise measurements, a small mass on one of the arms is adjusted to achieve balance. This allows measurements down to 0.001 g.

It takes some time for the balance arm to come to rest. Because speed of weighing can be important, many analytical balances have a device called a *damper*. The damper stops the movement of the balance arm that occurs while weighing the object.

**Other types of balances**   Several other types of balances have been developed for measuring mass.

The platform balance is a type of equal arm balance. It has two flat platforms attached to the top of the beam, one at each end.

The unequal arm balance has a fulcrum close to one end. The object to be measured is placed in a pan supported at this end. A small known mass is moved along the long arm until balance is obtained.

Another type of balance is a spring balance. The object to be measured is suspended from a hook on one end of the spring. The other end of the spring is fixed. The measurement of mass is read from scale. The movement of the spring is proportional to the object's mass.

The newest types of balances are electronic and do not rely on mechanical linkages and movements. This gives an electronic balance greater precision in measuring mass.

**Something to try**   Make your own equal arm balance using a coat hanger, two pie pans, and string. Hang the coat hanger on a hook so it swings freely. Attach the pie pans to the ends of the coat hanger with string. Adjust the pans so they are balanced. Place an object of known mass in one pan and something of unknown mass in the other. Can you estimate the mass of the object? How?

## Section 2 Review   Chapter 1

### Check Your Vocabulary

| | |
|---|---|
| 20°C | 60 L |
| 40°C | 200 L |
| 40 cm | 20 m |
| 100 g | 2 m$^3$ |
| 19 g/cm$^3$ | 300 mL |

*Match each measurement above with the numbered item most likely to have the value.*

 1. Length of a swimming pool
 2. Space inside a drinking glass
 3. Mass of an apple
 4. Temperature of a hot bath
 5. Temperature of a spring day
 6. Height of a seat
 7. Volume of water in a hot water heater
 8. Density of a gold ring
 9. Volume of gasoline that car tank can hold
10. Space inside a hall closet

### Check Your Knowledge

*Mutiple Choice: Choose the answer that best completes each of the following sentences.*

1. The mass of 50 mL of water is __?__.
   - a) 50 kg
   - b) 50 km
   - c) 50 mg
   - d) 50g

2. In the SI symbol km, the "m" stands for __?__.
   - a) minute
   - b) meter
   - c) milli-
   - d) metric

3. The SI unit for power is the watt (W). The symbol kW stands for __?__.
   - a) 1000 watts
   - b) 1000 meters
   - c) 1/1000 of a watt
   - d) 1/1000 of a meter

4. The SI symbol for cubic centimeter is __?__.
   - a) cc
   - b) cu cm
   - c) cm$^2$
   - d) cm$^3$

### Check Your Understanding

1. Why is it important for scientists in all countries to use the same system of measurement?

2. You are standing beside a high brick wall. You have no measuring instruments with you.
   - a. How could you estimate the height of a brick?
   - b. How could you measure the height of the wall indirectly?

3. a. How many small cubes 1 cm on a side fit along the side of a big cube 1 m on a side?
   - b. How many rows of the small cubes fit along the bottom of the big cube?
   - c. How many layers of the small cubes will fill up the big cube?
   - d. How many cubic centimeters equal one cubic meter?

4. A tank of water is being drained. The table shows the volume of water remaining after different times.

| Time (in s) | Volume of Water Remaining (in L) |
|---|---|
| 0 | 100 |
| 1 | 95 |
| 2 | 90 |
| 3 | 85 |
| 4 | 80 |
| 5 | 75 |
| 6 | 70 |

Make a graph of the data.
   - a. How long does it take to drain half of the water?
   - b. How long does it take to empty the tank?

### Practical Science

1. What property does an equal arm balance measure?

2. Where is the fulcrum of an equal arm balance located?

# Changes in Matter    Section 3

**Section 3 of Chapter 1 is divided into six parts:**

Changes in volume

Changes in phase

Changes in solubility

Chemical changes

Changes in mass and volume

Burning

*Practical Science: The Science of Baking*

### Learning Objectives

1. To distinguish between physical and chemical changes.

2. To predict the effect of changes in temperature on physical and chemical changes.

3. To recognize that even though substances are changed, mass remains unchanged in a chemical change.

4. To identify some common physical and chemical changes.

Figure 1-24. The photo shows iron rusting. The word *iron* is a label for a kind of matter. The word *rust* is a label for a change that happens to iron when it is exposed to air and moisture.

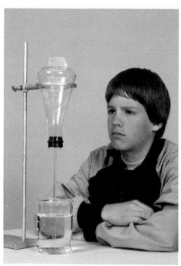

Figure 1-25. What causes the water level to move up and down in the glass tube?

Substances change. **Physical changes** are the changes in properties of a substance without a change in the substance. For example, ice melts and becomes liquid water. The ice and water are different forms of the same substance. When dry ice seems to disappear, it is changing directly to a gas. The dry ice and the gas formed are both the same substance, carbon dioxide. A balloon filled with air expands, or increases in volume, when heated. Salt and sugar seem to disappear when stirred into water. These are all physical changes.

### Changes in volume

A change in the volume of a substance is a physical change. The volume can be changed by changing the temperature.

The volume of a sample of air increases when its temperature increases. A decrease in temperature causes a decrease in volume. The results of temperature changes in air are shown in Figure 1-25. The flask is fitted with a one-hole rubber stopper. One end of a piece of glass tubing is inserted through the hole. The flask is turned upside down. The other end of the glass tubing is in a beaker of water. Air is trapped in the flask and in the glass tube. Then the air in the flask is warmed. The air expands, and some air is forced from the glass tube. Bubbles of air can be seen escaping into the water.

Cooling the flask with a few ice cubes reverses the result. The air contracts, or decreases in volume. Water moves up into the glass tube to fill the space left by the air.

Other gases also change volume with temperature change. They change in the same way as air does.

Liquids and solids also increase in volume when the temperature is increased. The changes in volume are not as easy to see as in gases. These changes, however, can be observed if you look carefully. Telephone and electric power lines sag on hot days. Cold temperatures cause them to tighten up.

Steel, too, changes in size as the temperature changes. You may have seen metal plates covering expansion joints on large bridges. The metal plates cover the openings that appear when the joints expand. Even though the volume changes in solids and liquids are small compared to gases, the changes are

## Activity 1–3A    Temperature and Air Volume

### Materials

jar or beaker          transparent tape
water                  test tube
food coloring          dishcloth
modeling clay          ice cubes
transparent
    drinking straw

### Purpose

To show how temperature changes affect the volume of a sample of air.

### Procedure

1. Fill the jar about halfway with water. Add several drops of food coloring and stir with the straw.
2. Let the straw rest on the bottom of the jar. Compare the water level in the straw with the water level in the jar. Record the data as you collect it.
3. Hold a test tube upside down over the top 4 to 5 cm of the straw. Keep the straw in the water to maintain the same water level and pack modeling clay tightly around the mouth of the test tube. Be sure to form an airtight seal. A sample of air is now trapped in the test tube.
4. Keep the bottom of the straw in the water and lift the test tube. Note the water level in the straw.
5. Now mark the water level in the straw by wrapping a piece of transparent tape around the straw. Place the top edge of the tape along the water level in the straw.
6. Put some ice in the dishcloth and press the cloth against the test tube to cool the air inside. Observe what happens to the water level in the straw.
7. Now let the straw rest on the bottom of the jar. Record the water level in the straw.
8. Put your hands around the test tube and warm the air sample. Record the water level in the straw.

### Questions

1. How does the water level in the straw compare to the water level in the jar when the straw is resting on the bottom of the jar?
2. After you form an airtight seal in the test tube, what happens to the water level in the straw when you lift the test tube?
3. What happens to the water level inside the straw when the air sample is cooled?
4. What happens to the volume of the air sample when it is cooled? Why?
5. When you warm the air sample with your hands, what happens to the water level inside the straw?
6. What happens to the volume of the air sample when it is warmed? Why?

### Conclusion

Explain how temperature changes affect the volume of an air sample.

Figure 1-26. What causes the two fastened strips to bend?

### Main Idea

What is a thermostat and how does it work?

Safety
Mercury is an extremely toxic substance. Any mercury spill, even the small amount in a thermometer, should be cleaned up with a mercury spill kit.

important. Engineers must plan for these changes or serious problems result.

Thermometers work because the volume of a substance changes when the temperature changes. The flask and tubing in Figure 1-25 could be used as a thermometer. The level of the water in the glass tubing could be marked with a temperature scale. In common thermometers, liquids such as mercury and alcohol are used to indicate temperature changes.

Some thermometers use the expansion and contraction of different metals. For example, devices to control heating and cooling are called **thermostats**. They consist of two strips of metal fastened together. The metals expand by different amounts for the same temperature change. As a result, the strips bend. As they bend, the strips act as a switch to turn on or off a heating or cooling unit.

### Check yourself

1. What happens to the volume of gases, liquids, and solids that are cooled?

2. Name two devices that work because a temperature change causes a change in volume.

## Changes in phase

A substance is classified as a solid, liquid, or gas at ordinary temperatures (around 20°C). It can change phase when its temperature changes. For example, water is a liquid at ordinary temperatures. When the temperature is lowered to 0°C, liquid water freezes, or changes to a solid (ice). When the temperature is increased to 100°C, liquid water boils, or changes to a gas. Water in the gas phase is known as **water vapor** (VAY′-per).

Other substances also change from one phase to another when their temperatures change. The phase of a substance depends on the temperature.

For any substance, **freezing** is the change in phase from liquid to solid. **Melting** is the reverse change, from solid to liquid. A pure substance will melt at a specific temperature. Water (ice) melts at 0°C. Lead melts at 327°C. Copper melts at 1083°C. The **melting point** does not change with the amount of the substance. Small amounts of ice melt at the same temperature as large amounts of ice. The melting point of a substance is a useful property in identifying the substance.

**Evaporation** (ih-vap′-uh-RAY′-shun) is the change in phase from liquid to gas. Some evaporation of a liquid takes place at any temperature. Water spilled on a desk top in an open room will soon dry up. The water changes from the liquid phase to the gas phase (water vapor). Warming a liquid speeds up evaporation.

**Condensation** (kon′-den-SAY′-shun) is the reverse change, from gas to liquid. Droplets of liquid water collect on a glass containing a cold drink. Where did these droplets come from? Water vapor in the air has condensed to a liquid on the cold surface. The cooling of a gas leads to condensation, and formation of a liquid.

When a liquid is heated to a high enough temperature, bubbles of gas of the same substance begin to form within the liquid itself. This process is called **boiling**. The **boiling point** is the temperature at which boiling begins. The boiling point, like the melting point, does not depend on the amount of the substance. Small amounts of a liquid boil at the same temperature as large amounts.

**Main Idea**

What is the reverse of freezing?

Figure 1-27. What caused the droplets of water to form on the outside of the glass?

Figure 1-28. If the temperature remains below 0°C, what can make the snow banks shrink in size?

### Data Search

The boiling point of a substance varies with elevation. How does the boiling point of water in Denver, Colorado compare to the boiling point of water in Vancouver, British Columbia? Search page 560.

### Main Idea

What phase of matter is not involved in sublimation?

The boiling point of water is 100°C. Other pure substances also have definite boiling points. Alcohol boils at 78°C. Mercury boils at 357°C. Boiling points vary with altitude, or height above sea level. The boiling point of a substance is usually given for locations at or near sea level.

**Sublimation** (sub′-lih-MAY′-shun) is the change from solid to gas or gas to solid without going through the liquid phase. Dry ice (solid carbon dioxide) is a familiar solid that sublimes. In the hottest weather, dry ice does not melt. Instead, it just seems to disappear. The solid carbon dioxide changes directly into a gas. Solid water in the form of ice and snow also sublimes. In cold, clear weather, snow banks will slowly disappear without melting. The snow changes directly into water vapor.

### Check yourself

1. What change is the reverse of melting?
2. What change is the reverse of condensation?
3. Explain why the melting and boiling points of a pure substance can be considered properties of the substance.

### Changes in solubility

Gases dissolve in water in varying amounts. The amount of a gas that dissolves depends on the kind of gas. Large amounts of carbon dioxide dissolve in water. Carbon dioxide is said to be very **soluble** (SOL′-yoo-bul) in water. Ammonia is also very soluble in water. Much smaller amounts of oxygen dissolve in water. Nevertheless, the small amounts of oxygen dissolved

---

**Activity 1–3B**        Dissolving Substances Faster

---

**Materials**
sugar cubes
2 250-mL beakers
100-mL graduated cylinder
watch or clock that measures seconds
water
hot plate
wire screen
2 thermometers
hot pad

**Purpose**

To show if a solid dissolves faster in hot water
or in cold water.

**Procedure**

1. Put 100 mL of cold water in each of the two
   beakers.
2. Place one of the beakers on the wire screen
   on the cold coil of the hot plate. Heat the
   water to boiling. SAFETY NOTE: Use the
   wire screen to prevent the beaker from
   breaking.
3. Using a hot pad, remove the beaker of
   boiling water from the heat. Immediately
   measure and record the temperature of
   both beakers. SAFETY NOTE: *Use care
   when handling a thermometer to avoid
   breaking it.*
4. Drop a sugar cube in each beaker. *Do
   not stir.*
5. Observe the beakers as the sugar dissolves. Record what happens in each beaker
   after (a) 30 seconds; (b) one minute; (c) two
   minutes.

**Questions**

1. After 30 seconds, what is the difference in
   the amount of sugar dissolved in the two
   beakers?
2. What is the difference in the amount of sugar
   dissolved in the two beakers after one minute? After two minutes?
3. What is the difference in the water temperature of the two beakers?
4. How does the temperature of the water affect
   the rate at which sugar dissolves?

**Conclusion**

What can you conclude about the effect temperature has on the rate at which a solid will
dissolve in water?

---

are important. Fish depend on the oxygen dissolved in water
just as land animals depend on oxygen from the atmosphere.

The amount of a gas that dissolves in water also depends
on the water temperature. Bubbles will form in cold water as
it warms up. This shows that warm water cannot hold as much
dissolved gas as cold water.

**Library research**

Find out the meaning of "hard"
and "soft" water. What does it
mean for water to be softened?
What methods are used to soften
water?

Carbonated beverages contain dissolved carbon dioxide gas. You may have tasted a carbonated beverage from a bottle left open in a warm room. How would you describe its taste? What has happened that affects the taste?

In some places water in streams and lakes is warmed by excess heat discarded by electric power plants. How does the warming of the water affect the amount of oxygen that remains dissolved? How might this change in temperature of the water affect the fish that live in the water?

The amount of a solid that dissolves in water depends both on the solid and on the water temperature. Unlike gases, most solids increase in solubility as the temperature increases.

The graph at the left compares the changes in solubility with temperature for several substances. Sodium chloride (table salt) is not much more soluble in hot water than in cold water. Potassium nitrate, on the other hand, is far more soluble in hot water than in cold water.

Deposits of minerals are found around geysers and hot springs. You may have visited locations where these are found. The hot water below the surface of the earth dissolves minerals in large quantities. The hot solution cools as it reaches the surface. The minerals are not as soluble in the cooler water. Some of the dissolved minerals leave the solution. More minerals are deposited as the water evaporates.

Sometimes you want to know not how much solid will dissolve but how fast it will. Suppose you were making iced tea for some people who liked sugar in it. To dissolve the sugar faster, should you put it in when the tea is still hot? Or should you add it after the ice cubes have cooled the tea?

The temperature of a liquid affects how fast a solid dissolves in it. At higher temperatures, most solids dissolve faster, as well as in greater amounts. Increasing the temperature increases the speed of dissolving of a solid.

Another way to increase the speed of dissolving is to break up the solid into smaller pieces. Granulated sugar will dissolve faster than a sugar cube. Superfine sugar will dissolve even faster. The smaller the particles, the more surface area is exposed to the liquid. Why does stirring the liquid speed up the dissolving process? Which kind of sugar would you choose for sweetening a cold drink?

Figure 1-29. How does temperature affect the solubility of solids in water?

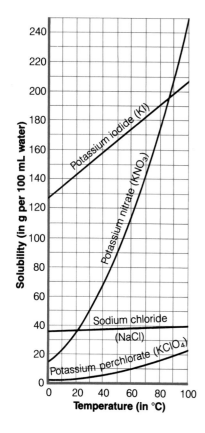

## Check yourself

1. Name two gases that are more soluble than oxygen is in water.

2. What effect does an increase in temperature have on the solubility of a gas in water?

3. Name two ways of making a solid dissolve more quickly in water.

Figure 1-30. What causes the build-up of mineral deposits around the edge of this hot spring?

## Chemical changes

The changes discussed so far have been physical changes. In physical changes, no new substances are formed.

**Chemical changes** are changes that produce new substances. For example, gasoline burns easily in air to form water and carbon dioxide. The properties of water and carbon dioxide are much different from those of gasoline. New substances have been formed. Iron rusts in air. The rust formed from iron crumbles and breaks apart. It no longer has the strength of the iron. A new substance has been formed. The change in cake batter as it bakes is a chemical change. The flour and other ingredients have been changed into new substances.

### Main Idea

How do chemical changes differ from physical changes?

## Activity 1–3C          Recognizing Chemical Changes

### Materials

safety goggles
2 test tubes
water
10 mL copper chloride ($CuCl_2$) solution
2 20-cm sections of wire
2 iron nails, each at least 4 cm in length
test tube rack
test tube holder
watch or clock with second hand

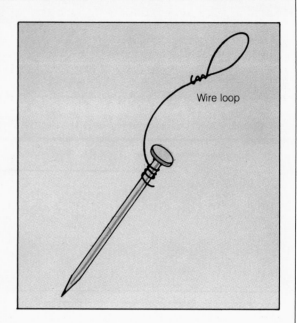

Wire loop

### Purpose

To determine when a chemical change has taken place.

### Procedure

1. Put on safety goggles.
2. Label one test tube "$CuCl_2$" and the other "water." Make a table like the one shown.
3. Fill one labeled test tube with 10 mL of the copper chloride ($CuCl_2$) solution. Fill the second labeled test tube three-quarters full of water. SAFETY NOTE: *Avoid touching the copper chloride. If you get any on your skin, wash the affected skin area with soap and water. If you get any in your eyes, flush them with large amounts of water.*
4. Wind a section of the wire securely around the nail. Leave enough wire to allow you to raise and lower the nail in the test tube.
5. Holding each nail by the wire, put the first nail halfway into the copper chloride solution for 30 seconds. Put the second nail halfway into the water for 30 seconds.
6. Remove the nails and record on the table any changes that took place on the two nails.
7. Unless directed otherwise, return the test tube with copper chloride to your teacher.

2. What happened to the nail dipped in the copper chloride solution for 30 seconds?
3. What evidence is there to show that new substances were formed when the nail was held in the copper chloride solution?
4. What kind of a change took place on the nail?
5. What happened to the nail that was put in plain water?
6. How do you know that the change in the first nail was not the rusting of wet iron?

|  | Description at start of experiment | Description after 30 seconds |
|---|---|---|
| Nail put in water |  |  |
| Nail put in copper chloride solution |  |  |

### Questions

1. What properties describe the copper chloride solution?

### Conclusion

Explain how you can recognize when a chemical change takes place in a substance.

Sometimes it is hard to tell whether a change is physical or chemical. Changes in properties accompany both kinds of change. When the changes in properties indicate that a new substance has been formed, a chemical change has taken place.

When paper burns, it gives off heat. The formation of new substances is often accompanied by the release of heat. The release of heat is sometimes used to help decide if a chemical change has taken place. However, some physical changes also release heat. Even in some chemical changes, the release of heat is slow and hard to detect. The heat released in the rusting of iron is not noticed. And some chemical changes produce a cooling effect rather than a release of heat.

Other clues indicate that a chemical change is happening. Suppose a solid or liquid is added to another liquid, and bubbles are produced. The bubbles indicate that a new substance, a gas, has formed. Another clue is the appearance of cloudiness when two clear liquids are mixed together. The cloudiness indicates that a new substance, a solid, has formed.

Figure 1-31. Why is it incorrect to say that this tablet is dissolving in the water?

### Check yourself

1. If two liquids are mixed together and bubbles are produced, what is happening?

2. If two clear liquids are mixed together and the mixture turns cloudy, what is happening?

### Changes in mass and volume

The volume of the new substances formed in a chemical change may be different from the volume of the original substances. When the chemical change results in the forming of a substance in a different phase, such as a gas, this is particularly true. The volume of the new substances may also be unchanged. Where the substances formed are in the same phase as the original substances, no change in volume may be noticed.

For a long time, scientists were not sure whether or not mass changes during a chemical change. Collecting the new substances formed was often a problem. Not until late in the eighteenth century was an acceptable answer found. Mass remains unchanged in a chemical change. New substances with new properties can be formed. But no gain or loss of mass can be detected.

### Check yourself

1. In a chemical change, how does the volume of the new substances compare to the volume of the original substances?

2. In a chemical change, how does the mass of the new substances compare to the mass of the original substances?

### Burning

Burning, or **combustion** (kum-BUS´-tyun), is a chemical change. Substances that will burn are said to be **combustible** (kum-BUS´-tih-bul). Some familiar combustible substances are paper, wood, coal, natural gas, and petroleum.

What changes accompany burning? Think about wood being burned in a fireplace or stove. Heat and light are released. Smoke is usually observed. The wood turns into ash. Only a small amount of ash is produced from a large supply of wood. These and other observations once led scientists to believe that a substance was released during burning. Substances that would burn were thought to contain this special substance. When burning took place, the special substance was thought to be released.

**Library research**

Find out the meaning of *spontaneous combustion.* Under what conditions does it occur? How can it be prevented?

Figure 1-32. A small fire in a kitchen may be stopped by covering it with baking soda. How does the baking soda prevent the fire from continuing?

Today burning is viewed as a combining of substances. The combustible substance combines with oxygen that is a part of the air. They combine in a chemical change that releases heat and light. Other new substances are produced as a result of the burning. Some are released into the air. When wood burns, ashes are only one of many new substances produced.

**Safety**
Be sure you know the location of the fire extinguisher in your classroom.

**Check yourself**

In burning, what substance combines with the combustible substance?

---

**Our Science Heritage**

The French scientist Antoine Lavoisier (1743–1794) changed the direction of chemical investigation. He used measurements to support his conclusions. He repeated his experiments many times with many different substances.

Prior to Lavoisier's work, it was believed that all burning things gave off something called *phlogiston*. Supposedly, only substances containing phlogiston would burn. The phlogiston that left a burning substance was absorbed by the surrounding air.

When burned, most substances lost mass. Some gained mass, however. Lavoisier wondered how a loss of phlogiston could cause a loss of mass sometimes and a gain in mass other times.

Lavoisier experimented with the burning of substances in air inside a closed container. He found that the change in mass of a substance after burning was always equal and opposite to the change in mass of the surrounding air. Lavoisier's explanation was that the burning substance combined with oxygen from the air. At the same time, if other gases were given off, they became part of the air.

Lavoisier did experiments that convinced others that the total mass of all the substances in a chemical reaction did not change. This result became the principle of conservation of mass.

Lavoisier's many contributions led to his being called the Father of Modern Chemistry.

**The Father of Modern Chemistry**

Antoine Lavoisier is observing mercury rise in the domed container. Air in the container is combining with the mercury being heated at his left.

# Practical Science

## The Science of Baking

Until about six thousand years ago, any kind of bread made from wheat flour was flat and hard. The leavened, or raised bread, was discovered probably by accident in the Near East. Leavened bread is light and filled with many holes. However, scientific understanding of leavened bread remained a mystery until a little more than 100 years ago.

### Leavening agents and the rising process
In the mid-19th century, Dr. Louis Pasteur solved the mystery with the discovery of yeast, a microscopic fungus that is a natural leavening agent.

Today, we still use yeast as a leavening agent for baked bread. We also use baking soda and baking powder as leavening agents in cakes, biscuits, and many other kinds of baked goods. These are known generally as quick breads. There are also other methods for getting bubbles in baked goods.

### How leavening agents work
Both physical and chemical processes are involved in the making of leavened breads. The physical processes involve mixing the ingredients, kneading the dough in the case of yeast breads, and baking the dough in an oven. The chemical processes involve the actions of the leavening agent and the hardening of the dough.

In raised breads, the leavening agent, yeast, reacts with the natural sugar in the wheat flour. The reaction forms carbon dioxide gas and alcohol. This reaction is called fermentation. The gas creates thousands of bubbles which cause the dough to expand or rise. The dough is kneaded to develop elastic strands formed by a substance called *gluten* in the wheat flour. Kneading the dough also evenly distributes the gas bubbles. The elastic strands of gluten allow the dough to rise without breaking, trapping the bubbles in the dough. The heat from baking the dough drives off the carbon dioxide and alcohol. The heat also sets the gluten, thereby fixing the bubbles in the dough.

In quick breads, the leavening agent, baking powder or baking soda, reacts during baking to create the carbon dioxide bubbles.

For baking soda to release carbon dioxide, an acid must be present. This can be sour milk, lemon juice or some other acid.

Baking powder is a mixture of baking soda and cream of tartar, along with other substances to control the reaction. The cream of tartar forms an acid when mixed with the liquids in the dough. This acid reacts with the baking soda to make carbon dioxide bubbles.

Raw dough          Baked dough

### Other ways to create bubbles in baked goods
Beaten egg whites contain thousands of tiny air bubbles. When these beaten egg whites are mixed into a batter and baked, they form a light, airy cake.

Steam generated during baking from the liquids in the batter creates the bubbles found in popovers. Usually, the bubbles are mostly large and not evenly distributed.

### Something to try
Use any quick bread recipe you like. Make three batches of the recipe. Use one half the listed amount of leavening in the first batch, twice as much leavening in the second batch, and the correct amount of leavening in the third batch. Compare the visible results after baking the three batches.

# Section 3 Review   Chapter 1

## Check Your Vocabulary

combustion            rusting

evaporation           sublimation

freezing              water vapor

melting

*Match each term above with the numbered phrase that best describes it.*

1. A physical change in which a liquid is formed
2. A chemical change in which the heat released is not noticeable
3. The burning of natural gas in a kitchen stove burner
4. The disappearance of dry ice
5. The gas phase of water
6. The drying up of water on a counter
7. The hardening of liquid copper when it cools to 1083°C

## Check Your Knowledge

*Multiple choice: Choose the answer that best completes each of the following sentences.*

1. _?_ is a physical change.
   a) The burning of paper
   b) The freezing of water
   c) The baking of bread
   d) The rusting of iron

2. The change of phase from gas to liquid is known as _?_.
   a) sublimation        c) evaporation
   b) freezing           d) condensation

3. As the temperature of water is increased, the solubility of _?_.
   a) both gases and solids increases
   b) both gases and solids decreases
   c) gases increases, while that of solids decreases
   d) gases decreases, while that of solids increases

4. All chemical changes are accompanied by _?_.
   a) a cooling effect
   b) new products
   c) explosions
   d) harmful effects

5. During all chemical changes, the _?_ remain(s) the same.
   a) temperature
   b) total volume
   c) total mass
   d) kinds of substances present

6. The volume of _?_ is most affected by temperature changes.
   a) gases              c) solids
   b) liquids            d) metals

## Check Your Understanding

1. Give three examples of changes in the volume of a substance that are caused by a temperature change.
2. How is the boiling of a liquid different from the evaporation of a liquid?
3. How does an increase in temperature affect the speed of dissolving?
4. What are some things to look for that will help you decide if a chemical change has taken place?

## Practical Science

1. Name three leavening agents used in baking.
2. When does fermentation occur in baking?
3. How does fermentation cause dough to rise?

# Chapter 1 Review

## Concept Summary

**Matter** is anything that has mass and takes up space.
□ Each substance, or kind of matter, has properties by which it is recognized.

The **classification of matter** is a grouping of matter according to its properties.
□ Substances can be put in order by differences in the same property.
□ Substances are classified as solids, liquids, or gases at ordinary temperatures; as metals or nonmetals; or as elements, compounds, or mixtures.
□ Elements are substances that cannot be broken down into other substances.
□ Compounds are substances made of two or more elements according to a fixed formula and have properties very different from those of the elements.

A **measurement** is an observation that describes the amount of a property and that includes both a number and a unit.
□ Measured values always include some error.
□ Graphing measurements can help reveal relationships between the quantities being measured.
□ Estimation can provide approximate measurements when direct measurement is impractical.
□ Very small or very large quantities can be measured indirectly.

A **physical change** is a change in which the properties of a substance change but no new substances are formed.
□ Substances generally increase in volume as their temperature increases.
□ The phase of a substance depends on the temperature of the substance.
□ Most solids become more soluble in water as the water temperature increases.
□ Breaking up a solid allows it to dissolve in a liquid more quickly.

A **chemical change** is a change in which one or more new substances are formed.
□ The total mass of substances before and after a chemical change does not change.
□ Burning is a chemical change that involves the combining of oxygen with another substance to produce new substances.

## Putting It All Together

1. Explain how two objects can have the same density but different masses.
2. What properties do paper and plastic share? What properties of paper and plastic are different?
3. How is classifying into groups different from classifying in order?
4. How are the properties of shape and volume used to distinguish among a solid, a liquid, and a gas?
5. What two properties could you use to decide whether or not a substance is a metal?
6. What property does a mixture have to have for it to be a solution?
7. In a solution of sugar dissolved in water, which substance is the solvent? Which substance is the solute?
8. What three important properties does a compound have that a mixture does not have?
9. How are the meter, kilometer, centimeter, and millimeter related to each other?
10. Name the basic SI units of length, mass, and time.
11. What can be done to reduce the effect of measurement errors?
12. Name three properties of a substance that can change when the temperature of the substance is changed.
13. How is a physical change different from a chemical change?
14. What property remains unchanged in all chemical changes?

## Apply Your Knowledge

1. Flour is sold by mass, not volume, even in the U.S., where recipes call for certain volume amounts of flour. Why is it fairer to sell flour by mass, rather than by volume?
2. Calculate the following, and show your calculations.
   a. How many centimeters are in a kilometer?
   b. How many millimeters are in 3.5 m?
   c. How many square centimeters are in a square meter?
   d. How many liters equal a cubic meter?
3. Estimate the number of basketballs that would be required to fill your classroom. Describe how you made your estimate.
4. Suppose you were given two unidentified samples and were asked to test whether they were made of the same substance.
   a. Name as many properties as you can that would have to be the same if the samples were of the same substance.
   b. Name as many properties as you can that could be different even if the samples were of the same substance.
5. Name three similarities between the dissolving of a solid in water and the melting of a solid.

## Find Out on Your Own

1. Interview a librarian in your school or public library. Find out what different systems are used to classify and locate books.
2. Examine a classification key used in biology or geology to identify plants, animals, or minerals. Describe the system used. What skills would you need to use such a key?
3. In a supermarket, make a list of the different sizes of bottles and/or cans of a single soft drink product. Record the stated volume (in L or mL) and the price for each size. Use your data to calculate the cost per milliliter for each size. (*Hint:* Divide the price by the volume of soft drink received for that price.)
4. Trap a soap bubble on the top of a flask or bottle. Warm the flask with your hands. What happens to the soap bubble? Cool the flask by placing it in cold water. What happens to the soap bubble?
5. An explosion is a very rapid chemical change. Conduct an interview with a firefighter or safety officer. Find out what precautions are taken to prevent the occurrence of an explosion.

## Reading Further

Arnov, Boris. *Water: Experiments to Understand It.* New York: Lothrop/Morrow, 1980
   Experiments to investigate 13 properties of water, including its ability as a solvent and the effects of evaporation are described.

Moore, William. *Metric Is Here!* New York: Putnam, 1974
   The history of the metric system and its use in sports, science, and industry is clearly explained.

O'Donnell, James J. *Fire! Its Many Faces and Moods.* New York: Messner, 1980
   The role of fire in ancient civilizations, how magicians use fire, and how to deal with forest fires and house fires are explained.

Paterson, Alan J. *How Glass Is Made.* New York: Facts on File, 1985
   This book explains the history of glassmaking, different varieties of glass, and the uses of glass.

Perrins, Lesley. *How Paper Is Made.* New York: Facts on File, 1985
   This interesting book explains how different kinds of paper are made and how to make your own paper.

# Chapter 2

# The Structure of Matter

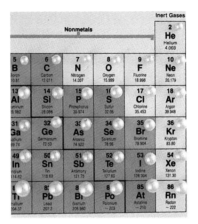

Section 1
## The Particle Model of Matter

The idea that all matter is made of very small particles can explain many observations of the behavior of matter. It can explain how elements, compounds, and mixtures differ from each other.

Section 2
## A Model of the Atom

The difference among elements can be explained by the idea that each element is made of a unique kind of particle. The uniqueness of each kind of particle can be explained by the idea that the particles are made of even smaller particles.

Section 3
## A Model for Chemical Compounds

The idea that matter is made of particles can be used to explain how elements combine to form compounds. It can also explain the behavior of certain groups of compounds known as acids and bases.

In this chapter you will learn how the behavior of matter can be explained. The perfume atomizer in the photo at the left is spraying perfume into the air. How does the perfume's scent travel to a person's nose?

# The Particle Model of Matter     Section 1

## Learning Objectives

1. To differentiate amount the science processes of observing, inferring, and hypothesizing.

2. To describe the nature of a scientific model and how a scientific model is developed and used.

3. To apply the particle model to the nature of matter.

4. To use the particle model of water to explain the differences in the properties of elements, compounds, and mixtures.

Figure 2-1. The structure of many solids is similar to a stack of oranges.

When you take notice of the properties of matter, you are making **observations**. You can use all five senses to make observations. But you probably use your sense of sight the most. For example, the shininess of metals or the dissolving of sugar in water can be seen. The ringing sound made by metal when struck can be heard. Grains of salt can be felt as well as seen.

Sometimes you extend your senses through the use of instruments. For example, you use a balance or a graduated cylinder. These instruments help you describe and compare the amounts of substances. A thermometer helps you describe temperatures and detect temperature changes. Instruments help you make better observations and measurements.

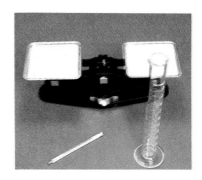

Figure 2-2. How do instruments help you make observations?

### The scientific method

Suppose you observe that the volume of a gas decreases when the gas is cooled. The same observation is made over and over again. Other observers make the same observation. They repeat the observation under different conditions. The observation might then be called a fact. A **fact** is an observation that has been confirmed by other observers in many different situations.

You may go beyond what you can observe and measure. You may suggest relationships to other observations. Suppose you do go beyond the observation. You suggest a relationship or possible cause. For example, you suggest that the change in volume is related to the change in temperature. You have then made an **inference** (IN′-fer-uns). You have **inferred** (in-FERD′) that the two changes are related.

Observations and inferences are often confused. You can observe the lowering of the temperature. You can observe the change in volume. You can observe that they occur at the same time. But when you suggest that the change in temperature *causes* the change in volume, you are making an inference.

You can observe sugar disappearing when it is stirred into water. If the water evaporates away, you can observe grains of sugar remaining in the container. You infer that the sugar was in the water the entire time.

**Main Idea**

How does making an inference differ from making a simple observation?

Figure 2-3. Use the hypothesis that sugar and water are made of tiny particles to explain how sugar dissolves.

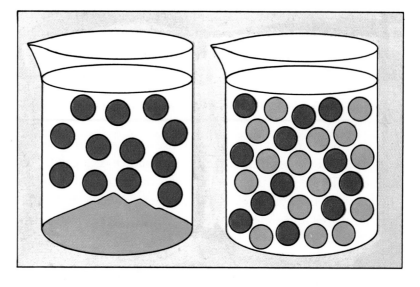

Figure 2-4. Facts and experiments depend on observations. Hypotheses and theories depend on inferences. Experiments make new facts available so that a hypothesis can be refined. A thoroughly tested hypothesis is a theory.

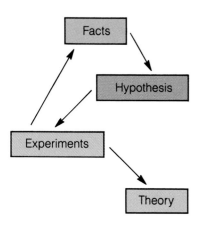

How can the dissolving of sugar in water be explained? Scientists may guess at explanations, but they have to check that they fit the facts. For example, a good explanation is that both sugar and water are made of very tiny particles. The particles are much too small to be seen even under a microscope. When sugar dissolves, it breaks up into particles. The sugar particles fit in between the water particles. So the solution can taste sweet even though the sugar cannot be seen.

An explanation based on a group of observations or facts is called a **hypothesis** (hi-POTH′-uh-sis). A hypothesis must be tested many times before it can become accepted. Such testing is often referred to as the scientific method. The **scientific method** is a way of solving problems by developing and testing hypotheses. To test a hypothesis, a controlled experiment must be used, where all conditions, or **variables**, remain the same except for one.

Hot water expands and takes up more space. Does more sugar dissolve in it? The hypothesis can be tested. The water temperature is the variable. If more sugar dissolves in hot water then the hypothesis is supported. When the particles of water move further apart, there must be more space for sugar particles. However, this does not prove for certain that the hypothesis is correct. Many more tests must be performed. Eventually, if the hypothesis is supported many times, it becomes a theory. A **theory** is a way of explaining a certain set of observations, based on considerable testing. But theories are not proved completely. They are sometimes changed by new evidence.

Theories are often developed through the following steps.

1. Recognizing a problem.
2. Selecting a hypothesis.
3. Testing the hypothesis.
4. Revising the hypothesis to agree with experimental results.

### Check yourself

1. Describe the difference between an observation and a fact.
2. Describe the difference between a fact and an inference.
3. Describe the scientific method.

### Particles of matter

The hypothesis that matter is made of particles must be tested and expanded to become a theory. It must explain how there can be different phases of matter. It must explain how there can be elements, compounds, and mixtures. It must explain physical and chemical changes.

In addition to further testing, a hypothesis is expanded by making more inferences from further observations. Observations of gases are helpful. For example, add air to a balloon. Can you fill the balloon with air? Keep adding air until the balloon seems ready to burst. Release the air from the balloon. You can get some idea of how much air was inside. A lot of air can be forced into a small space.

Large amounts of gas can be forced into a small space. This property of gases is called **compressibility**. Gases are very compressible. Liquids and solids cannot be compressed easily. They strongly resist being pushed into smaller spaces.

From these observations, you can infer that there is empty space between the tiny particles of a gas. When a gas is compressed, the particles are pushed closer together. You can infer that the particles in liquids and solids must be much closer together than in gases.

Figure 2-5. What can be inferred about the spacing between particles in gases and in liquids?

**Activity 2–1A** Compressibility of Air and Water

**Materials**

clear soft plastic bottle with cap
water

**Purpose**

To find which can be compressed more easily—air or water.

**Procedure**

1. Put the cap tightly on the "empty" plastic bottle.
2. Squeeze the bottle with your hands. Note whether or not it takes up less space (compresses).
3. Fill the bottle to the top with water and replace the cap tightly.
4. Squeeze the bottle and note how easy or difficult it is to compress.
5. Now pour out half of the water and replace the cap tightly.
6. Hold the bottle upright and predict what will happen if you squeeze the bottle below the water line. Then squeeze it and record your observation on a table like that shown.
7. Now predict what will happen if you squeeze the bottle above the water line. Then squeeze it and write down your observations.

**Questions**

1. What filled the "empty" bottle?
2. Could you compress the "empty" bottle after you put the cap on? Why?
3. Could you compress the bottle when it was filled with water and tightly capped? Why?
4. What happened to the water level of the half-filled bottle when you squeezed below the water line? Why?
5. What happened to the water level of the half-filled bottle when you squeezed above the water line? Why is there a difference?
6. In what way did your predictions about what would happen to the water level of the half-filled bottle differ from what you actually observed?

| Half-filled bottle | Prediction | Observation |
|---|---|---|
| Squeezed below water line | | |
| Squeezed above water line | | |

**Conclusion**

Explain how you can determine if there is space between the particles of a liquid or a solid.

**Main Idea**

When two substances are mixed together, is the volume of the mixture equal to the sum of the individual volumes?

Alcohol and water can be mixed together. The volume of the alcohol-water mixture is less than the sum of the individual volumes. For instance, if 50 mL of alcohol is mixed with 100 mL of water, the volume of the mixture is less than 150 mL. You can infer that there must be some space between the particles in a liquid. The dissolving of a solid in a liquid adds additional evidence. The particles of the solid must be able to move between the particles of the liquid.

A particle picture of matter seems consistent with observations. The particles must be very tiny. And they can move through very tiny openings.

When water is added to a clay flowerpot, the outside of the pot becomes damp. Water inside the clay pot moves to the outside through tiny openings in the clay.

Have you ever tried to save a filled balloon? The balloon eventually deflates. The air finds its way out through tiny openings in the material of the balloon.

There must be space between the particles of matter. The amount of space between particles must be greater in gases than in liquids and solids. This part of the hypothesis explains how gases are more easily compressed.

### Check yourself

1. Give two examples of evidence that supports the inference that there is space between the particles of matter.

2. Give two examples of evidence that supports the inference that the particles of matter are very tiny.

Figure 2-6. Explain why it is not a good idea to put a clay flowerpot and saucer directly on a wood floor.

### Particles called atoms

Matter can be classified as belonging to one of the following groups: elements, compounds, or mixtures. Elements are substances that cannot be broken down any further. Compounds are formed from elements and can be broken down into elements. The elements that form a compound have different properties from the compound. Also, the elements in a compound are combined according to a definite formula. Mixtures include two or more substances with the amounts of each varying. Substances in a mixture are more easily separated than the substances in a compound. How can a particle picture of matter explain these differences in substances?

John Dalton (1766–1844) was a British teacher who thought of a hypothesis that explained how particles formed elements, compounds, and mixtures. The idea that matter was made of particles had been introduced over 2000 years earlier by the Greeks. Dalton called his particles **atoms** (AT′-umz) after the Greek word for *indivisible*. In other words, Dalton believed that atoms were the smallest particles of matter possible and could not be broken up.

### Library research

Read about the life of John Dalton. Write a report about him, and present it to the class.

## Activity 2–1B        Space Between Particles

### Materials

marbles (enough to fill a 250-mL beaker)
sand
water
3 250-mL beakers

### Purpose

To show that there is space between the particles in a liquid or a solid.

### Procedure

1. Put 250 mL of marbles in a beaker.
2. Put 250 mL of sand in a second beaker.
3. Put 250 mL of water in a third beaker.
4. Observe how much of the space is taken up in each of the three beakers.
5. Add sand from the second beaker to the beaker of marbles. Mix the sand and marbles carefully to get as much sand as possible up to the 250-mL line. Measure the volume of sand left in the second beaker and record the data.
6. Now slowly add water from the third beaker to the beaker containing the sand and marbles. Measure the volume of water left in the third beaker and record the data.

### Questions

1. Before adding other materials, how much of the space is filled in the first beaker? Explain your answer.
2. How much sand did you add to the first beaker?
3. Explain how you can determine whether or not there is space in the first beaker after adding sand to the marbles.
4. How much water did you add to the first beaker?

### Conclusion

Explain how you can determine if there is space between the particles of a liquid or a solid.

Dalton suggested that each element consists of only one kind of atom. All the atoms of one element are alike. But the atoms of one element are different from the atoms of another element. Each element is made of its own kind of atom.

Dalton explained how compounds were formed from atoms. He said that atoms of one element combined with atoms of one or more other elements. For example, he said that water was made of particles that were combinations of hydrogen atoms and oxygen atoms. All water particles were the same. This explained why a compound always formed according to a definite formula.

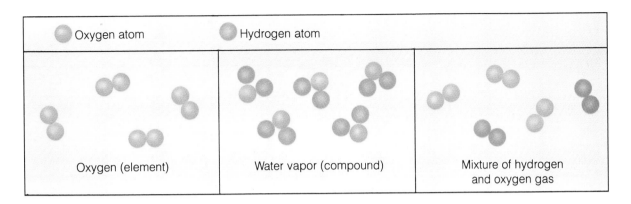

According to Dalton, a mixture, too, was made of two or more kinds of atoms. But the different kinds of atoms were not joined tightly together as in a compound. The number of one kind of atom could be changed without affecting the other atoms. This explained how varying amounts of substances could form a mixture. It also explained what made it easier to separate mixtures.

Dalton developed his hypothesis after making many observations of the behavior of gases in physical and chemical changes. Observations made since Dalton's time have shown that some of his details were incorrect. But his overall picture of particles of matter is still used today.

Figure 2-7. The atoms in an element, compound, and mixture. What is the difference between the particles in an element and in a compound? In a compound and in a mixture?

### Check yourself

How did Dalton explain the difference between elements and compounds?

### Element names and symbols

More than twenty elements had been identified when Dalton proposed his hypothesis. Just over a hundred elements are now known. The names of the elements have many different origins. Some elements are named for their properties. For example, hydrogen means *water former*. Hydrogen gas burns in air to form water. Bromine means *stench*. Bromine has a very disagreeable odor.

Some elements discovered after Dalton's time include germanium, californium, europium, and indium. Do you recognize the locations they are named after? Helium was first discovered by studying sunlight. Its name comes from the Greek word *helios*, meaning *sun*.

### Library research

Find out the meanings of the names of as many different elements as you can.

Dalton represented the different kinds of atoms by symbols he invented. He used circles filled in with different designs or letters. Some of Dalton's symbols for the elements are shown in Figure 2-8.

The number of known elements increased. The names for some of the elements were different in different countries. It became important that everyone agree on at least a common symbol for each element.

The symbols in use today are accepted by all countries. An element is represented by one or two letters. The first letter used is always capitalized. The second letter (when used) is always a lower-case letter.

The letters are chosen from the name of the element. The symbol for the element hydrogen is H. The symbol for the element helium is He. The element sodium takes its symbol, Na, from its Latin name, natrium.

Figure 2-8. Some of Dalton's symbols for the elements known during his time. Would such symbols be convenient today? Explain.

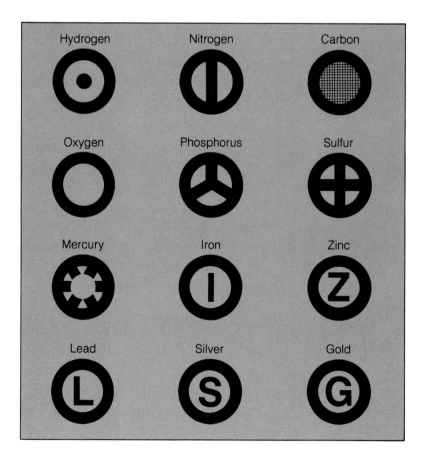

| Name | Symbol | Name | Symbol |
|------|--------|------|--------|
| aluminum | Al | mercury | Hg |
| arsenic | As | neon | Ne |
| bromine | Br | nickel | Ni |
| calcium | Ca | nitrogen | N |
| carbon | C | oxygen | O |
| chlorine | Cl | phosphorus | P |
| chromium | Cr | platinum | Pt |
| copper | Cu | potassium | K |
| fluorine | F | radium | Ra |
| gold | Au | silicon | Si |
| helium | He | silver | Ag |
| hydrogen | H | sodium | Na |
| iodine | I | sulfur | S |
| iron | Fe | tin | Sn |
| lead | Pb | tungsten | W |
| lithium | Li | uranium | U |
| magnesium | Mg | zinc | Zn |

Table 2-1. Names and symbols of some common elements.

The names and symbols of some common elements are given in Table 2-1. Which symbols do you think are based on the Latin name of the element?

## Check yourself

How do some elements happen to have symbols that are not the first letter of the name of the element?

## Models

Scientists often try to describe something unfamiliar in terms of familiar things. Such descriptions are called **models**. We can picture atoms as behaving much like small balls or marbles. This model of atoms can be used to explain the difference between solids, liquids, and gases.

**Main Idea**

What method do scientists often use to describe unfamiliar things?

A scientific model develops as the result of many observations, inferences, and hypotheses. The hypotheses have been tested and revised. Some have been discarded. The model must agree with observations. It is used to make predictions. As long as the model can be used to explain observations and make good predictions, it is used. Like a hypothesis, a model can never be proved correct. When it contradicts observations, it may be revised or discarded for a new or better model.

The model scientists use today to represent the atom is more complex than simple balls. The ball model is not consistent with all observations. Very likely, today's model of the atom will change, too. That is the nature of a scientific model. If a model is not consistent with new and old observations, it must change.

**Check yourself**

What is a scientific model?

**A model for elements**

Iron, copper, and lead are among the elements that are solids at normal temperatures. A model for the arrangement of atoms in a solid element is shown in Figure 2-9. The atoms are represented by oval balls. The balls are very close together in a regular pattern.

Other elements in the solid phase would be represented in much the same way. The atoms might be different in size. They might be packed together in a slightly different pattern. But the general picture would be similar.

Figure 2-9. Model of the arrangement of atoms in a solid element.

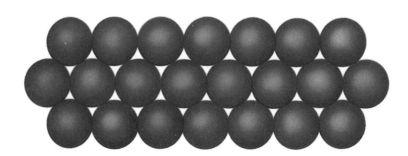

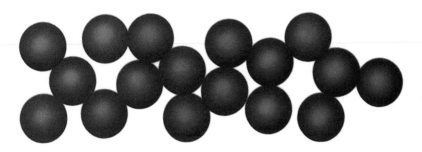

Figure 2-10. Model of the arrangement of atoms in a liquid element.

Mercury is among the elements that are liquids at normal temperatures. A model for the arrangement of atoms in a liquid element is shown in Figure 2-10. Although the balls are close together, they are not arranged in a regular pattern. In a liquid element, the atoms are free to move past each other. Thus, a liquid can take the shape of its container and can be poured. In a solid element, on the other hand, the atoms stay in the same location. This allows a solid to keep its shape.

Helium, neon, and oxygen are among the elements that are gases at normal temperatures. Figure 2-11 shows a model for the arrangement of atoms in a gas like helium. The spaces between the balls are much bigger than the balls themselves. The balls are free to move in all directions.

**Data Search**

Name three elements that melt between 0°C and 100°C. Search page 559.

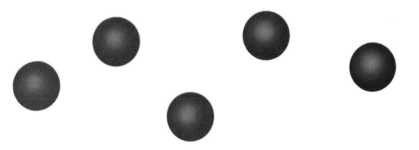

Figure 2-11. Model of the arrangement of atoms in a gaseous element like helium.

The simple model of solid, liquid, and gaseous elements does not fit all elements. Some elements seem to be made of particles containing more than one atom each. As the particles get moved, the atoms inside remain together. For example, the gas oxygen has particles that contain two oxygen atoms. So do the gases hydrogen, nitrogen, fluorine, and chlorine. And so do the liquid element bromine and the solid element iodine.

The particles with more than one atom are called **molecules** (MOL′-uh-kyoolz). Molecules with two atoms are called **diatomic** (dī′-uh-TOM′-ik) molecules. In a diatomic gas, the

**Main Idea**

How do molecules differ from atoms?

## Library research

Read about the current state of the ozone in the atmosphere. Is there still concern that the amount of ozone is decreasing, or does the problem seem to be under control? Is there disagreement about the seriousness of the problem?

Figure 2-12. The label on this can lets consumers know that this product will not destroy the ozone in the atmosphere.

molecules act like the single atoms in a gas like helium. Sometimes it is convenient to think of helium atoms as molecules with one atom each. Then you can think of all gases as made of molecules.

The symbol for oxygen gas is written $O_2$. The small number to the lower right indicates that there are two atoms of oxygen in every oxygen molecule. The symbol for hydrogen gas is $H_2$. What is the symbol for nitrogen gas?

Another form of oxygen is found in small amounts in the earth's atmosphere. It is made of molecules that have three oxygen atoms each. The symbol is $O_3$. This form of oxygen is given the special name of **ozone** (Ō′-zōn). Ozone absorbs dangerous rays from the sun. These rays are capable of causing skin cancer. Without the ozone, more of these rays could reach the earth. Increases in skin cancer would result from a decrease in ozone.

Certain chemicals react with ozone. These chemicals were used in some spray cans. Scientists were afraid that the amount of ozone could be decreased. Restrictions have been placed on the use of these chemicals. High-altitude jet aircraft may also be capable of affecting the amount of ozone. Their effect is being studied.

Phosphorus is a solid at normal temperatures. Phosphorus is made of molecules that have four atoms each. The symbol for solid phosphorus is $P_4$. Solid sulfur can have eight atoms in a molecule. The symbol for solid sulfur is $S_8$.

### Check yourself

1. How do the molecules of helium differ from the molecules of oxygen?

2. What is the difference in the way the atoms are grouped in ordinary oxygen and in ozone?

### A model for compounds

Compounds are special combinations of two or more different kinds of elements. Water is pictured as a combination of the elements hydrogen and oxygen. The smallest particle of

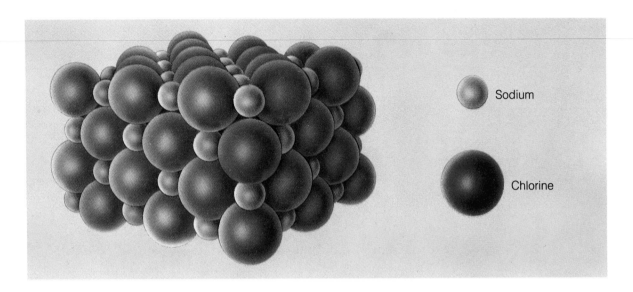

water is a water molecule. A water molecule consists of two atoms of hydrogen and one atom of oxygen. The three atoms are held tightly together. The formula for water is $H_2O$. This formula shows that there are two atoms of hydrogen for every atom of oxygen. The formula for carbon dioxide is $CO_2$. Sugar (sucrose) has a more complicated molecule. The formula for sucrose is $C_{12}H_{22}O_{11}$. How many atoms of hydrogen are in a molecule of sucrose?

The molecules of water are all the same. Similarly, the molecules of carbon dioxide are all the same. Molecules of a single compound are all alike.

Molecules do not change when a compound changes phase. The molecules of solid water (ice) are the same as the molecules of liquid water or of water vapor. Only the arrangement and movement of the molecules changes.

Some compounds are not made up of molecules. Sodium chloride (table salt) is one example. The compound is made from the elements sodium and chlorine. For every atom of sodium, there is one atom of chlorine. The formula for salt is written as NaCl. However, no molecule of sodium chloride exists. Instead, the atoms of sodium and chlorine are locked together in an alternating pattern.

Figure 2-13. Compounds such as sodium chloride are not made of molecules.

### Check yourself

1. How many atoms of carbon are in one molecule of sucrose?

2. Give an example of a compound that is not made of molecules.

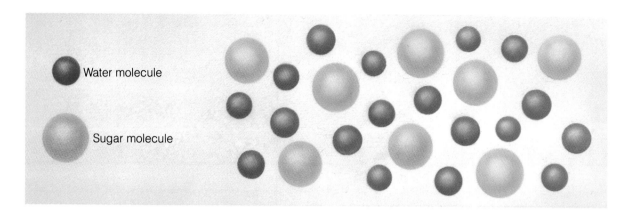

Figure 2-14. How is the model for a mixture different from that of a compound?

Water molecule

Sugar molecule

## A model for mixtures

In a mixture, the numbers of particles of each of the different substances can vary. The different particles are not held together tightly as in a compound. A mixture of sugar and water is pictured in Figure 2-14. The molecules of sugar are scattered among the molecules of water. More molecules of sugar can easily be added.

Clean air is a mixture. Molecules of oxygen and nitrogen make up most of this mixture. Molecules of water vapor are there in varying amounts. There are also molecules of carbon dioxide and several other gases.

Solids, liquids, and other gases can all mix with clean air and pollute it. For example, smoke consists mostly of bits of solid carbon. The carbon bits are collections of carbon atoms. Car engines give off gases such as carbon monoxide and nitrogen dioxide. These gases contribute to the haze in the air known as smog.

In a solid mixture, atoms or molecules of two different substances are mixed together. Even though they are not free to move about, as in a gas or liquid, there is no fixed recipe. This is what makes a solid mixture different from a compound. For example, in carbon steel, carbon atoms are mixed among iron atoms. In stainless steel, chromium and manganese atoms are mixed among iron atoms. Mixtures of metals are called **alloys** (AL′-oyz). Brass is another common alloy. It is a mixture of copper atoms and zinc atoms.

**Main Idea**

What are mixtures of metals called?

### Check yourself

Give two examples of mixtures that contain different kinds of molecules.

# Practical Science

## Water for Life

Water is vital to life. Without it, humans, animals, and birds will die within a few days. The water you drink is part of a cycle powered by the sun. The sun evaporates vast amounts of water from the oceans. This water vapor cools and condenses to form clouds. The clouds become increasingly heavy, and eventually drop their moisture in the form of rain and snow.

Some of the water runs off the land and forms rivers and lakes. This water is called *surface water*. The remaining water from the rain and snow is absorbed by the ground. This is called *ground water*. Drinking water comes from both sources.

**Types of pollutants**  Water is pure when it evaporates from the oceans into the air. From then on it is exposed to contaminating pollutants. Some of these are human and animal waste products. Other pollutants are produced by chemical manufacturing and processing plants. Sediments from building and road construction, are also water pollutants.

**Effects of pollutants**  Surface water is affected by all types of pollutants. Ground waters are cleaned naturally of sediments and organic pollutants by dirt, sand, and gravel. These substances work as a sieve to filter out solid pollutants. Unfortunately, they do not remove toxic substances that are dissolved in the water.

The effects of water pollutants on all forms of life can be devastating. Human and animal wastes can cause cholera, typhus and other diseases. These diseases kill thousands of people every year. Toxic waste materials can cause birth defects and cancer.

Another major source of waste is water discharged from sewage plants into the oceans. However, this water may be made safe to drink if harmful materials are removed.

**Water treatment**  In a water treatment plant, water first passes through several types of filters to remove solid pollutants. Next, chlorine is added to the water to kill harmful living organisms. Then the water is sprayed into the air to add oxygen to it. Water polluted with toxic wastes needs further treatment.

**Sewage treatment**  In a sewage treatment plant, raw sewage is first ground up to break up the solid matter. Next it is mixed with bacteria-rich water and oxygen. As the sewage is agitated, the bacteria change potentially harmful organic matter into harmless material. Most of this material settles out and is disposed of. The remaining water is filtered through large masses of sand and treated with chlorine to kill any remaining bacteria.

**Something to try**  After a rainstorm, collect some water from a puddle in a jar. Label the jar "rainwater" and cover it with a lid. Then put some water from your kitchen tap in a jar. Label the jar "tap water" and cover it with a lid. Compare the color and clarity of the water in both jars. Why might they be different? Why is tap water safe to drink?

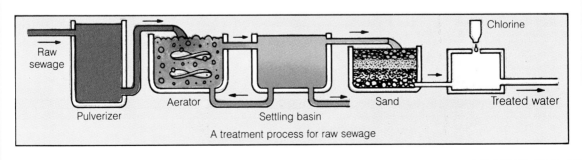

A treatment process for raw sewage

# Section 1 Review   Chapter 2

## Check Your Vocabulary

alloy                    inference

fact                     molecule

hypothesis               ozone

scientific method

*Match each term above with the numbered phrase that best describes it.*

1.  An element with three atoms in each molecule

2.  Explanation that can be used to make predictions

3.  The smallest particle of sugar

4.  Stainless steel

5.  Statement that relates observations

6.  Statement that sums up observations

7.  A way of solving problems

## Check Your Knowledge

*Mutiple Choice: Choose the answer that best completes each of the following sentences.*

1.  Of the following statements, the one that would be an inference rather than an observation is __?__.
    a) Ice melts at 0°C.
    b) Ice floats in water.
    c) Ice sinks in alcohol.
    d) If a solid sinks in a liquid, it is heavier than an equal volume of the liquid.

2.  A hypothesis __?__.
    a) can be tested
    b) is likely to be correct
    c) has been proved correct
    d) cannot be changed

3.  A substance made up of only one kind of atom is a(n) __?__.
    a) mixture          c) compound
    b) element          d) alloy

4.  The present-day international symbols for the elements are made up of __?__.
    a) circles with designs or letters inside
    b) the first letter of the name of the element
    c) two letters for every element
    d) either one or two letters

## Check Your Understanding

1.  List three observations that support the hypothesis that matter is made of tiny particles.

2.  Use the particle model to explain the difference between liquid water and water vapor.

3.  Use the particle model to explain how mixtures are different from compounds.

4.  The Spanish word for silver is *plata*, while the French word is *argent*. How is the use of the symbol Ag in all countries like the use of SI symbols of measurement?

5.  The formula for carbon dioxide is $CO_2$. Draw a model of a carbon dioxide molecule. Use different colored circles for each kind of atom. Be sure to explain your color scheme.

6.  Dalton thought that hydrogen and oxygen were made of individual atoms not joined together. He also thought that a water molecule had one atom each of hydrogen and oxygen. Draw a model that shows Dalton's idea of a) the element oxygen; b) the compound water vapor; and c) a mixture of hydrogen and oxygen gases.

## Practical Science

1.  How can water be made fit to drink?

2.  How can raw sewage be treated so that it will not pollute lakes and streams?

# A Model of the Atom   Section 2

**Section 2 of Chapter 2 is divided into five parts:**

Atomic mass

The periodic table of Mendeleev

The modern periodic table

Particles within the atom

Atomic models

*Practical Science:*

*Lighting Up the Night with Neon*

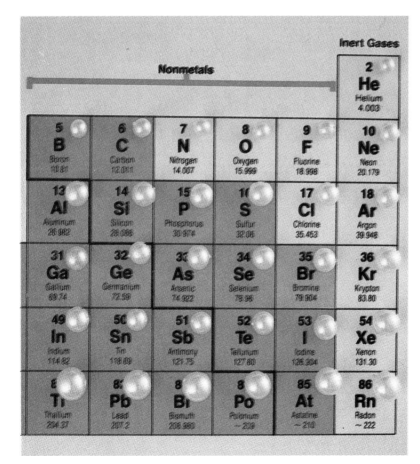

## Learning Objectives

1. To use the periodic table to identify elements with similarities in properties.

2. To describe the arrangement of protons, neutrons, and electrons in the atoms of the elements.

3. To relate the properties of the elements to the arrangement of the electrons in the atoms of the different elements.

Figure 2-15. The periodic table contains information on atoms of each of the elements. It also organizes the elements so that those with similar properties are close to each other.

Elements differ in their properties. At room temperature, some are gases, while others are solids or liquids. Some, such as oxygen, combine with many other elements to form compounds. Others, such as helium, rarely form compounds. Some, such as copper, conduct electricity. Others, such as sulfur, do not.

If the elements differ in properties, it is likely that their atoms differ also. A study of the properties of the elements has led to mental pictures of what the atoms are like.

## Atomic mass

A property of all matter is mass. Matter is made up of atoms. Therefore, all atoms must have mass.

Oxygen combines with many other elements. For example, oxygen combines with hydrogen. Eight grams of oxygen combines with one gram of hydrogen to form water. Oxygen combines with carbon to form carbon dioxide. Eight grams of oxygen combines with three grams of carbon. Oxygen combines with sulfur to form sulfur dioxide. Eight grams of oxygen combines with eight grams of sulfur. The same mass of oxygen combines with different masses of other elements.

Figure 2-16. In these compounds containing oxygen, the same mass of oxygen is combined with different masses of other elements.

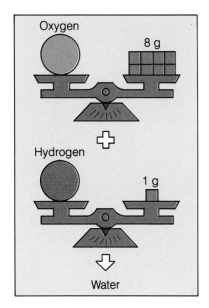

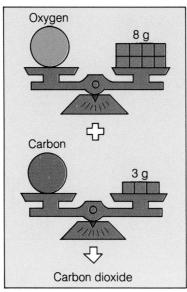

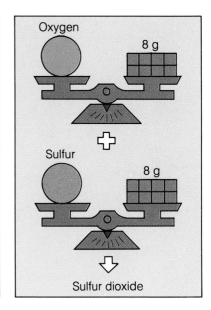

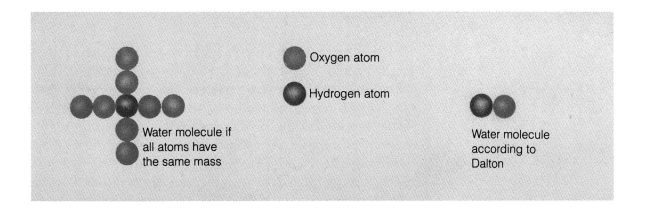

Suppose all atoms have the same mass. In water, the mass of the oxygen is eight times the mass of the hydrogen. There would have to be eight oxygen atoms for each hydrogen atom in a water molecule. Similarly, in carbon dioxide, there would have to be eight oxygen atoms for every *three* carbon atoms. And in sulfur dioxide, there would be equal numbers of oxygen and sulfur atoms.

Dalton thought that each molecule had the smallest possible number of atoms. He rejected the idea that a water molecule had eight atoms of oxygen and one of hydrogen. Instead, he assumed it had one atom of oxygen and one of hydrogen. Then the atoms would have to have different masses.

Evidence discovered after Dalton's time showed he was right about different masses for different kinds of atoms. But he was not completely right about water molecules. Each molecule actually has two hydrogen atoms and one oxygen atom. So the mass of an oxygen atom is 16 times the mass of a hydrogen atom.

Many measurements were made of the masses of elements that combine with each other to form compounds. The results of these measurements led to a table of masses for an atom of each different element. The mass of one atom of an element is called the **atomic mass** of the element.

Figure 2-17. If all atoms had the same mass, a water molecule would have eight oxygen atoms and one hydrogen atom. Dalton assumed a water molecule had one atom each of oxygen and hydrogen.

**Main Idea**

What is the mass of an oxygen atom, compared to the mass of a hydrogen atom?

**Check yourself**

Who developed the hypothesis that different kinds of atoms each have different masses?

**Main Idea**

What are groups of elements with similar properties called?

**Data Search**

Which element has the greater atomic mass, magnesium or sodium? Search page 559.

### The periodic table of Mendeleev

As scientists become more familiar with the elements, they began to look for similarities. They noticed groups of elements that had similar properties. For example, fluorine, chlorine, bromine, and iodine all react very easily with metals. The compounds they form with each metal have similar formulas. The formulas for the compounds of the metal magnesium are $MgF_2$, $MgCl_2$, $MgBr_2$ and $MgI_2$. The formulas for the compounds of the metal sodium are NaF, NaCl, NaBr, and NaI. Groups of elements with similar properties are called **families**. Fluorine, chlorine, bromine, and iodine are in the same family.

Scientists searched for ways to classify all the elements in one system. Many different arrangements were tried. Dmitri Mendeleev (MEN´-de-lay-ev) (1834–1907), a Russian scientist, developed a classification system in 1869 that, with some changes, is still used today.

Mendeleev first arranged all the known elements in order of increasing atomic mass. Hydrogen had the smallest atomic mass, so it was first. He compared additional properties of each of the elements. Then he made a chart that looked something like a monthly calendar.

Figure 2-18. What do the dates April 5, 12, 19, and 26 have in common?

| S | M | T | W | TH | F | S |
|---|---|---|---|----|---|---|
| | | | | | 1 | 2 |
| 3 | 4 | 5 | 6 | 7 | 8 | 9 |
| 10 | 11 | 12 | 13 | 14 | 15 | 16 |
| 17 | 18 | 19 | 20 | 21 | 22 | 23 |
| 24 | 25 | 26 | 27 | 28 | 29 | 30 |

APRIL

On a calendar, the days of the month are in numerical order. But dates for the same day of the week are in the same column. In Mendeleev's chart, the elements in the same family were in the same column.

Every seventh day on a calendar falls on the same day of the week. Mendeleev found a similar pattern of repeating properties among the elements. Things that repeat according to a pattern are said to be periodic. Mendeleev's chart is called the **periodic table** because it shows a periodic pattern for the elements.

### Check yourself

How did Mendeleev arrange the elements in his periodic table?

### The modern periodic table

A modern periodic table of the elements is shown in Table 2-2. It is something like a calendar with weeks that are not all the same length. The atomic mass of each element is given in units called **atomic mass units** (symbol u). It takes over 600 000 000 000 000 000 000 000 (6 with 23 zeroes after it) atomic mass units to make one gram. Atomic masses are extremely small!

The elements in the far right-hand column were unknown during Mendeleev's time. These elements form very few compounds. They are not likely to react with other elements. They are all gases at ordinary temperatures. Because of these properties, they are called the **inert** (ih-NERT´), or **noble gases.** The word *inert* means *unreactive.* It is to Mendeleev's credit that this new family fit easily into his table.

The elements just to the left of the inert gases are the **halogens** (HAL´-uh-jenz). The word *halogen* means *salt former.* The elements in this family form compounds known as salts when they combine with elements from the left-hand side of the periodic table. You are familiar with the compound sodium chloride, or table salt. Other salts can also be formed. Which elements are members of the halogen family?

**Main Idea**

What family of elements was overlooked by Mendeleev?

**Table 2–2.**

# Periodic Table of the Elements

The **period** number tells how many occupied energy levels are in each atom of the element.

Elements with the same **group** number are in the same family. In the traditional numbering system, groups are numbered from 1 through 8 and with the letter *A* or *B*. In the new system (shown in parentheses), groups are numbered from 1 through 18, without any letters.

**1A (1)**

| | 1 | 1 |
|---|---|---|
| 1 | **H** | |
| | Hydrogen | |
| | 1.008 | |

**Metals**

**2A (2)**

**Transition Elements**

**8B**

| Period | 1A (1) | 2A (2) | 3B (3) | 4B (4) | 5B (5) | 6B (6) | 7B (7) | (8) | (9) |
|---|---|---|---|---|---|---|---|---|---|
| 2 | 3 (2,1) **Li** Lithium 6.941 | 4 (2,2) **Be** Beryllium 9.012 | | | | | | | |
| 3 | 11 (2,8,1) **Na** Sodium 22.990 | 12 (2,8,2) **Mg** Magnesium 24.305 | | | | | | | |
| 4 | 19 (2,8,8,1) **K** Potassium 39.098 | 20 (2,8,8,2) **Ca** Calcium 40.08 | 21 (2,8,9,2) **Sc** Scandium 44.956 | 22 (2,8,10,2) **Ti** Titanium 47.90 | 23 (2,8,11,2) **V** Vanadium 50.942 | 24 (2,8,13,1) **Cr** Chromium 51.996 | 25 (2,8,13,2) **Mn** Manganese 54.938 | 26 (2,8,14,2) **Fe** Iron 55.847 | 27 (2,8,15,2) **Co** Cobalt 58.933 |
| 5 | 37 (2,8,18,8,1) **Rb** Rubidium 85.468 | 38 (2,8,18,8,2) **Sr** Strontium 87.62 | 39 (2,8,18,9,2) **Y** Yttrium 88.906 | 40 (2,8,18,10,2) **Zr** Zirconium 91.22 | 41 (2,8,18,12,1) **Nb** Niobium 92.906 | 42 (2,8,18,13,1) **Mo** Molybdenum 95.94 | 43 (2,8,18,14,1) **Tc** Technetium 98.906 | 44 (2,8,18,15,1) **Ru** Ruthenium 101.07 | 45 (2,8,18,16,1) **Rh** Rhodium 102.906 |
| 6 | 55 (2,8,18,18,8,1) **Cs** Cesium 132.905 | 56 (2,8,18,18,8,2) **Ba** Barium 137.33 | 71 (2,8,18,32,9,2) **Lu** Lutetium 174.967 | 72 (2,8,18,32,10,2) **Hf** Hafnium 178.49 | 73 (2,8,18,32,11,2) **Ta** Tantalum 180.948 | 74 (2,8,18,32,12,2) **W** Tungsten 183.85 | 75 (2,8,18,32,13,2) **Re** Rhenium 186.2 | 76 (2,8,18,32,14,2) **Os** Osmium 190.2 | 77 (2,8,18,32,15,2) **Ir** Iridium 192.22 |
| 7 | 87 (2,8,18,32,18,8,1) **Fr** Francium 223 | 88 (2,8,18,32,18,8,2) **Ra** Radium 226.025 | 103 (2,8,18,32,32,9,2) **Lr** Lawrencium 257 | 104 (2,8,18,32,32,10,2) **Unq** Unnilquadium 257 ? | 105 (2,8,18,32,32,?) **Unp** Unnilpentium 260 ? | 106 (2,8,18,32,32,?) **Unh** Unnilhexium 263 ? | 107 (2,8,18,32,32,?) **Uns** Unnilseptium 258 ? | 108 (2,8,18,32,32,?) **Uno*** Unniloctium ? | 109 (2,8,18,32,32,?) **Une** Unnilennium 266 ? |

*Not yet reported

**Rare Earth Elements**

**Lanthanoid Series**

| 57 (2,8,18,18,9,2) **La** Lanthanum 138.906 | 58 (2,8,18,20,8,2) **Ce** Cerium 140.12 | 59 (2,8,18,21,8,2) **Pr** Praseodymium 140.908 | 60 (2,8,18,22,8,2) **Nd** Neodymium 144.24 | 61 (2,8,18,23,8,2) **Pm** Promethium ~ 147 | 62 (2,8,18,24,8,2) **Sm** Samarium 150.4 |
|---|---|---|---|---|---|

**Actinoid Series**

| 89 (2,8,18,32,18,9,2) **Ac** Actinium 227 | 90 (2,8,18,32,18,10,2) **Th** Thorium 232.038 | 91 (2,8,18,32,20,9,2) **Pa** Protactinium 231.036 | 92 (2,8,18,32,21,9,2) **U** Uranium 238.029 | 93 (2,8,18,32,22,9,2) **Np** Neptunium 237.048 | 94 (2,8,18,32,24,8,2) **Pu** Plutonium ~239 |
|---|---|---|---|---|---|

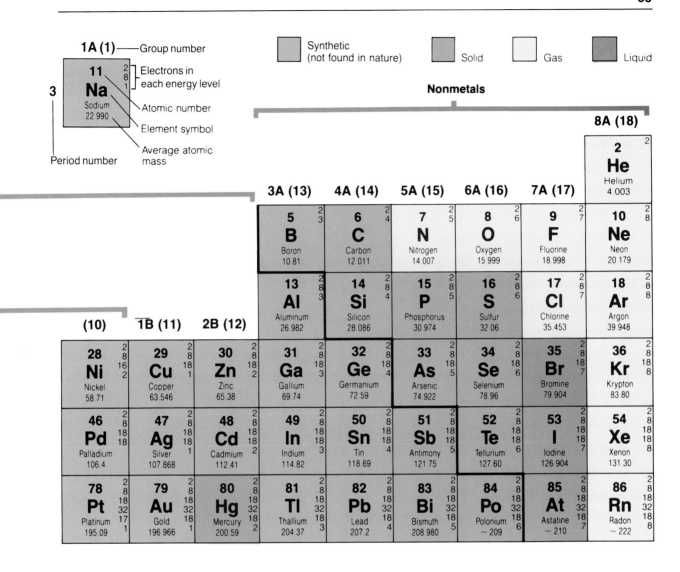

## Main Idea

What family of elements is located in the left-hand column of the periodic table? What are some of its properties?

The elements in the left-hand column of the periodic table are the **alkali** (AL´-kuh-lī) **metals**. The word *alkali* refers to the type of substance formed when these metals react with water. They also have the properties associated with metals. These elements are all solids at ordinary temperatures. Which elements are alkali metals?

Elements on the left-hand side of the periodic table (except hydrogen) have the properties of metals. Elements on the right-hand side have the properties of nonmetals. In the table on the previous page, a heavy black line separates the metals from the nonmetals. Most elements are solids at ordinary temperatures. Notice that all the gases (except hydrogen) are on the right-hand side.

Properties of the elements change as you go across the table. For example, the elements become less metallic as you

## Our Science Heritage

### The Discovery of the Periodic Relationship

Dmitri Mendeleev

The periodic table was suggested independently by two different people at about the same time. Dmitri Mendeleev (1834–1907), a professor of chemistry in St. Petersburg, Russia, is generally given credit for discovering the periodic relationship among the elements. He published the first version of his table in 1869. Julius Lothar Meyer (1830–1895), a professor of chemistry in Tuebingen, Germany, prepared a table relating atomic mass to properties in 1868 but did not publish it until 1870. Meyer's publication probably influenced Mendeleev's

revision of his table published in 1871.

At the time Mendeleev and Meyer discovered the periodic relationship, each was trying to write a chemistry textbook. There existed a large amount of information about the more than 60 elements known at that time. In trying to organize this information for students, each professor uncovered the periodic relationship.

Unlike Meyer, Mendeleev left spaces in his table and predicted that elements with certain properties would be discovered. When gallium, scandium, and germanium were found, their properties matched his predictions.

go from left to right. Neighboring elements in the center of the table are more alike than those near the sides.

Mendeleev based his table on the idea that the properties of an element are related to the mass of the atoms that make up that element. The properties of the elements repeat in a regular way with increasing atomic mass. Mendeleev was so convinced of the periodic properties of the elements that he left a few empty spaces in his table. He felt that none of the known elements belonged in those spaces. But he predicted the existence of elements with the correct properties to fit in the empty places. His convictions were confirmed when these elements were discovered.

More elements were discovered and atomic masses were measured more accurately. A few elements seemed to fit in the table out of order. For example, argon seems to be in the same family as helium. Yet argon's atomic mass is greater than potassium's. The reason for these "misfits" became clear as more was learned about atoms.

**Main Idea**

What problem did there seem to be about argon's position in the periodic table?

## Check yourself

1. Explain why Mendeleev left one family of elements out of his periodic table.

2. Why did Mendeleev leave some empty spaces in his periodic table?

## Particles within the atom

Dalton had assumed that atoms could not be broken apart. Observations that were made later contradicted this picture. Atoms must be made up of even smaller particles of matter. The first of these particles to be discovered was the **electron** (uh-LEK′-tron). All electrons are identical, no matter from which kind of element they come.

The relation of the electrons to the rest of the atom became an important question. Some experiments by Ernest Rutherford (1871–1937) in the early 1900s suggested a fascinating picture. The results of his experiments could be explained only as follows.

## Library research

Read about Maria Goeppert Mayer (1906–1972), who won a Nobel Prize in physics in 1963. Write a report about her life and her work on the nucleus.

Figure 2-19. Rutherford's model of an atom. The nucleus is shown much larger than it is in proportion to the whole atom. If an atom were really this size, the nucleus would still be too small to be seen.

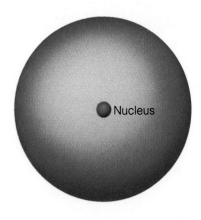

Nucleus

In the center of every atom is a **nucleus** (NEW′-klee-us). The electrons are in the space outside the nucleus. The nucleus is very small compared to the whole atom. Yet, it has almost all the mass of the atom.

Suppose a nucleus were as big as a tiny flea. Then the whole atom would be as big as a large baseball park. Yet, the individual electrons would be too small to be seen at all.

The nucleus was found to be made of two kinds of particles. One kind was called the **proton** (PRŌ′-ton). The other was called the **neutron** (NEW′-tron). All protons are identical, no matter from which kind of element they come. Similarly, all neutrons are identical. A neutron has slightly more mass than a proton. Each has almost 2000 times the mass of an electron.

All atoms, then, are made of three basic particles: electrons, protons, and neutrons. What makes atoms of different elements different? Evidence from experiments led to the following model for the atoms of different elements.

Each element has a specific number of protons in its atoms. A hydrogen atom always has one proton. A helium atom always has two protons. A lithium atom always has three protons, and so on. The number of protons in the nucleus of an atom determines the element. The number of protons in the atom came to be called the **atomic number** of the element.

In the modern periodic table, the elements are in order of atomic number. Argon may have a greater atomic mass than potassium, but it has a lower atomic number. The families line up in perfect columns when atomic number is used instead of atomic mass.

Most atoms have roughly as many neutrons as protons. A helium atom normally has two of each. An oxygen atom normally has eight of each. However, a hydrogen atom normally has one proton and no neutrons at all.

All atoms of one element have the same number of protons. Yet, they do not all have the same mass. Different numbers of neutrons cause the differences in mass. For example, most oxygen atoms have eight neutrons. But some have nine or even ten neutrons. Atoms of the same element with different numbers of neutrons are called **isotopes** (Ī′-suh-tōps).

When an atom is not combined with other atoms, it has the same number of electrons as protons. An oxygen atom would have eight electrons, no matter which isotope it is. In a chemical change, an atom may gain or lose electrons. However, the nucleus is not affected by a chemical change.

### Check yourself

1. Atoms are made of what three basic particles?
2. In the modern periodic table, the elements are in what order?

### Atomic models

The electrons of an atom play a major role in chemical changes. The chemical properties of an element are closely linked to the arrangement of its electrons.

In 1913 Niels Bohr proposed an atomic model that described the arrangement of electrons in atoms. This **planetary model** helped explain the properties of many elements. In the planetary model, electrons move in orbits at different distances from the nucleus. In this way, the electrons are like the planets which move around the sun.

A more recent and accurate model of atomic structure is known as the **electron cloud model**. In the electron cloud model, electrons do not move around the nucleus in fixed orbits. Instead, they move at random throughout a volume of space surrounding the nucleus. Their constant movement over a period of time produces a blurred, cloud-like appearance. This effect is similar to one produced by an electric fan. When the fan is turned off, you can see that it has distinct blades. When it is turned on, you see only a cloud-like blur.

The electron cloud model is based on complex mathematical equations. These equations predict that electrons have different **energy levels**. Electrons at low energy levels tend to be close to the nucleus most of the time. Electrons at higher energy levels spend more time further from the nucleus.

There is a limit to how many electrons can be in each energy level. The lowest energy level can never hold more than two electrons. The second level has more space. It can hold up to

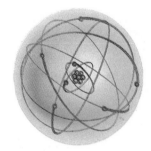

Figure 2–20. The planetary model described electrons as being in orbits around the nucleus.

Figure 2–21. Electrons are not restricted to orbits according to the electron cloud model. In this model the electrons move throughout a spherical volume close to the nucleus.

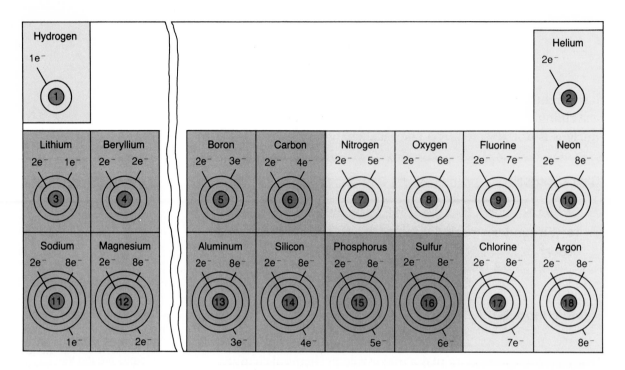

Figure 2-22 This portion of the periodic table shows the energy levels of electrons for the first 18 elements. The number in the center circle is the number of protons in the nucleus (the atomic number).

eight electrons. The third energy level can hold up to 18 electrons. The fourth energy level can hold up to 32 electrons.

There are two more limits to the number of electrons in an energy level. First, the number of electrons in a normal atom is the same as the number of protons in its nucleus. This limits the total number of electrons. Second, there are never more than eight electrons in the highest occupied energy level.

The arrangement of the electrons in energy levels matches the arrangement of the periodic table. Look at Figure 2–22. Hydrogen and helium are in the first row. Both have one energy level. Hydrogen has one electron and helium has two.

All elements in the second row have two energy levels. The first energy level has two electrons. The second energy level has from one to eight as you go to the right along the row.

All the elements in the third row have three energy levels. All have two electrons in the first energy level and eight in the second. How many electrons does each have in its third energy level?

Consider the inert gases at the right-hand end of each row in the periodic table. Helium has two electrons, the maximum the first energy level can hold. Neon's second energy level has eight, the maximum it can hold. Argon's third energy level has eight. This is the maximum an outer energy level can hold. Thus, each level is full. This fact seems to be related to the non-reactive properties of these elements.

## Activity 2-2        Using the Periodic Table

### Materials

periodic table

### Purpose

To use the periodic table to determine the identity of some mystery elements.

### Procedure

1. Make a table like the one shown. From the description given of each mystery element, use the periodic table to determine which element is being described. Write the name and the symbol of the element corresponding to each mystery element on your table.
2. Draw a model of mystery elements "L," "P," "W," and "Y." Show the number of protons in the nucleus and the number of electrons in each energy level. Give the name and the symbol of each mystery element you drew.

### Family 1

- Element "L" has 12 protons and 12 neutrons in the nucleus of each of its atoms.
- An atom of element "M" has two more electrons than an atom of argon.
- Element "N" has a total of 38 electrons in each normal atom.

- Element "P" has electrons in only two energy levels in each of its atoms.

### Family 2

Element "W" has a greater atomic number than carbon, but less than oxygen.
- Element "X" has 33 protons and 42 neutrons in each of its nuclei.
- An atom of element "Y" has electrons in three energy levels.
- An atom of element "Z" has 15 more electrons than an atom of krypton.

### Conclusion

What kinds of information are useful in identifying elements?

| Family 1 | | Family 2 | |
|---|---|---|---|
| Mystery element | Element from periodic table | Mystery element | Element from periodic table |
| "L" | | "W" | |
| "M" | | "X" | |
| "N" | | "Y" | |
| "P" | | "Z" | |

Now look at the outer energy levels of the halogens, just to the left of the inert gases. They each have one fewer electron than the inert gases to their right. The family in the first column is the alkali metal family. They each have only one electron in their outer energy level. Each column has elements with similar electron arrangements.

### Check yourself

What property do the outer energy levels of the atoms of all the elements of a family have in common?

# Practical Science

## Lighting Up the Night with Neon

The famous flashing neon lights of Times Square and Las Vegas owe their rainbow of colors to electrons and energy levels.

You have learned that electrons are arranged in energy levels outside the nucleus of an atom. Electrons in the lowest energy level are relatively close to the nucleus. Electrons in the higher energy levels spend more time further from the nucleus.

**Neon's electrons**  Neon has ten electrons. Two electrons are in the lowest energy level, and eight are in the second energy level. The electrons have the lowest possible energy when they are in these two lowest energy levels. This is called their *ground state*. The ground state is the most stable arrangement for the electrons in an atom.

The glass tube of a neon light contains a small amount of the noble gas, neon. When the atoms of neon are jolted by high voltage electricity, the electrons in the atoms absorb the electrical energy. With this energy they "jump" to higher energy levels. However, they do not remain long at these higher levels. They drop back to their stable ground state. As they drop back, they give off the extra energy that they absorbed. This energy is given off not as electricity, but as colored light. Every time an electron drops from a higher level to a lower one, a tiny flash of light is given off. Because many billions of electrons are doing this every second, the light that you see is steady and bright.

**A rainbow of colors**  The color of the light given off is characteristic of the gas used in the glass tube. The pattern of colors that is produced by a substance is called its *spectrum*. This pattern is unique for each gas as each person's fingerprints are unique. For example, neon produces orange light, sodium produces yellow light, and mercury produces bluish light.

When only neon is in the tube, the light given off is orange. A mixture of neon and argon gives a blue or green light. If mercury is added to the tube, its excited electrons give off ultraviolet energy. We cannot see this form of energy. However, the glass tube can be coated with a substance that will give off visible light when ultraviolet energy strikes it. Sometimes the glass itself is colored. Thus, by varying the substance in the tube, the coating on its inner surface, and the color of the glass, all colors of the rainbow can be captured in neon lights.

**Other types of lights**  If the street lights in your town give off a golden glow, they are probably sodium vapor lamps. Electric current produces heat that vaporizes the sodium in the lamp. The electrons in sodium atoms absorb energy and move to higher energy levels. When the electrons fall back to lower energy levels, they give off energy as light. Yellow light is characteristic of sodium.

Other street lamps contain mercury vapor instead of sodium. The light given off by these lamps is bluish-white. Vapor lamps produce bright light, and are long-lasting. The lamps are popular for lighting streets and parking lots.

**Something to try**  Look for different types of lights at night where you live. Make a list of the lights and their colors. Return to look at these lights during the day. Which of them use colored glass to make the light colored? Which of them have clear glass but produce colored light?

## Section 2 Review   Chapter 2

### Check Your Vocabulary

| | |
|---|---|
| alkali metal | inert gas |
| atomic number | isotope |
| electron | neutron |
| family | nucleus |
| halogen | proton |

*Match each term above with the numbered phrase that best describes it.*

1. Any group of elements with similar properties

2. Determines order of elements in modern periodic table

3. Element with one more electron than an inert gas

4. Has almost all the mass but occupies hardly any of the space of an atom

5. Particle outside the nucleus

6. Particle inside the nucleus whose number can vary between atoms of an element

7. Particle whose number is always the same for a particular element

8. Element that tends not to react with others

9. Family of elements that react very easily with metals

10. Atom that has a different mass from, but belongs to the same element as, another atom

### Check Your Knowledge

*Multiple Choice: Choose the answer that best completes each of the following sentences.*

1. In his perodic table, Mendeleev put the elements in order of __?__.
   a) atomic mass
   b) atomic number
   c) number of neutrons
   d) boiling point

2. Two atoms must belong to the same element if they have the same number of __?__.
   a) energy levels       c) protons
   b) electrons           d) neutrons

3. In the periodic table, all the gases except hydrogen are __?__.
   a) in the first row
   b) in the first column
   c) in the same family
   d) on the right-hand side

### Check Your Understanding

1. Compare the properties of elements in the halogen family with the properties of elements in the alkali metal family.

2. Compare the arrangement of the electrons in an atom of silicon with those of another element in the same family.

3. How many energy levels of electrons does every element in the third row of the periodic table have? How many energy levels would you expect every element in the fifth row to have?

4. The mass of both the proton and the neutron is approximately 1 u. One isotope of chlorine has an atomic mass of 36.97 u. How many neutrons does it have?

### Practical Science

1. In what ways can neon light be made to display different colors?

2. Name two other gases that can be mixed with neon to create different colors of light.

# A Model for Chemical Changes    Section 3

**Section 3 of Chapter 2 is divided into seven parts:**

## Learning Objectives

1. To interpret chemical equations by identifying the reactants and products and by identifying whether an equation is balanced.

2. To relate the charge of ions to the gain or loss of electrons.

3. To describe chemical bonds within compounds in terms of the transfer or sharing of electrons.

4. To identify the properties of acids, bases, and salts.

Figure 2-23. The structure in the photo is a ball-and-stick model of a molecule. The red balls represent oxygen atoms, the yellow balls represent hydrogen atoms, and the black balls represent carbon atoms. The sticks between the balls represent bonds between the atoms.

A good model explains a large number of observations. Dalton was able to explain how new substances are formed in chemical changes. According to his model, different substances are made from different combinations of atoms. In a chemical change, old combinations break up and new combinations form.

There are still some questions to be answered.

☐ What holds atoms together in combinations?

☐ What makes some pairs of atoms more likely to combine than other pairs?

☐ What makes elements in a family form compounds with similar formulas?

## Chemical equations

In one common chemical change, carbon combines with oxygen to form carbon dioxide. A short way to write this is

carbon + oxygen → carbon dioxide.

The substances on the left are called **reactants**. They are the substances that exist before the change. The substance on the right is the **product**. It is formed during the change. The arrow indicates the direction of the change.

A chemical change can be described even more briefly using formulas instead of names. The same chemical change would appear in this form as

$$C + O_2 \rightarrow CO_2.$$

This is a **chemical equation**. Chemical equations are a way of summarizing a chemical change.

In a chemical change, the total number of atoms of each element does not change. Only the arrangement of the atoms changes. Look at the chemical equation in the preceding paragraph. There is one carbon atom before the change. There is one carbon atom after the change. There are two oxygen atoms before the change. There are two oxygen atoms after the change. This equation is said to be **balanced** because the same number of atoms of each element are on the left and right sides.

**Main Idea**

What is a shorthand way of describing and summarizing a certain chemical change?

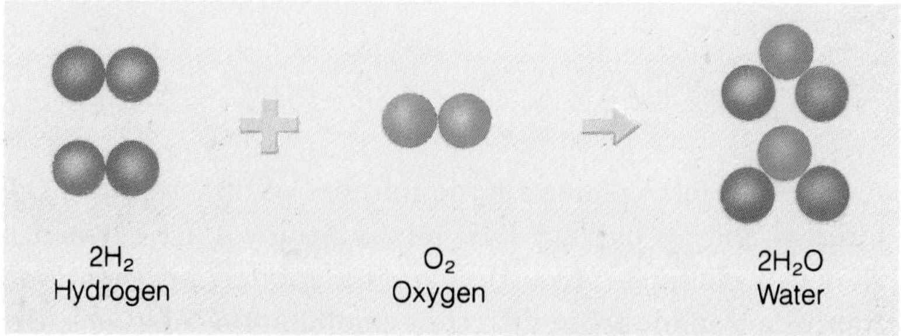

$$2H_2 \qquad O_2 \qquad 2H_2O$$
Hydrogen       Oxygen       Water

Figure 2-24. How many atoms of oxygen are present before and after the change shown?

Hydrogen and oxygen gases combine to form water. The balanced chemical equation that summarizes this change is

$$2H_2 + O_2 \rightarrow 2H_2O.$$

The 2s in front of the formulas for hydrogen and water are needed to balance the equation. In words, two molecules of hydrogen combine with one molecule of oxygen. The product of the reaction is two molecules of water.

### Check yourself

Answer each of the following for this chemical equation.

$$Zn + 2HCl \rightarrow ZnCl_2 + H_2$$

1. For each element, tell how many atoms of it appear on each side of the equation.

2. Is this equation balanced? How can you tell?

### Electric charges

Clothes stick together in a dryer. A sweater and a pillowcase crackle when they are pulled apart. The sticking and crackling are due to **electric charges**. Two different kinds of electric charges have been identified. Normally, an object has the same number of each kind. But charges can be removed by rubbing. When an object has unequal numbers of charges, it may push or pull on other objects.

For example, suppose a glass rod is rubbed with silk. The rod and the silk will then stick together. They pull on each other because of their electric charges. After the rubbing, the rod was left with more of one kind and the silk was left with more of the other kind. On the other hand, suppose the rod is rubbed with two pieces of silk. Then, the pieces of silk will push each other apart. They have the same kind of charges.

## Activity 2-3A    Charged Objects

### Materials

2 balloons                      wool flannel
string or thread                wood dowel
support stand with clamp

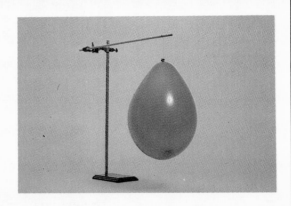

### Purpose

To observe the behavior of charged objects.

### Procedure

1. Clamp the wood dowel to the support stand.
2. Hang an inflated balloon from the dowel by thread. Check to be sure the balloon is not touching anything.
3. Hold a piece of wool flannel close to, but not touching, the balloon. Record whether the balloon is attracted, repelled, or unaffected by the flannel.
4. Rub the whole balloon with the wool flannel.
5. Slowly bring the wool flannel close to the balloon. Record whether the balloon is attracted, repelled, or unaffected by the flannel.
6. Rub the whole surface of a second inflated balloon with the wool flannel.
7. Bring the second balloon close to the first balloon. Record whether the first balloon is attracted, repelled or unaffected by the second balloon.

### Questions

1. Were the balloon and wool flannel charged before they were rubbed together?
2. Can an uncharged (neutral) object be made up of charged particles?
3. What happened to the two kinds of charges when the balloon and wool flannel were rubbed together?
4. Would you expect the charges on the two balloons to be the same or different after each was rubbed with the wool? Explain.

### Conclusion

How do objects with like charges and objects with unlike charges affect each other?

---

In general, an object with more of one kind of charge than another is said to be **charged**. Two charged objects pull each other together if they have different charges. Two charged objects push each other apart if they have the same charges. In short, opposites attract and likes repel.

The charges on objects can be traced to the particles that make up matter. The two kinds of charge are labeled positive and negative. A proton has a positive charge. An electron has a negative charge. The amount of charge on the proton and electron is the same. The positive charge on a proton cancels the negative charge on an electron.

### Main Idea

What condition exists in an object that is said to have an electric charge?

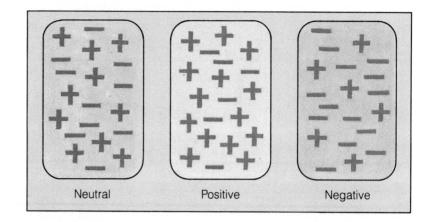

Figure 2-25. How can an object with both kinds of charges be neutral?

Objects that have equal numbers of protons and electrons seem to have no charge. They are **neutral** (NEW'-trul). Objects that have more electrons than protons have a negative charge. Objects that have more protons than electrons have a positive charge.

### Check yourself

1. What causes an object to have a negative charge?
2. What effect do two positively charged objects have on each other?

### Ions

Figure 2-26. How is a sodium ion different from a sodium atom?

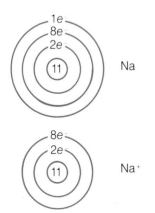

In a chemical change, the number of protons in an atom cannot change. If it did, the atom would become another element. However, the number of electrons can change.

In a chemical reaction, only some of the electrons of an atom are involved. The electrons that take part in a chemical reaction are the ones that belong to the highest energy level. Electrons that belong to the highest energy level are known as **valence electrons**. Valence electrons are the electrons of an atom that take part in a chemical change. For the most part, the chemical properties of the different elements depend on their number of valence electrons.

Atoms of some elements give up electrons easily. The elements in the left and middle portions of the periodic table have only one, two, or three valence electrons. These are the same elements that have metallic properties. So, metals are elements that give up electrons easily.

When atoms give up electrons, they become positively charged. The positively charged atoms are called **positive ions** (Ī′-unz). Atoms of elements in the alkali metal family have a single valence electron. If they lose this electron, they have one uncancelled positive charge. They become positive ions with a charge of 1+. An example is the sodium atom. The symbol for the sodium ion is $Na^+$. (Note that the 1 is understood but not written.)

Atoms of elements in the second family have two valence electrons. These atoms lose two electrons quite easily. They become positive ions with a charge of 2+. An example is the magnesium atom. The symbol for the magnesium ion is $Mg^{2+}$.

Atoms of elements in the halogen family accept extra electrons. The halogens have seven valence electrons. The atoms of these elements accept one extra electron easily. They then have one extra negative charge. Atoms with a negative charge are called **negative ions**. The names end in -*ide*.

Chlorine, for example, forms a negative ion. The symbol for the negative chloride ion is $Cl^-$. Iodine is another element in the same family as chlorine. The symbol for the iodide ion is $I^-$.

Figure 2-27. The electron structures of two ions and an atom are shown. How are they similar? How are they different?

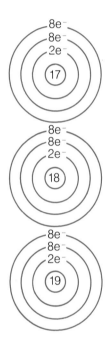

### Check yourself

1. What is the meaning of the symbol $H^+$?
2. What is the meaning of the symbol $Br^-$?

### Electron sharing

Atoms with four, five, and six valence electrons do not gain or lose electrons easily. Instead they tend to share electrons with other atoms. They often share electrons with atoms of the same element. For example, chlorine forms the diatomic molecule $Cl_2$. In this molecule, each atom shares one of its own electrons with the other atom.

Oxygen shares electrons with atoms of many other elements. For example, oxygen shares electrons with hydrogen in the compound water and with carbon in the compound carbon dioxide.

| Table 2-3 | | Electron Dot Structures of Some Elements | | | | | | |
|---|---|---|---|---|---|---|---|---|
| 1 | H· | | | | | | | He : |
| 2 | Li· | ·Be· | ·Ḃ· | ·Ċ· | ·N̈· | :Ö· | :F̈· | :N̈e : |
| 3 | Na· | ·Mg· | ·Al· | ·Si· | ·P̈· | :S̈· | :C̈l· | :Är : |
| 4 | K· | ·Ca· | ·Ga· | ·Ge· | ·Äs· | :S̈e· | :B̈r· | :K̈r : |

Figure 2-28. These electron dot structures of three molecules show the sharing of valence electrons in covalent bonding. Notice how many electrons surround each atom.

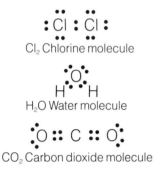

Cl₂ Chlorine molecule

H₂O Water molecule

CO₂ Carbon dioxide molecule

**Data Search**

In what year and to whom was a Nobel prize in physics awarded for research on the movement of electrons within the atom? Search page 558.

Many ions have the same electron structure as inert gases. For example, $Na^+$ and $Mg^{2+}$ both have the same electron structure as neon. So does $F^-$. Similarly, $K^+$, $Ca^{2+}$, and $Cl^-$ have the same electron structure as argon.

By sharing electrons, atoms may also acquire an electron structure of an inert gas. When an oxygen atom shares the electrons of two hydrogen atoms, it has as many electrons as neon. Thus, many atoms that lose, gain, or share electrons become more like inert gases. Inert gases, on the other hand, have very little tendency to lose, gain, or share electrons.

There are different ways to picture what happens to the electrons when they are being shared between atoms. One of the simpler ways to illustrate what is happening to electrons is with symbols that show only the valence electrons. An **electron dot structure** shows the valence electrons of an atom as dots. The inner electrons of the atom are represented by the atomic symbol of the element. The electron dot structures for various atoms are shown in Table 2-3. The electron dot structures for some of the molecules that have been mentioned are shown in Figure 2-28.

**Check yourself**

What is the difference between electron sharing and the formation of ions?

**Chemical bonds**

Dalton pictured compounds as made from atoms of different elements that had joined together. However, his theory did not explain what held atoms together. Nor did it explain why some combinations were more likely to occur than others.

As more became known about the atom, the theory behind combinations developed. Atoms that have lost electrons are positive ions. Atoms that have gained electrons are negative ions. Positive and negative ions pull on each other because of their opposite charges. The pull keeps the positive and negative ions together in a compound.

When atoms share electrons, there is also a pull between opposite charges. The positive nucleus of each atom pulls on the negative electrons being shared by the other atom. Again, the pull between positive and negative charges keeps the atoms together.

Thus, there is a sort of invisible attraction between two atoms that have transferred or shared electrons. The tie is called a **chemical bond.** When elements combine and form compounds, their atoms form chemical bonds. The bonds exist because of the pulls between opposite charges.

Sodium chloride (salt) is an example of a compound held together by bonds between oppositely charged ions. Such a compound is called an **ionic (ī-ON′-ik) compound**. When the compound forms, sodium atoms give up their outer electrons to chlorine atoms. Look at Figure 2-29. Each positive sodium ion ($Na^+$) in the compound is surrounded by six negative chlorine ions ($Cl^-$). And each $Cl^-$ ion is surrounded by six $Na^+$ ions. There are bonds between each ion and its neighbors. Since the bonds are between ions, they are called **ionic bonds**.

**Main Idea**

What is an ionic compound?

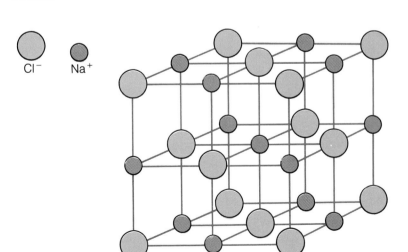

Cl⁻    Na⁺

Figure 2-29. Sodium chloride is an ionic compound. The straight lines between the ions represent ionic bonds.

Figure 2-30. Two different ways to represent covalent bonds are straight lines or pairs of shared electron dots. Notice that methane is a three-dimensional molecule but that carbon dioxide is linear.

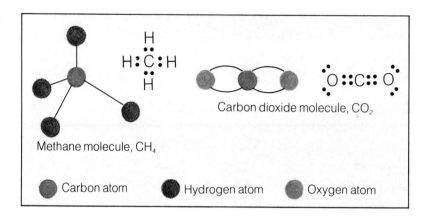

Carbon dioxide molecule, $CO_2$

Methane molecule, $CH_4$

Carbon atom          Hydrogen atom          Oxygen atom

Elements of the alkali metals form ionic compounds with elements of the halogen family. Potassium bromide (KBr), magnesium chloride ($MgCl_2$), and lithium chloride (LiCl) are some additional examples of ionic compounds. Ionic compounds are usually formed by a metal and a nonmetal.

Methane ($CH_4$) is an example of a compound formed of molecules. Within each molecule, one carbon atom shares electrons with four hydrogen atoms. There is a bond between each hydrogen atom and the carbon atom, as shown in Figure 2-30. Bonds like these, due to shared electrons, are called **covalent** (kō-VAYL'-unt) **bonds**. Covalent bonds usually form between atoms of nonmetals.

In diatomic gases such as oxygen, there are covalent bonds between the two atoms in the molecule. Each nucleus is exactly the same, so each pulls with the same strength on the shared electrons. In a compound, on the other hand, the covalent bonds are usually between two different kinds of atoms. The nucleus of one kind will pull more strongly on the shared electrons. The electrons will still be shared but they will be closer to the nucleus with the stronger pull.

Some compounds contain both ionic and covalent bonds. Silver nitrate, for example, is made of $Ag^+$ and $NO_3^-$ ions. The nitrate ion, $NO_3^-$, acts like a single atom that has gained one electron. But within the ion, the nitrogen and oxygen atoms share electrons and form covalent bonds. In chemical changes, the nitrate ion usually stays together. However, plants are able to take in nitrate ions from the soil and break them down.

**Main Idea**

Under what conditions do covalent bonds form?

The compound calcium nitrate contains $Ca^{2+}$ and $NO_3^-$ ions. Since the calcium ion has given up two electrons, there must be two nitrate ions for every calcium ion in the compound. The formula for calcium nitrate is $Ca(NO_3)_2$. The numeral 2 after the second parenthesis indicates that there are two of everything inside the parentheses. In other words, there are two nitrate ions for every calcium ion. If the formula were written $CaN_2O_6$, you would not realize the compound contained nitrate ions.

The formation of new substances always involves making and/or breaking chemical bonds. Thus, chemical changes are changes in chemical bonds. These changes occur when electrons are transferred from one atom to another. They also occur when electrons stop or start being shared between atoms.

**Main Idea**

What effect do chemical changes have on chemical bonds?

### Check yourself

1. How can the pull between atoms in a compound be explained?

2. Describe the difference between an ionic bond and a covalent bond.

3. The structure of potassium nitrate, $KNO_3$, is like that of silver nitrate. What ions make up potassium nitrate?

### Acids and bases

Citrus fruits such as oranges, grapefruit, and lemons have a sour taste. So do vinegar and tomatoes. These foods have something in common with the liquid inside an automobile battery. They will all make a substance known as litmus dye turn from blue to red. They all make another substance, bromthymol blue (BTB), turn from blue to yellow.

Citrus fruits and tomatoes contain citric acid. Vinegar contains acetic acid. A battery contains sulfuric acid. An **acid** (AS'-id) is a substance that makes litmus dye or BTB change color as described. Although edible acids can be recognized by their sour taste, it is very dangerous to taste unknown substances.

**Library research**

Find out what besides litmus and BTB are commonly used as acid indicators and at what pH value they each change in color.

Figure 2-31. Which glass of tea
has had lemon juice added to it?

## Main Idea

What are some common acid
indicators?

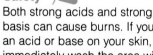

Safety

Both strong acids and strong
basis can cause burns. If you spill
an acid or base on your skin,
immediately wash the area with
running water. If you get an acid
or base in your eye, wash the eye
with running water for at least 15
minutes.

Substances that are changed in color by acids are called
**acid indicators**. Tea, as well as litmus dye and BTB, is an acid
indicator. It turns lighter in color when lemon juice or any
other acid is added.

There is another group of substances that can cancel, or
**neutralize** (NEW'-truh-līz), an acid. That is, when one of them
is added to an acid, it can prevent an acid indicator from
turning the color for an acid. These substances are called
**bases**. By themselves, bases have the opposite effect from
acids on indicators. They turn litmus dye from red to blue
and BTB from yellow to blue. Bases have a bitter taste and
feel slippery. Again, however, it is dangerous to taste unknown
substances. Many bases destroy skin and should not be felt.

Some substances will be more acidic or more basic than
others. A scale of acidity has been set up to rank substances.
A measure of the acidity of a substance is known as **pH**. A
substance with a pH value of 7 is neither acidic nor basic. It
can be called neutral. Substances with pH values less than 7

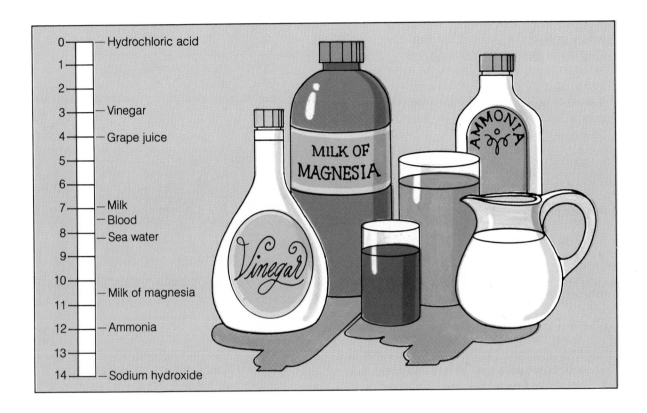

| | |
|---|---|
| 0 | Hydrochloric acid |
| 1 | |
| 2 | |
| 3 | Vinegar |
| 4 | Grape juice |
| 5 | |
| 6 | |
| 7 | Milk / Blood |
| 8 | Sea water |
| 9 | |
| 10 | Milk of magnesia |
| 11 | |
| 12 | Ammonia |
| 13 | |
| 14 | Sodium hydroxide |

are acidic. Substances with pH values greater than 7 are basic. The lower the pH value, the more acidic the substance is. The higher the pH value, the more basic the substance is.

If you studied the chemical formulas of different acids, you would notice that they all contain hydrogen. Common laboratory acids, as well as household acids, are in water solutions. In water solutions, acids break up into positive and negative ions. The positive ion is always a hydrogen ion, $H^+$. For example, vinegar is a solution of acetic acid ($HC_2H_3O_2$) and water. The acetic acid breaks up into $H^+$ and $C_2H_3O_2^-$ ions. Hydrochloric acid (HCl) breaks up into $H^+$ and $Cl^-$ ions.

Similarly, formulas for bases contain both oxygen and hydrogen. In water solutions, bases break up into ions. The negative ion is $OH^-$, which is known as the **hydroxide** (hī-DROK'-sīd) **ion**. Many bases have the word *hydroxide* in their names. The base sodium hydroxide (NaOH) breaks up into $Na^+$ and $OH^-$ ions. The base potassium hydroxide (KOH) breaks up into $K^+$ and $OH^-$ ions.

Figure 2-32. Substances are ranked for acidity on a pH scale from 0 to 14. Would a substance with a pH value of 2 be very acidic or very basic?

**Library research**

Two common household cleaning substances are ammonia (in a water solution) and liquid bleach. Find out why they should never be used together.

## Activity 2–3B    Identifying Acids and Bases

### Materials

safety goggles  
household ammonia  
vinegar  
lemon juice  
4 antacid tablets  
cola  
baking soda  
6 pieces each of red and blue litmus paper  
masking tape, labels, or grease pencil

table salt  
6 test tubes  
test tube rack  
6 stirring rods  
graduated cylinder  
distilled water

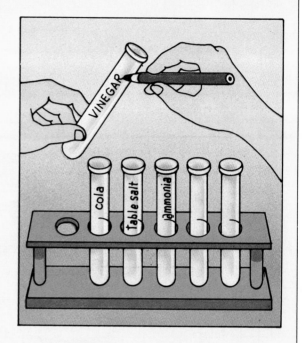

### Purpose

To develop a system for the identification of acids and bases.

### Procedure

1. Put on safety goggles.
2. Place the test tubes in the test tube rack.
3. Use a grease pencil or label to mark the test tubes with the names of the six substances to be tested from the materials list above.
4. Place 2 mL of the liquid substances to be tested into the labeled test tubes.
5. For each solid to be tested, place an amount equal to the size of a pea into the labeled test tubes. Dissolve the solid by adding 2 mL of distilled water and gently shaking the test tube.
6. Test the lemon juice with a piece of blue litmus paper by dipping a stirring rod into the juice and transferring a drop onto the litmus paper. Observe the results. Repeat the procedure using a piece of red litmus paper. Observe the results. Lemon juice is an acid.
7. Use a clean stirring rod and test the household ammonia in a similar manner, using red litmus paper first. Observe the results. Repeat the procedure with blue litmus paper. Ammonia is a base.
8. Continue to test the remaining substances, using a different stirring rod for each trial. Use separate pieces of red and blue litmus paper for each test.

### Questions

1. What color changes did you observe in the blue litmus paper in testing the lemon juice? In the red litmus paper?
2. What color changes did you observe in the red litmus paper in testing the household ammonia? In the blue litmus paper?
3. Which substances you tested were acids?
4. Which substances you tested were bases?
5. Were any substances you tested neither acid nor base? List them, if any. What word could you use to describe such substances?

### Conclusion

How can litmus papers be used to identify a substance as an acid or a base?

Pure water (such as distilled water) is not made up strictly of $H_2O$ molecules. Some of the $H_2O$ molecules have broken up into $H^+$ and $OH^-$ ions. There are equal numbers of these ions in pure water. When an acid is added to water, there will be more $H^+$ ions than $OH^-$ ions. When a base is added to water, there will be more $OH^-$ ions than $H^+$ ions.

### Check yourself

1. Name three foods that contain an acid.
2. Which is more acidic—a pH of 3 or a pH of 5?
3. What ion can be found in water solutions of bases?

### Neutralization and salts

Your stomach normally contains hydrochloric acid. Some people take drugs known as antacids when they feel discomfort due to too much acid in the stomach. Antacids contain a base. The base neutralizes some of the acid.

When a base neutralizes an acid, hydroxide ions from the base combine with hydrogen ions from the acid. Water is formed. The chemical equation is

$$OH^- + H^+ \rightarrow H_2O.$$

Another product is formed as well when an acid and base neutralize each other. For example, suppose HCl in the stomach is neutralized by an antacid containing magnesium hydroxide, $Mg(OH)_2$. The complete chemical equation is

$$2HCl + Mg(OH)_2 \rightarrow 2H_2O + MgCl_2.$$

The product magnesium chloride, $MgCl_2$, is formed from the positive ion $Mg^{2+}$ of the base and the negative ion $Cl^-$ of the acid. This kind of compound is known as a **salt**. Salts are always formed from the positive ion of a base and the negative ion of an acid. A salt usually contains a metal and a nonmetal.

**Safety**
Never take more than the recommended dose given in the directions on any package of medicine.

**Main Idea**

How can we recognize that a certain chemical is a salt?

Figure 2-33. The discomfort of an acid stomach can be relieved by taking an antacid such as magnesium hydroxide.

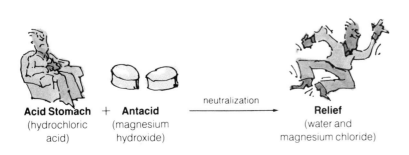

**Acid Stomach** + **Antacid**    —neutralization→    **Relief**
(hydrochloric      (magnesium                      (water and
acid)              hydroxide)                 magnesium chloride)

Common table salt, NaCl, is formed in the same way. Its sodium ion Na$^+$ comes from the base sodium hydroxide, NaOH. Its chloride ion Cl$^-$ comes from the acid hydrochloric acid, HCl. The complete equation is

$$HCl + NaOH \rightarrow H_2O + NaCl.$$

Which acid and base neutralize each other in the reaction that forms the salt potassium chloride, KCl?

All neutralization reactions between an acid and a base produce a salt and water.

$$acid + base \rightarrow salt + water$$

Although salts are all formed in the same standard way, they do not have the same properties. Some, but not all, are white like table salt. Some, but not all, dissolve in water. Some, but not all, taste salty.

**Check yourself**

1. What products are formed when an acid and a base neutralize each other?

2. What acid and what base form sodium chloride, NaCl, when they neutralize each other?

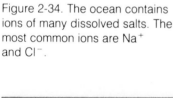

Figure 2-34. The ocean contains ions of many dissolved salts. The most common ions are Na$^+$ and Cl$^-$.

# Careers  Chemist / Medical Technologist

**Chemist**  Chemists usually perform some kind of research. They are employed by industry, by government agencies, and by universities and colleges. Some may investigate the basic properties and behaviors of matter. Others work on the development of new substances with desired properties. Still other chemists strive to improve existing products that can be used by industry or the public. Chemists play an important role in the petroleum and fuel industries, in agriculture, and in clothing industries. They may also be asked to participate in criminal investigations.

The chemical technician's job is to assist the chemist in doing research. Chemical technicians must understand the procedures needed to carry out the chemist's ideas. Chemical technicians work in every type of chemical laboratory and factory. They are usually part of a team engaged in chemical research, design, development, production, analysis or testing.

To become a chemical technician usually requires a strong high school science and math background, on-the-job training, and sometimes a two-year college program. Chemists have college degrees. Employment is possible with a bachelor's degree, but specialized areas may require advanced degrees.

In the laboratory, a chemist may make tests to try to identify the substances in a mixture.

**Medical Technologist**  The job of the medical technologist includes the analysis of blood, fluids, and tissues from the human body. The technologist relies on sensitive instruments and microscopes in making these analyses. The results of the technologist's work is helpful in the diagnosis and treatment of disease. Technologists may be employed in hospitals, independent laboratories, physician's offices, public health agencies, or in research institutions.

Accuracy, ability to work under pressure, manual dexterity, and normal color vision are important attributes of the medical technologist.

Medical technologists are usually trained in community colleges, trade schools, technical institutes, or in the armed forces. They must receive a professional license. High school biology, chemistry, and math courses provide a good preparation for training as a medical technologist.

A medical technologist uses sensitive instruments to analyze blood, fluid, and tissues.

# Practical Science

## How Soap Works

Soap is a cleansing agent from a mixture of sodium or other metallic salts and fatty acids from oils and fats.

Fats and oils are chemicals called *esters*. Esters are easily bonded to water in the presence of acids and bases. This type of bonding is called *saponification*. Saponification is the key process in making soap.

**How soap is made**   A Roman historian named Pliny described the method of soap manufacture used in the first century A.D. He noted that goat tallow, or fat, was boiled with wood ashes to produce a soapy paste. Then the paste was treated with salt. The result was a hard soap that, when rubbed with water, produced cleansing suds.

There was little change in this method of making soap for hundreds of years. Indeed, most people made their own soap, or did without it. In the early 19th century, more sophisticated chemical and industrial processes were discovered. Then large-scale soap manufacturing began.

Today, soap is made by heating beef tallow, coconut oil, or other fat in large kettles with an excess of sodium hydroxide. When sodium chloride (table salt) is added to the mixture, the sodium salts of the fatty acids separate as a thick curd of crude soap. The crude soap is then purified. Further processing creates a finished product that can range from a liquid to a decorative bar, and from flakes to powders. Pure soap is beige and has no smell. Perfumes and coloring agents are added by soap manufacturers. These additives do not increase a soap's cleansing power, but do serve to increase sales.

**Some types of soap**   The familiar, waxy bars you use for washing your hands and face are called *hard-milled* soaps. Hard-milled soaps are made by passing soap between rollers that make it compact, dense, and shiny. The rollers also may be used to press perfumes and other additives into the soap.

*Soap powder* is made by spraying liquid soap into a stream of heated air. The resulting puffy particles dissolve readily in your washing machine on laundry day.

**How soap does its work**   There is still some disagreement among scientists about how soap actually removes dirt. Most scientists believe that soap removes dirt in the following way. One end of each soap molecule becomes bonded to a water molecule. The other end of the soap molecule bonds to organic materials in dirt such as oil. This bonding serves to hook the organic material to the water molecule and pull it into solution. The soap-oil mixture forms droplets that disperse in the water and can then be readily washed away.

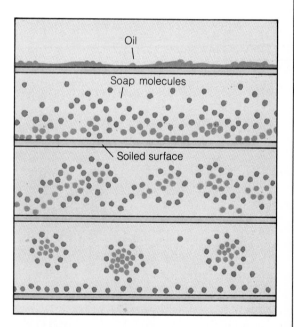

**Something to try**   Look at the ingredient lists for all the shampoos and detergents and soaps in your house. What is the most common ingredient in commercial soaps? Which ingredients do you think are doing the work? Which are there to improve the soap's color or smell?

## Section 3 Review   Chapter 2

### Check Your Vocabulary

| | |
|---|---|
| acid | hydroxide ion |
| base | ionic bond |
| chemical bond | pH |
| covalent bond | salt |

*Match each term above with the numbered phrase that best describes it.*

1. Exists when two atoms share one or more pairs of electrons
2. Formed when an acid and a base neutralize each other
3. Found in a solution of a base and water
4. Has a pH of less than 7
5. Measure of how acidic or basic a substance is
6. Is broken and/or formed in every chemical change
7. Turns red litmus paper blue
8. Exists between ions in a compound

### Check Your Knowledge

*Multiple Choice: Choose the answer that best completes each of the following sentences.*

1. Positive ions are formed when neutral atoms __?__.
   a) gain protons    c) lose protons
   b) gain electrons    d) lose electrons
2. Elements whose atoms are likely to form negative ions can be found in __?__.
   a) the alkali metal family
   b) the halogen family
   c) the inert gas family
   d) all families in the periodic table
3. Ionic compounds are a result of the __?__.
   a) transfer of electrons
   b) sharing of one electron by atoms in a molecule

c) sharing of a pair of electrons by atoms in a molecule
d) presence of more $OH^-$ ions than $H^+$ ions

### Check Your Understanding

1. For each of the following chemical equations, tell how many atoms of each element appear on each side and whether the equation is balanced.
   a. $O_2 + NO \rightarrow NO_2$
   b. $O_2 + C \rightarrow CO_2$
   c. $NO + O_2 \rightarrow 2NO_2$
   d. $2SO_2 + O_2 \rightarrow 2SO_3$
   e. $CH_4 + O_2 \rightarrow CO_2 + 2H_2O$
2. Explain why inert gases do not burn.
3. Explain why it is not wise to taste a substance in order to tell whether it is an acid or base. Describe two better ways to make such a test.
4. In the chemical equation
   $$NaOH + HNO_3 \rightarrow NaNO_3 + H_2O$$
   identify the acid, base, and salt and explain what clues helped you identify them.

### Practical Science

1. What is the method of making soap used by soap manufacturers today?
2. Many brands of soap, shampoo, and laundry powder are scented. How do they become scented?

# Chapter 2 Review

## Concept Summary

Processes of science include making repeated observations, inferring relationships between sets of observations, and forming theories by using the scientific method.

A scientific model is a description in terms of familiar things and is used to explain observations and predict behaviors.

The particle model of matter pictures matter as made of tiny particles with space between them.
- The particles of a gas are farther apart than those of a liquid or solid.
- An element is made of atoms, which are identical particles of that element.
- Compounds are made of two or more kinds of atoms joined in a fixed arrangement.
- In some elements and compounds, the atoms are grouped into particles known as molecules.
- Mixtures are made of two or more kinds of atoms that are not in a fixed arrangement.

The periodic table of the elements is an arrangement that is in order of increasing atomic number and in which elements with similar properties are in the same column.

The electron cloud model of the atom includes a nucleus containing protons and neutrons, surrounded by electrons at various energy levels.
- The elements in each row of the periodic table all have the same number of energy levels.
- The elements in each column of the periodic table all have the same number of electrons in the highest energy level.

Electric charges cause pushes and pulls between objects that do not have equal numbers of positive and negative charges.
- An electron has one negative charge.
- A proton has one positive charge.
- An atom that gives up electrons becomes a positive ion.
- An atom that accepts extra electrons becomes a negative ion.

A chemical bond is a tie between two atoms that have transferred or shared electrons.
- Chemical bonds result from the attraction between opposite charges.
- Chemical changes involve the forming and/or breaking of chemical bonds.

Acids and bases are substances that furnish hydrogen ions and hydroxide ions, respectively.
- The pH value of a substance is a measure of how acidic or basic the substance is.
- An acid and base can neutralize each other in a reaction that produces a salt and water.

## Putting It All Together

1. How does a theory differ from a hypothesis?
2. What property of gases supports the inference that there is more space between the particles in gases than in liquids or solids?
3. Describe how Dalton used the idea of atoms to explain the different properties of elements, compounds, and mixtures.
4. How does the particle model of a solid differ from the particle model of a liquid?
5. How do the individual molecules of the liquid form of water compare to those of water vapor?
6. What did Dalton assume about the number of atoms in a molecule?
7. What is a family of elements?
8. Which part of the periodic table contains the elements with metallic properties?
9. How is the atomic number of an element related to the structure of its atoms?
10. How are the structures of the elements in the same family similar?
11. How can you tell whether a chemical equation is balanced?
12. What is the difference between a charged object and a neutral object?
13. In which part of the periodic table are the elements that give up electrons easily?
14. What holds atoms together in a molecule?

15. How are covalent bonds different from ionic bonds?
16. What happens to chemical bonds during a chemical reaction?
17. What test could you use to identify a substance as an acid?
18. Would a substance with a pH of 9 be an acid, a base, or neutral?
19. What ions are present in pure water?

## Apply Your Knowledge

1. Dalton believed that all atoms of the same element were identical. How has the discovery of isotopes changed that view? In what way are atoms of the same element like each other?
2. Explain why a compound made of potassium and bromine is more likely to be like sodium chloride than like water. Would you expect the potassium-bromine compound to be molecular or ionic? Explain your reasoning.
3. The element astatine is in the sixth row down and the second column from the far right of the periodic table. How many energy levels are occupied by electrons in an atom of this element? How many electrons are in the highest energy level of these atoms? How do you know?
4. The atomic mass of lead is approximately two hundred times that of hydrogen. How would the number of atoms in a gram of hydrogen compare to the number in a gram of lead?

## Find Out on Your Own

1. Different antacids are sold for neutralizing excess acid in the stomach. Design and carry out an experiment to compare the effectiveness of two or more antacids.
2. Compare the effectiveness of two or more antistatic products in preventing clothes that are removed from a dryer from clinging to one another.
3. Place about 6 uncooked popcorn kernels in a plastic tumbler of water. Add an Alka-Seltzer tablet to the water. Observe what happens to the popcorn kernels. Look for two kernels stuck together. Do the kernels seem to be sharing a bubble between them? How is the sharing of a bubble similar to a covalent bond?
4. The colored liquid obtained from boiling a few leaves of purple cabbage in water can be used as an indicator. Add a few drops of the liquid to vinegar. What color change takes place? Add a few drops of the indicator to a solution of baking soda in water. What color change takes place?

## Reading Further

Asimov, Isaac. *How Did We Find Out About Atoms?* New York: Walker & Co., 1976
   From the ideas of the Greeks to the actual "pictures" of atoms from a field-emission microscope.

Chester, Michael. *Particles; An Introduction to Particle Physics.* New York: Macmillan Pub. Co., 1978.
   An introductory book on the structure of the atom and the atomic nucleus.

Cohen, Daniel. *Gold; The Fascinating Story of the Noble Metal Through the Ages.* New York: M. Evans & Co., 1976
   The story of gold from its discovery in ancient times, through the alchemists' search for how to make it, to its modern use.

# Chapter 3

# Motion

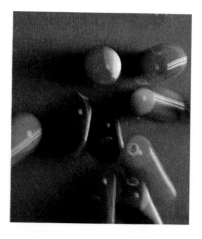

## Section 1
### Describing Motion

The speed of a moving object is related to how far it travels and how long it takes to travel that far. The speed of a moving object may change, or it may remain the same. An object may travel in a straight line, or its path may curve.

## Section 2
### Forces and Motion

Isaac Newton was the first person who realized the relation between forces and motion. He understood that an unbalanced force causes a change in speed or direction or both.

## Section 3
### Energy

Moving objects have energy, or the ability to cause change. Nonmoving objects have energy when they are in a position where a force can make them move. Each kind of energy can be changed into the other.

In this chapter you will learn how motion can be described and how it depends on forces. In the photo at the left, which objects are moving? How can you tell? What kinds of forces are affecting the windsurfers?

# Describing Motion    Section 1

**Section 1 of Chapter 3 is divided into five parts:**

Reference objects

Speed

Average speed

Constant speed

Acceleration

*Practical Science: Finding Your Way with Maps*

**Learning Objectives**

1. To describe the position and motion of an object with respect to a reference object.

2. To determine the speed of a moving object using time and distance measurements.

3. To recognize constant speed on a distance-time graph.

4. To differentiate between speed and acceleration.

5. To recognize changing speed (acceleration) on a distance-time graph.

Figure 3-1. Is the cyclist moving or are the bushes moving? What helps you decide?

Is the cyclist in Figure 3-1 moving? How do you explain the clear image of the cyclist? The blurred image of the bushes?

Now look at the three photos of a moving car in Figure 3-2. The photo on the left was taken first. The one on the right was taken last. The photos were taken with the same camera. Is the car coming toward or going away from the camera? What clues help you answer?

Figure 3-2. Can you be sure that the car, rather than the camera, is moving? What helps you decide?

## Reference objects

It is not always easy to decide which objects are moving. Clues are often found by looking at other objects in the surroundings. Normally, you think of signs or walls as stationary, not moving. You judge motion in relation to these apparently stationary objects. When you do this, you are using the signs or walls as **reference objects.**

When you are on a bus, you expect the bus to be moving and buildings to be still. You might see the wall of a building move by the window of the bus. Yet, you know it is the bus that is moving. You use the building as a reference object to judge the motion of the bus.

There are times you may be confused. Suppose your bus is parked close to a second bus. The bus next to you starts to move forward. You may think your bus is moving backward instead. You are fooled into thinking you are moving. This time your reference object is moving.

**Main Idea**

How can you judge whether something is moving?

Figure 3-3. Is the sun moving?

Imagine watching a beautiful sunset. The sun is slowly sinking below the horizon. But which is really moving—the sun or the earth? Even though the sun appears to move, you know it is really the earth that is moving. But wait! Is the sun perfectly still? Measurements made on distant stars indicate that the sun and all the planets are moving. The stars are also moving. In fact, there are no perfectly stationary objects to use as reference objects.

Even though buildings on the earth are moving, they can be perfectly good reference objects. Suppose you are studying a ball as it moves through the air. It makes sense to use a building as a reference object. It doesn't matter that the earth, to which the building is attached, is moving. On the other hand, suppose you were returning to the earth on a spacecraft. Then you should consider the movement of the earth. You might choose some stars as reference objects.

Generally, when you pick a reference object, you think of it as not moving. Then you compare the position of something else to that of the reference object. You study movement from the point of view of the reference object you choose.

Suppose you walk toward the rear of a moving bus. You are moving backward in relation to the bus. Yet, the bus is probably moving so fast that you are still moving forward in relation to the ground. The way you describe motion depends on the reference object you choose. Your description of motion will change as you change the reference object.

## Activity 3–1A    Describing Motion in Different Ways

### Materials

stick or pole 2 or 3 m in length
brightly-colored scarf or ribbon

### Purpose

To find out if the motion of an object can be described in different ways.

### Procedure

1. Choose a student to walk across the room with a long pole. The rest of the group observes.
2. Select a section of the wall in the room to act as the reference object. Tie the brightly-colored scarf around the pole near the top.
3. The first time, the student carrying the pole walks several steps across the room. Observe the change in the position of the pole in reference to the wall. Use the scarf to help you to make your observation.
4. The second time, the same student walks slowly across the room. This time, the student should move the pole slowly backwards at the same speed he or she is walking. Observe the position of the pole in relation to the wall and in relation to the student.

### Questions

1. In what direction does the pole move in relation to the reference section of the wall after the first walk?
2. After the first walk, what is the position of the pole in relation to the student carrying the pole?
3. After the second walk, what is the position of the pole in relation to the student carrying the pole?
4. What is the position of the pole in relation to the wall after the second walk?

### Conclusion

What are some of the ways the motion of an object can be described?

### Check yourself

How can a reference object be used to study the motion of something else?

### Speed

**Speed** describes how fast an object is moving in relation to a reference object. Objects in motion move at different speeds. That is, some objects move faster than others.

A car on a highway travels at about 90 kilometers per hour, which is the same as 25 meters per second. A very fast runner may reach a speed near 10 meters per second. Light travels at 300 million meters per second. Other objects move at very slow speeds. A glacier may move only a few centimeters per year.

Notice that speeds are described in units of distance *and* time. In the examples given, the distance units are kilometers, meters, or centimeters. The time units are years, hours, or seconds. Common units of speed are meters per second (m/s) and kilometers per hour (km/h). Note that when symbols are used for the distance and time units, the slash (/) means *per*.

You can measure the speed of a moving object. For example, you can measure how long it takes someone to bike a certain distance, such as 100 m. Or, you can measure how far the person can bike in a certain time, such as 10 s. In either case, the speed will be the distance traveled divided by the time it takes to travel that distance.

$$\text{speed} = \frac{\text{distance}}{\text{time}}$$

**Main Idea**

What are two common units of speed?

Figure 3-4. What two things must be known before the speed of an object can be known?

## Activity 3–1B        Measuring Speed

### Materials

watch or clock that indicates seconds
tape measure

### Purpose

To show how the speed of an object is measured.

### Procedure

1. Use a large activity field or a gymnasium. Establish a starting line. Use a tape measure to draw a finish line 50 meters from the starting line. Then measure and draw lines at 5-meter intervals between the start and finish lines. Label the lines 5 m, 10 m, 15 m, and so forth.
2. One student should act as a timer and another student should record the data. Select ten students to be runners.
3. For Trial 1, measure the time it takes each person to run 50 m. Record the time for each runner. List the five fastest runners.
4. Select a shorter time interval for running Trial 2. Use the 5-m lines to estimate the distance each person runs in this time interval. Record the data.
5. Calculate the speed of each runner. List the five runners with the best speed.

### Questions

1. Considering their running times, which runners have the higher speeds?
2. Considering their running distances, which runners have the higher speeds?
3. How does the list of the five fastest runners in the 50-meter trial compare to the list of the five fastest runners in the timed trial?

### Conclusion

How is the speed of an object measured?

| Name of student | Trial 1 | Trial 2 | Speed meters ÷ seconds | |
|---|---|---|---|---|
| | Running time for 50 meters | Running distance for ____ seconds | Trial 1 | Trial 2 |
| 1. | | | | |
| 2. | | | | |

You can see that speed is both distance *per* unit of time and distance *divided by* time. The word *per* means *divided by*.
    Suppose the biker went 100 m in 4 s. The speed was

$$\frac{100\,\text{m}}{4\,\text{s}} = 25 \text{ m/s}.$$

Or, suppose the biker went 250 m in 10 s. The speed was

$$\frac{250\,\text{m}}{10\,\text{s}} = 25 \text{ m/s}.$$

*Good Word Problem to show speed*

The speed of the biker in both examples was 25 m/s. This means that the biker traveled 25 m in each second. Does this agree with the measurement of 4 s to go 100 m? Does it agree with a measurement of 250 m traveled in 10 s? Here is how to find out.

When you know the speed of something, you can find how far it will travel in a certain time.

$$\text{distance} = \text{speed} \times \text{time}$$

The biker traveled for 4 s at 25 m/s.

$$(25 \text{ m/s}) \times (4 \text{ s}) = 100 \text{ m}$$

In the second measurement, the biker traveled for 10 s at 25 m/s.

$$(25 \text{ m/s}) \times (10 \text{ s}) = 250 \text{ m}$$

Both answers agree with the measurements.

### Check yourself

1. What two kinds of units make up all units of speed?

2. What is the speed of a skater who travels a distance of 210 m in a time of 10 s?

3. How far can a person run in 10 min at a speed of 260 m/min?

### Average speed

The speed found for the biker was an **average speed**. He or she may have biked faster at the beginning or near the end or in the middle. But overall, the speed was 25 m/s.

When you travel a long distance in an automobile, you probably change your speed often. You slow down in towns and going up hills or around curves. You speed up going downhill or on the open road.

Dividing total distance traveled by the total time on the road gives average speed. Suppose you travel a total distance of 800 km in 16 h. Your average speed equals

$$\frac{800 \text{ km}}{16 \text{ h}} = 50 \text{ km/h}.$$

But some of the time you may have traveled at 90 km/h. And some of the time you may have been stopped at a gas station or restaurant.

Figure 3-5. During a race, the speed of a swimmer usually changes. Is the winner the swimmer with the highest average speed?

### Check yourself

Does an average speed indicate how fast something travels at every moment during a trip? Explain.

### Constant speed

An object that does not change its speed is moving at **constant speed.** How does an automobile driver know when the car is traveling at constant speed?

Suppose you wanted to jog around a marked track at constant speed for half an hour. How could you check that your speed was constant? Constant speed means equal distances are covered in equal times. You could use a stopwatch to measure how long it takes to jog each lap of the track. It would be even better to measure how long it takes to travel very short distances of equal length. If all the times are the same, your speed must be constant.

Suppose you jogged each lap in 2 min. How long would it take to jog 14 laps? You could calculate the answer. But another way to find out is to make a distance-time graph. On a distance-time graph, distance is marked off on the vertical axis. Study Figure 3-6a. It shows distance marked in units of laps. Time is marked off along the horizontal axis. It is marked in units of minutes.

In Figure 3-6a, there is a point at zero time and zero distance. At zero time no distance had been covered. The point at the time of 2 min and the distance of one lap shows that it took 2 min to cover the first lap. There is another point for 2 min later. At that time another lap had been covered. The total distance after a total time of 4 min was 2 laps. After another 2 min (total time 6 min), another lap had been covered (total distance 3 laps). Similarly, after a total time of 8 min, a total distance of 4 laps had been covered.

Figure 3-6. A distance-time graph for a jogger who covers each lap in 2 min. How long does it take to cover 14 laps?

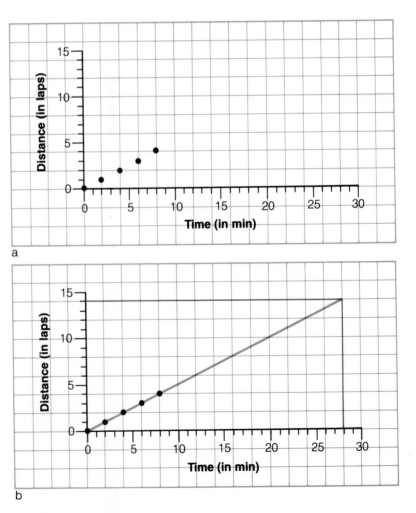

## Activity 3–1C          Recognizing Constant Speed

### Materials

toy vehicle (battery powered)
table top or flat surface
meter stick or tape measure
masking tape
watch or clock that indicates seconds

### Purpose

To recognize that an object is moving at constant speed.

### Procedure

1. Find a flat, smooth surface at least 2 m long.
2. Use a meter stick and masking tape to mark off distances at intervals of 20 cm on the surface.
3. Designate one student to be the timer. The timer will start the watch when the vehicle is released at the starting line. The timer should call out the time when the vehicle passes each of the distance markers.
4. Designate a second student to write down the time when the vehicle passes each of the distance markers.
5. Designate a third student to release the vehicle at the starting line.
6. Make at least one practice run before any data is recorded. (The speed of the vehicle may make it more convenient to use smaller or larger distance intervals.)
7. Make a distance–time graph like the one shown in Figure 3–6. Mark distance units on the vertical axis and time units on the horizontal axis. Plot your data.

### Question

1. Do the plotted points seem to line up along a straight line or nearly so? If they do, draw a straight line through the points.
   (A straight line indicates that the vehicle was traveling with constant speed.)

| Distance | Time |
|---|---|
|  |  |
|  |  |
|  |  |

### Conclusion

Was the speed of the vehicle constant? Explain how you can tell.

A straight line can be drawn through all five points in Figure 3-6a. In Figure 3-6b, the straight line has been drawn. Look at where the straight line crosses the distance line for 14 laps. What time line meets the distance line at this point? The answer tells you how long it took to jog 14 laps.

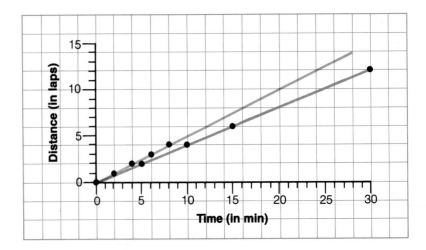

Figure 3-7. You know which jogger was faster. How do you recognize the faster jogger from the graphs?

Suppose you are jogging with a friend. Your friend can't keep up with you. He finds that it takes 2.5 min to complete each lap. Nevertheless, he is able to keep going for 12 laps. Each lap takes the same amount of time. After 5 min he has run two laps. After 10 min he has run four laps. After 15 min he has run six laps. He completes the 12 laps in 30 min. A distance-time graph describing your friend's jogging is shown in Figure 3-7. The first graph is included for comparison.

The line describing the motion of your friend is not as steep as the first line. He covered less distance in the same time. His speed was slower. You can compare speeds on a distance-time graph. The greater speed has a steeper line. The line representing the slower speed will have a less steep line. Suppose you time a member of your school track team. She is able to cover each lap in 1.5 min. How would a line describing her motion compare to the other two lines?

### Check yourself

1.  How is an average speed different from a constant speed?
2.  On a distance-time graph, how can you tell which of two lines represents a slower constant speed?

### Acceleration

A baseball rolls down a steep hill. What happens to its speed? An automobile driver places his or her foot on the brake pedal. What happens to the speed of the automobile? The gun sounds for the start of a race. What happens to the speed of the runners? In all these examples, the speed of something changes. The ball rolls faster and faster. The automobile slows down. The runners start moving and quickly reach top speed.

You most likely have felt the effects of changing speed. You lurch forward if you are on a bus that comes to a sudden stop. You get pressed back against your seat on an airplane that is taking off down the runway. The faster the speed changes, the more you feel it. If a bus gently slows down, you don't notice the change.

An object that is changing speed is **accelerating** (ak-SEL′-er-rayt′-ing). In common speech, an accelerating object is speeding up, but in science, objects slowing down are also said to be accelerating.

An object does not have to be changing its speed to be accelerating. Moving objects that change direction are also accelerating. **Acceleration** (ak-sel′-er-RAY′-shun) is the changing of the speed and/or direction of motion of an object. You feel the effects of acceleration in an automobile that is making a sharp turn. During the turn, you lurch to the side.

Suppose you are riding in an automobile. You fasten your seat belt, and the driver starts the car. You can see both the odometer (distance gauge) and the second hand of your watch.

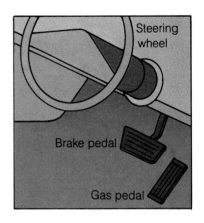

Figure 3-8. How do each of these three parts cause an automobile to accelerate?

Figure 3-9. Do the thrills in riding a roller coaster come from the speed or the acceleration? Explain.

| Time (in s) | Total distance (in km) |
|---|---|
| 0 | 0.0 |
| 30 | 0.1 |
| 60 | 0.3 |
| 90 | 0.6 |
| 120 | 1.0 |
| 150 | 1.5 |
| 180 | 2.0 |
| 210 | 2.5 |
| 240 | 3.0 |

Table 3-1. Time and distance data for a car ride.

Figure 3-10. When is the speed of the automobile changing? When is the speed of the automobile constant?

The odometer is set at zero when you start. Every 30 seconds you record how far the car has gone. At the end of 240 s, or 4 min, you have the data shown in Table 3-1.

Figure 3-10 shows a distance-time graph based on the data in Table 3-1. If you had actually been riding in the automobile, you would have recognized a change in speed. Can you recognize that the speed is changing from the graph? How does this graph compare with a graph of constant speed?

Constant speed is recognized on a distance-time graph by a straight line. Changing speed is recognized by a line that is not straight. Constant speed results in equal distances traveled in equal times. According to Table 3-1, how far did the car go in the first 30 s? during the next 30 s? Was it speeding up or slowing down? Explain how you know.

Lay a straight edge against the graph line in Figure 3-10. Find the portion of the line that is straight. Was the car traveling at constant speed during this time? To check your answer, use Table 3-1 to find out how far the car went every 30 s. When was it traveling equal distances in equal times?

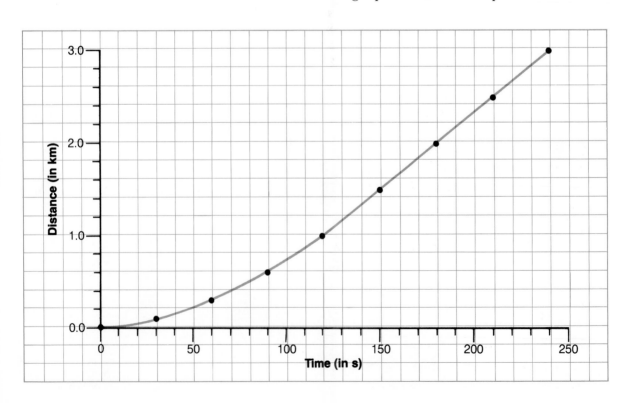

## Activity 3–1D          Detecting Changes in Speed and Direction

### Materials

vial with cap or small test tube with stopper
water
small cart or roller skate
masking tape

### Purpose

To determine how changes in speed and direction can be detected.

### Procedure

1. Fill a vial with water. Leave only a small space for an air bubble.
2. Cap the vial and turn it on its side. The small air bubble should be visible. Make sure the vial does not leak.
3. Tape the vial in this position to the side or top of a small cart or roller skate. Make sure that the bubble is in the middle of the upper side of the vial when the cart is not moving.
4. Give the cart a push. Record the direction the bubble moves.
5. When the cart is moving, quickly bring the cart to a stop. Record the direction the bubble moves.
6. Pull the cart at constant speed. Record what the bubble does.
7. While the cart is moving at constant speed, change its direction by giving it a twist. Record what the bubble does.

### Questions

1. What was happening to the cart when the bubble moved forward?
2. What was happening to the cart when the bubble moved backward?
3. What did the bubble do when the direction the cart was moving changed?
4. Under what conditions did the bubble remain in the center?

### Conclusion

Under what conditions did the bubble change its position?

### Check yourself

1. When an object is slowing down, is it accelerating? Explain your answer.

2. How is it possible for an object to be moving at constant speed and yet be accelerating?

3. On a distance-time graph, what kind of line represents motion that is not at constant speed?

# Practical Science

## Finding Your Way with Maps

The art and science of mapmaking is quite old. Mapmakers, also called cartographers, have been making maps since about 2000 B.C. The earliest maps were made in the Near East, in Babylonia and Egypt.

Gerhard Kremer, known as Mercator, was a famous sixteenth-century cartographer. He developed a method of projecting the earth on paper that was invaluable to navigators. Maps were especially important to navigators in search of new lands and trade routes. In turn, explorers of land and sea were important sources of information for cartographers.

Accuracy and precision are crucial elements in mapmaking. Today, mapmaking has become an even more exact study, thanks to information provided by airplanes and satellites.

**Types of maps**   There are many types of maps containing different kinds of information.

A political map shows the locations of county, state, and national boundaries. It may also show the locations of cities and towns.

A physical map depicts the natural features of the land, including mountains, lakes, and rivers. A topographic map indicates the elevations of those natural features, as well as the presence of roads, buildings, and other structures.

A map used for ship navigation is called a *chart*. A chart indicates water depths, currents, and other features needed to navigate a ship.

A good atlas will contain examples of these and other kinds of maps.

**Finding your way**   You have probably seen a road map at home or at a gas station. Road maps show highways, cities, and other features you need to know when traveling by car from place to place. With a road map you can find your starting and destination points, the distance to your destination, and the direction you must travel.

A road map, like any other map, is much smaller than the area of the earth it represents. The relationship between a distance measured on the map and the actual distance it represents is called the *scale* of the map. The scale may be given as a statement such as "one centimeter equals one kilometer" or "1 cm = 1 km." A small scale map covers a large area and shows only major features such as paved roads, large rivers, and cities. A large scale map covers a small area and shows much more detail than a small scale map.

A map may also have a scale bar which looks like a ruler. The scale bar is marked in equal units indicating distances they represent on the map. The scale bar is especially useful for measuring distances from place to place on a map.

Compass direction on a map—north, east, south, and west—is indicated by an arrow. The direction in which the arrow points always indicates north. If no arrow is present, you may assume north is at the top of the map. Once you know where north is, you can determine all the other compass points.

**Map symbols**   Cartographers use symbols to indicate railroads, roads, bridges, schools, dams, and other features. These symbols and their explanations are found in a separate area on a map. Together, they constitute the *legend* of the map.

**Something to try**   Look at any road map. Find the scale and the legend. Identify some of the symbols on the map using the legend.

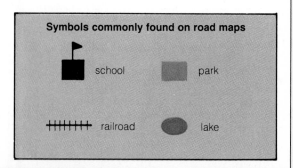

**Symbols commonly found on road maps**

school   park

railroad   lake

## Section 1 Review   Chapter 3

### Check Your Vocabulary

acceleration          reference object

average speed         speed

constant speed

*Match each term above with the numbered phrase that best describes it.*

1. Total distance traveled divided by total travel time

2. Considered nonmoving in relation to a moving object

3. How fast something moves

4. The changing of the speed or direction of a moving object

5. Describes motion of an object that always travels equal distances in equal times

### Check Your Knowledge

*Multiple Choice: Choose the answer that best completes each of the following sentences.*

1. The speed of a flight attendant walking down the aisle of a moving plane is NOT the same in relation to a seated passenger as in relation to ?.
   a) another seated passenger
   b) a person on the ground
   c) the cockpit of the plane
   d) the wings of the plane

2. An object is NOT accelerating in the scientific sense when it ?.
   a) speeds up
   b) slows down
   c) moves around a curve at constant speed
   d) moves in a straight line at constant speed

3. A runner travels 300 m in 150 s. The average speed of the runner is ?.
   a) 0.5 m/s          c) 2 km/h
   b) 2 m/s            d) 45 000 m/s

### Check Your Understanding

1. The graph shows distance-time lines for three cyclists during a race. Which one was going the fastest? Explain how you know.

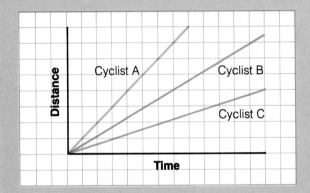

2. A cyclist averages 30 km/h on a cross-country trip. She plans to ride 10 hours a day.
   a. How far can she expect to go in one day?
   b. How many days will it take her to travel 4500 km?

3. Explain why an object moving in a circle at constant speed is considered to be accelerating.

### Practical Science

1. What does the scale of a map indicate?

2. In what ways can a scale be shown on a map?

3. How is compass direction indicated on a map?

# Forces and Motion    Section 2

**Section 2 of Chapter 3 is divided into eight parts:**

Forces

First law of motion

Second law of motion

Third law of motion

The law of gravitation

Weight and mass

Motion under gravity

Curved motion under gravity

*Practical Science: Flying with Bernoulli*

## Learning Objectives

1. To identify the forces acting on an object both when the forces are balanced and unbalanced.

2. To describe the effects of friction on a moving object.

3. To relate the acceleration of an object to the force applied and to the mass of the object.

4. To recognize that forces always come in pairs that are described as action and reaction forces.

5. To apply the law of gravitation to the motion of objects.

Figure 3-11. In this strobe photo, you can see multiple images of two bouncing balls. How does the force of gravity affect the motion of falling objects?

You have observed and described moving objects. You might be wondering, What causes objects to start moving? What must be done to stop moving objects? How do you change the motion of an object? These questions will be explored in this section.

## Forces

Suppose a book is resting on your desk. You can move it by lifting it. You can push it away from you. You can pull it toward you. The lift, push, or pull is called a **force**.

You use forces to make an object start moving. You also use forces to stop moving objects. You pull on the brake controls of a bicycle. You catch a baseball. Sometimes you use forces to change the direction of the motion of an object. When you hit a tennis ball or a baseball, it reverses direction. You change the direction of your bicycle with a force on the handlebars. Finally, forces can change the shape of objects. You can crumple a sheet of paper or an aluminum can with a force.

Forces can cause changes in the motion of objects. They can cause changes in the shape of objects. Sometimes, however, you can exert a force on an object and no change in motion or shape occurs. A force that produces no change must be balanced by another force. Forces that oppose each other with equal strength are **balanced forces**.

Suppose a book drops to the floor from the edge of your desk. A force must have caused the motion. You are well acquainted with this force. The force is gravity. Objects are pulled toward the center of the earth by gravity. In other words, gravity pulls objects downward.

Suppose the book is back on top of the desk. The book is again at rest. Is the force of gravity still acting on the book? Yes, the force of gravity is always present, pulling the book downward. Then why doesn't the book move?

There must be another force that balances the force of gravity. The desk top is pushing upward on the book. Since no motion results, the upward force must be exactly as strong as the downward force. The upward push of the desk and the downward pull of gravity are balanced forces.

Figure 3-12. In soccer, what do players do to start the ball moving? To stop it? To change its direction?

Figure 3-13. Why doesn't the book move?

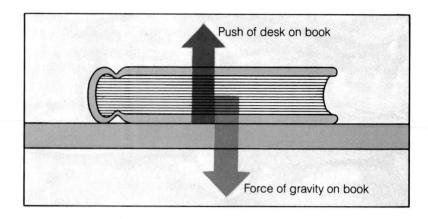

Push of desk on book

Force of gravity on book

## Main Idea

What is true about the strength and direction of two balanced forces?

Suppose two forces acting on an object are balanced. They must be equal in strength and opposite in direction. Figure 3-13 shows how the forces can be shown as arrows. The equal strength is represented by arrows of the same length. The direction of each force is represented by the direction of the arrows.

You may be seated at your desk as you read this sentence. Gravity is also pulling you downward. Since you are not moving downward, another force must be pushing you upward. Become aware of the chair seat pushing upward on you. This force must balance the force of gravity. As a result, you do not move.

### Check yourself

1. Does a force on an object always cause a change in the motion or shape of the object? Explain.
2. When a force is represented by an arrow, what do the length and the direction of the arrow represent?

### Newton's first law of motion

If something is not moving, you know the forces on it are balanced. But what about an object that is already moving? What about an object that starts to move? What about an object that stops moving?

Greek philosophers who lived about 2300 years ago studied motion. They thought matter should normally be at rest. They believed all objects in motion tended to stop moving. According to their thinking, an unbalanced force had to be present just to keep an object moving.

A ball thrown upward soon falls back down to earth and stops moving. A cart rolling on a level surface also soon stops. The early Greek philosophers believed that objects stopped because no force was present to keep them moving.

In the seventeenth century, Isaac Newton (1642–1727) suggested a different explanation. He believed that as long as the forces on an object are balanced, the object does not change its motion. This tendency of an object to resist changes in its motion is called the **inertia** (ih-NER'-shuh) of the object. Because of inertia, an object at rest tends to stay at rest. Because of inertia, a moving object tends to move in a straight line at constant speed. Changes in motion can take place only if the forces on an object are unbalanced. This is Newton's first law of motion. An unbalanced force is needed to change the motion of an object.

According to Newton, a ball thrown upward comes back down because the force of gravity is acting on the ball. A rolling cart stops because of a force known as **friction**. If there were no forces on the ball and cart, they would keep moving in one direction forever.

Figure 3-14. How did the early Greek philosophers explain why a rolling cart soon stops? How did Newton explain it?

## Library research

Read about sliding friction. How does it differ from static friction? Does sliding friction depend on the speed of the moving object? What about the friction between a liquid or gas and an object moving through it?

Figure 3-15. According to Newton's first law, an unbalanced force of any size can put an object in motion. Yet, this couch is not moving. Explain why it isn't.

One kind of friction acts on moving objects. It is caused by contact between the moving object and another substance. Friction always tends to slow down the moving object. For example, the wheels of a cart are in contact with the ground. Friction between the wheels and the ground makes the cart slow down.

A boat moving through the water is slowed by friction. Water is in contact with the lower part of the boat. Air is in contact with the upper part of the boat. The contacts of the boat with both the air and the water cause friction. The friction slows the boat.

Another kind of friction keeps objects from moving when they are pushed gently. Suppose you wish to move a heavy trunk across the floor. You would have to push hard to get it moving. Friction between the trunk and the floor balances your push up to a certain point. This kind of friction is called **static** (STAT'-ik) **friction**. The word *static* means *at rest*. Static friction tends to keep an object at rest. To move the trunk, you have to exert a force great enough to overcome the force of static friction.

Even if there is no static friction, some force is required to start an object moving. However, the force can be any size, even very small. Once an object is moving, if there is no friction nor any other force, the object keeps moving at the same speed in a straight line.

You have experienced the effect of Newton's first law of motion. When you are in an automobile, the force to start you moving is supplied by the engine. Once you are moving at constant speed, you keep moving. Even when the brakes are applied, you tend to keep moving forward. What keeps you from hitting the dashboard or windshield? If the braking is gentle, the friction of the car seat is enough to slow you down with the car. If the braking is sharp, only a fastened seat belt can slow you down in time.

What happens to you when the automobile turns a corner? You tend to continue moving in a straight line. A force is needed to keep you from hitting the door when the car changes direction. Again, a seat belt will keep you in place.

Figure 3-16. How do seat belts protect people against the effects of Newton's first law of motion?

### Check yourself

1. According to early Greek philosophers, what keeps an object in motion?

2. According to Isaac Newton, what keeps an object in motion?

3. What force balances your push when you try to push a heavy bookcase?

### Newton's second law of motion

Newton's first law of motion predicts what will happen to an object when no unbalanced force acts on it. His second law of motion predicts what will happen to an object when an unbalanced force does act on it.

Suppose two movers start out in an empty moving van. They drive on an expressway to reach the house whose goods they are to load. As they enter the expressway, they speed up quickly until they are at the speed limit. When they reach their exit, the van responds well to the brakes and slows quickly.

**Main Idea**

How do Newton's first and second laws of motion differ?

The driver has no trouble steering the van around the curve of the exit ramp.

At the house, the movers load up the van. Now the van is full of furniture and appliances. The movers drive back onto the expressway. They notice it is much harder to speed up, even with the pedal pressed to the floor. It takes a longer time than before to reach the speed limit. The driver realizes that he will have to start braking for the exit earlier than before. As he steers the van around the exit curve, he has to pull harder on the steering wheel than before. The loaded van seems to be more resistant to any changes in its motion than the empty van.

The same engine speeds up the van whether it is empty or full. The same brakes slow it down. So the forces that change the speed are about the same. But with the same forces, the speed changes less quickly when the van is full than when it is empty.

Newton realized that when the force is the same size, some objects change speed more quickly than others. He said that the mass of the object made the difference. A full van has more mass than an empty van. The more mass an object has, the less quickly it changes speed under the same force.

He also realized that objects of different mass can change speed equally quickly if the forces are adjusted. The object with more mass needs a greater force to change speed at the same rate. Automobiles with more mass are usually made with more powerful engines. Then they can get up to speed as quickly as smaller automobiles. Of course, they use more gasoline doing so.

When an object is changing direction, the mass makes a difference as well. More force is required to move the full van around the exit ramp curve at the same speed. If the driver had not been able to supply more force, what would have happened? The van would have changed direction less quickly. It would have moved on a wider curve and gone off the road. Automobiles with more mass are usually made with power steering. Power steering helps drivers steer around curves.

In Newton's second law, he showed how force was related to mass and acceleration. According to the second law, the

## Main Idea

How did Newton explain why different objects change speed at different rates under the same size force?

Figure 3-17. What should the driver of a fully loaded camper remember from Newton's second law?

greater the force is, the greater the acceleration. The greater the mass is, the smaller the acceleration. That is, the greater the force is, the more quickly an object changes speed or direction. And the greater the mass is, the less quickly an object changes speed or direction.

The SI unit of force is named after Isaac Newton. It is called the **newton** (symbol N). One newton is the amount of force required to speed up a 1-kg mass an additional 1 m/s every second. A 2-N force will speed up the same 1-kg mass by 2 m/s every second. Doubling the force doubles the acceleration. But a 2-N force will speed up a 2-kg mass by only 1 m/s every second. Doubling the mass cuts the acceleration in half.

The change in motion produced by a force depends on both the size and direction of the force. Pushing a bicycle in the direction it is moving will speed it up. Pushing a bicycle in a direction opposite to its direction of motion will slow it down. And pushing it from the side will make it change direction.

**Main Idea**

What is the SI unit of force?

### Check yourself

1. How is the mass of an object related to how quickly the object can change speed or direction when a force acts on it?

2. How is the amount of force on an object related to how quickly the object can change speed or direction?

3. What effect could a 2-N force have on a 1-kg mass? On a 2-kg mass?

## Newton's third law of motion

**Main Idea**

What property of forces is described in Newton's third law of motion?

3rd
Law

3rd
Law

Another property of forces was described by Newton. It is called the third law of motion. Newton realized that if one object pulls on another, the second object also pulls back on the first object. If one object pushes on another, the second pushes back on the first object. In other words, for every action by a force there is a reaction by another force. Forces always come in pairs.

Try pressing your finger against your desk. The desk pushes back against your finger. The harder you press, the harder the desk presses back. The force that the desk exerts on your finger is always the same size as the force your finger exerts on the desk. Another way to state the third law of motion is that for every force, there is an equal and opposite force. The two equal and opposite forces act on different objects. The force of your finger acts on the desk. The force exerted by the desk acts on your finger.

Suppose you jump from a boat to the dock. As you jump, you push against the boat. The boat pushes back against you. The two pushes make a pair of equal and opposite forces. Your push on the boat can be thought of as the action force. It makes the boat move away from the dock. The push of the boat on you can be thought of as the reaction force. It makes you move to the dock. The two motions are the result of the two forces acting on the different objects.

When you walk or run, you make use of reaction forces. With your feet, you push backward against the ground. The ground then pushes forward on you.

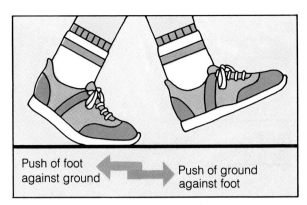

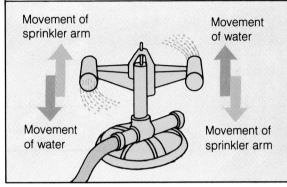

A rotating water sprinkler is another example of action and reaction. Water is forced from the sprinkler. This is the action. The reaction is the movement of the sprinkler arms away from the water. You feel the same kind of reaction when you hold a water hose and turn the water on quickly. You may have seen firefighters struggling to control a fire hose. The hose is forced backward when the water leaves it. This reaction makes the hose hard to handle.

Consider the pull of gravity on you. The earth pulls downward on you with a force. According to Newton's third law, you pull upward on the earth with the same size force. But if you jump off a diving board, you fall to the earth. Why

Figure 3-18. How do runners and water sprinklers make use of Newton's third law of motion?

Figure 3-19. Why doesn't the diver's pull on the earth make the earth move upward?

## Activity 3–2A    Action and Reaction

### Materials

2 skateboards
3-m rope with knot in center
meter stick or tape measure
protective clothing

### Purpose

To show that for an action force, there is an equal and opposite reaction force.

### Procedure

1. Have two students of equal mass stand on skateboards pointing straight at one another. Designate as Student A and Student B. SAFETY NOTE: *They should be wearing protective clothing.*
2. Have the students move apart with the rope fully extended between them. Mark the middle (beside the knot).
3. Mark the starting points of Students A and B. Predict the point where they will meet when Student B pulls on the rope.
4. Have Student B pull on the rope. Measure and record how far each student moves.
5. Return the skateboards to the starting points used in Step 4. Predict the point at which Students A and B will meet when Student A pulls on the rope.
6. Have Student A pull on the rope. Measure and record how far each student moves.
7. Repeat Steps 1 through 7 with two students with very different masses.

### Questions

1. Was the direction of motion of Student A opposite to the direction of motion of Student B in all trials?
2. How did the distances moved by Students A and B compare when they had similar masses and when they had different masses?
3. If you had only seen their starting and ending positions, could you have told which student did the pulling? Explain.

### Conclusion

How did the size and direction of the reaction force compare to the size and direction of the action force?

doesn't the earth rise toward you? The answer lies in the difference between your mass and the mass of the earth. The mass of the earth is so great that your pull on the earth produces an extremely small acceleration. The force you exert on the earth is the same as the force acting on you. But the force acting on you acts on a much smaller mass. Therefore, your acceleration toward the earth is much greater.

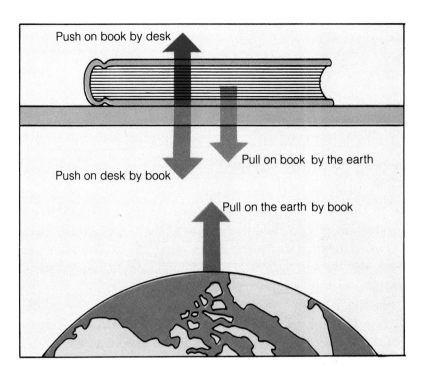

Push on book by desk

Pull on book by the earth

Push on desk by book

Pull on the earth by book

Figure 3-20. Which pairs of forces are balanced forces? Which pairs are action and reaction forces?

Action and reaction forces always act on *different* objects. They should not be confused with two balanced forces that act on the *same* object. For example, a book lying on a desk is acted on by the force of gravity. This force pulls downward. The desk exerts an equal but upward force on the book. The pull by the earth and push by the desk are equal and opposite forces. These are balanced forces. They both act on the same object—the book.

Where, then, are the action and reaction forces? The force of gravity pulls the book downward. The reaction to the earth's pull is the upward pull of the book *on the earth*. These forces are equal and opposite. And they act on different objects.

Another action force is the downward push of the book on the desk. The reaction force is the upward push of the desk on the book. These two forces are equal and opposite. Again, they act on different objects.

**Main Idea**

Can a pair of action and reaction forces act on the same object?

### Check yourself

1. If you push against a swinging door, what is the equal and opposite reaction force?

2. Explain the difference between a pair of balanced forces and a pair of action and reaction forces.

Figure 3-21. Which object has the greatest weight?

**Main Idea**

What did Newton predict about the weight of objects on the moon?

## The law of gravitation

All objects on or near the earth are pulled toward the earth by gravity. Gravity pulls harder on some objects than others. You can see this by hanging different objects from a spring. The pull of gravity makes some objects stretch the spring more than others. The pull of gravity on an object has a special name. It is called the **weight** of the object. Weight, like any other force, is measured in newtons. The heavier an object feels, the harder the earth is pulling on it. In other words, the greater is its weight.

During Newton's time, it was known that gravity makes objects fall toward the earth. But Newton was the first to realize that the earth pulls on the moon as well as on nearby objects. Newton proposed that the moon moves around the earth because the earth is pulling on it. He also proposed that the sun has its own pull of gravity. The sun pulls on the earth, moon, and all the planets. The sun's gravity, he said, is what causes the planets to move in curved paths around the sun. Otherwise, according to Newton's first law, the planets would move in straight lines at constant speed. They would leave the sun and never come near it again.

Newton summarized his conclusion in his law of gravitation. He said that there is a pull of gravity between every two objects in the universe. The size of the pull depends on the mass of each object. The greater the masses are, the greater the pull. The pull is extremely small unless one of the masses is very great. The pull of gravity between two buildings is too small to be measured. But the pull of gravity between one building and the earth can be measured.

Newton predicted that objects on the moon would have weight because the moon would pull on them. But because the mass of the moon is less than that of the earth, the weight of the objects would be less. Sure enough, the astronauts who visited the moon were much lighter there. They weighed only one sixth as much as they did on earth. They found they could jump much higher than on earth.

Newton studied measurements that had been made on the paths of the moon and other planets. He figured out how much force was needed to keep these bodies moving in their curved paths instead of straight lines. He found that the pull of gravity between two objects is weaker the farther apart they are. The pull of gravity depends on the distance between the centers of the objects as well as on their masses. Doubling the distance makes the pull only one fourth as strong.

Even on the earth, the weight of an object is slightly less on a mountaintop than at sea level. When space vehicles move away from the earth, they lose weight the farther out they go. When the astronauts were on the moon, the moon's pull on

## Our Science Heritage

Isaac Newton (1642–1727) made many important contributions to both mathematics and science. After receiving his degree from Cambridge University, England, he spent the next 18 months at home, working by himself. In those 18 months, he made discoveries about light and color, calculus, gravity, and motion. He returned to Cambridge and joined the faculty.

Newton did not publish his discoveries for a long time. As a result, he did not clearly establish that he was the first person to make them. He carried on quarrels with others who arrived at the same results independently of him as to who should have the credit.

Robert Hooke (1635–1703), for example, believed he should share in the recognition that Newton received

for stating the law of gravitation. He had come to some of the same conclusions by himself before Newton published his ideas. Newton, however, had a more complete description and had shown that his theory agreed with observations of the planets' motions.

Newton was so upset by his quarrels with Hooke that he did not publish his book about light until after Hooke had died. This work showed that he was as good in the laboratory as he was at theoretical explanations.

While Newton was unwilling to share the credit for things he had done by himself, he realized his dependence on the work of others. In a letter, he repeated a saying of the time, "If I have seen further than other men, it is by standing on the shoulders of giants."

**Isaac Newton**

them was much stronger than the earth's pull. Yet the earth has more mass than the moon. Can you explain how the moon had a stronger pull on them?

### Check yourself

1. How are the masses of two objects related to the size of the pull of gravity between them?
2. How is the distance between the centers of two objects related to the size of the pull of gravity between them?

### Weight and mass

In everyday speech, the word *weight* is commonly used instead of *mass*. Many people think they mean the same thing. It is true that on earth if one object has more mass than another, it also weighs more. The object with more mass feels heavier. That is, the earth is pulling harder on it—it has more weight.

But mass and weight are not the same thing. The mass of an object is a property of the object. An object has the same mass on earth as on the moon or in outer space. It does not matter whether another object is pulling on it because of gravity.

Weight, on the other hand, is a force. The SI unit of force is the newton, so weight is measured in newtons in SI. Weight

**Main Idea**

What is the difference between the mass and the weight of an object?

Figure 3-22. Why is "newton-burger" a good name for this hamburger?

depends on the mass of the object as well as on what is pulling on the object. On earth, everything is being pulled by the same object—the earth. And everything on the surface of the earth is about the same distance from the center of the earth. So differences in weight depend only on differences in mass.

But weight is not a property of an object. The weight depends on where the object is. For example, an object of mass 1 kg has a weight of about 10 N on earth. On the moon, that same object would still have a mass of 1 kg. But its weight would be less than 2 N. And on Jupiter, the planet with the greatest mass, the same object would weigh 26 N.

### Check yourself

Explain why weight is not considered to be a property of an object.

### Motion under gravity

Every object on earth is pulled downward by gravity. When an object moves, the pull of gravity usually affects its motion.

Galileo (1564–1642) studied the motion of objects falling toward the earth. He did not have instruments that could measure the speeds of objects falling straight down. The travel times were too short for him to measure. So he thought of a way to slow the motion. He had balls of different mass roll down ramps. On a ramp, part of the force of gravity is balanced by the upward push of the ramp. Only the remaining part of the force accelerates the balls. Since the balls move more slowly, it is easier to measure travel times.

Galileo did many experiments with balls on ramps. He concluded that objects of different mass accelerate under the earth's pull of gravity at the same rate. You may be puzzled by this conclusion. After all, if you drop a feather and a coin at the same time, the coin will reach the ground first. But when objects fall downward through the air, gravity is not the only force acting. The air produces a friction force that pushes upward against falling objects. The friction force is greater on a feather than on a coin. As a result, the coin accelerates

Figure 3-23. On Jupiter, you would weigh two and a half times what you weigh on earth. Would your mass be the same as on earth?

Figure 3-24. Do objects of different mass accelerate at the same rate?

**Data Search**

U.S. Olympic athlete Platt Adams jumped 1.63 meters in the standing high jump. Would he have been able to jump higher on Uranus or on Mars than he did on Earth? Search page 560.

more than the feather. To show that gravity accelerates all objects equally, you must drop them where there is no air. A glass tube with most of the air removed from it can be used.

A similar demonstration was performed on the moon by the astronauts. A hammer and feather were dropped at the same time. The moon's gravity was the only force acting, as the moon has no air. Both objects hit the surface of the moon at the same instant.

On the moon, the hammer and feather accelerated together. But they did not accelerate as much as they would have on earth (in a tube with no air). Acceleration due to gravity does not depend on the mass of the falling object. But it does depend on two other things. One is the mass of the large object pulling on the falling object. The moon's mass is much less than the earth's mass. The second thing is the distance from the falling object to the center of the pulling object. The moon is smaller than the earth, so its center is closer to its surface. The effect of the smaller distance partly cancels out the effect of the smaller mass. Still, the acceleration due to gravity on the moon is only about one sixth what it is on earth.

Suppose a baseball is thrown straight upward at a certain speed. As soon as the ball is released, gravity starts slowing it down. Eventually the ball stops moving upward. The ball then starts to fall back down. It speeds up until, when it reaches the thrower's hand, it is moving as fast as when leaving the hand, assuming there is no air resistance.

## Activity 3–2B    Motion Down a Ramp

### Materials

2 long, metal or wood, grooved ramps of
    equal length, with a metal stop at one end
steel ball and aluminum ball of same
    diameter but different mass
2 books or blocks of wood
ruler

### Purpose

To determine whether the mass of a ball affects
the length of time it takes to roll down a ramp.

### Procedure

1. Set up two ramps side by side. Raise one
   end of each of the ramps slightly. Support
   the raised end with a book or block of wood.
   The angle of the ramps must be the same—
   about 5° from the horizontal.
2. Determine whether the steel ball or aluminum ball has more mass.
3. Make a table like the one shown. Predict
   which ball will take the least time to roll down
   one of the ramps. Record your prediction.
4. Place one ball at the top of each ramp. Hold
   the balls with a ruler.
5. Release the balls at the same time by quickly
   raising the ruler. Listen for the sound of the
   metal balls striking the stop. Record your
   results.
6. Complete at least three trials.
7. Reverse the balls used on each of the ramps.
8. Complete at least three more trials.

### Questions

1. Which ball has more mass?
2. Does one ball consistently reach the end of
   the ramp before the other one?
3. What sources of error might make the results
   of these tests uncertain?

### Conclusion

How does the mass of a ball affect the length
of time it takes to roll down a ramp?

|  |  | Which ball hits first | |
|---|---|---|---|
|  |  | Prediction | Observation |
| Steel ball on ramp A Alum. ball on ramp B | Trial 1 |  |  |
|  | Trial 2 |  |  |
|  | Trial 3 |  |  |
| Alum. ball on ramp A Steel ball on ramp B | Trial 1 |  |  |
|  | Trial 2 |  |  |
|  | Trial 3 |  |  |

If the ball had been moving faster at the beginning, it could
have risen higher before falling back down. The faster it starts
out, the higher it can go. If the ball can start upward with
enough speed, it can keep moving upward from the earth

forever. At a speed of about 40 000 km/h, an object can escape from the earth's gravity. This speed is the **escape speed** for the earth's gravity.

### Check yourself

1. How did the use of a ramp help Galileo study falling objects?
2. What two forces act on objects that fall to the ground?
3. Under what condition could something leave the earth's surface and keep moving forever?

### Curved motion under gravity

Suppose an object is thrown horizontally. What path will it follow? The earth's gravity pulls the object toward the earth. The object will be accelerated toward the ground. However, it will continue to move horizontally. Its path will curve.

Does horizontal motion affect the time for a thrown object to hit the ground? Suppose three balls are released at the same time from the same height above ground. The first is simply dropped. The second is thrown horizontally at 10 m/s. The third is thrown horizontally at 20 m/s. Which will hit the ground first?

If friction of the air does not slow down the balls, all three should hit the ground at the same time. The horizontal motion does not affect the vertical acceleration. The balls accelerate toward the ground under the pull of gravity in the same way. They travel the same vertical distance in the same time.

Figure 3-25. A ball thrown horizontally falls downward while

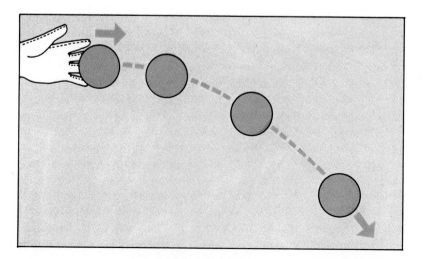

## Activity 3–2C     Falling Coins

### Materials

5 coins (same kind)
ruler or meter stick
table

### Purpose

To find out if objects with different horizontal speed fall at different rates.

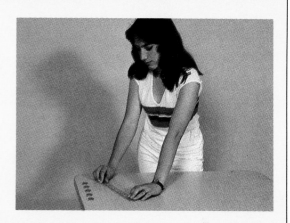

### Procedure

1.  Arrange five coins of the same kind along the edge of a table. Place a ruler or meter stick behind them.
2.  Hold one end of the ruler firmly against the table. Swing the other end of the ruler away from the coins as shown. Reverse the motion and let the ruler strike the coins, pushing all of them off the table at once. Watch how they fall.
3.  Repeat the trial. This time, listen carefully to the coins striking the floor. Listen for when each coin hits the ground.
4.  Repeat the trial once more. Have someone watch the coins from the side.

### Questions

1.  Which of the coins had the greatest horizontal speed?
2.  Which of the coins reached the floor at the same time?
3.  Are all the coins accelerated downward at the same rate? Why?

### Conclusion

How does the horizontal speed of an object affect its acceleration downward under gravity?

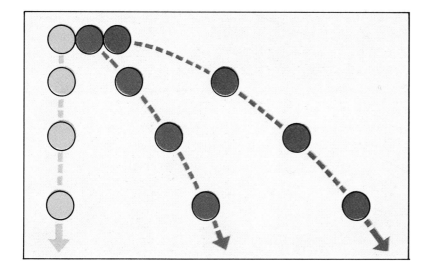

Figure 3-26. Which ball will reach the ground first?

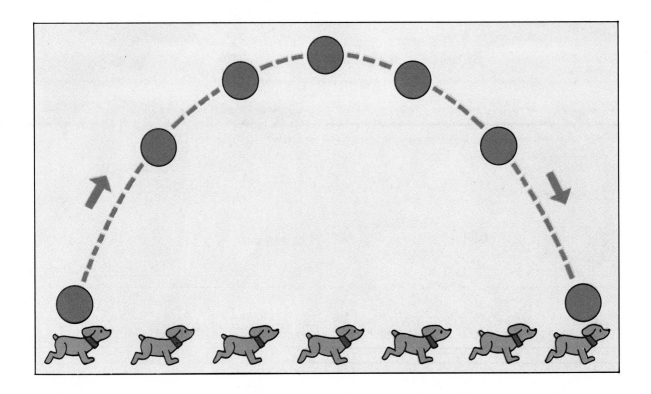

Figure 3-27. Even though the speed of a thrown ball changes, it moves the same horizontal distance in equal lengths of time.

**Main Idea**

What shape is the path of a ball that is thrown upward at an angle?

Suppose you throw a ball upward at an angle. What will its motion be after you release it? The easiest way to think about the motion is to separate it into two parts. There is a horizontal part that does not change. The ball moves horizontally at constant speed. At the same time, there is a vertical part of the motion. The ball starts out moving upward. Gravity slows down the upward motion. The ball goes to a certain height and then falls. Gravity speeds it up as it falls. It hits the ground some distance away from you.

The path of motion is an arch-shaped curve. The ball slows down on the upward portion and speeds up on the downward portion. But it moves the same horizontal distance each second. A dog racing under the ball would have to travel at constant speed to keep the ball directly overhead.

**Check yourself**

What effect does horizontal motion have on the time it takes an object to fall to the ground?

# Practical Science

## Flying with Bernoulli

Matter can exist at normal temperatures in one of three states: solid, liquid, or gas. Gases and liquids are both fluids and behave alike except in one respect. While a gas will expand to fill a closed container, a liquid will not.

Fluid mechanics is the study of the properties and behavior of fluids (liquids and gases). Hydrodynamics is the branch of fluid mechanics dealing with liquids, and aerodynamics is the branch of fluid mechanics dealing with gases. Because an airplane is an airborne vehicle, you need to know something about aerodynamics to understand how it flies.

**Bernoulli's principle**   In 1738, a Swiss mathematician named Daniel Bernoulli published a paper called *Hydrodynamica*. In it, he discussed the forces exerted by fluids in motion. One part contained a formula, now known as Bernoulli's principle. The formula explained why the pressure of a moving liquid decreases as the speed of the liquid increases. Though Bernoulli did not know it at the time, his principle also applies to gases and is used to help explain how an airplane flies.

**How an airplane flies**   You can lower the pressure at a particular place on a garden hose by pinching it. This causes the water to speed up. You could achieve the same effect by inserting an object into the hose.

An airplane in flight is an object inserted into a stream of air. An airplane wing is designed so that the distance across the top of the wing is greater than the distance across the bottom. Therefore, air molecules move faster across the top of the wing than across the bottom of the wing. With Bernoulli's principle you know that if the air on top of the wing is moving faster than the air on the bottom of the wing, the pressure on the top of the wing is lower than that on the bottom. The pressure difference causes the wing to lift.

Four forces act on an airplane when it is flying: thrust, drag, lift, and gravity. The thrust of the engine moves the airplane forward. Drag, caused by the resistance of air molecules on the surfaces of the airplane, holds it back. When the thrust exceeds the drag, the airplane moves forward. You have already learned about lift and you know that the force of gravity is pulling the airplane down. When the lift exceeds gravity, the airplane will rise.

**Something to try**   Cut a strip of loose-leaf paper lengthwise. Make the strip about an inch wide. Put one end of paper across your lower lip, letting most of the paper hang down. Hold the strip in place, and gently blow across the top of the paper. What happens? Why?

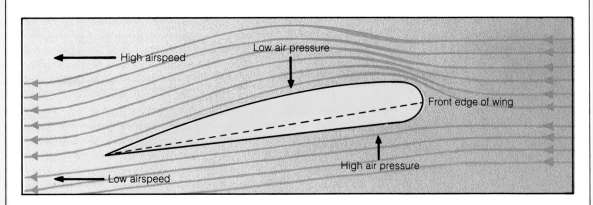

High airspeed

Low air pressure

Front edge of wing

High air pressure

Low airspeed

## Section 2 Review   Chapter 3

### Check Your Vocabulary

| | |
|---|---|
| balanced force | newton |
| escape speed | static friction |
| force | weight |
| friction | |

*Match each term above with the numbered phrase that best describes it.*

1. Unit of force
2. Depends on both the mass and the location of an object
3. Always tends to slow down moving objects
4. Causes no change in speed or direction
5. Enables object to keep moving away from the earth
6. Causes greater change in motion of objects of less mass
7. Prevents object from moving when weak force is acting on it

### Check Your Knowledge

*Multiple Choice: Choose the answer that best completes each of the following sentences.*

1. A change in the motion of an object is evidence that ?.
   a) the forces on the object are balanced
   b) an unbalanced force is acting on the object
   c) no forces are acting on the object
   d) Newton's law about equal and opposite forces is correct

2. A force that exists because of the motion of matter through or against other matter is ?.
   a) weight
   b) gravity
   c) mass
   d) friction

3. The pairs of forces referred to in Newton's third law are equal in strength and opposite in direction and ?.
   a) act on different objects
   b) are balanced forces
   c) produce no motion
   d) act independently of one another

4. The mass of an object is ?.
   a) greater at sea level than on a mountaintop
   b) greater on Jupiter than on earth
   c) smaller the farther it is from Earth
   d) the same everywhere

5. When an object is falling to the ground, ?.
   a) it has no mass
   b) it has no weight
   c) no forces are acting on it
   d) gravity causes it to accelerate

6. When objects of different mass fall to the ground, they ?.
   a) are pulled toward the earth by the same size force
   b) accelerate at the same rate
   c) have the same weight
   d) pull upward on the earth with equal reaction forces

### Check Your Understanding

1. The sun has a much greater mass than the earth does. How can the earth have a stronger pull of gravity on you than the sun does?

2. Explain the observation that a hammer and a feather fall at the same rate on the moon but at different rates on earth.

### Practical Science

1. How does Bernoulli's principle relate the speed and pressure of a moving fluid?

2. How is Bernoulli's principle used by aircraft?

# Energy   Section 3

**Section 3 of Chapter 3 is divided into four parts:**

Energy of moving objects

Stored energy

Energy conversion

Friction and mechanical energy

*Practical Science: Brake Action*

## Learning Objectives

1. To relate the kinetic energy of an object to its mass and speed.

2. To relate the potential energy of an object to its position.

3. To describe changes in the kinetic energy and potential energy of an object as it changes position.

4. To associate increases in the temperature of moving objects with the presence of friction.

Figure 3-28. A moving ball has energy. What happens to the energy when the ball collides with a group of balls?

**Main Idea**

What is energy?

Forces can set objects in motion. Objects in motion can cause changes. For example, suppose you throw a baseball. The force you exert on the ball causes the ball to move. The moving ball can break a window or cause other things to move. It has the ability to cause change. The ability of an object to cause change is referred to as its **energy**. The energy of an object in motion is called **kinetic** (kih-NET'-ik) **energy**. The word *kinetic* comes from the Greek word for *moving*.

### Energy of moving objects

The more force you use on a baseball before it leaves your hand, the faster it moves. The greater the speed of a moving object, the greater the kinetic energy.

Suppose a golf ball and baseball are traveling at the same speed. If both hit the same thing, the golf ball will do less damage. The kinetic energy of the golf ball is less than the kinetic energy of the baseball. The greater the mass of a moving object is, the greater the kinetic energy.

The kinetic energy of a moving object can be transferred to another object. Suppose a ball is rolling on a table. The ball strikes a similar ball head-on. The second ball is set into motion, while the first ball stops. The kinetic energy of the first ball has been transferred to the second ball.

Moving objects have kinetic energy. Nonmoving objects have no kinetic energy. If the speed of something changes, its kinetic energy changes. Suppose you start riding your bicycle at the top of a hill. Before you start, your kinetic energy is zero. As you move down the hill your speed increases rapidly. Your kinetic energy also increases.

Figure 3-29. Can kinetic energy be transferred from one object to another object?

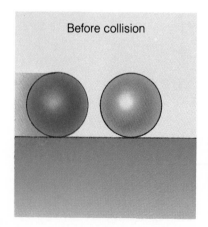
Before collision

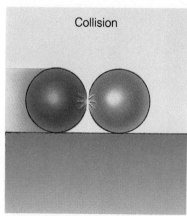
Collision

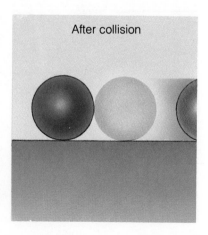
After collision

## Activity 3–3A          Kinetic Energy

### Materials

2 identical grooved ramps or grooved rulers
book
2 steel balls with different masses
2 identical, small cardboard boxes (about
    5 cm on a side) with one end open
meter stick or ruler

### Purpose

To determine whether the kinetic energy of a
moving object depends on its mass.

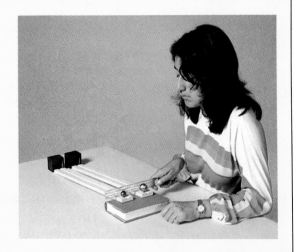

### Procedure

1. Place two ramps side by side.
2. Raise them at the same angle by placing a
   book under one end of each ramp.
3. Place a box at the lower end of each ramp
   to catch a ball as it leaves the ramp. Mark
   the position of the box.
4. Use a ruler to hold a ball on each ramp at
   its upper end.
5. Quickly lift the ruler to release the two balls
   at the same time.
6. Measure and record the distance each box
   moved.
7. Return the boxes to their original positions.
   Repeat Steps 4, 5, and 6 two more times.
8. Calculate the average distance each box
   was moved.

### Questions

1. What was the average distance each ball
   moved its box?

2. Did the two balls have the same kinetic
   energy? Explain how you can tell.
3. Did both balls have the same speed?

### Conclusion

Does the kinetic energy of a moving object
depend on its mass?

|         | Distance the box moved | |
|---------|----------------|----------------|
|         | With light ball | With heavy ball |
| Trial 1 |                |                |
| Trial 2 |                |                |
| Trial 3 |                |                |
| Total   |                |                |
| Average |                |                |

### Check yourself

1. What is the relation between the speed of a moving object
   and its kinetic energy?

2. What is the relation between the mass of a moving object
   and its kinetic energy?

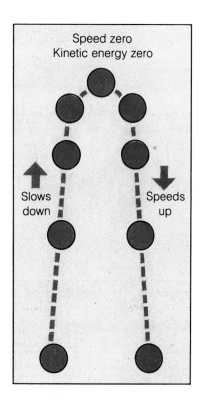

Speed zero
Kinetic energy zero

Slows down

Speeds up

Figure 3-30. When is the ball losing kinetic energy? When is it gaining kinetic energy?

## Stored energy

Suppose you toss a baseball straight up. The ball soon stops going up and falls back toward the ground. You catch it at the same height as you release it.

While the ball is moving upward, the earth's pull of gravity is making it slow down. If there were no pull of gravity, it could keep going at constant speed. Because of gravity, the ball can go only so high and then come down. When the ball reaches the highest point, it is no longer moving upward. Its speed is zero. It has no kinetic energy. In moving upward, the ball uses up its kinetic energy. Its original kinetic energy has allowed it to move farther from the earth. As the ball starts back downward, the pull of gravity makes it speed up. Its kinetic energy increases. Just before you catch it, it is going about as fast as it was when you first threw it. So its kinetic energy is about the same now as it was then.

When the ball is at its highest point, it has no kinetic energy. Yet, it can still cause damage to something below by falling on it. It still has the ability to cause change. That is, it still has energy. But now the energy is due to its position above the ground, not its motion. The ability of an object to cause change by its position is a form of **potential** (pu-TEN´-shul) **energy.**

If a coin is pushed over the edge of a table, it will fall to the ground. As it falls, it has kinetic energy. Where does the kinetic energy come from? When the coin was on the table, it had potential energy because it was above the ground. It had the ability to fall to a lower position. As the coin fell, the potential energy changed into kinetic energy.

Hold a rubber band loosely between your hands. If you let go of one end, you feel nothing. But now stretch the rubber band. If you again let go of one end, your other hand will be stung by the snap. Where did the rubber band get the energy to sting you? When you stretched the rubber band, you changed the position of its ends. You gave the rubber band potential energy. Then it was able to sting your hand.

You can think of potential energy as stored energy. It is energy that can be used to do something. It is stored up, ready to make something move or cause some other change. It exists even when nothing is happening.

Figure 3-31. In which picture is the potential energy changing?

You give something potential energy whenever you push it farther apart from something that is pulling on it. The earth's pull of gravity pulls everything downward. If you lift something, you are pushing it farther from the earth. Similarly, when you stretch a rubber band, you push its ends farther apart. But the rubber band is pulling the ends together. So stretching the rubber band gives it potential energy. On the other hand, sliding a book across a table does not change its potential energy. Even though its position has changed, the book is no closer or farther from the earth.

Suppose you were putting a book into a bookcase. Another book falls out and hits your foot. Which would hurt more—a paperback or a large dictionary? The dictionary would; it has more mass. Even though it is just as high on the shelf as a paperback, it has a greater ability to hurt your foot. It has more potential energy because of its greater mass.

Do you think it would make a difference whether the book was on the top shelf or the bottom shelf? A book falling from the top shelf has a greater ability to hurt your foot. It has more potential energy because it is farther above the ground.

In general, the potential energy increases when an object is pushed farther away from the object pulling on it. The higher an object is above the earth, the greater its potential energy. And the potential energy, like the kinetic energy, is greater for objects of greater mass.

**Data Search**

During an earthquake potential energy is released. What amount of TNT contains the same amount of energy as is released by an earthquake that measures 6.5 on the Richter scale? Search page 558.

### Check yourself

1. How can you give something potential energy?

2. Does a change in position always cause a change in potential energy? Explain.

## Library research

Find out how the energy of moving water in rivers and streams has been used for centuries to run mills and factories.

Figure 3-32. Identify the energy conversion that takes place in a waterfall.

## Energy conversion

As a ball falls, its potential energy decreases. The closer it gets to the ground, the less potential energy it has. At the same time, it is speeding up. Its kinetic energy is increasing. Potential energy is being converted, or changed, into kinetic energy.

When a ball is thrown upward, its potential energy increases. What happens to its speed and its kinetic energy? Is kinetic energy being converted into potential energy?

The change of energy from one form to another is called **energy conversion** (kun-VER'-zhun). Any change from kinetic to potential or potential to kinetic is energy conversion. When anything falls, energy is converted from potential to kinetic.

## Activity 3–3B    Energy of a Pendulum

### Materials

string about 1 m in length
lead ball with hole
2 or 3 books
masking tape
small wood block
metric ruler or meter stick

### Purpose

To determine when a pendulum has the most kinetic energy and when it has the most potential energy.

### Procedure

1. Make a pendulum by tying a piece of string to a lead ball with a hole in it.
2. Hang the pendulum over the edge of a desk or table so that the ball just clears a book placed on the floor.
3. Tape the upper end of the string to the top of the desk.
4. Place a block on the book under the pendulum. The pendulum ball should hit the block at the bottom of its first swing.
5. Release the pendulum ball from a point 30 cm above the floor. Observe what happens when it hits the block.
6. Predict in what part of the swing the pendulum has the most kinetic energy.
7. To test your predictions, move the book and block closer to the release point of the pendulum. Raise the block by adding more books. Release the pendulum ball and observe what happens. Use the same release point you used in Step 5.

### Questions

1. What happens to the block of wood when it is hit by the pendulum?
2. What kind of energy does the force of the pendulum ball give to the block?
3. During what part of the swing is the pendulum highest above the ground?
4. During what part of the swing does the pendulum have the least potential energy? Explain how you know.
5. Where in the swing does the pendulum move the block the farthest?

### Conclusions

Where is the potential energy of the pendulum greatest? Explain.
Where is the kinetic energy of the pendulum greatest? Explain.

For example, at the top of a waterfall, water usually moves slowly. It has little kinetic energy. As it goes over the fall, potential energy is converted to kinetic energy. At the bottom of the fall, the water is moving much faster.

Figure 3-33. Where does a pendulum have the most potential energy? Kinetic energy?

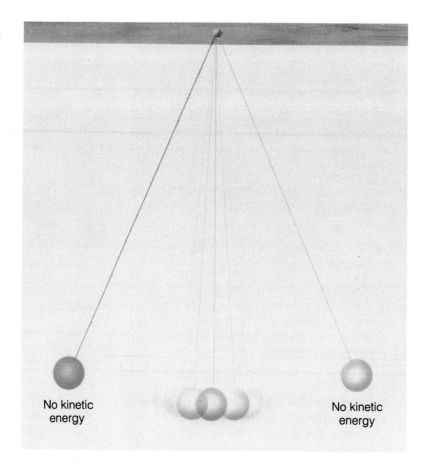

No kinetic energy

No kinetic energy

When a pendulum swings back and forth, energy is continually being converted. At the end of each swing, the pendulum reverses direction. Like a ball thrown up in the air, it stops for an instant and then moves the other way. At the end of a swing, the pendulum has no kinetic energy. But it has potential energy because it is higher up than at the bottom of the swing. What energy conversion takes place as the pendulum moves downward? What energy conversion takes place as it keeps moving and swings upward?

When you stretch a rubber band or spring and let go, energy is converted. The potential energy of the rubber band or spring is converted into kinetic energy. An archer has to stretch the bow to put the arrow in it. When the archer lets go, the potential energy of the bow is converted into kinetic energy for the arrow.

## Check yourself

1. Give an example of a conversion from kinetic energy to potential energy.

2. Give an example of a conversion from potential energy to kinetic energy.

## Friction and energy

Kinetic energy and potential energy are the two forms of what is called **mechanical energy**. Mechanical energy is energy due to motion or position. Sometimes it seems that mechanical energy is disappearing. For example, in each swing of a pendulum, it goes almost as high up as on the previous swing. It has almost the same amount of potential energy after every swing. But if you watch it long enough, the swings get shorter. Finally, the pendulum comes to a stop. It has lost both its kinetic and its potential energy.

If you stop peddling on a bicycle, you'll coast to a stop. Your kinetic energy becomes zero. But you have no more potential energy than before.

Can mechanical energy disappear? Or is it just converted to another form?

It is friction that brings most moving objects to a stop. When friction is reduced, the motion continues longer. Objects continue moving longer on smooth surfaces than on rough ones. Lubricants such as oil and grease cut down on friction. But friction cannot be totally eliminated in the real world on earth. And so nothing on earth keeps moving forever without an energy boost from the outside.

What, then, is the relation between friction and energy? One clue is that where there is friction, there are changes in temperature.

Place the palms of your hands on your face. Notice how warm or cold they feel. Then rub your palms together and place them on your face again. Can you feel any change in temperature?

You may have seen a fire started from friction. A stick is turned rapidly in a small opening in another piece of wood.

**Main Idea**

What happens to a swinging pendulum that is left alone?

Figure 3-34. What makes the wood hot enough to catch on fire?

Friction raises the temperature of the wood to the kindling point. A spark is caught on some wood shavings. The wood shavings burst into flame.

Friction can be used to melt pieces of ice. When two pieces of ice are rubbed together, friction increases the temperature of the ice. The ice melts. This method works even when the surrounding air is colder than 0°C.

The chemicals in the end of a match are ignited by friction. The friction of the match head with another surface causes an increase in the temperature. The increase in temperature causes the chemicals to ignite.

Temperature increases are found wherever friction is present. In fact, the presence of friction is often identifed by increases in temperature. Large temperature increases may be a clue to locating unwanted frictional forces.

Large amounts of energy seem to be used up whenever large temperature increases occur. Is there a relationship between the energy used up and the temperature increases? This question will be explored in the next chapter.

### Check yourself

1.  What is mechanical energy?

2.  When there is friction, what happens to the kinetic and potential energy of a moving object?

3.  When there is friction between objects that are rubbed together, what happens to their temperature?

**Careers** Construction Machinery Operator / Airplane Pilot

**Construction Machinery Operator** Bulldozers and tower cranes are familiar equipment at major construction sites. The men and women who manipulate this powerful equipment are called construction machinery operators. Construction machinery operators work outdoors, in all seasons.

Operators usually acquire their skills by working with experienced operators. Nick-named "oilers," novices to this work learn to clean and lubricate heavy machinery, and eventually to operate it.

Tower cranes, which lift and position building materials, are especially difficult to pilot. Operators must judge distances accurately and follow verbal commands. The construction machinery operator must always be aware of and comply with safety rules to prevent accidents.

Construction contractors prefer to hire high school graduates who have had mechanics classes or experience. Operators must have stamina and excellent eye–hand–foot coordination.

Construction machinery operators work in cities and remote locations. Their work is essential to the erection of new skyscrapers, dams, and other large structures.

**Airplane Pilot** Pilots may fly planes that carry passengers or cargo. They may do crop dusting, aerial photography, or perform other flying services. Many serve as members of one of the armed forces.

A career as a pilot demands good judgment, the ability to make quick decisions, and calmness under pressure. The pilot on a commercial airliner carries a heavy responsibility for the lives of the passengers and crew.

Commercial pilots are licensed only after success-fully passing both a physical exam and a written exam, and after demon-strating their flying ability. Flight training is taught in both military and civilian schools. A background of high school science and mathematics is valuable. Pilots must know how to read maps and flight instruments, how to interpret weather reports, and how to calculate distances accurately.

The pilot of a high-altitude plane must wear a protective flight suit.

# Practical Science

## Brake Action

A moving bicycle has lots of kinetic energy. To stop it from moving, you must get rid of that kinetic energy. This is what brakes do.

**How brakes work** All brakes work by pressing brake pads against one or both wheels to create friction. The friction turns the kinetic energy into heat energy. Cooler air surrounding the brakes removes most of the friction-generated heat from the brake pads. As the bicycle loses kinetic energy, it slows down and stops.

**Types of brakes** There are three types of bicycle brakes. They are known as *coaster brakes, disc brakes,* and *rim* or *caliper brakes.* Forms of coaster and disk brakes are used in automobiles and other vehicles.

Coaster brakes were the first type of brake used on bicycles. The coaster brake mechanism is inside the rear hub. To brake, you step back on the brake pedal. The chain transfers this reverse force from the front to the rear sprocket. The force on the rear sprocket activates the brake mechanism.

Rim or caliper brakes are used on both front and rear wheels. They consist of two brake pads mounted in a device known as a *caliper assembly.* The caliper assembly acts like a pair of pliers to create pressure on the brake pads. The brake pads are mounted on the tire so that they can press against the edge of the rim when

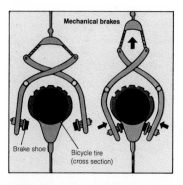

Mechanical brakes

Brake shoe

Bicycle tire (cross section)

you apply pressure to the brake lever. When you apply pressure to the brake lever, it pulls on a cable attached to the caliper assembly. When the cable pulls on the assembly, the calipers squeeze the brake pads against the rim.

Disk brakes are a more efficient version of caliper brakes. They are very expensive and are used more often on motorcycles and automobiles than on bicycles.

**Why brakes can fail to work properly** While brakes in good working order can save you from an accident, they can also get you into trouble if they are damaged or used in dangerous situations. For example, you should avoid riding through deep puddles whenever possible. This is because water reduces friction between braking surfaces. With little or no friction between the braking surfaces, you will not be able to quickly stop your bicycle.

Another dangerous situation may occur if you brake continuously while riding down a long hill. The enormous amount of friction created by continuous hard braking may cause the brake pads to overheat, deteriorate, and stop working. To avoid overheating your bicycle brakes, ease up on the pressure you apply to the brake levers from time to time.

One other dangerous situation may occur if you apply the brakes hard to the front wheel only. Doing this causes your bicycle to become one big lever. The front axle acts as the fulcrum. The frame and rear wheel pivot around the front axle, lifting the rear wheel off the ground. This may result in your sailing over the handlebars and experiencing serious injury.

Bicycle brakes kept in good working order and used properly will make bicycling experiences safe, as well as fun.

**Something to try** Turn a bicycle upside down, and use your hands to turn the pedals as fast as you can. Then use hard pressure on the brake lever to quickly stop the wheel from turning. Put your hand next to the area around the tire where the brake was applied. How does the air feel? Why?

## Section 3 Review    Chapter 3

### Check Your Vocabulary

energy                    kinetic energy

energy conversion         potential energy

*Match each term above with the numbered phrase that best describes it.*

1. Occurs when a pencil rolls along a desk

2. Increases whenever an object moves farther from another object pulling on it

3. Increases whenever an object speeds up

4. The ability to cause changes in matter

### Check Your Knowledge

*Multiple Choice: Choose the answer that best completes each of the following sentences.*

1. Energy that exists even when nothing is happening is _?_.
   a) kinetic energy     c) energy conversion
   b) energy of motion   d) potential energy

2. The potential energy of an object is a result of _?_.
   a) its motion
   b) the pull of another object
   c) friction
   d) changes in its temperature

3. Kinetic energy is converted to potential energy when _?_.
   a) a ball is thrown upward
   b) a pendulum stops moving after a while
   c) a rock hits the ground and stops
   d) a skater coasts to a stop

4. If a bicycle and a car are moving at the same speed, the bicycle has _?_.
   a) more kinetic energy than the car
   b) less kinetic energy than the car
   c) the same amount of kinetic energy as the car
   d) no kinetic energy

5. At the top of a swing, a pendulum has _?_.
   a) all kinetic energy and no potential energy
   b) neither kinetic nor potential energy
   c) all potential energy and no kinetic energy
   d) the most potential and the most kinetic energy

### Check Your Understanding

1. Can an object have both kinetic and potential energy at the same time? Explain.

2. As the earth goes around the sun, it is closest to the sun in January and farthest from the sun in July.
   a. The earth has potential energy because of the sun's pull of gravity on it. When is the earth's potential energy greatest?
   b. If the total amount of energy does not change, when is the earth's kinetic energy greatest?
   c. When does the earth move the fastest?

3. When a car is driven, its tires get hot, even on a cold day. Explain how the tires get hot.

### Practical Science

1. What is the force created by bicycle brakes that causes a bicycle to slow down or stop?

2. What can cause brakes to fail to work properly?

# Chapter 3 Review

## Concept Summary

**Motion** is the movement or changing of position of an object with respect to a reference object.
- The description of motion may change with a change in the reference object.

**Speed** is how fast an object changes its position with respect to a reference object.
- Speed is described in units of distance divided by units of time.
- Average speed is the total distance traveled divided by the total time taken to travel that distance.
- An object traveling at constant speed always travels equal distances in equal times.
- On a distance-time graph, a slanting straight line indicates constant speed.

**Acceleration** is a change in the speed or in the direction of motion of an object.
- On a distance-time graph, a curving line indicates changing speed.

A **force** is a push or pull.
- Balanced forces act on the same object without producing any changes in its motion.
- An unbalanced force acting on an object produces a change in the speed or direction of the object.
- Friction forces prevent or slow down the movement of objects.
- The greater the unbalanced force on an object is, the greater the acceleration of the object.
- The greater the mass of an object is, the smaller the acceleration of the object.
- When a force acts on an object, the object exerts a reaction force of equal strength but opposite in direction.

The **force of gravity** acts between any two objects.
- Weight is the pull of gravity on an object.
- The force of gravity increases as the masses of the objects increase.
- The force of gravity decreases as the distance between the objects increases.
- The acceleration of a falling object does not depend on the mass of the object.

**Energy** is the ability to cause change.
- Kinetic energy is the energy of an object due to its motion.
- The kinetic energy of an object depends on both its mass and its speed.
- The kinetic energy of an object can be transferred to other objects.
- Potential energy is stored energy due to the position of an object that is acted on by a force.
- Energy can be converted from one form to another.

## Putting It All Together

1. How do people usually decide whether an object is moving?
2. What is the speed of a cyclist who travels 80 m in 5 s?
3. What information would you need to determine whether a rolling ball is moving at constant speed?
4. Suppose you took an express elevator to the top of a tall building. During what parts of the ride would you be accelerating? What would you feel as you accelerated?
5. When two forces are balanced, what is true for their strengths and directions?
6. Which of Newton's three laws of motion is best illustrated when you fly forward as the automobile brakes are suddenly applied?
7. If the force on an object is doubled, how does its acceleration change?
8. What force has the ability to slow down moving objects?
9. Explain how the weight of an object can be different on the moon and on the earth.
10. Describe the path of a ball that is thrown horizontally off a high cliff.
11. How can something have energy when it is not moving?

12. How does the kinetic energy of an object change as the object slows down?
13. What happens to the temperature of something that experiences large frictional forces?

## Apply Your Knowledge

1. If you were describing the path of a space probe traveling from the earth to Mars, what would you use as a reference object? Explain your choice.
2. A raindrop falls at constant speed for most of its trip from a cloud to the ground. Explain why the force of gravity does not cause it to move faster and faster.
3. Many small cars are without power brakes and power steering. Why do large cars need to have both power brakes and power steering?
4. Suppose a ball were thrown by an astronaut on the surface of the moon.
   a. What two conditions on the moon would affect the motion of the ball?
   b. What effect would each of these conditions have on the distance the ball would travel before reaching the moon's surface?

## Find Out on Your Own

1. A standard 33⅓ rpm record makes 33⅓ turns in one minute. A 45 rpm record makes 45 turns in one minute. Determine how fast a spot on the edge of each type of record moves when it is on the turntable. What must you measure before you can determine the speeds?
2. Use a reference book or text to find out the speed required for a satellite to escape the pull of the earth's gravitational force. What would be the escape speed on the moon? On Jupiter?
3. Place about 500 grams of lead shot in one end of a meter-long cardboard mailing tube. Stopper both ends. Read the room temperature

from a thermometer. Invert the tube so that the lead shot falls to the other end. Repeat the inverting about one hundred times. Pour the lead shot into a plastic foam cup. Place the bulb of the thermometer in the lead shot. The lead shot was originally at room temperature. What happened to its temperature? Explain the change.

## Reading Further

Berger, Melvin. *Space Shots, Shuttles and Satellites*. New York: Putnam, 1983
    The history of satellites and manned space flight and possibilities for their future development is presented.

Gardner, Robert, and David Webster. *Moving Right Along; A Book of Science Experiments and Puzzlers About Motion*. Garden City, NY: Doubleday, 1978
    Various speed records are given. Experiments for measuring speed are suggested, and puzzles about motion are presented.

Ipsen, D. C. *Isaac Newton: Reluctant Genius*. Hillside, NJ: Enslow, 1985
    The personal story and scientific achievements of this great scientist are recounted.

Jollands, David, ed. *Energy, Forces and Resources*. New York: Arco, 1984
    Topics about energy and forces are simply explained and clearly illustrated.

O'Connor, Karen. *Sally Ride and the New Astronauts: Scientists in Space*. New York: Franklin Watts, 1983
    How to become an astronaut and what it is like to be part of an astronaut team are described.

Vogt, Gregory. *A Twenty-Fifth Anniversary Album of NASA*. New York: Franklin Watts, 1983
    The history of U.S. space exploration is chronologically detailed with photographs and brief text.

# Chapter 4

# Work and Heat

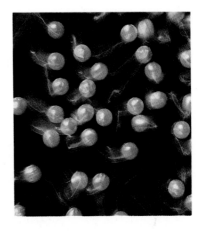

Section 1
**Doing Work**

Scientists use the term *work* in a special way that relates it to forces and motion. Work can be made easier to do by changing the force required or changing the distance something must move. Things often become warmer when work is done on them.

Section 2
**Heat and Internal Energy**

Heat moves from warmer to cooler substances. When something takes in heat, either it rises in temperature or it changes phase. Heat can be transferred in different ways.

Section 3
**The Kinetic Theory of Matter**

The particle model of matter can be expanded by the idea that the particles are in constant motion. This improved model of matter can be used to explain the behavior of solids, liquids, and gases.

In this chapter you will learn how both work and heat can change the energy of something. In the photo at the left, where is heat being given off? Where is heat being taken in? Where is heat changing energy levels?

# Doing Work Section 1

**Section 1 of Chapter 4 is divided into eight parts:**

Defining work

Inclined planes

Wedges and screws

Levers

Other simple machines

Efficiency

Power

Work and energy

*Practical Science: Gearing Up for Fun*

## Learning Objectives

1. To define work in terms of a force moving through a distance.

2. To explain the specific advantages of several simple machines that assist in doing work.

3. To measure the mechanical advantage and efficiency of different machines.

4. To differentiate between work and power.

5. To relate work to energy.

Figure 4-1. The design of a screw makes it possible for a person to push a screw into solid wood without using much force. A screw is considered a simple machine because it makes it easier to do work.

How much work have you done today? That should be a simple question. But how do you describe the amount of work you have done? By how tired you are? By the number of hours you have spent doing something? By what you have accomplished? You may have used all of these descriptions at one time or another.

What is work? This question may be just as difficult to answer. The same activity may be work one day and fun the next. Work is used to describe many different things. Its meaning changes from one person to another.

## Defining work

Scientists use the term **work** in a special way. They relate work to forces and motion. Work is done on an object when two conditions are met. First, the object must move. Second, a force must be acting on the object partly or entirely in the direction of motion. When you lift a rock off the ground, you are doing work. If you slide the rock along the ground, you are also doing work. But if you push on the rock and it does not move, you have not done any work. You may feel exhausted from pushing on the rock. But because the rock does not move, you have not done any work on the rock.

Pushing a lawn mower is work. You exert a force and the lawn mower moves. When you push a lawn mower, you push downward at a slant, along the handle. Your push moves the

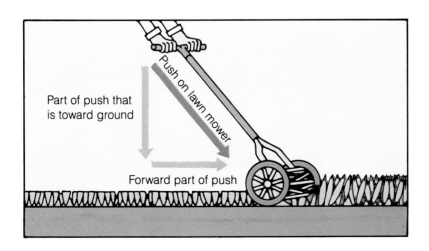

Figure 4-2. Only part of the push on a lawn mower moves the lawn mower forward.

Part of push that is toward ground

Push on lawn mower

Forward part of push

Figure 4-3. Explain why it is easier for a short person than for a tall person to mow the same grass with the same lawn mower.

lawn mower forward. But part of the push is toward the ground and does not make the lawn mower move. Another part of the push is in the forward direction. Only this second part does any work.

Suppose you are having trouble mowing some thick grass. You lower the handle. Now more of the push you exert is in the forward direction. Without pushing any harder, you can cut the grass more easily. The force in the direction of motion of the lawn mower has increased. The greater the force in the direction of motion, the more work is done.

Mowing a large lawn is more work than mowing a small lawn. The farther you push the lawn mower, the more work is done.

The amount of work done depends on two things. One thing is the amount of force in the direction of motion. The other is the distance moved while the force is acting. The amount of work equals the product of these quantities:

$$\text{work} = \text{force} \times \text{distance}.$$

Force is measured in newtons, and distance is measured in meters. The unit for work is sometimes called the newton meter. But this unit also has its own name, the **joule** (JOOL). One joule (symbol J) equals the work done by a force of 1 N that moves an object a distance of 1 m. The joule is named after James Joule, a nineteenth-century English scientist. A force of 10 N that moves an object 15 m does 150 J of work. How much work is done by a force of 20 N that moves an object 5 m?

## Activity 4–1A    Measuring Work

### Materials

meter stick
table more than 1 m in length
wood block with screw eye hook
spring balance calibrated in newtons

### Purpose

To show how work is measured.

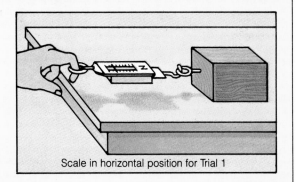

Scale in horizontal position for Trial 1

### Procedure

1. Attach the spring balance to the wood block and place the block on a smooth table.
2. For Trial 1, hold the spring balance in a horizontal position, and slowly move the block at a constant speed. Record the force reading on a table like the one shown.
3. Using the spring balance to pull it, move the block one meter. Calculate the amount of work that was done.
4. For Trial 2, hold the spring balance at an upward slant, and slide the block slowly at a constant speed. Record the force reading.
5. For Trial 3, lift the spring balance with the block attached to a height of one meter from the floor. Record the amount of force.
6. For Trial 4, hold the block one meter above the floor for one minute. Record the force.

### Questions

1. What force balances the force that is required to pull the block across the table during the first and second trials?

2. How much work is done during Trial 1 when the block is moved one meter? When the block is moved two meters?
3. Compared to the first trial, is more or less force applied during the second trial? Is more or less work being done? Explain why.
4. How much force is required to lift the block one meter? How much work is being done?
5. How much work is being done to hold the block above the floor for one minute?

### Conclusion

How is work measured?

| Trial | Spring scale | Force | Work |
|-------|-------------|-------|------|
| 1 | Horizontal position | N | J |
| 2 | Slant position | N | J |
| 3 | Vertical position | N | J |
| 4 | Holding block | N | J |

### Check yourself

1. How much work do you do if you push with a force of 100 N on a desk that does not move?

2. How much work do you do if you push with a force of 30 N on a box while sliding it 0.6 m?

Figure 4-4. Why is a ramp considered to be a machine?

## Inclined planes

Suppose you are helping to lift a couch into the back of a truck. You place a long board at a slant from the ground to the back of the truck. You slide the couch up the board. The board allows you to apply less force in lifting the couch. In exchange, you have to move the couch a greater distance.

Anything that changes the size or direction of forces used in doing work is a **machine**. The board is a machine because it allows you to apply less force than is needed to do the work. Slanting boards and other ramps are called **inclined planes**. A plane is a flat surface. The term *inclined* means *slanting*. An inclined plane is one type of machine.

Most machines reduce the amount of force you have to apply. The applied force is usually less than the force used to move the object directly. The **mechanical advantage** of the machine describes how these two forces compare.

A machine with a mechanical advantage, or M.A., of 1 does not change the force you have to apply. A machine with an M.A. of 2 can double your force, so you have to apply only half the force needed. A machine with an M.A. of 3 can triple your force. You have to apply only one third the force needed. In general,

$$\text{mechanical advantage} = \frac{\text{force needed to do work directly}}{\text{force applied to machine}}$$

This equation can be applied to an inclined plane. The force needed to do the work directly is the force needed to lift the object. It equals the weight of the object. The force

**Main Idea**

What is the mechanical advantage of a machine?

## Activity 4–1B          Using an Inclined Plane

### Materials

spring balance calibrated in newtons
roller skate or skateboard
board about 2 m in length
chair
meter stick

Inclined plane

### Purpose

To show how the amount of work is changed
when an inclined plane is used.

### Procedure

1. Measure the distance in meters from the
   floor to the seat of a chair.
2. Attach a spring balance to a roller skate or
   a skateboard. Hold the skate by the spring
   balance and lift it to the same height as the
   chair. Measure the amount of force shown
   on the spring balance. Record your data on
   a table like the one shown.
3. With one end of a long board resting on the
   floor, place the other end on the edge of the
   chair seat. The board is now an inclined
   plane.
4. Use the spring balance to pull the skate up
   the inclined plane from the floor to the chair
   seat. Keep the spring balance parallel to
   the board, and keep the speed constant as
   you pull. Read the force needed to move
   the skate.
5. Measure the total distance you moved the
   skate along the board. Record the data on
   your table.

### Questions

1. How much work is being done when you lift
   the skate from the floor to the chair seat?
2. How much work is being done on the skate
   when it is moved along the inclined plane
   from the floor to the chair seat?
3. In which case is a greater force used?
4. In which case is a greater distance traveled?
5. What is the advantage of using an inclined
   plane?

### Conclusion

How is the amount of work done changed when
an inclined plane is used?

| Method | Force | Distance | Work done |
|--------|-------|----------|-----------|
| Direct lift | N | m | J |
| Inclined plane | N | m | J |

applied to the machine is the force used to move the object
along the inclined plane. The mechanical advantage can also
be found from the distances the object moves. For an inclined
plane:

$$\text{mechanical advantage} = \frac{\text{length of the inclined plane}}{\text{height of the inclined plane}}$$

Figure 4-5. What advantage do switchbacks provide the traveler compared to a direct route to the top?

Roads that take you to the top of a hill are examples of inclined planes. Mountain roads often have zigzags, or switchbacks, that make the climb more gradual. But a road with switchbacks is longer than one that goes straight up the side of the mountain.

### Check yourself

1. What effect does an inclined plane have on the amount of force you must apply to do work?

2. What effect does an inclined plane have on the distance you have to move something to do work?

### Wedges and screws

The blade of an ax, a knife blade, a razor blade, and a door stop are all similar. They all taper from a thick end to a very thin end. They are all examples of a **wedge**, a form of inclined plane. A force is applied to the thick end of a wedge. The thin end of the wedge is driven into something which is to be cut. The sides of the wedge push apart the object being cut. They exert a much greater force than the force applied to the thick end. To make the cut, they have to move the object

## Activity 4–1C        The Screw

### Materials

paper
metric ruler
scissors
pencil
transparent tape

### Purpose

To find out how a screw is related to an inclined plane.

### Procedure

1. Draw a full-size right triangle on a sheet of paper using the measurements shown for Triangle 1. Color the longest edge of the triangle. This edge represents an inclined plane.
2. Cut out the paper triangle. Place the colored side down. Place the pencil on top of it as shown in the diagram. Then tightly wrap the entire paper around the pencil. Tape the wrapped triangle to itself.
3. Note the pattern made by the edge of the colored side of the triangle that is wrapped around the pencil. The pattern represents the threads of a screw. You can see how a screw is an inclined plane.
4. Make a second right triangle with a 4-cm side like the one shown. Use a different color on the longest edge of this triangle. Wrap the paper triangle tightly around the same pencil and over the first triangle. Tape it securely in place.
5. On each triangle, draw a line 3-cm long down the length of the pencil. Observe how many times this 3-cm line crosses both of the "screws."

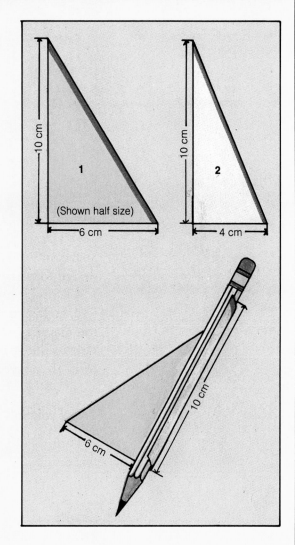

### Questions

1. In which triangle are the slanted edges closer together?

2. How many times does the 3-cm line you drew down the length of the pencil cross the edge of each triangle?
3. How many times would you have to turn each "screw" to move it 3 cm?
4. Which "screw" has the larger mechanical advantage?

### Conclusion

What can you conclude about how a screw is related to an inclined plane?

Figure 4-6. How is a wedge like an inclined plane?

apart only a short distance. The applied force pushes the wedge forward a much greater distance.

A screw is another form of inclined plane. When a screw is turned, it moves forward. At the same time, it presses against the material around it. Many turns are needed to move the screw a short distance. But the screw produces a far greater force than the force needed to turn it.

### Check yourself

A knife blade and a screw are both forms of what kind of machine?

### Levers

The oars of a rowboat, a wheelbarrow, and a rake are all machines. They all have a straight part that turns when a force is applied. And they all have one point that does not turn. On an oar, the point is where the oar touches the boat. On a wheelbarrow, it is at the center of the wheel. On a rake, it is beside the upper hand of the person holding it. The point that does not turn is called the **fulcrum** (FUL′-krum). Machines that do work by turning around a fulcrum are known as **levers** (LEE′-verz).

The three levers in Figure 4-7 are of three different types. An oar is a **first-class lever**. A force is applied at one end by a person's hand. The oar applies a force to the water at the

**Main Idea**

On a lever, what is the name of the point that does not turn?

other end. On a first-class lever, the fulcrum is always between the two forces. A first-class lever changes the direction of a force. When you move one end in a certain direction, the other end moves in the opposite direction.

A spading fork can be used as a first-class lever to lift a dead plant from the ground. The fulcrum is among the tines of the fork. When a small downward force is applied at the handle, the plant is pushed upward with a greater force. The amount of downward force needed to move the plant can be changed. If the handle is lengthened, then less downward force is needed to move the plant. If the handle is shortened, then more force is needed.

A wheelbarrow is an example of a **second-class lever**. The force is applied at the handles. Somewhere between the wheel and the handle is the load being lifted. When you lift the handles, you apply less force than the weight of the load. In return, you have to move the handles a greater distance than the load is raised. Does the wheelbarrow change the direction of the force? Where is the fulcrum on a wheelbarrow?

On a second-class lever, the fulcrum is always at one end. The force is applied to the lever at the other end. The lever applies a force to something between the two ends. This force is always greater than the force applied to the lever. That is, the mechanical advantage is greater than 1.

A rake is an example of a **third-class lever**. When you rake leaves, the fulcrum is beside the wrist of your upper hand. You move the rake by pushing or pulling with your lower hand. The rake applies a force to the leaves at its bottom end.

Figure 4-7. On these three examples of levers, what do the white circles mark?

Figure 4-8. A spading fork can be used as a first-class lever. At which end of the fork is the force greater? Which end moves farther as the fork rotates?

## Activity 4–1D      First-Class Levers

### Materials

1-kg standard mass
spring balance calibrated in newtons
wire or strong cord
wood dowel, 1 m in length, 2 cm in diameter
meter stick
chair with straight back

### Purpose

To show how the mechanical advantage of a first-class lever can be changed.

### Procedure

1. Use a spring balance to measure the weight in newtons of the 1-kg standard mass. Record the weight.
2. Mark the 1-m dowel in five places: 3 cm from each end, 23 cm from each end, and in the center. Attach a short piece of wire or strong cord to the 1-kg mass.
3. Hang the 1-kg mass at the 3-cm mark at one end of the dowel. Hang the spring balance at the 3-cm mark on the other end of the dowel. Place the dowel on the chair back at the 23-cm mark that is closest to the mass. Carefully balance the dowel by pulling downward on the spring balance. Record the force needed to balance the mass. SAFETY NOTE: *Stand so that the 1-kg mass cannot hit you if it falls or slides.*

4. Move the dowel so that it rests on the center mark. Read and record the force needed to balance the 1-kg mass.
5. Move the dowel again so that it rests on the 23-cm mark closest to the spring balance. Read and record the amount of force needed to balance the 1-kg mass.
6. Calculate the mechanical advantage (weight ÷ force) for each trial.

### Questions

1. When the fulcrum is close to the mass, how does the force needed to balance the mass compare to the weight of the mass?
2. When the fulcrum is at the center of the dowel, how does the force needed to balance the mass compare to the weight of the mass? Why?
3. When the fulcrum is far from the mass, how does the force needed to balance the mass compare to the weight of the mass?
4. Where is the fulcrum located when the mechanical advantage is the greatest?
5. Where is the fulcrum when the least force is needed to balance the mass?

### Conclusion

How can the mechanical advantage of a first-class lever be changed?

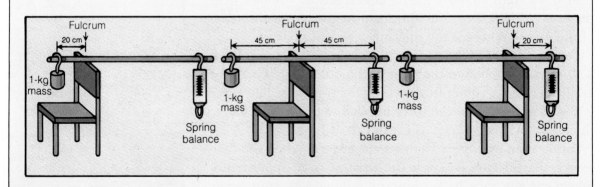

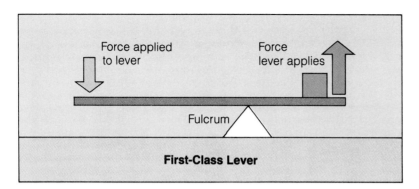

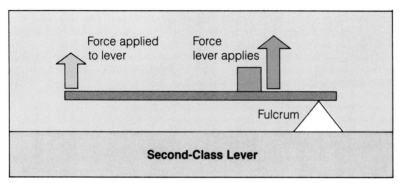

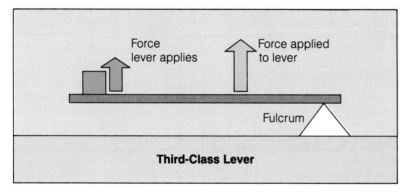

Figure 4-9. The three classes of levers. Which class changes the direction of the force?

On a third-class lever, the fulcrum is always at one end. The lever applies a force to something at the other end. A force is applied to the lever between the two ends. This force is always greater than the force the lever applies. The mechanical advantage is less than 1. The reason for using a third-class lever is to increase the distance moved, not the force. The tooth end of a rake moves much farther than the hand pulling the rake. You can reach more leaves this way.

### Check yourself

Where is the fulcrum on each of the three classes of levers?

Figure 4-10. A combination of pulleys can be used to lift a very heavy object.

**Library research**

The pyramids in Egypt and Central America must have been built with the use of simple machines. The giant stone heads on Easter Island in the Pacific must have been raised into position by simple machines. Find out what types of machines are likely to have been used.

## Other simple machines

A steering wheel on an automobile is an example of another simple machine: the **wheel and axle**. It is really a form of the lever. The steering wheel and its shaft, which is the axle, turn together. The spoke of a wheel is like the straight part of other levers. The fulcrum is located at the axle. As the wheel and axle turn together, a point on the wheel moves farther than a point on the axle. In return, the force exerted by the axle is greater than the force applied to the wheel. The wheel and axle allow you to use less force to do work. The larger the wheel, compared to the axle, the greater is the mechanical advantage.

A **pulley** is a wheel with a groove in its rim. It is turned by a rope or chain that lies against the groove. A pulley, too, is a simple machine that is a type of lever. It changes the direction of a force and can reduce the force needed.

A combination of pulleys can be used to provide a large mechanical advantage. Such a combination is called a **block and tackle**. A block and tackle can produce a great enough

## Activity 4–1E    Using Pulleys

### Materials

1 pulley with attachment points at one end
1 pulley with attachment points at both ends
support (ring stand, clamp, bar)
cord about 1 m in length
spring balance calibrated in newtons
500-g standard mass
metric ruler

### Purpose

To determine the mechanical advantage of different pulleys.

### Procedure

1. Use a spring balance to find the weight in newtons of a 500-g mass. Record its weight on a chart like the one shown.
2. Hang the pulley with two attachment points from the support. Attach one end of the cord to the mass. Run the other end of the cord over the pulley wheel. Attach this end to the spring balance.
3. Lift the mass slowly by pulling down on the spring balance. Record the force needed.
4. Now attach one end of the cord directly to the support. Hang the mass from the pulley with one attachment point. Run the cord under the pulley wheel. Tie the balance to the free end of the cord.
5. Pull straight up on the balance to lift the mass slowly. The pulley should move along the cord. Record the force needed.

6. Move the spring balance a distance of 20 cm. Record how far the mass is lifted.
7. Remove the end of the cord from the support. Tie this to the bottom attachment point of the pulley used in Steps 2–4. Run the other end of the cord over this pulley's wheel. Attach this end of the cord to the balance. Repeat Steps 4 and 7.

### Questions

1. What is the mechanical advantage of the attached pulley used in Step 2?
2. In what way did the attached pulley make it easier for you to lift the mass?
3. What is the mechanical advantage of the moving pulley used in Steps 5–6?
4. Divide the distance the spring balance moved in Step 6 by the distance the mass moved. Is your answer the same as the pulley's mechanical advantage?
5. What is the mechanical advantage of the two-pulley machine (Step 7)?
6. Divide the distance the spring balance moved in Step 7 by the distance the mass moved. Is your answer the same as the pulley's mechanical advantage?
7. How does the mechanical advantage of a pulley system compare to the number of lines supporting the load?

### Conclusion

Describe three ways to determine the mechanical advantage of a pulley system.

| Type of pulley | Weight lifted in N | Force needed in N | Mechanical advantage (weight ÷ force) | Distance weight was lifted | Distance balance moved | Mechanical advantage (distance weight was lifted ÷ distance balance moved) |
|---|---|---|---|---|---|---|
| Attached | | | | | | |
| Moving | | | | | | |
| Double | | | | | | |

force to lift an automobile engine or a piano. A block and tackle is also used to tighten wires and cables.

### Check yourself

1. On a wheel and axle, how does the force applied to the wheel compare to the force exerted by the axle?
2. What two things can a pulley do to a force?

### Efficiency

A machine makes it easier to do work. You might think that a machine does more work than you put into it. In fact, the reverse is always the case. The work put into a machine is always greater than the work done by the machine. Whenever you apply less force to a machine than what is needed to do the work, you must move something farther. Force times distance is even greater for you than for the machine.

Some of the work input is always used to overcome friction. The rest does the task required. In an efficient machine, almost all of the work input is changed to useful work. Very little is used to overcome friction. The machine's **efficiency** is the work output divided by the work input. Efficiency is usually described in percentages.

$$\text{efficiency} = \frac{\text{work output}}{\text{work input}} \times 100 \text{ percent}$$

Since the work output is always less than the work input, the efficiency is less than 100 percent.

### Check yourself

Which is greater—the work put into a machine or the work done by the machine?

### Power

Often, people are interested in how fast work is done, or **power**. Power is the rate at which the work is done. It is equal

---

**Library research**

Find out what a "perpetual motion" machine is. Describe how one or two of these machines are supposed to work. Explain why they cannot really work.

Figure 4-11. Which person has the greater power in moving up a hill?

to the work done divided by the time required to do the work.

$$\text{power} = \frac{\text{work}}{\text{time}}$$

When the work is in joules and the time in seconds, the power is in joules per second (symbol J/s). Another name for a joule per second is the **watt** (symbol W). The watt is named after James Watt, an eighteenth-century Scottish engineer. Watt became known for inventing a steam engine that could do work faster and more efficiently than previous engines. One watt equals 1 J/s. One hundred joules of work done per second is equal to 100 watts of power.

**Library research**

Electric motors and gasoline engines are often rated in units of horsepower. Find out the origin of the horsepower unit and how it is related to the watt, the SI unit of power.

### Check yourself

What is the relation among the following units: joules, watts, and seconds?

### Work and energy

When you toss a ball, you do work on the ball. While it is in your hand, you push on it and move it in the direction of your push. After you let go, the ball keeps moving. It has kinetic energy. You also do work in stretching a rubber band. A stretched rubber band has potential, or stored, energy. By doing work on a ball and a rubber band, you increase their

Figure 4-12. Suppose you lift a box that weighs 90 N from the floor to a surface 0.9 m high. By how much do you increase the potential energy of the box?

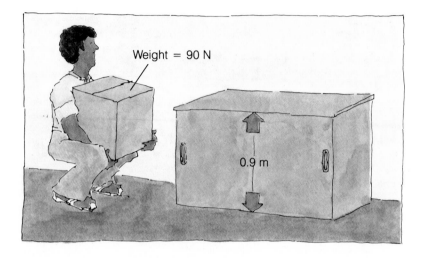

Weight = 90 N

0.9 m

**Data Search**

How much power in joules is given off when 846 kg of TNT is exploded? Use the Mercalli scale to describe an earthquake of equal power. Search page 558.

energy. Scientists look at work as the transfer of energy from one object to another. When you do work on an object, you transfer energy from yourself to the object.

The units for measuring work and energy are the same. If you do one joule of work on an object, you give it one joule of energy. Suppose you lift an object of weight 20 N a distance of 2 m. You do 40 J of work and increase its potential energy by 40 J.

The rate of using energy is called *power*, just as is the rate of doing work. Electric bulbs and appliances are rated by their power use. A 100-W light bulb uses 100 J of energy each second that it is operating. A hair dryer that is rated at 1200 W uses 1200 J of energy every second.

Sometimes work is done on an object but the object does not seem to gain energy. Suppose you put a screw into a piece of wood. You do work to spread apart the fibers of wood and force the screw in. When you are done, neither the screw nor the wood moves. Neither seems to have the ability to cause change. But both the screw and the wood would be warmer. Often, things get warmer when work is done on them. The next section will explore how temperature and energy are related.

**Check yourself**

How do scientists view the relation between work and energy?

# Practical Science

## Gearing Up for Fun

Take a look at a bicycle. At first glance, it looks rather complex. Now, look at it more closely. It is really a collection of simple machines.

**Levers** You will see several examples of levers. These include handlebars, rim brake and gearshift controls, and pedal cranks.

The handlebars act together as a lever with the fulcrum, or steering head, in the center between them. Turning the handlebars causes the steering head to rotate. The force exerted by the rotating steering head allows the tire to overcome friction between itself and the ground.

Rim brakes use three levers. One is the brake lever that you control. The other two are the caliper levers that press the brake pad against the wheel rim.

Gear levers let you change the gear ratio in the rear hub of a three-speed bicycle or operate the derailleur in a ten-speed bicycle.

The pedal cranks are a pair of levers with the crank axle acting as a common fulcrum.

**Wheels** Wheels are rotating lever systems. A wheel exchanges distance for mechanical advantage, or the reverse.

The rear wheel exchanges the mechanical advantage applied to the axle for distance on the tire. The front wheel transfers part of the weight to the ground and changes the direction of the bicycle.

The pedals are wheels, too. An axle is attached to one end of each pedal crank. As you pedal, the cranks rotate and the axles rotate in the pedals.

**Pulleys** Like wheels, pulleys are rotating lever systems that exchange mechanical advantage for distance, or the reverse. Two pulleys called *sprockets* are used on a bicycle.

The front sprocket is attached to the crank axle and the rear sprocket is attached to the rear wheel. Teeth on the sprockets engage a chain. When the front sprocket rotates, it pulls on the chain. The chain then pulls on the rear sprocket, rotating it and the wheel.

When the rear sprocket is smaller than the front sprocket, it rotates faster. Most of the mechanical advantage is exchanged for increased distance on the ground. This is good for riding on a flat surface.

To ride up a hill, you must apply a greater mechanical advantage to the rear wheel. You do this by making the sprockets more nearly the same size.

On a ten-speed, or derailleur, bicycle, you have a choice of sprocket sizes. This lets you choose the best combination for mechanical advantage or distance. Several sizes of sprockets are mounted on both the rear wheel and the crank pedal axles. By using the gear changing levers, you can shift the chain between pairs of sprockets.

**Gears** A gear is a wheel with teeth along its circumference. These teeth engage the teeth of another gear. Like pulleys, they exchange mechanical advantage for distance. Three-speed bicycles use a geared transmission in the rear hub. With the gear lever, you can change the ratio between the rotations of the pedal cranks and the rear wheel.

**Something to try** Find examples of other simple machines on a bicycle, such as screws, wedges, or inclined planes. How are they used?

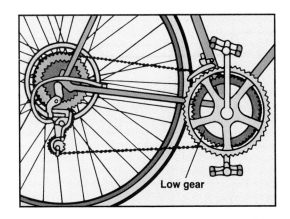
Low gear

## Check Your Vocabulary

| | |
|---|---|
| block and tackle | mechanical advantage |
| efficiency | power |
| fulcrum | watt |
| inclined plane | wedge |
| joule | wheel and axle |
| lever | work |
| machine | |

*Match each term above with the numbered phrase that best describes it.*

1. SI unit of work and energy
2. SI unit of power
3. Type of machine a knife blade is
4. Type of machine a steering wheel is
5. Type of machine a broom is
6. Used to lift a car's engine
7. Type of machine a playground slide is
8. Close to 100% when there is little friction
9. Transfer of energy when an object moves in the direction of a force
10. Point on lever that does not rotate
11. Anything that changes the size or direction of a force
12. Indicates how fast work is done
13. Indicates how much a force has been multiplied by a machine

## Check Your Knowledge

*Multiple Choice: Choose the answer that best completes each of the following sentences.*

1. The amount of work done on an object is equal to the ?.
   a) force applied to the object
   b) distance the object moves in the direction of the force
   c) product of the force and the distance the object moves in the direction of the force
   d) product of the force and the time the force acts on the object
2. Machines are used to do all of the following EXCEPT ?.
   a) increase the amount of work done on an object
   b) change the direction of a force
   c) reduce the force necessary to accomplish the work
   d) make it easier to do work

## Check Your Understanding

1. Describe the difference between a second-class lever and a third-class lever. Give an example of each.
2. Give an example of a machine with a mechanical advantage greater than 1. Describe how this machine makes it easier to do work.
3. Give an example of a machine with a mechanical advantage less than 1. Describe how this machine makes it easier to do work.
4. What is meant by the efficiency of a machine? Why is the efficiency always less than 100%?
5. A pen or pencil is used as a lever in writing.
   a. Identify the fulcrum, the point where your hand applies a force, and the point where the pen or pencil applies a force.
   b. Which class lever is a pen or pencil? Explain how you can tell.
   c. In what way does a pen or pencil make it easier to do the work of making marks on paper?

## Practical Science

Name some of the simple machines found on a bicycle. Discuss how they are used.

# Heat and Internal Energy    Section 2

**Section 2 of Chapter 4 is divided into six parts:**

Temperature changes and heat

Specific heat

Phase changes and heat

Theories about heat

Heat transfer

Insulation

*Practical Science: Home Heating Systems*

**Learning Objectives**

1. To relate heat to the energy transfer because of differences in temperature.

2. To recognize that the amount of heat gained or lost by a substance depends on the kind of substance, the amount of the substance, and the change in temperature of the substance.

3. To differentiate among temperature, heat, and internal energy.

4. To describe the different methods by which heat is transferred and how heat is prevented from being transferred.

Figure 4-13. Glass is being shaped by a glassblower. Glass softens when it absorbs heat and hardens when it gives off heat.

Figure 4-14. How can you make one finger feel the water to be cold and another feel the same water to be warm?

**Main Idea**

What is temperature a measure of?

You dip your finger in water to test how hot or cold the water is. Parents feel a child's forehead with their hand to see if the child seems to have a fever.

**Temperature** is a measure of how hot or cold something is. Your skin is not always an accurate judge of temperature. To prove this to yourself, put a bowl of cold tap water next to an ice cube. Place one finger on the ice cube for a few seconds. Then dip that finger and another finger in the water at the same time. The water will feel much warmer to the finger that was on the ice. Thermometers are not fooled. They measure temperatures much more accurately than your skin can.

In everyday metric units, temperatures are measured in degrees Celsius. Your body temperature is about 37°C. People try to keep the temperature of rooms at about 20°C.

### Temperature changes and heat

When something is warmer than its surroundings, it tends to cool down. For instance, a bathtub of hot water cools to room temperature. Colder things tend to warm up. A cold drink left on the kitchen counter will warm to room temperature.

Something that cools down is said to lose heat. Does something that warms up lose cold? Suppose milk is warmed "to take the chill out of it." Is "chill" something real that leaves the milk? Or does milk take in heat from the stove? People

## Activity 4−2A    Predicting Temperature Changes

### Materials

3 plastic foam cups
thermometer
2 100-mL graduated cylinders
cold water
hot water
stirring rod

### Purpose

To predict the final temperature when hot and cold water are mixed.

### Procedure

1. Place 30 mL of cold water in a plastic foam cup.
2. Place 30 mL of hot water in another cup.
3. Make a table like the one shown.
4. Measure and record the temperature of the water in each cup. SAFETY NOTE: *Use care when handling a thermometer to avoid breaking it.*
5. Predict the temperature of a mixture of the hot and cold water. Record your prediction. Explain your prediction.
6. Pour the hot and cold water together into a third cup and stir well.
7. Measure and record the temperature of the mixture. Compare your results to your prediction.
8. Repeat Steps 4 through 7 with 30 mL of cold water and 60 mL of hot water.
9. Repeat Steps 4 through 7. This time use 60 mL of cold water and 30 mL of hot water.

### Questions

1. How did the temperature of the mixture compare to the starting temperatures when equal volumes of hot and cold water were mixed?
2. When different volumes of hot and cold water were mixed, was the temperature of the mixture closer to that of the larger or smaller sample?

### Conclusion

How can the temperature be predicted when hot and cold water are mixed?

| Cold Water | | Hot water | | Mixture | | |
|---|---|---|---|---|---|---|
| | | | | | Temperature | |
| Volume | Temperature | Volume | Temperature | Volume | Predicted | Measured |
| 30 mL | | 30 mL | | | | |
| 30 mL | | 60 mL | | | | |
| 60 mL | | 30 mL | | | | |

have been thinking about the meaning of heat for a long time. At first heat was thought to be a fluid. But ideas about what heat is have changed a lot. Cold is now thought to be just a lack of heat. So milk that is warmed on the stove takes in heat, instead of losing cold.

What is heat? For a start, you can think of heat as what a substance loses when it cools down. Heat tends to move from a hotter substance to a colder substance. The colder substance takes in heat lost by the hotter substance. As a result, the colder substance warms up. When the two substances are at the same temperature, no movement of heat is observed.

Hot and cold water are often mixed. You know that the temperature of the mixture will be somewhere in between. If a bathtub of water is too hot, you add cold water. The more cold water you add, the cooler the tub of water gets. The temperature of the mixture depends on how much hot water and how much cold water are mixed. Of course, it also depends on the temperatures of the hot and cold water. You can cool the tub with less water if you use very cold water.

Suppose equal amounts of hot and cold water are mixed. The hot water gives up heat to the cold water until they are the same temperature. The temperature of the mixture will be halfway between the temperatures of the cold and hot water. The hot water should cool down and the cold water should warm up by the same number of degrees.

What happens when the amounts of hot and cold water are not equal? Think of the bathtub of hot water. Suppose you add a cup of ice-cold water to the hot water. The hot water will cool only a little. The temperature of the mixture is closer to the temperature of the larger amount of water.

Figure 4-15. How much will the lake be warmed by the warm cans of fruit juice?

### Check yourself

1. Explain why it is incorrect to think that when something is warmed, the chill leaves it.

2. When hot water and cold water are mixed, what besides the original temperatures determines the final temperature of the mixture?

3. What will a mixture of water at 20°C and water at 30°C equal?

### Specific heat

In general, the temperature change of a substance that gains or loses heat depends on the amount of the substance. The amounts of different types of substances are best described by mass. Suppose a certain amount of heat is gained or lost by a substance. The greater the mass of the substance, the

## Activity 4–2B    Temperature Changes of Different Substances

### Materials

safety goggles
balance
metal cylinder (solid aluminum, copper, lead, or iron)
100-mL graduated cylinder
water at room temperature
3 250-mL heat-resistant beakers
thermometer
hot plate
tongs or forceps
hot pad
wire gauze

### Purpose

To find out which gives up more heat, hot metal or an equal mass of water at the same temperature.

### Procedure

1. Put on safety goggles.
2. Make two tables like the ones shown to record your data. Use a balance to measure the mass of the metal cylinder. Record the data on your table.
3. Calculate the volume of water that equals the mass of the metal cylinder. Remember, each gram of water has a volume of 1 mL. Use a graduated cylinder to measure the water, then pour it into Beaker 1. Record the volume of the water on your table.
4. Put 100 mL of water in each of the other two beakers. Measure and record the water temperatures in Beakers 2 and 3. SAFETY NOTE: *Use care when handling a thermometer to avoid breaking it.*
5. Place the metal cylinder in Beaker 1. Place this beaker on the hot plate and bring the water to a boil. SAFETY NOTE: *Use a wire gauze between the beaker and the coil to avoid breaking the beaker. Use a hot pad when handling the hot beaker.*
6. Turn off the hot plate. Using the tongs, transfer the hot metal cylinder to Beaker 2.
7. Pour the boiling water from Beaker 1 into Beaker 3. Immediately measure the temperature of the water in Beaker 3. Record the data on your table.
8. Stir the water in Beaker 2. Measure the temperature. Watch this reading until the water temperature starts to fall. Record the highest temperature of the water in Beaker 2.

### Questions

1. What is the difference in temperature between the metal cylinder and the boiling water?
2. Which of the beakers took in more heat, Beaker 2 or Beaker 3? What was added to the beaker taking in more heat?
3. Which substance lost more heat, the boiling water or the metal cylinder?

### Conclusion

What can you conclude about the amount of heat that is given up by equal masses of hot metal and hot water?

|  | Mass |
|---|---|
| Metal cylinder |  |
| Volume of water equal to mass of metal |  |

|  | Water temperature at start of experiment | Highest water temperature |
|---|---|---|
| Beaker 1 |  |  |
| Beaker 2 |  |  |
| Beaker 3 |  |  |

less its temperature changes. The smaller the mass of the substance, the more its temperature changes.

If you put a solid metal block on a hot plate, it would soon be too hot to touch. But if you put the same mass of water on a hot plate, it would take much longer to get that hot. Water requires more heat than metal does to warm up by the same amount. Different kinds of substances require different amounts of heat to make the same temperature change.

The amount of heat gained or lost by a substance is determined by three factors:

(1)  the kind of substance;

(2)  the amount of the substance;

(3)  the temperature change that takes place.

The amount of heat gained or lost by a substance is commonly measured in **calories** (KAL'-uh-reez). A calorie (symbol cal) is the amount of heat needed to raise the temperature

**Main Idea**

What three factors determine the amount of heat gained or lost by a substance?

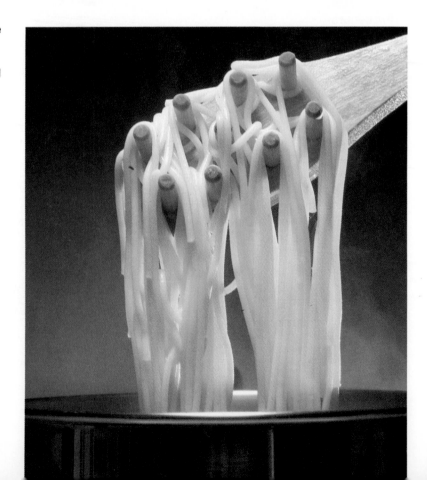

Figure 4-16. The spaghetti can be eaten almost immediately without burning your tongue. It doesn't give up as much heat as an equal mass of boiling water.

of 1 g of water by 1°C. Compared to other substances, water absorbs a large amount of heat when it warms up by 1°C. Only 0.11 calorie of heat is needed to raise the temperature of 1 g of iron by 1°C. And only 0.03 calorie of heat will raise the temperature of 1 g of lead by 1°C. The amount of heat absorbed or given up per gram of a substance and per degree Celsius of temperature change is different for each substance. This property is the **specific heat** of the substance.

Many uses of water depend on water's high specific heat. Most automobile engines use water for cooling. A lot of excess heat from the engine can be absorbed by the water. Yet, the increase in the temperature of the water will be small. Electric generating plants often use water to absorb some of the excess heat. Many of these electric plants are located near large lakes or rivers. These large bodies of water can absorb a lot of heat with only a small temperature increase.

Some heating systems in homes use hot water heat. Pipes carry the hot water through the house. Heat is given up to the room as the hot water cools down. The water delivers a lot of heat to the room. The water is recirculated through a furnace. Here it again gains heat from the burning fuel.

### Check yourself

1. If the same amount of heat is added to equal masses of water and iron, which will become hotter?

2. What substance has a relatively high specific heat?

### Phase changes and heat

Temperature changes are not the only kind of changes that result from the gain or loss of heat. When heat is added to ice at 0°C, the ice melts. The liquid water that is produced remains at 0°C until all the ice is melted. All pure substances act the same way during melting. When heat is added, the only change is that the solid changes phase to a liquid. There is no temperature increase until all the solid has melted.

Similarly, when heat is added to water at its boiling temperature (normally 100°C), the water boils. The water vapor

---

**Data Search**

The specific heat capacity of water is 1.00. The specific heat of which element, lithium, or helium, is closer to that of water? Search page 559.

---

**Safety**

Hot water can cause serious burns because of the high specific heat of water.

that is produced remains at the boiling temperature until all the liquid has boiled away. All pure substances act the same way during boiling. As heat is added, the only change is that the liquid becomes a gas. There is no temperature increase until all the liquid has boiled off.

Each gram of a pure solid substance requires a certain amount of heat to melt completely. This amount is called the **heat of fusion** (FYOO′-zhun). The heat of fusion of water is about 80 cal/g. That is, ice at 0°C must take in 80 cal of heat for each gram that melts. An equal amount of heat is released for each gram of liquid water at 0°C that freezes. Each pure substance has its own heat of fusion.

You add ice when you want to cool your drink. Why not use just cold water? The ice absorbs 80 calories from the drink for each gram of ice that melts. Just a few grams of ice can absorb a lot of heat. The cooling effect of the ice is much

Figure 4-17. During which changes of phase is heat released? During which changes of phase is heat taken in?

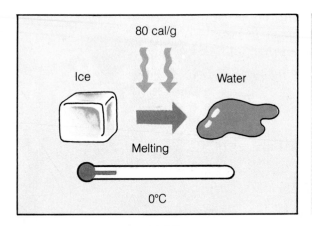

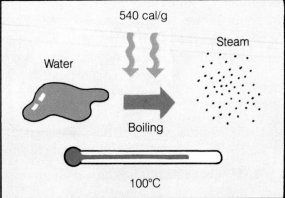

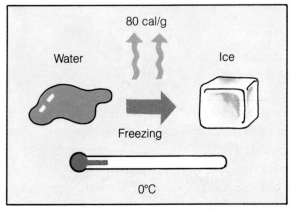

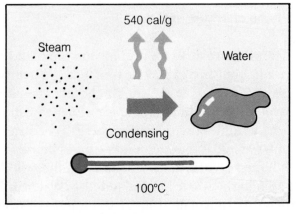

greater than just cold water—even water at 0°C. Water at 0°C absorbs only 20 calories for each gram of water that warms up to 20°C. And after the water has absorbed this heat, it is warm itself.

Each gram of a pure liquid substance requires a certain amount of heat to become a gas. This amount of heat is called the **heat of vaporization** (vay-per-uh-ZAY'-shun). The heat of vaporization of water at 100°C is 540 cal/g. That is, each gram of boiling water that changes to steam must take in 540 cal of heat.

During evaporation, a liquid below the boiling temperature changes to a gas. The gas formed when water evaporates is water vapor. The heat of vaporization for the formation of water vapor is about the same as for steam.

An equal amount of heat is released when a gram of water vapor condenses, or becomes liquid. When water vapor in the air condenses, a cloud is formed. The condensation releases much heat to the air. This extra heating from condensation is a major cause of some severe thunderstorms and even tornadoes.

## Check yourself

1.  Under what circumstances is there no temperature change in water even though it is absorbing heat?

2.  Which requires more heat—to melt 10 g of ice at 0°C or to boil off 10 g of water at 100°C?

## Theories about heat

Early scientists had a hard time explaining what heat was. Heat was not visible. Yet, it could cause changes in both phase and temperature.

One early model of heat was used for nearly a hundred years. Heat was pictured as an invisible fluid. The fluid was named **caloric** (kuh-LOR'-ik). According to the model, caloric could be transferred from one substance to another. A hot substance warmed a cold substance by giving it some of its own caloric. It was known that iron gave off heat when it was

**Main Idea**

What was named *caloric*?

## Activity 4–2C        Work and Temperature

### Materials

100-mL graduated cylinder
water
plastic foam bowl large enough to hold
    200 mL of water
thermometer
eggbeater, hand-held
watch or clock that indicates seconds
graph paper

### Purpose

To show how the temperature of water can be raised by doing work on it.

### Procedure

1. Put 200 mL of water in a plastic foam bowl. Measure the temperature of the water. SAFETY NOTE: *Use care when handling a thermometer to avoid breaking it.* Record the temperature reading on a table like the one shown.
2. Beat the water vigorously with a hand-held eggbeater for one full minute. Have your lab partner hold the bowl so that it does not slip and spill the water. Immediately measure the temperature of the water and record the reading.
3. Beat the water again for a full minute. Measure the temperature of the water and record the reading.
4. Repeat Step 3. Measure and record the water temperature.
5. Plot your temperature readings on graph paper. Label the horizontal axis *Minutes* and the vertical axis *Temperature (in °C)*. Connect the points and study the graph.

### Questions

1. What is the temperature of the water at the beginning of this activity?
2. How does the temperature change after the water has been beaten for one minute?
3. How does the temperature change after the water has been beaten again for one minute?
4. Calculate the average change in water temperature per minute of beating.

### Conclusion

How much can you raise the temperature of water by doing work on it?

|  | Temperature of water °C |
|---|---|
| At start |  |
| After 1 minute |  |
| After 2 minutes |  |
| After 3 minutes |  |

hammered. The model explained this by saying that caloric was being pressed out of the iron. It was believed that caloric could not be created or destroyed. Although it could leave or enter a substance, the total amount remained the same.

Benjamin Thompson (1753–1814) was an American who lived in Europe and became known as Count Rumford. Rumford became famous for his measurements of heat. He was supervising the making of brass cannon barrels. Holes were bored in solid brass to make hollow barrels. The leftover metal chips were very hot. The barrel itself also was hot. According to the caloric model, caloric was being pressed out of the barrel. Apparently, as long as the process continued, caloric was released. There seemed no end to the supply of caloric, even though less and less metal remained in the barrel. Rumford became convinced that heat was not a fluid.

Over 40 years after Rumford's experiments, James Joule (1818–1889) carefully measured temperature changes caused by doing work. He showed that a certain amount of work always produces the same temperature change as adding a certain amount of heat. As more work is done, the temperature rises more. He measured temperature changes in different substances: water, mercury, oil, and iron. Because of his experiments, the unit of energy, the joule (J), is now named after him. He concluded that doing 4.2 J of work produces the same temperature rise as adding 1 cal of heat.

Work can have the same effect as heat. A certain amount of work raises the temperature of a substance the same as a certain amount of heat. Joule repeated his measurements many times. Each time he was led to the same result. Scientists soon became convinced that heat, like work, is a form of energy. The SI unit for heat, as well as work, is the joule.

The modern definition of heat is that heat is the form of energy transferred because of a temperature difference. Heat always moves from warmer to cooler substances.

A substance may give off heat or take in heat. However, it does not contain heat. The energy is called heat only when it is moving from one substance to another. The energy has another name when it is inside a substance—**internal energy**.

Internal energy does not produce visible motion. Nor does it reflect a change in position of the substance. But a rise in

## Library research

Read about the life of Count Rumford (Benjamin Thompson). Write a report describing some of the many inventions and improvements he is responsible for.

Figure 4-18. When you pump up a tire, it gets warmer than the surrounding air. Where does the energy come from that warms the tire?

## Main Idea

When are energy and heat the same?

temperature is a sign of increased internal energy. A change in phase from solid to liquid or from liquid to gas is also a sign of increased internal energy.

A substance can lose internal energy either by giving off heat or by doing work. In electric power plants, steam engines do work that drives the generator. First, water is boiled and changes to steam. As the steam expands, it pushes some blades and makes them rotate. In doing this work, the steam loses some internal energy. As a result, it cools.

Joule's work led scientists to a very important conclusion: *Energy cannot be created or destroyed.* Instead, it can only change from one form to another.

**Main Idea**

What did scientists conclude about the creation of energy?

### Check yourself

1. What is the modern definition of heat?

2. What is the difference between heat and internal energy?

3. How can a substance lose internal energy?

### Heat transfer

Heat moves from matter at a higher temperature to matter at a lower temperature. Think about all the movements of heat when you light a wood fire. First, you put a burning match against some kindling wood. Heat moves from the flame to the kindling. The kindling reaches a high enough temperature to ignite. Heat is transferred to bigger pieces of wood. These pieces also start to burn. You stand close to the fire. The heat reaches you.

Heat moves in three basic ways. First, heat can move through a material without the material itself moving. This type of heat movement is called **conduction** (kun-DUK'-shun). For example, if a metal spoon is placed in a hot drink, the handle becomes warm. Heat travels easily through metals by conduction. It warms the metal as it travels. Metals are good conductors of heat. Glass, wood, and air are not as good conductors of heat as are metals. Substances that are poor conductors of heat are called **insulators** (IN'-suh-lay-terz). Would you call plastic foam a conductor or an insulator?

Figure 4-19. What creates the convection currents that move heat to the top of water heated from below?

Heat can also move through a material by actual movement of the material. This type of heat movement is called **convection** (kun-VEK′-shun). Heat usually moves through liquids and gases by convection. For example, water at the bottom of a pot takes in heat from the burner on a stove. This water expands as it warms. The water at the bottom is then less dense than the cooler water above it. That is, each cubic centimeter of warm water at the bottom is lighter than each cubic centimeter of cooler water above. As a result, the cooler water moves downward. The warmer water is forced upward. The cooler water is now closer to the burner. It too takes in heat, expands, and is forced upward. The movements of the material itself, due to temperature differences, are called **convection currents**.

Breezes are caused by convection currents in the atmosphere. Air is heated near the surface of the earth. The heated air expands. It is forced upward as the surrounding colder air sinks.

**Main Idea**

What is convection?

## Activity 4–2D    Transfer of Heat

### Materials

safety goggles
hot plate
water
250-mL heat-resistant beaker
aluminum foil
thermometer
metal spoon
glass stirring rod

### Purpose

To determine how heat moves from one place to another.

### Procedure

1. Put on safety goggles.
2. Plug in a hot plate. Turn the setting to high. SAFETY NOTE: *Do not touch hot plate to avoid being burned.*
3. Hold your hand about 10 cm to the side and slightly above the hot plate. Do you feel the heat?
4. Turn the hot plate setting to low.
5. Fill the beaker a little more than half full with water. *Carefully* place the beaker on the hot plate.
6. Roll very tiny pieces of aluminum foil into small, tightly-packed balls.
7. Drop the foil balls into the water. Observe what happens to them as the water warms.
8. Leave the water on the hot plate for about 5 minutes. Then, hold a thermometer so that the bulb is just below the surface of the water. SAFETY NOTE: *Use care when handling a thermometer to avoid breaking it.* Read and record the temperature of the water near the top.
9. Next, hold the thermometer so that the bulb is near the bottom of the beaker. Record the water temperature near the bottom.
10. Hold a metal spoon in one hand. Hold a glass stirring rod in the other hand. Place

the end of each in the heated water. Which transfers heat to your hand first—the glass or the metal?
11. Turn off the hot plate. Allow it to cool.

### Questions

1. What process transferred heat to your hand when it was held beside the hot plate?
2. Which was hotter, the water near the top of the beaker or the water near the bottom?
3. What does the movement of the pieces of foil suggest to you about the movement of water within the beaker?
4. a) How is the water near the top warmed?
   b) What is this process called?
5. a) Did the glass or metal transfer heat to your hand first?
   b) Which is the better heat conductor?

### Conclusion

Name three different ways that heat can be transferred and give an example of each.

Figure 4-20. Quartz heaters give off infrared. If you are in the path of the radiation, you can feel the heat. But if you move out of the path, you may feel cold. Air does not absorb infrared as well as human skin does. The room air remains cold.

The third way heat moves is as pure energy that moves through empty space. Heat from the sun reaches the earth this way. Energy that moves through space, and is not carried by matter, is known as **radiant** (RAY'-dee-unt) **energy,** or **radiation** (ray-dee-AY'-shun). Light, X-rays, and microwaves, as well as heat, are radiation. Although radiation is not carried by matter, it can travel through some kinds of matter. Heat from a fireplace travels through air as radiation.

Heat radiation is called **infrared** (in-fruh-RED'). Quartz heaters give off infrared. Infrared is invisible to the human eye, but special film and instruments can detect it.

**Safety**
Invisible infrared radiation can damage the eyes.

### Check yourself

1. What is the difference between conduction and convection?
2. Can heat travel through empty space?

### Insulation

Heat is transferred through the walls, windows, and roofs of buildings. When it is very cold outside, large amounts of heat are wasted if a building is poorly insulated. The heat is conducted by the materials in the walls, windows, and roofs to the outside. From the outside it radiates into the air. There are several ways to cut down on heat loss. Attics and walls can

Figure 4-21. Jackets filled with down or polyester fiberfill are lightweight and yet warm. How do they keep body heat from escaping?

**Library research**

Insulating materials are rated by R values. Find out what the R is based on. What R values are recommended for homes in your area?

be lined with insulating materials. Storm windows can be placed over existing windows. Cracks around doors and windows can be sealed.

When it is very hot outside, heat moves readily through the walls, windows, and roof to the inside of buildings. Again, insulating materials reduce the amount of heat transferred. Roof overhangs, awnings, and shade trees cut down on heat from direct sunlight. Then the need for air conditioning is reduced. Valuable energy is conserved. Understanding how heat is transferred can help save energy.

Insulating materials have long fibers that trap air between them. Heat transfer is prevented in two ways. First, since air is a poor conductor, the material does not conduct heat well. Second, the fibers hold the air in place. Heat cannot be transferred by convection currents through the air.

### Check yourself

What are the qualities of a good heat insulator?

# Practical Science

## Home Heating Systems

Imagine yourself indoors on a cold day in an unheated house. Of course you would really rather be someplace warm. To make your house warm requires a centralized heating system.

**Your choices**   You need to decide whether you want a system which requires a furnace or one which does not. If you decide to use a system which requires a furnace you will have two options. These are *hot water or steam heating,* and *forced or warm air heating.*

Hot water heating systems use the heat generated by hot water to warm a house. The system requires a furnace to heat the water and small pipes to carry the heated water to the various rooms of the house. The pipes lead to metal room radiators. These radiators conduct the heat from the hot water. The heat is spread throughout the room by convection.

Forced air heating uses a furnace to heat air. The heated air is carried through large rectangular pipes called ducts. These ducts lead to vents in the floor of the house. The hot air is forced through the vents to heat the house.

Radiant electric heat uses electric wires in the walls, ceiling, or in baseboards along the floor to radiate heat energy. Radiant electric heat does not require a furnace.

**How to decide**   Heating systems using a furnace require fuel to burn in order to create heat energy. These fuels can be coal, wood, oil, or gas. The heating system you choose may depend upon the cost of fuel where you live.

Other criteria for choosing one heating system over another are efficiency and convenience. Hot water or steam heating is the most efficient method of your three options for home heating. The small pipes take up less space and are easier to install than the ducts required for forced air heating. However, once the ducts are in place for forced air heating, they can be used for both central heating and air-conditioning. The room radiators for hot water heating take up space, while the duct vents in the floor do not.

Both hot water and forced air heating produce soot and dust as a result of burning fuel in the furnace. Radiant electric heating is a cleaner heating system since it does not use a furnace. However, the system is slow to heat up and cool down. Repairs may involve tearing down a wall where the electric wires are.

**Reducing costs**   As an adult, you will probably spend ten to fifteen cents of every dollar you earn to pay utility bills. These bills are for the services that heat and cool your house and supply it with gas and electricity. Costs for operating home appliances may be small compared to the expenses of heating and cooling your house. You may also waste thousands of dollars because of poor insulation in your house. Make sure your house is well insulated to keep you warmer in the winter and cooler in the summer.

**Something to try**   Identify the types of heating systems used at your house and at school.

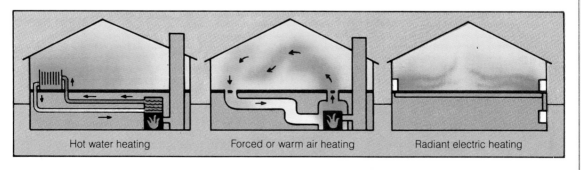

Hot water heating       Forced or warm air heating       Radiant electric heating

## Section 2 Review  Chapter 4

### Check Your Vocabulary

| | |
|---|---|
| calorie | heat of vaporization |
| conduction | insulator |
| conductor | internal energy |
| convection | radiant energy |
| convection current | specific heat |
| heat of fusion | temperature |

*Match each term above with the numbered phrase that best describes it.*

1. Material through which heat easily moves
2. Material through which heat does not easily move
3. Measure of how hot or cold something is
4. Transfer of heat involving movement of a liquid or gas
5. Transfer of heat through a material but with no movement of the material
6. Movement within liquid or gas caused by temperature differences
7. Unit of energy equal to 4.2 J
8. Energy that travels through empty space
9. Energy required per gram of solid for the solid to melt
10. Energy required per gram of liquid for the liquid to evaporate or boil
11. Energy required per gram and per degree for a substance to warm up
12. Energy inside matter

### Check Your Knowledge

*Multiple Choice: Choose the answer that best completes each of the following sentences.*

1. Heat tends to move from a __?__.
   a) conductor to an insulator
   b) liquid to a solid
   c) substance with greater mass to one with less mass
   d) warmer to a cooler substance

2. The greater the specific heat of a substance, the __?__.
   a) faster it will cool down
   b) more slowly it will warm up
   c) higher its temperature will be
   d) faster it will melt

3. The amount of work that can raise the temperature of 1 g of water by 1°C is about __?__.
   a) 1 J          c) 80 J
   b) 4 J          d) 540 J

### Check Your Understanding

1. In a refrigerator, there are pipes containing a liquid. This liquid evaporates easily at refrigerator temperature. Explain how the evaporation of the liquid within the pipes can keep the food in the refrigerator cold.

2. In a hot-air heating system, air heated by a furnace enters a room through a hot-air vent. Will the room be heated better if the vent is closer to the ceiling or to the floor? Explain.

3. People place food in picnic coolers to keep the food cold on a warm day. Does a cooler really cool the food? If not, how does it work?

4. Double-paned windows have two panes of glass with an air space between them. Explain what makes them better than single-paned windows at keeping heat from passing through.

### Practical Science

What are some standards by which to choose an appropriate central heating system for your house?

# The Kinetic Theory of Matter     Section 3

**Section 3 of Chapter 4 is divided into nine parts:**

Motion in matter

An improved model for gases

An improved model for solids

An improved model for liquids

Explaining temperature increases

Explaining heat transfer

Explaining phase changes

Explaining evaporation

Explaining specific heat

*Practical Science: Hot-Air Ballooning*

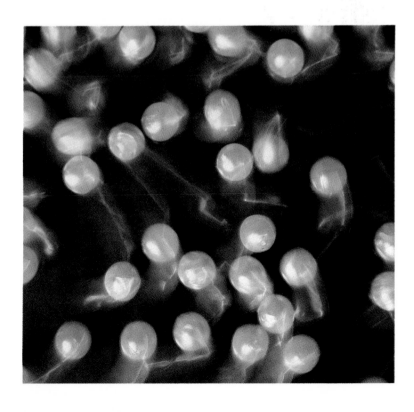

### Learning Objectives

1. To apply the kinetic theory of matter to the behavior of gases, solids, and liquids.

2. To relate the internal energy of a substance to the potential and kinetic energy of its particles.

3. To use the kinetic theory of matter to explain phase changes, heat transfer, and specific heat.

Figure 4-22. The moving beads represent particles of matter in motion. Note how the beads are moving in different directions. When the balls collide, they change direction. Particles of matter also move in different directions and change directions when they collide.

According to the particle model of matter, all matter is made of tiny particles. The particles are separated from each other by space. In a gas, the amount of space between particles is relatively large. In liquids and solids, the amount of space between particles is much smaller.

You have learned that when matter takes in heat, its internal energy increases. When matter gives off heat, its internal energy decreases. How do changes in internal energy affect the particles of matter? In this section, you will learn about a model for matter that takes internal energy into account.

**Motion in matter**

Odors quickly spread throughout a room. If a bottle of perfume is opened, the odor is soon noticed all over the room. Onions frying on the stove can be smelled beyond the kitchen. For odors to spread, particles carrying the odor must move through the surrounding air.

Food coloring spreads through water even if the water is not stirred. When crystals of copper sulfate dissolve in water, they form a blue-green solution. The blue-green color spreads through the water, even with no stirring. For the color to spread, particles carrying the color must move through the surrounding water.

The natural movement within gases and liquids that spreads out odors and colors is called **diffusion** (dih-FYOO'-zhun). Diffusion occurs even when there are no temperature differences that would cause convection currents. It occurs in gases and liquids that appear to be perfectly still.

Figure 4-23. From left to right, the photos below show copper sulfate crystals just after they have been placed in water; after 4 hr; after a day; and after 2 days. How can the spreading of the color be explained?

Diffusion can be explained by thinking of the particles in gases and liquids as constantly moving. The motion is **random**, or without pattern. At any time there are as many particles moving in one direction as in the opposite direction. All the individual motions balance each other. There is no visible motion within the gas or liquid. But because the particles themselves move, odors and colors spread out.

Diffusion takes place faster in gases than in liquids. To understand why, think of moving through a crowd of people to catch up with a friend. It is easier to move through a thin crowd than through a tightly packed crowd. There is much more space between particles in a gas than in a liquid. A gas is like a very thin crowd, while a liquid is like a tightly packed crowd.

**Main Idea**

In what direction do particles move in a gas or liquid?

Figure 4-24. Will the sugar dissolve faster in the hot tea or in the iced tea?

## Activity 4–3A    Diffusion at Different Temperatures

### Materials

2 250-mL beakers or similar containers
food coloring
hot water
cold water
watch or clock with second hand

### Purpose

To determine if the speed of diffusion differs at different temperatures.

### Procedure

1. Fill one beaker with hot water. Fill the second beaker with an equal volume of cold water.

2. Add two or three drops of food coloring to each of the beakers. Do NOT stir.
3. Make a table like the one shown and record your observations.

### Questions

1. Does the color diffuse faster in hot water or in cold water?
2. What is the difference in the amount of diffusion in the beakers after 1 minute? After 5 minutes? After 15 minutes?

### Conclusion

How is the speed of diffusion affected by temperature?

| | Amount of diffusion after 1 minute | Amount of diffusion after 5 minutes | Amount of diffusion after 15 minutes |
|---|---|---|---|
| Hot water | | | |
| Cold water | | | |

### Library research

Find out what John Dalton thought about the question of whether the particles of matter are in motion.

Increasing the temperature increases the speed of diffusion. A drop of food coloring diffuses through warm water faster than through cold water. Substances also dissolve faster in warm water than in cold water. A cube of sugar will disappear faster in warm water.

The increased speed of dissolving and diffusion can be explained. You would make your way through a crowd in less time if you were moving faster. Similarly, the particles are moving faster at the higher temperature.

Something that is moving has kinetic energy, or energy of motion. The faster it moves, the more kinetic energy it has. When a substance becomes warmer, its particles move faster. The kinetic energy of the particles increases. The temperature of a substance measures how warm the substance is. An increase in temperature means an increase in the kinetic energy of the average particle.

These ideas are part of the **kinetic theory of matter**. This theory can be summarized as follows.

1. All matter is made of particles which are in constant motion.
2. As a substance becomes warmer, its particles move with greater energy. As a substance cools, its particles move with less energy.

Adding motion to the particles of matter leads to an improved model of matter. More observations can be explained. Better predictions of the behavior of matter can be made.

### Main Idea

What are the main ideas of the kinetic theory of matter?

### Check yourself

When a substance cools down, what happens to the speed of its particles?

### An improved model for gases

Common gases, such as oxygen, carbon dioxide, and clean air, are made of molecules. Each molecule is made of atoms that remain close together. The molecules, on the other hand, are relatively far apart. But they are so tiny that a cubic centimeter of air contains more than a million times a million times a million of them! Despite the large number of molecules, a gas is 99.9% empty space.

The molecules of a gas are in constant, random motion. At room temperature they move at about 100 m/s, on the average. Yet they rarely move very far before they collide with

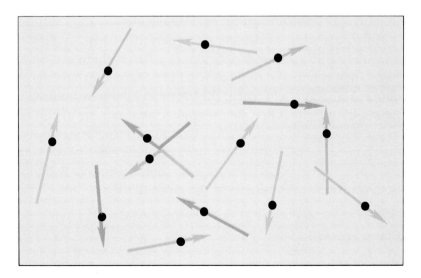

Figure 4-25. In a gas, what makes the directions and speeds of molecules keep changing?

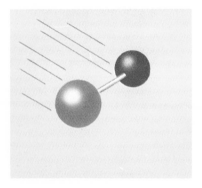

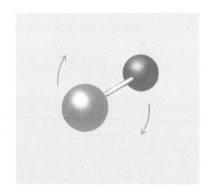

Figure 4-26. A molecule can move as a whole (left). In addition, its atoms can vibrate (center) or rotate around each other (right).

each other or with their container. After a collision, a molecule goes off in a different direction. One molecule may give up some of its kinetic energy to another molecule in a collision. The first molecule will then move more slowly, while the second will move faster. The total amount of kinetic energy stays the same. Because of collisions, both the speed and the direction of a molecule keep changing. But the average kinetic energy of all the molecules does not change.

Within a molecule, the atoms can **vibrate**, or move back and forth. They can also rotate around each other. Thus, a molecule can have additional energy due to the vibration and rotation of its atoms.

The internal energy of a gas is the sum of the energies of all the molecules. This sum includes the total kinetic energy of the moving molecules. It also includes the energy from the motions of the atoms within each molecule.

If two gases are at the same temperature, their molecules have the same average kinetic energy. But if there are more molecules in one gas, that gas will have more internal energy altogether. You could warm the air in a balloon by holding it near a light bulb. Then the average kinetic energy of the air in the balloon would be greater than that of the room air. But the room air would have so many more molecules that it would still have more internal energy. The internal energy depends both on the temperature and the amount of gas.

### Check yourself

What three types of motion can a molecule in a gas have?

## An improved model for solids

Some solids are made of molecules, but many are not. Ice is made of water molecules, and dry ice is made of carbon dioxide molecules. But metals are made of separate atoms. And salts, including sodium chloride, are made of ions, or atoms with extra or missing electrons. In a discussion of solids, then, the word *particle* can mean molecule, atom, or ion.

The particles in a solid are not free to move throughout the solid. They are held together by forces that keep them close to each other. However, even in a solid, the particles are in constant motion. They each vibrate back and forth around a "home" position. They move as if they were attached to little springs.

The vibrating particles in a solid have both kinetic and potential energy. To understand this, think of a bouncing ball. Whenever the ball is moving toward the ground, it is losing potential energy. At the same time, it is gaining kinetic energy. On the other hand, when it bounces away from the ground, it is gaining potential energy. And it is losing kinetic energy.

Figure 4-27. Particle motions in a solid. How are the motions of particles different in a solid and in a gas?

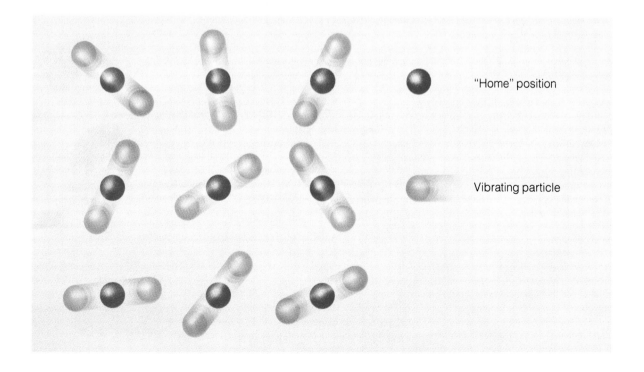

"Home" position

Vibrating particle

The total energy of the ball remains almost unchanged. (The ball loses some energy each time it touches the ground, and it stops moving after a while.)

A bouncing ball has potential energy because the earth is pulling on it with the force of gravity. A particle in a solid has potential energy because its neighbors exert forces on it. As the particle vibrates, potential energy is changed to kinetic and back to potential. But the total energy stays the same. For a solid, the internal energy is the sum of all the energies of its particles. That is, the internal energy includes both the kinetic and the potential energies of the particles.

The kinetic energy of a single vibrating particle keeps changing. But the sum for all the particles does not change. The temperature of a solid depends on the average kinetic energy of the particles. This average does not change as long as no heat enters or leaves and no work is done. When two substances are at the same temperature, the particles have the same average kinetic energy. The potential energy does not contribute to the temperature.

When a solid warms up, its particles receive more energy. They move in bigger vibrations. That is, they move farther

## Our Science Heritage

**The Contributions
of Boyle and Black
to the Theory of Heat**

Many persons contributed to the development of the present theory of heat. Robert Boyle (1627–1691) became one of England's first experimental scientists. He is known for Boyle's Law, which describes how the volume of a gas changes when the pressure on it changes. Boyle suggested that when a gas is heated, the particles of the gas move faster. Boyle published his hypothesis more than 150 years before the

Robert Boyle

from the "home" position on each swing. They are like a ball that can make higher bounces when it has more energy. The average kinetic energy of the particles of the solid is greater. The particles are moving faster, on the average.

If the solid happens to be made of molecules, the atoms within the molecules are moving. As in a gas, the atoms can vibrate or rotate inside each molecule. A solid object that appears to be at rest is full of motion!

### Check yourself

When two substances are at the same temperature, how do the values of the average kinetic energy of their particles compare?

### An improved model for liquids

A liquid can be thought of as a cross between a solid and a gas. As in a solid, the particles remain close to each other. As in a gas, the particles can move past each other.

experiments of Count Rumford and James Joule led scientists to accept this view relating heat to motion.

A century after Boyle's work, the Scottish scientist Joseph Black (1728–1799) was demonstrating that equal amounts of heat produced different temperature changes in different substances. He found that when ice was heated, it melted but did not change temperature. When the same water froze, an equal amount of heat was given off. Black, like other scientists of his day, believed that heat was a fluid. However, this hypothesis could not be used to explain his experiments very easily.

The contributions of Joseph Black have been preserved primarily through the notes of his students, since Black published very little. He founded one of the first chemical societies to be formed.

Joseph Black

## Activity 4–3B        Particle Movement

### Materials

transparent plastic container with top
glass marbles
transparent tape

### Purpose

To show the movement of particles in the different phases of matter.

### Procedure

1. Place enough marbles in a plastic container to make a layer at least two marbles deep. Place the top on the container and seal it with tape.
2. Gently move the container back and forth. Move it just enough for the marbles to keep clicking. Observe the movement of the marbles.
3. Turn the container gently in different directions. At the same time, gently shake the container back and forth. Observe the changes in the movement of the marbles.
4. Increase the shaking and turning until the marbles move freely throughout the container.

### Questions

1. When do the marbles act more like the particles of a solid? Explain your answer.
2. When do the marbles act more like the particles of a liquid? Explain your answer.
3. When do the marbles act more like the particles of a gas? Explain your answer.

### Conclusion

How does the movement of the particles of matter differ in the three phases of matter?

The particles in a liquid are in constant motion. Some of the particles may group together for a time. Within the group, the particles vibrate as in a solid. But the whole group of particles moves. After a short time, the group breaks apart.

On the average, the particles have enough energy to keep from being held in a fixed position. Yet, they do not have enough to free themselves from the forces between particles. They are always close to other particles.

In a liquid, as in a gas and solid, temperature is related to the average kinetic energy of the particles. The potential energy does not contribute to the temperature. At higher temperatures, the particles move faster. The vibrations are bigger. In addition, the particles move faster past each other.

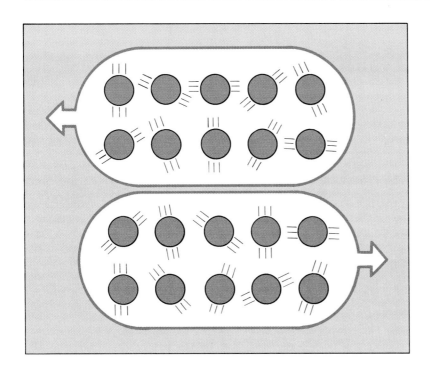

Figure 4-28. How are the motions of particles in a liquid different from the motion of particles in a solid? In a gas?

### Check yourself

What kind of motion is similar for particles in liquids and in solids?

### Explaining temperature increases

The usefulness of a model in science is its ability to explain and predict. The model of matter based on the kinetic theory explains many observations of the behavior of matter.

For example, suppose work is done on a substance or heat is added to it. What does the kinetic theory predict will happen to the substance? The internal energy increases when the work is done or the heat is added. In a gas, the internal energy is mainly due to the kinetic energy of the moving molecules. The theory predicts that the molecules will move faster, on the average. The average kinetic energy of the molecules will increase. And the temperature of the gas will increase.

On the other hand, suppose the gas does work on something else or gives off heat. It loses internal energy this way. The theory predicts that the molecules will slow down and have less kinetic energy. The temperature will fall.

In a solid and liquid, the internal energy consists of both kinetic and potential energy. The potential energy comes from

### Library research

Air that rises cools about 1°C for every 100 m that it rises. Find out how the lowering of the temperature can be explained with the kinetic theory.

the forces between the particles. When the internal energy increases, both the kinetic and potential energies increase. This is true except during melting or boiling, which will be discussed later. When the average kinetic energy of the particles increases, the temperature rises. The increase in potential energy has no effect on the temperature. What happens to the temperature when the internal energy decreases?

### Check yourself

If work is done on a solid, what happens to the kinetic energy of its particles?

### Explaining heat transfer

Suppose one end of a metal bar is placed in a flame. Heat is absorbed by the metal bar at that end. The temperature of the end of the bar increases. The kinetic theory can explain how heat is conducted through the bar. The particles at the hot end have more kinetic energy on the average than other particles in the bar. Particles at the hot end of the bar collide with nearby particles in the bar. In the collisions, particles with more energy lose some energy to particles with less energy.

Figure 4-29. In which direction will heat move through this rod?

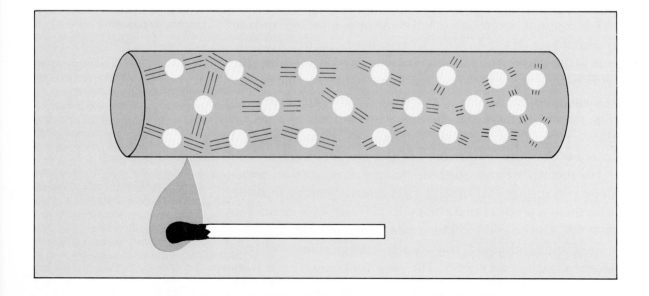

As a result, the nearby part of the bar becomes warmer. The process continues along the bar. Finally, particles all over the bar have the same average kinetic energy. The entire bar is hot.

Suppose a hot cup of tea is sitting on the kitchen counter. How does the kinetic theory explain how heat is conducted away from the tea? Particles in the warmer tea have more kinetic energy on the average than particles in the cooler air. Particles of tea and air collide with each other at the top surface of the tea. The tea particles give up some kinetic energy to the air particles. Collisions continue between the particles of tea and air. Finally, the tea and air particles have the same average kinetic energy. The tea and air then have the same temperature.

You may be wondering how the hot tea lower down in the cup cools down. When the tea near the top cools a little, its particles move in smaller vibrations. The particles take up less space than the particles of the warmer tea below. The cooler tea is now more dense and sinks below the warmer tea. Now the warmer tea is near the surface and its particles collide with the air particles. Thus, the kinetic theory can explain convection as well as conduction.

### Check yourself

When particles of something warm collide with particles of something cool, what happens to their kinetic energies?

### Explaining phase changes

Boiling can be understood by thinking about the launching of spacecraft. How are spacecraft able to overcome the pull of the earth's gravity? During launching, the spacecraft's rockets give off tremendous amounts of burning gases at high speeds. The gases, in an equal and opposite reaction, push forward on the spacecraft. The forces are exerted by the gases for some distance. They do work on the spacecraft. The work done on the spacecraft is changed to kinetic energy. The spacecraft is able to move upward at high speed.

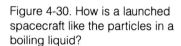

Figure 4-30. How is a launched spacecraft like the particles in a boiling liquid?

As the spacecraft moves away from the earth, some of its kinetic energy is changed into potential energy. But it has so much kinetic energy that it keeps moving upward.

Particles in a liquid can be thought of as tiny spacecraft. Adding heat to a liquid increases the energy of the particles. The temperature of the liquid increases until the boiling point is reached. Any additional heat gives the particles energy to break away from each other. They form bubbles of gas that escape from the liquid.

The average kinetic energy of the particles of gas is the same as in the liquid. The gas and liquid have the same temperature until all the liquid has boiled away.

The particles of gas have more potential energy than they did in the liquid. They are like spacecraft that have more potential energy after they have left the earth. The extra potential energy came from the heat added to the liquid after it reached the boiling temperature.

## Activity 4–3C     Melting

### Materials

| | |
|---|---|
| sharpened pencil | 2 250-mL beakers |
| 2 thermometers | crushed ice |
| clear tape | glass stirring rod |
| water | 2 wire gauzes |
| hot plate | |

2 cardboard circles, each 9 cm in diameter
watch or clock that indicates seconds

### Purpose

To show the temperature changes that occur during the melting of ice.

### Procedure

1. Use a sharpened pencil to poke a hole in the center of the cardboard disk. Gently ease the bulb of a thermometer through the hole. SAFETY NOTE: *Be sure the hole in the cardboard disk is large enough so the thermometer can be pushed through without breaking. If a thermometer is broken, avoid touching the mercury and notify your teacher.* Slide the bulb down so that when the cardboard rests on the rim of the beaker, the bulb is suspended inside the beaker. Tape the thermometer in this position. Do this for both beakers. Make a table like the one shown with spaces for 15 minutes.
2. Fill the first 250-mL beaker half-full of water. Add enough crushed ice to fill the beaker. Stir the ice and water. When the water temperature reaches 0°C, remove any remaining ice and transfer it to the second beaker.
3. Add enough ice to the second beaker to make the volume in the two beakers equal.
4. Put a cardboard disk with a thermometer set in it over each of the beakers. Make sure the bulbs of the thermometers are set in the middle of the water and in the middle of the ice. Place both beakers on a wire gauze on the cold coils of the same hot plate. Set the hot plate control to low heat. Record the temperature of both beakers.

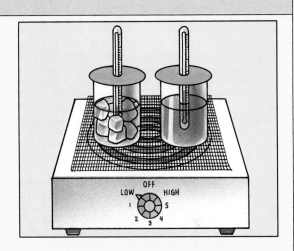

5. Take a temperature reading for each beaker every minute until the ice melts completely. Record all the data.
6. Periodically remove the cardboard and thermometer for a few seconds and stir the ice and water mixture.
7. Use two colored pencils to plot the data for both beakers on the same graph.

### Questions

1. How did the temperatures of the two beakers compare at the start?
2. Was the same amount of heat added to each of the beakers? Explain your answer.
3. How did the temperatures of the two beakers compare when all the ice melted? Why?

### Conclusion

How does the temperature change in an ice-water mixture as heat is added?

| Temperature | Beaker #1 | Beaker #2 |
|---|---|---|
| At start | | |
| Minute 1 | | |
| Minute 2 | | |

**Main Idea**

Compare the average kinetic energy of the particles in a freezing liquid and in the resulting solid.

Particles in a solid are held together by forces between them. They vibrate but they are not free to move past each other. When heat is added to a solid at its melting temperature, no change in temperature occurs. The average kinetic energy of the particles does not change. All of the heat is changed into potential energy. The particles receive enough energy to overcome the forces holding them in place. In the liquid formed from the melted solid, the particles are free to move past each other.

At the end of the melting, the particles have the same average kinetic energy as they did in the solid. The liquid is at the same temperature as the solid was when melting began. But the particles have more potential energy.

The reverse of boiling is condensation. The reverse of melting is freezing. No temperature change takes place during these phase changes either. The average kinetic energy of the particles does not change. But heat is given off. During condensation and freezing, the particles lose potential energy. This potential energy is released as heat.

**Check yourself**

When a solid melts, what happens to the kinetic and potential energies of its particles?

**Explaining evaporation**

A puddle of water dries up. Freshly washed dishes dry in a dish rack. Liquids evaporate even at temperatures way below their boiling temperature. How can the kinetic theory explain evaporation?

The temperature of a liquid is related to the average kinetic energy of the particles. But not all particles in the liquid have the same kinetic energy. During collisions, individual particles gain and lose energy. A few particles may gain very large amounts of energy. Some of them will have enough energy to overcome the forces between the particles. When they reach the surface of the liquid, they escape.

What effect does the escape of the high-energy particles have on the rest of the liquid? To understand, think about the following. Suppose your teacher announced that all the "A" students would be excused from taking the next test. What would happen to the class average on the next test? Without the high scores of the "A" students, the class average would go down.

In the same way, the average kinetic energy of the remaining particles in the liquid is less. The temperature of the liquid is reduced. The liquid becomes cooler than its surroundings. As a result, heat moves into the liquid from its surroundings. Because of this, evaporation has a cooling effect. When drops of water or alcohol evaporate from your skin, your skin feels much cooler. Heat moves from your skin into the evaporating water or alcohol.

Figure 4-31. Cologne contains alcohol. What makes alcohol at room temperature feel so cool on the skin?

Your body maintains its constant temperature in warm weather using this cooling method. Perspiration is evaporated from the surface of the skin. The body cools as a result.

### Check yourself

What particles of a liquid are the most likely to escape?

### Explaining specific heat

It takes different amounts of heat to raise the temperature of equal masses of different substances by the same number of degrees. Water requires the most heat. Copper requires

Figure 4-32. The tub of golf balls has the same mass as the tub of table tennis balls. Which tub must contain more balls? Explain how you know.

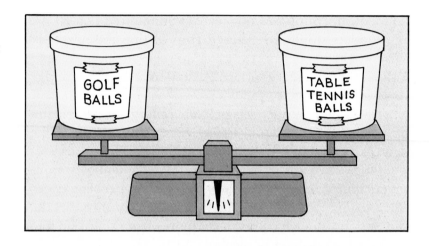

### Data Search

What is the atomic mass of lead? of copper? What is the specific heat capacity of lead? of copper? Search page 559.

### Main Idea

In what way does water absorb energy that has no effect on the temperature of the water?

much less heat. And lead requires even less than copper. How can the kinetic theory explain these differences?

The mass of a copper atom is only a third of that of a lead atom. As a result, in a gram of copper there are three times as many atoms as in a gram of lead. For the same temperature increase, the average kinetic energy of the atoms must rise by the same amount. But with three times as many copper atoms, three times as much total energy is required. Just as the kinetic theory predicts, the specific heat for copper is three times the specific heat for lead.

A water molecule has even less mass than a copper atom. A gram of water has more than three times as many water molecules as a gram of copper has copper atoms. Furthermore, some of the energy absorbed by water increases the motions of the atoms of oxygen and hydrogen within the molecules. These motions within the molecules do not increase the motion of the total molecule. They have no effect on the kinetic energy of the water molecules. Thus, the energy absorbed in this way does not affect the temperature. As predicted, water absorbs much more heat than an equal mass of copper during the same temperature change.

### Check yourself

What is the relation between the number of particles in a gram of a substance and the specific heat of that substance?

**Careers** Refrigeration and Heating Mechanic / Machinist

**Refrigeration and Heating Mechanic** Most refrigeration and heating mechanics work for companies that sell and service cooling and heating equipment. In some cases individuals may operate their own repair and installation service. Mechanics in this field receive their training either by working with experienced mechanics or by attending a trade school offering this specialty. A high school education is preferred for either apprenticeship training or for admittance to the trade school. Science and math courses in high school offer valuable background for such training.

The work can challenge the mechanic's ability to solve problems. Long, irregular hours may be required. Demands are seasonal and, of course, vary with location.

Increasing awareness of the need for conserving valuable energy resources has led to expanded opportunities in this career field. New technological developments and greater use of solar energy promise continued growth in the years ahead.

A refrigeration and heating mechanic may be called into a home to repair a heater.

**Machinist** A person employed as a machinist may be trained in one of a variety of specialized machine tooling operations. The precise job title is related to the type of machine operated, such as metal lathe operator, milling machine operator, drill press operator, or grinding machine operator. In general, a machinist follows specific guidelines in cutting and shaping metal to a certain size to produce metal parts. Machined parts are used in transportation equipment and a wide range of manufacturing machinery.

Most machinists work in factories where parts are mass produced. Often they work in a hazardous work environment and must wear safety glasses or goggles to protect their eyes from flying metal particles. Operators of noisy machinery wear ear plugs.

Most training for machinists takes place on the job, often through a formal apprenticeship program. Useful courses in high school to prepare for this occupation include mathematics, machine shop, and blueprint reading.

Machinists must follow specifications exactly so that the parts they make will function smoothly.

# Practical Science

## Hot-Air Ballooning

Everyone has wondered what it would be like to be "free as a bird" and fly. For centuries, many inventors tried to design "flying machines" that had wings. Yet the first aircraft that succeeded in flying did not even have wings! Two brothers from France, Jacques and Joseph Montgolfier, launched a large balloon filled with hot air in 1783. The balloon floated in air like a boat floats in water.

**Why balloons float in air**   In a way, gravity makes things float! You know that a table tennis ball will float in water. The combined mass of the table tennis ball and the air inside it is less than the mass of the same volume of water. Gravity attracts the water with a greater force than it pulls down on the plastic ball filled with air. As the water surrounding the ball is pulled downward by gravity, the table tennis ball is pushed upward by the water.

A hot air balloon floats for the same reason. The combined mass of the balloon, the hot air inside, the basket, and the people is less than the mass of the same volume of air. Gravity attracts the colder air surrounding the balloon with a greater force than it pulls down on the balloon, its hot air, basket, and passengers. As the heavier air around the balloon is pulled to the surface of the earth, the balloon and its cargo are pushed upward. In other words, less dense materials float in more dense fluids (liquids or gases).

**The air in the balloon**   The Montgolfier brothers used hot air because it has less mass than the same volume of cold air. This is because it takes fewer hot air particles to fill the same sized balloon. Hot air particles collide with each other more often than cold air particles. This causes some of them to "spill out" of the balloon. Rapidly moving air particles take up the same amount of space as more slowly moving particles. In the diagram at the right, both balloons are the same size. Which one is filled with hot air? Which one has more particles? Which one has the greater mass?

**Controlling altitude**   The pilot of the balloon uses a gas burner to keep the air hot. It is not necessary to keep the flame burning all the time. What do you think happens to the altitude of the balloon when the burner heats the air in the balloon? After the heater has been off for a while, is the size of the balloon larger, smaller, or the same? What will happen to the altitude of the balloon as a result?

**Something to try**   Fill a bowl halfway with water. Place an object that will float, such as an ice cube or plastic ball, in the bowl. Push the object to the bottom of the bowl of water. Can you feel the force of the water pushing the object upward? Release the object and watch how it moves to the top of the water. How much of the object floats above the water level? Do all floating objects have the same amount of material above the water level? The force pushing the object up is small because the object is small. Have you ever tried to hold a large beach ball under water in a swimming pool? In that case the force pushing the ball up is much greater. Why?

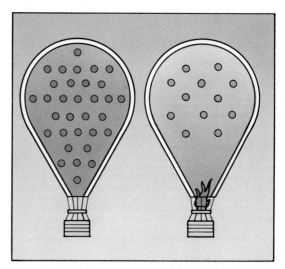

# Section 3 Review   Chapter 4

## Check Your Vocabulary

diffusion                    random

kinetic theory of            vibrate
  matter

*Match each term above with the numbered phrase that best describes it.*

1. Describes what atoms in a piece of metal do

2. Causes smell of burnt toast to spread out

3. Explains how a liquid below its boiling temperature can change into a gas

4. Describes direction of motion of gas molecules

## Check Your Knowledge

*Multiple Choice: Choose the answer that best completes each of the following sentences.*

1. The temperature of a substance is most closely related to the __?__.
   a) volume of the substance
   b) mass of the substance
   c) internal energy of the substance
   d) average kinetic energy of the particles

2. The particles in a liquid __?__.
   a) vibrate as well as move past each other
   b) all move with the same speed
   c) all have the same kinetic energy
   d) exert no forces on each other

3. During melting, the effect of adding heat is to increase the __?__.
   a) kinetic energy of the particles
   b) potential energy of the particles
   c) size of the particles
   d) forces between the particles

## Check Your Understanding

1. Explain what makes gases diffuse faster than liquids do.

2. What effect does an increase in temperature have on the motion of the particles of a substance?

3. Compare the motion of particles in a solid with the motion of particles in a liquid.

4. When a substance absorbs heat, is all the energy converted into kinetic energy of the particles? Explain your answer.

5. Use the kinetic theory to explain how heat moves from a heated pot to the soup inside.

6. Use the kinetic theory to explain why a puddle dries up more quickly in the sun than in the shade.

7. Helium and neon are both gases with only one atom in each molecule. The mass of a neon atom is five times that of a helium atom. Predict how the specific heats of the two gases should compare.

## Practical Science

1. Why does hot air cause a balloon to rise?

2. Explain why a hot air balloon carrying a basket filled with people and supplies can still float in the air.

## Chapter 4 Review

### Concept Summary

**Work** is the transfer of energy to an object when the object moves in the direction of a force acting on it.
- The amount of work done is equal to the amount of force in the direction of motion multiplied by the distance moved.
- No work is done when the object does not move.

A **machine** is something that changes the size and/or direction of a force used to do work.
- Examples of machines include the inclined plane, wedge, screw, lever, wheel and axle, and pulley.
- The mechanical advantage of a machine equals the force needed to do the work directly divided by the force applied to the machine.
- The efficiency of a machine equals the work done by the machine divided by the work put into the machine, expressed as a percentage.
- The efficiency of any machine is always less than 100% because some of the work is used to overcome friction.

**Power** is a measure of how fast work is being done or how fast energy is being used.

**Heat** is energy that is transferred as a result of differences in temperature.
- Temperature is a measure of how hot or cold a substance is.
- Heat moves from a warmer to a cooler substance.
- Substances usually become warmer when they take in heat and cooler when they give it off.
- When a substance is changing phase, it gains or loses heat but remains at a constant temperature.
- The amount of heat gained or lost by a substance depends on the amount of substance, the type of substance, and the temperature change.
- Heat is transferred by conduction, convection, and radiation.

The **internal energy** of a substance is the energy inside it.
- A substance may gain internal energy either by taking in heat or by having work done on it.
- When a substance gains internal energy, either its temperature increases or it changes phase.

**Forms of energy** are different kinds of energy, such as kinetic energy, potential energy, work, heat, and internal energy.
- Energy can be changed from one form to another.
- Energy cannot be created or destroyed.

The **kinetic theory of matter** is a model that pictures matter as made of particles that are in constant, random motion.
- The temperature of a substance is related to the average kinetic energy of the particles.
- When a substance becomes hotter, its particles move faster, on the average.
- Models for solids, liquids, and gases picture the particles as having potential energy because of the forces between them.
- Changes in phase are explained by changes in the potential energy of the particles.
- The internal energy of a substance equals the sum of all the energies of the particles.

### Putting It All Together

1. What two conditions must be met for work to be done on an object?
2. Why is it that an inclined plane can be called a machine?
3. How does a second-class lever differ from a first-class lever?
4. What advantage is gained by using a third-class lever?
5. What limits the efficiency of a machine?
6. What is the power of a machine that does 50 J of work in 5 s?

7. When a substance gains heat, how is the temperature change related to the mass of the substance?

8. Why would ice at 0°C cool a pitcher of lemonade more than the same amount of water at 0°C would?

9. How does the amount of heat taken in during evaporation of a liquid compare to the amount of heat released during condensation?

10. What changes suggest that a substance has gained internal energy?

11. How does the average kinetic energy of the particles in a substance change with an increase in temperature?

12. How can the kinetic theory be used to explain the conduction of heat in a solid?

13. The evaporation of a liquid produces a cooling effect. How can the kinetic theory be used to explain this effect?

## Apply Your Knowledge

1. To open a swinging door, you usually push on the part of the door farthest from the hinges. Use your knowledge of levers to explain why it would be harder to open the door if you pushed on the center of the door.

2. A hot, dry climate is generally more comfortable than a hot, humid climate. Use your understanding of evaporation to explain why.

3. Suggest an explanation for the good insulation properties of plastic foam. (*Hint:* What causes plastic foam to be so light for its size?)

4. Use your knowledge of solids, liquids, and gases to explain why solids are generally the best conductors of heat.

## Find Out on Your Own

1. Compare the dissolving times of a fixed amount of granulated sugar in water at different tem-peratures. Use water samples of equal volume. On a graph, plot the dissolving time vs. the water temperature. How does the dissolving time change with temperature?

2. Measure the heat of fusion of water as follows. Measure the temperature of a known volume of warm water (50°C to 60°C) that half fills its container. Add ice to the warm water and wait until the temperature is just lowered to 0°C. Remove any remaining ice and remeasure the volume of the water. How many grams of ice were melted? (*Hint:* Assume each milliliter of water added to the original sample to be from one gram of ice that melted.) How many calories of heat were lost by the original sample of warm water? How many calories were used to melt each gram of ice?

3. Experiment with keeping an ice cube in surroundings that are at room temperature. What kinds and combinations of materials keep the ice the longest?

## Reading Further

Adler, Irving. *Hot and Cold.* New York: John Day, 1975

This book explains the nature of heat and cold; examines theories of heat and its behavior; describes how very high and very low temperatures can be produced.

Jollands, David, ed, *Machines, Power and Transportation.* New York: Arco, 1984

The book explains how modern technology works in the machines seen and used everyday.

Kingston, Jeremy. *How Bridges Are Made.* New York: Facts on File, 1985

Great bridges of the world and principles governing their design are described and illustrated.

# Chapter 5

# Energy and Changes in Matter

## Section 1
### Energy and Chemical Changes

In a chemical change, energy may be absorbed or given off. The energy given off can be used for warming or to do work. Although the energy is useful, undesired products may be produced.

## Section 2
### Energy and Materials in Industry

Chemical and physical changes are used to convert raw materials to finished products. Industries use large amounts of energy to carry out these processes.

In this chapter you will learn about the absorption and release of energy in chemical reactions. Fireworks are the result of spectacular chemical reactions. In what ways do they absorb or release energy?

# Energy and Chemical Changes    Section 1

**Section 1 of Chapter 5 is divided into seven parts:**

Starting a reaction

Catalysts

Burning fuels for heat

Controlling the rate of burning

Burning fuels to do work

The products of burning fuels

Energy and chemical bonds

*Practical Science: Two-Stroke Engines*

## Learning Objectives

1. To recognize that chemical changes involve changes in energy.

2. To explain how catalysts increase the speed of a chemical reaction.

3. To describe how the energy released from the burning of fuels is controlled and used.

4. To identify the products of the burning of fuels and their effects on the atmosphere.

5. To relate the release and absorption of energy in chemical reactions to the forming and breaking of chemical bonds.

Figure 5-1. The oven releases the heat that provides the energy for the bread dough to bake.

Imagine that you are in a group crowded around a campfire. The heat from the fire is keeping you warm. The release of heat is a common sign that a chemical reaction is taking place. You may not think of the burning of wood as a chemical reaction, but it is one. When wood is at a high enough temperature, it combines with oxygen from the air. Ashes and some gases are produced. Great amounts of heat are released. Light is given off as well.

Heat and light are both forms of energy. Burning is a chemical reaction in which energy is released rapidly. There are many chemical reactions in which energy is released more slowly. A compost heap containing grass clippings, vegetable scraps, and soil warms up from the energy released as the plant material breaks down. Wet concrete warms up in the reaction that makes it harden. The warming up is a sign that energy is being released.

Figure 5-2. A quick way to stop vegetables from overcooking is to run cold water over them. What would happen if they were left in the hot cooking water but the pan was removed from the stove?

Some reactions, on the other hand, require energy to be added continually or they will stop. Water can be separated into hydrogen and oxygen. The reaction continues only as long as energy is supplied by an electric current through the water. Vegetables cook as long as they get energy from hot water. If they are removed and placed under running cold water, they stop cooking immediately.

### Starting a reaction

You know that wood will not start to burn by itself. It must
first be brought to a high enough temperature. It takes energy
to raise the temperature of the wood to this temperature.
Once it burns, however, the wood gives off a greater amount
of energy.

Burning is something like getting out of a valley between
two hills at the edge of a plain. The valley is higher than the
plain. But to reach the plain from the valley, you must first
go to the top of the hill between them. From there, it is all
downhill.

Figure 5-3. How is the burning of
wood like reaching a plain from a
valley?

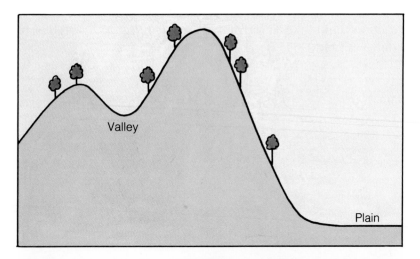

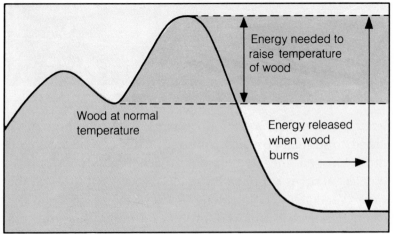

Figure 5-4. How does paint protect a car from rust spots like these?

Most reactions will not start when the reactants are simply brought together. They must be heated before any change takes place. Heating supplies the "uphill push." Some reactions do start without the addition of energy from outside. Unprotected iron rusts easily when wet or even when exposed to humid air. Rusting is a chemical reaction in which iron combines with oxygen from the air, forming the reddish compound iron oxide. The hardening of cement is another reaction that needs no energy push to start it.

### Check yourself

1. Give an example of a reaction that stops when energy is no longer supplied.

2. Give an example of a reaction that needs some energy to get started and then releases much more energy.

### Catalysts

Some reactions happen quickly. In explosions and burning, it is easy to see that a change is taking place. Other reactions happen over so long a time that you are not aware of the change. Silver slowly loses its shine and tarnishes. The tarnish is a black compound, silver sulfide, formed when silver reacts with sulfur compounds in the air.

Many reactions can be speeded by the addition of a substance that is left unchanged at the end of the reaction. A substance which can speed up a reaction without being changed itself is called a **catalyst** (KAT'-uh-list). Catalytic converters on automobiles speed up the conversion of harmful gases in the exhaust system into harmless gases.

Figure 5-5. A catalyst speeds up a reaction by lowering the amount of energy needed for the reaction to start.

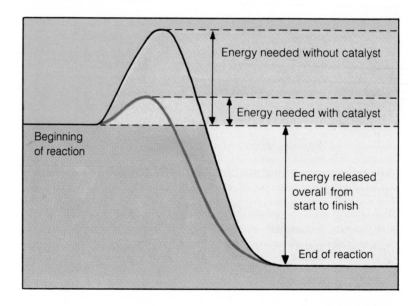

Catalysts work by lowering the amount of energy needed to make a reaction start. They act like a tunnel through the energy "hill." They do not change the overall amount of energy released from start to finish in the reaction.

### Check yourself

What is a catalyst?

## Burning fuels for heat

Many buildings are heated through the burning of substances. Substances burned to supply energy are known as **fuels**. Many different fuels can be used to supply heat.

Natural gas is one such fuel. It consists mostly of the gas methane, $CH_4$. Natural gas is found in gas wells underground and carried by pipelines to cities and towns. It is the gas normally burned in gas stoves. Although natural gas is odorless, the utility company adds a strong smelling chemical to make people aware of leaks.

Some homes use bottled gas, which consists of butane ($C_4H_{10}$), propane ($C_3H_8$), or a mixture of the two. Butane and propane are normally gases, but they are stored as liquids by compressing them into steel cylinders. Bottled gas is used by people located away from natural gas lines.

Fuel oil is another common fuel formed from petroleum. It is a mixture of compounds of two elements: carbon and hydrogen. Such compounds are called **hydrocarbons** (HĪ'-drō-kar-bunz). Hydrocarbons are our most widely used fuels. Methane, butane, and propane are also hydrocarbons.

The branch of chemistry that deals with hydrocarbons is known as organic chemistry. **Organic chemistry** deals with carbon-containing compounds. It includes the chemistry of living things.

Wood and coal once were the most widely used fuels. They also contain compounds of carbon. As fuel oil has risen in price and shortages of natural gas have developed, wood and coal are again becoming popular.

### Check yourself

Name three fuels that are hydrocarbons.

### Controlling the rate of burning

Using fuels for heat requires that the rate of burning be controlled. It cannot be too rapid or too slow. What are the conditions that affect the rate of burning?

Figure 5-6. For what reasons might people use bottled gas (upper photo) or wood (lower photo), rather than natural gas or fuel oil, as fuels?

## Main Idea

How does the amount of fuel used affect the amount of heat given off?

**Safety**

If you smell gas at home or in the laboratory, do not light a flame or spark. A flame or spark may ignite the gas and cause an explosion.

You know that when a wood fire seems to be dying down, you can make it hotter by adding more logs. In a barbecue, you add more charcoal. Increasing the amount of fuel increases the amount of heat released. On a gas stove, you can change the amount of gas released by turning the burner control. Decreasing the amount of fuel decreases the heat.

In burning, a fuel combines with oxygen. Thus, the rate of burning can be controlled by increasing or decreasing the oxygen supply. In a fireplace, the damper in the chimney controls the amount of air that passes through the chimney.

---

## Our Science Heritage

### Alfred Nobel

Winners of the Nobel Prize receive a gold medal like this as well as a large cash award.

Alfred Nobel (1833–1896) is now most well known for the world-famous prizes he established in the fields of peace, chemistry, physics, medicine, and literature. In his own time, he was known as the inventor of dynamite and other explosives.

The son of a Swedish inventor and manufacturer of explosives, Nobel saw how explosives could help people blast roads through mountains, dig canals, and excavate for building construction. He himself started a factory that made the highly dangerous explosive nitroglycerine. His younger brother and four others were killed when the factory blew up. He decided to find a way to control explosives so that they could be used more safely.

Nobel experimented until he found a way to package nitroglycerine fairly safely in sticks he called dynamite. He also invented blasting gelatin and a smokeless powder that was used by the military. His inventions made him wealthy, but people saw him as responsible for large-scale death and destruction in warfare. To show his concern for humanity, he left all his money toward the establishment of prizes for advancements toward peace as well as toward science. Today, the Nobel Prize is probably the most prestigious award a person can receive.

The Nobel Institute, a research institute in Sweden, is named after Alfred Nobel. Element 102, which was first isolated at the Nobel Institute, was named nobelium.

Covered barbecues have adjustable vent openings. Since oxygen is part of the air, changing the air supply changes the oxygen supply.

There is a problem with controlling burning by limiting the oxygen supply. When a hydrocarbon fuel burns in the presence of plenty of oxygen, the products are carbon dioxide and water vapor. This reaction is known as **complete burning**. However, when there is not enough oxygen, carbon monoxide and soot are formed, in addition to carbon dioxide and water vapor. This reaction is known as **incomplete burning**.

The less oxygen there is, the more carbon monoxide and soot are formed. Carbon monoxide is a colorless, odorless gas. It can cause death if it is allowed to build up. For this reason, a fireplace should never be used with the damper closed. Soot, which is powdered carbon, can coat chimney flues and later catch on fire.

There is a third way of controlling the amount of heat given off. In a gas furnace or water heater, the gas supply is closed off when no more heat is needed. It is opened when heat is needed. Thus, the burning itself is stopped and started as needed. The length of time of the burning controls the amount of heat.

Solid and liquid fuels can be made to burn faster in yet another way. When they are broken up into small pieces or small drops, more of their surface is exposed to oxygen in the air. Twigs catch on fire more easily than heavy logs. Wood shavings and sawdust burn much more rapidly than twigs. Very little heat is needed to start a sawdust particle burning. As it burns, it releases enough heat for the particles around it to burn. Some materials that are not considered fuels can burn rapidly in powdered form. Dust from flour in a mill can set off an explosion if set on fire by a spark.

**Safety**

No flames should be used around oxygen supplies.

Figure 5-7. If the coals in a barbecue are giving off too much heat, how can they be cooled easily?

### Check yourself

1. Explain the difference between complete burning and incomplete burning.

2. List four ways of controlling the amount of heat given off by a fuel.

## Burning fuels to do work

Heat released in burning can be used not only to warm things but to do work. For example, most automobile engines run on the energy from burning gasoline vapor. The burning takes place in the cylinders of the engine.

Figure 5-8 shows what happens inside one cylinder. A mixture of air and gasoline vapor enters the cylinder. The mixture is compressed into a smaller space by the piston. Then it is ignited by an electric spark from the spark plug. Burning occurs so rapidly that an explosion results. The gases produced from the burning gasoline vapors expand because of

Figure 5-8. The four steps in the burning of gasoline vapor in one cylinder of a gasoline engine. The engine does work only in the third step. Explain why an engine runs more smoothly if it has more than one cylinder.

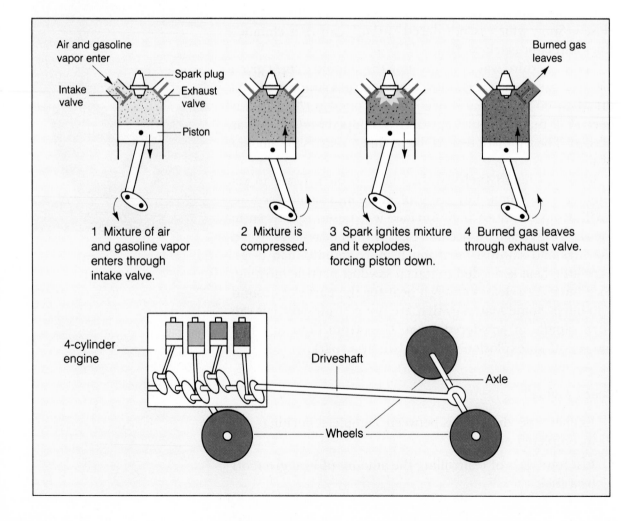

1  Mixture of air and gasoline vapor enters through intake valve.

2  Mixture is compressed.

3  Spark ignites mixture and it explodes, forcing piston down.

4  Burned gas leaves through exhaust valve.

the heat released. The expanding gases move the piston down in the cylinder. Finally, the burned gases are pushed out.

Automobile engines are also known as four-stroke engines. Four steps are needed to complete each cycle. Most automobiles have four or six cylinders. The explosion in each cylinder occurs at a different time.

In an automobile engine, the burning, or combustion, takes place inside the engine. For this reason, the engine is called an **internal combustion engine**. Some internal combustion engines use other fuels instead of gasoline. Alcohol, as well as gasohol (a mixture of alcohol and gasoline) may be used.

Diesel engines use diesel oil. These engines have cylinders, but they operate differently than those of gasoline engines. First, air with no fuel mixed with it enters the cylinder. The air is compressed much more than the air and gasoline mixture in a gasoline engine. The compressed air becomes so hot that when fuel is sprayed into the cylinder, the fuel explodes at once. No spark plug is needed.

A steam engine does work as a result of the burning of fuel outside the engine itself. It is an example of an **external combustion engine**. The fuel is burned to boil water. The water

**Main Idea**

In an automobile, where does the burning of the fuel take place?

**Library research**

Find out the advantages and disadvantages of diesel fuel over gasoline fuel for an automobile or truck.

Figure 5-9. A steam turbine.

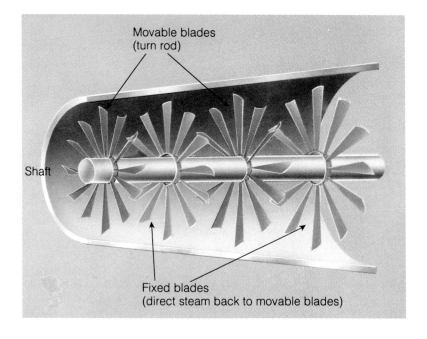

Movable blades (turn rod)

Shaft

Fixed blades (direct steam back to movable blades)

## Activity 5–1A    Making a Steam Turbine

### Materials

2 aluminum foil pie pans
scissors
ballpoint pen cap
tape
modeling clay
large paper clip
hot plate
water
flowerpot
teakettle with narrow spout

### Purpose

To show how a steam engine works.

### Procedure

1. Cut off the sides of an aluminum foil pan to make a flat circle. Make a $\frac{1}{2}$ cm hole in the center of the pan with the tips of the scissors. SAFETY NOTE: *Hold the scissors so that you will not be cut.*
2. Using the diagram shown as a model, measure eight evenly-spaced sections. Make eight cuts from the edge toward the center, stopping 2 cm from the hole.
3. Bend up each section 2 cm from the next cutting line. Turn the turbine over.
4. Push the cap of a ball point pen through the hole in the turbine and tape it in place.
5. Put a small lump of clay in the center of the second aluminum pan. Straighten out the large paper clip and stand it in the clay. Place the "turbine" over the paper clip.
6. Now set up the steaming teakettle and turbine as seen in the diagram. SAFETY NOTE: *Keep the spout of the teakettle pointed away from you. Steam can scald your skin.*

### Questions

1. Describe what happens to the steam turbine when steam is directed at the blades?
2. In what direction do the blades move in relation to the direction of the steam?

### Conclusion

How does a steam turbine work?

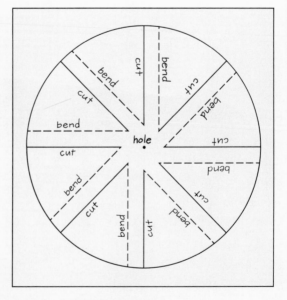

changes to steam (water vapor at 100°C or higher). Normally, a vapor takes up much more space than the liquid phase. However, the steam is confined to a small space, and pressure builds up. The steam is then allowed to move through an opening and expand.

In one widely used type of steam engine, there are several sets of fanlike blades. The blades are attached to a shaft that can rotate. The expanding steam enters the chamber containing the blades. It pushes against the blades and causes them and the shaft to rotate. This type of engine is known as a steam **turbine** (TER′-bin). Steam turbines are used to generate most of our electrical energy.

### Check yourself

1. What is an internal combustion engine?
2. List three ways in which a diesel engine differs from a gasoline engine.
3. Describe how a steam turbine works.

### The products of burning fuels

When a fuel burns, it combines with oxygen in a chemical reaction. Not only is heat released, but substances are formed. Most fuels contain hydrocarbons. The complete burning of a hydrocarbon produces water and carbon dioxide. For example, the burning of methane, $CH_4$, is summarized in the following chemical equation.

$$CH_4 + 2O_2 \rightarrow CO_2 + 2H_2O$$

Gasoline is a mixture of hydrocarbons. The complete burning of one of them, $C_8H_{18}$, is summarized in the following chemical equation.

$$2C_8H_{18} + 25O_2 \rightarrow 16CO_2 + 18H_2O$$

Both water vapor and carbon dioxide are normally present in the air. Burning large amounts of hydrocarbons increases the amount of water vapor and carbon dioxide present in the air.

**Main Idea**

What is gasoline made of?

Hydrocarbon fuels normally contain impurities such as sulfur. Sulfur combines with oxygen to form a colorless gas, sulfur dioxide ($SO_2$). The chemical equation summarizing this reaction is

$$S + O_2 \rightarrow SO_2$$

Sulfur dioxide irritates the lungs and is especially harmful to people with lung disease. In addition, it combines further with oxygen in the air to form sulfur trioxide, $SO_3$.

$$2SO_2 + O_2 \rightarrow 2SO_3$$

Sulfur trioxide combines with water vapor to form sulfuric acid, $H_2SO_4$.

$$SO_3 + H_2O \rightarrow H_2SO_4$$

When sulfuric acid forms in the air, it washes down during the next rain. Sulfuric acid is a very corrosive substance, damaging both living and nonliving things. For instance, the acid in rain kills off the fish in lakes and attacks limestone build-

Figure 5-10. How does the burning of fuel contribute to pollution problems?

ings. One way to prevent the problems caused by sulfur compounds is to use fuels with a low sulfur content.

The high temperatures in automobile engines allow nitrogen from the air to react with oxygen from the air. Many different compounds of nitrogen and oxygen, known as oxides of nitrogen, are formed. They contribute to the brownish smog that often pollutes the air over cities. Also, some of the oxides react with water vapor to form acids that increase the acid rain problem.

All fuels burn incompletely to some degree. The incomplete burning of hydrocarbons results in the production of carbon and carbon monoxide. It also puts some unchanged hydrocarbons into the air. The energy from sunlight causes the unchanged hydrocarbons to react with the oxides of nitrogen and with oxygen to form smog. Antismog devices on automobiles trap hydrocarbons before they can enter the air. In cars with catalytic converters, the hydrocarbons and carbon monoxide react with oxygen and form carbon dioxide and water. In effect, the converters make gasoline burn more completely.

When hydrogen gas burns in air, only water vapor is formed.

$$2H_2 + O_2 \rightarrow 2H_2O$$

No dangerous pollutants are produced. Thus, hydrogen can be thought of as a clean fuel. It is being suggested by many as a substitute for both gasoline and methane. To produce the same amount of heat, however, larger volumes of hydrogen than of gasoline must be burned. Difficulties in the storing and transporting of hydrogen may also be encountered.

Which fuels are best? You can see that each fuel has advantages and disadvantages. Many factors must be considered. These include cost, the amount of the fuel available, and the ease of storing and obtaining it. They also include the ease of burning the fuel and the products produced by the burning.

### Main Idea

What causes the formation of the brownish smog made of oxides of nitrogen?

### Data Search

How did the average amount of carbon monoxide in the air change between 1975 and 1983? Search page 561.

### Check yourself

1. List some harmful effects caused by sulfur in fuels.

2. Describe how antismog devices and catalytic converters help reduce the formation of smog.

## Energy and chemical bonds

Burning is a chemical reaction in which energy is released overall. That is, it takes less energy to start the reaction than what is released during the reaction.

Every chemical reaction, not just burning, involves the absorption and/or release of energy. How can these changes in energy be explained in terms of the atoms involved in the reaction?

In any chemical reaction, atoms join together or break away from each other. New substances are formed as a result. When atoms join together, a chemical bond is said to form. When they break away, the chemical bond is broken. Thus, in a chemical reaction, bonds are formed and/or broken.

Every atom is made up of electrically charged particles. There are positvely charged protons in the nucleus and negatively charged electrons outside the nucleus. Since opposite charges attract, the positive nucleus of one atom is attracted to the negative electrons of another atom close by.

When two atoms attract, there is a force between them. If the atoms get very close and form a chemical bond, energy is released. To understand why, think of a book falling to the floor. There is a force between the book and the earth. When the book hits the floor, it has less potential energy than it had up in the air. It is not moving, so it has no kinetic energy. Overall, the book seems to lose energy. (The energy has been converted to internal energy. The book and the floor are a little warmer after the collision.)

To break a chemical bond and separate two atoms requires energy. Again, to understand why, think of separating a book from the floor on which it is lying. To raise the book, you must do work on it. When you do work on something, you are giving it energy.

When a bond is broken, the same amount of energy is required as was released when the bond formed. But some bonds require more energy than other bonds. For example, about 12% more energy is required to break the bond between the oxygen atom and one hydrogen atom in $H_2O$ than to break the bond between the carbon atom and one hydrogen atom in $CH_4$.

### Main Idea

Is energy required or released when a chemical bond is formed?

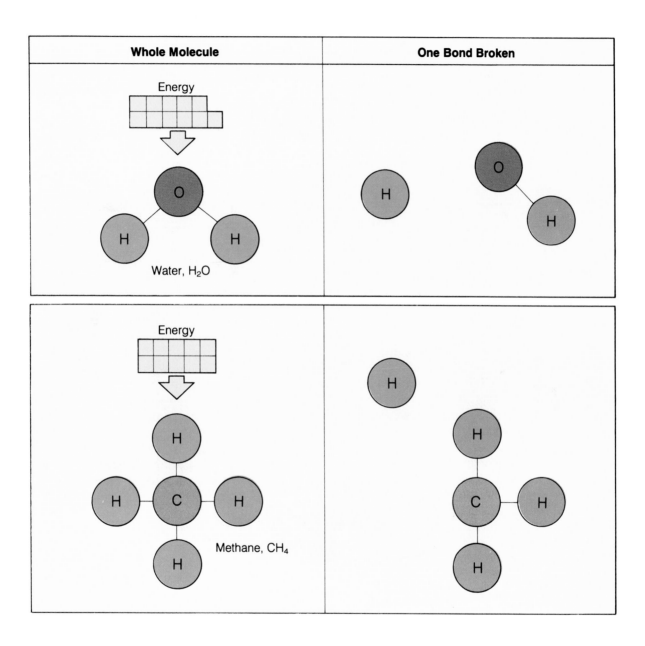

| Whole Molecule | One Bond Broken |
|---|---|
| Energy | |
| Water, H$_2$O | |
| Energy | |
| Methane, CH$_4$ | |

When a fuel burns, bonds within the fuel are first broken. Also, bonds between the oxygen atoms in oxygen molecules are broken. Breaking these bonds requires energy—the energy needed to start the fuel burning. Once these bonds are broken, new bonds form between atoms in the fuel and oxygen atoms. Forming these bonds releases energy—much more energy than was needed to break the original bonds.

Figure 5-11. More energy is required to break one of the oxygen-hydrogen bonds in water than to break one of the carbon-hydrogen bonds in methane.

## Activity 5–1B        Energy Changes in a Chemical Reaction

### Materials

safety goggles
small beaker (50-mL or 100-mL)
metric measuring spoons
2-3 large copper sulfate crystals ($CuSO_4$)
water at room temperature
hot pad
paper
hot plate
wire gauze

### Purpose

To show how the energy changes in a chemical reaction can be observed.

### Procedure

1. Put on safety goggles.
2. Put about one metric teaspoonful (2-3 large crystals) of copper sulfate ($CuSO_4$) crystals in a beaker. SAFETY NOTE: *Avoid touching the copper sulfate. If you get any on your skin, wash the affected skin area with soap and water. If you get any in your eyes, flush them with large amounts of water.* Record the color of the crystals.
3. Place the beaker on a wire gauze on the hot plate. Heat until the crystals become a powder and drops of liquid form on the sides of the beaker. Turn off the hot plate. Record the color of the powder.
4. Use a hot pad to remove the beaker from the hot plate. Allow about 15 minutes for the beaker to cool completely.
5. Add one metric tablespoon (15 mL) of water to the powder. Record the color of the solution that results.
6. Feel the beaker. Note any temperature changes that occur.
7. When you finish the activity, put the copper sulfate solution into the container provided by the teacher. Thoroughly wash your hands and the beaker.

### Questions

1. What is the color of the copper sulfate crystals?
2. After heating, what color is the copper sulfate powder?
3. What color is the copper sulfate and water solution?
4. The water at room temperature was mixed with the copper sulfate powder. How does the temperature of the resulting solution compare to the temperature of the powder and water?
5. What evidence seems to indicate that the droplets of liquid that appeared when the crystals were heated must be water?
6. During what part of the activity was energy required for a reaction to take place?
7. When was chemical energy being released during this activity?

### Conclusion

How were energy changes observed during this chemical reaction?

Figure 5-12 shows the breaking and formation of bonds when methane burns. The chemical equation is

$$CH_4 + 2O_2 \rightarrow CO_2 + 2H_2O.$$

The first diagram shows that energy is needed to break the bonds within the methane and oxygen molecules. The second diagram shows all the bonds broken. The atoms can now

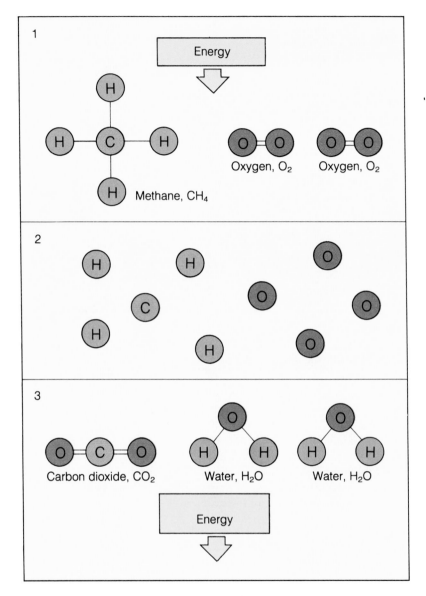

Figure 5-12. (1) For methane to burn, energy must be supplied to break the bonds in methane and oxygen. (2) The bonds have been broken and the atoms can rearrange themselves. (3) New bonds are formed and a greater amount of energy is released.

rearrange themselves and form different molecules. The third diagram shows that new bonds have formed and energy has been released. Overall, energy was released.

People sometimes speak of the energy stored in fuel. Energy must be added to fuel to make it burn. But much more energy is released when the new bonds are formed. Fuel has the potential to burn and release a lot of energy.

### Check yourself

Describe the pattern of energy input and release in a chemical reaction in terms of the bonds formed and broken.

# Practical Science

## Two-Stroke Engines

The two-stroke engine is an internal combustion engine. You will find two-stroke engines in chain saws, lawn mowers, lawn edgers, tillers, lightweight motorcycles, mopeds, outboard motors, electric generators, snow blowers, and other small equipment.

**How a two-stroke engine works** A four-stroke engine has four strokes: intake, compression, power, and exhaust. A two-stroke engine has only two strokes: power and compression.

The power stroke starts when the air-fuel mixture in the combustion cylinder ignites. The force of the resulting burning gases drives the piston down. The hot exhaust gases escape when the piston passes the exhaust port. The intake port opens as the piston continues down. This allows the air-fuel mixture to enter the cylinder. The downward movement of the piston drives the connecting rod and the crankshaft to produce rotary motion.

The compression stroke starts when the piston passes its bottom position. The upward motion of the piston compresses the air-fuel mixture. When the piston reaches its top position, a spark jumps between the two electrodes of the spark plug. This causes the air-fuel mixture to explode and the next power stroke begins.

**Method of operation and control** A two-stroke engine requires the proper mixture of gasoline and oil. The oil lubricates moving engine parts. Fuel should never be added to the gas tank while the engine is hot. The heat could ignite any spilled fuel.

Overloading the engine will make it overheat and cause rapid wear of the engine parts. An example of overloading an engine is a lawn mower being forced through tall grass faster than the blade can cut.

**Two-stroke versus four-stroke engines** Compared to a four-stroke engine, a two-stroke engine is lighter, has fewer parts, and is cheaper. It is simple in operation, as it has only three moving parts: piston, connecting rod, and crankshaft. A two-stroke is more powerful than a four-stroke engine having the same weight.

The engine parts are always lubricated in a two-stroke engine. This is because the oil is mixed with the gas. The oil in a four-stroke engine is in a crankcase. If it is not kept level, the oil pump will not be able to supply oil to the engine parts.

A two-stroke engine does run hotter than a four-stroke engine. This causes the parts to wear out faster.

**Something to try** A gasoline-powered lawn mower uses a two-stroke engine. Learn how to operate a gasoline-powered lawn mower correctly and safely from an experienced person.

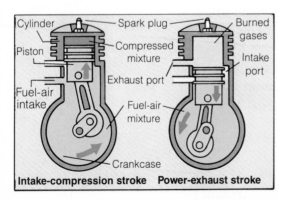

Intake-compression stroke   Power-exhaust stroke

## Section 1 Review   Chapter 5

### Check Your Vocabulary

| catalyst | hydrocarbon |
|---|---|
| complete burning | incomplete burning |
| external combustion engine | internal combustion engine |
| fuel | turbine |

*Match each term above with the numbered phrase that best describes it.*

1. Does work when fuel is burned inside it
2. Does work when fuel is burned outside it
3. Compound containing only carbon and hydrogen
4. Has blades that turn when hot water vapor expands
5. When burned, releases great amount of energy
6. Occurs when there is enough oxygen available
7. Results in the production of carbon monoxide
8. Helps speed up a reaction without being changed itself

### Check Your Knowledge

*Multiple Choice: Choose the answer that best completes each of the following sentences.*

1. Burning is a chemical change in which a substance combines with ?.
   a) carbon          c) carbon dioxide
   b) carbon monoxide  d) oxygen
2. Natural gas consists primarily of ?.
   a) hydrogen   c) butane
   b) propane    d) methane
3. The rate of burning can be reduced by ?.
   a) breaking the fuel into smaller pieces or drops
   b) decreasing the air supply
   c) using a catalyst
   d) raising the temperature of the fuel

4. Both a gasoline engine and a diesel engine ?.
   a) use energy from burning fuel for heating
   b) use energy from burning fuel to do work
   c) rely on spark plugs
   d) are external combustion engines
5. ? is added to the air as a result of incomplete burning.
   a) Carbon monoxide  c) Sulfur dioxide
   b) Carbon dioxide   d) Water vapor
6. When chemical bonds are formed, energy is ?.
   a) always absorbed
   b) always released
   c) sometimes absorbed and sometimes released
   d) never absorbed nor released

### Check Your Understanding

1. Describe what effect a catalyst has on the energy changes in a chemical reaction.
2. In some fireplaces, the hot air from the fire seems to escape up the chimney opening. Why is it dangerous to solve this problem by keeping the chimney opening closed?
3. The engine walls of a diesel engine are much thicker than those of a gasoline engine. Explain why the thicker walls are needed.
4. Explain how rain becomes acid and what can be done about this problem.

### Practical Science

1. What are the two strokes of a two-stroke engine?
2. Name some kinds of machines which use two-stroke engines.

# Energy and Materials in Industry    Section 2

**Section 2 of Chapter 5 is divided into six parts:**

Processing materials

Metals and alloys

Ceramics

Plastics

Composites

Waste management

*Practical Science: The Art of Ceramics*

**Learning Objectives**

1. To describe how processing is used to alter raw materials into manufactured products.

2. To explain how materials are processed to give them specific properties.

3. To describe the manufacture and use of alloys, ceramics, plastics, and composites.

4. To explain the importance of safe waste management in materials processing.

Figure 5-13. Industrial processes use physical and chemical changes to transform raw materials into finished products.

You get up in the morning. You look in the mirror, wash your face, eat breakfast, and brush your teeth. Already you have used many of the materials produced by modern industry. The mirror is glass, the faucet and cooking utensils contain metal, the toothbrush is plastic. The stove is made of a combination of materials, probably metal and plastic. Throughout the day you will use many more items made of these and other materials.

## Processing materials

Every material you use is manufactured to have properties that meet specific needs. For example, the stainless steel in a knife must be hard enough to keep a sharp edge. It must resist rust and wear well. The concrete in a driveway must be strong enough to withstand heavy loads, and flexible enough so that it will not crack when the temperature changes. Such physical properties are developed while a material is being processed from raw material to finished product.

Processing materials takes several steps. At each step, the material is altered physically, chemically, or both ways. The first step in processing is to obtain the raw material. If the material is metal, for example, it would be mined from the earth. Next, the raw material is **refined** to separate the unwanted substances from the pure material. The pure material then enters the manufacturing stage. During manufacturing, the material is formed into a product or parts for a product. Steel, for instance, might be rolled into sheets for the body of an automobile. It may also be shaped into bolts, nuts, and screws to hold the automobile together. The final step in manufacturing is assembling all the parts into the finished product. Quite often, the parts are of several different materials.

The ways a material is used in industry depends somewhat on cost. Every step in materials processing costs money. Equipment is often expensive. There are transportation costs for hauling the material from the mine to the refinement plant, and then to the manufacturing plant. Putting materials through numerous physical and chemical changes requires

**Main Idea**

Why are raw materials refined?

**Main Idea**

What factors contribute to the cost of processing materials?

energy, and this can be very costly. Also, each step produces wastes that must be disposed of. All of these costs are reflected in the price of the final product.

### Check yourself

In what ways is a material altered during processing?

### Metals and alloys

The earth's crust forms a vast storehouse of metals that is used by industry. Usually, metals do not occur in their pure state. Instead, most metals are found in compounds with other elements. These rock-like compounds are called **ores.** In the process of **metallurgy,** metals are separated from their ores.

The story of metallurgy can be told in the production of steel, the most widely used metal. Steel begins as iron ore found in the earth's crust. Iron ore is a mixture of the metal iron, oxygen, sand, and a few other substances. Once the ore has been mined, the process of refinement begins. First, the ore is crushed and washed to remove as much sand and rock as possible. These physical changes do not alter the ore's chemical composition.

The next step is to break down the ore chemically in order to separate the iron. This is done in a tall structure called a **blast furnace.** A mixture of ore, limestone, and a carbon-based fuel called *coke* is dumped in the top. Blasts of hot air cause the coke to burn. The burning coke produces carbon monoxide, which combines with the oxygen from the ore to produce carbon dioxide. This gas is vented out the top of the furnace.

The oxygen-free ore then settles to the bottom of the furnace, where it is melted by the great heat from the burning coke. There, the limestone combines with unwanted materials in the ore to produce a waste called *slag* that floats on top of the melted iron.

The iron produced by the blast furnace is not yet pure. It contains carbon and other impurities. The iron must go through yet another refinement to be converted to steel.

---

**Data Search**

What is the melting point of iron? Search page 559

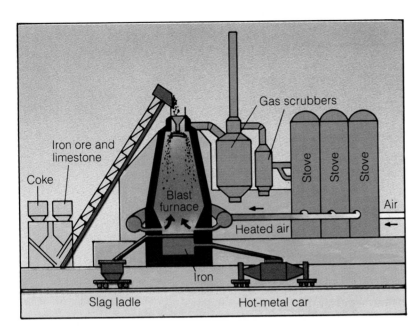

Iron ore and limestone

Coke

Gas scrubbers

Blast furnace

Stove · Stove · Stove

Air

Heated air

Iron

Slag ladle

Hot-metal car

Figure 5-14. How do you think a blast furnace got its name?

The first major method for making steel was the Bessemer process. In this process, a blast of hot air removed the excess carbon and impurities. However, it was not possible to control the properties of the steel produced. Today, steelmakers use other methods that give them better control. The most widely used steel making technique is the **basic oxygen process.** This method is fast and inexpensive, because it requires no fuel to create heat. Molten iron and scrap steel are placed in a furnace and pure oxygen is blown into the mixture. The oxygen combines with the carbon and other impurities in the iron. These chemical reactions create the heat necessary for the refining process. The waste gases are trapped in a hood, and remaining impurities combine with limestone to form a slag.

At this point, other metals are added to the molten steel in order to produce the desired physical properties in the finished material. Such a mixture of metals is called an **alloy.** For example, an alloy of steel and titanium can be manufactured into extremely sharp blades. Such blades are used to cut steel parts. An alloy of manganese and steel is nonmagnetic and hardens with repeated impact. These properties make the alloy a useful material in earth-moving equipment. A silicon–steel alloy has properties which make it useful as a component material in electric generators.

One of the most familiar alloys is made of steel, chromium, and nickel. This alloy is called *stainless steel*. On contact with oxygen in the air, the chromium forms a thin protective film

### Library Research

Find out about Sir Henry Bessemer, inventor of the Bessemer process for creating steel.

Figure 5-15. Molten iron emerges from a blast furnace, ready to be processed further.

### Main Idea

From what materials is stainless steel made?

## Activity 5-2A          Slowing Corrosion

### Materials

15 iron nails
200 mL 10% salt solution
4 250-mL glass containers
200 mL vinegar
metal file
petroleum jelly
fingernail polish
paraffin

### Purpose

To observe how the rate of corrosion of iron placed in various liquids is affected by having different surface textures and different protective coatings.

### Procedure

1. Label four 250-mL containers "A," "B," and "C." Put 200 mL of water in Container A. Put 200 mL of vinegar into Container B. Put 200 mL of 10% salt solution into Container C. Put one nail into each of the containers.
2. With a metal file, make some deep scratches in three of the iron nails. Place a scratched nail in Containers A, B, and C.
3. Coat three nails with petroleum jelly. Coat three more nails with nail polish and allow the polish to dry. Coat three nails with a layer of wax by rubbing them with paraffin. Place one of each of the three types of coated nails into Containers A, B, and C.
4. After three days, remove the nails from the container of water and compare the amount of corrosion on each nail. Rate each coating, using a scale of 1 to 5. Use the number 1 to indicate the most corroded and the number 5 to indicate the least corroded. Record your date on a table like the one shown.
5. Repeat Step 4 on the nails you had placed in the other two containers.

### Questions

1. Is water more corrosive to the scratched nail or the unscratched nail? What role does water play in the corrosion of metals?
2. What effect does the vinegar have on the corrosion of iron?
3. How does salt affect the rate at which iron corrodes?
4. Which coating provides the best protection against corrosion in most of the liquids?
5. Which coating is the most effective under acidic conditions? Under salty conditions?
6. What are some kinds of coatings that might be used by manufacturers of iron products to prevent corrosion?

### Conclusion

How do the different surface textures and protective coatings on the iron nails affect their rate of corrosion when they are placed in various liquids?

|  | Container A (water) | Container B (vinegar) | Container C (10% salt solution) |
|---|---|---|---|
| Unscratched nail |  |  |  |
| Scratched nail |  |  |  |
| Nail with petroleum jelly |  |  |  |
| Nail with paraffin wax |  |  |  |
| Nail with nail polish |  |  |  |

| Alloy | Composition | Property | Uses |
|---|---|---|---|
| Duraluminum | aluminum<br>magnesium<br>copper<br>manganese | strong<br>lightweight |  |
| Brass | copper<br>tin | strong<br>resistant to corrosion | 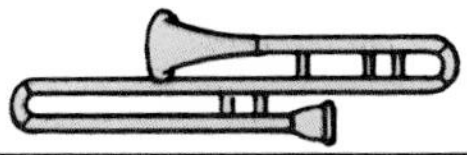 |
| Bronze | copper<br>zinc | strong<br>attractive | 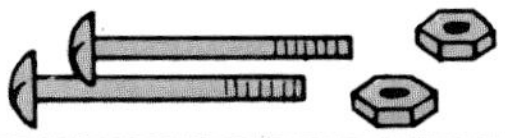 |
| Stainless steel | iron<br>carbon<br>chromium | does not rust |  |
| Dentist's amalgam | mercury<br>silver | nonporous<br>able to be molded | 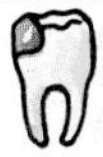 |
| Tungsten steel | iron<br>carbon<br>tungsten | strong<br>maintains sharpness<br>when hot | 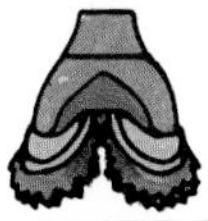 |

Figure 5-16. Alloys having different properties are used in a wide variety of products.

on the metal's surface, making it resistant to rust. Stainless steel is also stable at very low temperatures. This property makes it useful as a storage vessel for liquid gases.

The properties of steel are also determined by the way it is processed into final form. The most common method of shaping steel is called *rolling*. Rolling is the process of turning molten or hardened block steel into thin sheets or bars. This process breaks down and stretches the metal crystals so that they become a thick bundle of fibers. The process of rolling gives steel added toughness and strength. Most steel sheets are used for automobile bodies. Steel bar products include auto parts and hand tools.

In other shaping processes, steel is formed into products ranging from nails to wire to rigid beams used in buildings and bridges. Finally, some types of steel are given a special coating of zinc or tin to prevent rust. The "tin" can in the supermarket is really a steel can coated with tin.

### Check yourself

1. In the blast furnace, how is oxygen removed from the iron ore?

2. What is slag?

3. What is an alloy?

Figure 5-17. Ceramics are manufactured for both industrial and home uses.

Figure 5-18. The photo shows a jiggering, or shaping machine. It is used to evenly distribute the ceramic material in a mold.

# Ceramics

Ceramic products are as commonplace as dinnerware and as out of the ordinary as rocket nose cones. Indeed, the physical properties of ceramics make them useful in a wide variety of products. Manufacturers use very hard ceramic tools for cutting and grinding metal surfaces. Because ceramics can withstand exposure to acids, gases, salts, water, and temperature extremes, they are useful as construction materials. These same properties make them good containers for foods and beverages. Some ceramics do not conduct electricity, and are used as insulators in spark plugs and televisions. Because of their heat resistance, ceramics are used to make industrial furnaces and boilers, and parts for space vehicles. Glass is one of the most important ceramic materials, mainly because of its property of transparency.

Ceramics, like metals, come from the earth. The word, *ceramic,* comes from the Greek word, *keramos,* which means "potter's clay." Ceramics are made from materials called silicates, which include clay, feldspar, quartz, and sand. These raw materials occur abundantly throughout the earth's crust and are inexpensive to obtain. Most ceramic materials are made of clay and other silicates, along with carbon, oxygen, and nitrogen. Porcelain is an example of a type of ceramic material. It is made of clay, feldspar, and quartz. Products made of porcelain include fine dinnerware, sinks, art objects, and insulators.

The processing of ceramics begins with mining the raw materials. The raw materials are crushed to form a powder. Powdered raw materials are then mixed together in order to obtain particular ceramic properties.

Next, water is added to the powdered raw material mixture. This allows the ceramic material to be shaped into an object. Shaping may be done by hand, on a potter's wheel, in a press, or in a jiggering, or shaping, machine. The object is then dried by using heat to remove excess water from the ceramic material. The temperature and rate of this process must be controlled. If the object is heated too much or too quickly, large holes may develop in the ceramic material as the water vaporizes.

---

**Activity 5-2B**       Properties of a Material

**Materials**

200 mL liquid cornstarch
a clear plastic cup
container 5 cm larger in diameter than the cup
crushed ice
hot water
thermometer
paper towels
old newspapers
watch or clock

**Purpose**

To observe how fluid cornstarch responds to changes in pressure and temperature.

**Procedure**

1. Cover your desk with old newspapers. Pour some of the prepared fluid cornstarch into your hand. Observe the properties of this material. Hold your hand over the container and apply pressure to the cornstarch by squeezing it in your hand. Observe what happens.
2. Fill a container with crushed ice. Place a cup containing 50 mL of the liquid corn starch into the ice. At the end of five min-

utes, record the temperature. Observe the properties of this material when it is cooled by squeezing it. Empty the container.
3. Fill the container with very hot water. Place a cup containing 50 mL of the fluid cornstarch into the hot water. At the end of 5 minutes record the temperature. Describe the effect heat has on the properties of the material.

**Questions**

1. What are the properties of the liquid cornstarch at room temperature?
2. What effect does pressure have on liquid cornstarch?
3. How does cooling the material affect its properties?
4. How does heating the material affect its properties?
5. How does the way the cooled liquid cornstarch responds to pressure differ from the way it responds to pressure after it is heated?

**Conclusion**

How are the properties of liquid cornstarch affected by changes in temperature and pressure?

---

The final step is **firing,** meaning heating at very high temperatures. Like drying, this process must be closely controlled. As the heat is slowly increased, the ceramic object undergoes different physical and chemical changes. First, any remaining moisture is dried out. Then, the carbon and other impurities are burned off. At the highest temperature, the ceramic crystals become bound together in a solid mass. This hardens the ceramic object so that it will keep its shape. The higher the firing temperature, the more dense the ceramic object becomes.

The properties of the finished ceramic object depend on the firing temperatures and the raw materials used. In firing

**Main Idea**

What changes does a ceramic object undergo as it is being fired?

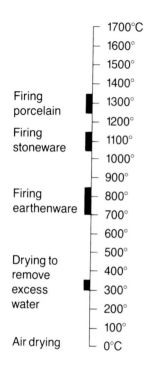

| | |
|---|---|
| Firing porcelain | 1700°C |
| | 1600° |
| | 1500° |
| | 1400° |
| | 1300° |
| | 1200° |
| Firing stoneware | 1100° |
| | 1000° |
| | 900° |
| Firing earthenware | 800° |
| | 700° |
| | 600° |
| Drying to remove excess water | 500° |
| | 400° |
| | 300° |
| | 200° |
| | 100° |
| Air drying | 0°C |

Figure 5-19. The scale shows the temperatures necessary to fire different kinds of ceramic objects. Why do you think porcelain has a higher firing temperature than stoneware?

### Main Idea

Are plastic products natural or synthetic?

porcelain, for example, the feldspar melts and coats the ceramic object. The grains of quartz are partly dissolved. As the porcelain cools, the feldspar–quartz mixture changes from a crystalline to a glassy state. This process gives the finished porcelain a smooth, waterproof surface. The higher the firing temperature, the more dense the ceramic object becomes.

Glass is processed by a different method. The materials are first heated and then shaped. Ordinary glass is made from sand, soda, limestone, and small amounts of other materials. The materials are heated at a high temperature in a huge tank. The sand and soda melt and blend, and the limestone combines with impurities. The gases produced by chemical reactions form bubbles. The molten glass is kept in constant motion for five days to allow all the bubbles to escape. Then the glass is slowly cooled so that it will not crystallize.

The molten glass can be shaped in several ways. For windows, it is rolled into sheets. Objects such as bowls are formed by pressing glass in a mold. Glass is pulled around a metal rod to form tubing for laboratory pipes and neon lighting. For art objects and glass containers, glass can be blown into many different sizes and shapes. Special types of glass, such as shock-resistant glass, can be made by varying the raw materials and the processing.

### Check yourself

What are the major raw materials of ceramics?

### Plastics

Plastic materials are *synthetic*. This means they are created in the laboratory. Because scientists have great control over the chemical structure of plastics, these materials can be manufactured to meet many different needs. For example, a tough, shock-resistant plastic is made for tool handles and household appliances. Another clear, glass-like plastic is made for windows, skylights, and lenses. Yet another plastic that can resist chemicals and high temperatures is made for gaskets and protective coatings. There are dozens of other kinds of plastic materials.

One of the most familiar kinds of plastic is called *polystyrene*. This is a rigid, somewhat brittle plastic that is inexpensive to process. These properties make it useful for disposal items like picnic utensils. Foamed polystyrene is a good insulator, and is made into such products as building insulation and the common white foam cups.

Plastics are also used to make fibers. *Polyester*, a strong and durable plastic, can be made to form a fiber having similar properties. Polyester fibers are used to make fabrics that resist wrinkling, fading and mildew. These fibers are also used to make carpets that resist abrasion, as well as the tough cord fabric in tires.

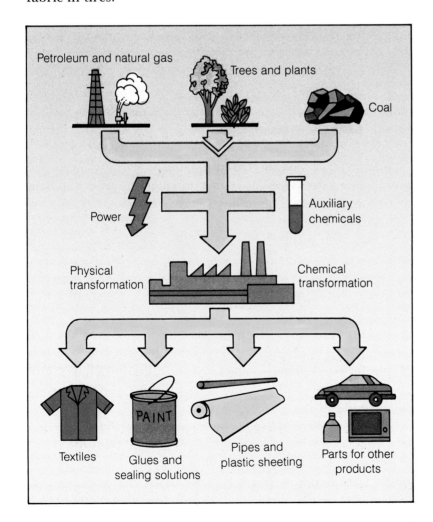

Figure 5-20. By what processes are raw materials changed to create plastics?

Figure 5-21. How does an injection-molding machine work?

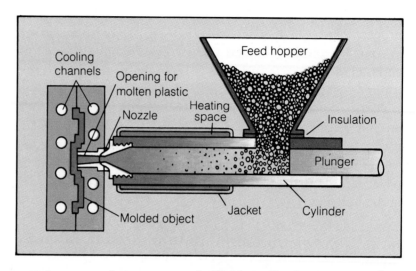

Polyester, polystyrene, and all other plastics are manufactured in two major stages. First, the basic plastic materials must be created. This is a chemical process. Raw materials such as petroleum, coal tar, and wood are broken down into their basic molecules and atoms. Then, they are reassembled into molecules of plastic called polymers. Various chemicals are added to the plastic-forming polymers to give them the desired properties. The basic plastic materials are then produced in such forms as grains, pellets, and liquids.

In the second stage, the basic materials are shaped into usable forms. The word *plastic* comes from the Greek word, *plastikos,* meaning "to form." There are several processes for forming plastics. Polystyrene is formed by a process known as **injection molding.** This process involves feeding polystyrene pellets into a hot cylinder. The heated walls of the cylinder melt the plastic pellets. A large plunger then pushes the hot liquid plastic through a nozzle. This action injects the plastic into a mold. The mold is then cooled and opened to produce the finished article.

Polystyrene foam is used in such products as the white cups used to hold hot beverages. The polystyrene used for these products is most often produced by foaming the plastic in a mold. The plastic is processed into beads that contain gas. The beads are then placed in a closed mold and heated. The heat softens the plastic and causes the gas in the beads to expand. The expanding beads are pressed firmly together to form the bubble-like foam structure. The product is then removed from the mold.

Polyester fibers are created from hot liquid plastic. The molten polyester is forced through the tiny holes of a metal disk and emerges as hair-like fibers. After the fibers have cooled to a solid state, they are stretched. Stretching makes the polymer molecules lie parallel and gives the plastic fibers greater strength.

While some plastic products, like foam cups, are finished in the shaping stage, others must be worked further. They may be cut, drilled, smoothed, or polished. Plastic parts are assembled by gluing or bonding. Plastics can be bonded by softening or heating their surfaces until the molecules inter-mix. Polyester fibers are woven into finished products.

### Check yourself

1. What is a polymer?
2. What causes polystyrene beads to expand and press together to form a foam?

### Composites

Often, a single material does not have the properties to meet the needs of industry. Joining materials in a form called a **composite** can answer those needs. Composites are used for products in which the properties high strength, low weight, and heat resistance are needed. These properties are particularly important in the aviation and space industries.

In composites, fibers of one material are embedded in another material called a **matrix.** The matrix determines the composite material's density, heat resistance, and electrical properties. The embedded fibers determine the composite material's strength.

Composites with a plastic matrix are lightweight. Metal matrix composites are more resistant to heat than plastic composites. They are strong and tough, but heavy. Due to the need for complex processing, metal matrix composites tend

**Main Idea**

For what properties are composite materials needed?

**Library Research**

Find out about the composite materials that made it possible for the aircraft *Voyager* to circle the Earth without refueling in 1986.

to be expensive. Ceramic matrix composites can withstand the extreme heat. Some of them grow stronger as the temperature increases.

Fibers for composites are made of several different materials. Glass fibers are stronger than steel. Even stronger fibers are made from carbon. These tough fibers retain their strength at very high temperatures. This property makes them ideal for composites used in the construction of aircraft and spacecraft.

Methods of producing composites depend on the nature of the materials and the use to which the composites will be put. One familiar example is glass-reinforced plastic, commonly called **fiberglass.** The glass fibers are made by melting glass marbles in a furnace. The glass flows through tiny holes at the furnace bottom, emerging in the form of fibers.

The fibers are then woven or matted together. The resultant fiber mat is then laid in a mold of the desired shape and coated with liquid plastic, usually polyester. A roller is used to squeeze out air bubbles and smooth the plastic. A chemical is added to *cure,* or set, the fiberglass. The final composite material is strong, lightweight, and inexpensive because production costs are low. It is used to make auto bodies, boat hulls, fishing rods, aircraft parts, and many other products.

Figure 5-22. Fiberglass is one type of composite. From what is it made?

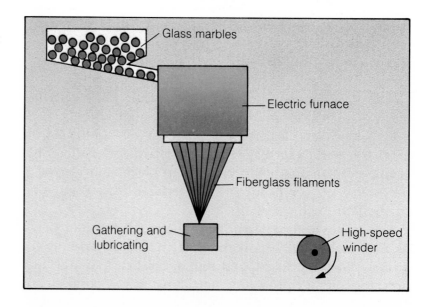

Figure 5-23. Fiber-optic lights are another use of composite materials.

**Check yourself**

1. What contributes strength to a composite?

2. What is fiberglass?

## Waste Management

Scientists estimate that, on average, every American requires the processing of about 9000 kilograms of material yearly. While material processing creates the products we use, it also produces wastes and harmful substances. Part of industry's job is to control these pollutants.

Every stage of material processing can create pollutants. During the mining of earth materials, minerals may drain into and harm nearby water systems. Mining and crushing materials produce dust in the air and piles of unwanted rock and sand. In addition, the energy used in both mining and processing often comes from burning fuels. Burning these fuels produces polluting gases and particles such as soot.

Refining processes also give off pollutants. Refining steel, for example, produces carbon monoxide. Cement-making creates sulfur dioxide. These and other gas pollutants can cause health problems and damage plant life, water systems, buildings, and finished materials. Many manufacturing processes create polluting solid wastes in the form of slag, ash, scraps, and other byproducts. Some solid wastes, such as lead and mercury, are poisonous. Decomposing plastics may give off poisonous gases and particles.

**Main Idea**

When are pollutants produced?

**Library Research**

Throughout the manufacturing process, many substances are used and created which are toxic. Find out how workers in manufacturing plants can protect themselves from such substances.

Figure 5-24. Industrial wastes can produce toxic and unsightly pollution. What must industry do to reduce or eliminate such wastes?

Industry uses a variety of methods to manage pollutants. Filters placed in smokestacks can remove particles and some harmful gases from the exhaust. *Wet scrubbers* are also used by industry to clean exhaust gases. They use a spray of water to absorb polluting particles and gases.

Water used by factories is cleaned in sludge ponds. Buoyant wastes such as oil float to the top of the water and are skimmed off. Heavy wastes sink to the bottom, where they are decomposed by bacteria. Sometimes, chemicals are used to remove the wastes.

Solid wastes may be burned or dumped in landfills, abandoned mines, rivers, and wells. However, these wastes can often be reused. Slag produced by refining iron ore is used in the manufacture of cement. Sulfuric acid produced by refining copper is reused in ore processing.

In some cases, there is no effective way to remove pollutants. For example, nitrogen oxides produced by burning coke in a blast furnace cannot be controlled. New fuels, new production processes, and new control methods are needed to eliminate such pollutants.

However, the added expense for installing pollution control systems increases manufacturing costs. The challenge to find affordable and effective new ways to handle wastes is an important one for materials processing industries.

**Check yourself**

1. Name two gas pollutants created in materials processing.

2. How does a wet scrubber clean exhaust gas?

## Careers  Firefighter / Welder

**Firefighter**  When the fire station alarm sounds, firefighters must respond immediately. They quickly put on protective clothing and drive to the site of the fire. When they arrive, the company lieutenant assigns specific tasks to each firefighter. These tasks include connecting fire hoses to fire hydrants and getting ladders in place.

Firefighters may enter burning buildings to save people or property. They may encounter collapsing roofs and toxic smoke. They must ignore foul weather and fatigue.

Extinguishing destructive fires is only one of a firefighter's many jobs. Firefighters also inspect buildings for fire hazards, and educate community and school groups about fire prevention.

Calmness in emergency situations and the ability to work in a team are two of firefighters' most important attributes. They must be dependable, alert, and show good judgment.

Only high school graduates are eligible for professional firefighting careers. Candidates must pass both written and physical exams. High school students interested in this work should have a strong science background and an interest in public service.

Firefighters work outdoors, at any hour, and in all weather conditions to control destructive fires.

**Welder**  Welders are highly skilled workers who have a practical understanding of properties of metals and alloys. The process of welding is used to join metal parts to form a permanent bond. Welders work on ships, automobiles, spacecraft, and nuclear reactors, to name a few of the many products requiring welded parts.

Good eyesight, eye–hand coordination, good physical condition, and manual dexterity are important attributes for a welder. Safety gear such as goggles and helmets are worn while welding to protect the welder from burns and eye injuries.

A skilled welder has usually spent several years of on-the-job training. Entry level welding skills are taught in vocational/technical institutions and many community colleges. High school training in welding as well as courses in physics, chemistry, mechanical drawing, and blueprint reading are helpful in preparing for this career.

Welders wear protective eye gear to shield their eyes from flying sparks, metal fragments, and extremely bright light.

# Practical Science

## The Art of Ceramics

Ceramics is the art and science of making things from fired clay. Artists since prehistoric times have used clay to make objects which are beautiful as well as useful.

**Why use clay?**   Clay is a simple, abundant, and amazingly versatile material. It is formed over millions of years from decomposed rocks composed of silica and alumina.

Clay has always attracted artists because of its two special properties: it is plastic, or easily modeled when wet, and it becomes rock hard after being intensely heated.

**How clay is prepared**   Clay is mined from the earth, dried, then pounded into a powder. Rocks and other impurities are sifted out. The clay is then soaked in water and poured through a sieve. Finally, after any excess water is poured off, the clay is partially dried and kneaded. Kneading mixes the clay and drives out air bubbles. The finished clay is dense and plastic. About one fourth of its weight is from water.

**Types of ceramic art**   Ceramic artists use different types of clay to create their work. The two main types of ceramic objects created from these clays are called *earthenware* and *stoneware*.

Earthenware is made from mineral-rich clays mined directly from the ground, hence its name. Earthenware is usually fired at about 982°C. It is porous, meaning it will absorb liquids unless it is glazed. A clay flowerpot is a good example of pottery made from earthenware clay.

Stoneware gets its name because it is rock-hard. The hardness comes from the intense firing heat of 1260°C. Stoneware is made from natural or specially refined clays. These clays have fewer mineral impurities than earthenware clays. Stoneware is used for durable bowls and dishes, and for art pieces such as vases and sculpture. Most stoneware objects are nonporous, meaning they will not absorb liquids even if they are not glazed.

**The firing process**   Firing was probably discovered by accident. Perhaps a clay-lined basket was left near a cooking fire and fused enough to form a pot. Today, special gas or electric ovens called *kilns* are used to fire ceramic objects.

Most fine pottery is fired twice. The first firing is called the *bisque firing,* and the second is called the *glaze firing.* Bisque firing physically and chemically alters the clay to make it permanently hard. Glaze firing causes a glaze to become physically and chemically a part of the ceramic object to which it was applied.

**What is a glaze?**   A glaze is a glassy coating applied to a ceramic object. It may add color and texture. It may also make a ceramic object smooth and nonporous. Glazes are made mostly of silica, to which small amounts of other materials are added. These added materials determine the color, gloss, hardness, and texture of the glaze.

After firing, a glaze can be opaque, transparent, or translucent. Almost any color can be achieved by adding the appropriate materials.

**Something to try**   Try to find examples of ceramic art at home. Look for stoneware and earthenware objects, and observe the variety of glazes they have.

## Section 2 Review   Chapter 5

### Check Your Vocabulary

| | |
|---|---|
| alloy | metallurgy |
| basic oxygen process | polymers |
| composite | silicates |
| firing | slag |

*Match each term above with the numbered phrase that best describes it.*

1. Heating materials at very high temperature
2. A mixture of metals
3. The molecules of plastic
4. A waste formed during the processing of steel
5. Minerals used as raw materials for ceramics
6. The process of separating metals from their ores
7. Material in which fibers of one material are embedded in another
8. The most widely used steel-making method

### Check Your Knowledge

*Multiple Choice: Choose the answer that best completes each of the following sentences.*

1. In a blast furnace, carbon monoxide from burning coke combines with __?__ in the ore.
   a. iron
   b. oxygen
   c. limestone
   d. carbon dioxide

2. The __?__ in stainless steel forms a protective film on the metal's surface.
   a. nickel
   b. rust
   c. chromium
   d. oxygen

3. At the highest firing temperature, ceramics are hardened by __?__ .
   a. the removal of excess water.
   b. the crystals binding together
   c. molten feldspar coating the surface
   d. fast heating

4. Polystyrene is shaped by __?__ .
   a. injection molding
   b. being forced through the holes of a metal disk
   c. rolling
   d. blowing air into the plastic

5. __?__ add(s) strength to composite materials.
   a. Metals
   b. Fibers
   c. The matrix
   d. Heating

6. Wet scrubbers __?__ .
   a. wash mined materials to remove the rocks and sand
   b. clean water used by factories
   c. decompose wastes in a sludge pond
   d. absorb pollutants from exhaust gases.

### Check Your Understanding

1. At what stages in the production of steel are physical properties of the finished product determined? Give examples.
2. Brick is made primarily from clay. In what category of materials does brick belong? What would be the general steps for processing clay into finished brick?
3. In a composite, why are the matrix and fibers made of different materials?

### Practical Science

What properties make clay an especially good material for artists?

# Chapter 5 Review

## Concept Summary

A **chemical reaction** is a change in which one or more new substances are formed.

- Most reactions result in the overall release of energy.
- Most reactions will not start unless energy is added.
- Burning is a reaction that requires energy to get started but results in the rapid release of a far greater amount of energy.
- Catalysts allow reactions to occur more quickly by lowering the amount of energy needed to start the reaction.
- When a chemical bond is formed, energy is released.
- When a chemical bond is broken, energy is absorbed.

A **fuel** is a substance that burns easily and is burned to supply energy.

- The most widely used fuels are hydrocarbons, which are compounds of carbon and hydrogen.
- Most of the energy released when a fuel burns is in the form of heat.
- The amount of heat released can be controlled by changing the amount of fuel, the amount of oxygen, the length of time that burning takes place, or the surface area of solid and liquid fuels.
- The heat released by burning can be used to do work in an engine.
- The burning of fuels adds substances to the atmosphere, some of which are responsible for pollution problems.

**Metallurgy** is the process of separating metals from their ores.

- Most metals are compounded with other elements in rock-like ores.
- The first step in metallurgy is to crush and wash the ore and to remove sand and rock.

- The next step is to chemically break down the ore to separate the metal.
- The final step is to remove any remaining impurities in order to obtain the pure metal.

**Firing** is a process of heating materials at very high temperatures used to create ceramic objects.

- The first stage in firing is drying the ceramic object to remove excess moisture.
- As the temperature increases, impurities are burned off.
- At the hottest temperature, the ceramic crystals are bound into a solid mass. This hardens the ceramic object so that it will keep its shape.
- Firing must be carefully controlled so that the ceramic object does not crack.

**Plastic** is made of molecules called **polymers.**

- Polymers are created from such raw materials as petroleum, coal tar, and wood.
- The raw materials are chemically broken down into their basic molecules and atoms, then reassembled into polymers.
- Various chemicals are added to the polymers to make different kinds of plastics.

A **composite** is a material in which fibers of one material are embedded in a matrix of another material.

- The matrix material determines the composite's weight, heat resistence, and electrical properties. The fibers determine its strength.
- The matrix can be plastic, ceramic, or metal.
- The fibers can be made of several different materials, including glass and carbon.

## Putting It All Together

1. What must usually be added to the reactants before a chemical reaction will start?
2. Why is it easier to start a fire with twigs than it would be with heavy logs?

3. What causes a piston to move up and down in an automobile engine?
4. How is the fuel in a diesel engine ignited?
5. What are some of the disadvantages of using hydrogen as a fuel?
6. Energy is added to start a fuel burning. In terms of chemical bonds, what happens to this added energy?
7. What creates the heat in the basic oxygen process of making steel?
8. How is a steel alloy produced?
9. What properties make ceramics good construction material?
10. What are the two major steps in processing glass?
11. How are polyester fibers made?
12. What is an advantage of ceramic matrix composites?
13. What kinds of solid wastes are created by manufacturing processes?
14. How does a sludge pond work?

## Apply Your Knowledge

1. A kerosene heater is a portable heater that burns kerosene to provide heat. What precautions should a person take to avoid carbon monoxide poisoning when a kerosene heater is used in a home?
2. Methane ($CH_4$) and butane ($C_4H_{10}$) are two simple hydrocarbons.
   a. Which fuel has more chemical bonds in a molecule? Explain your reasoning.
   b. Which of the two hydrocarbons would need more energy added to start burning?
3. Suppose you are interested in manufacturing and marketing a new product with great sales potential. What factors in the processing of your new product would you need to consider in order to determine your total manufacturing costs?

4. Foamed plastics are made of bubble-like cells. The cells can be either closed off from each other by thin walls of plastic, or open to each other. Are foamed plastic cups open-cell or closed-cell? Why?

## Find Out On Your Own

1. The hardening of cement releases energy during the chemical reactions that take place. Use a chemistry text to find out the nature of the changes that occur. How might you measure the amount of heat released?
2. The properties of low weight, high strength, and heat resistance make composites useful in the aviation and space industries. Find out how composites are used in these industries, and why these physical properties are desirable.
3. Interview some car salespeople about catalytic converters. Find out whether people who want to buy a car are interested in whether the car has a catalytic converter. Do the salespeople present catalytic converters in a positive or negative light?
4. Find out what kinds of pollutants and wastes are produced by a factory in your community. How are the pollutants controlled?

## Reading Further

Millard, Reed, and the editors of Science Book Associates. *Clean Air—Clean Water for Tomorrow's World.* New York: Messner/Simon and Schuster, 1977

This is a well-organized account of what has happened, what is now being done, and what must still be done about air and water pollution.

# Chapter 6

# Sound

Section 1
**Properties of Sound**

Sound can travel through different substances. Properties such as loudness and pitch can be used to distinguish sounds. The properties of a sound can be changed by making changes in the object that produces the sound.

Section 2
**The Wave Model of Sound**

A good model for sound must be able to explain how the properties of a sound can be changed. It must also explain how sound behaves as it travels through matter. The wave model of sound can explain these things.

Section 3
**Listening to Sound**

The ear is able to detect and distinguish different sounds. A knowledge of sound helps people understand how music is produced. It also allows people to control unwanted sound—noise—and to make desirable sounds easier to hear.

In this chapter you will learn how sound can be described, explained, and controlled. The photo at the left shows the pipes of a pipe organ. Why do the pipes have different lengths?

# Properties of Sound   Section 1

**Section 1 of Chapter 6 is divided into seven parts:**

Producing sound

Carriers of sound

The speed of sound

Pitch

Loudness and noise level

Amplifying sound

Quality

*Practical Science: Sonar and Echolocation*

## Learning Objectives

1. To recognize that sound is a form of energy produced by vibrations.
2. To compare the effect of different materials on the speed of sound.
3. To relate the pitch of sound to the length and thickness of the vibrating object.
4. To identify the conditions that affect the loudness of sound.
5. To describe the sources of differences in the quality of sounds.

Figure 6-1. The strings of a cello vibrate when they are bowed. Can they be made to vibrate in other ways?

Cut a rubber band and stretch it between your hands. Then pluck it with a free finger. You will see it vibrate, or move back and forth. At the same time, you will hear a humming sound.

Whistle a note. While you are whistling, place a finger on the center of either your upper or lower lip. Can you still whistle? Do you think your lips vibrate when you whistle? Explain the reason for your answer.

Figure 6-2. When a rubber band is plucked, the vibration can be seen and a humming sound can be heard.

## Producing sound

Place one hand around the front of your throat. Rest your fingers lightly against the skin. Hum a low note and feel the vibrations within your throat. What happens to the vibrations when you stop humming? Do you feel vibrations when you breathe in and out?

The vibrations in your throat are produced by your **vocal cords**. When you use your voice, your vocal cords vibrate. Sometimes when people have bad colds, they lose their voice. This happens because the vocal cords have become swollen and can no longer vibrate. When the swelling goes away, the voice comes back.

A guitar is played by plucking the strings. When a guitar string is plucked, it vibrates. When the wind blows through a tree, the leaves vibrate and make a rustling sound. All sounds are caused by vibrations.

### Check yourself

What is the relation between sound and vibrations?

### Carriers of sound

When you talk to someone, the sound travels through the air from your throat to the other person. Sound from a jet airplane can travel through the air to you from far away.

Can sound travel through anything besides air? Put your ear against your desk and tap the opposite side of the desk.

## Activity 6–1A          Sounds in Solids

### Materials

watch that ticks
wood dowel, about 80 cm in length
metal rod, about 80 cm in length

### Purpose

To compare sound transmission in air to that in wood, metal, and string.

### Procedure

1. Hold a ticking watch as far from your body as you can. Record whether or not you hear ticking.
2. Press one end of a wood dowel against the metal back of the watch. Press the other end against the little flap that is beside your ear. Record whether you hear ticking and/or other sounds from the watch.
3. Repeat Step 3 using the metal rod instead of the wooden dowel.

### Questions

1. Could you hear the watch ticking when you held it at arm's length?
2. Could you hear the watch ticking when you held it against the wood dowel? Did you hear any other noises through the dowel?
3. Could you hear the watch ticking when you held it against the metal rod? Did you hear any other noises through the rod?
4. Based on what you heard, is air, metal, or wood a better carrier of sound? Which one is second best?

### Conclusion

Rank the materials you tested—air, metal, and wood—from best to worst as carriers of sound.

You can hear the sound clearly through the desk top. Even when swimming underwater, you can hear sounds. Sounds travel through gases, solids, and liquids.

Some solids are not good carriers of sound. Sounds tend to be muffled in rooms with thick carpets and heavy drapes. Special tiles are often placed on ceilings to reduce the noise level. Materials which carry sound poorly are called **sound insulators**. All sound insulators have something in common. They are made of materials which trap air.

Some kinds of matter carry sound better than others. But

### Main Idea

What characteristics do all sound insulators have in common?

all matter carries sound. Is matter needed for sound? Or can sound travel through empty space, just as sunlight does?

Look at Figure 6-3. It shows a setup that can be used to answer this question. An electric doorbell is placed inside a piece of glass known as a bell jar. When the doorbell is connected to a battery on the outside of the jar, it starts to ring. Then a vacuum pump is connected to the jar. As the air is removed from the jar, the sound of the bell gets fainter and fainter. When air is allowed to enter the jar again, the sound of the bell gets louder.

It seems as if matter must be present for sound to travel from one place to another. Sound does not travel through empty space.

Figure 6-3. What happens to the sound of the bell when the air is removed from the jar?

### Check yourself

1. Through what else besides air can sound travel?
2. Can sound travel through empty space?

### The speed of sound

It may seem that sound gets from one place to another in no time at all. When you talk to someone, you don't have to wait for your voice to reach the person. But an echo is proof that it does take some time for sound to get someplace. When you hear an echo, sound has traveled to a distant wall or hillside, then bounced back to you. You hear the echo after the original sound. The time difference equals the length of time it took the sound to reach the wall and come back to you.

Do sounds travel in all kinds of matter at the same rate? One can hear the sound of footsteps through the ground before they can be heard through the air. The sound of a motorboat can be heard underwater earlier than through air.

In general, sound travels faster in solids than in liquids, and faster in liquids than in gases. As Table 6-1 shows, sound depends on temperature as well as on the kind of matter. The warmer the matter, the faster it carries sound.

Table 6-1. The speed of sound in different kinds of materials.

**Data Search**

Name a liquid through which sound travels more slowly than it travels through water. Search page 560.

| Material | Speed of sound, in m/s |
|----------|------------------------|
| Air at 0°C | 331 |
| Air at 20°C | 344 |
| Air at 100°C | 390 |
| Water at 25°C | 1498 |
| Wood (oak) | 3850 |
| Steel | 5200 |

**Our Science Heritage**

**Breaking the Sound Barrier**

The first flight faster than the speed of sound was in October 1947. A Bell X-1 aircraft made a diving flight from a B-29 aircraft that had carried it to a high altitude. The X-1 reached a speed of more than 300 m/s, greater than the speed of sound in the high-altitude air.

Flying aircraft at supersonic speeds—greater than that of sound—created problems beyond just how to go faster.

A supersonic aircraft produces a shock wave similar to the wake a motorboat makes in water. A cone-shaped high-pressure region spreads out from the nose of the aircraft. Aircraft had to be redesigned to withstand the forces produced by the shock wave. The swept-back wings on an aircraft are the mark of its supersonic capabilities.

When a shock wave reaches the ground, it produces a sonic boom that is like loud thunder. In addition, the shock wave can cause damage to buildings. Supersonic passenger transports such as the Concorde are restricted to certain flight paths to avoid shock wave problems.

The speeds of aircraft are often described by Mach numbers. An aircraft that cruises at Mach 2.7 travels at 2.7 times the speed of sound. Mach numbers are named in honor of the work done by Austrian physicist Ernst Mach (1838–1916), who studied the flow of air over objects moving at high speed.

## Activity 6–1B          Measuring the Speed of Sound in Air

### Materials

2 wood blocks, 10 cm × 20 cm × 2 cm
metric tape measure or meter stick
hygrometer (to measure humidity)
thermometer

### Purpose

To find out how to measure the speed of sound
traveling through air.

### Procedure

1. Use an outside wall that faces an open area.
   Measure 25 meters from the wall.
2. Take the readings of the hygrometer and
   the thermometer. Record the data.
3. Stand facing the wall and clap the two wood
   blocks together. Listen for an echo. If you
   can hear the echo, move in closer a few
   meters, and clap the blocks together again.
   Listen for the echo.
4. Continue to move closer a few meters each
   time, until the echo can no longer be heard.
5. Measure from this location to the wall. The
   time needed for sound to travel from this
   point to the wall and back again is about
   0.10 second.

### Questions

1. At what distance from the wall can the echo
   no longer be heard? What is the total distance the sound travels?

2. In what way does the time of day cause the
   speed of sound to vary? Why?
3. Describe the weather conditions at the time
   of day you did this activity.
4. Calculate the speed of sound through the
   air during this time of day. To do this, divide
   the total distance by 0.10 second. Your
   answer will be in m/sec.

### Conclusion

How can the speed of sound traveling through
the air be measured?

### Check yourself

1. If you make a sound that echoes off a wall 75 m away, how
   far did the sound travel before you heard the echo?

2. Would sound travel through air faster in the winter or the
   summer? Explain.

## Activity 6–1C    Pitch and Length

### Materials

safety goggles
plastic ruler
rubber band

### Purpose

To compare the length of a vibrating object with the pitch of the sound it makes.

### Procedure

1. Wear safety goggles.
2. Press a ruler tightly against a desk or table top. Allow most of the ruler to stick out beyond the edge.
3. With the other hand, *gently* pull down and release the free end. Listen to the sound made by the vibrating ruler.
4. Slide a little more of the ruler onto the desk or table. Press the ruler near the edge of the desk. Again, make it vibrate and listen.
5. Continue to shorten the portion of the ruler that can vibrate. Listen to the pitch.
6. Slide the ruler back toward the edge. Again, press the ruler against the desk and listen to what happens to the pitch when you make the ruler vibrate.
7. Stretch a rubber band over the ruler lengthwise. SAFETY NOTE: *Exercise caution when using stretched rubber bands. Be sure that the ruler and rubber band are aimed at the floor and away from other students.*

8. Put your thumb under the rubber band at the 8-cm mark.
9. Pluck the short side of the stretched rubber band and listen to the sound it makes.
10. Pluck the long side of the stretched rubber band and listen to the sound it makes.

### Questions

1. Does the pitch rise, fall, or stay the same as the length of the vibrating ruler increases?
2. Does the pitch rise, fall, or stay the same as the length of the vibrating stretched rubber band decreases?

### Conclusion

How did the length of the vibrating ruler and the length of the vibrating rubber band affect the pitch of the sounds they made?

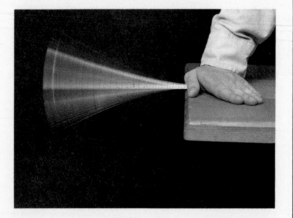

### Pitch

When you sing a high note and then a low note, you are changing **pitch**. Pitch refers to how high or low a sound is. When two sounds seem equally high, they have the same pitch.

How can the pitch of a sound be changed? One way is to change the length of the vibrating object. On a guitar or violin the pitch of one string can be changed by pressing down on the string at a different place. This changes the length of the part that can vibrate. When the length of the vibrating string is shortened, the pitch rises.

Some of the strings on a guitar are thicker than others. When a thick string vibrates, it produces a lower sound than a thinner string of the same length would.

The tightness of a string also affects the pitch. A stringed instrument is tuned by tightening or loosening the strings. The tighter the string, the higher will be the sounds it makes. The looser the string, the lower the sounds will be.

**Check yourself**

What effect does tightening the strings on a piano have?

Figure 6-4. Which hand controls the pitch of the sounds?

**Loudness and noise level**

If you lightly tap your desk, you will produce a softer sound than if you bang your fist. The amount of energy used to make the sound is one factor that affects the loudness.

A ringing telephone sounds louder when you are beside it than when you are in another room. Distance from the source of the sound affects loudness.

Table 6-2. Noise levels of various sounds.

The amount of sound energy received per second is called the **intensity** (in-TEN'-sit-ee) of a sound. Intensity, which is measured by instruments, is similar to loudness but not exactly the same. The human ear is more sensitive to certain pitches than others. One sound may seem louder than another of the same intensity if they differ in pitch.

**Noise level** compares the intensity of a sound with that of the quietest sound the ear can hear. Noise level is measured in units called **decibels** (DES'-uh-belz). A sound of 0 decibel is the quietest sound that can be detected by the human ear. A sound of 120 decibels is the loudest the ear can hear without pain. However, a sound of only 85 decibels can cause damage to the ear.

| Sound | Noise level in decibels |
|---|---|
| Jet 30 m away | 140 |
| Rock music | 120 |
| Riveting | 95 |
| Busy traffic | 70 |
| Conversation | 65 |
| Quiet car | 50 |
| Quiet radio | 40 |
| Whisper | 20 |
| Rustle of leaves | 10 |

**Check yourself**

According to Table 6-2, which would sound louder—a whisper or the rustling of leaves?

Figure 6-5. How do megaphones help cheerleaders communicate with the crowd?

## Amplifying sound

**Main Idea**

What is meant by amplifying sound?

At a sports event, cheerleaders will often yell through megaphones in order to make their voices heard. Megaphones seem to make sounds louder. That is, they **amplify** (AMP′-lif-fī) the sound.

Sounds coming through a megaphone are best heard directly in line with the megaphone. Therefore, if several cheerleaders are leading the cheer, they will point their megaphones in different directions. That way, the people spread out in the crowd can hear.

Megaphone-shaped objects are used in receiving as well as sending sound. The fleshy part of the ear itself is something like a megaphone. It gathers sound and directs it inside the skull. Many years ago, a person with a hearing loss would hold to the ear a hollow ram's horn. The horn was called an ear trumpet. Sounds entering the ear were amplified by the horn. Nowadays, sound is usually amplified by changing it into an electrical signal before changing it back to sound. Greater amplification can be achieved by using electrical signals.

### Check yourself

What effect does a megaphone have on sound?

## Quality

Sounds which have the same loudness and pitch may sound quite different. A tune played on a piano does not sound the same as on a violin. These sounds are said to differ in **quality**.

Some sounds have a metallic quality. Others may be mellow, harsh, or shrill. Objects made from different materials produce sounds of different quality. The shape of the vibrating object also affects the quality of sound.

**Main Idea**

How do sounds differ in quality?

### Check yourself

What is meant by the statement that two instruments produce sounds of different quality?

Figure 6-6. Composers of music for groups of instruments take into account that the quality of a sound depends on the instrument that makes it.

# Practical Science

## Sonar and Echolocation

Sonar is an acronym, or abbreviation, for Sound Navigation And Ranging. It is a method of using sounds to determine the position of objects. Sonar originally referred to a system for locating enemy submarines. Now the term is applied to any method that uses sound to locate objects in either water or air.

**How sonar works** There are two types of sonar: active and passive. In active sonar, a short pulse of sound is transmitted as a narrow beam. When that pulse strikes an object, part of it is reflected back and picked up by a receiver. This is like an echo. The direction the reflected pulse comes from can be used to locate the object's direction. The time for the pulse to be reflected back can be used to determine the distance to the object. Active sonar is also known as *echolocation*. It uses echos to locate objects.

In passive sonar, a sensitive receiver with a directional microphone is used to listen for underwater sounds. By slowly rotating the microphone, an operator can determine the direction of the sound source. Signals from two receivers can be used to calculate the distance to the object.

**Uses for sonar** Sonar can be used for many purposes. Ships use sonar to measure the depth of the water and locate underwater obstacles. Fishing vessels use sonar to locate schools of fish. Research ships use echolocation to map the contours of the ocean floor.

Some mammals use echolocation. Sonar enables bats to catch dinner on the wing and navigate around obstacles even in total darkness. Whales and dolphins also use sonar to navigate underwater, search for food, and communicate with their own species.

Blind persons who use canes use echolocation. They tap the cane and listen for echos from objects. This helps them find their way.

**Factors that interfere with sonar** The propellers of ships and submarines often create high noise levels which render sonar useless.

Marine organisms can also adversely affect sonar. A large school of shrimp may completely absorb the sonar pulse or its echo. Thus a submarine or reef might go undetected.

Masses of cold water also can deflect sonar waves aimed into them. This is because the boundary between warm and cold water appears as a mirror to the sonar beam.

**Radar is similar but different** Both radar and sonar operate on the same principle. They both produce a signal and receive an echo from it. They use the echo to determine the direction and distance of the object. Sonar uses sound waves because they travel well underwater. Radar, on the other hand, uses radio waves because they travel well through air.

**Something to try** Run some water into a bathtub or large pan. Turn your head sideways and place your ear in the water. SAFETY NOTE *Keep your face out of the water.* Listen for sounds as you tap the water or the container. Can you hear the sounds better with your ear in the water or with your ear out of the water?

## Section 1 Review   Chapter 6

### Check Your Vocabulary

| | |
|---|---|
| amplify | pitch |
| decibel | quality |
| intensity | sound insulator |
| noise level | vocal cord |

*Match each term above with the numbered phrase that best describes it.*

1. Is different for sounds made by a trumpet and by a piano.
2. Vibrates in the throat.
3. Unit for measuring noise level.
4. Absorbs sound instead of carrying it.
5. How high or low a note sounds.
6. Amount of energy being received per second because of a sound.
7. Make louder.
8. Intensity of a sound compared to intensity of quietest sound ear can hear.

### Check Your Knowledge

*Multiple Choice: Choose the answer that best completes each of the following sentences.*

1. Sound can travel through each of the following EXCEPT FOR _?_.
   a) air        c) water
   b) empty space    d) wood
2. Of the following, sound travels fastest in _?_.
   a) air        c) water
   b) empty space    d) wood
3. The pitch of the sound made by a guitar string can be lowered by _?_.
   a) shortening the part that can vibrate
   b) tightening the string
   c) replacing the string by a thicker string
   d) plucking the string more vigorously

4. A sound of 65 decibels _?_.
   a) can be heard without discomfort or damage
   b) cannot be heard by anyone
   c) can cause permanent damage to the ear
   d) causes intense pain

### Check Your Understanding

1. Explain why placing a hand on a bell that has just been rung will stop the sound immediately.
2. Suppose there was an enormous explosion on the sun. The sun is 150 000 000 km from the earth. How long would it take for the sound of the explosion to reach the earth?
3. People who work on the ground near jet runways wear big ear muffs filled with a sound insulator. Explain why they wear the earmuffs.

### Practical Science

1. What is another term for active sonar? How does it work?
2. Which animals use active sonar? Why do they use it?

# The Wave Model of Sound   Section 2

**Section 2 of Chapter 6 is divided into six parts:**

Compressions in springs and air

Compressional waves

Sound as wave energy

Frequency and pitch

Loudness and amplitude

The Doppler effect

*Practical Science: Records of Sounds*

**Learning Objectives**

1. To describe compressional waves as they relate to the behavior of sound.

2. To relate the pitch of a sound to the frequency of the sound wave.

3. To associate the loudness of sound with the amplitude of the sound wave.

4. To use the wave model of sound to explain the Doppler effect.

Figure 6-7. Energy travels along a row of dominoes from one end to the other as one domino falls on the next. Do the dominoes themselves travel with the energy?

Sound travels through matter. If there is no matter—only empty space—sound cannot travel. Yet, the matter itself does not travel. Sound can travel through air when there is no breeze. It can travel through a wooden table top while the table remains in place.

What is sound? A model for sound must explain how it can travel through matter.

Figure 6-8. Does sound travel when the air is still? Or does sound have to be carried by a breeze?

## Compressions in springs and air

When the coils at one end of a long, loose wire spring are compressed, or squeezed together, they spread apart again. At the same time, the coils next to them move together. Then these coils spread apart and the next ones move together. The **compression**, or "squeeze," travels along the spring to the other end. Although the compression travels, the coils do not. Each coil simply moves away from and back to its original position.

Suppose there were two compressions, one shortly after the other. Then both would travel along the spring. Look at

**Main Idea**

How do compressional waves travel along a spring?

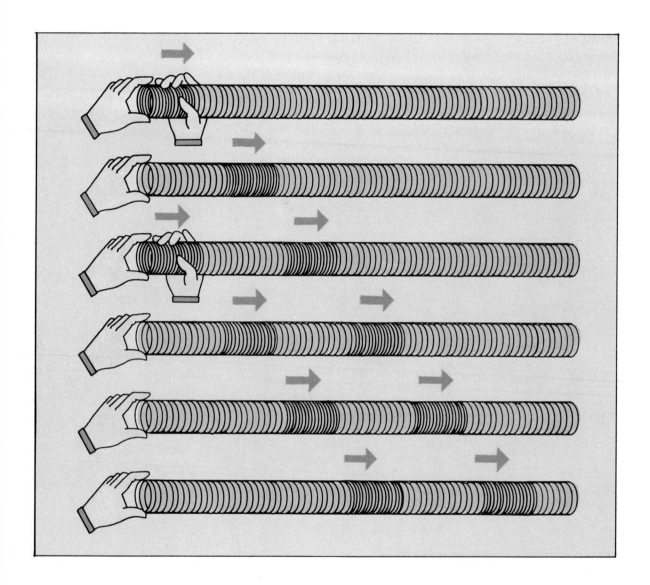

Figure 6-9. This spring has been given two squeezes, one after the other. Each drawing shows the spring at a later time, looking from top to bottom.

Figure 6-9. From top to bottom, it shows how the spring would look as the compressions were traveling to the right.

Sound is produced by the vibration of some matter. As matter vibrates, it pushes again and again on the surrounding air. Each time, it must push the nearby particles of air closer together.

When you push against a filled balloon, you can compress it somewhat. As soon as you let go, however, the balloon fills out again. In the same way, the air compressed by a sound vibration spreads apart again.

**Activity 6–2A**          Travel Through Matter

### Materials

4 marbles
book
pencil
long, loose, wire or plastic spring (such as a
   Slinky)
small piece of yarn

### Purpose

To observe something traveling through matter
without making the matter travel.

### Procedure

**Part 1**

1. Place four marbles next to each other in the
   groove along the front cover of a book. The
   marbles must touch each other.
2. Press three fingers on the three closest
   marbles. Do not touch the fourth marble.
3. Hold the end of a pencil in your hand. Swing
   the pencil so that it strikes the front of the
   first marble. The first three marbles cannot
   move because you are holding them.
4. Record what happens to the fourth marble
   when you hit the first marble.

**Part 2**

5. Place a long, loose wire spring on an uncar-
   peted floor or long table. Stretch it just
   enough so that all the coils of wire are separated. SAFETY NOTE: *Keep loose wire
   away from eyes to prevent eye injury.*
6. Tie a piece of yarn to one of the center coils.
7. Squeeze together the coils near one end
   and quickly let go. Observe what happens.

8. Predict what would happen if you squeezed
   the coils twice. Test your prediction.

### Questions

1. What happened to the fourth marble when
   you hit the first one?
2. How did the coils move as the compression
   traveled through them?
3. Did the whole spring travel with the
   compression?
4. What happened when you squeezed the
   coils at one end twice?

### Conclusion

What traveled through the coils of the spring
and through the marbles?

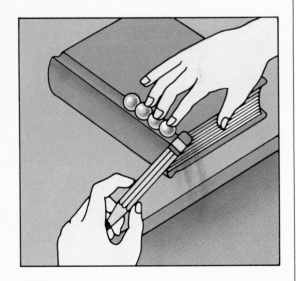

Can a compression travel through air? Suppose the window
is open and there are curtains hanging in front of it. If you
quickly open the door to the room, the curtains will swing
toward the outside. Opening the door compresses the air near
the door. The compression travels through the air and pushes
the curtains out.

Figure 6-10. What causes the curtains to move when the door is opened and closed?

Now suppose the door is quickly closed. The curtains will swing into the room. Closing the door pushes some air out of the room. The air remaining near the door is thinner, or less dense. There is said to be a **rarefaction** (rayr-uh-FAK′-shun) near the door. Since the curtains get sucked into the room, the rarefaction must travel toward the window.

When a source of sound vibrates, it acts like a door being opened and closed over and over again. Many compressions, one after the other, travel through the surrounding air. Traveling in between each two compressions is a rarefaction. In

Figure 6-11. The compressions created by playing a trumpet move outward in all directions.

other words, air acts like a spring. Of course, on a spring compressions travel in one direction—along the spring. In air, compressions travel outward in all directions.

## Check yourself

1. How is the movement of one coil on a spring different from the movement of a compression on the spring?

2. What evidence is there that compressions and rarefactions travel through air?

## Compressional waves

A vibrating sound source sends many compressions and rarefactions through the air. They form what is called a **compressional wave**. The compressional wave disturbs the air as it passes through. It makes the air particles move back and forth. They move together and spread apart, over and over again. But they do not travel with the wave.

A wave causes many compressions to pass through one place. The number of compressions arriving per second is called the **frequency** (FREE'-kwen-see) of the wave. The faster the source vibrates, the higher is the frequency of the wave it sends out. The SI unit for frequency is the **hertz** (HERTS),

**Main Idea**

How is the frequency of a wave determined?

Figure 6-12. The compressions are closer together in the wave on the right than in the wave on the left. More compressions will reach the person in one second from the wave on the right. Which wave has the higher frequency?

## Activity 6–2B          A Model for a Compressional Wave

### Materials

scissors
index card
metric ruler
clear tape

### Purpose

To make a model of a compressional wave.

### Procedure

1. Cut an index card in half.
2. Draw a rectangle 1 cm × 6 cm along one cut edge. Cut it out and discard it.
3. Use the cards to form a slit 6 cm in length but only 1 mm in width. Tape the two pieces in this position.
4. Place the slit vertically at the left edge of the drawing of wavy lines. Through the slit you should see short lines which are closest together near the center of the slit. These lines represent a compression.
5. Slide the card from left to right. Count the number of compressions to reach the center of the slit. Record the direction the compressions moved.

6. Predict what will happen to the compressions if you slide the card from right to left. Test your prediction.
7. Watch how the short colored line moves as you slide the card. Describe the motion of the colored line.
8. Mark a spot somewhere between the end and the center of the slit. Count how many compressions arrive at this spot as you slide the card across the drawing.
9. Assume that it took one second to move the card, and calculate the frequency of the compressional wave.

### Questions

1. What happened to the compressions when you slid the card from left to right?
2. What happened to the compressions when you slid the card from right to left?
3. What do you think the short colored line represents?

### Conclusion

What was the frequency of your compressional wave if you took one second to move the card?

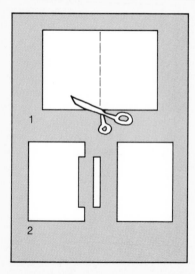

whose symbol is Hz. A frequency of one hertz means that one compression is arriving each second. A frequency of one hertz also means that one rarefaction is arriving each second. What frequency means that 15 compressions and 15 rarefactions are arriving each second?

Even though matter does not move with a wave, energy does. When a wave reaches a place, the particles there receive enough energy to move back and forth. As the wave passes on, the particles give up their energy to the next group of particles. Thus, the energy travels along with the compressions. The energy can also travel much farther than the individual particles.

> **Data Search**
> A bat has a hearing range from 1000 Hz to 120 000 Hz. Name four musical instruments that a bat cannot hear. Search page 560.

### Check yourself

1.  What effect does a compressional wave have on the matter it travels through?

2.  What does it mean for a compressional wave to have a frequency of 120 Hz?

### Sound as wave energy

It is reasonable to think that sound is the energy that travels in a compressional wave. After all, sound is produced by vibrating matter, which sends out a compressional wave. And compressional waves carry energy.

The theory that sound is the energy that travels in a compressional wave is known as the **wave model of sound**. It explains many observations. First, it explains how people in different locations can hear the same sound. When your teacher talks, the compressional wave spreads out into the classroom.

Second, it explains why sound stops when air is removed by a vacuum pump. There can be no compressional wave where there is no matter.

Third, the wave model of sound explains "dead spots" in auditoriums. A "dead spot" is a place where sound coming from the stage is much weaker than in other places. It is very hard to hear if you are sitting in a "dead spot." Sound from the stage not only goes directly out to the audience but also

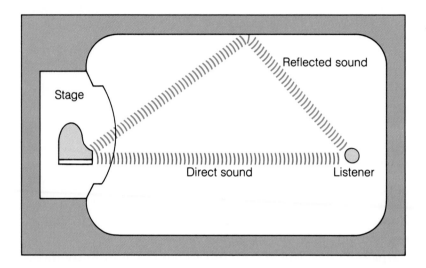

Figure 6-13. In a "dead spot" direct sound from the stage is cancelled out by sound that first bounces off the walls or ceiling. How can the wave model of sound be used to explain the cancelling of sound?

bounces off the walls and ceilings. In a "dead spot," compressions from direct sound arrive at the same time as rarefactions from bounced sound. And rarefactions from direct sound arrive at the same time as compressions from bounced sound. The compressions and rarefactions cancel each other out. As a result, the sound is faint.

Sound can travel through liquids and solids as well as through gases. Gases are easily compressed. Although it is harder to compress a liquid or solid than a gas, it is not impossible. Sound does compress a liquid or solid. A compressional wave can travel through the liquids and solids that are carriers of sound. The best carriers are materials that return quickly to their original state after the compression has passed. Metals are excellent sound carriers.

## Check yourself

1. What is the wave model of sound?
2. What happens if compressions from direct sound arrive at the same time as rarefactions from bounced sound.

## Frequency and pitch

**Main Idea**

How does pitch depend on the length of a vibrating object?

How can the wave model of sound explain pitch? Suppose the end of a ruler is made to vibrate. The pitch of the sound depends on the length of the end free to vibrate. The longer that end, the lower is the pitch.

## Activity 6–2C    Length and Frequency

### Materials

ball of string
scissors
washer for each student
watch or clock that indicates seconds
masking tape

### Purpose

To determine the relation between length and frequency for a pendulum.

### Procedure

1. Take a piece of string betwen 15 cm and 150 cm in length. Each student should have a string of a different length.
2. Tie a washer to one end of the string. Tie a knot close to the other end.
3. Hold the knot and make sure that the washer is free to swing. The string and washer make a pendulum.
4. Have someone be the timekeeper and call out the beginning and end of one minute.
5. Each person should silently count the number of complete back-and-forth swings his or her pendulum makes in one minute. The number of complete back-and-forth swings per minute is the frequency of the pendulum.
6. Measure and record the frequency of your pendulum three times. Find the average frequency.
7. Put a piece of masking tape below the knot. Write the average frequency of your pendulum on the masking tape.
8. Have someone draw a horizontal line near the top of the chalkboard. Number along the line by units of 5, starting at 0 and ending with 100. Label the line *Frequency in swings per minute.*
9. Using masking tape, each person should stick his or her pendulum to the chalkboard so that the knot is on the line at the proper frequency. Notice the pattern.

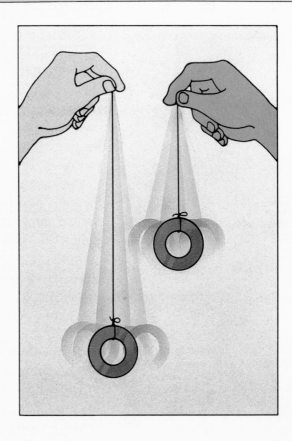

### Questions

1. Are all the pendulums in order of length? Do you see any that perhaps should be tested again?
2. Do the bottoms of the pendulums lie along a straight line? If so, how long a pendulum would have a frequency of one swing per minute?
3. Do the longest pendulums have the lowest or the highest frequencies?

### Conclusion

How does the frequency of a pendulum depend upon its length?

Figure 6-14. When a tuning fork is struck, it vibrates at a single frequency. Tuning forks are used by piano tuners to set the frequency of the first set of strings they tune.

A ruler vibrates too quickly for you to count the number of back-and-forth movements in a time period. A pendulum, made by hanging a small object from a string, swings more slowly than a ruler vibrates. You can find the frequency of a pendulum by counting how many back-and-forth swings it makes in a minute. The shorter the pendulum, the higher is its frequency. A ruler behaves similarly. The shorter the vibrating part, the higher is the frequency of the vibration.

The shorter the vibrating part of the ruler, the higher is the pitch of the sound it gives off. In other words, the higher the frequency of the vibration, the higher is the pitch of the sound.

Other sound sources behave the same way. The frequency of the vibration is the same as the frequency of the sound wave it produces. Thus, the higher the pitch of the sound, the higher is the frequency of the sound wave. Conversely, the lower the pitch, the lower is the frequency.

Some sounds seem to have a definite pitch, while others do not. A tuning fork vibrates at a single frequency. The sound it produces has a very pure quality. Most sounds do not have this pure quality. They are a combination of several different frequencies at once. When different musical instruments play the same note, each produces a different combination of frequencies. This is what gives each musical instrument its own quality.

**Check yourself**

1. How is the frequency of vibration of a sound source related to the pitch of the sound it produces?

2. How can the different sound qualities of musical instruments be explained?

**Loudness and amplitude**

Suppose you had an extremely long spring. You could send a compressional wave down the spring by moving one end in and out. As the wave moved, it would make the spring coils move back and forth.

The distance each coil moves from its original position is called the **amplitude** (AMP′-lih-tewd) of the wave. You could change the amplitude by moving the end of the spring more gently or more vigorously. What would you expect more vigorous movements to do to the amplitude?

When you move the end more vigorously, you give the spring more energy with each push. The wave must carry more energy. Thus, the greater the amplitude of the wave, the more energy it carries.

A sound wave is similar to a wave on a spring. Bigger vibrations of the sound source produce a sound wave with a bigger amplitude. A sound wave carries energy away from the source. The bigger the vibrations of the source, the more energy the sound wave carries. Thus, a sound wave with a bigger amplitude carries more energy.

The sound energy that reaches a place per second is the intensity of the sound wave. For the same pitch, louder sounds are produced when the intensity is greater. Thus, the greater the amplitude, the louder the sound. When sound is amplified, or made louder, the amplitude of the wave is increased.

Sound waves move out from the source something like an expanding balloon. However, a sound wave expands without ever breaking. As a balloon gets larger and larger, the rubber wall of the balloon gets thinner and thinner because it must cover a larger area. The "wall" of a sound wave is energy. As the wave gets larger, the energy gets spread out over a larger area.

The farther you are from the source, the "thinner" is the wall of sound energy that reaches you. The particles of air or other matter move with a smaller amplitude the farther they are from the sound source. At great distances from the source, the energy wall is so "thin" the sound cannot be heard. You are not even aware that an energy wall is striking your ear.

Figure 6-15. The energy carried by a sound wave gets spread over a larger area as the sound wave spreads out like a balloon. What happens to the amplitude of the wave?

**Library research**

Read about and prepare a report on how high-frequency sound, or ultrasound, is used in the medical field. How does ultrasound compare to x rays? Has ultrasound been used successfully in the treatment of disease as well as in diagnosis?

The amplitude of the wave is not great enough for your ear to detect the sound.

Figure 6-16. How is a megaphone able to affect the loudness of a sound?

A megaphone focuses the sound in one general direction. It keeps the sound from spreading out very much. As a result, the amplitude does not decrease as rapidly when the sound travels outward. The sound can be heard a greater distance from the source.

**Check yourself**

1. What is the relation between the amplitude of a sound wave and the loudness of the sound?
2. How is a sound wave like an expanding balloon?

**The Doppler effect**

A very interesting effect can be heard when a train blows its whistle at a railroad crossing. To a person at the crossing, the train whistle seems to be at one pitch as the train is approaching. However, as the engine passes the crossing, the pitch seems to drop. The person hears a lower pitch as the train moves away from the crossing.

The wave model of sound can explain this change of pitch. If the whistle blew when the train was not moving, the sound wave would have a certain frequency. It would be the same frequency as that of the whistle's vibration. When the train moves, each compression is sent out from a different point.

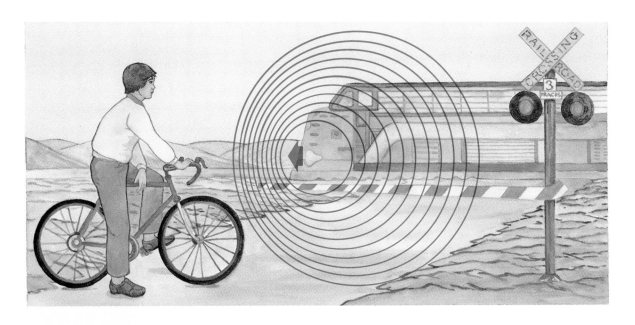

Look at Figure 6-17. Ahead of the train, the compressions get crowded together. Behind the train, the compressions get spread out. Thus, a person ahead of the train hears a higher frequency sound than for a nonmoving train. A person behind the train hears a lower frequency sound.

What happens if the listener is moving but the sound source is not? Suppose you were on a moving train and a bell was ringing at the crossing. When you were moving toward the crossing, you would meet each compression a little sooner. Thus, you would receive more compressions in one second. The frequency of the bell would sound higher than if you were not moving. After you passed the crossing, you would meet each compression a little later. You would receive fewer compressions in one second. The frequency of the bell would sound lower than if you were not moving.

As you can see, the apparent frequency of the sound depends on whether either the source or the listener is moving. The apparent change in frequency due to motion is called the **Doppler shift**. It is named after the Austrian scientist Christian Doppler (1803–1853). The sudden drop in pitch when the source and the listener pass each other is called the **Doppler effect**.

### Check yourself

If you were on a moving train, how would the pitch of the ringing bell at a crossing seem to change as you passed by?

Figure 6-17. As the train passes, the person on the bicycle hears a sudden drop in pitch of the train whistle. How can this be explained?

### Main Idea

What is meant by the Doppler shift?

**Careers**  Acoustical Engineer / Sound Mixer

**Acoustical Engineer**  Acoustical engineers help to control sound. Some work on ways to reduce sound pollution. Others try to find new ways to conduct sounds over long distances. Architectural and design firms hire acoustical engineers to help in the design of buildings.

Acoustical engineers must know a lot about sound. They must be familiar with how various materials affect sound. They also must know how to measure and record different properties of sound. Acoustical engineers usually have a college degree and on-the-job training.

An acoustical engineer might have to decide whether construction noise is within allowed limits.

**Sound Mixer**  In a recording studio, different types of sound are recorded on separate tapes, or tracks. In preparing the final recording, sound mixers put together the different tracks to produce a mixture they think sounds best.

Sound mixers must have a good ear for music. They must be able to operate electronic equipment. They must have some knowledge of the technical aspects of sound. A sound mixer may receive on-the-job training by working as an apprentice for several years.

A sound mixer uses sophisticated equipment to blend sound tracks recorded separately.

# Practical Science

## Records of Sounds

A phonograph record is a thin, flat, vinyl disk "structurally coded" to reproduce sound. A closer look at the wave model of sound will explain how this structural coding works.

**Complex waves**   So far, you have studied the wave model of a single sound. You also have read that each musical instrument produces a unique quality of sound. The quality of sound is due to the combination of frequencies produced for each note played. As each primary note is produced, several others, called *overtones*, are generated. The primary tone and the overtones each have a distinct pitch, or frequency.

The combination of sounds produced by a single instrument as it generates a note and its overtones can be pictured as a complex wave. In a complex wave, the waves from all the different simultaneous overtones are superimposed on each other.

In a band or orchestra, each instrument's complex wave is superimposed on the complex waves created by the other instruments. This results in a very complex wave.

**Recording music on records**   Technicians record these extremely complex waves in the spiral groove that runs from the outer edge to the center of a record. During a recording session, special equipment engraves the complex waves of music in the sides of the groove of a master record. This gives the groove a roughened surface. The engraved groove is what is meant by "structural coding." The sound is physically represented in the structure of the record.

**Reproducing the music on records**   A mold is made from the master record, and pressings (the records you buy) are made from the mold. When the needle of the turntable arm runs in the record groove, the engraved surface causes the needle to vibrate. The vibrations recreate the sounds on the record, but very faintly. They must be *amplified*, or made louder.

As the needle vibrates it causes tiny electrical signals to be produced in the phonograph cartridge. These signals are then sent to the *amplifier*, which greatly boosts them. Finally, the amplified signals are sent to a *speaker*, which makes the amplified signals audible.

**Stereo**   Recording in stereo means that two channels of sound are created. Each channel is recorded on a separate side of the groove in the record. When a stereo record is played, the stereo phonograph cartridge thus sends two signals to the amplifier.

A stereo amplifier is really two amplifiers. Each amplifier handles one channel, boosting it and sending it on to a speaker. At least two speakers are required, one for each channel.

Music recorded in stereo sounds more realistic than music recorded on one channel (mono). This is because two channels can reproduce the original recording locations of individual instruments better than one channel.

**Something to try**   Use a microscope to look at the spiral groove in a record. Does the groove appear smooth or rough? Does it have a uniform appearance over the entire record? Why?

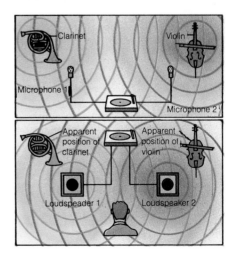

## Section 2 Review   Chapter 6

### Check Your Vocabulary

| | |
|---|---|
| amplitude | frequency |
| compression | hertz |
| compressional wave | rarefaction |
| Doppler effect | wave model of sound |
| Doppler shift | |

*Match each term above with the numbered phrase that best describes it.*

1. Drop in pitch when sound source and observer pass each other.

2. SI unit of frequency.

3. A thinning out.

4. The number of times per second that something happens.

5. Formed when something like a spring is squeezed.

6. A traveling disturbance that carries energy and that makes matter compress and spread apart.

7. Theory that sound is the energy that travels in a compressional wave.

8. Distance something moves from its original position as it moves back and forth.

9. Apparent change in frequency due to motion of source or observer.

### Check Your Knowledge

*Multiple Choice: Choose the answer that best completes each of the following sentences.*

1. Compressions and rarefactions can move through ?.
   a) empty space
   b) gases but not liquids nor solids
   c) gases and liquids but not solids
   d) gases, liquids, and solids

2. When a compressional wave moves through matter, the particles of matter ?.
   a) do not move at all
   b) move back and forth but are not carried along with the wave
   c) move back and forth and are carried along with the wave
   d) spread farther and farther apart like an expanding balloon

3. The greater the number of compressions that arrive per second, the greater is the ?.
   a) amplitude of the wave
   b) energy carried by the wave
   c) frequency of the wave
   d) speed of the wave

4. When the amplitude of a sound wave changes, a person would hear a change in ?.
   a) pitch
   b) loudness
   c) quality
   d) length of time for echo to return

### Check Your Understanding

1. If a pendulum makes 60 complete swings in one minute, how many swings does it make per second? What is its frequency in hertz?

2. If a ruler makes 10 vibrations per second, what is its frequency in hertz? How many vibrations does it make in one minute?

3. Suppose a long metal pipe is banged at one end. Would you expect the sound to be heard farther away through the pipe or through the air? Explain.

### Practical Science

1. Where is the structural coding of a phonograph record located?

2. What does the structural coding contain?

# Listening to Sound    Section 3

**Section 3 of Chapter 6 is divided into five parts:**

The human ear

Hearing in animals

Music

Noise pollution

Controlling sound

*Practical Science: Noise Control at Airports*

## Learning Objectives

1. To explain how sound is sensed in humans.

2. To describe the hearing organs and hearing capabilities of some animals.

3. To recognize ways in which noise can be controlled.

Figure 6-18. Hearing and speech are important ways people use to communicate with each other. A hearing aid helps the boy in the left of the photo to hear the spoken words of the boy at the right. Hearing aids amplify sound waves for hearing-impaired people.

We think of sound as something that is heard. For a sound to be heard, three things are needed. First, there must be a sound source that produces the sound. Second, there must be some matter that carries the sound. Third, there must be an organ of the body that can detect sound. In the human, this organ is the ear.

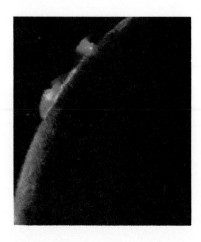

Figure 6-19. If a volcano erupts on Jupiter's innermost moon, Io, and no one is around to hear it, does it make a sound?

### The human ear

Only part of the human ear is visible. This part receives sound waves and directs them through an opening in the skull known as the **ear canal**. The visible part and the ear canal form the **outer ear**. The outer ear is shaped like a funnel with the wider part outward.

At the end of the ear canal is the **eardrum**. The eardrum is a membrane which vibrates when sound waves reach it. Beyond the eardrum is an air-filled space called the **middle ear**. Three small bones reach across the middle ear. They vibrate when the eardrum does.

Further inside the head is the **inner ear**. It is separated from the middle ear by a membrane that lies against one of the three small bones. Part of the inner ear controls the person's sense of balance. The part affected by sound waves is called the **cochlea** (KOK′-lee-uh). It is shaped like a snail shell and contains liquid. Inside the cochlea are special cells attached to nerve fibers. The nerve fibers join together to form one main nerve to the brain.

When sound waves enter the inner ear, they move through the liquid. Movements in the liquid cause the special cells to move. These cells then send nerve messages along the nerve fibers. The messages travel to the main nerve and on to the brain. The brain interprets them as sound.

There are many theories about how different frequencies are sensed. It is likely that different parts of the cochlea are sensitive to different frequencies. A particular frequency stimulates a particular part of the cochlea. That part sends a message to the brain through the nerve.

The human ear can detect sound frequencies between 20 Hz and 20 000 Hz. It is most sensitive to frequencies between

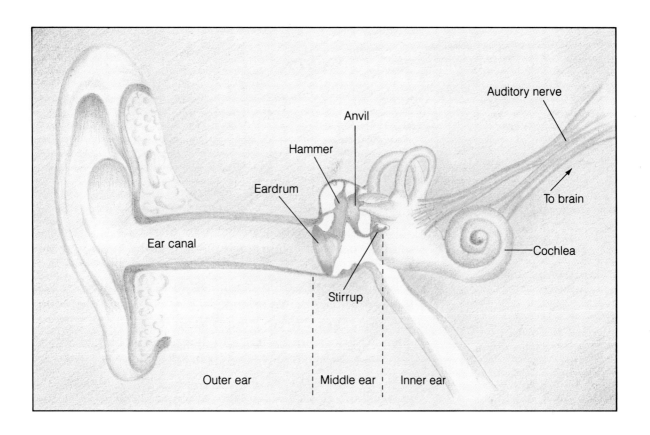

Auditory nerve

Anvil

Hammer

Eardrum

To brain

Ear canal

Cochlea

Stirrup

Outer ear    Middle ear    Inner ear

1000 Hz and 4000 Hz. These are the frequencies of the high notes on a piano. Sounds in this range can be detected at a lower intensity than sounds outside the range.

Figure 6-20. The human ear. What happens after sound waves enter the ear canal?

## Check yourself

1. Describe the path of sound from the time it enters the ear until a message is sent to the brain.

2. What is the frequency range that the normal human ear can hear?

## Hearing in animals

All mammals have ears, but some do not have a visible part of the ear. For example, there are many different kinds of seals. Seals can be divided into two groups. One group is

Figure 6-21. (Left) harbor seal; (right) California sea lion. Which of these seals has a visible ear? Can both seals hear? Explain.

known as earless seals because the animals have no visible ear. Yet, they can hear because they have all the parts that detect sound. The other group has visible ears and is known as eared seals.

Bats are small, flying mammals. Most kinds sleep during the day and are active at night. They use sound to find out the position of objects around them in the dark. The frequency of the sound is much higher than the human ear can hear—between 50 000 Hz and 100 000 Hz. Bats give off sounds in this range and listen for the echo. The sooner the echo returns, the closer the bat is to an object.

Dogs, too, can hear **ultrasound**, or high-frequency sound beyond the range of human hearing. Dog owners may use ultrasonic dog whistles to call their pets. To people, the whistle seems to be silent, but dogs can hear it.

Birds can hear, although their ears are not as complex as mammal ears. In place of a visible ear, there is a small opening behind the eye.

Some kinds of animals can sense sound through hearing organs that do not resemble human ears. Fish have hearing organs along their bodies that can detect low-frequency vibrations. Some kinds of grasshoppers have a hearing organ on each front leg. Other kinds have one on each side of the lower body. Grasshoppers probably hear the intensity of sound but not pitch.

## Library research

Animals such as whales, wolves, and birds are believed to communicate with each other through sound. Read and write a report about how one kind of animal uses sound to communicate.

### Check yourself

1. How can earless seals hear?
2. How do bats use ultrasound?

## Activity 6–3A          Musical Bottles

### Materials

8 identical bottles
water
metric ruler
grease pencil

### Purpose

To make eight bottles play a musical scale.

### Procedure

1. Put a little water in one of eight identical bottles.
2. Number the bottles 1 through 8 with a grease pencil.
3. Without touching the bottle, blow across the opening until the bottle hums.
4. Predict what will happen if you hold the bottle as you blow across the opening. Test your prediction.
5. Predict what will happen to the pitch of the hum if you add water to the bottle. Test your prediction.
6. Adjust the water levels in two bottles until their hums are one octave apart. Adjust the water levels in the other six bottles to fill in the remaining notes of a musical scale.
7. Record the height of the water and the height of the air column for each bottle. (Your readings should be to the nearest tenth of a centimeter.)

### Questions

1. Was the bottle vibrating or was the air inside it vibrating? Explain how you know.
2. How did increasing the height of water affect the pitch of the sound produced?
3. How does increasing the height of a vibrating column of air affect the pitch produced?

### Conclusion

In what way does the vibrating air column act like a vibrating string or rubber band?

## Music

When you sing *do, re, mi, fa, sol, la, ti, do,* you are singing a musical scale. Each note has a higher pitch than the previous one. The high *do* and the low *do* sound the "same" except that one is higher. The reason they sound the "same" is that the high *do* has a frequency exactly twice that of the low *do*.

Middle C

| do | re | mi | fa | sol | la | ti | do |
|----|----|----|----|-----|----|----|----|
| C  | D  | E  | F  | G   | A  | B  | C  |

Figure 6-22. Near the center of the piano keyboard is the white key called middle C. Playing the eight white keys starting with middle C produces a musical scale.

---

**Data Search**

What instruments cannot match the pitch of the oboe's note A? Search page 560.

---

Whenever one note has double the frequency of another note, the two are said to be an **octave** (OK'-tiv) apart. The word *octave* comes from the Latin for *eight*. There are eight different pitches on the scale within one octave.

Musical instruments are tuned, or adjusted, to play a certain note, called A, at 440 Hz. At the beginning of an orchestra performance, the oboe player sounds an A. The string players tighten or loosen their strings until their A's have the same pitch.

The wind instruments, such as the flute and trombone, all contain columns of air. They are played by blowing at one end to make the air vibrate. The pitch is changed by changing the length of the air columns. The lowest notes are produced by the longest air column.

Every musical instrument has its own quality of sound. The quality is produced by the combination of frequencies heard for each note played. A violin note contains not only the

Figure 6-23. These people are playing recorders of different sizes. Which would you expect to play notes of the highest pitch? Of the lowest pitch?

frequency of the pitch heard but double, triple, four times, and so on that frequency. The higher frequencies are called **overtones.** Each kind of instrument produces a different combination of overtones at different intensities.

**Main Idea**

What causes different instruments to have different sounds at the same frequency?

**Check yourself**

1. What is the frequency relationship between two notes one octave apart?
2. What vibrates in a wind instrument?

---

**Activity 6–3B**    Noisy Backgrounds

**Materials**

ticking portable clock
metric tape measure or meter stick

**Purpose**

To compare how different background noises affect your ability to detect a particular sound.

**Procedure**

1. With a partner, take a ticking alarm clock and a metric measuring tape or meter stick to a quiet place. One person should hold the clock.
2. Move far enough apart so that the clock cannot be heard by the other person.
3. Measure how close together you must be for the clock to be heard. Repeat.
4. Trade places and make two more trials.
5. Calculate the average distance where you can just hear the clock.
6. Repeat Steps 2 through 5 for two noisy backgrounds. You might try a sidewalk or yard near traffic, the cafeteria during lunchtime, or a bandroom during practice.
7. Divide your average distance for the quietest place by your average distance for the noisiest place.

8. Estimate the intensity level of the "quiet" and "noisy" places you tested by using the table on page 281. Record your estimate.

**Questions**

1. How many times farther away were you when you heard the clock against a quiet background as compared to a noisy background?
2. What happens when you try to talk to someone against a noisy background?
3. What other unpleasant effects have you experienced due to a noisy background?

**Conclusion**

Did both the kind and intensity of the background noise affect your ability to hear your test sound? Explain.

| Trial | Place | Distance in m | Decibels (estimated) |
|---|---|---|---|
|  |  |  |  |
|  |  |  |  |
|  |  |  |  |
|  |  |  |  |

## Noise pollution

Noise is any sound that is unwanted. The noise level in our society increases each year. Highway and air traffic, industrial noise, and amplified music are a few of the causes.

Too much sound can be harmful. Sound causes the ear to work. Loud sounds overwork the ear. As the noise level increases, people are more likely to suffer hearing loss.

Moderately loud sounds over a long period of time may also cause ear damage. Many people suffer hearing loss without being aware of it. They do not hear quiet sounds.

Sounds with decibel ratings between 60 and 100 can be annoying. Such sounds include a garbage disposal, food blender, subway train, and freeway traffic. Sounds above 100 decibels can cause temporary or permanent loss of hearing. A snowmobile, power mower, rock band, and a jet flying 300 m above ground make sounds over 100 decibels.

### Check yourself

What, besides the loudness of a sound, can make sound cause ear damage?

### Controlling sound

There are many things that can be done to cut down on noise. At the same time, people can be helped to hear sounds they want to hear.

One way to cut down on noise is to pass laws that set limits on the loudness of sounds. For example, there are laws that set limits on noise by new motors. The motors are made quieter by surrounding them by materials that absorb sound. In many communities near airports, there are laws about how close to the ground planes may fly and about hours of takeoff and landing. People who must work near loud noises are required to wear ear protectors. Heavy trucks may not be allowed on residential streets.

Unwanted sound can be reduced by different sound absorbing materials. You may not have thought of bushes and trees as sound absorbers. But they are effective in sheltering a community from highway noise. Does your school have carpeting or rough-textured ceiling tiles? They absorb sound. So does insulation between the walls of rooms.

**Main Idea**

What kind of sound tends to overwork the ear?

**Safety**
Wear ear protection if you must work in a noisy environment.

Figure 6-24. How do earphones help reduce noise pollution?

Figure 6-25. What design features in this concert hall help to control the sound the audience hears?

You can help control the amount of noise others must hear. When you listen to a recording or broadcast, keep the sound volume as low as you can hear comfortably. Before making loud noises, think of people nearby who may be disturbed by the noise.

Auditoriums can be designed so that speech or music can be easily heard from every seat. The word *auditorium* comes from the Latin words meaning *hear* and *place for*. Reflecting panels behind and above the stage can prevent the sound from being lost backstage. They bounce the sound back out to the audience.

On the other hand, sound should go out from the stage or loudspeakers to the audience without too much echo. Echo makes speech hard to understand. For music, some echo is desirable as it makes the music sound smoother and richer. But too much echo covers up the music. Echo can be controlled through the use of materials that absorb sound.

### Library research

Read about the sound problems encountered when modern concert halls first open. Write a report about what steps have been taken to improve the sound in a hall after it has opened. One hall which had to be totally changed was Avery Fisher Hall (formerly Philharmonic Hall) in New York City.

### Check yourself

1. List three ways noise can be reduced.

2. What sound problems have to be solved in designing an auditorium?

# Practical Science

## Noise Control at Airports

You have learned that prolonged exposure to loud noise can result in hearing loss. Too much noise may also cause physical and psychological stress. People living or working near airports are especially vulnerable to these effects. Airplane takeoffs and landings produce extremely high noise levels that may cause loss of hearing. Airplanes in flight produce lower noise levels that may also cause some hearing loss.

**Who is affected**  People working at airports are the most affected by airplane noise. For example, an airplane lands or takes off every minute at O'Hare Airport in Chicago. Therefore, people working at O'Hare are exposed to almost continuous noise.

Airplane passengers are exposed to lower noise levels than the workers. This is because they are usually inside the terminal building or the airplane cabin. However, even the noise level in the cabin of an older jet is loud enough to cause stress. Passengers walking outside between the terminal and their planes are exposed to the same noise levels as the workers.

People living or working under the paths that airplanes follow during takeoffs and landings are affected by airplane noise. They cannot hear a radio, television, or each other when a plane passes overhead. People in offices cannot concentrate on their work and find telephone conversations impossible. Students at schools near airports have difficulty hearing their teachers or concentrating on their work.

**Types of ear protection**  There are two basic kinds of ear protectors: ear muffs and ear plugs. Some workers wear both for more protection.

Ear muffs look like stereo headphones. They are filled with sound-absorbing material and enclose the ear. Some are designed so a worker can hear normal conversation.

Ear plugs fit inside the ear canal. They do not provide as much protection as ear muffs and are used in less noisy places.

**Noise abatement programs**  The harm caused by excessive noise caused the Federal government to recognize the need to search for ways to reduce airport noise levels. There are now noise abatement (reduction) programs which attempt to bring about airport noise reduction by creating strict noise limits.

As a result, airplane manufacturers have designed and built quieter jet airplanes. A major part of this noise reduction comes from new, quieter jet engines. Airlines are replacing the engines in their older jets with the new engines.

Airplanes now land and take off at much steeper angles. At many airports the angles are even steeper during the night. Jets must also reduce the thrust from their engines shortly after takeoff. This lessens the noise for people living and working near the end of a runway. Airplanes may also be required to make a turn shortly after takeoff to avoid populated areas.

Some local governments have purchased houses under airport approach and takeoff patterns. The houses were moved or destroyed to provide an unpopulated noise buffer zone near the airports.

**Something to try**  If there is a nearby airport you can visit, go to it and observe the ear protection airport workers use. Do all airport workers use ear protection? Should they?

## Section 3 Review   Chapter 6

### Check Your Vocabulary

cochlea         octave

ear canal       outer ear

eardrum         overtone

inner ear       ultrasound

middle ear

*Match each term above with the numbered phrase that best describes it.*

1. Includes the visible part of the ear as well as the ear canal.
2. Sound whose frequency is too high for the human ear to hear.
3. Relation between two pitches, one with double the frequency of the other.
4. Air-filled space containing three small bones that vibrate in response to sound.
5. Snail-shaped part of inner ear that converts sounds to nerve messages.
6. Opening in the skull through which sound passes from outside.
7. Membrane that separates the outer from the middle ear.
8. Part of the ear that not only controls a person's sense of balance but also contains the nerve fibers that send sound messages to the brain.
9. A higher frequency produced when a note is played on an instrument.

### Check Your Knowledge

*Multiple Choice: Choose the answer that best completes each of the following sentences.*

1. The normal human ear cannot hear sounds at frequencies above ?.
   - a) 20 Hz
   - b) 1000 Hz
   - c) 4000 Hz
   - d) 20 000 Hz

2. The ? has a hearing organ that is not in the head.
   - a) bat
   - b) earless seal
   - c) grasshopper
   - d) dog

3. The overtones that are produced when a note is played on an instrument ?.
   - a) form a musical scale
   - b) give the instrument its own quality
   - c) are eliminated when the instrument is tuned
   - d) are caused by changing the length of the vibrating air column

4. The echo in an auditorium could be cut down by using ?.
   - a) sound-absorbing materials
   - b) reflecting panels at the back of the stage
   - c) a more powerful amplifying system
   - d) sound insulation in the walls

### Check Your Understanding

1. People have been known to suffer permanent hearing loss as a result of sticking sharp objects into the ear. Explain how a sharp object can cause such damage.
2. What are the frequencies of the notes one octave below and one octave above the A (440 Hz) used in tuning up an orchestra?
3. Imagine that you have been hired by your school to reduce the amount of noise that can be heard in the classrooms. What recommendations would you make?

### Practical Science

1. What does an airport noise abatement program attempt to do?
2. How does a noise abatement program work?

# Chapter 6 Review

## Concept Summary

Sound is energy that is produced and transferred by vibrating matter.
- All sounds are caused by vibrations.
- Sound can travel through solids, liquids, and gases.
- Some materials transmit sound better than others do.
- Sound cannot travel where matter is absent.
- The speed of sound depends on the temperature and on the kind of matter carrying the sound.
- Pitch refers to how high or low a sound is.
- Loudness depends on the amount of energy used to make the sound, distance from the source, and pitch.
- Quality of sound refers to the difference in sounds from two sources even when the loudness and pitch are the same.

The wave model of sound is the theory that sound is energy that travels in a compressional wave.
- As a compressional wave moves through matter, the particles move back and forth but do not move with the wave.
- Amplitude is the distance a particle moves from its normal positon.
- Amplitude is related to loudness.
- Frequency is the number of compressions passing a point per second.
- Frequency is related to pitch.
- Combinations of frequencies are related to quality.
- The frequency of a sound wave appears to change when either the source or the listener is moving.

The ear is the detector of sound in humans and other mammals.
- Each kind of mammal has different limits on the lowest and highest frequency it can hear.
- Some other kinds of animals have simple hearing organs other than ears.

The control of sound is the reduction of unwanted sound and the adjustment of desired sound.
- Noise can be controlled by restricting the use of its sources and by using materials that absorb sound.
- Lecture halls and concert halls can be designed so that listeners can hear sounds the way they are most acceptable.

## Putting It All Together

1. How is sound produced?
2. What are some materials that are good carriers of sound?
3. Does sound travel faster in cold or warm air?
4. How can you increase the pitch of the sound produced by a vibrating wire?
5. What property of sound is measured in decibels?
6. What is the difference between a compression and a rarefaction?
7. What is meant by the frequency of a wave?
8. What property of sound is the result of the frequency?
9. What property of a sound wave is associated with the intensity of the sound?
10. How does a megaphone help to make sound travel a greater distance?
11. What happens to the pitch of the sound of an automobile horn as the car passes you?
12. Compare the frequency of sound waves reaching your ear when the source moves away from you and when the source is stationary.
13. What three things are needed for sound to be heard?
14. What part of the ear transmits the sound through a nerve connected to the brain?
15. What frequencies is the human ear most sensitive to?
16. What animal uses high-frequency sound to locate objects?

17. What are ultrasonic sounds?
18. What can be the danger of prolonged exposure to loud sounds?
19. What can be done to reduce noise pollution?

## Apply Your Knowledge

1. Vibrations caused by earthquakes travel through the solid earth as waves that are similar to sound waves. How might differences in the composition of the earth's interior affect these waves?
2. Describe what happens to the particles in a material when a sound wave moves through the material.
3. The energy in a sound wave is like an expanding soap bubble as it spreads out in all directions. What property of a sound wave changes in the same way as the thickness of the surface of the soap bubble?
4. Do you think that singers produce overtones when they sing? Explain your reasoning.
5. How might noises from a busy highway be reduced within a nearby office building?

## Find Out on Your Own

1. Examine a musical instrument. Determine what it is in the instrument that vibrates to produce the sound. Find out what the player of the instrument must do to change the pitch of the sound.
2. Compare several samples of acoustical tile that are sold in a building materials center. What properties do the samples have that would prevent the transfer of sound energy?
3. Add water to a plastic foam cup until it is about three-fourths filled. Slide the cup slowly across the surface of a desk or table. Observe the movement of the surface of the water. What is the evidence that the cup is vibrating?

4. Find out what regulations related to noise are enforced in your city. Interview a number of community residents to find out if additional steps are needed to reduce noise pollution.

## Reading Further

Kavaler, Lucy. *The Dangers of Noise*. New York: Crowell/Harper & Row, 1978
  This is a description of how we hear, the effects of noise on people and wildlife, and what people can do to control noise.

Lutrell, Guy L. *The Instruments of Music*. New York: Lodestar, 1978
  The book explains how different instruments make their sounds, their roles in an orchestra, and information about their origins.

Tannenbaum, Beulah, and Myra Stillman. *Understanding Sound*. New York: McGraw-Hill, 1973
  A clear and interesting outline of the physics of sound, production of animal sounds, hearing in mammals, and uses of sound waves is given. Suggestions for demonstrations and experiments are described.

# Chapter 7

# Light

Section 1
**Properties of Light**

Light can pass through, bounce off, and be absorbed by matter. Images of objects are formed when the direction of light is changed by its interaction with matter. Light travels extremely fast. The brightness of light from a source depends on the distance to that source.

Section 2
**Color**

The color of something that does not give off its own light depends on two factors. One is the thing itself and the other is the light that strikes it. Sunlight is a combination of light of different colors. The human eye is sensitive to colors in light, but we see a combination of colors as a single color.

Section 3
**Models for Light**

A model of light as energy carried by a wave can explain many observations. However, when light falls on a metal and causes electrons to be released, it does not act like a wave. Instead, it acts like a stream of particles. Scientists now realize that light has both wave and particle properties.

In this chapter you will learn about the properties of light and how they can be explained. The photo at the left shows a stained glass window in a spiral pattern. Do stained glass windows create light?

# Properties of Light   Section 1

**Section 1 of Chapter 7 is divided into six parts:**

Light and matter

Reflection and mirrors

Refraction and lenses

The human eye

The speed of light

Brightness and distance

*Practical Science: The Camera's Eye*

## Learning Objectives

1. To identify the different ways in which light interacts with matter.

2. To describe how images are formed by mirrored surfaces.

3. To describe how images are formed by lenses, including the lens of the human eye.

4. To recognize that the bending of light (refraction) is the result of the changing of the speed of light in different substances.

5. To relate the brightness of a light source to its distance from an observer.

Figure 7-1. What are the sources of light in this picture?

Just as your ears detect sound, your eyes detect light. Some things are sources of light. They give off light by themselves. Sources of light include the sun, light bulbs, and flames. Most things do not give off their own light. You can see them only when a source of light throws light on them. For instance, you cannnot see a chair in a dark room. But if you turn on a lamp, light from the lamp lets you see the chair.

**Library research**

Among the objects visible in the night sky are the moon, stars, planets, and galaxies. Find out which of these are sources of light and which can be seen only because of reflected light.

## Light and matter

There are three ways light can interact with matter. One is for the light to pass right through the matter. Light easily passes through air, for example. It can pass through glass and

Figure 7-2. What three sub-stances transmit the light that travels from the fish to this person's eyes?

water as well. Matter is said to **transmit** (trans-MIT′) light that passes through the matter. Matter that transmits most of the light that strikes it is said to be **transparent** (trans-PA′-rent). If you can see through something, it is transparent.

Second, light can bounce off, or reflect from, matter. We can see things that are not sources of light because of reflected light. Light from a source bounces off such objects and travels to our eyes. Dark-colored objects do not reflect as much light as do light-colored objects. Snow, for example, reflects enough light to give skiers a sunburn.

**Main Idea**

What term describes matter that transmits most of the light that strikes it?

**Data Search**

Some solar radiation is reflected from the earth's surface. What percentage is reflected from freshly fallen snow? Search page 560.

Figure 7-3. The etched glass shown here has both transparent and translucent areas.

Third, light can be absorbed by matter. Dark-colored objects absorb more light than light-colored objects do. Solar collectors for buildings usually have black coverings so that they will collect the most sunlight.

No kind of matter transmits 100 percent of the light that strikes it. Even air absorbs some light. Nor does any matter reflect 100 percent or absorb 100 percent of the light. Matter that reflects and absorbs but does not transmit is said to be **opaque** (ō-PAYK′). Most solids are opaque. If a book, for example, is held in front of a flashlight, the light cannnot be seen. A book is opaque.

If the book is replaced by a piece of waxed paper, on the other hand, some of the light can be seen. Yet, details of the flashlight cannnot be seen. Waxed paper is neither transparent nor opaque. It is **translucent** (trans-LOO′-sent). It transmits some light but also reflects and absorbs a good deal of light. Other examples of translucent matter include frosted glass, sheets of paper, and thin fabrics.

**Check yourself**

1. List three ways light can interact with matter.

2. How do dark-colored objects differ from light-colored objects in their interactions with light?

**Reflection and mirrors**

**Main Idea**

What can be seen by looking at a shiny surface?

Rough, light-colored surfaces such as sand and paper reflect much light. Smooth, shiny surfaces also reflect much light but in a different way. When you look at a shiny surface, you can see a likeness, or **image**, of objects facing the surface.

Silver, aluminum, and other metals have smooth, shiny surfaces. Mirrors are made by coating a piece of glass with silver or aluminum. Light that strikes the glass is transmitted through the glass but is reflected by the metal coating.

If you hit a tennis ball toward a wall at an angle, the ball will not come straight back to you. It will bounce off the wall and move away from you. It acts very much like light that strikes a mirror.

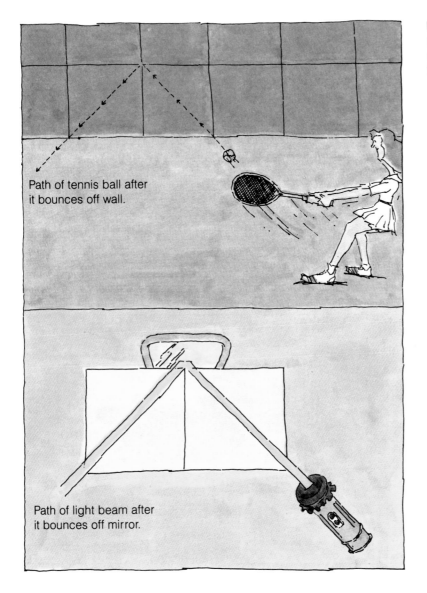

Figure 7-4. Just as a tennis ball is reflected from a smooth wall, a narrow beam of light is reflected from a mirror.

Path of tennis ball after it bounces off wall.

Path of light beam after it bounces off mirror.

A narrow beam of light is used in studying the path of light that strikes a mirror. Black paper with a narrow slit can be put over the front end of a flashlight. A narrow beam of light comes through this slit. Look at Figure 7-4. The beam is aimed toward the mirror at the point where it touches the line on the paper. The beam lights up the paper along its path. Look at the angle between the line and the path of the beam after it is reflected. How does this angle compare to the angle between the line and the original path of the beam?

## Main Idea

What is the difference between an incident ray and a reflected ray?

In drawings the path of a very narrow beam of light is shown as a line called a **ray**. Light rays are drawn with arrows that show in which direction the light is moving. The path of light moving towards something is called an **incident** (IN′-sid-ent) **ray**. The path of light after it has been reflected from a surface is called a **reflected ray.**

Figure 7-5 shows light rays that start at the end of a pencil. The pencil is to the left of a mirror. The mirror is shown as a heavy black line, as if you were looking down on its upper edge. Three incident rays, which hit the mirror at different angles, are shown. For each incident ray, there is a reflected ray. The dotted lines extend the reflected rays backwards, to the right of the mirror. Notice that the dotted lines all meet at one point. The reflected rays *seem* to start from this point, in back of the mirror. This point is where the image of the end of the pencil is located.

Figure 7-5. Reflection of light from a pencil tip by a flat mirror. The reflected rays all appear to come from the same point behind the mirror. The mirror image of the pencil tip is at this point.

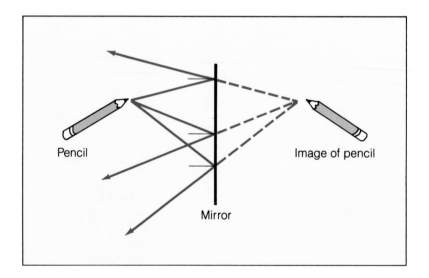

The image formed by a flat mirror always seems to be behind the mirror. However, light from the object does not really travel behind the mirror. The image from a flat mirror is called a **virtual** (VERCH′-uh-wul) **image.** A virtual image cannot be projected on a screen the way a real image can be. The light from the object does not really meet at the image. It only appears to.

## Activity 7–1A        Mirror Images

### Materials

sheet of lined paper
lined index card
scissors
small, flat mirror
modeling clay

### Purpose

To determine how the image distance is related to the object distance for a flat mirror.

### Procedure

1. Darken the center line on a sheet of lined paper. Number the other lines downward and upward to show how far each line is from the darkened center line.
2. Trim an index card along the top and bottom lines. Cut the wider trimming in half crosswise. Fold each piece in half to form two V's. Save the V's for Step 5.
3. If the card has an even number of ruled spaces, cut it in half lengthwise along the center line. If not, first trim off one space and then cut the card in half.
4. At one end of each piece of index card, cut two slits, each 1 cm in length, along the lines next to each edge.
5. Fit the V's you made in Step 2 into the slits of each card so that the cards stand up.
6. Place a piece of modeling clay at the center of the darkened line on the paper. Stand the mirror upright in the clay so that the reflecting surface is on the line.
7. Place one card behind and the other card in front of the mirror, with the lines toward the mirror. Have a partner check that the mirror and cards are vertical.
8. Bend down and look straight into the mirror as your partner aligns the rear card along a numbered line. You should see the top of this card over the mirror.
9. Move the front card until its image in the mirror is the same width as the top of the

rear card. The lines on the image on the front card should line up with the lines on the rear card.
10. Record the positions of the front and rear cards in terms of the numbered lines. Repeat the measurement for two other positions of the rear card.
11. Slowly back away from the mirror. Check to see if the image and the rear card remain the same size as each other as you move.

### Questions

1. Does the position of an image depend on the position of the observer?
2. When the object is moved farther from the mirror, what happens to the position of the image?

### Conclusion

How is the position of an image related to the position of the object whose image it is?

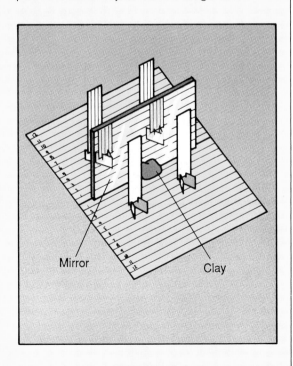

Figure 7-6. Reflection of light from a pencil tip by a concrete wall. The reflected rays do not appear to come from a single point behind the wall. No image is formed.

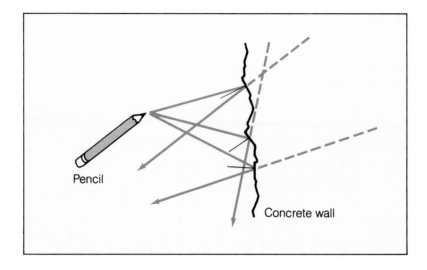

Suppose the mirror is replaced by a white concrete wall. The surface of the wall is rough, not smooth. It reflects light like many mirrors, all at different angles. Look at Figure 7-6. The reflected light does not all seem to come from the same point beyond the wall. No image is formed.

Curved, as well as flat, smooth surfaces reflect images. You have seen images reflected from shiny metal surfaces.

Surfaces that curve outward in the center, like the back side of a spoon, are said to be **convex**. Convex mirrors are used in stores. They help clerks watch a large area of the store at once. A convex mirror reflects beams of light in a way that causes them to spread out. See Figure 7-7. The image is a virtual image that is smaller than the original object.

Figure 7-7. A convex mirror, like the ones used in stores, produces smaller images that appear to be behind the mirror.

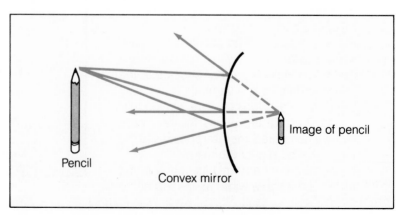

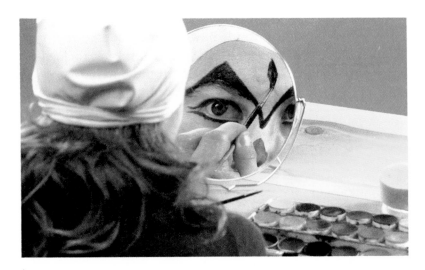

Figure 7-8. A concave mirror, like the ones used for shaving or makeup, magnifies close objects but reflects a smaller, upside-down image if the object is far enough from the mirror.

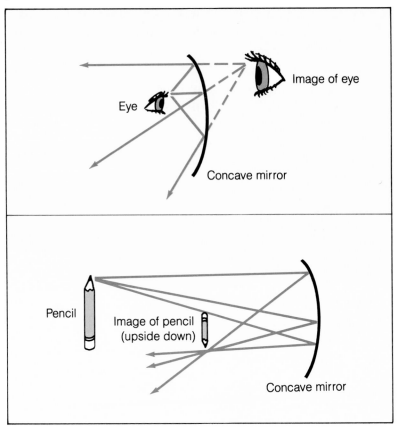

Surfaces that curve inward in the center, like the bowl of a spoon, are called **concave**. Concave mirrors are used as shaving or makeup mirrors. When you hold one close to your face, you see an enlarged image. See Figure 7-8. A curious thing happens if you back away from a concave mirror. When you are more than a certain distance away (depending on the

**Main Idea**

What is meant by a concave surface?

## Main Idea

What is meant by a real image?

mirror), your image is upside down. The upside-down image can be focused on a small card. It is a **real image**, formed by light rays that actually meet in front of the mirror.

### Check yourself

1. Where does the image formed by a flat mirror seem to be?
2. How can an image form in front of a mirror?

### Refraction and lenses

A straw or spoon in a glass of water will appear to be broken in two at the water line. Another strange effect of water on light can be seen if you place a coin in the bottom of an empty opaque cup. Slowly back away until the coin is just cut off from view by the top of the cup. Have someone carefully add water to the cup without disturbing the coin. As the water level in the cup rises, the coin will reappear!

Light travels in a straight line as long as it is moving through one substance (or empty space). When it passes from one substance to another—as from water to air—it changes direction. Its path bends. The bending of light as it moves from one substance to another is called **refraction** (ree-FRAK′-shun).

The amount of bending depends on the two substances. Light is bent more when it passes from air to glass than when it passes from air to water. The path of the light does not depend on the direction in which the light travels. It is the same whether the light is moving *from* air or *into* air. For example, suppose a gull in the air and a fish in the water are

Figure 7-9. A coin that is blocked from view by the top of an empty cup can be seen when water is added to the cup. How is this possible?

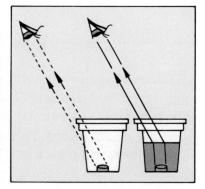

## Activity 7–1B          Bending of Light

### Materials

transparent rectangular container at least 4
   cm deep
water
cardboard at least 10 cm longer and wider
   than container
4 pins
ruler
protractor

### Purpose

To measure the way light bends as it moves
from one substance to another.

### Procedure

1. Place water in a transparent rectangular
   container to a depth of at least 3 cm.
2. Mark the outline of the container on the
   cardboard.
3. Place a pin in the cardboard behind the
   container. The pin should be as close to
   the container as possible.
4. Place a second pin 4 to 5 cm behind the
   first. The two pins should form a line that
   is at an angle less than 45° with the side
   of the container.
5. Lean over so that you are viewing the pins
   through the water in the container. Place
   a third pin close to the front of the container. This pin should appear to line up
   with the pins behind the container.
6. Place a fourth pin 4 to 5 cm in front of the
   third pin so that it lines up with the other
   pins. Readjust the position of any of the
   pins to make certain that they all appear
   to be in line when you look along the pins
   through the water in the container.
7. Carefully remove the container of water,
   leaving the pins in their positions.
8. Use a ruler to draw a line connecting the
   positions of the two pins that were behind
   the container. Repeat for the two pins that
   were in front of the container.

9. Draw a third line connecting the two lines
   already drawn. These three lines represent the path the light followed to your eye.
10. Measure the angle between the side of the
    container and the line connecting the two
    pins that were behind the container.
11. Repeat Step 10 for the line connecting the
    two pins that were in front of the container.

### Questions

1. Did the light bend toward or away from the
   side of the container as it entered the water?
2. Did the light bend toward or away from the
   side of the container as it left the water?
3. Were the angles measured in Steps 10 and
   11 equal?
4. How did the direction of the light entering
   the water compare to the direction of the
   light leaving?

### Conclusion

Did the light bend the same way as it went from
water to air as when it went from air to water?
Explain.

Air

Water

Figure 7-10. Light moves back and forth between the eyes of the gull and the fish along the same path.

watching each other. The gull sees the fish with light that moves from water to air. The fish sees the gull with light that moves along the same path in the reverse direction.

Curved, transparent objects known as **lenses** (LENZ'-uz) form images through refraction of light. Magnifying glasses, cameras, and binoculars all contain lenses. Lenses are usually made of glass or plastic.

A lens that is thicker in the middle than at the edge is called a **convex lens**. A convex lens makes parallel rays of light come together at one point. The distance between this point and the center of the lens is called the **focal** (FŌ'-kul) **length** of the lens.

Slide projectors contain convex lenses. The lens produces an image of the slide on a screen. The image can be seen without looking through the lens. Is such an image a real or virtual image?

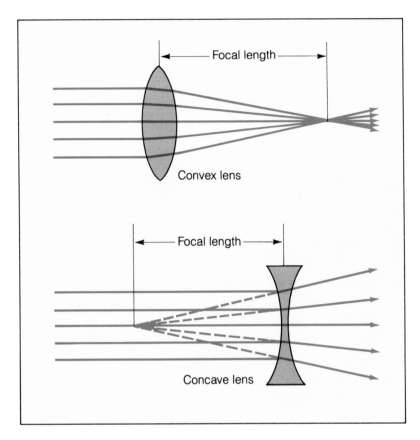

Figure 7-11. The focal length of a convex lens (top) and a concave lens (bottom).

A convex lens can be used as a magnifying glass. When it is held close to an object, an enlarged image is seen. The image is on the same side of the lens as the object and is a virtual image. In order to see a virtual image, you must look through the lens.

A lens that is thinner in the middle than at the edge is called a **concave lens**. A concave lens makes parallel rays of light spread out as if they were coming from a single point. The distance between this point and the center of the lens is the focal length of the lens. Whether the object is close to or far from a concave lens, the image is always virtual. It is also closer to the lens and smaller than the object.

### Library research

Read about telescopes and write a report about them. Include a description of the difference between refracting and reflecting telescopes. Explain why the largest telescopes are reflecting telescopes.

### Check yourself

What type of lens can form a real image of an object?

### The human eye

Light that enters the human eye is refracted so that real images form on the **retina** (RET′-ih-nuh) at the back of the eye. The retina contains nerve cells sensitive to light. Messages about the images are carried to the brain by a nerve attached to the retina.

The front of the eye is covered by tough, transparent tissue called the **cornea** (KOR′-nee-uh). Light is refracted as it passes through the cornea. In a person with perfect eyesight, the cornea forms images of distant objects on the retina.

The colored part of the eye is called the **iris** (Ī′-ris). In the center of the iris is an opening, called the **pupil**, which appears black. The pupil can change size, and this affects how much light can enter the eye. Would you expect a person's pupils to be larger in bright sunlight or in a dim room?

Just behind the pupil is a sac of jelly known as the **lens**. Muscles attached to the lens can cause it to thicken when a

**Main Idea**

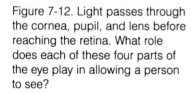

What is the cornea, and what is its function?

Figure 7-12. Light passes through the cornea, pupil, and lens before reaching the retina. What role does each of these four parts of the eye play in allowing a person to see?

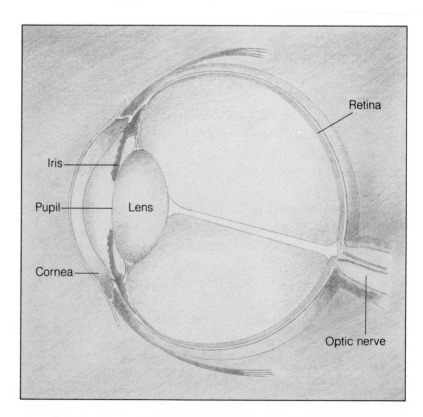

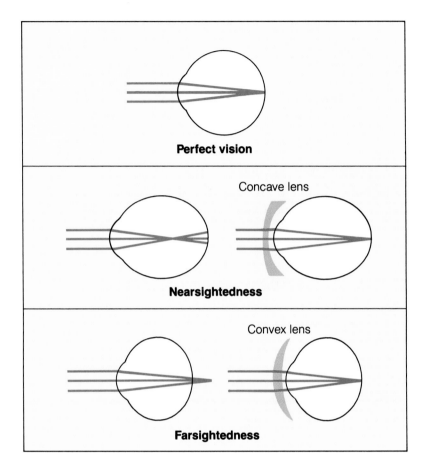

Perfect vision

Concave lens

**Nearsightedness**

Convex lens

**Farsightedness**

Figure 7-13. If the eyeball is too long, images form in front of the retina (nearsightedness). If the eyeball is too short, images form behind the retina (farsightedness). What shape lens can correct each problem?

person is looking at nearby objects. Refraction of light by the thickened lens allows images of nearby objects to form on the retina. The thickening changes the focal length of the cornea and lens combination.

Persons who are **nearsighted** have eyeballs that are too long. See Figure 7-13. Images of distant objects form in front of the retina. Persons who are **farsighted** have eyeballs that are too short. Images of distant objects form behind the retina. Eyeglasses or contact lenses can correct a person's vision so that the images form right on the retina.

### Check yourself

What two parts of the eye refract light and form images on the retina?

## The speed of light

How fast does light travel? Light seems to take no time at all to get from one point to another. It is now known that it does take some time for light to travel. Light travels so fast, however, that it is difficult to measure the time unless the distance is very great.

Light travels fastest in empty space. Its speed in empty space is about 300 000 000 m/s. It moves very slightly slower in gases, such as air. In liquids and transparent solids, the change in speed is more marked. Even so, the speed is always very great.

Light travels so fast that its speed is difficult to comprehend. A beam of light could travel more than seven times the distance around the equator in one second. It takes only a little over a second for light to travel from the moon to the earth. Light from the sun reaches the earth in just over eight minutes.

**Main Idea**

Where does light travel fastest?

## Our Science Heritage

### Measuring the Speed of Light

Measuring the speed of a moving object is normally quite easy. The distance traveled by the object during some time interval is determined. Measuring the speed of light, however, presents problems. Light travels so fast that early observers thought it took no time at all for light to get from one place to another.

The first evidence that light had a travel time was found by Olaus Roemer (1633–1710). Roemer was a Danish astronomer who was observing the four large moons of Jupiter. A moon would disappear from view, or be eclipsed, when it moved behind Jupiter. Several days later, as it traveled around the planet, the moon would be eclipsed again. Roemer discovered that the time between eclipses of the same moon was greater during the months when the earth was moving away from Jupiter. He concluded that light from Jupiter's moons was taking longer to reach the earth because the light had farther to travel. He said that it took 22 min for light to cross the earth's orbit around the sun. (We now know it takes only 16 min.) Another scientist divided his own value for the distance by Roemer's time value. He concluded that light traveled at 200 000 km/s.

In the 1920s, Albert A. Michelson (1852–1931), an American physicist, made a very accurate measurement of the speed of light. He used a rotating eight-sided mirror. One side of the mirror reflected a beam of light to a flat mirror 35 km away. The

| Substance | Speed of light, in millions of m/s | Percent of speed in empty space |
|---|---|---|
| Empty space | 300 | 100% |
| Air | 300 | 99 + % |
| Water | 223 | 74% |
| Glass | 200 | 67% |
| Diamond | 124 | 41% |

Table 7-1. The speed of light in different substances.

The speed of sound in air is about 300 m/s. The speed of light is about one million times the speed of sound. Can you explain why you see lightning before you hear the thunder that accompanies it?

When light passes from air into water or glass, it slows down. At the same time, it changes direction. The reason for the change in direction can be explained by the following analogy. Suppose there is a piece of carpet in the center of a

reflected beam returned to a different side of the eight-sided mirror and was reflected to the observer. The mirror was rotated at a speed so that it would make one-eighth of a revolution while the light traveled the 70-km distance. The rate of revolution of the mirror could be determined. The small interval of time needed for light to travel the 70-km distance could be found from the rate of revolution. Dividing 70 km by this time interval gave the speed of light as just under 300 000 km/s.

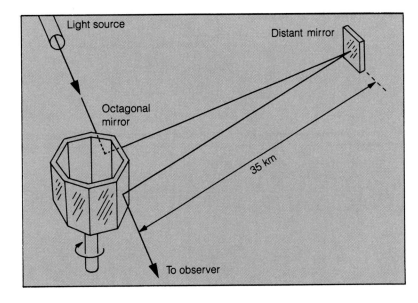

Michelson's eight-sided mirror rotated as light traveled 70 km round trip.

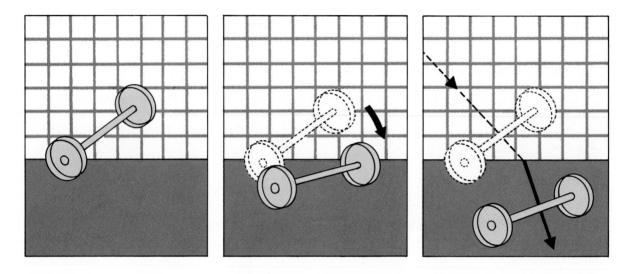

Figure 7-14. The stroller wheel that reaches the carpet first is slowed down and causes the stroller to turn. How is this like the refraction of light passing from air into water?

linoleum floor. You wheel a stroller on its two rear wheels across the linoleum toward the carpet. There is more friction when you reach the carpet, and the wheels slow down. If you cross the carpet at an angle, one wheel rolls onto the carpet before the other. The wheel on the carpet moves more slowly than the one on the floor. The stroller turns because the wheel remaining on the floor moves in a curve around the wheel on the carpet.

For a light beam that crosses from air into water at an angle, air is like the linoleum floor. Water is like the carpet. The light beam is turned just as the stroller wheels are.

### Check yourself

How does the speed of light compare with the speed of sound in air?

### Brightness and distance

Imagine that you are in a room lit only by a candle. You find a note on the floor. In order to read the note, you hold it close to the candle. Otherwise, there would not be enough light on the note. The brightness of the light depends on how far you are from the candle.

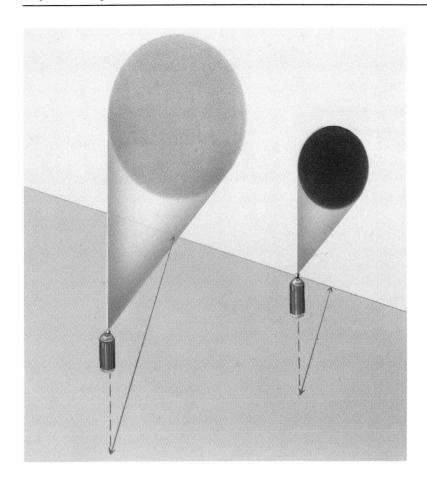

Figure 7-15. In what way is light that reaches a surface like paint that is sprayed on the surface?

Light, like sound, spreads out equally in all directions. As it does, the same amount of light spreads over a much greater area. Light acts like paint that is sprayed on a wall. The farther the sprayer is from the wall, the more spread out and thin the coating of paint will be. The farther a surface is from a light source, the dimmer the light is that reaches that surface.

A light meter can be used to measure the change in brightness of light at different distances from the source. Moving twice as far from the source decreases the brightness to, not half, but only one fourth the first brightness. Moving ten times as far away decreases the brightness to only one hundredth. Light from a source becomes very much dimmer as you move away from the source.

### Check yourself

Suppose you measure the brightness of a light source when you are 50 cm from the source. How far from the source would you expect to find the light only one fourth as bright?

Photographers rely on lenses and light meters in photographing subjects.

**Photographer** Photographers find work in many locations. Some work in commercial studios, while others work for newspapers and magazines or for government agencies. Many photographers work freelance, selling their pictures to magazines and other customers. Some colleges and universities employ photographers as teachers. About one-third of all photographers are self-employed.

Artistic and creative skills, along with the ability to meet the public, are requirements for the work of a photographer. Good color vision and manual dexterity are also necessary assets for a person working in this field.

The possibilities for preparing to become a photographer are extremely varied. Some aspiring photographers may work as assistants in on-the-job training for two to three years. Others attend art schools and colleges that offer special programs. Specialized training is needed where photography is to be used in a field such as science or medicine. High school chemistry and physics courses provide good background for the specialized training and for understanding the photographic process.

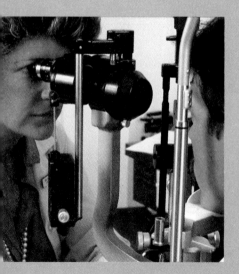

The condition of a person's eye can be studied by looking through an instrument like the one shown.

**Optometrist** Optometrists do eye examinations. They can prescribe glasses, contact lenses, or other treatment that does not involve drugs or surgery. Many optometrists have their own practice. Some work in partnership with one or more other members of the profession. Others may work in hospitals. Some have a practice for particular groups, such as the elderly.

Many demands are placed on an optometrist. He or she must be able to work with detail and with precision. Problem-solving ability is necessary for success. The capacity to deal effectively with individual patients is required. Maintaining a private practice requires additional business skills.

Preparation for a career as an optometrist is accomplished by completing an accredited four-year program in a college of optometry. A state board examination must be passed before a person may practice optometry. Specialized work in the field usually requires an advanced degree. High school biology and physics courses are good preparation for a career in optometry.

# Practical Science

## The Camera's Eye

A camera provides the means to record visual images. It directs the light energy that passes through it onto light-sensitive film. By means of chemical processing, the images on the film can be transferred to special paper. Visual images can then be preserved.

Cameras have been in use for centuries. Modern cameras range from pocket-size and fully automatic to large ones requiring expert manipulation.

Every camera has four basic parts: the body, the film holder, the shutter, and the lens.

The body is a light-proof black box that keeps unwanted light away from the film.

The film holder keeps the film in place.

The shutter acts like an eyelid. The rate at which it "blinks" is called the *shutter speed.* Shutter speed controls exposure time. Exposure time is the amount of time the shutter is open and allowing light to enter the camera. Exposure time can be varied on most cameras from a thousandth of a second to half a second. Being able to vary exposure time helps a photographer compensate for variable levels of available light. The longer the exposure time, the longer light can enter the camera.

The lens of a camera is like the lens of an eye. It focuses the light let in by the shutter.

Behind the lens is a shield called the *iris.* The iris of a camera functions like the iris of an eye. It contains a hole called the *aperture.* The size of the aperture can be made larger and smaller. Most cameras have a control to choose the appropriate aperture size. The aperture control settings are called *f-stops.*

Many cameras have a photoelectric cell, or light meter. Light striking this battery-powered device causes a needle to move along an indicator scale. The scale usually has f-stop markings and also sometimes shutter speed markings. The light meter indicates the appropriate f-stop and shutter speed settings to use to take a properly exposed photo.

**From camera to film** Once light has passed through the aperture it strikes the film. The film is coated with light-sensitive silver compounds. More chemical changes occur in the film when more light energy strikes it. Light-colored objects reflect more light energy than dark-colored objects. Therefore, more chemical changes occur on the part of the film where the light-colored image is focused than where the dark-colored image is focused.

**From film to paper** Film must be developed in total darkness. Any additional light would ruin the images already on it. Chemicals are used to further develop the film. The images on the film are called negatives. The film negatives are translated into positives by shining light through the film onto light sensitive paper. The visual images seen through the camera's eye then become permanent photographs.

**Something to try** Look at your camera or one belonging to a friend. Identify as many parts as you can. Note if there is a light meter. If there is, does it indicate both f-stop and shutter speed settings? Does your camera focus automatically or do you have to adjust the lens? When and why do you need to use a flash?

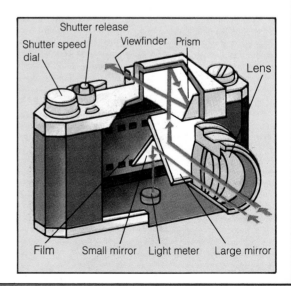

Shutter release
Shutter speed dial
Viewfinder  Prism
Lens
Film  Small mirror  Light meter  Large mirror

## Section 1 Review   Chapter 7

### Check Your Vocabulary

| | |
|---|---|
| concave lens | real image |
| convex lens | refraction |
| cornea, lens | retina |
| opaque | translucent |
| pupil | virtual image |
| ray | |

*Match each term above with the numbered phrase that best describes it.*

1. Line that shows the path a narrow beam of light takes
2. Bending of the path of light when it enters a different substance
3. Formed by both flat and concave mirrors
4. Controls the amount of light that enters the eye
5. The parts of the eye that refract light
6. The part of the eye that contains nerve cells sensitive to light
7. Unable to transmit light
8. Transmits some but not all light that arrives
9. Is thicker in the middle than at the edge
10. Can be seen on a screen
11. Spreads out parallel rays so that they appear to be coming from a single point

### Check Your Knowledge

*Multiple Choice: Choose the answer that best completes each of the following sentences.*

1. Compared to dark-colored objects, light-colored objects _?_.
   a) transmit more light
   b) transmit less light
   c) reflect more light
   d) reflect less light

2. When an object is in front of a flat mirror, _?_.
   a) a virtual image is formed in front of the mirror
   b) a virtual image is formed behind the mirror
   c) a real image is formed in front of the mirror
   d) a real image is formed behind the mirror

3. Light is refracted when it _?_.
   a) passes from water to air
   b) bounces off a flat surface
   c) bounces off a curved surface
   d) moves through empty space

4. Compared to the speed of sound, the speed of light is _?_.
   a) slightly less
   b) about the same
   c) slightly greater
   d) much greater

### Check Your Understanding

1. Are you more likely to get sunburned if you sunbathe on a light-colored or dark-colored blanket? Explain.
2. If you look into a store window on a sunny day, you will see your reflection. How can glass act like a mirror if it is transparent to light?
3. Describe what happens to light from the time it reaches the eye until it reaches the nerve cells sensitive to light.
4. What happens to a stroller when it rolls from a carpet to a linoleum floor at an angle? What behavior of light is like the behavior of the stroller?

### Practical Science

1. What does the lens of a camera do?
2. What does a light meter of a camera indicate?

# **Color**   Section 2

**Section 2 of Chapter 7 is divided into five parts:**

Colored and white light

The color spectrum

Seeing color

Animals and color

Colors from scattered light

*Practical Science: The Printer's Ink*

**Learning Objectives**

1. To recognize that an object's color, in most cases, is due to the light reflected by the object.

2. To explain how the human eye "sees" colored objects.

3. To describe how the blue appearance of the sky and water is produced.

Figure 7-16. Imagine how much harder it would be to describe the flowers in the field if you could not mention what color they were.

One of the first things you notice when you look at something is its color. You choose clothing for its color as well as its style and fit. You refer to things by their colors—the green book, the blue car, the yellow house on the corner.

## Colored and white light

**Data Search**

What percent of solar radiation is reflected from a green forest? Search page 560.

Most objects reflect light, rather than give off their own light. The light reflected from an object makes the object appear to have a color. The color depends not only on the object but on the light that strikes the object. Objects look different in bright sunlight and inside stores. They look different under fluorescent lighting and under incandescent lighting (the kind provided by common light bulbs).

In a photo taken under red light, the lightest objects are those that reflect the most red light. When the same objects are photographed under green light, the lightest objects are those that reflect the most green light. The objects that reflect the most red are not the same as the ones that reflect the most green. An object that normally looks red reflects more red light than green light.

A single colored light makes objects appear either black or the same color as the light. Sunlight, on the other hand, allows all the colors to be seen. Sunlight is an example of **white light,** a mixture of all colors of light. Under white light, different colors are reflected from objects. A red object reflects red light, while a green object reflects green light.

Figure 7-17. These photos were taken with (left) no filter; (center) a green filter; (right) a red filter. How do the tomatoes appear in the three photos?

## Activity 7–2A          Using Colored Light

### Materials

flashlight
construction paper of all the following colors:
    white, black, red, green, blue
cellophane of the following colors: red,
    green, blue
transparent tape

### Purpose

To show how colored objects appear under colored light.

### Procedure

1. In large lettering, write the name of the color of each piece of construction paper on the paper itself. Overlap the red, green, and blue pieces of paper. Place the white and black pieces on either side of them as shown. Tape the papers together in place.
2. Make a table like the one shown. Tape red cellophane over the lens of a flashlight. Carry out the rest of this activity in a dark room.
3. Shine the flashlight with the red cellophane cover onto the colored papers you taped together. Observe what color each of the papers appears to be. Indicate if the colored paper appears darker. Record your observations on your table.
4. Replace the red cellophane with green cellophane. Predict what color each piece of paper will be under the green flashlight beam. Test your predictions, and record on the table the color each piece of paper appears to be.
5. Replace the green cellophane with blue cellophane, and repeat Step 4.

### Questions

1. What color light is transmitted by the red cellophane? The blue cellophane? The green cellophane?

2. Under the red beam of light, does the red paper appear to be more like the white paper or the black paper? Why?
3. What color change takes place in the white paper under the green light? Under the blue light? Why?
4. What color change takes place in the black paper under each of the different colored lights? Why?
5. How do the green and blue papers appear under the red light? Why?

### Conclusion

How do colored objects appear under different colored lights?

| Paper color | Apparent color of paper | | |
| --- | --- | --- | --- |
| | With red cellophane | With green cellophane | With blue cellophane |
| White | | | |
| Black | | | |
| Red | | | |
| Green | | | |
| Blue | | | |

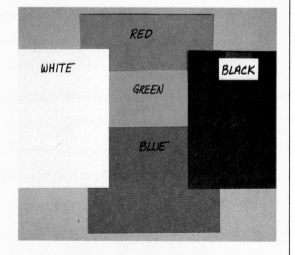

Colored cellophane acts like a filter for colors. Red cellophane, for example, transmits red light but filters out other colors. What would green cellophane do to red light? How would a red strawberry look if you put green cellophane in front of your eye?

### Check yourself

1. What color light does a blue object reflect?
2. What color does a green object appear under red light?

### The color spectrum

Objects appear colored when they reflect colored light. Since they look colored under white light, white light must contain colors. It is possible to split white light into a group of colors called the **color spectrum** (SPEK'-trum). The spectrum is a band of colors starting with red and including orange, yellow, green, blue, and violet.

Figure 7-18. When white light passes through a prism, it is split into a band of colored light.

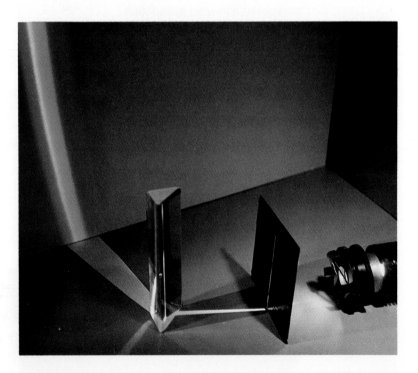

Figure 7-19. In a rainbow, which color is on the outside of the curve? Which color is on the inside?

An easy way to split white light into a spectrum is to pass the light through a **prism** (PRIZ′-um). Commonly, prisms are made of solid glass or plastic and have triangular ends. Light is refracted when it enters one side and again when it comes out another side. The colors in white light do not refract equally. Red light bends the least, while violet light bends the most. The colors leave the prism at slightly different angles. They can be seen if a white surface is placed in their path.

A rainbow is a color spectrum that is caused by refraction of sunlight by water drops in the air. For you to see a rainbow, the sun must be behind you, and the air ahead of you must be moist. Each point on the rainbow you see is caused by the interaction of sunlight with a different drop of water. Sometimes only a short length of rainbow is visible. In these cases, there are not any water drops in the right positions to create the missing portions.

You do not have to wait until it rains in order to see a rainbow. On a sunny day, you can make a rainbow with the spray from a garden hose. Direct the spray into the air, away from the sun, and look for the rainbow. Try this in the early morning or late afternoon, when the sun is low in the sky.

**Main Idea**

What is a prism, and what does it do to white light?

Figure 7-20. Beams of red light, green light, and blue light can produce white light where they come together.

If white light can be split into colors, can colored light be mixed to make white light? Look at Figure 7-20. Three projectors are throwing light on a screen. One projects red light. The other two project green and blue light. The projectors can be moved closer or farther to adjust the brightness of each beam on the screen. Projector positions can be found so that the red, green, and blue beams will produce a spot of white light.

### Check yourself

1. Name two ways light can be split into a band of colors.
2. How can beams of blue, red, and green light be used to make white light?

### Seeing color

Light that enters the eye is absorbed by the retina, at the back of the eye. The cells in the retina which are sensitive to color are the **cones**. The cones are closest together near the center of the retina. Thus, the center is most sensitive to color.

## Activity 7–2B    Combining Colors

### Materials

3 flashlights or slide projectors
cellophane or filters: red, green, blue
transparent tape
white screen or wall
colored pencils (optional)

### Purpose

To show if white light can be made from colored light.

### Procedure

1. Cover each flashlight lens with a different color cellophane or filter. Tape the cellophane or filters securely in place.
2. Direct the three beams of colored light to the same spot on a white wall or screen. Observe the color where all three beams overlap. If it seems reddish, move the red light source farther back. If the spot seems greenish or bluish, move that color back.
3. Move the beams of light so that only two of them overlap. Record the results.

### Questions

1. What color light appears on the screen where the three beams of colored light overlap?
2. What color appears on the screen where the blue and green light beams overlap? Where the red and blue light beams overlap?
3. What combination of colored lights make the screen appear orange?

### Conclusion

How can white light be made from colored lights?

| Colors of light beams | Color where light beams overlap on screen |
|---|---|
| Red, green, blue | |
| Blue, green | |
| Red, blue | |
| | Orange |

There are materials in the cones sensitive to red, green, or blue light. Each cone contains only one kind of this material. Thus, some cones absorb red light, some absorb green light, and some absorb blue light.

When a mixture of light of different colors enters our eyes, we see the mixture as a single color. For example, a mixture of red light and blue light looks purple. In contrast, we can hear two distinct notes played on a piano at the same time. If our sight were like our hearing, we would see the red and blue, not the purple. We would not need to use a prism in order to see the colors in white light.

Most colors that we see around us are really mixtures. The cones in the retina respond to the red, green, and blue in the mixture. The brain interprets the cones' response as a single color.

### Library research

During the late nineteenth century, a style of painting known as impressionism developed among artists in France. Find out how the impressionist painters used color differently from other artists.

## Library research

When you enter a dark movie theater, you probably have trouble seeing the seats at first. After a while, your eyes adjust to the darkness and you can see much better. Find out what happens inside your eyes that allows them to adjust to darkness.

About 8 percent of males and 1.5 percent of females have trouble telling red from green. They are said to be **colorblind**. Their condition seems to be due to a lack of either red-absorbing or green-absorbing material in the cones. A few people lack the blue-absorbing material and have a different kind of colorblindness.

The retina also contains **rods**, cells which are very sensitive to low levels of light but not to color. In dim light, you use your rods to see. You can see light and dark but you cannot see color. Almost all the objects in the night sky appear colorless to the eye, even through telescopes, because the eye receives so little light from them. Yet, when they are photographed through telescopes and exposed to color film for a long time, beautiful colors can be seen.

The cones are more sensitive than the rods to detail. That is why you see most clearly out of the center of your eyes. But the rods are very quick to detect motion. You can notice something moving out of the side of your eye even if you cannot tell what it is or what color it is.

Because of the way the human eye sees color, color pictures can be printed in books with only four colors of ink. All the pictures in this book are printed in tiny dots of these four ink colors. One ink color is a purple-pink known as magenta.

Figure 7-21. The dots of colored ink in printed pictures look like these under magnification. What combination of the four ink colors produces green? Red-orange?

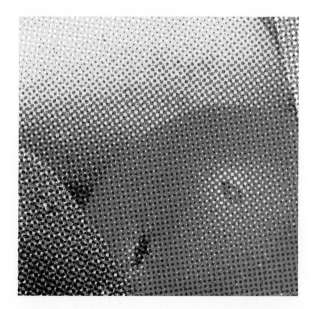

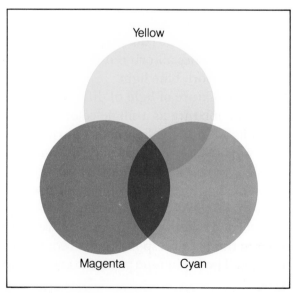

Magenta ink absorbs green light but reflects other colors. One ink color is a yellow that absorbs blue light but reflects other colors. One ink color is a blue-green known as cyan. Cyan ink absorbs red light but reflects other colors. The fourth ink color is black, which absorbs all colors.

When the ink colors overlap, more than one color is absorbed. The light that is reflected combines to look different from either ink color. For example, the overlap of magenta and cyan absorbs both green and red. The result looks blue-purple. Figure 7-21 shows how magenta, cyan, and yellow look when they overlap. All three together produce a brownish black. Black ink is used when a purer black is desired.

Paints work just a little differently from inks. You may have been taught that you could make all colors from red, yellow, and blue paint. In truth, you can make most, but not all, colors from these three.

Your impression of the color of a surface is affected by more than the colors of light the surface reflects. It is strongly affected by the surrounding background, as well. Look at the purple squares in Figure 7-22. Does one look darker than the other? Which one?

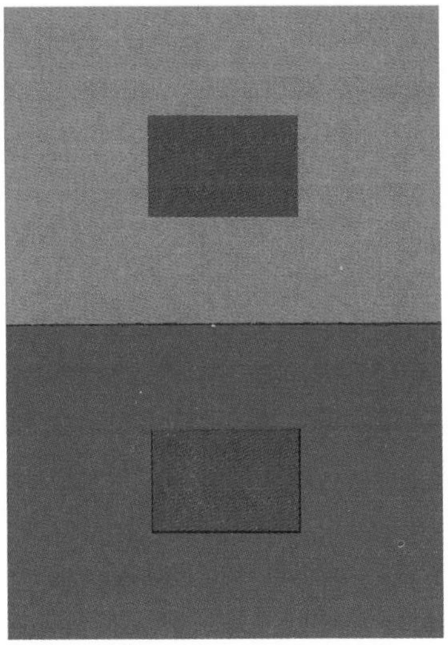

Figure 7-22. What differences do you see in the two purple squares? Does the background affect how you see color?

## Check yourself

1. What things are cone, but not rod, cells sensitive to?

2. What four colors of ink are used in printing colored pictures in books?

## Animals and color

Although humans can see color, most mammals cannot. The only other mammals whose eyes can distinguish color are the apes, monkeys, and other primates.

Bees, butterflies, fish, reptiles, and birds can see color. Bees do not see the same range of colors that humans do. They cannot see red. However, they can see **ultraviolet**, which is light beyond violet. The ultraviolet in the sun's radiation is what tans (or sunburns) our skin. Bees can see differences in two white flowers that reflect different amounts of ultraviolet.

## Main Idea

What is ultraviolet, and what effect does it have on humans?

Figure 7-23. The color of flowers enables bees to find flowers.

Why do bees visit red roses if they cannot see red? Most red flowers reflect blue light as well as red. The bees see the blue. There are a few red flowers that do not reflect blue or even ultraviolet. These flowers would look black to a bee, just like a dark shadow. The bees do not visit these flowers, but hummingbirds, which do see red, visit them.

The color patterns of butterflies, fish, reptiles, and birds enable them to find their own kind. Some animals have colors that make them blend with their background. Such colors protect them from their enemies. The viceroy butterfly is protected by the fact that it looks like the monarch butterfly. The monarch tastes unpleasant to birds, but the viceroy does not. Birds learn to avoid anything with that color pattern.

**Check yourself**

1. How does a bee's ability to see color differ from a human's?
2. Name two ways body color can be helpful to an animal.

**Colors from scattered light**

On a clear day, the sky is blue. Why does it have a color, when sunlight contains all colors? The atmosphere contains molecules of air and water, as well as tiny dust particles. The molecules and dust particles **scatter** light, or redirect it in all directions. As sunlight passes through the atmosphere, more blue and violet light is scattered than other colors. Thus, much of the blue and violet light reaches our eyes from all directions in the atmosphere. This produces a blue sky. The sun looks yellow, but we are really seeing a mixture of green, yellow, orange, and red light coming from the sun.

Clouds are made of small drops of water. These drops are much bigger than air and water molecules. The drops scatter all colors of sunlight equally. As a result, clouds appear white.

When the sun is very low in the sky, at sunrise or sunset, it looks orange or red. Sunlight must travel through a thicker layer of atmosphere to reach us at these times. The green and yellow light is scattered out, as well as the blue and violet. Only the orange and red light remains.

**Main Idea**

What causes sunlight to be scattered?

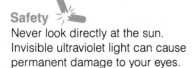

Safety
Never look directly at the sun. Invisible ultraviolet light can cause permanent damage to your eyes.

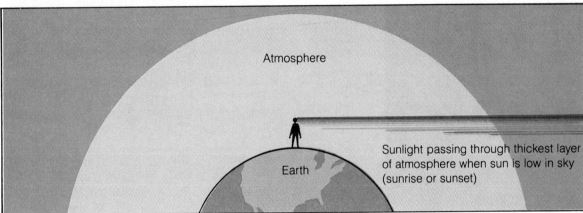

The sky at sunrise or sunset looks spectacular when there are clouds near (but not in front of) the sun. The orange and red light from the sun is reflected off the clouds. The clouds appear bright orange, pink, and red.

Figure 7-24. What makes the sun and clouds look orange and red when the sun is very low in the sky?

Water, like air, is colorless in small amounts. Deep lakes, however, are a brilliant blue. Water absorbs most colors of sunlight to some extent. The deeper the water, the more sunlight is absorbed. Blue is the last color to be absorbed. In a deep lake, the blue light that is not absorbed is scattered by the water molecules. Some is scattered upward and can be seen by someone looking at the lake.

When the water is full of microscopic living things or mud, light cannot pass deeply. Water that has these things may take on their color, which is often green or brown.

### Check yourself

What colors of sunlight are best able to pass through the atmosphere without being scattered?

# Practical Science

## The Printer's Ink

If you were a printer, which color ink would you choose to print black words on a sheet of paper? You would choose black ink, of course. Suppose you want to print the headlines in some other color. You would then choose an ink color from a color chart. These are called *mechanical colors*. There are hundreds of mechanical, or standard colors of inks available to printers. These mechanical colors are selected from a catalogue. The catalogue contains a printed chip of each color. The chips are similar to the paint color samples you see in a paint store.

How would you print a picture in full color like the ones in this book? You would use inks that are colored cyan, yellow, magenta, and black. These are called *process colors*. Process colors are the color elements of four color printing.

**Halftone screens** Look at some of the full-color pictures in this book with a magnifying glass. Notice that the color you see depends both on the colors and sizes of the dots. A *halftone screen* creates the dots you see in the pictures. It has a mesh pattern like a window screen, but much finer. A small mesh pattern will produce sharp pictures like the ones in this book. A larger mesh produces fuzzier pictures like those seen in newspapers.

The actual screen can be lines ruled on glass or a photographic image made from a glass screen. The photographic image is called a contact screen and is used for four-color separations.

**Color separation** There are several steps to four-color printing, which can be seen in the diagram. The first step in four-color printing is to make four photographic color negatives from a color slide of the picture. All the negatives are exposed using a halftone screen to make the dot pattern. One negative is exposed through a special filter that produces a black-and-white negative. The negative is used to make a positive printing plate. This plate prints with black ink in the shadow areas of the picture. The shadows would have a brownish color without the black ink.

The other three negatives are made by exposing them separately through red, green, and blue filters. The blue filter produces a negative that records all the blue light. The positive printing plate made from this will record the red and green colors in the picture. These are additive colors that produce yellow, so the plate prints with yellow ink.

Similarly, the negative exposed through the red filter produces a positive plate that records blue and green. This plate prints with cyan ink. The negative exposed through the green filter produces a plate that records blue and red. This plate prints with magenta ink.

**Something to try** Look at the drawing in Figure 7-24 through a magnifying glass. Notice the size of the blue dots in the atmosphere. They are much smaller than the blue dots in the Earth's ocean. This is why the blue of the atmosphere seems paler than the blue of the oceans even though the dots are the same color blue.

The amount of light passing through a contact screen determines the dot area. Light areas on the original picture will print with small dots, or a low percentage of dot area. Dark areas will print with large dots, or a large percentage of dot area. In the language of printers, this is called the *screen percentage*.

90%

50%

10%

**Three halftone screens of cyan**

# Section 2 Review   Chapter 7

## Check Your Vocabulary

| | |
|---|---|
| color spectrum | rod |
| colorblind | scatter |
| cone | ultraviolet |
| prism | white light |

*Match each term above with the numbered phrase that best describes it.*

1. Redirect in all directions

2. Can split white light into colors

3. The band of colors in white light

4. Unable to see all colors

5. Is not totally absorbed by any color filter

6. Cell in the retina that is sensitive to color but not to dim light

7. Cell in the retina that is sensitive to dim light but not to color

8. The part of sunlight that can be seen by bees but not humans

## Check Your Knowledge

*Multiple Choice: Choose the answer that best completes each of the following sentences.*

1. Objects that produce no light of their own but appear red must ?.
   a) absorb red light
   b) absorb all colors of light equally
   c) reflect or transmit red light
   d) reflect or transmit green and blue light

2. White light separates into colors when it enters a prism because ?.
   a) the colors in white light are bent different amounts
   b) the colors in white light are reflected in different directions
   c) some colors in white light are scattered more easily than others
   d) the colors in white light speed up by different amounts when they move from air into glass

3. Under blue light, a piece of red paper will appear ?.
   a) red            c) white
   b) blue           d) black

4. Besides black, the colors of ink used in printing color pictures are ?.
   a) red, yellow, and blue
   b) red, green, and blue
   c) magenta, yellow, and cyan
   d) magenta, green, and cyan

5. The sky looks blue because the atmosphere ?.
   a) transmits only blue light
   b) absorbs blue and violet light
   c) scatters blue and violet light
   d) scatters all colors of light except blue and violet

## Check Your Understanding

1. In some supermarkets, the lighting over the produce is green, and the lighting over the meat is red. How does this affect the appearance of the produce and meat?

2. Clear glass transmits all the colors in sunlight that humans can see, but it filters out ultraviolet. Can you get sunburned through a closed glass window? Explain your answer.

3. To astronauts above the earth's atmosphere, the sky appears black, even when the sun is visible. Explain what causes the sky to be black.

## Practical Science

1. Name the four process colors.

2. For what kind of printing are process colors used?

# Models for Light    Section 3

**Section 3 of Chapter 7 is divided into seven parts:**

Light as energy

Transverse waves

How water waves behave

Evidence for light as a wave

Polarized light

Electromagnetic energy

The nature of light

*Practical Science: Radio Waves*

## Learning Objectives

1.  To recognize that light is a form of energy and travels from one place to another.

2.  To describe the characteristics and behaviors of transverse waves.

3.  To compare the particle and wave models of light and the properties of light that support each model.

4.  To identify the types of radiation that are a part of the electromagnetic spectrum.

Figure 7-25. One model for light describes light as the movement of waves against the shore.

What is light? Is there a model that can explain the behavior of light? The behavior of light can be summarized as follows.

☐ Light travels in straight lines until it comes to a surface.

☐ When light strikes a smooth surface, it is reflected at an equal angle.

☐ When light crosses the boundary between one transparent material and another at an angle, it is refracted; that is, it changes direction.

☐ Sunlight and other white light can be broken up into several colors.

☐ The colors in sunlight are refracted by different amounts, with red refracted least and violet most.

☐ Light can travel through empty space.

## Light as energy

In some ways, light is similar to heat. Heat and light are released together in some chemical reactions, including burning. When an electric light bulb is turned on, the wires inside give off both heat and light.

Heat is a form of energy. Is there evidence that light, too, is a form of energy? Energy causes changes in things. There are changes that happen only when light is present. Plants need light in order to make food from carbon dioxide and water. They cannot make food in darkness. Light causes a change in photographic film, so that an image is recorded. Sunlight triggers reactions that change some of the products in auto exhausts into poisons.

Light, then, like heat, must be a form of energy. Like heat, it can travel from one place to another.

There are two basic ways energy can travel. Energy can be carried by moving objects. A baseball carries energy from the batter toward the fielder. Energy can also be carried by a wave. When sound moves through air, the air molecules move back and forth but do not move with the wave.

Light, unlike sound, can travel through empty space. Light from the stars—including the closest star, the sun—travels

Figure 7-26. When an electric heating element is turned on, it gives off both heat and light.

through empty space to the earth. Is the energy of light carried by moving particles? Or is there some kind of wave that can travel through empty space? A model for light must answer these questions.

### Check yourself

In what two ways can energy travel?

### Transverse waves

Before one can decide whether light can be a wave, one must know more about waves. Sound waves are an example of compressional waves. In a compressional wave, particles move back and forth along the direction of a wave motion.

There is another kind of wave. In a **transverse** (trans-VERS′) wave, particles move perpendicular, or crosswise, to

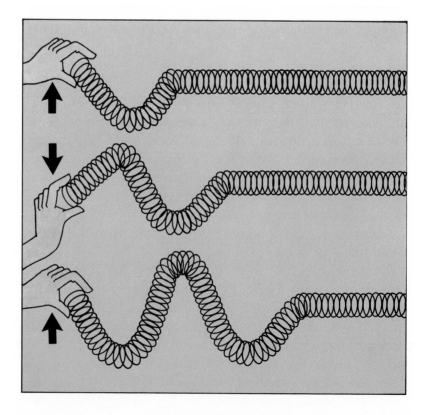

Figure 7-27. The motion of a transverse wave on a spring. From top to bottom, the wave is shown as it moves to the right.

the direction of the wave motion. Look at Figure 7-27. It shows a transverse wave in a loose wire spring. As the wave passes down the spring, the coils move from side to side. They do not move with the wave.

Water waves show how transverse waves behave. If you toss a pebble into water, a circular ripple moves outward from the pebble. As it moves, the circle gets larger. A leaf floating in the water will bob up and down as the ripple passes. But the leaf will not move outward with the ripple.

Water waves can be studied in a device called a **ripple tank**. The tank is usually a rectangular or circular transparent container on legs. A strong light source is above the tank and a white screen or paper is below it. Images of water ripples in the tank are visible on the screen or paper. The images form because the water acts like lenses when its surface is curved by the ripples.

When a metal or wood strip is dipped in the water, a straight ripple moves away from it. An electric motor can move the

**Main Idea**

What happens to a ripple that is created when a pebble is tossed into water.

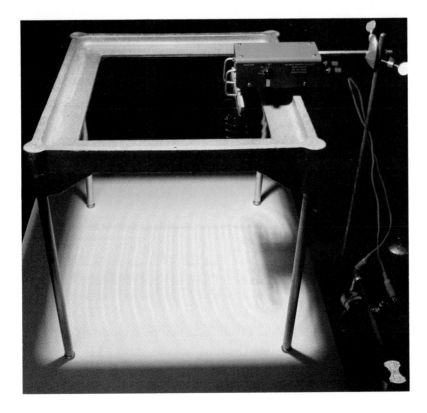

Figure 7-28. A ripple tank. An electric motor can make a metal ball or strip dip up and down at regular intervals. An image of the water wave can be seen on the screen under the tank.

## Activity 7–3A   Water Waves

### Materials

clear pan (20 cm to 30 cm across and at
    least 3 cm deep)
water
white paper
pencil
small bits of paper

### Purpose

To observe the behavior of water waves.

### Procedure

1. Place a sheet of white paper under a clear
   pan in bright light.
2. Pour water into the pan to a depth of 1 to 2
   cm. Dip the eraser end of a pencil in the
   water once. Observe the ripple that moves
   along the surface of the water. You can see
   the image of the ripple on the paper under
   the pan. The image is produced because
   light is refracted as it passes through the
   ripple. Record the shape of the ripple.
3. Dip the pencil again. Record what happens
   when the ripple reaches the side of the pan.
4. Predict how you would make a series of
   evenly spaced ripples. Test your prediction.
   If your method does not work, keep changing it until you create a series of evenly
   spaced ripples.
5. Sprinkle the surface of the water with small

bits of paper. Dip the pencil into the water.
Observe what happens to the paper.

### Questions

1. Did the ripple change shape when it hit the
   side of the pan?
2. How did the direction of motion of the ripple
   change after it hit the side of the pan?
3. How did the water at a point on the surface
   move as a ripple moved past that point?
4. Did the ripple carry the paper to the edge
   of the pan, or did the ripple move right past
   the paper?

### Conclusion

Does the water move along with a wave, or
does a wave move through the water?

**Main Idea**

What is the difference between a
crest and a trough?

strip up and down at regular intervals. A wave made of a
series of straight ripples will move away from the strip.

In a water wave, the places where the water surface is highest are the **crests**. The places where the water surface is the
lowest are the **troughs** (TROFS). The crests appear bright in
a ripple tank, while the troughs appear dark. The distance
between two neighboring crests in a wave is called the **wavelength**. The troughs are the same distance apart as the crests

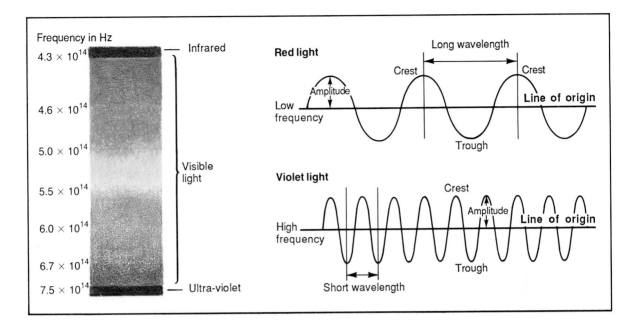

Figure 7-29. The parts of a transverse wave. A wavelength is the distance between two neighboring crests or troughs. As frequency increases, the wavelength becomes shorter.

are. The height of a crest above the normal water surface is the **amplitude** of the wave. The troughs are usually the same distance below the normal water surface.

One can count the number of crests that pass a point on the screen per second. This quantity is the **frequency** of the wave. Suppose that 18 crests pass a point in 10 s. The frequency is 18 crests divided by 10 s, or 1.8 crests per second. The SI unit for the number of things per second is the hertz (Hz). The frequency would be 1.8 Hz.

The frequency of a wave is related to the wavelength. The more crests that pass a point per second, the closer together they must be. Thus, the higher the frequency is, the shorter the wavelength must be. The waves with lower frequencies have longer wavelengths. For example, in the visible light spectrum in Figure 7-29, violet light has a shorter wavelength and a higher frequency than red light. Ultraviolet light has a shorter wavelength and a higher frequency than violet light. Infrared light has a longer wavelength and a lower frequency than red light.

**Data Search**

What color of light has a frequency of $5.3 \times 10^{14}$ Hz? Search this page.

**Check yourself**

1. Distinguish between the wavelength and the amplitude of a water wave.

2. Give the frequency, in hertz, for a wave in which 21 crests pass a point in 5 s.

## How water waves behave

When a wave in a ripple tank strikes a barrier, it is reflected. It moves away from the barrier in a different direction. A wave made by a straight strip has crests and troughs that look like straight lines. The wave moves perpendicular to the straight lines of the crests and troughs.

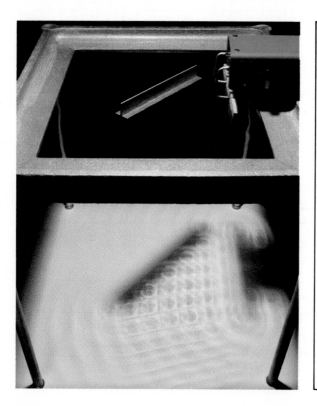

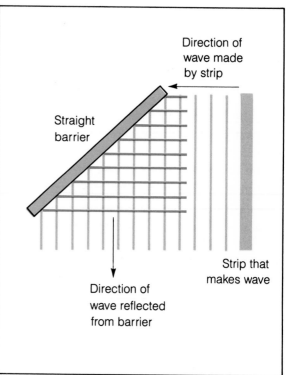

Figure 7-30 A straight water wave moves toward a barrier from the right. The reflected wave moves away from the barrier and crosses the first wave.

Look at Figure 7-30. Compare the direction of the wave before and after it strikes the straight barrier. Does the direction change in the same way as it does for a light ray that strikes a flat mirror?

A glass plate can be placed over part of the bottom of a ripple tank. In the shallow water over the glass plate, the wave slows down. Each crest does not travel as far by the time the next crest arrives at a point. As a result, the crests are closer together. If the crest is at an angle to the edge of the plate, it bends at the plate. The wave is refracted.

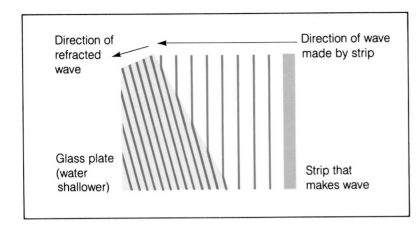

Direction of refracted wave

Direction of wave made by strip

Glass plate (water shallower)

Strip that makes wave

Figure 7-31. When a straight wave passes over a glass plate in the tank, it slows down. What happens to its direction of motion?

Look at Figure 7-31. Does the direction of the wave change in the same way as it does for light that passes from air into water?

The bending of water waves can be noticed along a beach. The water close to the beach is shallower than the water farther out. The waves moving toward the shoreline at an angle are changed in direction. This causes the wave to bend as in a ripple tank.

An interesting wave pattern is produced as follows. A piece of wood with a small notch in the top reaching below the water line is placed in the ripple tank. When a wave with straight crests reaches the wood, most of the wave is reflected. However, a wave with circular crests spreads out beyond the notch. See Figure 7-32. The notch acts like a small ball dipping into the water at regular intervals. A hole can act like a source of a circular wave.

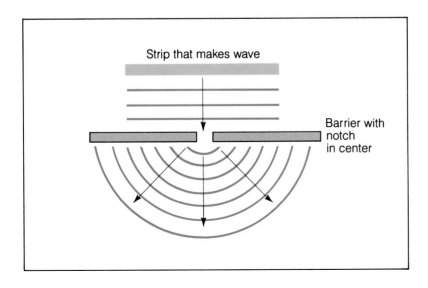

Strip that makes wave

Barrier with notch in center

Figure 7-32. A straight wave is moving toward a barrier with a small notch in it. A circular wave spreads out from the notch. The part of the wave that goes through the notch looks just like a wave made by dipping a small ball into the water.

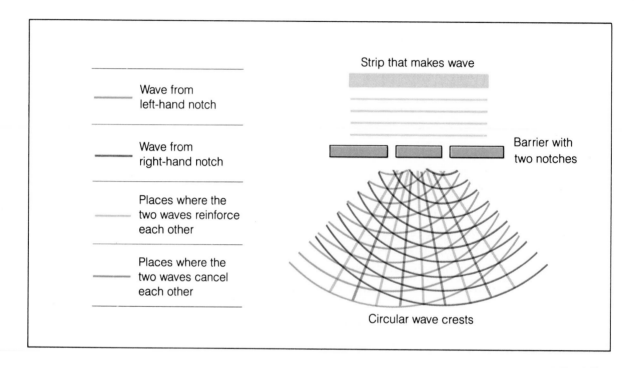

Wave from left-hand notch

Wave from right-hand notch

Places where the two waves reinforce each other

Places where the two waves cancel each other

Strip that makes wave

Barrier with two notches

Circular wave crests

Figure 7–33. The two notches create two circular waves that pass through each other. The blue lines show places where two crests or troughs reinforce each other. In between are gray lines, which show areas where a crest and a trough cancel each other.

When two notches are in a similar piece of wood, a circular wave spreads out from each notch. See Figure 7-33. The crests and troughs from each notch pass right through each other. Where two crests reach the same point, the water is twice as high. Where two troughs reach the same point, the water is twice as low. In both these cases, the two waves are said to **reinforce** (ree-in-FORS′) each other at these points. And where a crest and a trough reach the same point, the water is at its normal level. The crest and trough cancel each other.

The reinforcement or cancellation of two waves as they pass through each other is called **interference**. Despite the name, interference has no effect on the waves themselves. Each wave continues to move with the same frequency, wavelength, amplitude, and speed.

### Check yourself

1. How can refraction of water waves be demonstrated in a ripple tank?

2. What happens to two circular waves that meet?

## Evidence for light as a wave

The English scientist Thomas Young (1773–1829) was able to show that light behaves the same way as water waves. In 1800 he let light of one color pass through two tiny slits that were very close together. When the light reached a screen, dark lines could be seen within a lighted band. The dark lines were evidence that light could be cancelled. Young's experiment can be explained by the theory that light is a wave.

Have you ever noticed colors glistening from the top of a puddle of water? The colors are produced when there is some oil (or gasoline) on the ground. Oil and gasoline float on water and form a thin layer at the top of the water. The colors are additional evidence that light acts like a wave. They can be explained as follows.

When light strikes the oil surface, some is reflected from the top of the oil layer. Some passes through the oil and is then reflected from the water surface. The oil layer is very

**Main Idea**

Who was able to show that light behaves like water waves?

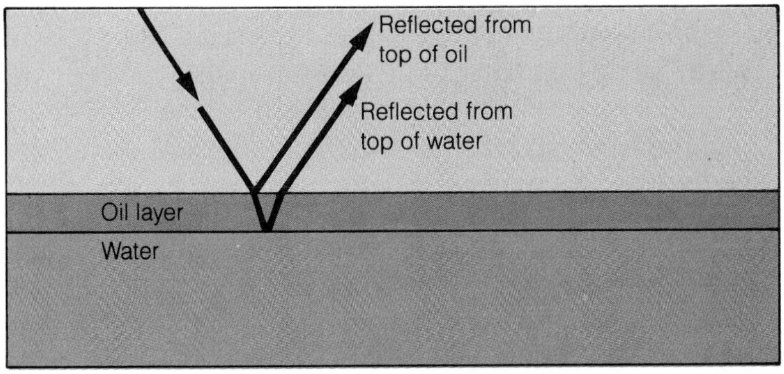

Figure 7-34. All or part of a color spectrum can be seen when a thin layer of oil or gasoline floats on water. The colors are caused by the interference of two slightly different reflected light waves— one from the top of the oil and one from the top of the water.

thin. The light reflected from the water travels only slightly farther than the light reflected from the oil. Light reflected from the water surface interferes with light reflected from the oil surface. At some places, colors are cancelled out. At other places, colors are reinforced. These are the colors you see when you look at the puddle.

The colors are not all cancelled out at the same place. Some are cancelled where others are reinforced. This observation can be explained by assuming that each color of light in white light has a different wavelength. Red light has the longest wavelength, violet the shortest. Cancellation and reinforcement depend on the wavelength of the wave. They occur at different places for the different colors in white light.

The hypothesis that each color in white light has a different wavelength can explain how a prism makes the colors visible. Recall how water waves are refracted when they slow down. Water waves slow down when they pass into a region where the water is shallower. A tiny change in water depth slows the water only slightly. The direction of the wave changes only slightly. The greater the change in depth, the more the water slows down and the more the wave is refracted.

When light passes from air into glass or water, it slows down. The colors with the shortest wavelengths (violet and blue) happen to be slowed the most. Because they are slowed the most, they are refracted the most. Each color of light is refracted differently and comes out of a prism in a slightly different direction.

**Library research**

Find out what a diffraction grating is. How does it separate white light into a color spectrum?

### Check yourself

1. How could the dark lines that appeared in Young's experiment be explained?
2. Which color in white light has the longest wavelength?

### Polarized light

Some sunglasses and filters are made of a transparent material that reduces glare from shiny surfaces. This material is called a **polarizing** (PŌ′-ler-ī-zing) **filter**.

## Activity 7–3B    Polarizing Filters

### Materials

2 polarizing filters or 2 pairs of polarizing sun glasses
book or magazine with shiny cover

### Purpose

To observe the effect polarizing filters have on light.

### Procedure

1. Look at a light source through a single polarizing filter. The light source can be a candle, light fixture, or flashlight. SAFETY NOTE: *Do not look at the sun. Looking at the sun, even through a polarizing filter, can cause permanent eye damage.*
2. Rotate the filter. Observe any changes in the brightness of the light source.
3. Place a second polarizing filter in front of the first. Look through both filters as you rotate one of them.
4. Find the position which lets the least light through the filters. Then find the position which lets the most light through the filters.
5. Place a book or magazine with a shiny cover on the desk or table in front of you. Move your head until the cover appears very shiny. Now look at the cover through a single polarizing filter.
6. Slowly rotate the filter. Find the position for which the shine disappears. Find the position for which the cover appears shiniest.

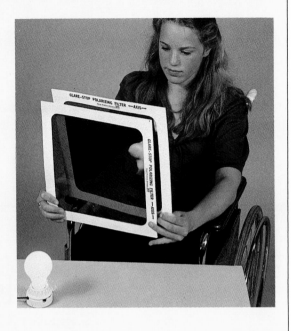

### Questions

1. Was the light from your light source polarized? How do you know?
2. Was the light reflected from the shiny cover polarized? How do you know?
3. Polarizing sunglasses are helpful in cutting the glare from the surface of roads and water. Does it matter whether the filter material is placed in the frames in a particular direction? Explain.

### Conclusion

Describe two ways that light can be polarized.

The most widely used polarizing filters consist of thin plastic sheets. Some natural mineral crystals can also polarize light. Polarizing filters are powerful tools used in science, industry, and daily life.

The effect of a polarizing filter on light can be explained in terms of a wave model of light. In this model, light moves as a transverse wave. That is, the vibrations are perpendicular, or crosswise to the direction of wave motion.

Figure 7-35. The picture at the right was shot with a polarizing filter. What effect did the filter have on the reflections?

A polarizing filter acts like a picket fence. Think of a long, loose wire spring with its center between two of the pickets in such a fence. You could send a transverse wave all the way down the spring only if you shook the spring up and down. Then the crests and troughs could move through the space in the fence. Suppose you shook the spring from side to side. When the crests and troughs reached the fence, the pickets would not let them pass through.

Light seems to move as a transverse wave with vibrations in all directions perpendicular to the direction of motion. A

Figure 7-36. A vertical wave can pass through the space between the pickets, but a horizontal wave is stopped.

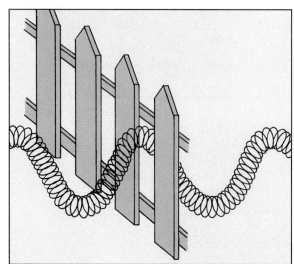
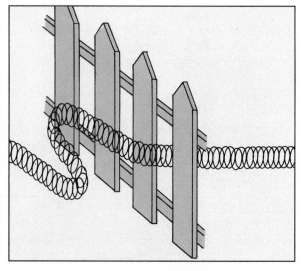

polarizing filter allows vibrations in only one direction. When light goes through the filter, only the vibrations in that direction can pass through. When the light has passed through, it is said to be **polarized**. All its vibrations are in the same direction.

What happens when polarized light strikes another polarizing filter? It can go right through if the second filter is aligned in the same direction. If it is crosswise to the original direction, the light will be stopped.

A single polarizing filter has an effect on light reflected from a shiny surface. Reflection polarizes light. It makes all the vibrations parallel to the surface. When the polarizing filter is aligned so that parallel vibrations cannot pass through, the reflected light is stopped. In this way, reflected glare is cut down.

Sound moves as a compressional wave. Its vibrations are back and forth in the direction of wave motion. A compressional wave, such as sound, cannot be polarized.

**Main Idea**

What is polarized light?

### Check yourself

What evidence supports the model that light is a transverse wave and not a compressional wave?

### Electromagnetic energy

Ultraviolet light is invisible to humans but visible to bees. It can expose camera film like ordinary light. It has all the properties of ordinary light. The only difference is that it acts like a wave with a higher frequency than visible violet.

Similarly, infrared radiation acts like a wave with a lower frequency than visible red. Humans detect it with their skin, as heat, not with their eyes. But otherwise, it acts like light. It moves from the sun to the earth like visible sunlight.

With instruments sensitive to different frequencies, scientists have been able to detect many kinds of energy similar to light. All of this energy moves as transverse waves. It all moves at the same speed as light. It can all move through empty space. The general name for energy with these properties is

**Main Idea**

How does the frequency of ultraviolet light compare to that of visible violet light?

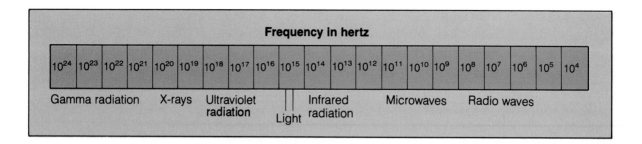

**Frequency in hertz**

| $10^{24}$ | $10^{23}$ | $10^{22}$ | $10^{21}$ | $10^{20}$ | $10^{19}$ | $10^{18}$ | $10^{17}$ | $10^{16}$ | $10^{15}$ | $10^{14}$ | $10^{13}$ | $10^{12}$ | $10^{11}$ | $10^{10}$ | $10^{9}$ | $10^{8}$ | $10^{7}$ | $10^{6}$ | $10^{5}$ | $10^{4}$ |

Gamma radiation     X-rays    Ultraviolet radiation    Light    Infrared radiation    Microwaves    Radio waves

Figure 7-37. The electromagnetic spectrum. Each mark on the frequency scale represents a frequency ten times higher than the mark to its right. The small numbers after the 10s tell how many zeros are in the number. For example, $10^8$ is 1 followed by eight zeros (100 million).

**electromagnetic** (ih-lek′-trō-mag-NET′-ik) **radiation**. The name comes from the fact that this radiation has electric and magnetic properties.

The **electromagnetic spectrum** is made up of the whole range of electromagnetic radiation from the highest to lowest frequency. Different names are applied to radiation in different frequency ranges.

At the high-frequency end is **gamma radiation**. It was originally discovered in the radiation that comes to the earth from

Figure 7-38. This radio telescope collects low-frequency electromagnetic waves. The waves are focused at the point where the three straight supports meet. The supports hold a feed antenna at that point. The feed antenna can send out radio waves as well as receive them.

This telescope has been used during space missions and for studying the moon and the upper atmosphere.

**Data Search**

When and to whom was a Nobel prize in physics awarded for using radiotelescopes to probe outer space? Search page 558.

outer space (cosmic radiation). It is used in the treatment of cancer, as it destroys cancer cells more easily than normal cells.

**X-rays** are just lower than gamma radiation in frequency. X-ray pictures of the teeth and bones are used by dentists and doctors to identify problems.

**Microwaves** have a lower frequency than infrared. Microwave ovens send microwaves into food. The food absorbs the energy of the microwaves and cooks. Since metal reflects microwaves, metal cooking pans cannot be used. Paper and china dishes transmit microwaves without absorbing the energy. The dishes remain much cooler than the food.

The lowest frequency electromagnetic waves are **radio waves**. These are the waves that carry broadcast signals to radios and televisions. Each station broadcasts at its own frequency. When you tune into an FM station at 88.5 megahertz (MHz), your radio is picking up 88.5 million crests per second from the station. AM stations broadcast in the kilohertz (kHz) range. Which broadcast at higher frequencies—AM or FM stations?

**Safety**

Gamma rays, x-rays, and microwaves are all health hazards. Avoid unnecessary exposure to these types of radiation.

**Library research**

Find out the origin of the word *radar*. How are radar waves used? What frequency range do radar waves have?

### Check yourself

1. Name the three types of electromagnetic radiation that have higher frequencies than visible light.

2. Name the three types of electromagnetic radiation that have lower frequencies than visible light.

### The nature of light

The wave model of light can be used to explain much of the behavior of light. But one difficulty remains. It cannot explain what happens when light shines on a metal and electrons are released.

In the ocean, the biggest waves can do the most damage. They are the ones that have the most energy.

The energy of light causes electrons to be released from the surface of metals. You would expect that if the light were bright enough, it would provide enough energy to release the electrons. In reality, the release of electrons depends on the color of the light. Light at the red end of the color spectrum does not seem to have enough energy to release electrons at all.

The release of electrons due to light is called the **photoelectric effect**. Albert Einstein (1879–1955), the great German-born American physicist, proposed an explanation for the photoelectric effect in 1905. He said that light acted like a group of energy particles, which are now called **photons** (FŌ′-tonz). The energy of a photon is related to the frequency of the light in the wave model. A photon of violet

Figure 7-39. Electrons are released from the surface of a metal when they receive enough energy from light. Light with too low a frequency does not provide enough energy, no matter how bright the light is. Yet, weak light with a high enough frequency seems to have enough energy to release electrons.

**Library research**

A laser is an instrument that strengthens, or amplifies, light. The word *laser* stands for *l*ight *a*mplification by *s*timulated *e*mission of *r*adiation. Find out how light produced by a laser differs from light produced by other sources, such as electric bulbs and the sun.

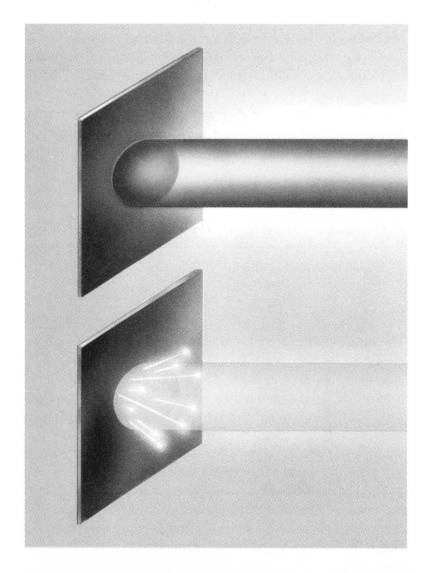

light has more energy than a photon of red light. The higher the frequency of the light in the wave model, the more energy each photon has in the particle model. The brighter the light, the more photons it has.

Einstein suggested that no electrons could be released from a metal unless the photons each had enough energy to release an electron. The photons at the red end do not have enough energy. Although Einstein's idea was very controversial at the time, it came to be accepted. He was awarded the 1921 Nobel Prize for it, not for his even more controversial theory of relativity.

A photon is different from a particle of matter in one important way. A photon always moves at the speed of light. When it is absorbed by matter, it ceases to exist. A particle of matter can be at rest or it can move at a speed less than that of light.

What about the wave properties of light? Is light really made of energy particles and not waves? This question cannot be answered yes or no.

In science, models are developed to explain observations. The models are based on the behavior of familiar things. Models are never exactly like the thing they are supposed to describe.

Light has both wave and particle properties. A wave model describes light as a wave and not particles. A particle model describes light as particles and not a wave. The problem is with the models we can imagine. We cannot think of anything else that acts like both waves and particles.

Light seems to act like a wave when it is traveling. It seems to act like particles when it is being absorbed by or given off by matter. Light should not be thought of as switching back and forth from particle to wave. Rather, it has the properties of both.

**Main Idea**

What is the relation between the frequency of light and the energy of the photons?

**Library research**

The smallest particles of matter, namely electrons, have observable wave properties themselves. Read about the experiments of Davisson and Germer in 1927. Report on how they discovered the wave properties of electrons.

## Check yourself

1. What fact about the photoelectric effect could not be explained in terms of the wave model of light?

2. Which has more energy—a photon of orange light or a photon of blue light?

# Practical Science

## Radio Waves

You have just learned about light waves. Radio waves are similar and also are a part of the electromagnetic spectrum. They bring radio and television to your home.

**Properties of radio waves**   Radio waves travel at the same speed as light waves. They have shapes similar to ocean waves. Some radio waves are large and far apart. Others are smaller and closer together.

Radio waves are reflected from the ionosphere and the earth itself. The ionosphere consists of several ionized layers high in the earth's atmosphere. The part of the wave that travels along the earth is called the *ground wave*. The part that goes above the horizon is called the *sky wave*. Part of the sky wave is reflected by the ionosphere. These reflected waves allow radio signals to be heard over long distances.

As radio waves spread out in all directions, they become weaker. A signal received two miles away from the transmitter is only 1/4 as strong as the signal received one mile away. The same signal received ten miles away is only 1/100 as strong.

**Broadcasting the signal**   A radio or television station broadcasts on a specific assigned frequency different from every other station in its broadcast area.

The assigned frequency of a station is called the *carrier frequency*, or *carrier signal*. The sounds of voices and music are also converted to electrical waves. These waves are added to the carrier signal. This is called *modulation*.

When the crests of two waves of the same size come together, the crest of the resulting wave will be twice as high. If a crest and a trough of two equal waves come together, they cancel each other out. Waves of this type are used to create an *amplitude modulated signal*. AM stations broadcast using this kind of signal.

FM stations broadcast using a *frequency modulated signal*. The varying frequencies of the voices or music modulate the constant frequency of the carrier signal.

**Types of antennas**   The design of the antenna depends on whether the signal is amplitude modulated (AM) or frequency modulated (FM). Its length depends on the frequency of the radio waves and their wavelengths. The length of an ideal antenna is equal to or is a multiple of wavelength. Your radio or television antenna receives a wide range of frequencies, so its length is a compromise.

The wavelengths of AM signals are long. This makes an AM radio require a long antenna.

The waves used in television and FM radio have much higher frequencies than AM waves. Because FM wavelengths are short, the antennas to receive them are also short. FM antennas consist of antenna rods that pick up the signal directly from the transmitter.

**Causes of interference**   Interference may result in static on your radio or strange patterns on your television screen. Electromagnetic waves cause this interference.

**Something to try**   Fully extend the antenna on a radio. Turn on the radio, and point the antenna in different directions. Does the clarity of sound reception remain constant? Why?

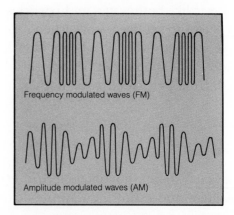

Frequency modulated waves (FM)

Amplitude modulated waves (AM)

## Section 3 Review   Chapter 7

### Check Your Vocabulary

electromagnetic    photon
  spectrum    polarized
gamma radiation    transverse
interference    wavelength
microwave

*Match each term above with the numbered phrase that best describes it.*

1. Has a higher frequency than light
2. Has a lower frequency than light
3. The distance between two neighboring crests or two neighboring troughs
4. Energy particle
5. Type of wave in which vibrations are crosswise to the direction of motion
6. The cancellation and reinforcement of two waves that are passing through each other
7. Describes a transverse wave whose vibrations are back and forth in only one direction
8. The range of radiation that travels at the speed of light

### Check Your Knowledge

*Multiple Choice: Choose the answer that best completes each of the following sentences.*

1. When water waves in a ripple tank strike a solid barrier, they are ?.
   a) reflected
   b) refracted
   c) polarized
   d) absorbed
2. Young's experiment showed that light ?.
   a) could be polarized
   b) could be cancelled
   c) was made of energy particles
   d) traveled through empty space

3. The properties of polarized light are evidence for a model of light as ?.
   a) particles
   b) compressional waves
   c) transverse waves
   d) the highest frequency radiation in the electromagnetic spectrum

### Check Your Understanding

1. Name three ways in which light behaves like water waves.
2. What do radio waves and light have in common? How are they different?
3. The photon model of light applies to all electromagnetic radiation. How would you expect photons of infrared radiation and ultraviolet light to compare in energy?
4. Explain why light is said to have both wave and particle properties.

### Practical Science

1. What kind of signals do AM radio stations use for broadcasting? What kind of signals do FM stations use?
2. What do radio antennas do?

# Chapter 7 Review

## Concept Summary

**Light** is energy that can be detected by the eye.
- Matter may be a source of light, or it may transmit, reflect, or absorb light.
- Light is reflected from a mirror or shiny surface at an angle equal to the angle at which the light strikes the surface.
- The path of light bends as light moves from one substance into another.
- Light travels at extremely high speed—close to 300 000 000 m/s in empty space.
- Light appears dimmer as a person moves farther from the source.

**White light** is a combination of light of all colors.
- The color of an object depends on both the object itself and on the colors of the light striking the object.
- The ability to distinguish among colors of light is limited to humans and only a few other animals.
- Colored light can be separated out of white light because of the way different colors are refracted or scattered.

The **wave model of light** is the theory that light is energy that travels as a transverse wave.
- The pattern produced when light passes through a tiny double slit is evidence for light as a wave.
- The polarization of light is evidence for light as a transverse wave.
- The colors of light can be explained by the hypothesis that each color in white light has a different wavelength and, therefore, a different frequency.

**Electromagnetic radiation** is any kind of energy that behaves like light and travels at the speed of light but may have a frequency higher or lower than visible light.
- Electromagnetic radiation includes gamma radiation, X-rays, ultraviolet light, visible light, infared radiation, microwaves, and radio waves.

The **particle model of light** is the theory that light is a group of energy particles called photons.
- The photoelectric effect is evidence for light as particles.
- The colors of light can be explained by the hypothesis that each color corresponds to photons of a different energy.
- Neither the wave model alone nor the particle model alone can explain all the known behaviors of light.

## Putting It All Together

1. Explain the difference between transparent matter and translucent matter.
2. What are some practical ways in which convex and concave mirrors are used?
3. Explain the difference between reflection and refraction.
4. What is meant by the focal length of a lens?
5. What can cause light to slow down?
6. Which of the colors in white light is bent the most in passing through a prism?
7. How does the function of the cones of the retina differ from that of the rods?
8. How is it possible for a bee to see some red flowers but not others?
9. Explain the red appearance of the sun when it is near the horizon.
10. What evidence is there that light is a form of energy?
11. How is a transverse wave different from a compressional wave?
12. What happens to the frequency of a wave if the wavelength increases?
13. Which model of light can be used in explaining the colors seen in a puddle with a layer of gasoline on top?
14. What do microwaves and X-rays have in common?
15. Explain why light is thought of as having both wave and particle properties.

## Apply Your Knowledge

1. Is it always true that light travels in a straight line? Explain.
2. Explain why it would be incorrect to assume that the brighter a star appears in the sky, the closer it is to the earth.
3. Why might it be wise to examine clothing or other colored goods you plan to buy under different lighting than that in the store?
4. How might you arrange polarizing filters in headlights and windshields of automobiles to reduce the glare of oncoming traffic? Remember, the driver must still see the light on the road ahead from his or her own headlights.

## Find Out on Your Own

1. Set up two cups as shown in Figure 7-9 on page 326. Put a coin in the bottom of each cup. Put water in one cup and an equal volume of mineral oil in the other. In which cup is light bent more when it travels from the liquid into air?
2. Use a prism to break a beam of white light into the colors of the spectrum. Experiment with a second prism to see if the colors can be recombined to form white light. Trace the paths of the colors as they separate and recombine.
3. Bring a book or magazine with colored pictures to a place where the light is very dim. Look at the pictures. Are some colors easier to identify in dim light than others?
4. Many check-out counters have laser scanners that can "read" the price and identity of groceries. Find out some other practical uses for lasers.
5. Obtain a set of cards used to determine whether or not a person is colorblind. Test your classmates to determine the percentage that are colorblind. How does the percentage compare with the figures given in this textbook?

## Reading Further

Adler, Irving. *Color in Your Life.* New York: John Day, 1967

Clear and simple explanations about how things appear the color they do and how light interacts with matter.

Adler, Irving. *The Story of Light* (revised edition). New York: Harvey House, 1971

This is an easy-to-understand description of light and the entire electromagnetic spectrum.

Branley, Franklin M. *The Electromagnetic Spectrum; Key to the Universe.* New York: Crowell/Harper & Row, 1979

The author discusses light and the other parts of the electromagnetic spectrum. He explains theories of the nature of this radiation.

Filson, Brent. *Exploring with Lasers.* New York: Messner/Simon and Schuster, 1984

This book clearly explains the complex subject of lasers and holographs and details their applications.

Hellman, Hal. *The Art and Science of Color.* New York: McGraw-Hill, 1967

This is an informative, nontechnical discussion of all aspects of color, from the science of light to photography, holography, and television.

Jollands, David, ed. *Sight, Light and Color.* New York: Arco, 1984

A clear and beautiful explanation of light and color and how we see them is given.

Simon, Hilda. *The Magic of Color.* New York: Lothrop/Morrow, 1981

This book explains how colored inks are used to print illustrations. It gives examples of colorblindness, magic with color, and color illusions.

# Chapter 8

# Electric Charges and Currents

Section 1
### Electric Charges

All matter is made of particles that have electric charges. There are two kinds of charge, negative and positive. They may be separated from each other so that an object has more of one kind than the other. Charged objects exert forces on each other.

Section 2
### Electric Currents

Moving charges create an electric current. The current flows in a closed path called a circuit. The charges receive energy from a cell or battery in the circuit. They lose energy as they travel through the rest of the circuit.

Section 3
### Electric Circuits

The conductors in a circuit may be connected in a row or in separate branches. The current in a circuit depends upon what things are in the circuit and on how they are connected. Safety devices shut off the current when it starts to become too high.

In this chapter you will learn about the behavior of electric charges. The photo at the left shows the lighted marquee of a movie theater. All the lights require electric current to remain lit.

# Electric Charges    Section 1

**Section 1 of Chapter 8 is divided into five parts:**

Charging by friction

Charging by contact

Charging by induction

Lightning

Avoiding a buildup of charges

*Practical Science: Anti-Static Agents*

## Learning Objectives

1. To explain the charging of objects by friction, by contact, and by induction.

2. To describe how lightning and thunder occur in clouds.

3. To relate the electric force between charged objects to the kinds of charges, to the amount of charge, and to the distance between the charges.

Figure 8-1. Large amounts of electric charge build up on clouds during thunderstorms. Finally, charged particles move off the clouds to the ground, producing flashes of lightning.

All matter is made of particles that have electric charges. The effects of these charges are both familiar and mysterious. For example, a hard rubber comb is run through your hair. Afterward, the comb picks up small pieces of paper. A balloon is rubbed against your sweater. Afterward, the balloon sticks to the wall. A charged balloon can bend a stream of water from the faucet.

The effects of electric charges were observed more than 2500 years ago. However, explanations did not develop until about 200 years ago. At first, charge was explained as a fluid. No one knew that matter was made of charged particles—electrons and protons.

Figure 8-2. Hair is sometimes attracted toward a comb that has just been run through it. This attraction is due to electric charges.

## Charging by friction

It is now known that electrons are negatively charged. Protons are positively charged. Matter that has equal numbers of electrons and protons is electrically neutral. Negatively charged matter has more electrons than protons. Positively charged matter has more protons than electrons.

Electric charges that are not moving are called **static charges**. A static charge can be positive or negative. Some objects can gain a static charge by rubbing. Friction between unlike materials can cause electrons to move from one to the other. A balloon and a piece of wool flannel work well. Many other materials can also be used.

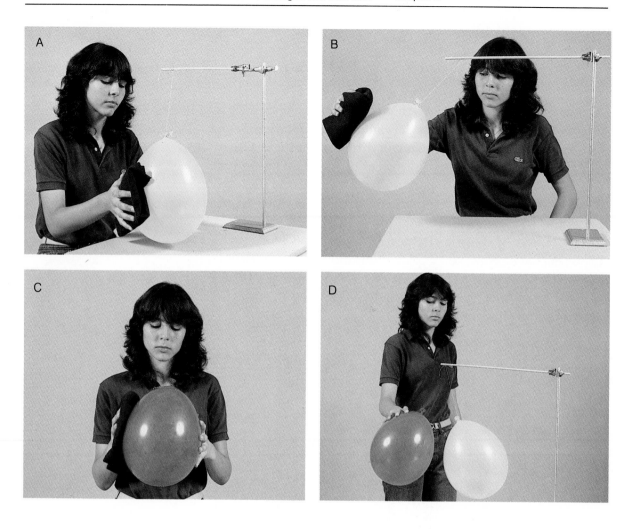

Figure 8-3. When a balloon is rubbed with wool flannel, they stick together. A second balloon is rubbed with the flannel. The balloons push each other away. Explain these observations.

The photos in Figure 8-3 show how a balloon interacts with flannel after they are rubbed together. The balloon sticks to the flannel. A second balloon is rubbed with the same flannel. The two balloons now push each other away, or **repel** (ree-PEL') each other.

Figure 8-4. What happens to the positive and negative charges on a balloon and wool flannel after they are rubbed together?

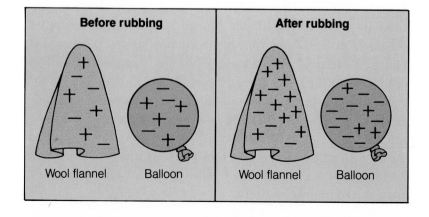

---

**Activity 8–1A**          Identifying Positively and Negatively Charged Objects

**Materials**

| | |
|---|---|
| balloon | silk |
| piece of thread | solid glass rod |
| wood dowel | hard rubber comb |
| wool flannel | plastic bag |

**Purpose**

To demonstrate how the electric charge on an object can be identified.

**Procedure**

1. Inflate a balloon. Suspend it from a wood dowel by a piece of thread.
2. Rub the balloon with wool flannel. The balloon is now negatively charged.
3. Rub a glass rod with a piece of silk. Without touching the balloon, bring the rod toward the balloon. Record whether the rod attracts or repels the balloon.
4. Bring the silk toward the balloon. Record whether the silk attracts or repels the balloon.
5. Rub a hard rubber comb with the flannel. Bring each one near the balloon. Record what happens to the balloon.
6. Test other combinations of the materials available. Record how each material affects the balloon.

**Questions**

1. What is the charge on a balloon that has been rubbed with wool flannel?
2. What is the charge on a material that repels a balloon rubbed with wool flannel?
3. What is the charge on a material that attracts a balloon rubbed with wool flannel?
4. What charge did each of the materials you used have after rubbing?

**Conclusion**

How can a charged balloon be used to identify the electric charge on an object?

---

The diagram in Figure 8-4 shows the static charges on the balloon and flannel. Rubbing causes electrons to come off the flannel onto the balloon.

Opposite charges attract. An object with a positive charge attracts an object with a negative charge. Like charges repel. Two objects with the same charge repel each other.

**Check yourself**

How can charging by friction be explained?

**Charging by contact**

Metals are good **conductors** of electric charge. That is, electrons are able to move through them easily. Other materials, such as glass, wood, hard rubber, and plastic, are good **insulators.** Few, if any, electrons move through them.

---

**Data Search**

Which metal listed in the table on electric conductivity is the best electrical conductor? Search page 560.

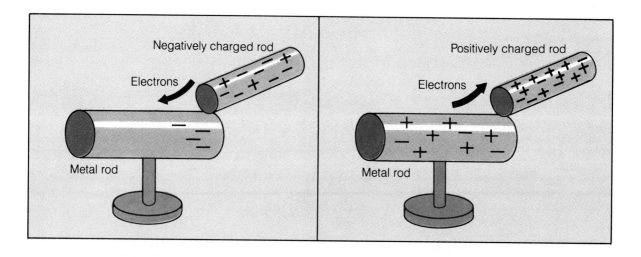

Figure 8-5 The metal rod on the insulator is being charged by contact with a charged rod. When does the metal rod become positively charged? When does it become negatively charged?

### Library research

The SI unit of charge is the coulomb (KOO′-lōm), named after the French scientist Charles Augustin de Coulomb (1736–1806). Find out what scientific contribution Coulomb made that led to the honor of having a unit named after him.

Suppose a metal rod is attached to an insulator. A charged object touches the rod. What happens to the charge? If the object has extra electrons, some will move onto the rod. The rod is now negatively charged.

On the other hand, suppose the object has more protons than electrons. Electrons will move from the rod onto the object. The negative electrons are attracted by the positively charged object. The metal now becomes positively charged.

Conductors can be charged by contact with a charged object. The charge on the conductor always has the same sign (positive or negative) as the charge on the object.

Dry air is a good insulator. Moist air is a fair conductor of electric charge. In wet weather, it is hard to charge objects. The air conducts the charge away from them so that they do not stay charged. In dry weather, objects become charged more easily. You may have felt an electric shock after walking across a rug and touching a metal doorknob. You yourself had become charged by friction between your shoes and the rug. Then you charged the doorknob by contact.

### Check yourself

How can charging by contact be explained?

### Charging by induction

Bits of paper will stick to a negatively charged rubber comb. They will also stick to a positively charged glass rod. How can the same objects be attracted to both types of charge?

## Activity 8–1B          Charging Without Touching

### Materials

foil gum wrapper
scissors
jar with narrow neck
15-cm stiff wire with uninsulated ends

modeling clay
plastic bag
wool flannel

### Purpose

To charge an object without touching it.

### Procedure

1. Make an electroscope, or charge detector, as follows.
   a. Carefully strip the paper backing off a foil gum wrapper. Cut a lengthwise strip of foil about 1 cm in width. Fold the foil strip in half.
   b. Bend one end of a stiff wire to form a hook. SAFETY NOTE: *Keep loose wire away from eyes to prevent eye injuries.*
   c. Poke the hook into the foil just below the fold. The two ends of the foil should hang straight down, or nearly so, from the hook. Be sure that the foil is in contact with the uninsulated part of the wire.
   d. Lower the hook and foil into a jar with a narrow neck. Use modeling clay to seal the wire in the neck of the jar.
2. Lay a plastic bag flat on a desk or table.
3. Rub the bag with wool flannel.
4. Bring the flannel close to the top end of the wire. Do not touch the wire. Record whether the foil ends spread apart or stay close together.

5. Move the flannel away from the wire. Record what happens to the electroscope.
6. Bring the flannel back again. Record what the foil ends do.
7. Repeat Steps 3, 4, 5 and 6 using the plastic bag instead of the flannel.

### Questions

1. What charges do the wool and plastic have after they have been rubbed together?
2. Was the induced charge on the foil ends positive or negative when the charged wool flannel was near the top of the electroscope?
3. Was the induced charge on the foil ends positive or negative when the charged plastic bag was near the electroscope?

### Conclusion

What is a hypothesis that explains the behavior of the electroscope when the charged flannel and plastic were close by and far away?

The bits of paper are neutral. They have equal numbers of electrons and protons. The charged rubber comb is brought near the bits of paper. The electrons in the paper are somewhat free to move away from the comb. They remain in the paper. But now the part of the paper closest to the comb is positively charged. The part farthest from the comb is negatively charged. The comb attracts the positively charged part.

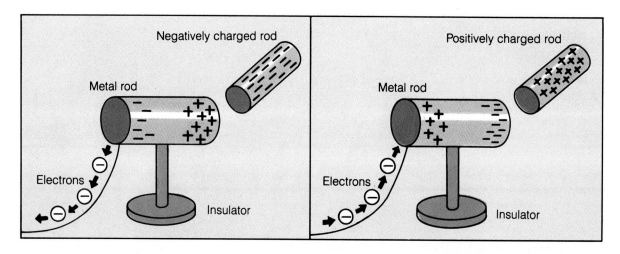

Figure 8-6. The metal rod is being charged by induction because a charged rod is nearby. When does the metal rod become positively charged? When does it become negatively charged?

**Main Idea**

When a metal object that is near a charged object is connected to a conductor, what motion of electrons results?

This is why charged objects attract noncharged objects.

The process of charging an object by bringing a charged object nearby is called **induction** (in-DUK'-shun). An object that is charged by induction is not touched by the charged object. When an object is charged by induction it has a charge that is opposite to that of the charging object.

For example, an insulated metal rod can be charged by induction. A charged object is brought near. The electrons in the metal rod move toward the charged object if its charge is positive. The electrons in the metal rod move away from the charged object if its charge is negative. They cannot leave the metal. Induction causes only a temporary movement of charges. An object that is charged by induction will become neutral when the charged object is taken away.

An induced charge can become permanent if a conductor is touched briefly to the metal rod. Electrons move in the direction that will give the metal rod an opposite charge from that of the charged object. When the conductor is taken away, the metal rod is left charged.

**Check yourself**

How can charging by induction be explained?

**Lightning**

Lightning is a result of charges that become separated in thunder clouds. The top of the cloud becomes positively charged. The bottom of the cloud becomes negatively charged.

The ground under the negative part of the cloud becomes positively charged by induction.

When the charge is great enough, the air becomes a conductor. Electrons move toward the positively charged ground. The interaction of the electrons with the air causes the glowing spark we call lightning. The air becomes greatly heated by the lightning and expands rapidly. An exploding noise that we call thunder is heard. Lightning also occurs within a thunder cloud or between one cloud and another.

Benjamin Franklin (1706–1790) was an American statesman who enjoyed experimenting with electricity. He discovered that sparks leave a sharply pointed object more readily than a rounded one. He invented the **lightning rod**. The lightning rod is a pointed rod that is attached at the top of a building. It is connected by a cable to the ground.

In a thunderstorm, charge builds up in the ground. The charge can leave from the point of the lightning rod. Even if lightning does strike, it will hit the lightning rod and protect the building.

Lightning tends to strike the highest nearby point. Suppose you are riding in a car out in the country during a thunderstorm. What is the best thing to do? Avoid taking shelter

**Library research**

Benjamin Franklin is famous for flying a kite during a thunderstorm. Find out what he was trying to determine. Explain why his experiment was so dangerous that he is lucky to have survived.

Figure 8-7. When the bottom of a cloud becomes negatively charged, what causes the ground underneath it to become positively charged?

**Safety**
Get out of water and seek shelter during a lightning storm. If no shelter is nearby, lie down away from trees and other high points.

under a tall tree. The tree could be hit by lightning and fall on you. On the other hand, you will be safe inside the car, even on an open road. Charge moves freely on the outside of a metal surface such as a car. No charge will build up inside.

### Check yourself

What condition in clouds leads to lightning and thunder?

### Avoiding a buildup of charges

Have you ever received an electric shock by touching an operating electric appliance? This can happen with older, metal appliances that have electric motors in them. Charges can build up on the metal case of a fast-turning electric motor. This is much the same as when charges build up on an object that is being rubbed by a cloth.

When electric charges build up, they will always follow the easiest path to the ground. This is usually through a conductor. A conductor that allows excess electrons to leave or enter an object is called a **ground**. A ground keeps a charge from building up on an object.

When you touch a fast-turning motor, you also provide a path to the ground, like the wire in Figure 8-6. This can cause a shock. In order to prevent shocking, most newer appliances are already connected to the ground by a third prong in the plug. These appliances are said to be *grounded*. Electric charges do not build up on a grounded appliance because the charges are conducted to the ground.

Older appliances with two-prong plugs are usually not grounded. If necessary, they can be grounded by running a wire from the case of the appliance to a cold-water pipe, which goes underground. Appliances that should be grounded include electric drills, washers, and dryers.

Figure 8-8. A three-prong plug. Which prong is the ground?

### Check yourself

What is the best way to prevent charges from building up on an electric appliance?

# Practical Science

## Anti-Static Agents

You have often seen and felt the presence of static electricity. For example, you often get a shock as you reach for the doorknob after you walk across a carpet. Your hair is attracted to a comb on a dry day. When you remove clothes from the dryer, they cling together.

It is annoying to have your laundry all stuck together, or to get a shock when you walk across the living room carpet and reach for the doorknob. But there are times when the effects of static electricity are much more serious, or even dangerous.

**Potentially dangerous situations involving static electricity**   Textiles, paper, and plastic are all good insulators. In factories, these materials travel at high speeds through various machines. The friction created as they move through the air can result in a buildup of static electricity. The result may be a product that will not sell because it is covered with clinging bits of dust and dirt. The charged material may jam a machine. If the air of the factory is full of fine lint or dust, a spark could even cause an explosion.

Another potentially dangerous situation involving static electricity occurs while fueling a jet. Jet fuel travels at high speed through fuel lines, filters, and valves. The substances in this fuel are good insulators and are very explosive. If friction causes a build up of charge in the liquid fuel, a spark could be disastrous.

**Reducing the risks of static electricity**
Scientists and engineers have developed products and techniques to help get rid of static charge safely. Machines can be grounded so that the charge will not build up. The air in a factory can be made more humid, so that the charge can "leak out" to the air more easily. Plastics can be coated or mixed with substances that are good electrical conductors. Substances that increase electrical conductivity can be mixed with jet fuel.

**The development of anti-static agents**
Many brands of carpets are advertised as having anti-static qualities. The individual fibers in some of these carpets may contain conducting substances. Other supposedly anti-static carpets may only be coated with a substance that will reduce friction between your feet and the carpet. Of course, anti-static agents that are just applied to the surface will not last as long as those that are actually part of the fibers of the carpet.

Fabric softeners and hair rinses also act as anti-static agents. They consist of molecules having negatively and positively charged ends. The negatively charged end is soluble in water. The positively charged ends are not soluble in water. The negative end allows part of the molecule to mix well with water. The positive end allows the other part of the molecule to cling to a negative surface, like hair or clothes, rather than just being washed out with the water. Coating your hair or clothes with these anti-static agents increases the conductivity of your hair or clothes and reduces static charge.

**Something to try**   Put on a pair of shoes with leather soles. Rub your feet vigorously on a carpet. Touch a metal doorknob. What happens? Now put on a pair of rubber-soled shoes. Again rub your feet vigorously on a carpet. What happens? Why?

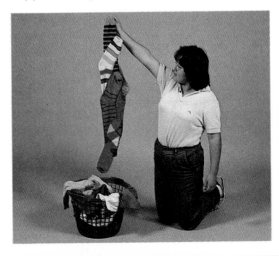

## Section 1 Review    Chapter 8

### Check Your Vocabulary

| | |
|---|---|
| conductor | lightning rod |
| induction | static charge |
| insulator | ground |

*Match each term above with the numbered phrase that best describes it.*

1. An electric charge that is not moving
2. Material through which charge can move easily
3. Material through which charge cannot move easily
4. Process of charging an object by bringing it near a charged object
5. Pointed piece of metal attached to top of building
6. A conductor that keeps a charge from building up

### Check Your Knowledge

*Multiple Choice: Choose the answer that best completes each of the following sentences.*

1. When two materials are charged by friction between them, __?__.
   a) both lose electrons
   b) both gain electrons
   c) one loses electrons to the other
   d) there is no change in the number of electrons each has
2. When an object is charged by contact with a charged object, __?__.
   a) both lose electrons
   b) both gain electrons
   c) one loses electrons to the other
   d) there is no change in the number of electrons each has
3. When an insulated object is charged by induction because of a nearby charged object, __?__.
   a) both lose electrons
   b) both gain electrons
   c) one loses electrons to the other
   d) there is no change in the number of electrons each has
4. When electric charges build up, __?__.
   a) they are always caused by induction
   b) they repel objects
   c) they always follow the easiest path to the ground.
   d) they tend to stay put

### Check Your Understanding

1. How do conductors differ from insulators?
2. If you hold a charged balloon near your arm, you will feel a tickle as the hair on your arm reaches toward the balloon. Explain what might cause your hair to do this.
3. Trucks that carry gasoline and other flammable substances often have a chain underneath that drags along the street. How does the chain prevent dangerous electric charges from building up on the truck?

### Practical Science

1. What kind of substance will build up a static charge?
2. What are the conditions in a clothes dryer that cause static charges to build up?
3. Give an example of a situation in which static electricity can be dangerous.

# Electric Currents    Section 2

**Section 2 of Chapter 8 is divided into five parts:**

Making charges move

Direct and alternating current

Measuring current

Resistance and voltage drop

Electric power

*Practical Science: Controlling Electricity*

## Learning Objectives

1. To identify the necessary conditions for an electric current to exist.

2. To differentiate between direct and alternating current.

3. To describe the measures of current, voltage drop, and resistance.

4. To relate the power rating of an electric appliance to the energy used.

Figure 8-9. Light is produced in an incandescent bulb when the filament contained in the bulb is heated by an electric current.

Moving electric charges do work. They are a source of energy. The energy of moving charges is used to light buildings and to transport people. It puts people in touch with each other through telephones, radio, and television.

## Making charges move

The movement of electric charges creates an **electric current**. Moving electric charges cannot be seen. The movement must be inferred from indirect observations. The presence of an electric current is usually indicated by its effects.

Charges move only when energy is supplied to them. The energy can come from a dry cell. Chemical reactions within the cell supply energy to electrons. Electrons inside the cell collect at the **negative terminal** of the cell. In the common flashlight cell, the negative terminal is the metal base of the cell. When the top and bottom of the cell are connected by wires, electrons move through the wires toward the **positive terminal**. The positive terminal is at the center of the top.

Dry cells are sometimes called **batteries**. A true battery is a series of cells. The chemical reactions that make cells work are described in Section 1 of Chapter 10.

Cells and batteries are marked with the **voltage** (VŌL′-tuj) they supply to the charge that passes through them. Voltage is the amount of energy supplied per unit of charge. The SI unit of voltage is the **volt** (symbol V). A 1.5-V flashlight cell supplies one joule of energy for every four million million

## Main Idea

In what direction do electrons move when the top and bottom of a dry cell are connected by wires?

## Library research

After whom is the volt named? What did this person accomplish that led to such an honor?

Figure 8-10. Explain why one bulb is lit but the other is not.

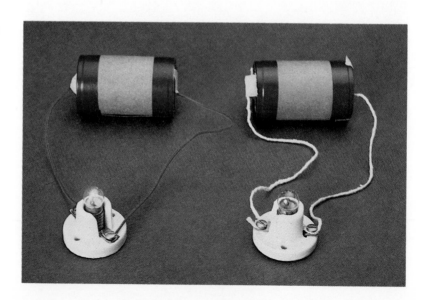

## Activity 8–2A    Detecting Electric Currents

### Materials

masking tape          flashlight bulb
"D" cell              magnetic compass
2 30-cm lengths of wire with uninsulated
  ends

### Purpose

To show how electric currents can be detected.

### Procedure

1. Use masking tape to attach the two 30-cm wires to the "D" cell. Attach one wire to the base of the cell. Attach the second wire to the knob at the top of the cell.
2. Touch the free end of one wire to the bottom of the metal base of the flashlight bulb. Touch the free end of the second wire to the side of the base of the bulb. Watch the bulb.
3. Switch the locations of the two wires. Watch the flashlight bulb. Set the bulb aside.
4. Place the magnetic compass on the table. Arrange the wires so that they are lined up in the same direction as the compass needle. With the wires held over the compass, briefly touch the free ends of the wire together. Watch what happens to the compass needle.

### Questions

1. What evidence is there to show that an electric current is moving through the bulb?
2. What happens to the current when you switch the wires on the base of the bulb?
3. What happens to the compass needle when the wires from the "D" cell touch?
4. How does the compass needle indicate an electric current in the wires?

### Conclusion

How can electric currents be detected?

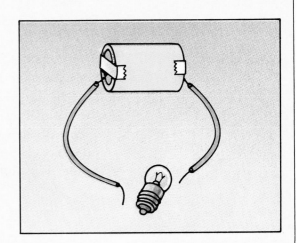

million electrons that pass through it. This is about the number of electrons that might pass through the cell each second.

A cell will operate for only a limited time, until the chemical reactants inside it are used up. A cell will wear out quickly if the top and bottom are directly connected by wires, with no bulb in between. Electrons can move through a wire more easily than through a bulb. They move more quickly when there is no bulb and use up the cell's energy faster.

For charges to move through a cell, there must be an unbroken path of conductors between the positive and negative terminals of the cell. The path is called a **circuit** (SER´-kit). Figure 8-10 shows a cell and a bulb connected by wire and by string. The bulb lights up when wire is used but not when string is used. Wire is a conductor, but string is not.

## Main Idea

What happens to the current when a circuit is opened?

The circuit must be unbroken, or **closed**. If any of the wires is disconnected, the current stops. An **open circuit** is one in which there is an opening in the path. A switch may be connected into the circuit. The switch makes it easy to open and close the circuit.

### Check yourself

1. What role does a dry cell play in a circuit?
2. What conditions must be met for current to exist in a circuit?

### Direct and alternating current

There are two kinds of current. In a **direct current**, the electrons move in one direction. They leave the cell or battery at the negative terminal. They travel through the circuit toward the positive terminal.

Any of the conductors in the circuit can be reversed with no effect on the direction of the electrons. For instance, the connections to the bottom and side of the base of a bulb can

Figure 8-11. Electrons leave the negative terminal of the cell or battery. They travel through the bulb and wires toward the positive terminal.

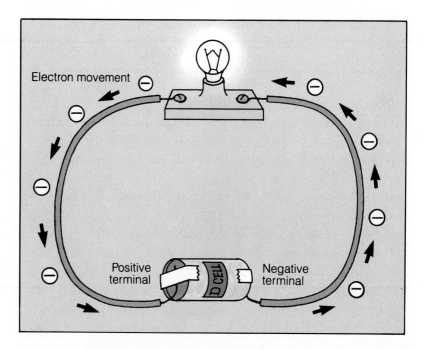

be switched. Wires can be turned around. The electrons will still move toward the positive terminal.

The same amount of charge passes through each part of the circuit each second. Charge does not build up in any part. The same amount of charge that leaves the negative terminal enters the positive terminal.

Direct current is provided by cells and batteries. Cars use direct current to run their lights and radios. In older cars, a direct-current (dc) generator supplies the direct current.

In the second kind of current, the electrons move back and forth in a regular repeating cycle. This kind of current is called **alternating current** (ac).

Household current in North America is alternating current that reverses direction every 1/120 second. The current makes a complete back-and-forth cycle every 1/60 second. In one second, it makes 60 cycles. It has a frequency of 60 cycles per second, or 60 Hz (hertz). In some parts of the world, the common household current has a frequency of 50 Hz.

An ac circuit must be closed, just like a dc circuit. It may seem as though electric appliances have only one wire to connect to the wall outlet. However, the cord has two wires, side

**Library research**

Find out what voltage and what frequency current are standard for three countries on different continents. What can a traveler do to be able to use an appliance designed for a different voltage or frequency of current?

**Safety**
Remember, your body will conduct electricity! You can receive a serious shock from the voltage in the electrical wiring of your house.

Figure 8-12. The electrons in a standard 60-Hz alternating current change direction 120 times in each second.

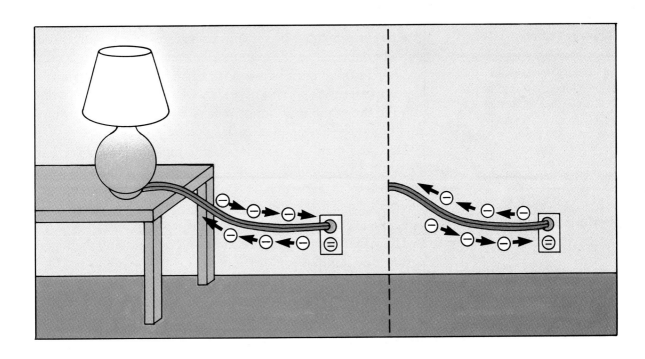

by side. They are separated from each other by the plastic insulation you see. When the electrons in one wire are moving away from the outlet, the electrons in the other wire are moving toward it. They change direction at the same time. No charge builds up anywhere in the circuit.

Alternating current has some advantages over direct current. Today, most electric energy is generated at large power plants. The energy has to be transported large distances. Alternating current can carry the energy with less energy loss along the way than direct current.

In modern cars, alternating current is produced by the generator. The current is changed to direct current before it passes through the rest of the car's electrical system.

### Main Idea

What is one advantage that alternating current has over direct current?

### Check yourself

1.  What are the two kinds of current?
2.  What does it mean for a current to have a frequency of 60 Hz?

### Measuring current

### Library research

After whom is the ampere named? What did this person accomplish that led to such an honor?

A current is created by moving charges. The amount of the current depends on the amount of electric charge that passes a point in the circuit in a second. The SI unit of current is the **ampere** (AM'-pihr), whose symbol is A. People commonly refer to the number of "amps" in a circuit. Most of the circuits in a home are designed to carry a current of 15 to 20 A.

Electric current can be compared to the movement of water. Figure 8-13 has a diagram of the path of water that falls over some rocks in a garden. A pump gives the water enough energy to reach the top of the rocks. When the water goes over the rocks, it is carried back to the pump.

The water current could be increased by pumping the water faster. The pump would use more energy. The pump acts like a cell in a circuit. An electric current can be increased by using more cells in the circuit. The electrons would get more energy and would move faster. More electrons would pass a point in the circuit in a second.

Figure 8-13. The water moves around and around in this garden waterfall system. The pump gives the water enough energy to reach the top. Compare the parts of this system with an electric circuit.

Electric current is measured by an **ammeter** (AM'-mee-ter). The ammeter is connected into the circuit. It is important to use only a dc meter in a dc circuit and an ac meter in an ac circuit, unless the meter is designed for both. On a dc meter, the negative terminal of the meter should be connected toward the negative terminal of the cell or battery.

Meters are built to read within different ampere ranges. If the range is much higher than the current, the meter will not be sensitive enough to read the current. On the other hand, the meter can be ruined if the range is too low for the current.

### Check yourself

What three things should be checked on an ammeter that is connected into a dc circuit?

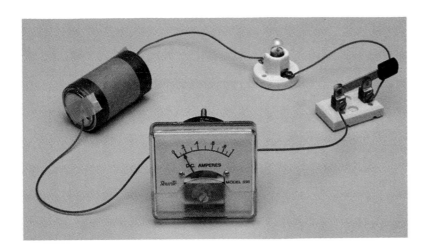

Figure 8-14. An ammeter measures the amount of current passing through it.

## Activity 8–2B          Using an Ammeter

### Materials

2 "D" cells
flashlight bulb and socket
dc ammeter of range 0 A to 1 A
switch
4 20-cm lengths of bell wire
masking tape

### Purposes

To learn how to use an ammeter.
To measure current in a circuit.

### Procedure

1. Make a circuit like the one in Figure 8–14. SAFETY NOTE: *Keep loose wires away from eyes to prevent eye injuries.* Be sure that the negative terminal of the ammeter is connected to the negative terminal (bottom) of the cell. The positive terminal of the ammeter must be connected to the positive terminal (top) of the cell.
2. Make a table. Record the reading on the ammeter when the switch is open.
3. Close the switch and record the reading on the ammeter.
4. Predict whether the ammeter reading will be different if the bulb and ammeter are switched in the circuit. Record your prediction.
5. Test your prediction by reconnecting the bulb and ammeter in the switched positions. Be sure that the positive terminal of the ammeter is connected toward the positive terminal (top) of the cell.
6. Record the reading on the ammeter. Compare the brightness of the bulb to its previous brightness.
7. Predict whether the ammeter reading will be different if another cell is added to the circuit. Record your prediction.
8. Test your prediction by adding another cell to the circuit. Be sure that the top of one cell is in good contact with the bottom of the other cell. Use masking tape to hold them together firmly.
9. Record the reading on the ammeter. Compare the brightness of the bulb to its previous brightness.

### Questions

1. According to the cell label, what is the voltage of one "D" cell?
2. What was the current reading when one cell was used?
3. Did the current reading change when the bulb and ammeter were switched?
4. Did the brightness of the bulb change when a second cell was added to the circuit?
5. What is the total voltage of two "D" cells?
6. What was the current reading when two cells were used?
7. From your data, what relation can you see between the voltage supplied to a circuit and the current in a circuit?

### Conclusion

How should an ammeter be connected to a light bulb to measure the current through the bulb?

| | |
|---|---|
| Step 2 | Reading when switch is open: |
| Step 3 | Reading when switch is closed: |
| Step 4 | Prediction: |
| Step 5 | Test of prediction: |
| Step 6 | Reading on ammeter: |
| Step 7 | Prediction: |
| Step 8 | Test of prediction: |
| Step 9 | Final reading on ammeter: |

## Resistance and voltage drop

Electrons move through metal wires easily. They give up only a small amount of energy as they move. This energy makes the wires warm.

It is easier for electrons to move through thicker wires than thinner wires. To understand why, think of water moving through a pipe. The wider the pipe, the easier it is for the water to flow.

The **resistance** of a conductor is a measure of how hard it is for charge to move through it. The greater the resistance, the harder it is for charge to move through the conductor. The SI unit of resistance is the **ohm** (ŌM). Light bulbs contain a very thin wire called a filament. Electrons move through the filament as they travel between the side and bottom of the base of the bulb. The filament has a high resistance. The electrons lose more energy as they move through the filament than when they move through the base. The filament becomes very hot. It gives off both heat and light.

Consider a simple circuit containing a flashlight cell, a flashlight bulb, and wires connecting them. The cell supplies energy to the electrons. As they move through the circuit, they lose most of that energy in the bulb. They lose an additional, but small, amount of energy in the wires.

**Main Idea**

What does the unit known as the ohm measure?

Figure 8-15. The resistance of a wire depends on the material of the wire as well as the thickness.

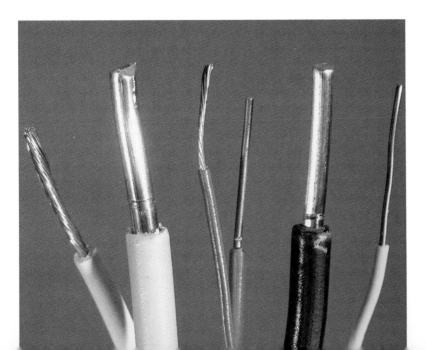

**Data Search**

Which kind of wire is a better conductor of electricity, aluminum or copper? What is the IACS percentage for each? Search page 560.

Figure 8-16. The voltmeter is connected so that it measures the voltage drop across the bulb.

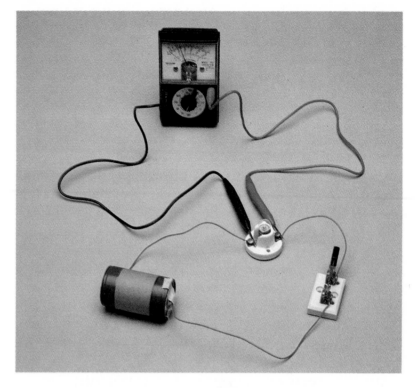

**Main Idea**

How is the voltage drop across a conductor measured?

The voltage of a cell is the energy it supplies per unit of charge passing through it. The **voltage drop** across a conductor is the energy removed per unit of charge passing through it. Like voltage, voltage drop is measured in volts. The total voltage drop of all the conductors in a circuit equals the total voltage of the cells in the circuit.

Voltage drop is measured with a **voltmeter**. A voltmeter is connected differently from an ammeter. The voltmeter is connected across the conductor being measured. The current has a choice between passing through the conductor or passing through the voltmeter. Figure 8-16 shows a voltmeter that has been connected across a flashlight bulb.

There are both ac and dc voltmeters. The type of voltmeter must match the type of circuit it will be used in. Like ammeters, voltmeters can measure different ranges. The correct range must be chosen. Finally, in a dc circuit the voltmeter is connected so that its negative terminal is toward the negative terminal of the cell or battery.

The voltage drop across a conductor depends on two things. One is the resistance of the conductor. The higher the resistance is, the harder it is for electrons to move through the conductor. Thus, the electrons give up more energy as they pass through it. The voltage drop is greater.

---

**Activity 8–2C**    Using a Voltmeter

**Materials**

2 "D" cells
flashlight bulb and socket
dc voltmeter of range 0 V to 5 V
switch
5 20-cm lengths of bell wire
masking tape

**Purposes**

To learn how to use a voltmeter.
To measure the voltage drop across a conductor.

**Procedure**

1. Make a circuit like the one in Figure 8-16. SAFETY NOTE: *Keep loose wires away from eyes to prevent eye injuries.* Be sure that the negative terminal of the voltmeter is connected to the negative terminal (bottom) of the cell. The positive terminal of the voltmeter must be connected to the positive terminal (top) of the cell.
2. Record the reading on the voltmeter when the switch is open.
3. Close the switch and record the reading on the voltmeter. Open the switch.
4. Add another cell to the circuit. Use masking tape to hold them together firmly.
5. Close the switch. Record the reading on the voltmeter. Open the switch.
6. Connect the voltmeter across the wire between the switch and the bulb.
7. Close the switch. Record the voltmeter reading. Open the switch.

**Questions**

1. What was the voltmeter reading when the switch was open.
2. According to the cell label, what is the voltage of the cell?
3. When the switch was closed, how did the voltage drop across the bulb compare with the voltage of the cell?
4. How did the voltmeter reading change when the second cell was added to the circuit?
5. How does the voltage drop across a conductor depend on the total voltage of the cells in the circuit?
6. How did the voltage drop across the wire compare with the voltage drop across the bulb.

**Conclusion**

How should a voltmeter be connected in order to measure the voltage drop across part of a circuit?

---

The voltage drop also depends upon the current. In bulbs and wires, the voltage drop increases when the current increases. A bulb becomes brighter when more current passes through it. The increase in brightness is a sign that the bulb is taking more energy from the electrons that pass through its filament. The voltage drop across the bulb is greater.

**Check yourself**

Suppose two copper wires have the same length but different thicknesses. Which should have the greater resistance?

### Electric power

The energy of moving charges is converted to heat, light, and motion in electric appliances. Heat is the desired product in electric stoves, toasters, and clothes dryers. Light is the desired product in light bulbs. Motion is the desired product in blenders, fans, and typewriters.

The total amount of energy an appliance uses is measured in joules. The amount of energy it uses per second is its power.

$$\text{power} = \frac{\text{energy}}{\text{time}}$$

Power is measured in joules per second, or watts.

Appliances are often marked with the power in watts that they use. They use their rated power only when the standard voltage (110 V or 220 V) is supplied. In North America, clothes dryers and electric stoves are expected to run on 220 V. All other appliances are expected to run on 110 V.

The electric power company charges customers for the amount of energy they use. The amount of energy on the bill is stated in kilowatt-hours. A typical home might use 500 kilowatt-hours of electricity in a month.

One kilowatt is equal to 1000 watts. It is a unit of power. If a kilowatt of power is used for one second, the amount of energy used is 1000 joules. There are 60 seconds in a minute and 60 minutes in an hour. Thus there are 60 × 60, or 3600, seconds in an hour. A kilowatt of power used for one hour is equal to 3600 × 1000, or 3 600 000, joules of energy.

1 kilowatt-hour = 3 600 000 joules

Why are electric bills stated in kilowatt-hours instead of joules?

**Main Idea**

What condition must be met for the power use of an appliance to be the same as the rated power marked on it?

Figure 8-17. Appliances that heat (or cool) things tend to have higher power ratings than appliances that only move things.

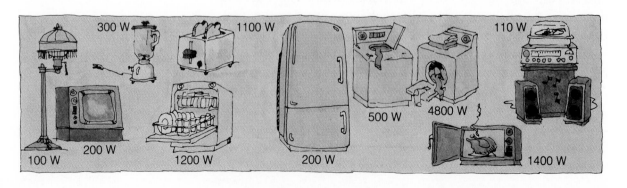

300 W    1100 W    110 W

100 W    200 W    1200 W    200 W    500 W    4800 W    1400 W

The amount of energy an appliance uses depends both on the power rating and on how long it is used.

$$\text{energy} = \text{power} \times \text{time}$$

An 1100-W toaster may be used for two minutes each day. A 400-W refrigerator runs all the time. Which uses more energy?

### Check yourself

How is the amount of energy an appliance uses related to the power rating of the appliance?

---

**Our Science Heritage**

Thomas Edison (1847–1931) is remembered as the greatest of inventors. More than a thousand patents were issued in his name. The phonograph, the electric light bulb, and the motion picture are probably his most famous contributions.

Edison concentrated on making items immediately useful to society. In only one instance is he credited with a scientific discovery. He was the first to use a vacuum tube to permit negative charges to move in only one direction.

The inventor received only a limited formal education. He admitted to having great difficulty with mathematics. His curiosity and hard work helped overcome these limitations. By accident, he came across some of the descriptions of the findings of Michael Faraday. They provided Edison with ideas and background for some of his later inventions. Edison put the results of the work of scientists into practical use.

Edison developed his inventions chiefly by trial and error. He is famous for being an extremely hard worker. He sometimes worked as many as twenty hours a day. He had a large number of people working for him. At times his staff would be working on fifty different inventions.

The interests of Edison encompassed many different fields. As an illustration, at one time he worked on problems related to cement, storage batteries, flamethrowers, periscopes, and the production of rubber from domestic sources. No other inventor has had such an impact on our daily lives.

**Thomas Edison**

Thomas Edison listening to the dictating machine he invented.

# Practical Science

## Controlling Electricity

You start the flow of electricity by closing a switch in the circuit. This allows electrons to flow. You stop the flow of electrons by opening the switch. You can slow down the flow of electrons with a device called a *rheostat*. A rheostat is like a tap on a sink. With it, you can turn on the current full force or slow it down.

**Common appliances that use rheostats**
Do you have an electric range? Rheostats control the heat from the burners. Do you have an electric mixer? The rheostat changes the mixing speeds. Rheostats also control the volume and tone of your radio, television, and stereo. Some dimmer switches for lights may also be controlled by rheostats.

**How a rheostat is constructed**  There are two types of rheostats in your home. Both are circular in shape and usually have three terminals. There is a terminal at each end of the resistance element, or *resistor*. Another terminal is attached to a contact that slides along the length of the resistor.

One type of rheostat is used in heavy-duty motors, electric ranges, and other large appliances. It is called a *wire-wound rheostat*. This type of rheostat must control considerable power. The resistor is made of a coiled wire.

The other type of rheostat is used in low-power appliances such as televisions and stereos. It is called a *potentiometer*. The resistor is made of a thin layer of carbon.

**How does it work?**  A rheostat is an electrical control containing a variable resistor. You slow down a motor or dim a light bulb by turning the rheostat knob in a clockwise direction. This moves the sliding contact along the resistor. The resistance is increased and fewer electrons flow through the rheostat. When you turn the knob in the opposite direction, the resistance is lowered and more electrons flow through the circuit. This causes the motor to speed up or the light to become brighter.

**Save electricity with the new rheostats**  A wire-wound rheostat wastes electricity. This happens because part of the electricity is converted to heat by the resistance of the rheostat.

Modern motor controls and dimmer switches are much more energy efficient than wire-wound rheostats. They use a device called a *semiconductor-controlled rectifier* (SCR) to control the flow of electrons. An SCR does this by turning the current on and off very rapidly. A small potentiometer controls the speed of the on-and-off action. Reducing the speed of this action slows a motor or dims a light. Increasing the speed has the opposite effect.

**Something to try**  You can save money by replacing a regular switch with a dimmer switch. By dimming a light you use less electricity and make the bulb last longer. When you reduce the voltage by ten per cent, you double the bulb life. In which areas of your house would dimmer switches be appropriate?

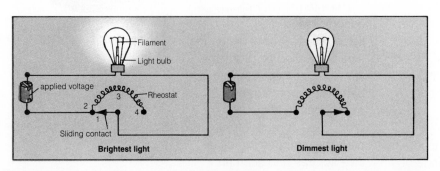

**Brightest light** — Filament, Light bulb, applied voltage, Rheostat, Sliding contact — 1 2 3 4

**Dimmest light**

## Section 2 Review   Chapter 8

### Check Your Vocabulary

| | |
|---|---|
| alternating current | ohm |
| ammeter | positive terminal |
| ampere | resistance |
| battery | voltage |
| direct current | voltage drop |
| negative terminal | voltmeter |

*Match each term above with the numbered phrase that best describes it.*

1. Part of cell where electrons come out
2. Part of cell where electrons enter
3. SI unit of current
4. SI unit of resistance
5. Energy supplied per unit of charge passing through a cell
6. Energy removed per unit of charge passing through a conductor
7. Used to measure current
8. Used to measure voltage drop
9. Contains two or more cells
10. Kind of current commonly used for household appliances
11. Kind of current in which electrons move in one direction
12. Measure of how hard it is for electrons to move through a conductor

### Check Your Knowledge

*Multiple Choice: Choose the answer that best completes each of the following sentences.*

1. In a dc circuit, the positive terminal of an ammeter must be connected ?.
   a) to a flashlight bulb socket
   b) toward the positive terminal of the cell or battery
   c) toward the negative terminal of the cell or battery
   d) directly to the base of the cell or battery
2. For an electric current to exist in a circuit, the circuit must ?.
   a) be closed
   b) contain a light bulb
   c) contain an ammeter
   d) contain a voltmeter

### Check Your Understanding

1. A flashlight bulb is connected to a cell, as shown in the diagram below. Why won't the bulb light?

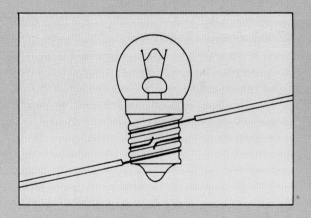

2. Silver is a better conductor than aluminum. If a silver wire and an aluminum wire have the same length and same diameter, which should have a higher resistance? Explain.
3. How much energy, in kilowatt-hours, is used by a 100-W light bulb that is on for 24 hours?

### Practical Science

1. What does a rheostat do?
2. Name some appliances which use a potentiometer and explain why they do.

# Electric Circuits    Section 3

**Section 3 of Chapter 8 is divided into four parts:**

Ohm's law

Series circuits

Parallel circuits

Fuses and other safety devices

*Practical Science: Amateur Radio*

## Learning Objectives

1. To apply Ohm's Law to simple electric circuits.

2. To describe the characteristics of series circuits.

3. To describe the characteristics of parallel circuits.

4. To explain how fuses, circuit breakers, and ground-fault interrupters act as safety devices.

Figure 8-18. The photo of the inside of a hairdryer clearly shows how wires carry electric current to different parts of the hairdryer. Controls on the outside of the hairdryer are connected to the wires. The controls allow you to direct the flow of electric current through the hairdryer.

Any complex circuit is made of simple circuits put together. Learning more about simple circuits is the first step toward understanding complex circuits.

## Ohm's law

Georg Simon Ohm (1789–1854) was a high school teacher in Cologne, Germany. He wanted to find out how the current through a wire was related to the voltage of the battery attached to it. He tested wires of different materials.

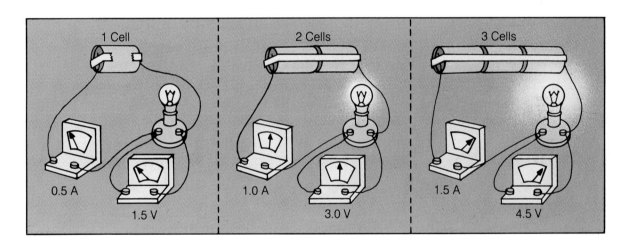

Ohm discovered that the current depended on the material of the wire. It also depended upon the thickness and length of the wire. He kept the material, thickness, and length the same and changed only the voltage. He found that the voltage divided by the current always had the same value. When the voltage doubled, the current doubled. When the voltage tripled, the current tripled. Ohm called this constant value the resistance of the wire.

$$\frac{\text{voltage}}{\text{current}} = \text{resistance}$$

This relation came to known as Ohm's law. In honor of Ohm, the unit of resistance was named the ohm. If a voltage of one volt causes a current of one ampere, the resistance of the wire is one ohm.

Figure 8-19. Putting more cells in a circuit increases the current. When the current increases, the voltage drop across the bulb increases. In this circuit, is the voltage drop divided by the current always the same?

### Library research

Find out what semiconductors are. How are they different from conductors? Why are they so important nowadays?

Ohm's law can be expressed in other forms. In Ohm's simple circuit, the voltage of the battery equaled the voltage drop across the wire. Even when there are other conductors in a circuit, Ohm's law holds for each conductor.

$$\frac{\text{voltage drop}}{\text{current}} = \text{resistance}$$

That is, the voltage drop across a conductor divided by the current through the conductor equals the resistance of the conductor. For example, if a voltmeter across the conductor reads 6 V and an ammeter reads 3 A, then the resistance is 2 ohms.

Another way to express Ohm's law is

$$\text{voltage drop} = \text{current} \times \text{resistance}.$$

For example, if you know that the current is 4 A and the resistance is 3 ohms, the voltage drop is 12 V.

Ohm thought that the resistance of a wire was a property of that wire and did not change. We know that when wires heat up, their resistance increases. Ohm's law describes an ideal situation. It works fairly well for metals. It does not work at all at very low temperatures or for semiconductors such as silicon.

### Check yourself

1. What is Ohm's law?

2. If the voltage drop across a bulb is 3 V and the current through it is 2 A, what is the resistance of the bulb?

Figure 8-20. The three bulbs are connected in series. The same current passes through all three.

### Series circuits

Suppose you wanted to put more than one flashlight bulb in a circuit. Figure 8-20 shows three bulbs connected so that the same current goes through all three bulbs. The bulbs are said to be connected **in series**.

In a series circuit, there is only one path for the current. The same current flows through all parts of the circuit. Breaking the circuit at any point reduces the current to zero. The current is measured by connecting an ammeter in series

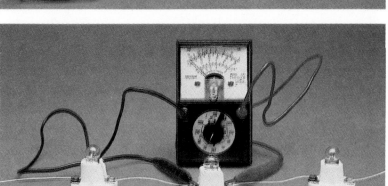

Figure 8-21. In a series circuit, the current is measured by connecting an ammeter in series with the other conductors (top). The voltage drop across one bulb is measured by connecting a voltmeter across the bulb (bottom).

**Data Search**

Give the names of the three men who were awarded the Nobel prize in physics for development of solid-state electronic devices. Search page 558.

with the other conductors in the circuit. See the upper photo in Figure 8-21. Does it make any difference which conductor the ammeter is placed next to?

The voltage drop across one conductor is measured by connecting a voltmeter across the conductor. See the lower photo in Figure 8-21. The total voltage drop in a series circuit is the sum of the voltage drops across each of the conductors. The electrons give up some energy as they move through each conductor.

The total voltage drop is approximately equal to the voltage supplied by the cell or battery. Any difference is due to the resistance of the cell or battery itself. The electrons must use some of their energy in passing through it.

If one of the conductors is removed from the series circuit, the total voltage drop will be the same as before. It still is about equal to the voltage of the cell or battery. However, there will be less resistance in the circuit. According to Ohm's law, the current should be greater. If the conductors are bulbs, they will light more brightly than before. What would happen to the brightness of the bulbs if two more bulbs were added in series to the circuit?

Figure 8-22. A circuit diagram for the circuit pictured in the photo of Figure 8-20. The symbols for many common circuit parts are shown in the key.

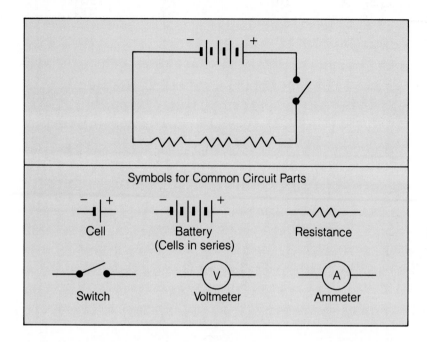

Circuits are represented in diagrams that use symbols for each part of the circuit. A circuit diagram for the series circuit shown in the photo of Figure 8-20 is shown in Figure 8-22. The bulbs are each represented by the symbol for resistance. They provide almost all the resistance in the circuit. The wires are shown by straight or curved lines.

### Check yourself

1. In a series circuit, is the current through each conductor the same as the current through the cell or battery?

2. In a series circuit, when there are fewer conductors in series, how does the current change?

3. Draw a circuit diagram that shows an ammeter and two bulbs in series with a battery. Use the symbols shown in Figure 8-22.

### Parallel circuits

In a series circuit, the current flows through everything in the circuit. Bulbs in series are either all on or all off. Imagine if your home were wired in a series circuit. Shutting off one lamp would shut off everything at once.

## Activity 8–3A    Bulbs in Series

### Materials

3 flashlight bulbs and sockets
switch
2 "D" cells
masking tape
7 10-cm pieces of bell wire
dc ammeter of range 0 A to 1 A
dc voltmeter of range 0 V to 5 V

### Purpose

To study properties of a series circuit.

### Procedure

1. Connect three bulbs in sockets in series with a switch, an ammeter, and two "D" cells that are firmly taped together top to bottom. SAFETY NOTE: *Keep loose wires away from eyes to prevent eye injuries.* The ammeter should be between the switch and the two-cell battery. Connect the negative terminal of the ammeter to the negative terminal of the battery.
2. Close the switch. Read and record the amount of current. Open the switch.
3. Reconnect the ammeter between two of the bulbs. Close the switch. Read and record the amount of current. Open the switch.
4. Reconnect the ammeter as in Step 1.
5. Connect a voltmeter across one of the bulbs. Be sure that the negative terminal of the voltmeter is connected toward the negative terminal of the battery.
6. Close the switch. Read and record the voltage drop. Open the switch.
7. Repeat Steps 5 and 6 with the voltmeter connected across two bulbs.
8. Predict what will happen to the voltage drop if the voltmeter is connected across all three bulbs. Repeat Steps 5 and 6 with the voltmeter connected across all three bulbs.
9. Remove one of the bulbs from its socket without disconnecting the socket. Remove

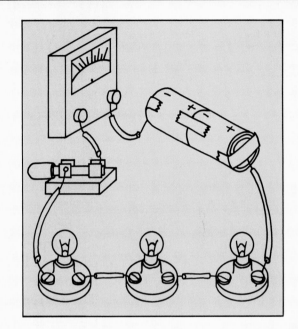

the voltmeter. Close the switch. Record the ammeter reading. Open the switch.
10. Reconnect the circuit so that there are only two bulbs and sockets in series with the ammeter, switch, and battery. Reconnect the voltmeter across one bulb. Close the switch. Record the current value and voltage drop. Open the switch.

### Questions

1. Is the current between the switch and the 2-cell battery the same as the current between two of the bulbs?
2. Compare the voltage drop across two bulbs or three bulbs to that across one bulb.
3. Do the other bulbs remain lit when one bulb is removed from a series circuit? Explain.
4. Compare the current in a "two-bulb" circuit to the current in a "three-bulb" circuit.

### Conclusion

Describe the current and voltage in a series circuit.

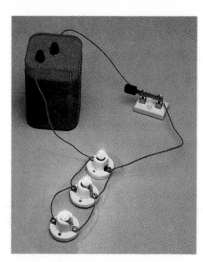

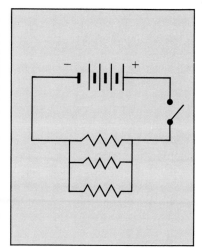

Figure 8-23. The three bulbs are connected in parallel. The current splits up among the three branches.

There is a way to connect conductors so that each can operate independently in a circuit. Figure 8-23 shows three bulbs connected **in parallel**. The bulbs are in separate branches of the circuit. The branches are alternate paths for the current. The current divides up among the branches. Some of the current flows through the first branch. Some flows through the second. The rest flows through the third.

A voltmeter is always connected in parallel with the conductor whose voltage drop is being measured. The voltmeter is an alternate path for the current. An ammeter, on the other hand, is connected in series. The same current must flow through the ammeter as flows through the part of the circuit whose current is being measured.

When one branch in a parallel circuit is open, current can still go through the other branches. A lamp can be shut off by opening a switch in the branch. The current in the other branches does not change. In homes and other buildings, all lights and appliances are connected in parallel.

The voltage drop across each of the branches is the same. The same amount of energy is used per unit of charge no matter which path the current follows. In a home the voltage drop across each branch is the standard 110 V or 220 V.

Figure 8-24 The cells at the left are connected in series. The cells at the right are connected in parallel. Which type of connection supplies the greater voltage to the circuit?

## Activity 8–3B    Bulbs in Parallel

### Materials

3 flashlight bulbs and sockets
switch
2 "D" cells
masking tape
10 10-cm pieces of bell wire
dc ammeter of range 0 A to 1 A
dc voltmeter of range 0 V to 5 V

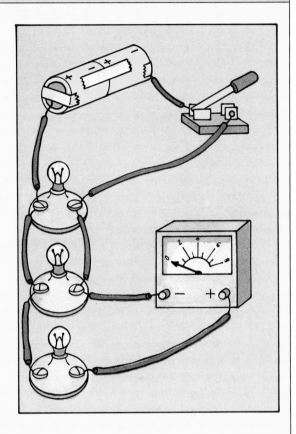

### Purpose

To study properties of a parallel circuit.

### Procedure

1. Connect three flashlight bulbs in sockets in parallel. SAFETY NOTE: *Keep loose wires away from eyes to prevent eye injuries.*
2. Connect them in series with a 2-"D" cell battery, a switch, and an ammeter. Be sure that the negative terminal of the ammeter is toward the negative terminal of the battery.
3. Close the switch. Read and record the current value. Notice how bright the bulbs are. Open the switch.
4. Without disconnecting the socket, remove one bulb. Close the switch. Record the current value. Compare the brightness of the remaining bulbs to their brightness before. Open the switch. Replace the bulb.
5. Connect the ammeter in a branch next to a bulb. Predict how the current will compare to the previous reading.
6. Test your prediction by closing the switch. Record the current and open the switch.
7. Remove a bulb in a different branch from the ammeter. Close the switch; read and record the current value. Open the switch.
8. Connect a voltmeter across one socket. Close the switch, read the meter, and record the voltage drop. Open the switch.
9. Reconnect the voltmeter across a different socket. Close the switch, read the meter. Record the voltage drop. Open the switch.

### Questions

1. Did the brightness of the other light bulbs increase, decrease, or remain the same when a bulb was removed from the circuit?
2. How did the current in one branch compare to the current in the main part of the circuit?
3. Does breaking one branch of the circuit affect the amount of current in the other branches?
4. How do the voltage drops across bulbs in different branches compare?
5. How does the voltage drop in a branch compare to the voltage of the battery?

### Conclusion

Describe the current and voltage in a parallel circuit.

## Library research

Calculators, digital watches, and computers use integrated circuits. Integrated circuits contain no wires. Find out how they are made. What great advantage do they have over circuits made with wires?

Cells, as well as conductors, can be connected in series or parallel. Cells connected in series increase the voltage supplied to the circuit. When "D" cells are connected top to bottom, they are in series. The total voltage is the sum of the voltages of each cell.

Cells connected in parallel have the same voltage as a single cell. However, they last longer than a single cell would. Each supplies energy to only part of the charge moving through the circuit.

### Check yourself

1. In a parallel circuit, is the current through each branch the same as the current through the cell or battery?

2. In a parallel circuit, what happens to the current in the other branches when one branch is opened?

3. In what way do cells connected in parallel act like a single cell? In what way do they act differently?

### Fuses and other safety devices

Wires get hot when they carry current. The greater the current, the hotter the wire becomes. Each wire can safely carry up to a certain amount of current. If it carries more than that amount, it may burn.

A cord designed for alternating current has two groups of wires side by side. The two groups are separated from each other by plastic insulation. If the insulation should crack open, the two groups could touch. Then current would go directly through the opening. It would bypass the appliance at the end of the cord. The resistance in the circuit would be far less than normal. The current would be much greater than normal. The cord could start a fire.

## Main Idea

What is a short circuit?

When the part of a circuit with the most resistance is bypassed, a **short circuit** is said to exist. Short circuits are dangerous because of the heating of the wires. Circuits in buildings contain safety devices that immediately open the circuit if the current becomes too great.

A **fuse** (FYOOZ) is a safety device that contains a substance with a low melting temperature. Should the current increase beyond a safe limit, the heat melts the fuse. The circuit is broken. The potential danger is avoided.

Fuses are rated according to the number of amperes of current that the circuit can safely carry. Fuses should be chosen to match the kind of wiring in the circuit. A fuse with too high a rating for the wiring cannot protect the wiring.

In a building, several wall sockets are connected in parallel in one of the main building circuits. The current in the main circuit is the sum of the currents in the parallel branches. If many appliances that draw high currents are used at the same time, the fuse on the main circuit will burn out. Simply replacing the burned-out fuse does not solve the problem. Instead, some of the appliances should be disconnected.

**Main Idea**

What is a fuse, and how does it work?

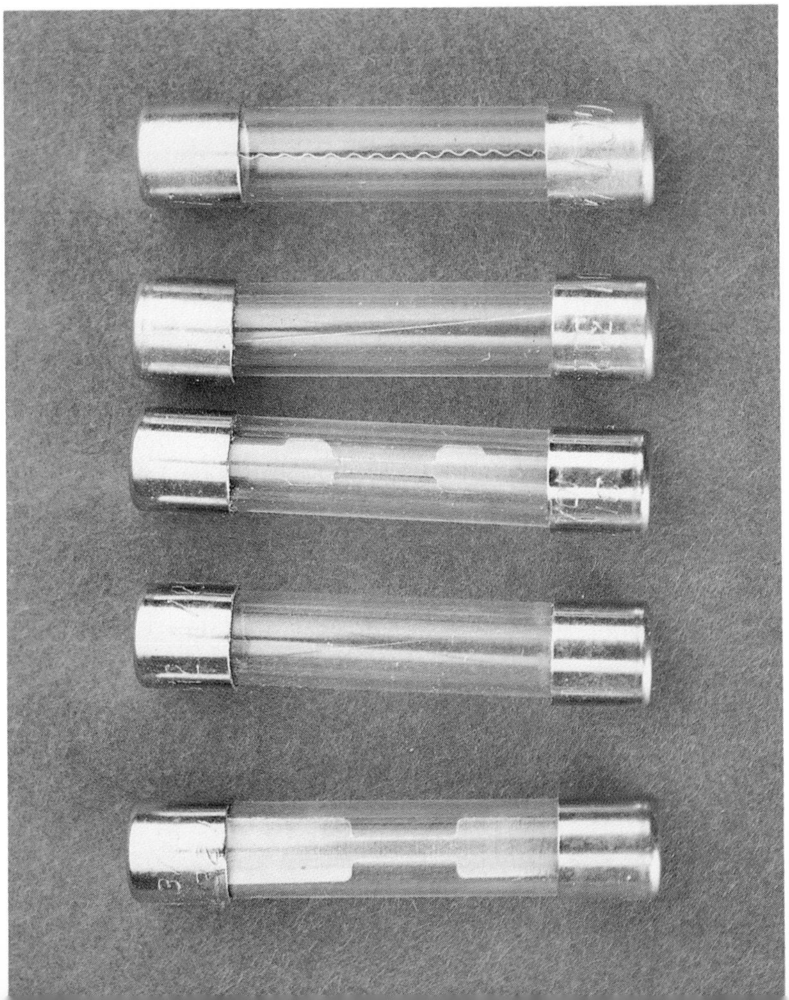

Figure 8-25. Fuses come with different ratings. It is important to check what maximum number of amperes the fuse will permit in a circuit. The fuse should never have a greater rating than the circuit it is protecting.

Figure 8-26. (Left) The fuses for the main circuits in a building are found in the fuse box.

(Right) In modern buildings, circuit breakers are used instead of fuses.

Figure 8-27. The ground-fault interrupter is placed in sockets used around water.

A **circuit breaker** is an alternative to a fuse. It works because a current produces a force on a magnet. When the current becomes too large for safety, the force is great enough to operate a switch. The switch opens the circuit.

One advantage of circuit breakers over fuses is that they do not have to be replaced each time the circuit is opened. The switch can simply be moved back to the "on" position. First, though, the problem that made the circuit open must be found and corrected.

A safety device that may be found in newer circuits is the **ground-fault interrupter**. It is designed for bathrooms, around pools, or in places where there is water. The human body conducts current more easily when it is wet than when it is dry. The interrupter opens the circuit if it senses that some current is passing through a person instead of all going through an appliance. The circuit can be closed again by pressing a reset button.

### Check yourself

What is the first thing that should be done when a safety device opens a circuit?

## Careers  Electrical Engineer / Electrician

**Assembler**  Assemblers are people who put together the parts of manufactured goods. Assemblers' jobs can vary from repetitive tasks which require minimal skills, to intricate jobs that demand specialized training and experience.

Accuracy, judgment, and the ability to read and follow complicated instructions are crucial to precision assembly. As these workers gain experience, they may work with engineers and designers, helping build prototypes of new products.

Classes in drafting, electronics, and mechanics are helpful to an assembler's work. Because assemblers use hand tools and hand-held power tools, they must have good eyesight and eye–hand coordination.

Precision assemblers may be promoted from the ranks of less-skilled laborers. Alternatively, they can acquire skills in junior colleges and technical and vocational schools.

Precision assemblers who build test products must be able to interpret engineering specifications.

**Electrician**  Electricians install and repair electrical systems that operate heating, lighting, air conditioning, communications, or anything needing electric power. Some electricians are self-employed. Others work for electrical contractors or power companies. While construction work is seasonal, the electrician generally works indoors. As a result, the electrician usually has year-round employment.

Special skills in dexterity and physical stamina are often needed in doing the work of an electrician. The work can be hazardous, and extra care must always be exercised. Outdoor work under adverse weather conditions may be required. The electrical needs of the general public are such that even short interruptions in electric power can cause hardship. The power company electrician can be called upon at any time.

The training needed to be an electrician is normally gained through a three- or four-year apprenticeship program. Some training is offered in high school or trade school course work. In some cities, electricians must be licensed before they can work. A high school physics course can provide a good background for the training required to be an electrician.

An electrician may be called on to change the wiring in a building.

# Practical Science

## Amateur Radio

Amateur radio is a hobby enjoyed by thousands of people all over the world. People who operate amateur radios are known as *hams*. Many hams provide vital communications during floods, tornadoes, hurricanes, earthquakes, and other natural disasters. Amateur radio has sometimes been the only way to provide communication with an area for several days after a major natural disaster has struck.

With a ham radio station, it is possible to communicate with people all over the world. Some hams use their own voice as if talking on a telephone. Others send and receive messages using a system of audible sounds called *Morse code*.

Many hams enjoy talking with other hams. Being able to contact hams in distant and out-of-the-way places is a goal for many. Hams specializing in long-distance contacts are known as *"DX'ers"*. This is because DX is the code for distance.

**How amateur radio works**  A ham operator must have both a receiver and a transmitter. Some buy their equipment, while others build their own.

The transmitter produces a single frequency signal. This is called the *carrier frequency*. It must be in an approved ham frequency band. The carrier frequency is set with a tuner.

In voice communications, the transmitter combines the signals from the microphone with the carrier frequency. The transmitter then amplifies the combined, or *modulated,* signal and sends it to the transmitting antenna. This radiates the signal into the air.

The transmitted signal, along with hundreds of others, is picked up by the receiving antenna. To receive a particular signal, the receiver then separates the voice signals from the carrier frequency. The receiver amplifies the voice signals before sending them to the loudspeaker.

A ham uses a special transmitting key to send the long and short signals of Morse code. Hams refer to them as *dits* and *dahs* because of the way they sound. The dits and dahs are made by using the transmitting key to rapidly turn the carrier frequency on and off.

**The language of amateur radio**  Radio operators using code adopted a system of two and three letter signals to speed up code transmissions. Now these are used by both code and voice hams. For example, "QRA" means "What is your station?"

**Citizens' band radio**  Citizens' band, or CB, radio is similar to amateur radio, but has some important differences. CB uses a number of specific frequencies. There are 23 of these frequencies. The legal maximum power of a CB transmitter is only five watts compared with up to two thousand watts for an amateur transmitter. Because of its low power, CB can be heard for only a few miles. You can apply for a CB license without any special training.

**How to become an amateur radio operator**  You must have a Federal Communications System license to operate an amateur radio station. There are five classes of licenses: novice, technician, general, advanced, and amateur extra. You must pass a licensing examination for each class.

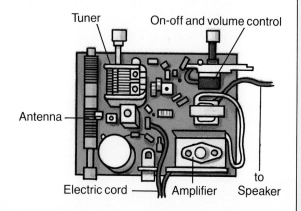

Tuner · On-off and volume control · Antenna · Electric cord · Amplifier · to Speaker

## Section 3 Review    Chapter 8

### Check Your Vocabulary

| | |
|---|---|
| circuit breaker | in parallel |
| fuse | in series |
| ground-fault interrupter | short circuit |

*Match each term above with the numbered phrase that best describes it.*

1. Exists when part of a circuit with most resistance is bypassed
2. Describes conductors that are in the same current path
3. Describes conductors that provide alternate paths for the current
4. Used in circuits that are in places where there is water
5. Opens a switch when the current is too large
6. Burns out when the current is too large

### Check Your Knowledge

*Multiple Choice: Choose the answer that best completes each of the following sentences.*

1. According to Ohm's law, when the voltage in a circuit is doubled, the current ?.
   a) is doubled
   b) is four times as great
   c) is reduced by half
   d) does not change

2. According to Ohm's law, when the resistance is doubled, the current ?.
   a) is doubled
   b) is four times as great
   c) is reduced by half
   d) does not change.

3. When the switch in the circuit shown at the top of the next column is closed, the ammeter measures 0.8 A. The current through bulb 2 is ?.

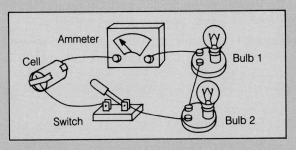

a) 0.4 A
b) 0.8 A
c) 1.6 A
d) impossible to determine from the information given

### Check Your Understanding

1. Suppose you plug a portable heater into the wall. As soon as you turn it on, all the lights in the room go out. Explain what must have happened.
2. Common flashlights require two "D" cells. The cells are pressed against each other by a spring. Explain what advantage two cells have over a single cell.

### Practical Science

1. What are amateur radio operators called?
2. What are dits and dahs?

# Chapter 8 Review

## Concept Summary

**Electric charges** cause pushes and pulls between objects that do not have equal numbers of positive and negative charges.

- □ Neutral objects have equal numbers of protons and electrons.
- □ Objects that gain electrons are negatively charged.
- □ Objects that lose electrons are positively charged.
- □ Opposite charges attract; like charges repel.
- □ Electrons move easily through conductors of electric charge but do not move through insulators.
- □ Objects can be charged by friction, by contact, and by induction.
- □ The force between charged objects depends on the amount of charge on each object and the distance between them.
- □ Energy is required to separate opposite charges or to bring together like charges.

An **electric current** is created by the movement of electric charges.

- □ Electric charges move only when energy is supplied to them.
- □ A current will flow when there is an unbroken path of conductors connected between the negative and positive terminals of an energy source such as a cell or battery.
- □ The size of a current is measured in terms of the amount of charge that passes a point per second.
- □ In a direct current, electrons move in only one direction.
- □ In an alternating current, electrons move back and forth in a regular cycle.
- □ The resistance of a conductor is a measure of how hard it is for charge to move through the conductor.
- □ The amount of energy removed per unit of charge passing through a conductor is the voltage drop across the conductor.

- □ The voltage drop across a conductor equals the resistance times the current through it.
- □ The amount of electric energy used per second by an electric appliance is its power.

An **electric circuit** is a conducting path or set of paths through which current can flow.

- □ A closed circuit is an unbroken loop, while an open circuit has a break in the path.
- □ A series circuit provides only one path for all the charges moving through the circuit.
- □ A parallel circuit provides branches, or alternate paths, so that the moving charges divide up among the branches.
- □ Fuses, circuit breakers, and ground-fault interrupters open a circuit when the current becomes too high for safety.

## Putting It All Together

1. How can the charge on an object be neutral if the object contains both positive and negative charges?
2. What effect do two negatively charged objects have on each other?
3. List two differences between the processes of charging by induction and charging by contact.
4. What causes the lightning that is associated with a thunderstorm?
5. List two ways in which electric forces differ from gravitational forces.
6. What happens at the positive terminal of a cell that is connected within a circuit?
7. When current flows in a circuit, where in the circuit is the build-up of charge the greatest?
8. Identify each of the SI units used to describe current, voltage, resistance, and power.
9. Moving electric charges carry energy. In the home, electric energy is changed into what different forms of energy?
10. How does the current in an electric circuit change when the voltage changes?

11. What happens to the current in a series circuit when another bulb (more resistance) is added? (The voltage stays the same.)
12. How is the diagram of a parallel circuit different from that of a series circuit?
13. What is the combined voltage of two 1.5-V cells connected in series? In parallel?
14. Why is it dangerous to use a fuse that is rated 30 A in a circuit calling for a 15-A fuse?
15. Identify two effects of electric currents that are used to operate or control safety devices.

## Apply Your Knowledge

1. When rubbed with flannel, a balloon becomes negatively charged. Which must have a greater ability to attract electrons?
2. You may have tried to clean a vinyl plastic record by rubbing it with a cloth. Results were probably discouraging. Explain why the record collects lint and dust again almost immediately.
3. Compare the ways in which voltmeters and ammeters are connected in a circuit. How would you expect the resistance of a voltmeter to compare with the resistance of an ammeter? Explain your answer.
4. Using your understanding of the effect of increased temperature, explain why the resistance of a wire increases as its temperature increases.

## Find Out on Your Own

1. Charge a filled balloon by rubbing it with flannel. Bring the charged balloon close to a fine stream of water from a faucet. Note what happens to the stream of water. Does the wool flannel have any effect on the stream of water? Find out what causes charged objects to affect the stream of water.

2. Add some pieces of plastic foam used as packing to a plastic container. Find out how the plastic foam pieces behave when rubbed with a piece of wool flannel. Find out what kind of charge is present on the pieces of plastic foam.
3. Examine a monthly electric bill for your home. Record the number of kilowatt-hours used. Determine the average cost of electricity per kilowatt-hour and the cost per joule. Note whether the bill indicates that the cost per kilowatt-hour changes when the usage is over a certain amount.
4. An ammeter can easily be damaged if excess current flows through it. Examine an ammeter. Find out what effect of the moving electric charges causes the needle to move. Find out what characteristics of the ammeter make it so susceptible to being damaged.
5. Find out from a physics text or other source how different amounts of electric current affect the human body. How much current is "harmless" to the human body? How much current is enough to cause death?

## Reading Further

Boltz, C.L. *How Electricity Is Made*. New York: Facts on File, 1985
  This book relates electricity to modern electron theory, and explores natural and man-made sources of electricity.

Cosner, Sharon. *The Light Bulb: Inventions that Changed Our Lives*. New York: Walker, 1984
  This is an informative biography of Thomas Alva Edison, who, with little formal education, changed the way we live.

Math, Irwin. *Wires and Watts; Understanding and Using Electricity*. New York: Scribner, 1981
  This book describes imaginative do-it-yourself projects using easily obtained materials.

# Chapter 9

# Electromagnetism

Section 1
**Properties of Magnets**

There are two kinds of magnetic poles on a magnet. Like poles repel, while unlike poles attract. Electric currents produce magnetic effects, and magnets produce electric effects.

Section 2
**Electric Energy**

Electric energy is produced by a conversion from other forms of energy. It is usually transported over large distances. Most often, it is used to make things move or converted to heat or light.

In this chapter you will learn about the relationship between magnets and electric currents. The photo at the left shows the inside of an electric bell. Most electric bells contain electromagnets.

# Properties of Magnets     Section 1

**Section 1 of Chapter 9 is divided into five parts:**

Magnetic poles

Magnetic fields

Magnetic fields from electric currents

Electromagnets

Electric currents from magnets

*Practical Science: Microphones and Speakers*

## Learning Objectives

1. To describe the behavior of magnets and their interaction with other magnetic materials.

2. To define a magnetic field and explain the behavior of magnetic materials in a magnetic field.

3. To demonstrate the magnetic effects of an electric current.

4. To illustrate how a changing magnetic field can be used to produce an electric current.

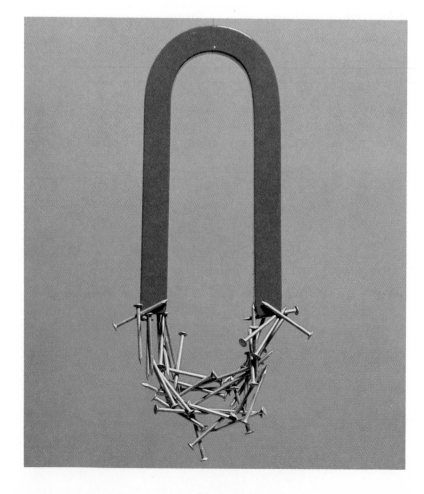

Figure 9-1. Iron tacks are attracted to the end of a bar magnet. The magnetic forces are strongest at the two ends of the magnet.

Magnets are fascinating. A small magnet can pick up many paper clips or tacks. People have known about magnets for thousands of years. Yet, a real understanding of them has developed only in the last two centuries.

## Magnetic poles

Paper clips and tacks cluster at the ends of a straight, or bar, magnet. The places on a magnet where the magnetic forces are strongest are called the **poles**. The poles of a bar magnet are at either end. The poles of a horseshoe magnet are at the ends of the "legs."

The two poles of a magnet respond differently to one of the poles of a second magnet. One pole pulls on the third pole, and the other pole pushes it away. This is evidence that the two poles of a magnet are different.

If a bar magnet is allowed to swing freely, one pole will line up toward the north, more or less. This pole is called the north-seeking pole, or simply the north pole. The other pole lines up toward the south. It is called the south-seeking pole or south pole.

The north poles of different magnets push each other away. So do the south poles of different magnets. They act just like two positive or two negative electric charges. The south pole of one magnet and the north pole of another magnet attract each other. They act just like a positive and a negative electric charge. In sum, like magnetic poles repel. Unlike magnetic poles attract.

Positive charges can be separated from negative charges. Can the poles of magnets be separated? Breaking a bar magnet produces two magnets. Each of the magnets has a north and a south pole. Breaking each of these magnets in half produces twice as many complete magnets. Each smaller magnet has a north and a south pole. This process can be continued until the magnets are very, very tiny.

The forces between poles are greatest when the poles are closest together. Separating the poles reduces the forces. In this way, too, magnetic poles behave in the same way as electric charges.

**Main Idea**

What are the poles of a magnet?

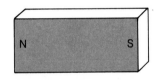

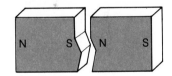

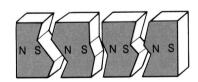

Figure 9-2. When a magnet is broken, each piece has both a south and a north pole.

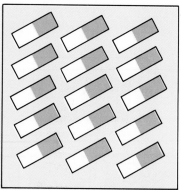

Figure 9-3. (Top) In nonmagnetic iron, the tiny magnets are lined up in all directions.

(Bottom) When iron is made into a magnet, the tiny magnets line up with their north poles all pointing in the same direction.

A magnet attracts paper clips even though the clips are not magnets themselves. Here, a magnet acts like a charged balloon that sticks to the wall. A charged balloon can make a wall act as though it is temporarily charged. A magnet can make a paper clip act as though it is temporarily a magnet.

The properties of a magnet can be explained by the following model. A magnet is pictured as a collection of many tiny magnets. In a magnet, the tiny magnets are all lined up so that their north poles point in the same direction.

Nonmagnets are also made of tiny magnets, but the tiny magnets are in all different directions. In some materials, the tiny magnets will temporarily line up if they are near a large magnet. These materials are the ones that are attracted to magnets. They include iron, cobalt, and nickel. When the large magnet is removed, the tiny magnets return to their original positions.

The same materials that are attracted to magnets can be made into magnets. This is done by stroking the material many times with a magnet. The tiny magnets line up because of the stroking.

The magnetic properties of a magnet can be destroyed by heating. When the temperature of a substance rises, its particles move faster. The tiny magnets move around and get out of order. Banging a magnet can also destroy its magnetic properties. The tiny magnets are pushed out of order.

### Check yourself

1. What happens when the south poles of two magnets are brought close to each other?

2. How can the attraction between a magnet and an iron nail be explained?

### Magnetic fields

A magnet does not have to touch something to push or pull on it. Magnetic forces, like electric and gravitational forces, act at a distance. Two magnets repel or attract each other without direct contact.

**Activity 9–1A**    Mapping a Magnetic Field

### Materials

bar magnet
sheet of unlined paper
small compass
meter stick or ruler

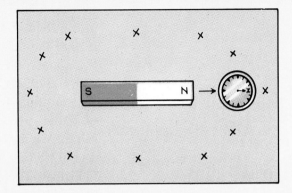

### Purpose

To map the magnetic field around a bar magnet.

### Procedure

1. Place a bar magnet near the center of a piece of unlined paper.
2. Outline the position of the magnet with a pencil. Label the poles: "N" and "S."
3. Place a small compass one cm from the north end of the magnet. Draw a small arrow pointing the same direction as the compass needle.
4. Move the compass straight away from the end of the magnet. Every 1–2 cm, make an arrow to show the direction of the compass needle.
5. Start at each of the points marked with an X in the drawing above. Move the compass away from the magnet, marking arrows every 1–2 cm.
6. Next, fill in the spaces between the arrows.
7. Starting at the south end of the magnet, draw a smooth line through nearby arrows. Con-

tinue the line, curving it when necessary to keep the line parallel to arrows near it.
8. Draw at least five lines on each side of the magnet.

### Questions

1. Are the magnetic field lines closer together at the poles or at the center of the magnet?
2. Where is the direction of the field parallel to the magnet?
3. Where is the direction of the field directly toward or away from the magnet?

### Conclusion

Describe the magnetic field around a bar magnet.

---

The region around a magnet is where magnetic forces can act. A region where magnetic forces can act is said to be filled with a **magnetic field**. The field is strongest where an object would feel the strongest force.

At each position around the magnet, the field has a direction as well as a strength. The direction is the direction that a compass needle at that position points.

A magnetic field can be represented by curving lines. These lines are called **magnetic field lines**. A tiny compass needle would line up along the magnetic field line through any place

**Main Idea**

What is a magnetic field?

in the field. The magnetic field lines around a magnet are a map of the magnetic field. Where the lines are closest together, the magnetic field is strongest. Where the lines are farthest apart, the field is weakest.

Iron filings may be used to outline a magnetic field. A piece of paper, glass, or plastic is placed over the magnet. Iron filings are sprinkled on the paper. Each of the iron filings acts like a tiny, temporary magnet. The filings line up in the field like little compass needles. The positions of the filings show the direction of the magnetic field of the magnet.

The iron filings are closest together where the magnetic field is the strongest. They are farthest apart where the magnetic field is the weakest. Thus, they show the positions of the magnetic field lines for the magnet.

## Main Idea

What can iron filings show about a magnetic field?

Figure 9-4. Iron filings outlining the magnetic field of a bar magnet (top) and horseshoe magnet (bottom). How can you tell where the poles of the magnets must be?

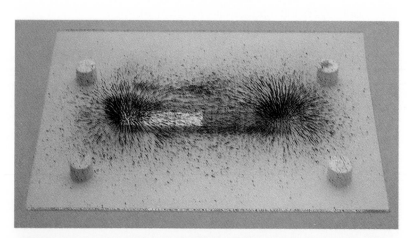

The needle in a compass is a magnetized needle that is free to turn. It tends to point north because the earth itself has a magnetic field. A compass needle lines up with the magnetic field lines of the earth's own field.

The earth's magnetic field is nearly the same as that produced by a large bar magnet. The earth acts as though there were a bar magnet deep inside, near the earth's center.

A compass needle does not point to the earth's true north pole. This is because the imaginary bar magnet does not point directly north and south. Instead, it points northward to what is called the earth's magnetic north pole. The earth's magnetic north pole is in northern Canada, just north of the Arctic Circle. Similarly, the earth's magnetic south pole is right near the Antarctic Circle, south of Australia. The earth's magnetic

**Data Search**

Suppose you are standing at the point where South Dakota, Wyoming, and Nebraska meet. How many degrees would you adjust your magnetic compass to find true north? Search page 561.

Figure 9-5. The earth's magnetic field is like that of a bar magnet near the earth's center. The imaginary bar magnet points toward the earth's magnetic poles, which are different from the true north and south poles.

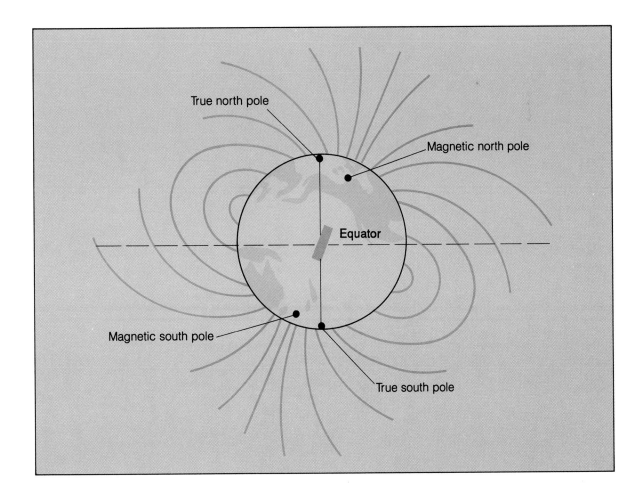

## Library research

Read about the hypotheses to explain what causes the earth's magnetic field. What seems to be the most widely accepted hypothesis?

## Main Idea

What is the evidence that a current can produce a magnetic field?

Figure 9-6. When there is no current in a wire, a nearby compass needle points toward the north. A current causes the needle to line up at right angles to the wire. What happens to the compass needle when the direction of the current is reversed?

poles slowly move. Studies indicate that there have been major changes in the earth's magnetic field over long time periods.

Pieces of iron can be magnetized. A piece of iron is lined up with the earth's field. The iron is hit with a hammer. The tiny magnets inside the iron realign in the direction of the earth's field. Now the piece of iron is a magnet.

### Check yourself

How do magnetic field lines represent the strength of a magnetic field?

## Magnetic fields from electric currents

A compass can be used to detect whether a wire is carrying an electric current. The needle of the compass is deflected, or turned, away from north when an electric current is present. A magnetic field is caused by the current.

The discovery that a current produces a magnetic field caused great excitement. It was the first evidence of a link between electric charges and magnetic effects. The discovery was made by a Danish physics professor, Hans Christian Oersted (1777–1851). He was giving a classroom demonstration. He had a wire lying above a compass. He noticed that when the circuit was closed, the compass needle moved. It

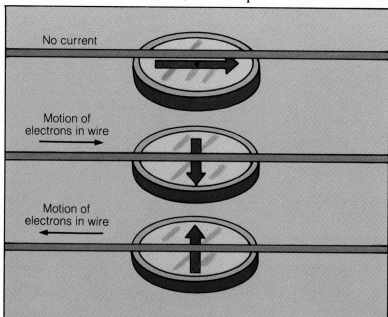

## Activity 9–1B    The Magnetic Field of a Current-Carrying Wire

### Materials

2 "D" cells
masking tape
heavy cardboard, about 30 cm × 30 cm
insulated wire, 60 cm, with ends exposed
4 small compasses
5 thick books

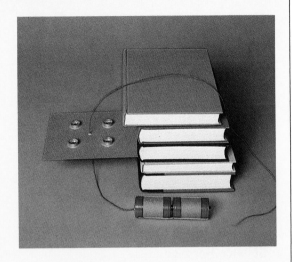

### Purpose

To map the magnetic field around a straight, current-carrying wire.

### Procedure

1. Tape together two "D" cells top to bottom to form a battery.
2. Punch a small hole in the center of a 30 cm × 30 cm piece of cardboard.
3. Push one end of the wire through the hole and tape it to the negative terminal (flat end) of your battery. SAFETY NOTE: *Keep loose wire away from eyes.*
4. Place one edge of the cardboard in the center of a pile of five books. Most of the cardboard should stick out.
5. Lay the upper end of the wire over the top book. The wire should pass straight up and down through the cardboard.
6. Put compasses on the cardboard around the wire.
7. On a sheet of paper make 3 large drawings. In each one show the wire surrounded by the 4 compasses. Label one drawing Step 7. Record the direction each needle points.
8. Label one drawing Step 8. Close the circuit for a few seconds by touching the free end of the wire to the positive terminal of the battery. Record the direction each compass needle points when current flows through the wire.
9. Label one drawing Step 9. Reverse the direction of the current through the wire by reversing the connections to the battery. Again record the direction each compass needle points.
10. Electrons were moving from the negative terminal of the battery to the positive terminal when current was flowing through the wire. Place your left hand around the wire so that your thumb points in the direction the electrons were moving. Compare the direction your fingers are pointing to the direction the compass needles pointed.

### Questions

1. Are all the compass needles pointing in the same direction when no current is flowing?
2. What happens to the compass needles when current flows through the wire?
3. What was your thumb indicating when the fingers of your left hand were pointing around the wire in the direction of the magnetic field.

### Conclusions

1. What is the shape of the magnetic field lines around a straight current carrying wire?
2. How is the direction of the magnetic field related to the direction of electron flow?

lined up at a right angle to the wire. He reversed the connections, so that the current moved in the opposite direction. The needle reversed its direction. It lined up in the opposite direction from before.

### Check yourself

How can the interaction between a compass needle and a wire that is carrying a current be explained?

## Our Science Heritage

### Hans Christian Oersted

The Danish scientist Hans Christian Oersted (1777–1851) discovered somewhat by accident that a current exerts a force on a magnet. He was lecturing to students at the time. Because of his background, he was able to realize the importance of his discovery. He repeated and refined the experiment outside of class. Then he demonstrated the effect for other scientists and published his findings.

Prior to the discovery, Oersted believed that electricity and magnetism were connected. As many as ten years earlier, he had suggested the connection in a paper he wrote. One reason the connection may not have been discovered earlier is that the direction of the force is unusual. The current neither pulls the needle toward itself nor pushes it directly away.

Instead, the current makes the needle align at a right angle to the wire.

Many important scientific discoveries have been made by accident. They might have been overlooked had they not been observed by a person with the right training to notice the unexpected. Before a discovery is accepted by other scientists, it must be observed many other times.

Oersted made other contributions to science. He was the first to determine the compressibility of water accurately. He experimented with the use of thermocouples. He also improved the tension balance used to measure electric forces.

Oersted was very interested in making the public aware of new findings in science. He founded a society to promote science in Denmark.

## Electromagnets

A wire that carries a current has a magnetic field around it. Increasing the current makes the magnetic field stronger. Another way to make the magnetic field stronger is to put many wires side by side. A coil of wire is like many wires side by side. The same current goes through each loop of the coil. The magnetic field is much stronger than it would be if the wire were straight.

The magnetic field of a coil of wire can be made stronger by inserting an iron bar in the coil. The iron bar with the coil around it is then an **electromagnet** (ih-lek′-trō-MAG′-net). The tiny magnets in the iron line up in the magnetic field. When the current stops, the tiny magnets return to their original positions.

Increasing the number of turns in the coil makes the magnetic field stronger. The fields of all the turns add together to make up the field of the whole coil.

Another way to increase the magnetic field of an electromagnet is to increase the current in the coil. This can be done by increasing the voltage supplied to the coil.

A **galvanometer** (gal-vuh-NOM′-uh-ter) is an instrument that can detect small currents. It has a needle that is deflected by the magnetic field of a coil of wire. Greater currents produce stronger magnetic fields. The stronger the magnetic field is, the more the needle is deflected.

A simple galvanometer can be made with a coil of wire and a compass. Figure 9-7 shows such a galvanometer. The coil is vertical. A compass fits horizontally inside it.

The ends of the coil can be connected into a circuit. When current flows through the coil, a magnetic field is produced. The needle is deflected in the direction of the field. When the current reverses direction, the needle is deflected toward the other side. Thus, a galvanometer can measure the direction of a current.

**Main Idea**

What is the effect of placing an iron bar inside a coil of wire carrying a current?

Figure 9-7. A simple galvanometer can be made with a coil of wire and a compass. When the coil is connected to a circuit, current flows through it. The magnetic field inside the coil makes the compass needle turn.

## Check yourself

Name two ways to make the magnetic field of an electromagnet stronger.

## Activity 9–1C Making an Electromagnet

### Materials

meter stick or ruler    2 "D" cells
pen or pencil    iron tacks or brads
masking tape    iron bolt
insulated wire, 1 m, with ends exposed

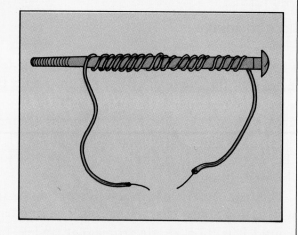

### Purpose

To make an electromagnet and determine how its strength can be changed.

### Procedure

1. Prepare a narrow coil of wire by winding the central portion of a one-meter-long insulated wire around a pencil or pen. Leave about 30 cm free at each end. SAFETY NOTE: *Keep loose wire away from eyes to prevent eye injuries.*
2. Using masking tape, attach one end of the wire to the negative (flat) end of a "D" cell.
3. Place a pile of tacks or brads near one end of the coil.
4. Briefly touch the free end of the wire to the positive (top) end of the cell. Record what happens to the tacks.
5. Place an iron bolt inside the coil.
6. Hold the end of the bolt over the tacks.
7. Again, briefly touch the free end of the wire to the top of the cell. Record the number of tacks picked up.
8. Increase the number of turns in the coil. Leave only 3–5 cm of wire free at each end. Leave the bolt in the cell.
9. Record the number of tacks picked up when you briefly close the circuit.
10. Tape a second cell to the first, top to bottom.
11. Predict how a second cell will effect the electromagnet. Record your prediction.
12. Briefly close the circuit. Record how many tacks are picked up by the electromagnet.

### Questions

1. Was there any evidence that the empty coil of wire had a magnetic field?
2. How did putting an iron bolt in the coil change the magnetic field?
3. How did increasing the number of turns in the coil change the magnetic field?
4. What happened to the strength of the magnetic field when the second "D" cell was added?

### Conclusions

1. What factors change the strength of an electromagnet?
2. What advantage does an electromagnet have over a permanent magnet?

## Electric currents from magnets

A wire with a current through it has a magnetic field. A coil of wire with a current through it acts like a bar magnet.

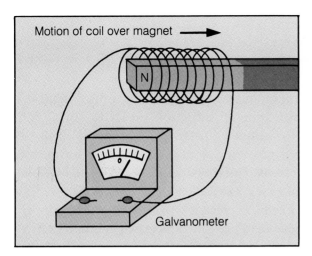

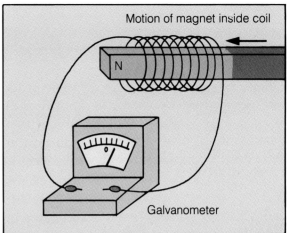

If a magnet can be made by using a current, can a current be made by using a magnet? Michael Faraday (1791–1867), an Englishman, was the first person to announce that it could be done. An American physics professor, Joseph Henry (1797–1878), had discovered it on his own. However, he had been too busy teaching to publish his results.

A coil of wire is attached to a galvanometer to make a closed circuit. There is no cell or battery in the circuit. The coil is placed around the end of a bar magnet. When neither the coil nor the magnet is moving, no current is detected. However, as the coil is moved, there is a current. The current changes direction when the coil is moved in the opposite direction.

The wire coil contains electrons that can move easily. When the coil is not moving, the electrons feel no magnetic force. They do not move within the coil and form a current.

When the coil is moving, the electrons do feel a magnetic force. The magnetic force makes the electrons move through the coil. Now there is a current in the coil.

Moving the coil in the opposite direction reverses the direction of the force on the electrons. They move through the coil in the opposite direction.

Another way to change the direction of the current is to change the direction of the magnetic field. This is done by using the other end of the bar magnet.

Moving a coil over the end of a bar magnet produces a current. So does moving a bar magnet through a coil. It makes no difference whether it is the coil or the magnet that is moving. The important thing is the motion. When the motion stops, the current stops.

Figure 9-8. A current can be detected in a coil when either the coil moves through the field of a magnet (left) or a magnet moves through the coil (right).

**Library research**

Both Michael Faraday and Joseph Henry were important scientists who made interesting discoveries. Choose one of these scientists and prepare a report about his life and achievements.

The production of an electric current by using a magnet is known as **electromagnetic induction** (in-DUK′-shun). The current is said to **induced** (in-DEWST′). The discovery of induction made it possible for every home and business to have electric currents. Currents could be produced without using cells and at much less cost.

Devices that produce electric current by turning a coil through a magnetic field are called **electric generators** (JEN′-er-rayt-erz). In most communities, the current is supplied by large generators, which may be far away.

At the generating plant, energy to turn the coils of wire is supplied by one of several kinds of sources. Sometimes falling water turns the coils. More often, large steam turbines turn the coils. Water is changed into steam by heat produced from burning fossil fuels such as natural gas or coal. Nuclear reactions are used in some generating plants to produce the heat needed to make steam. Sunlight is being tried as the source in a few experimental plants with solar collectors.

Faraday made another important discovery about electric currents. A changing current in one circuit produces a cur-

Figure 9-9. A large electric generator. It uses steam turbines to turn coils within a magnetic field, thereby producing electric current.

rent in another circuit, even though the circuits are not connected.

Look at Figure 9-10. It shows a circuit containing a battery and a coil of wire wound around an iron bar. A second circuit with no battery has a coil that is wound over the first coil. The two coils are separated by insulation. Electrons cannot move from one circuit to the other. The second circuit contains a galvanometer.

When the first circuit is opened or closed, a current is observed in the second circuit. When the first circuit has a steady current, there is no current in the second circuit. Only a *changing* current in the first circuit produces a current in the second circuit.

Closing the circuit creates a magnetic field around the first coil. Since there is no field when the circuit is open, closing the circuit changes the magnetic field. Similarly, opening the circuit changes the magnetic field. The second coil is then in a changing magnetic field. The changing field has the same effect as motion through a field. Even though there is no motion, the change in the field induces a current in the second coil.

Thus, electric currents can be induced three ways. A coil in a closed circuit can be moved within a magnetic field. A magnetic field can be moved in relation to the coil. Or the magnetic field around the coil can be changed.

With a cell or battery, the only way to change the current is to open or close the circuit. However, alternating current is constantly changing its direction of flow. If one coil is connected to a source of alternating current, there will always be a current in the second coil. The second current will be an alternating current, too.

Moving electrons produce magnetic fields. Changing magnetic fields produce electric currents. Clearly, electric and magnetic forces are linked. The branch of physics that deals with both electric and magnetic effects is called **electromagnetism** (ih-lek′-trō-MAG′-neh-tizm).

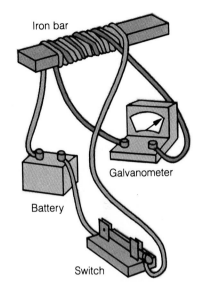

Figure 9-10. A current can be induced in the circuit connected to the galvanometer. The current is induced when the circuit connected to the battery is opened or closed. The changing magnetic field of the inner coil induces a current in the outer coil.

### Check yourself

Describe three ways that a current can be induced in a circuit.

A computer specialist may do much of her own work at a computer keyboard.

## Computer Specialist

Employment for computer specialists is available in many varied situations. Firms that have large computer systems hire computer programmers, systems analysts, computer operators, and service technicians. System analysts plan and develop methods for computerizing business and scientific tasks. Computer programmers write the directions, or software, that tell the computer exactly what to do. Computer operators actually work the computer consoles, printers, disk drives, and tape readers using operating instructions from programmers.

The level of education and training required for these jobs varies greatly. Systems analysts generally have at least a bachelor's degree in computer science. Computer programmers need a specialized vocational degree or appropriate college courses with a bachelor's degree. Computer operators usually get much of their training on the job or by vocational training in high school or junior college. Computer service technicians need one to two years of specialized training beyond high school in basic electronics and data processing equipment maintenance.

Competition among computer firms and the rapid growth of the field ensure excellent job opportunities to any type of computer specialist.

In repairing part of a stereo system, a technician uses test equipment to find the problem.

## Radio and Television Technician

Radio and television technicians repair radios, television sets, and other electronic products. Many own their own repair shops and are self-employed. Others work for repair shops or for stores that both sell and repair these products.

The ability to use tools and certain test instruments is needed. Technicians must be able to diagnose problems and correct them. They must also be able to work with precision. The changing design of products provides variety and new challenges in the work.

Entry into the field usually requires two or more years of technical training. The training may be obtained in a trade school, a community college, or in vocational courses in high school. Two to four years of on-the-job training are needed after the schooling.

# Practical Science

## Microphones and Speakers

Microphones and loudspeakers convert one form of energy into another. A microphone converts sound energy into electric energy. A loudspeaker converts electric energy into sound energy. Both use the principle you learned about in this chapter. When a coil of wire moves in a magnetic field, an electric current is created. The reverse is also true. When an electric current is applied to a coil of wire in a magnetic field, the coil will move.

**How a moving-coil microphone works**  A moving-coil microphone, also called a dynamic microphone, has a strong magnet, a nonmetallic diaphragm, and a voice coil. The voice coil consists of a few turns of fine wire. One end of the voice coil is attached to the center of the diaphragm. The diaphragm is supported along its outer edge by stiff material.

When you speak into a moving-coil microphone, the center of the diaphragm moves back and forth. The diaphragm moves the voice coil, causing it to slide along the arm of the magnet. This movement creates electric energy in the coil. There are also other types of microphones: carbon, ceramic, piezoelectric, ribbon, and condenser. All work on the same principle. Sound energy causes a part in the microphone to move and create an electric current.

**How loudspeakers work**  A loudspeaker works in a similar manner to a moving-coil microphone. The most common type of loudspeaker used in sound systems is the moving-coil loudspeaker. It is built similarly to a moving-coil microphone, but is much larger.

A loudspeaker has a magnet and a voice coil attached to a diaphragm. The magnet is circular and surrounds the voice coil. The diaphragm in a loudspeaker is called a *cone*. When electrical current comes from an amplifier, it energizes the voice coil. The voice coil moves the cone back and forth and creates sound.

**Sound systems**  A sound system consists of one or more microphones, loudspeakers, amplifiers, and volume controls. The microphone converts sound energy into electric currents, or signals. These signals have the same wave shapes as the sounds that created them. Signals can also come from a record player or a tape deck.

The signal is amplified or increased many times by an amplifier. The amplifier also has tone and volume controls. The amplified signal then goes to a loudspeaker which converts it into sound.

**Something to try**  Find an old loudspeaker. Take it apart and find the voice coil, the magnet, and the cone diaphragm. See how they are connected. If you can obtain an old microphone, take it apart also.

Look around your house and your school for microphones and loudspeakers. How many different microphones and speakers can you find? Where are they used?

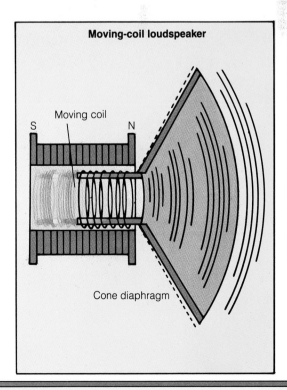

**Moving-coil loudspeaker**

Moving coil

S    N

Cone diaphragm

# Section 1 Review    Chapter 9

## Check Your Vocabulary

| | |
|---|---|
| electric generator | galvanometer |
| electromagnet | magnetic field |
| electromagnetic induction | magnetic field line |
| | pole |
| electromagnetism | |

*Match each term above with the numbered phrase that best describes it.*

1. Fills the region around a magnet

2. Becomes a magnet when a current passes through it

3. Produces electric current by turning a coil through a magnetic field

4. Shows how a compass needle would line up

5. Is used to measure the size and direction of small currents

6. One of the places on a magnet where the magnetic forces are strongest

7. Production of a current by a magnetic field

8. Branch of physics dealing with both electric and magnetic effects

## Check Your Knowledge

*Multiple Choice: Choose the answer that best completes each of the following sentences.*

1. One way that magnetic poles differ from electric charges is that _?_.
   a) like poles push each other away
   b) unlike poles attract each other
   c) the force between poles becomes weaker as the poles are moved farther apart
   d) a single pole cannot be removed from a magnet

2. The magnetic field of the earth is _?_.
   a) strongest at the equator
   b) much like that of a bar magnet

   c) unchanging according to very sensitive measurements
   d) what makes objects fall to the earth

3. Current will be induced in a circuit containing a coil that is _?_.
   a) near a magnet
   b) touching a magnet
   c) around a moving magnet
   d) connected to a galvanometer

4. A current in one circuit can induce a current in a second circuit when _?_.
   a) the current in the first circuit is constant
   b) the current in the first circuit is alternating
   c) both circuits are in a constant magnetic field
   d) the field due to the current in the first circuit is at right angles to the earth's magnetic field

## Check Your Understanding

1. Brass is not attracted to a magnet, but steel is. How could you use a magnet to test whether a brass bed was solid brass or brass-coated steel?

2. If you were on an Arctic expedition and were trying to find the true geographic north pole, could you use a compass? Explain.

3. Alnico is an alloy made of steel, aluminum, nickel, and cobalt. It is hard to magnetize. However, once magnetized, it remains magnetic for a long time. Explain why it would not be a good choice for the core of an electromagnet.

## Practical Science

Name the three major components of a moving-coil microphone.

# Electric Energy    Section 2

**Section 2 of Chapter 9 is divided into four parts:**

Generating electric energy

Other sources of electric energy

Transporting electric energy

Using electric energy

*Practical Science: Audio and Video on Magnetic Tape*

## Learning Objectives

1. To identify the sources of electric energy.

2. To describe the procedures used to transfer electric energy over large distances.

3. To identify and describe the ways in which electric energy is put to use.

Figure 9-11. A dam controls the flow of water that powers a hydroelectric plant. The moving water causes powerful engines to turn. These engines then produce electricity.

## Library research

One of the first electric power plants was the Pearl Street Station, constructed by Thomas Edison in New York City. Find out how power plants have changed over the years. Why is it no longer feasible for each community to have its own power plant?

The use of energy from electric currents has increased dramatically all over the world during the past few decades. This trend is expected to continue in the years ahead.

Existing electric generating plants are being expanded. New electric generating plants are being built each year. They all require energy from an outside source. This energy is used to produce electric currents. The energy carried by currents can be thought of as electric energy.

## Generating electric energy

An electric current can be induced when a coil of wire is moved in the magnetic field of a magnet. Large electric generators operate on this principle. Coils of wire are rotated in a strong magnetic field. The magnetic field is generally supplied by large stationary electromagnets.

The rotating coils are usually on a shaft connected to the blades of steam turbines. The turbine blades are turned by steam formed from the heating of water (Chapter 5, Section 1). When the turbine blades turn, the coils rotate in the magnetic field. Current is induced.

As the steam does work by turning the blades, it cools and becomes a liquid. The liquid water is reheated and the process continues. The steam again does the work of turning the blades of the turbine.

The heat needed to change water to steam can come from different sources. Most generating plants now burn coal, oil, or natural gas. Shortages of these fossil fuels have resulted in a wider use of nuclear reactions.

The heat from the nuclear reactions is used in the same way as heat from the burning of fossil fuels. Safeguards are provided to prevent dangerous radiation from leaving the nuclear reactor. Nuclear reactions are described in detail in Chapter 10, Section 2.

A small but important part of the electric energy we use is generated by falling water. Water moves downhill in rivers. When a dam is built across a river, water is held back at the higher level. A small amount of water is allowed to leave the higher level. As it falls, it turns turbine blades for an electric

## Data Search

Of the energy consumed in 1983, what percent came from water power? Search page 558.

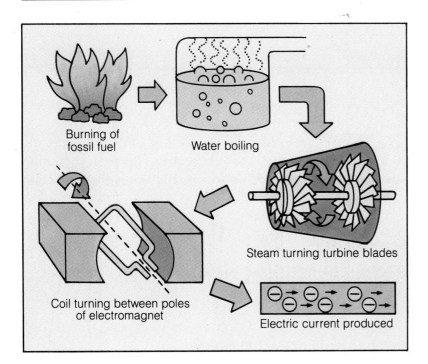

Figure 9-12. What are the steps that convert the energy released in burning a fossil fuel into electric energy in a generating plant?

generator. The potential energy of the falling water is converted to kinetic energy and then to electric energy.

A generating plant that gets energy from falling water is referred to as **hydroelectric**. The prefix *hydro-* comes from the Greek word for *water*. Hydroelectric plants can provide an inexpensive source of electric energy. Pollution problems that accompany the use of fossil fuels and nuclear reactions

Figure 9-13. Hydroelectric plants are built near large dams. What is the source of energy that is used in turning the generator coils?

can be avoided. However, dams can create other problems because they affect the wildlife that lives in the rivers.

Large solar generating plants are just starting to operate. Rows of mirrors gather and concentrate the sun's radiation. The energy in the radiation heats the water for the steam turbine.

### Check yourself

Besides fossil fuels, what can be used as a source of energy in electric generating plants?

### Other sources of electric energy

Using magnetic fields and coils of wire is the most common method of generating electric current. There are other methods that are less common. They are used in some very specific situations. They are interesting because they illustrate some very important principles.

Contact between two different metals that are at different temperatures causes a flow of electrons. The amount of current produced depends on the difference in temperature. A device that produces current in this way is a **thermocouple** (THER′-mō-kuh-pul).

A simple thermocouple is shown in Figure 9-14. Copper wire and iron wire are twisted together at the ends. The ends, where the two kinds of wire meet, are called junctions. The copper wire has been cut so that a galvanometer could be connected in the middle. The galvanometer can measure any current in the circuit.

One junction is in ice water, at 0°C. The other junction is being heated by a candle. As the second junction becomes hotter, the current in the circuit increases.

Thermocouples are often used as safety devices in furnaces. Suppose the temperature above the burner becomes too high for safety. The thermocouple either can operate the switch for a blower fan or turn off the fuel supply. Thermocouples are also used to indicate the temperature in an automobile engine. Should the temperature reach a danger

**Main Idea**

What is a thermocouple?

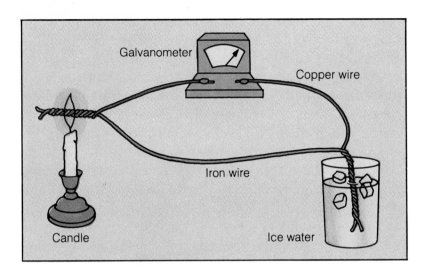

Figure 9-14. A simple thermocouple. What would happen to the current if the candle were blown out?

level, a warning light is turned on. Thermocouples are used to measure temperatures where use of other devices may be difficult. One such example is in very high-temperature furnaces.

Some crystals, such as quartz, produce a flow of electrons when they are compressed under forces. The compression causes changes in the shape of the crystal. The electrons are moved from their normal positions. When the forces are removed, the electrons return to their normal positions. Varying the forces on the crystal varies the current produced.

Sound produces compressions. Crystals have been used in microphones. The compressions in the sound wave change the shape of the crystal. These shape changes are converted into a varying electric current. The current can be carried through conductors. Then it can be converted back to sound at a distant location.

Up until the last decade, crystals were common in phonograph cartridges. As the needle moved through the grooves on a record, it changed the shape of the crystal in the cartridge. The changes in shape produced a varying current. The varying current was converted back into the original sounds at the speaker. Modern phonograph cartridges use electromagnetic induction to change motion into current.

Some materials release electrons when light shines on them. Selenium, silicon, and germanium have this property. Cells

Figure 9-15. The energy that runs this pocket calculator comes from the sun.

made of these materials are called **solar cells**. When sunlight falls on a solar cell, electrons move and create a current. The energy of the current comes from the sunlight.

Orbiting satellites and spacecraft rely to a large extent on this source of energy to operate their controls and to send communications. The amount of electric energy produced in a solar cell is small. However, several solar cells can be connected in series to provide the energy needed.

Solar cells have been used in exposure meters for photographers for many years. New uses for them have been found recently. They are the source of energy in many wristwatches and pocket calculators. The energy of light is used to recharge a battery that operates the watch or calculator. The use of solar cells to provide electric energy for the home may soon be possible.

### Check yourself

1. How does a thermocouple produce a current?
2. How does a crystal produce a current?
3. How does a solar cell produce a current?

### Transporting electric energy

Electric generating plants normally serve large areas. Some of the electric energy must be transported great distances. Electric energy cannot be stored very efficiently. It must be produced as it is needed.

The transmission lines that carry the electric energy must heat up as little as possible. The heating of the lines reduces the amount of electric energy available at the receiving end. Thus, the lines should be made of good conductors, which have the lowest resistance.

Silver and copper are the best conducting materials. Copper is used most often. Due to its high cost, silver is used only in special cases. Although not as good a conductor, aluminum is also used because it is cheap and lightweight.

The resistance of a conductor increases with its length. Resistance decreases with the thickness of the wire. Using short, large-diameter wires is not possible. The heat loss must be reduced in other ways.

The amount of electric energy transported per unit of time is the power. The power depends on the voltage as well as on the current in the transmission lines. The same amount of electric power can be transported at high voltage and low current, or at high current and low voltage.

A low current is preferable. The amount of energy lost in heating increases rapidly as the current increases. When the current is low, large-diameter wires do not need to be used. Thus, electric power is transported at high voltage and low current.

Voltages of more than 300 000 V are used in some transmission lines. Voltages can be raised and lowered by using

Figure 9-16. Power transmission lines transport electric energy at high voltage to make the energy loss as small as possible.

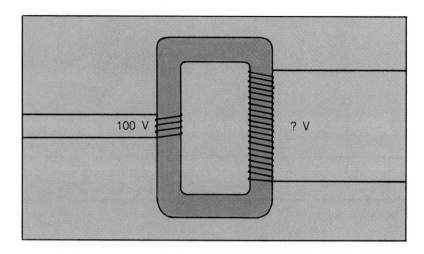

Figure 9-17. In this transformer, the second coil has five times as many turns as the first coil. If the voltage drop across the first coil is 100 V, what voltage will be induced in the second coil?

**Main Idea**

What does a transformer consist of?

**transformers.** A transformer consists of two separate coils of wire that are wound on the same piece of iron. The coils are insulated from each other and are in separate circuits. An alternating current in one circuit induces an alternating current in the other circuit.

The voltage drops across the two coils are related in a simple way. They depend on the number of turns in each coil. If one coil has three times as many turns, it will have three times the voltage drop of the other coil. If it has one tenth as many turns, it will have only one tenth the voltage drop. A very high voltage can be created by using a much greater number of turns on the second coil. How can a high voltage be lowered?

Tranformers that increase the voltage are called **step-up transformers.** They are used at generating plants to raise the voltage for transmission. Transformers that lower the voltage are called **step-down transformers.** The voltage is stepped-down in stages.

High-voltage transmission lines enter substations, which serve particular areas. Transformers in the substations lower the voltage to several thousand volts. From the substations, the power is distributed to the places where it will be used. The voltage is lowered again (to 110 V in North America) outside small groups of buildings.

In some communities, underground distribution lines are used. Underground lines improve the appearance of the area, but are more expensive. The lines must be surrounded by heavy insulation. The ground is a better conductor than air and would absorb energy from the lines. The heavily insulated lines are known as cables.

Many overhead power lines are not covered with insulation. Air itself is a poor conductor. Where the lines are supported by towers or poles, insulators keep the lines from making direct contact.

Power lines and transformers are protected from lightning by lightning arrestors. A lightning discharge near a power line causes a sharp increase in the current. The arrestors then become conductors. The large current is carried through connecting cables to the ground. The protection offered by arrestors is not complete. Some lightning discharges do cause damage to the lines and transformers. Electric storms sometimes do interrupt electric service.

Other types of weather can also do damage. Winter ice storms are especially dangerous. Rain or drizzle falling through cooler air near the ground freezes on the power lines. The weight of the ice may snap the lines. Sometimes tree branches give way and fall across power lines. Wind storms may have

Figure 9-18. A severe storm can cause power lines to fall and electric service to be interrupted.

the same effects by either directly or indirectly bringing down portions of the lines. Removing nearby trees and branches is about the only way to protect the lines from these weather hazards.

### Check yourself

1.  What is done to reduce energy loss in power lines?
2.  What changes in voltage are made between the time a current is generated and the time the energy is used by the consumer?

## Using electric energy

**Main Idea**

Into which forms of energy do we commonly convert electric energy?

Electric energy is produced from other forms of energy. In similar ways, electric energy is used to provide energy in other forms. Electric motors provide the energy of motion. Light bulbs provide us with light. Electric energy is frequently used as a source of heat. It is even used to make chemicals react. Electric energy is a convenient form of energy. It is relatively easy to change it to forms which are directly useful.

All of the changes in energy include "loss" of energy. That is, some of the energy changes into a form that cannot be recovered. Some of the energy is also "lost" because of the inconvenience of reusing it. Considerable heat is "lost" in the process of generating the electricity. Methods of using this heat may have to be considered in the future. At present, devices such as cooling towers are built to help dispose of the excess heat.

**Electric motors** are devices that convert electric energy to energy of motion. Heat is also a product of the conversion. The electric motor is an application of familiar principles. Electromagnets are a part of most electric motors. Two electromagnets interact. Like poles repel and unlike poles attract. The forces of attraction and repulsion provide the means of turning the shaft of an electric motor.

**Library Research**

The Amish are a group of people with a distinctive way of life. By choice, they do not use any appliances or machines which require electricity. Find out how the Amish people live and work without using electricity.

Electric motors have many different uses. They are found in blenders, fans, refrigerators, and vacuum cleaners.

Electric energy is frequently used in heating as well as to create motion. Coils of high-resistance wire are used in toasters, irons, curling irons, ovens, and portable heaters. High-resistance wire warms up rapidly. Electric energy is converted

## Activity 9-2A   Converting Electrical Energy to Energy of Motion

### Materials

meter stick or ruler      fine sandpaper
2 books      masking tape
new pencil      "D" cell
lacquered wire (#22–26), 4 m in length
horseshoe or bar magnet
ring stand and clamp
15 cm × 3 cm wood dowel

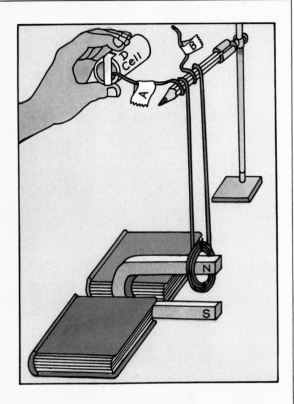

### Purpose

To convert electrical energy to energy of motion.

### Procedure

1. Use sandpaper to remove the insulation from the ends of the wire. Make sure that the copper is bare and shiny. SAFETY NOTE: *Keep loose wire away from eyes to prevent eye injuries.*
2. Wrap the wire around the 3-cm diameter wood dowel 30 times to make a coil. Leave 40 cm of uncoiled wire at each end.
3. Slide the coil off the dowel and tape the turns of wire together with masking tape.
4. Mount the pencil on the ring stand.
5. Wrap the ends of the coil around the pencil three or four times. The coil should be about 20 cm below the pencil. Leave about 10 cm of wire free at each end.
6. Use tape to label the wires "A" and "B."
7. Place the horseshoe magnet on its side with the N pole in the air. Stabilize the magnet with a book on each side. If you have a bar magnet, mount it between the books so that the N half of the magnet is sticking out between the books.
8. Adjust the height and position of the coil so that it hangs freely around the magnet but does not touch it.
9. Hold end "A" of the wire against the bottom of the "D" cell. Briefly touch end "B" of the wire to the top of the "D" cell. Record what direction the coil moves.

10. Reverse the direction of the current through the coil by holding end "B" against the bottom of the cell. Briefly touch end "A" to the top. Record the direction the coil moves.
11. Change the magnet so that the S pole is in the coil. Repeat Steps 9 and 10.

### Questions

1. Did reversing the current through the coil reverse the direction the coil moved?
2. Under what conditions did the coil move in the same direction?

### Conclusions

1. What did the direction the coil moved depend on?
2. How can a magnet and a current-carrying coil be used to convert electrical energy to energy of motion?

Figure 9-19. The high-resistance wire in a toaster gives off red light as well as heat when electric current passes through it.

to internal energy. This energy leaves the wire as heat. The wire may give off light, also, if it is hot enough.

Heating devices often use more electric energy than devices with motors. First, they usually have higher power ratings. A portable heater uses about 1500 W. A toaster may use 1100 W. On the other hand, a blender uses about 300 W. An electric toothbrush uses about 1 W. Second, heating devices may be used for longer time periods than devices with motors.

High-resistance wires are also used as a source of light. The common **incandescent** (in-kun-DES'-ent) light bulb uses a very thin filament of high resistance. The filament glows when an electric current moves through it. Even more energy is given off as heat than as light. In fact, *incandescent* means *glowing with intense heat*. A 100-W light bulb gives off 97 J of heat and only 3 J of light each second.

Incandescent light bulbs use tungsten filaments. Tungsten filaments have a high resistance but do not melt at the high temperatures produced. Ordinary air is also removed from the bulb. The air is replaced by nitrogen and argon gases. These gases do not react with the metal filament. Oxygen, which is part of ordinary air, does react with metals at high temperatures. The presence of oxygen would reduce the life of the light bulb.

**Library research**

Read about the problems Thomas Edison had in trying to make an incandescent light bulb. Write a report that describes his failures and successes in making a light bulb that would last.

## Activity 9–2B      Making a Model of an Incandescent Light Bulb

### Materials

3 pieces of copper wire
2-hole rubber stopper
iron picture wire, 2 cm in length
narrow-neck glass jar or flask that fits the
    rubber stopper
switch
2-"D"-cell battery
masking tape
several clear incandescent light bulbs of
    different wattages

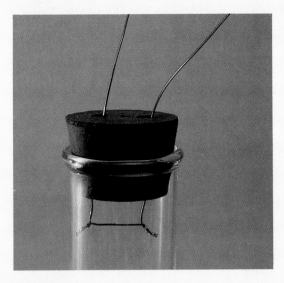

### Purpose

To make a model of an incandescent light bulb.

### Procedure

1. Insert two copper wires through the holes
   in a 2-hole rubber stopper. SAFETY NOTE:
   *Keep loose wires away from eyes to prevent
   eye injuries.*
2. Attach a single strand of picture wire to the
   lower ends of the copper wires by twisting.
3. Place the stopper in the neck of a glass jar.
   The picture wire should be inside the jar.
4. Connect the other ends of the copper wires
   to a two-cell battery and a switch in series.
   Use the third copper wire and masking tape.
5. Close the switch. Record what happens to
   the picture wire.
6. Compare the thickness of the filaments in
   several clear incandescent light bulbs with
   different wattages.

### Questions

1. How does the thickness of the picture wire
   compare to that of the copper wire?
2. What happened when the switch was
   closed?
3. In the light bulbs you examined, did bulbs
   with higher wattages have thicker or thinner
   filaments?

### Conclusions

1. Would you expect low-wattage or high-wattage bulbs to have filaments with a higher
   resistance?
2. In what important ways did your light bulb
   differ from the commercial light bulbs? How
   are these differences necessary for the
   success of the commercial light bulb?

### Check yourself

1. What kind of force makes something move in an electric
   motor?

2. What is the function of high-resistance wire in a circuit?

3. What prevents the filament of an incandescent light bulb
   from melting or wearing out quickly?

# Practical Science

## Audio and Video on Magnetic Tape

Many shows you watch on television are recorded on magnetic tape. With an audio or video cassette recorder (VCR), you can make and listen to magnetic tape recordings. Magnetic tape revolutionized the way sounds and sights can be reproduced.

**How magnetic tape is made**   Magnetic tape is made by mixing fine magnetic particles with a soft, sticky, semi-solid called *resin*. The types of magnetic particles most commonly used to make magnetic tape are iron oxide ($Fe_2O_3$) and chromium dioxide ($CrO_2$).

**Making an audio recording on tape**   Sound waves vary both in *amplitude*, or loudness, and *frequency*, or pitch. A diaphragm in a microphone converts sound waves into electric current. A loud sound moves the diaphragm more than a soft sound. This causes more current to flow through the wires from the microphone. A high-pitched sound causes the diaphragm to move faster than a low-pitched sound. Because of this, a high-pitched sound changes the flow of current more times per second than does a low-pitched sound.

The current goes through an amplifier to a coil of wire in an electromagnet. This electromagnet is called a *recording head*. As the tape moves across the recording head, the head pulls on the magnetic particles. Some magnetic particles line up in the same direction, making magnetic bands on the tape. Loud sounds create a strong pull from the magnet. This makes strong magnetic bands on the tape. The weak pull from soft sounds makes weak magnetic bands.

The rapidly changing pull from high-pitched sounds causes the magnetic bands to form close together. Low-pitched sounds causes them to form farther apart.

As the tape moves away from the coil, the magnetic bands become permanently magnetized. The sounds are now recorded in a magnetic pattern, or code.

**Playing back an audio tape**   When you play back the tape, it passes over another electromagnet. This is called the *playback head*. The magnetic bands of the tape create currents in the playback head. The harder a magnetic band pulls on the electromagnet, the more current flows through the coil. The closer together are the bands, the higher will be the frequency of the current.

This constantly changing current is strengthened by the amplifier. Then the current goes through the coil of an electromagnet in the loudspeaker. This moves a diaphragm in and out, creating the same sounds that went into the microphone.

**Erasing a tape**   You can erase the information stored on a tape by passing it under an erase head. An alternating current with steady amplitude and a very high frequency is emitted by the erase head. This current scrambles the magnetic particles and "erases" the tape.

**Video recording and playback**   Video recording is similar to audio recording except that much more information is recorded. In addition to sound, a video tape must contain all the magnetic bands that represent the picture information.

**Something to try**   Make a recording of yourself talking on a cassette tape. Then erase the tape. Record yourself talking using the same section of tape. Why is it possible to reuse a tape?

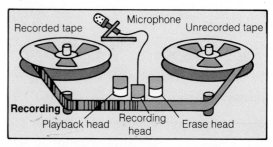

# Section 2 Review   Chapter 9

## Check Your Vocabulary

| | |
|---|---|
| electric motor | step-down transformer |
| hydroelectric | step-up transformer |
| incandescent | thermocouple |
| solar cell | transformer |

*Match each term above with the numbered phrase that best describes it.*

1. Glowing with intense heat
2. Converts electric energy to the energy of motion
3. Involving the conversion of the potential energy of falling water to electric energy
4. Provides a way to raise or lower a voltage
5. Used at generating plants
6. Used at substations
7. Produces current because of the contact of two metals at different temperatures
8. Produces current when light strikes it

## Check Your Knowledge

*Multiple Choice: Choose the answer that best completes each of the following sentences.*

1. Most electric energy used today is generated by  ? .
   a) thermocouples
   b) electromagnetic induction
   c) solar cells
   d) compression of crystals

2. An electric motor and an electric generator  ? .
   a) both use electric energy
   b) both convert another kind of energy to electric energy
   c) are both found in many common household appliances
   d) convert energy in opposite ways

3. Most of the energy for generating electric current today is supplied by  ? .
   a) the burning of fossil fuels
   b) falling water
   c) nuclear reactions
   d) solar radiation

4. The energy in light is converted directly into electric energy by  ? .
   a) quartz         c) germanium
   b) tungsten       d) copper

5. A filament in an incandescent light bulb should have  ? .
   a) long life and low resistance
   b) long life and high resistance
   c) short life and low resistance
   d) short life and high resistance

## Check Your Understanding

1. For each energy source used in an electric generating plant, list one advantage and one disadvantage.
2. Power lines are often linked together so that a community may receive electric power from different plants at different times. Suggest as many reasons as you can for why this is done.
3. List five ways in which you have made use of electric energy recently. For each way, what form was the electric energy converted to?

## Practical Science

1. What does a tape recording head contain?
2. How does a tape recording head operate?

# Chapter 9 Review

## Concept Summary

**Magnets** exert forces on each other and on materials such as iron, cobalt, and nickel.

□ The poles of a magnet are the places on the opposite ends of the magnet where the magnetic forces are strongest.

□ There are two kinds of poles—north poles and south poles; like poles repel and unlike poles attract.

□ A magnet can be pictured as a collection of tiny bar magnets all lined up with their north poles in the same direction.

A **magnetic field** is said to exist in a region where magnetic forces can act.

□ A magnetic field can be represented by curving lines known as magnetic field lines.

□ The earth has a magnetic field similar to that of a large bar magnet deep inside the earth.

□ A magnetic field is produced by an electric current as well as by a magnet.

□ A temporary magnet known as an electromagnet consists of a coil of wire with an iron bar inside it; a magnetic field is produced only when there is current in the coil.

□ The strength of an electromagnet increases as the number of turns in the coil and the current through the coil increase.

**Electromagnetic induction** is the production of an electric current by a changing magnetic field.

□ A current is induced in a circuit that is in a magnetic field that is either moving in relation to the circuit or is changing in strength.

**Electric energy** is the energy carried by electric currents.

□ Electric generators convert energy from other sources—fossil fuels, nuclear reactions, falling water, solar energy—into electric energy.

□ Electric energy is also obtained from thermocouples, crystals, and solar cells.

□ Electric energy is transported most efficiently at high voltage and low current.

□ Electric motors convert electric energy into energy of motion.

□ High-resistance wires convert electric energy into heat and light.

## Putting It All Together

1. In what two ways is the behavior of magnetic poles similar to the behavior of electric charges?

2. In what way does the behavior of magnetic poles differ from the behavior of electric charges?

3. What two kinds of information are revealed about a magnetic field by iron filings sprinkled near a magnet?

4. How was the magnetic effect of an electric current discovered?

5. What changes could you make to decrease the strength of an electromagnet?

6. What is necessary to induce a current in a coil of wire?

7. What are the essential parts of a large electric generator?

8. What produces the electric current in a thermocouple?

9. How are solar cells used to produce an electric current?

10. Why are transformers important in the transportation of electric energy between a generating plant and the users?

11. What three forms of energy used in the home are produced from electric energy?

12. In what form is most of the energy that is given off by an incandescent light bulb?

## Apply Your Knowledge

1. The earth's magnetic south pole is located near the edge of Antarctica. Explain why a compass is not very reliable on Antarctica.

2. What is the major advantage of an electro-magnet over a permanent magnet? Give an example of a use that demonstrates this advantage.
3. What advantage does alternating current have over direct current to induce a current in a second circuit?
4. Electric energy is sometimes used to pump water to an elevated storage area. Later the water is released, and the falling water is used to generate electric energy. Under what conditions would you expect this might be done?
5. How might some of the extra heat released during the generation of electricity be used?
6. Why is the presence of oxygen in an incandescent light bulb undesirable?

## Find Out on Your Own

1. Place several kinds of materials between a magnet and some iron nails or tacks. Which ones allow the magnetic force to pass through them?
2. Magnetic declination is the difference between the direction of true north and magnetic north. Find out the magnetic declination for your location by using a compass and a map of your city or locale showing true north.
3. Find out the location of the electric generating plant that is the major supplier of your electricity. What is the source of energy used to generate the electric energy?
4. Examine a bulb used in automobiles as a combination brake and tail light. Look closely, also, at a 3-way bulb used in some table and floor lamps. Find out how many filaments are included in each bulb and how the filaments differ from each other.
5. Look for the wattage rating on several home appliances. Find out which appliances would use the most energy in the same interval of time and which would use the least.

6. Set up the thermocouple described on pages 440 and 441. Find out if another combination of wires, such as aluminum and copper, produces a different amount of current for the same temperature difference.

## Reading Further

Cooper, Alan. *Electricity*. Morristown, NJ: Silver Burdett, 1983
　The principles, applications, and possible future uses of electricity and magnetism are described.

Lachenbruch, David. *Television*. Milwaukee: Raintree, 1985
　This is an excellent history of television and its uses in manufacturing and research.

Renner, Al G. *How to Make and Use Electronic Motors*. New York: Putnam, 1974
　Detailed instructions for constructing three types of battery-powered motors are given.

Ryder, John D. and Donald G. Fink. *Engineers and Electrons: A Century of Electrical Progress*. New York: IEEE Press, 1984
　This is a history of the electrical engineering profession and some important electrical engineers and their contributions.

Sootin, Harry. *Michael Faraday; from Errand Boy to Master Physicist*. New York: Messner/Simon and Schuster, 1954
　This is a biography of an extraordinary scientist who was largely self-educated.

Vogt, Gregory. *Electricity and Magnetism*. New York: Franklin Watts, 1985
　This book describes how people have learned about electricity and magnetism and gives ideas for experiments you can do.

Weiss, Harvey. *Motors and Engines and How They Work*. New York: Crowell/Harper & Row, 1969
　A clear and simple overview of many types of motors and engines is given.

# Chapter 10

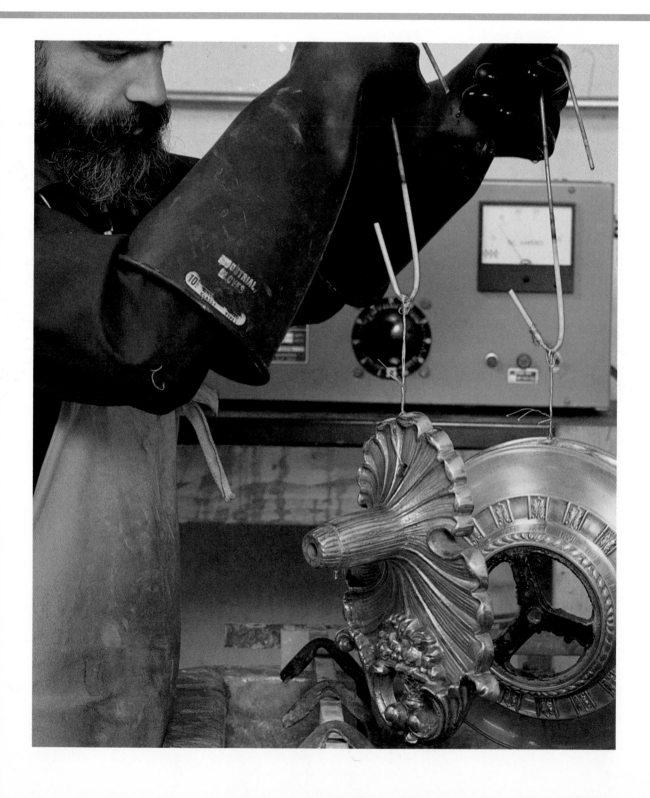

# Electrochemical and Nuclear Energy

## Section 1
### Energy from Electrochemical Changes

Electrons are transferred from one atom to another during certain chemical changes. Sometimes it is possible to make these electrons move along a wire outside the reaction. The electric energy in the wire can then be used for many purposes.

Some chemical reactions, such as the separation of metals from ores and the electroplating of one metal onto another, can be made to occur by using an electric current.

## Section 2
### Energy from Nuclear Changes

Some substances give off radiation from the nuclei of their atoms. These substances are radioactive and are constantly breaking down.

The nuclei of large atoms can be split, giving off enormous amounts of energy. Energy can also be produced by the nuclei of small atoms fusing together.

In this chapter you will learn how electric energy can be obtained from certain chemical reactions. You will also learn about reactions involving the nuclei of atoms that produce huge amounts of energy. The photo at the left shows an object which has just been electroplated. This means that a chemical reaction has been used to coat the original metal object with a different metal.

# Energy from Electrochemical Changes    Section 1

**Section 1 of Chapter 10 is divided into six parts:**

Oxidation and reduction

Electric energy from chemical changes

Activity of metals

Types of electrochemical cells

Using electric energy to produce chemical changes

Electroplating

*Practical Science: New Improved Flashlight Cells*

## Learning Objectives

1. To describe chemical changes that involve the transfer of electrons.

2. To explain the operation of an electrochemical cell.

3. To compare electrolysis reactions with the reactions taking place in an electrochemical cell.

4. To describe the procedures used and the reactions occurring during the electroplating of a metal.

Figure 10-1. Many silver objects are not sterling (solid) silver. Instead, they have a thin coating of silver over another metal. The coating is applied in a process that uses electric energy to create a chemical change.

Many chemical changes release energy. The energy released is often in the form of heat. The burning of fuels releases heat. Sometimes the heat released is used to generate electric energy. Some chemical changes can be used to produce electric energy without first producing heat. These chemical changes produce electric energy by causing electric charges to move. The moving electric charges have energy and can do work. Some very common chemical changes cause the movement of electric charges. How do they do this? Can electric energy produce chemical changes? These questions will be explored in this section.

## Oxidation and reduction

You already know what happens when iron rusts. Rusting is a familiar chemical change. The iron combines with oxygen in the air. The compound formed is iron oxide, which is commonly called rust. The rust is weak and crumbles. The properties of rust are much different from those of iron. The iron in the compound has lost its shinyness and strength.

The combining of a metal with water, air, or other materials in the atmosphere is called **corrosion** (kuh-RŌ′-zhun). Many other metals also corrode. Copper combines with carbon dioxide and water vapor in the air. The compound formed is copper carbonate, which has a pale green color. Even aluminum combines with oxygen, forming aluminum oxide. However, aluminum oxide does not crumble away as does iron oxide. A thin layer of aluminum oxide quickly forms on the aluminum. This thin layer protects the aluminum underneath from further corrosion. Chromium behaves in a way similar to aluminum. Both aluminum and chromium are used on automobiles. The oxides formed protect against further corrosion.

Corrosion is a chemical change. New substances with new properties are formed. It is a chemical change in which electrons are transferred. The metal iron loses electrons when it rusts. It changes from $Fe^0$ (balanced + and − charges) to $Fe^{3+}$. The iron atoms now are positively charged ions. The iron has been oxidized. **Oxidation** (oks′-ih-DAY′-shun) is the loss of

Figure 10-2. What causes the Statue of Liberty to have this green color? Of what metal is the statue made?

## Activity 10–1A          Corrosion of Metals

### Materials

iron nail
galvanized nail
silver-plated spoon
silver polish
penny
aluminum foil
open container
steel wool, fine
water

### Purpose

To find out what changes take place in metals exposed to air.

### Procedure

1. Polish the iron nail, galvanized nail, and aluminum foil with fine steel wool. Use the silver polish to shine the spoon.
2. Place each of the metals in an open container. Wet each with water. Leave the container exposed to the air for several days.
3. Notice the changes that took place on the metals.

### Questions

1. Describe the changes that took place on the metal objects.
2. How do you know the changes that took place are chemical ones?
3. What methods of protecting metals from corrosion are suggested by this activity?

### Conclusion

What can you conclude about the changes that take place in metals that are exposed to air?

### Main Idea

What happens to oxygen atoms when they combine with iron atoms?

electrons. The oxygen atoms that combine with the iron gain electrons. They now have a negative charge. The oxygen has been reduced. **Reduction** (ree-DUK′-shun) is the gain of electrons.

Aluminum foil reacts with solutions of copper sulfate or copper chloride. The reaction produces a reddish brown deposit on the foil. This deposit is copper metal. The copper ions ($Cu^{2+}$) in the solution gain electrons ($e^-$) to form neutral copper ($Cu^0$) metal. The copper ions are reduced.

$$Cu^{2+} + 2e^- \rightarrow Cu^0 \text{ (reduction = gain of electrons)}$$

The aluminum metal ($Al^0$) loses electrons to form aluminum ions ($Al^{3+}$). The aluminum metal is oxidized.

$$Al^0 \rightarrow Al^{3+} + 3e^- \text{ (oxidation = loss of electrons)}$$

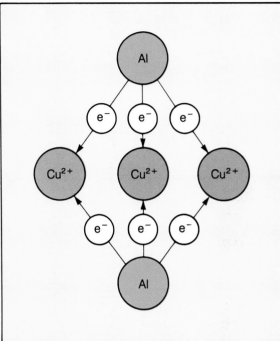

The aluminum metal gives up its electrons to the copper ions in the solution. As this happens, the mass of the foil decreases because aluminum ions enter the solution. At the same time, copper atoms come out of solution and collect on the foil.

Figure 10-3. How many electrons are needed by each copper ion to form a copper atom?

## Check yourself

1. What happens to metals that corrode?

2. What happens to a metal that becomes oxidized?

3. What happens to copper ions when they are reduced?

## Electric energy from chemical changes

When aluminum is in a solution containing copper ions, electrons move from the aluminum atoms to the copper ions. A conducting wire can provide a path for the electrons outside the solution. The electrons moving through the wire can be

Figure 10-4. How does this electrochemical cell produce electric energy?

detected with a sensitive electric meter. A galvanometer or a milliammeter (which measures thousandths of an ampere) can be used.

For example, a copper strip and an aluminum strip can be placed in a copper sulfate solution. See Figure 10-4. One end of a wire is attached to the aluminum strip. The other end of the wire is attached to a meter. A second wire is attached to the second terminal of the meter and to the copper strip. A complete path is provided for the electrons through the wires. The reading on the meter indicates there is a current.

The aluminum, copper, and copper sulfate solution make an **electrochemical** (ih-lek′-trō-KEM′-ih-kul) **cell.** An electrochemical cell uses chemical changes to produce electric energy. In a chemical change, electrons may be transferred from one substance to another. The electrons that are transferred have energy. They move through conductors. These moving electric charges are a source of electric energy. Because of their energy they can do work or produce light or heat.

**Main Idea**

What energy changes occur in an electrochemical cell?

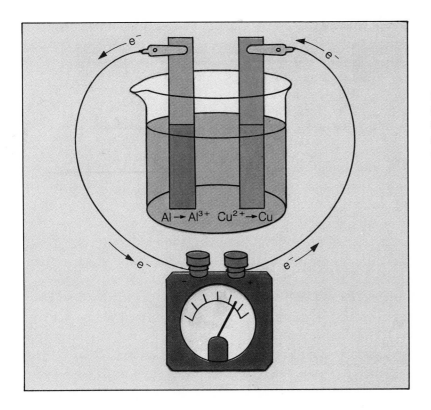

Figure 10-5. Movement of charges in an electrochemical cell. Why does the blue copper sulfate solution gradually turn clear?

The ability of metals to furnish electrons is different for different metals. For example, aluminum, zinc, and iron all give up electrons more easily than copper does. Two metals that have different abilities to give up electrons can be used to make an electrochemical cell.

Electrochemical cells are made of two different metals separated in a liquid or moist paste. The liquid or paste has to be a conductor of electricity and is called an **electrolyte** (ih-LEK´-truh-līt). An electrolyte contains ions. These ions move through the liquid or paste, giving up or taking on electrons at the two poles. When the cell contains a liquid, it is called a **wet cell.** Common flashlight cells are known as **dry cells** because they contain a paste instead of a liquid.

A simple cell can be made from very common substances. A piece of aluminum foil and a copper penny will work. The surface of the coin needs to be polished with sandpaper to make sure the copper metal is exposed. A folded piece of paper towel soaked in salt water is placed between the metals. The salt water serves as the electrolyte. Wires from a galvanometer are touched to the outside of the two metals. The galvanometer needle will be deflected in the direction that the charges are moving.

**Library research**

The SI unit of voltage, the volt, was named after Count Alessandro Volta. Find out what important contributions Volta made to the field of electricity. What was Volta's pile?

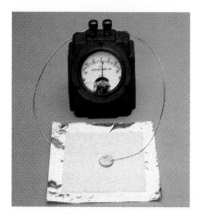

Figure 10-6. From which metal to which metal do the electrons move?

**Main Idea**

What is meant by the activity of a metal?

Table 10-1. Order of activity of some metals.

**Data Search**

Of the metals listed in Table 10-1, name in order five that are the highest in electrical conductivity. Search page 560.

### Check yourself

1.  What makes up an electrochemical cell?
2.  What is an electrolyte?

### Activity of metals

The metals that give up electrons more easily are said to be more active than metals that give up electrons less easily. In an electrochemical cell, the more active metal furnishes electrons and the less active metal receives electrons. When the metals are aluminum and copper, the electrons move from the aluminum to the copper. Aluminum is more active than copper. The **activity** of a metal refers to its tendency to furnish electrons. The activity of all metals is different. These differences for some metals are summarized in the activity table shown in Table 10-1. The most active metal in the group is at the top. The least active is at the bottom.

A metal gives up electrons to any of the metals below it in the table. Magnesium, for example, furnishes electrons to any of the other metals in the table. Gold receives electrons from any of the other elements in the table. Any two of the metals

| Metal | Activity |
|---|---|
| Magnesium | Most active |
| Aluminum | |
| Zinc | |
| Chromium | |
| Iron | |
| Nickel | |
| Tin | |
| Lead | |
| Hydrogen | |
| Copper | |
| Arsenic | |
| Mercury | |
| Silver | |
| Platinum | |
| Gold | Least active |

## Activity 10–1B          A Wet Cell

### Materials

masking tape
2 20-cm pieces of bell wire
zinc strip (1 cm × 10 cm)
aluminum strip (1 cm × 10 cm)
copper strip (1 cm × 10 cm)
iron strip (1 cm × 10 cm)
100-mL beaker or transparent container
copper sulfate ($CuSO_4$) solution (saturated)
dc voltmeter of range 0 V to 3 V
1.5 V flashlight bulb in socket

### Purpose

To find out how the voltage changes when different metals are used in a wet cell.

### Procedure

1. Fill the beaker two-thirds full with the copper sulfate ($CuSO_4$) solution. SAFETY NOTE: *Avoid touching the copper sulfate. If you get any on your skin, wash the affected skin area with soap and water. If you get any in your eyes, flush them with water.*
2. Tape one section of bell wire to the aluminum strip. Tape a second section of bell wire to the copper strip. Connect the other ends of the wire to the voltmeter as shown.
3. Place the two strips of metal in the solution. Note the reading on the voltmeter. If the reading is zero, reverse the connections.
4. Remove the wires from the voltmeter and connect them to the socket of the flashlight bulb. Note if the bulb is lit.
5. Remove the strips from the solution. Replace the aluminum strip with a zinc strip. Place the zinc and copper strips in the solution. Reattach the voltmeter and record the new reading. Now test the flashlight bulb.
6. Remove the strips from the solution. Replace the zinc strip with an iron strip. Place the iron and copper strips in the solution and record the voltmeter reading. Again test the flashlight bulb. Record the results.

7. Remove the metal strips from the solution. Rinse all the strips with water and dry thoroughly. Pour the copper sulfate solution into the container provided by your teacher.

### Questions

1. Which combination of metals gave the highest voltage?
2. Which combination of metals gave the lowest voltage?
3. Which of the combinations of metals caused the flashlight bulb to light?

### Conclusion

Compare the voltages produced by a wet cell when different combinations of metals are used.

can be used to make an electrochemical cell. Which combination would make the best cell? What else is needed to make the cell operate?

### Check yourself

What effect does the difference in activity of two metals have on the movement of electrons?

### Types of electrochemical cells

The voltage of a cell depends on the combination of metals used. (Voltage was discussed in Chapter 8, Section 2.) The greater the difference in the activity of the metals in the cell, the greater the voltage. When zinc and copper are used in a particular solution, the voltage is about 1.1 V. Suppose magnesium metal were used in place of zinc. Would you expect the voltage to increase or decrease?

The common flashlight cell is a dry cell that uses zinc and carbon. The zinc and carbon act as **electrodes** (ih-LEK′-trōdz). Electrodes are conductors that carry electrons into or out of a cell. The zinc is in the form of a can. The can holds a moist paste with a carbon rod in the center. The paste is a mixture of ammonium chloride, manganese dioxide, and water. The ammonium chloride serves as the electrolyte. The carbon, which is a nonmetal, does not take part in the chemical reaction.

The zinc gives up electrons and enters the paste as zinc ions. The electrons travel through the outside circuit and enter the cell through the carbon rod. The manganese dioxide accepts the electrons, and a substance called manganous oxide is formed. When the cell is fresh, it produces a voltage of 1.5 V. The voltage decreases as the manganese dioxide is used up, until the cell is finally "dead."

An **alkaline** (AL′-kuh-lin) **cell** is a type of dry cell. It provides longer and better service than the common flashlight cell. The electrolyte in an alkaline call is potassium hydroxide, a strong base. The voltage of this cell is also 1.5 V.

Cells can be combined to produce batteries of larger voltage. A battery consists of two or more cells wired together.

Figure 10-7. A standard flashlight cell. What chemical reactions produce the electric current?

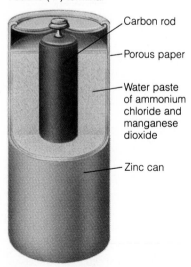

Positive ( + ) terminal

Carbon rod

Porous paper

Water paste of ammonium chloride and manganese dioxide

Zinc can

Negative ( − ) terminal (bottom of can)

Figure 10-8. What are some common uses for cells and batteries like these?

Two flashlight cells can be used together to make a battery of 3 V. Single flashlight cells are often called batteries by mistake. The manufacturers sometimes print the name "battery" on their labels. Even though it is incorrect, they feel that more people are familiar with this term. However, some batteries are correctly labeled. The common 6-V lantern battery contains four separate 1.5-V cells. How many of these cells would you expect to find in a 9-V battery?

The chemical reactions in all these cells and batteries will sooner or later "use up" the initial substances. Then the cells and batteries can no longer be used. The products cannot be easily changed back into the original substances. The chemical reactions that produce the electric current often are not easily reversed.

Some electrochemical cells are put together so that the reaction can be easily reversed. Batteries made of these cells are called **storage batteries.** You are probably most familiar with the storage battery in an automobile. The automobile storage battery uses lead and lead dioxide plates. These plates are separated by an electrolyte of sulfuric acid and water. Six of these cells connected together in series produce a voltage of 12 V. Most of today's automobile storage batteries are of this size. How many volts are produced by each cell in the automobile storage battery?

**Main Idea**

How does a storage battery differ from other batteries?

Safety
The sulfuric acid in an automobile battery is very corrosive. Handle these batteries with care.

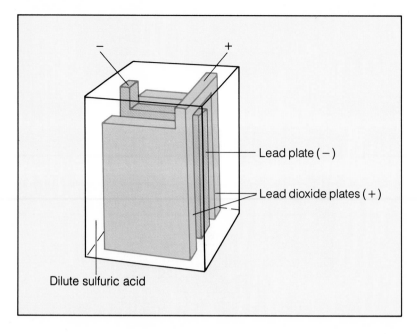

Figure 10-9. One cell of a storage battery. How is the storage battery recharged?

Lead plate ($-$)

Lead dioxide plates ($+$)

Dilute sulfuric acid

## Library research

The famous inventor, Thomas Alva Edison, devoted much of his time to the development of a certain type of storage battery. Find out what Edison's storage battery was like and how it worked. How does it differ from storage batteries of today? For what purpose did Edison first use his storage battery?

As the storage battery supplies electric energy, the lead plates give up electrons. The electrons move to the lead dioxide plates through an outer electric circuit. The sulfate from the sulfuric acid combines with lead on the plates. Water is also formed by the reaction. As the reaction continues, the amount of sulfuric acid in the electrolyte decreases. At the same time, the amount of water increases. The battery is discharging.

The battery is recharged by connecting it to a source of electric current moving in the opposite direction (usually from the car's generator). The chemical reactions are reversed. The sulfate is returned to the electrolyte. The lead and lead dioxide plates are restored. The battery can again be used to supply electric current. The battery can be recharged many times. Eventually, other chemical changes and loss of material from the plates make the battery wear out.

The storage battery is a very convenient device in an automobile. Electric current from the battery works the starter. Once the engine is running, electric current is produced by the generator, which recharges the battery. Before the storage battery was used, cars had to be started with cranks. Cranking a car was not an easy task, and the person cranking was sometimes injured from "kick-back" by the engine.

Some alkaline cells are also designed so that they can be recharged. These may be used in some calculators, flash cameras, and electronic games.

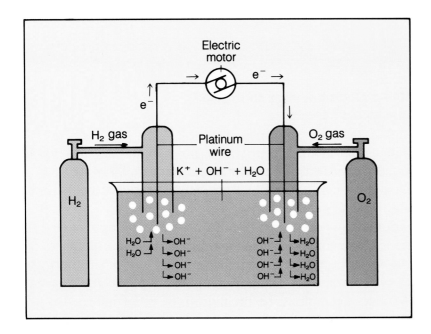

Figure 10-10. A fuel cell. The current it produces can be used to run an electric motor. What substance is produced in this cell?

Another source of electric current, which has been used in the spacecraft flights, is the **fuel cell.** It differs from other cells in one important way. Some of the materials that react are supplied from outside the cell.

In one type of fuel cell, two electrodes are in an electrolyte of potassium hydroxide. The electrodes are connected by an outside circuit. Hydrogen gas is released at one electrode. The hydrogen combines with hydroxide ions and releases electrons.

$$H_2 + 2OH^- \rightarrow 2H_2O + 2e^-$$

Oxygen gas is released at the other electrode. The oxygen accepts the electrons, which have traveled through the outside circuit. It reacts with water to form more hydroxide ions.

$$O_2 + 2H_2O + 4e^- \rightarrow 4OH^-$$

For every four electrons that travel from one electrode to another, two molecules of hydrogen and one molecule of oxygen are used. The net result is that water is formed, and an electric current is produced.

**Main Idea**

How does a fuel cell differ from other electrochemical cells?

### Check yourself

1. What substance is oxidized in a carbon and zinc cell? What substance is reduced?

2. What happens to the auto storage battery while the engine is running?

## Using electric energy to produce chemical changes

**Main Idea**

What constitutes a spontaneous chemical reaction?

The chemical changes that take place in an electrochemical cell do not need any energy to get started. They are said to be **spontaneous** (spon-TAYN'-ee-us). As a result of the changes, electric energy is released.

Some chemical changes require a continuous input of energy in order to continue. One example of this kind of change is the recharging of a storage battery. Here, electric energy is used to reverse the changes that produce an electric current. Another example is the breakdown of water into hydrogen gas and oxygen gas. This change, which happens when an electric current passes through water, also uses electric energy. It is just the reverse of the reaction inside a fuel cell that uses hydrogen and oxygen gas.

The breakdown of any compound by use of an electric current is called **electrolysis** (ih-lek-TROL'-uh-sis). Compounds other than water can also be separated into elements by electrolysis.

Figure 10-11. What two dangerous substances are formed when an electric current splits table salt apart?

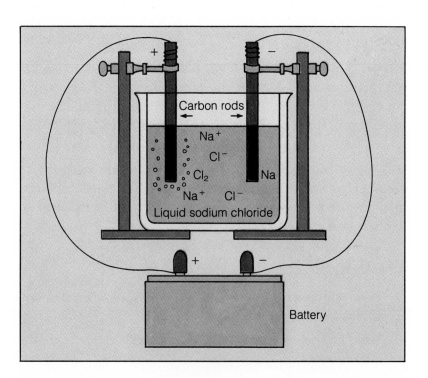

Table salt (sodium chloride) forms a liquid at a very high temperature. The liquid is made up of sodium ions ($Na^+$) and chloride ions ($Cl^-$). Two carbon electrodes are placed in the container of liquid sodium chloride. A battery is connected to the two carbon electrodes. Bubbles soon start appearing near one of the electrodes. The electrode connected to the positive end of the battery attracts the chloride ions. The chloride ions give up electrons and form chlorine gas ($Cl_2$). For every two chloride ions that are oxidized, one chlorine molecule is formed.

$$2Cl^- \rightarrow 2e^- + Cl_2^{\ 0}$$

The sodium ions ($Na^+$) are attracted to the electrode connected to the negative post of the battery. Each sodium ion gains a single electron. The sodium ions are reduced to form sodium metal.

$$Na^+ + e^- \rightarrow Na^0$$

Both sodium and chlorine are dangerous substances with very different properties from those of table salt.

Most metals are found in nature as part of a compound. Electrolysis can be used to separate some pure metals from the substances they are combined with. Aluminum is an example. It is found combined with oxygen in an ore called bauxite.

The modern method by which aluminum is separated from bauxite was developed by Charles Martin Hall. When Hall was a young chemistry student at Oberlin College in 1886, his professor told him there was no inexpensive way of extracting aluminum. Hall decided that he would try to find a way. Some time later he came into class with a handful of small aluminum pellets, which he had obtained from bauxite. Hall's process for obtaining inexpensive aluminum has been used ever since!

In Hall's process, the bauxite ($Al_2O_3$) is melted and placed in a graphite (carbon) container. The graphite is connected to the negative terminal of an outside source. It serves as the negative electrode, or **cathode** (KATH'-ōd). The aluminum ions ($Al^{3+}$) in the melted ore are attracted to the cathode. At the cathode, the aluminum ions gain electrons and form aluminum metal. The temperature must be kept very high so

Figure 10-12. Charles Martin Hall

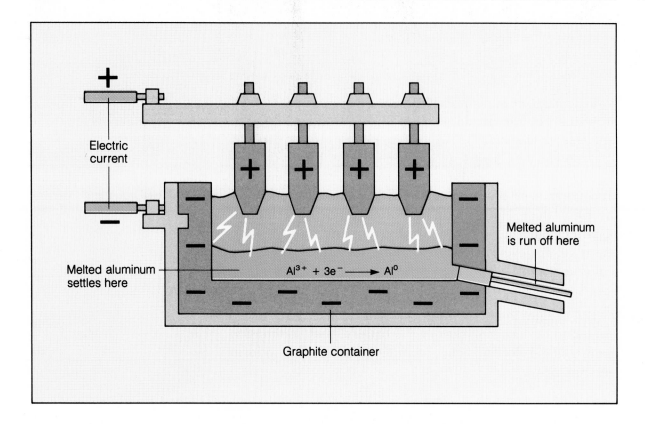

Figure 10-13. Separating aluminum from its ore. Why are large amounts of energy needed?

that the aluminum can be liquid and run off the bottom of the container.

$$Al^{3+} + 3e^- \rightarrow Al^0$$

Are the aluminum ions oxidized or reduced?

Other electrodes are immersed in the melted bauxite. They are connected to the positive terminal of the outside source. They serve as positive electrodes, or **anodes** (AN′-ōdz). The oxygen ions ($O^{2-}$) are attracted to the anodes. They give up electrons, and oxygen gas is formed.

$$2O^{2-} \rightarrow O_2 + 4e^-$$

Are the oxygen ions oxidized or reduced?

Even though Hall's process is relatively inexpensive, it still requires enormous amounts of electric energy. Far less energy is required to recycle old aluminum products. Returning aluminum cans for recycling is an important way of saving energy!

Additional steps are necessary in the refining of some metals from their ores. But the idea is the same. The metal can be separated from its ore using an electric current. The addition of electric energy causes the compound to break down. What energy change must have taken place when the compound was formed?

## Check yourself

1. Name one important use for electrolysis.
2. What kind of chemical reaction takes place at the anode?
3. What kind of chemical reaction takes place at the cathode?

## Electroplating

Metals can also be deposited on a conducting material. This process is called **electroplating** (ih-LEK′-trō-play′-ting). Electroplating is also an application of electrolysis. You probably know of many materials that have been electroplated. The less expensive metals such as iron corrode easily. Covering them with a thin coat of metal that does not corrode makes the metal last much longer.

Gold does not corrode. But gold is a very expensive metal. Gold can be added in a very thin layer to another metal by electroplating. Silver, too, can be plated on another metallic surface. Silver does tarnish. That is, it combines with sulfur in the air to form silver sulfide. But the deposit of silver sulfide can be removed quite easily.

Chromium metal is often plated on steel or iron surfaces. Chromium protects the iron from exposure to the oxygen of the air. Chromium also reacts with air to form a thin layer of chromium oxide. The layer of chromium oxide prevents any further reaction of chromium with the oxygen of the air. And it protects the iron from rusting.

A battery supplies electrons to the metal to be electroplated, which is always attached to the negative terminal. It serves as the cathode. The metal is in a salt solution that contains positive ions of the metal that forms the plating. These positive metal ions move toward the extra electrons on the metal to be plated. At the same time, negative ions in the salt solution move toward the anode. The anode is connected to the positive terminal of the battery. It is made of the metal that forms the plating.

The metal ions in the solution combine with the extra electrons on the object to be plated. For example, suppose a piece of iron is to be plated with copper. Copper ions from the

### Library research

Find out when electroplating was first used. What were some of the early products that were electroplated? Can metals be plated any other way than by electroplating? What is anodized aluminum?

### Main Idea

What happens to the extra electrons on an object that is to be electroplated?

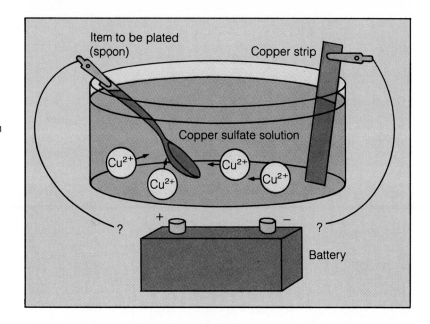

Figure 10-14. Which terminal of the cell should be connected to the spoon that is to be plated with copper? Does oxidation or reduction take place at the spoon?

**Safety**

Many metal ions, including nickel, chromium, and silver, are toxic.

solution combine with electrons on the surface of the iron, and form a copper plating.

$$Cu^{2+} + 2e^- \rightarrow Cu^0$$

At the anode, copper atoms give up electrons and enter the solution.

$$Cu^0 \rightarrow 2e^- + Cu^{2+}$$

The speed at which electroplating takes place is determined by the electric current. Each copper atom that is plated on the iron requires two electrons. Increasing the number of electrons that move to the iron increases the number of atoms of copper that form. Thus, increasing the current increases the speed of the electroplating. Increasing the length of time the current flows also increases the amount of copper that is plated.

Nickel, chromium, silver, and gold are frequently used for electroplating. What kinds of products would you expect to be plated with these metals? Brass, an alloy of copper and zinc, is also frequently used. Products such as nails, screws, door knobs, and fireplace screens are often plated with brass.

### Check yourself

1. What must the battery supply to a metal that is to be electroplated?

2. Name five metals that are frequently used for electroplating.

# Practical Science

## New Improved Flashlight Cells

You have quite a choice of dry cells for your flashlight, tape player, or other cell-powered devices. Look at the racks in a store. You will see heavy-duty, alkaline, and rechargeable nickel-cadmium dry cells in addition to regular zinc-carbon dry cells. They all produce electricity in ways similar to the zinc-carbon cell described in this chapter.

**The new dry cells** The most obvious difference between the various types of batteries is price. Less obvious differences affect the way a dry cell performs and how long it will last. Heavy-duty (zinc-chloride) dry cells are improved versions of zinc-carbon dry cells. They are more expensive but can store more energy. Zinc-chloride dry cells operate in a wider range of temperature. Like zinc-carbon dry cells, zinc-chloride dry cells can leak corrosive materials.

Alkaline (alkaline manganese) dry cells differ chemically and physically from both zinc-carbon and zinc-chloride dry cells. The alkaline chemicals give them the ability to produce more electricity. Alkaline dry cells have longer storage and operating lives than other types of dry cells. They perform better in extreme temperatures. They are also less likely to leak.

Rechargeable (nickel-cadmium) dry cells can be recharged with electric current. They can be reused hundreds of times. However, they are much more expensive than zinc-carbon dry cells, and you must buy a cell charger. The charge in a nickel-cadmium dry cell being used continuously lasts about as long as a heavy-duty dry cell. When a nickel-cadmium cell is used only occasionally, the charge lasts only as long as a regular dry cell. The charge in an unused rechargeable dry cell soon leaks away.

**Balancing the cost and efficiency of dry cells** To choose the best type of dry cell to use, you must balance cost with both how long the dry cell will operate and how you use it.

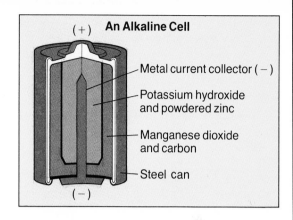

An Alkaline Cell
(+)
Metal current collector (−)
Potassium hydroxide and powdered zinc
Manganese dioxide and carbon
Steel can
(−)

For example, a dry cell-powered device might run for one hour on regular dry cells, two hours on heavy-duty, and four or five on alkaline. Although alkaline dry cells can cost about three times as much as regular dry cells, they last much longer.

Alkaline dry cells are a good choice for a car flashlight. They have a long shelf life. They will not deteriorate in the heat of summer, and are more likely to work in the cold of winter.

Heavy-duty dry cells are a good choice for a house flashlight. This is because the flashlight will probably rest between uses and temperatures are less extreme inside a house.

Rechargeable dry cells may be the best choice for a portable radio. The cost per year might be about $56.00, compared with $5.00 to $8.00 for rechargeable dry cells plus $12.00 for a cell charger. However, you would not want to use rechargeable batteries in an emergency radio or flashlight because rechargeable dry cells lose their charge quickly.

**Something to try** Buy one set each of regular, heavy-duty, and alkaline dry cells for a device that you use regularly. Write down the price you paid for each set. Every time you use the device, write down the starting and stopping times. Use each set of dry cells until it stops operating. Add up the total hours you used each set. Divide the total hours by the price for each set. The answers you get are the operating cost per hour of each dry cell set.

## Section 1 Review   Chapter 10

### Check Your Vocabulary

activity             electrolysis

anode                electrolyte

cathode              oxidation

corrosion            reduction

electrochemical cell

*Match each term above with the numbered phrase that best describes it.*

1. Combining of a metal with a part of the air
2. Gain of electrons by a substance
3. Produces an electric current from a chemical reaction
4. Separating of a compound using electric energy
5. The tendency of a metal to give up electrons
6. Loss of electrons by a substance
7. A liquid or a paste containing ions
8. Place where electrons are given up
9. Place where electrons are gained

### Check Your Knowledge

*Multiple Choice: Choose the answer that best completes each of the following sentences.*

1. In an electrochemical cell, _?_.
   a) chemical change produces an electric current
   b) electric current produces heat
   c) electric current is increased
   d) metals combine to form alloys

2. Electrons move from zinc to copper in one cell but from copper to silver in another cell. The arrangement of these metals from most active to least active is _?_.
   a) zinc-copper-silver
   b) silver-copper-zinc
   c) copper-silver-zinc
   d) copper-zinc-silver

3. A chemical change that releases energy as the change takes place is _?_.
   a) electrolysis
   b) electroplating
   c) battery recharging
   d) battery discharging

4. Objects to be electroplated should be connected to _?_.
   a) the positive terminal of the battery
   b) the negative terminal of the battery
   c) either the positive or negative terminal
   d) both the positive and negative terminals

5. A reaction that takes place at the cathode (negative terminal) is _?_.
   a) oxidation of copper ions
   b) reduction of copper ions
   c) oxidation of copper metal
   d) reduction of copper metal

### Check Your Understanding

1. Both iron and aluminum corrode in air. Why is the corrosion of iron more of a problem than the corrosion of aluminum?
2. What three substances are normally needed to make an electrochemical cell?
3. How is a fuel cell different from other types of electrochemical cells?
4. What procedures would you follow to increase the thickness of a copper layer that is being plated on a piece of iron?
5. What is the advantage of a storage battery?

### Practical Science

1. What kind of dry cell is rechargeable?
2. How do alkaline dry cells differ from other dry cells?

# Energy from Nuclear Changes    Section 2

**Section 2 of Chapter 10 is divided into eight parts:**

Natural radioactivity

Describing radiation

Detecting radiation

Changes in the nucleus

Using radioisotopes

Rate of nuclear decay

Fission of the nucleus

Nuclear fusion

*Practical Science: Nuclear Wastes*

### Learning Objectives

1. To compare the properties of alpha, beta, and gamma radiation.

2. To identify the nuclear change that accompanies each kind of radiation.

3. To illustrate the concept of half-life used in describing the rate of decay of a radioactive substance.

4. To relate the energy involved in nuclear reactions to the change in mass of the substances.

5. To compare the changes taking place in nuclear fission and nuclear fusion.

Figure 10-15. A worker uses an isolation chamber to handle highly radioactive material.

Just as chemical changes are accompanied by changes in energy, so are nuclear changes. Nuclear changes, too, are used as sources of energy. You have heard a great deal about nuclear energy. Still, nuclear changes have not been known to scientists for very long. What is nuclear energy? How did nuclear energy become known? How is nuclear energy released? What amounts of energy are released by nuclear changes? These questions will be explored in this section.

## Natural radioactivity

**Radioactivity** (ray′-dee-ō-ak-TIV′-uh-tee) refers to the release of particles and/or energy from the nucleus of an atom. Some atoms are naturally radioactive. Many other atoms can be made radioactive.

Radioactivity was first noticed in 1896. A French scientist, Henri Becquerel, was experimenting with uranium ore. He

---

## Our Science Heritage

**Marie Curie**

Marie Sklodowska was born in Poland in 1867. As a student in school she had a great interest in science. After graduation from high school she went to work in order to save money for further education. Her older brother and sister were studying in Paris, and after she had saved enough money, she joined them there. She entered the great French university, the Sorbonne. She studied and worked very hard, just barely supporting herself, but graduated at the top of her class in 1894.

After graduation she married a French scientist, Pierre Curie, who had been working with electricity. She became very interested in Becquerel's discovery and decided that she, herself, would investigate radioactivity.

She used some of her husband's findings in developing a method to measure radioactivity and to separate radioactive ores into several parts. She found that certain uranium ores seemed to be more radioactive than others. She guessed that there must be radioactive elements found that photographic plates left close by but covered up were exposed. Becquerel was puzzled. No visible light could have reached the plates. The mysterious radiation was evidently able to penetrate where visible light could not. With further study he became convinced that atoms of uranium were responsible. Uranium atoms must be giving off invisible radiation that had reached the photographic plates.

Becquerel had discovered that uranium was radioactive. His discovery led to more experiments. Marie and Pierre Curie soon discovered two more radioactive elements, radium and polonium. Now, many radioactive elements are known. In fact, many common elements, such as hydrogen, carbon, and nitrogen, have radioactive isotopes.

**Check yourself**

What strange effect led Becquerel to discover natural radioactivity?

---

other than uranium in these ores.

She and her husband separated many ores, looking for these other elements. They found samples of the element thorium which were radioactive but not as radioactive as they had expected. They decided that there must be something else. Then they discovered a new element, polonium, which was highly radioactive. But they still believed that some ores contained minute quantities of an even more radioactive substance. After separating enormous amounts of ore, they finally had a tiny sample of an even more radioactive element that they called radium.

In 1903, the third Nobel Prize in physics was awarded to Pierre and Marie Curie and to Henri Becquerel. In 1911, she received a second Nobel Prize, this time in chemistry.

Among other things, radium has been used as a treatment for some kinds of cancer. Ironically, Marie Curie died of cancer in 1934. Her death was caused by too much exposure to radiation.

Marie Curie in her laboratory

## Describing radiation

Scientists began to study the radiation given off by these radioactive elements. It was soon found that more than one kind of radiation seemed to be given off. Each different kind of radiation produced different effects. The mystery became more challenging. Not only did the nuclei of atoms give off radiation, but they gave off different kinds of radiation.

Three kinds of radiation were described. One kind behaved as if it had a positive electric charge. It was called **alpha** (AL′-fuh) **radiation**. Further studies identified the characteristics of alpha radiation more closely. Alpha radiation was found to consist of particles. The amount of positive charge and the mass of the particles are equal to those of the second smallest atomic nucleus—the helium nucleus. Alpha radiation has the same properties as helium nuclei.

A second kind of radiation was found to have a negative charge. It became known as **beta** (BAY′-tuh) **radiation**. It, too, consists of particles. The mass and charge of the particles are the same as those of electrons.

Figure 10-16. What difference among the three kinds of radiation causes them to separate when passing electrically charged objects?

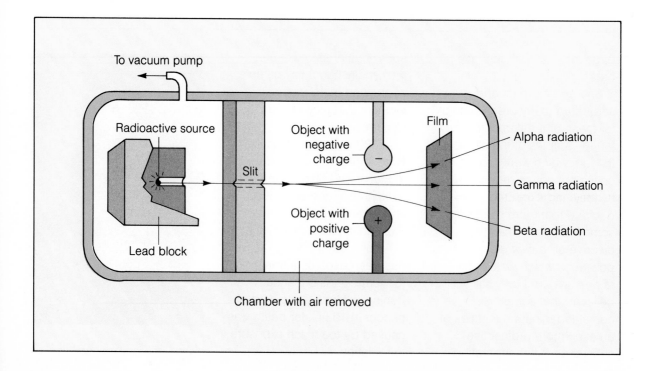

The third kind of radiation was found to have no charge. Its properties are similar in some ways to visible light and X-rays. This type of radiation became known as gamma radiation. It is now known to be electromagnetic radiation of a very high frequency.

Figure 10-16 shows how nuclear radiation becomes divided when it passes between two electrically charged objects—one negative and the other positive. Positively charged alpha particles are attracted toward the object with the negative charge. Negatively charged beta particles are attracted toward the object with the positive charge. Gamma radiation, having no electric charge, is not attracted toward either object; it continues to move straight ahead.

Gamma radiation is the most dangerous form of nuclear radiation. It is even more dangerous than X-rays. Gamma radiation has enough energy to pass through several centimeters of lead. It is very damaging to the skin and body tissue of living organisms. Beta radiation is less damaging than gamma radiation but does penetrate the skin and even thin sheets of metal. Alpha radiation is the least penetrating of

**Main Idea**

What are the principal properties of gamma radiation?

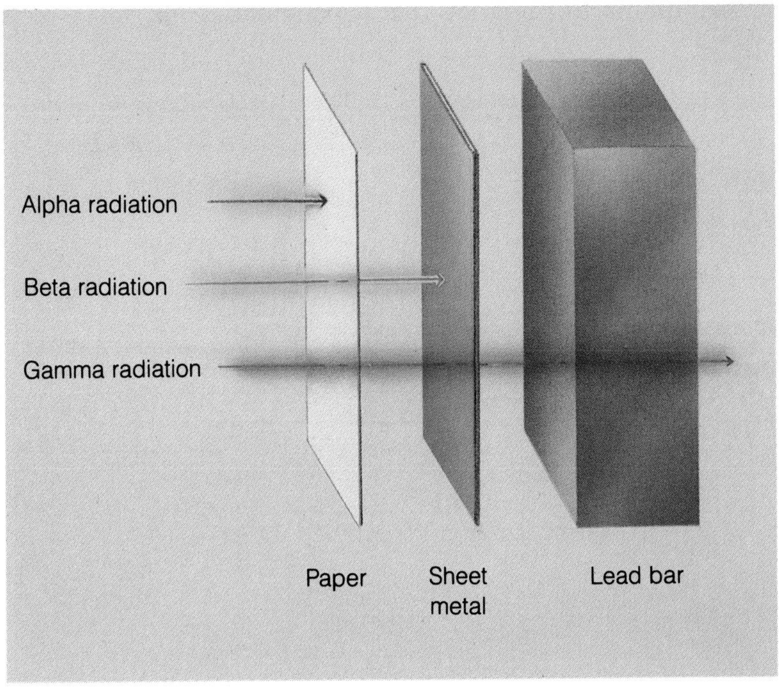

Figure 10-17. Which of the three types of radiation is most dangerous? Why?

Alpha radiation

Beta radiation

Gamma radiation

Paper    Sheet metal    Lead bar

the three types. Most alpha particles can be stopped by a thin sheet of paper.

### Check yourself

1. Describe the three different kinds of radiation.
2. Which kind of radiation is the most dangerous? Why?

### Detecting radiation

Nuclear radiation cannot be seen. But its effects can be made visible. Badges worn by workers in areas of possible radiation contain film. The film is protected from ordinary visible light. But dangerous radiation will expose the film. The worker then knows if he or she has been exposed to any dangerous radiation.

Some chemicals produce a flash of visible light when the invisible radiation strikes them. These flashes of light can be picked up by a photoelectric cell. The amount of current produced can be measured. The current is then a measure of the amount of radiation that is present.

Figure 10-18. The Geiger tube for detecting radiation.

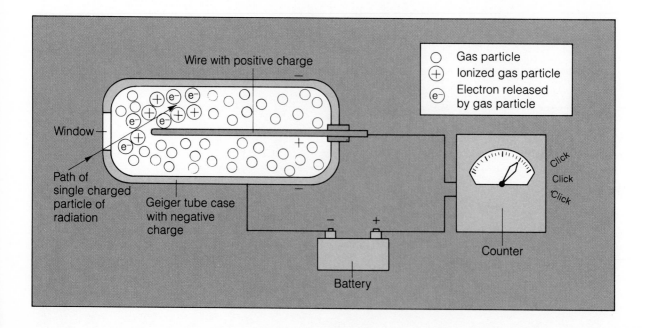

Probably the most familiar device for detecting radiation is the **Geiger** (GĪ'-ger) **tube**. Gas particles in the tube are ionized, or changed into ions, by the radiation that strikes them. The more radiation, the more gas particles are ionized. An electric current flows through the tube. The amount of current depends on the amount of ionized gas particles, and is therefore a measure of the amount of radiation. A counter is usually attached to the tube, and the entire device is called a Geiger counter. The counter registers the amount of radiation. It also produces the audible "clicks" that you hear when a radioactive source is nearby.

### Check yourself

What happens inside a Geiger tube when radiation strikes the tube?

### Changes in the nucleus

Radioactive elements release both particles and energy. The release is accompanied by changes in the nucleus. You are already familiar with two kinds of particles found in the nucleus of an atom. These particles are protons and neutrons.

The number of protons in the nucleus determines the kind of element. For example, any nucleus with 6 protons is carbon. Or, any nucleus with 7 protons is nitrogen. Protons have a positive charge.

Neutrons have no charge, but they add mass to the atom. The number of neutrons in the nucleus determines what isotope is present. The isotope carbon-12 has 6 protons and 6 neutrons. Carbon-13 has 6 protons and 7 neutrons. Both are isotopes of the same element—carbon. The number written after the name of the element is the **mass number** of the isotope. The mass number equals the sum of the numbers of protons and neutrons.

A change in the number of protons changes the element to a different element. A change in the number of neutrons changes the original isotope to a different isotope of the same element. Both of these changes are nuclear changes.

### Main Idea

What change in a nucleus is brought about by a change in the number of protons it contains?

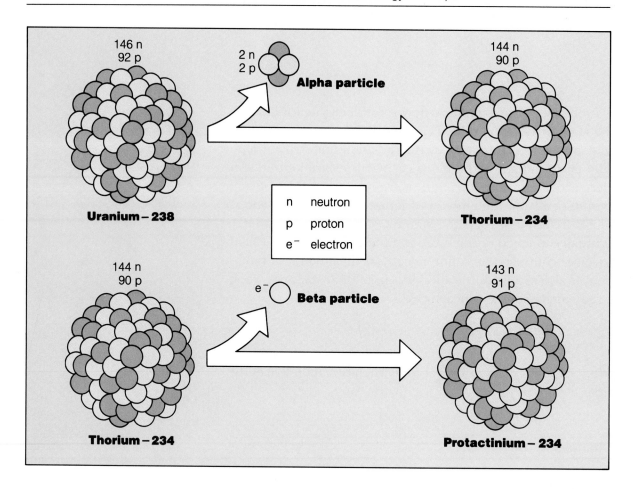

Figure 10-19. Uranium-238 decays to thorium-234 by giving off an alpha particle. Thorium-234 decays, in turn, by giving off a beta particle. What isotope results?

Isotopes of elements with more neutrons than protons in the nucleus are often naturally radioactive. Hydrogen atoms with a mass number of three have two neutrons and one proton. The isotope is called tritium. It is naturally radioactive. Carbon atoms with a mass number of 14 are also radioactive. These atoms have 6 protons and 8 neutrons.

Sometimes isotopes with more protons than neutrons are associated with natural radioactivity, too. Nitrogen atoms with a mass number of 13 are radioactive. How many protons and neutrons does an atom of this isotope have?

Most of the heavier elements have radioactive isotopes. Uranium-238 is an example. Its atomic number is 92. Each atom has 92 protons. How many neutrons does each atom of uranium-238 have? Uranium-238 breaks down, or decays, by giving off an alpha particle. An alpha particle, like a helium nucleus, has two protons and two neutrons. Therefore, the uranium-238 nucleus changes to another nucleus having two fewer protons and two fewer neutrons. What will be the number of protons in the new nucleus? Will it still be uranium?

If not, what element will it be? How many neutrons does it have?

Nuclei that give off a beta particle change in a different way. When an electron is given off as beta radiation, the number of protons increases by one. The mass of the nucleus stays about the same. Scientists have theorized that a neutron can break into a proton and an electron. Electrons have very little mass compared to a proton or neutron. Thus, the loss of an electron does not have much effect on the total mass of the nucleus.

## Check yourself

1. What kinds of isotopes are likely to be radioactive?

2. What does a nucleus become when it loses one or more protons?

3. When a nucleus loses a beta particle, what does it gain?

## Using radioisotopes

Isotopes of some of the common elements can be artificially made. Some are also produced in nuclear reactions used for other purposes. Many of these isotopes are radioactive. Phosphorus-32 is one example. It has the same properties as ordinary phosphorus-31. But it is also radioactive. Plants and animals both use small amounts of phosphorus. The path that the phosphorus takes through a plant or animal can be followed by a detector such as a Geiger counter. Much can be learned about the way the plant or animal uses phosphorus by following the tagged, or radioactive, isotope. Isotopes of other elements can be used in a similar way.

Some isotopes are used in the treatment of disease. Cancer cells can be destroyed by radiation from certain atoms. The radiation must be carefully controlled and directed. Otherwise, healthy cells are destroyed at the same time.

Radioactive isotopes, or radioisotopes, are also used in industry. Leaks in pipes can be detected by tagging some of the material that flows through the pipes with radioactive

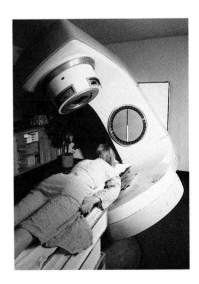

Figure 10-20. How are radioactive isotopes used in the treatment of disease?

Table 10-2. Uses of some radioisotopes.

| Radioisotope | Use of Isotope |
|---|---|
| Calcium-45 | Observing plant nutrition |
| Carbon-14 | Treating brain tumors, measuring age of ancient objects |
| Cobalt-60 | Treating cancer, irradiating food |
| Iodine-131 | Studying and treating the thyroid gland, finding leaks in water pipes |
| Iron-59 | Examining the blood circulation |
| Phosphorus-32 | Studying plants' use of fertilizer |
| Sodium-24 | Diagnosing circulatory diseases |
| Strontium-90 | Treating small lesions |
| Sulfur-35 | Studying body's use of certain amino acids |

**Library research**

Investigate the use of nuclear substances in medicine. What radioisotopes are most used, and for what purposes? What is the rate of success of such treatments?

isotopes. Changes in thickness of a material such as sheet metal can be measured by the changes in the amount of radiation that passes through it.

The ability to detect the movement of otherwise invisible atoms makes it possible to understand chemical changes even better. For example, in a certain experiment some green algae were exposed to carbon dioxide containing radioactive carbon. With detectors scientists could then tell how the green algae used the carbon in their food-making process.

**Check yourself**

How does radioactivity cure some kinds of cancer? What caution must be followed?

**Rate of nuclear decay**

Any sample of a radioactive substance, even a very tiny amount, contains many, many atoms. Predicting which nucleus will break down at a certain time is not possible. But a prediction of the percentage of a sample that will break down in any time period is possible. The breakdown of a nucleus is called **nuclear decay**.

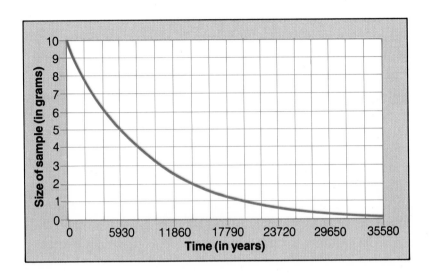

Figure 10-21. How long a time will pass before all the carbon-14 in the 10-gram sample is gone?

The decay rate, or number of nuclei that decay per second, depends only on the type and amount of the sample. Factors such as temperature or pressure do not change the decay rate for an isotope. However, as the sample decays, less of the radioactive isotope remains. This means that the number of nuclei that decay will decrease. The rate of decay decreases as the amount of the remaining radioactive isotope decreases. The rate of decay therefore slows down with time.

The rate of decay of a radioactive isotope can also be described using the term **half-life.** Half-life refers to the time required for half of the nuclei in a sample of a radioactive isotope to decay. For example, the half-life of carbon-14 is about 5930 years. This means that a 10-gram sample of carbon-14 will diminish to a 5-gram sample of carbon-14 in 5930 years. After another 5930 years there will remain only 2.5 grams. How much will remain after another 5930 years?

Suppose you were given a jar of peanuts. You are told that each day you are to eat one-half of the peanuts that remain. The first day you eat half the jar of peanuts. The second day you would be able to eat only half of the peanuts that remain. That would be only one-fourth of a jar. What fraction of a jar would you be able to eat the third day? What is the half-life of the jar of peanuts? The number of peanuts you could eat each day would certainly change. How many days do you think it would take you to finish the jar of peanuts?

**Main Idea**

What is meant by the half-life of a radioactive isotope?

Figure 10-22. The age of the wood used in old buildings, such as this one in Chaco Canyon, New Mexico, can be determined by measuring the percentage of carbon-14 in it.

The radioactive carbon-14 isotope has been used to determine the age of materials that were once living. Products made from the wood in trees contain carbon. The carbon came from the carbon dioxide the tree absorbed from the atmosphere. A small percentage of the carbon dioxide in the atmosphere is made of carbon-14. While a tree is still alive, it keeps replacing the carbon inside it with carbon from the atmosphere. The percentage of carbon-14 in the tree is the same as in the atmosphere. When the tree dies, the carbon-14 inside it decays but is not replaced. So the percentage of carbon-14 in the wood decreases as the wood gets older. By careful measurement scientists can estimate how long ago the tree was killed or cut down. Some animals eat plant materials containing carbon-14. The age of their remains can be determined in the same way.

Several other isotopes are used to determine the age of rocks. Uranium-238 has a half-life of 4.5 billion years. Rocks formed billions of years ago still contain U-238. The percentage of U-238 that has not decayed gives away the age of the rock being studied. Uranium-235, potassium-40, and rubidium-87 also are used in determining the age of rocks.

Table 10-3. Half-lives of some common radioisotopes.

| Radioisotope | Half-Life | Radioisotope | Half-Life |
|---|---|---|---|
| Bismuth-212 | 60.5 minutes | Polonium-215 | 0.0018 second |
| Carbon-14 | 5930 years | Polonium-216 | 0.16 second |
| Chlorine-36 | 400 000 years | Radium-226 | 1620 years |
| Cobalt-60 | 5.26 years | Sodium-24 | 15.0 hours |
| Iodine-131 | 8.14 days | Strontium-90 | 19.9 years |
| Iron-59 | 46.3 days | Uranium-235 | 710 million years |
| Phosphorus-32 | 14.3 days | Uranium-238 | 4.5 billion years |

**Data Search**

Who won the Nobel prize in physics in 1960 for developing a method of age-dating materials using the carbon-14 isotope? Search page 558.

**Check yourself**

1. What is meant when it is said that the half-life of a substance is 2500 years?

2. What isotope is used to determine the age of things that were once living?

## Fission of the nucleus

Energy is released when the nucleus of an atom decays. The amount of energy can be very large. Efforts to tap this source of energy led to scientists finding a way of splitting a nucleus. The nucleus was split by adding neutrons, which were shot at the nuclei of uranium-235 atoms. Some of these nuclei absorbed an extra neutron. The nucleus became unstable. As a result, it broke up into two smaller nuclei. Energy was released. Other neutrons were also released. This process of breaking a nucleus into two or more smaller nuclei is called **nuclear fission** (FISH'-un).

In one such fission process, the nucleus of uranium-235 splits into barium and krypton nuclei. Uranium atoms have 92 protons. The atomic number of barium is 56 and that of krypton is 36. The total number of protons is still 92 (= 56 + 36). The number of protons has not changed. One neutron is added to the uranium-235 nucleus. The mass number of the barium nucleus formed is 144. The mass number of the krypton nucleus formed is 90. The total mass number

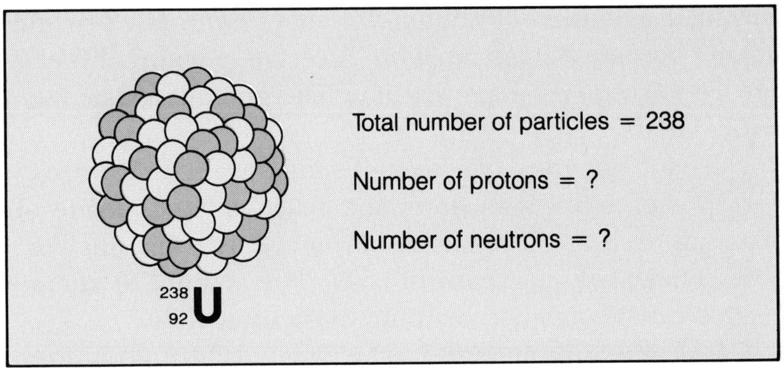

**Main Idea**

How did scientists split the atomic nucleus?

Total number of particles = 238

Number of protons = ?

Number of neutrons = ?

$^{238}_{92}\text{U}$

Figure 10-23. How many neutrons and how many protons are found in the nucleus of a uranium-238 atom?

of barium and krypton is 234. Two additional neutrons are released. The total mass number remains unchanged at 236.

The nuclear change can be summarized in a nuclear equation. Equations for nuclear reactions are similar to chemical equations. The total mass number is unchanged in a nuclear reaction. When no beta particles are given off, the total number of protons is also unchanged. The number of protons is indicated to the lower left of the element's symbol. The mass number is placed to the upper left of the same symbol. The symbol $_0^1$n stands for a neutron (zero charge and mass number of 1).

$$_{92}^{235}\text{U} + _0^1\text{n} \rightarrow _{56}^{144}\text{Ba} + _{36}^{90}\text{Kr} + 2\,_0^1\text{n}$$

The extra neutrons can be absorbed by other uranium-235 nuclei. If they are absorbed, the same reaction is repeated. More uranium-235 nuclei split. A chain reaction is said to take place. A **chain reaction** is a series of repeated reactions that occur very rapidly. You may have heard of a chain reaction on the road. A number of cars collide in rapid succession. One car collides with the one in front of it. The car following does the same, and so on. The series of collisions is sometimes called a chain reaction.

If each car that is hit were to hit two others, the reaction would be even faster. If the road were very crowded, a large number of cars would be involved in a very short time. How can these chain reactions be avoided? One way is to leave space between the cars. Under these conditions the chain reaction may be stopped completely.

Nuclear chain reactions can also be controlled. Suppose only small amounts of uranium-235 are present. The reaction will not become a chain reaction. A certain amount of fuel is needed to sustain a chain reaction. This amount is called the **critical mass**.

The neutrons given off during fission can also be captured. This prevents or slows down the reaction. Rods made of materials such as cadmium or boron are used for this purpose. They are called **control rods**. The amount of energy needed can be obtained by using the control rods.

A nuclear reactor must also include material that slows down the neutrons released. Natural uranium contains 140 times more uranium-238 than uranium-235. Only uranium-235 is likely to split. Both isotopes absorb fast neutrons, but only uranium-235 also absorbs slow neutrons. The neutrons must be slowed down or they will be absorbed by the wrong nuclei. Materials that slow down the neutrons are called **moderators** (MOD′-er-ray-terz). Graphite and water are often used as moderators.

## Library research

The first controlled nuclear chain reaction was accomplished December 2, 1942, under an old stadium at the University of Chicago. Find out the circumstances that led the scientists Leo Szilard and Enrico Fermi to undertake this project. Why was it a top secret project? What was Albert Einstein's involvement?

## Activity 10–2        Chain Reaction

### Materials

15 to 20 dominoes
watch or clock that indicates seconds

### Purpose

To illustrate a chain reaction by using dominoes.

### Procedure

1. For Trial 1, set a domino upright on its short-est edge. Stand a second domino upright directly in front of the first. The dominoes should be set apart about one-half of their length. Place the rest of the dominoes along the same line and the same distance apart.
2. Tap the first domino so that it falls onto the second and knocks it over. Time how long it takes for all the dominoes to fall.
3. For Trial 2, use the same number of domi-noes as before. Arrange them so that each domino will knock over two others. Time how long it takes for all the dominoes to fall.

### Questions

1. How many seconds did it take for all the dominoes to fall in Trial 1?
2. How many seconds did it take for all the dominoes to fall in Trial 2?
3. How does the speed of the reaction time in the two trials compare?
4. What would happen if each domino knocked down three dominoes?

### Conclusion

How can dominoes be used to illustrate a chain reaction?

A small amount of nuclear fuel releases tremendous amounts of energy. One kilogram of uranium that undergoes fission produces about 100 trillion joules of energy. To produce the same amount of energy would require the burning of about 4 000 000 kg of coal.

Where does the energy released in fission come from? Albert Einstein had theorized that mass and energy are related. That is, the more mass something has, the more energy it has, and vice versa. If *m* is the mass, *E* is the energy, and *c* is the speed of light, energy and mass are related by Einstein's famous equation:

$$E = mc^2$$

Now, when fission takes place, the total mass of the products seems to be slightly less than the total mass of the reactants. Only about one thousandth of the mass seems to have disappeared. When 1 kg of uranium undergoes fission, 1 g of mass disappears. According to Einstein, the 100 trillion joules of energy released is equivalent to a mass of 1 g. When the uranium releases energy, it also gives up a little mass.

Energy from nuclear fission is used to generate electricity. Heat energy given off by the nuclear reaction changes water into steam. The steam drives a turbine which generates the electricity. The electric generators work the same as in conventional plants. Only the fuel is different.

Safety practices must be followed strictly in the use of nuclear reactors. Excessive heat can lead to meltdown of the reactor.

Figure 10-24. A nuclear reactor is a place where nuclear fission occurs under controlled conditions. How is the reaction controlled?

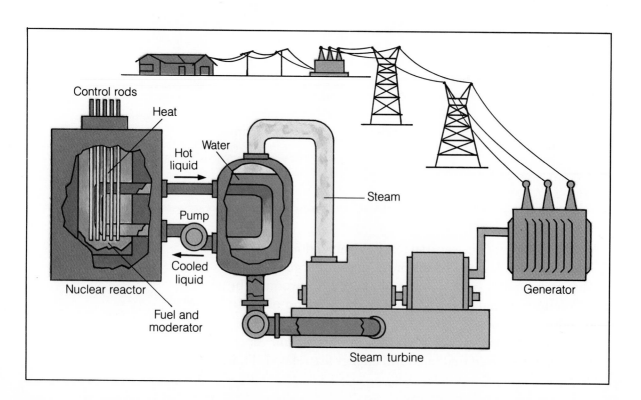

Radioactive substances can escape. Safety considerations have so far restricted the use of fission reactions to produce electric energy.

Another problem with nuclear fission is the waste materials that are produced. Many will remain dangerously radioactive for centuries to come. No one yet has developed a completely safe way of disposing of these wastes. For this reason, many people oppose the use of nuclear fission. Others favor careful use and continued scientific investigation into the waste disposal problem.

### Check yourself

1. What occurs during nuclear fission?
2. What are some of the problems caused by nuclear fission?

### Nuclear fusion

The sun and other stars are sources of even greater amounts of energy. This energy release is the result of the fusion of nuclei. **Nuclear fusion** (FYOO'-zhun) is the joining together of two or more nuclei. Most fusion reactions involve the joining of hydrogen atoms to form helium atoms. Some mass again seems to disappear, as in a fission reaction. But the reaction is the reverse. The heavier elements release energy when they split. The lighter elements release energy when they fuse.

Fusion takes place only at very high temperatures. The temperature has to be several million degrees Celsius. Temperatures that high are found only in the center of stars. They are difficult to produce in a laboratory. At such high temperatures electrons have been removed from the atoms. Under these conditions matter consists of bare nuclei and free electrons. This form of matter is sometimes referred to as **plasma** (PLAZ'-muh). In this form of matter the nuclei can be close enough to fuse.

The heavy isotopes of hydrogen—deuterium and tritium—can be used as the fuel in a nuclear fusion reaction. Deuterium has one proton and one neutron in its nucleus. Tritium

**Library research**

Find out about the accident that occurred in the nuclear power plant on Three-Mile Island in Pennsylvania. What was the probable cause? What were the damages and casualties?

**Main Idea**

How does plasma differ from other forms of matter?

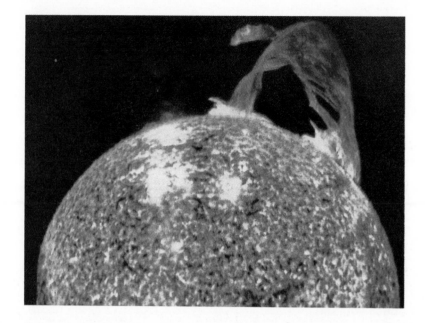

Figure 10-25. This huge flare coming from the sun's surface is many times larger than the earth. How is the sun's energy produced?

**Main Idea**

What would be a useful product of a fusion reaction?

has one proton and two neutrons in its nucleus. The fusion reaction forms helium and releases one neutron.

$$\,_1^2\mathrm{H} + \,_1^3\mathrm{H} \rightarrow \,_2^4\mathrm{He} + \,_0^1\mathrm{n}$$

Once the reaction is started, more heat energy is released than is used to start the reaction. Again, this heat can be used to generate electricity.

Fusion does not produce as many dangerous wastes as fission. Also, it can be controlled more easily. The reaction does take place at very high temperatures. But it can be more easily stopped by removing the fuel for the reaction.

Fusion has another advantage. There is an almost unlimited supply of fuel. Deuterium makes up a part of the hydrogen in sea water, which is very plentiful. Tritium can be prepared from lithium. Lithium also is available in quantities large enough to supply energy needs for a long, long time.

The use of nuclear fusion to supply energy may not be possible for quite some time. Still, its advantages are great enough to encourage researchers in their efforts. It may someday be possible to overcome the problems in putting fusion to a peaceful use.

**Check yourself**

1. What elements are involved in most fusion reactions?

2. What are three advantages of using nuclear fusion instead of nuclear fission for generating electricity?

## Radiologic Technologist

Radiologic technologists use X-rays, radioisotopes, and sound waves to help diagnose and treat medical patients.

Although some radiologic technologists work regular business hours, many work evenings or are "on call." Technologists check equipment, update medical records, read prescriptions, and position patients and equipment. They must know and comply with safety regulations.

Patients are often ill and anxious. Radiologic technologists ease patient fears by being sympathetic listeners, and by explaining procedures and their possible side-effects. Technologists must be able to work well with a variety of people. Precision, moderate strength, and the ability to work carefully and quickly under pressure are required in this field.

Programs in radiologic technology are offered at colleges, trade schools, hospitals, and medical centers. Classes in biology, chemistry, physics, and math are excellent preparation for a career in radiologic technology.

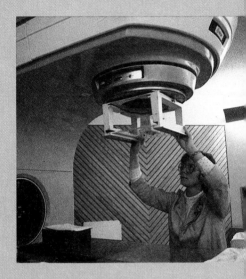

Radiologic technologies such as ultrasound and fluoroscopy allow doctors to see inside a living body without performing surgery.

## Electroplater

About half of all electroplaters work in shops that specialize in metal plating and polishing. Others work in plants that manufacture plumbing fixtures, cooking utensils, household appliances, electronic components, automobiles, and other metal products.

Work as an electroplater can be hazardous. Toxic fumes and acid spills may be part of the workers' environment. Protective masks and clothing may have to be worn. Patience, concern for detail, and attention to job specifications are important qualities of successful electroplaters.

Most electroplaters learn their skills by helping experienced workers in an on-the-job type apprenticeship. Some workers complete a one- to two-year electroplating course in a technical institute or in a vocational school. High school chemistry and physics courses provide students with an understanding of the process of electroplating. Experience in shop courses can provide a good general background for the field.

Electroplating involves the use of strong chemicals as well as electric current.

# Practical Science

## Nuclear Wastes

Science and industry are producing and using increasing amounts of nuclear energy for research and practical applications. However, production of nuclear energy also creates nuclear wastes. Many of these wastes are highly radioactive and can cause death as well as genetic damage. Many will be dangerously radioactive thousands of years from now.

As yet, there are no ways to dispose of nuclear wastes safely and permanently. Some experts say that these wastes can be safely stored for two centuries. As a result, the wastes are being stored "temporarily" around the country.

**Types of nuclear wastes**  Nuclear wastes come from many sources, and vary in the amount of contaminating radiation they emit.

*Low-level* wastes come from all activities using radioactive materials, except nuclear reactors and the reprocessing of spent fuels from nuclear reactors. These wastes occur in materials ranging from contaminated protective clothing and tools to industrial and medical wastes. Low-level refers to the source of the wastes and not to the level of radioactivity.

Another source of nuclear wastes is uranium mining and processing. The mining and milling of uranium ore produces fine sands called *tailings*. These tailings emit radon gas which may cause cancer. For many years, tailings were used in the construction of roads and buildings. Now, such use of tailings is banned.

*Transuranic wastes* contain the highly radioactive elements plutonium, neptunium, and americium. These wastes result from the production of nuclear weapons and the reprocessing of spent fuel. Some of them remain toxic for hundreds of thousands of years.

*Spent nuclear fuel* assemblies from nuclear reactors are stored temporarily by the thousands in water-cooling tanks. They await a federal government decision to reprocess or dispose of them. Reprocessing will produce more transuranic and high-level wastes.

*High-level wastes* are produced during the reprocessing of spent nuclear fuel. These wastes are intensely radioactive and must be handled without human contact.

**How big is the problem?**  The safe disposal of radioactive wastes is one of the most urgent problems facing this country. High-level liquid nuclear wastes remain intensely radioactive for 600 to 1000 years. Some of the transuranic wastes maintain toxic levels of radiation for up to 500,000 years.

**Disposal of nuclear wastes**  The disposal of such large amounts of nuclear wastes requires that they be concentrated and solidified. Then places must be found to safely dispose of the concentrated radioactive material.

The solution to the problem of how to safely and permanently dispose of nuclear wastes is only partly technical. For example, nobody wants nuclear wastes stored near them. Remote disposal sites have been proposed, including deep underground, underneath the sea floor, beneath the Antarctic ice cap, and in outer space. Many people are concerned about the unknown long-term effects of even remote nuclear wastes disposal sites on life and the environment. They are also concerned about the economic costs of safe nuclear waste disposal.

It is important that these concerns be solved soon to ensure a safe and healthy environment for future generations.

# Section 2 Review   Chapter 10

## Check Your Vocabulary

| | |
|---|---|
| alpha radiation | mass number |
| beta radiation | moderator |
| chain reaction | nuclear fission |
| control rod | nuclear fusion |
| Geiger tube | plasma |
| half-life | radioactivity |

*Match each term above with the numbered phrase that best describes it.*

1. Splitting of nucleus into two or more fragments

2. Release of particles and/or energy from the nucleus of an atom

3. Describes rate of decay of radioactive substance

4. Joining of smaller nuclei to form a larger nucleus

5. Series of repeated reactions that occur very rapidly

6. Form of matter with bare nuclei and free electrons

7. Device for detecting radiation

8. Slows or prevents a nuclear reaction

9. Material that slows down neutrons

10. Stream of electrons

11. Stream of helium nuclei

12. Total number of protons and neutrons

## Check Your Knowledge

*Multiple Choice: Choose the answer that best completes each of the following sentences.*

1. A type of nuclear radiation that has no charge but is very damaging is ?.
   a) alpha radiation     c) gamma radiation
   b) beta radiation      d) delta radiation

2. Beta radiation from the nucleus of an atom changes the nucleus by ?.
   a) increasing the number of protons
   b) increasing the number of neutrons
   c) decreasing the number of protons
   d) decreasing the total number of protons and neutrons

3. If a radioactive material has a half-life of 10 years, the fraction of the material that will remain after 30 years is ?.
   a) one-half        c) one-fourth
   b) one-third       d) one-eighth

4. The most practical device for detecting the presence of harmful radiation is a ?.
   a) Geiger tube     c) magnet
   b) moderator       d) control rod

## Check Your Understanding

1. What property of radioactivity was responsible for its discovery?

2. Give two examples of how radioisotopes are used.

3. What two factors determine the rate of decay of a sample of radioactive material?

4. What is the source of the energy that is released in a nuclear reaction?

5. What advantages does the use of nuclear fusion have over nuclear fission as a source of energy for the future?

## Practical Science

1. Is there a safe and permanent way to dispose of nuclear wastes?

2. How are nuclear wastes currently disposed?

3. What are the concerns about nuclear waste?

# Chapter 10 Review

## Concept Summary

**Oxidation** is the loss of electrons in a chemical change; **reduction** is the gain of electrons in a chemical change.
- Corrosion is the combining of a metal with water, air, or other materials in the atmosphere
- When a metal corrodes, it loses electrons.
- Metals differ in their tendency to give up electrons.
- An electrochemical cell uses a chemical change involving oxidation and reduction to produce electric energy.
- A storage battery can be recharged by using electric energy to run a current through it in the reverse direction.
- In a fuel cell, the materials that react are supplied from outside the cell.
- Electric energy can be used to produce chemical changes such as the separation of metals from their ores and the electroplating of metals.

**Radioactivity** is the release of particles and/or energy from the nucleus of an atom.
- Three kinds of radiation can be given off by radioactive atoms: alpha radiation, beta radiation, and gamma radiation.
- The number of nuclei in a sample of a radioactive isotope that decay per second depends only on the type and amount of the sample.
- The half-life of a radioactive isotope is the time required for half of the nuclei in a sample of that isotope to decay.

**Nuclear fission** is the breaking up of a nucleus into two or more smaller nuclei.
- Uranium-235 is commonly used for fission.
- A chain reaction is a series of fission reactions that occur when the neutrons released in one fission reaction cause another fission reaction.
- Einstein explained the energy released in a nuclear change by saying it was the equivalent of the mass that is given up in the reaction.
- Fission reactions can be controlled; the heat energy can be used to generate electricity.

- Safety considerations and the production of radioactive waste materials have restricted the use of nuclear fission for generating electricity.

**Nuclear fusion** is the joining together of two or more nuclei.
- Fusion most commonly involves the joining of hydrogen nuclei to form helium nuclei.
- Fusion occurs only where the temperatures are very high, such as in stars.
- The heat released by fusion may someday be used to generate electricity.
- The use of nuclear fusion to supply energy has many potential advantages over nuclear fission.

## Putting It All Together

1. What evidence is there that corrosion is a chemical change?
2. Why are most electrochemical cells made of two different metals?
3. What is the difference between a wet cell and a dry cell?
4. What is the difference between a battery and a cell?
5. How is an electrolysis reaction different from the reaction in an electrochemical cell?
6. What is the purpose of electroplating iron with chromium?
7. At which electrode would you place the metal to be electroplated?
8. In what way was the radiation that Becquerel discovered different from ordinary light?
9. What causes alpha, beta, and gamma radiation to behave differently when they pass between positive and negative charges?
10. What are three ways in which nuclear radiation can be detected?
11. How can a different element be produced as the result of the radioactivity of an isotope of one element?
12. What is the difference between nuclear fission and nuclear fusion?

13. How does the total mass of the products of a fission reaction compare with the total mass of the reactants?

14. What is one of the major difficulties in the harnessing of nuclear fusion to produce electric energy?

## Apply Your Knowledge

1. Some cells and batteries can be recharged. Describe what takes place during the recharging of a battery. What are the advantages of a rechargeable battery?

2. Suppose you wished to separate a metal from its ore by electrolysis. At which electrode would you expect the metal to be collected? Would the metal ion be reduced or oxidized?

3. The radioactive dating of once-living materials using carbon-14 is based on an assumption that the percentage of radioactive carbon in the atmosphere remains the same over long periods of time. Suppose that scientists found evidence that the percentage of radioactive carbon in the atmosphere has been increasing. How would this affect the estimates of the ages of materials that have already been dated by carbon-14?

4. In a nuclear reactor, how is the chain reaction controlled? What kind of dangers exist if the reaction should for some reason get out of control?

5. When a nucleus decays by giving off a beta particle, the number of protons in it increases. Explain how it is possible for the nucleus to lose a particle and yet show an increase in the number of protons.

## Find Out on Your Own

1. Find out if water increases the speed at which iron rusts by setting up a controlled experiment. Decide what variables you need to control and how you will measure the rate of the reaction.

2. Use a hacksaw to cut a standard carbon-zinc flashlight cell in half. Identify the electrodes and the electrolyte.

3. Obtain a strip of zinc, a strip of copper, and a sensitive galvanometer. Place the metal strips through the skin of a lemon, taking care that they do not touch. Connect the strips to the galvanometer and look for evidence of a current. Replace the lemon by a potato. Is there any difference in the amount of current?

4. Look through newspapers and magazines to find stories about any controversies over the use of nuclear fission reactors to generate electricity. What arguments do the proponents use? What arguments do the opponents use?

## Reading Further

Fermi, Laura. *The Story of Atomic Energy.* New York: Random House, 1961
   This book gives a dramatic account of the research on the atomic nucleus and the men and women who took part in it. It is written by the wife of Enrico Fermi, who won a Nobel Prize for his work on bombarding uranium with neutrons.

Hawkes, Nigel. *Nuclear Power.* New York: Gloucester Press, 1984
   This is a clear, well-diagrammed book describing what nuclear power is and how it is used.

Moché, Dinah. *Radiation: Benefits/Dangers.* New York: Franklin Watts, 1979
   A clear discussion of the many uses of nuclear radiation is presented.

Morgan, Alfred. *Adventures in Electrochemistry.* New York: Scribner, 1977
   This book describes experiments you can do and gives an interesting historical overview of electrochemistry.

# Chapter 11

# Our Energy Needs

### Section 1
**Present Energy Resources**

Energy comes from the sun to the earth along various pathways. The pathway we use most is one in which energy has been stored for a long period in fossil fuels. The world supply of fossil fuels is being used up at an increasing rate. Sooner or later, we will have to find other sources of energy.

### Section 2
**Alternative Energy Resources**

Some people are now using energy from alternative sources. These include fossil fuels from other places; energy that comes directly from the sun; wind; and flowing water. In the future more and more energy is likely to come from these alternative sources.

### Section 3
**Energy Conservation**

It is going to take a long time to convert to alternative energy sources. In the meantime, we can conserve the energy we are now using. This will give us the time we need to develop new energy resources. It will also help to cut down on pollution that has been caused by excessive use of fossil fuels.

In order for life to exist on this planet, we need water, air, and energy. Water and air are limited; we have no more than when the earth began. Energy is not limited. We get huge amounts of energy every day from the sun. We get more energy than we could ever use, and expect to keep getting it for billions of years to come. Yet, we are told that we have a problem in meeting our energy needs. In this chapter, you will explore our energy problem, what is causing it, and some possible solutions.

# Present Energy Resources    Section 1

**Section 1 of Chapter 11 is divided into seven parts:**

Our dependence on energy

Energy in the universe

Energy pathways

Fossil fuel pathways

The fossil fuel dilemma

Environmental problems

Nuclear pathways

*Practical Science: Energy Use at Home*

## Learning Objectives

1. To recognize that we depend on energy and that energy supplies are limited.

2. To recognize that changes in the form of energy reduce the amount of available energy.

3. To identify the steps in several energy pathways.

4. To describe the rate of growth of energy usage.

5. To relate energy usage to our current and future environmental problems.

Figure 11-1. Much of our energy comes from under the ground. How did it get there? When did the energy problem start?

The cave dwellers' demand for energy was small. They used only a small amount of energy to cook their food and make their tools. When they first tamed animals, more energy was made available to them. They then began to grow their food on fields plowed by animals. They also used animals to carry heavy objects.

For many years energy usage increased at about the same rate as the population grew. After the invention of the steam engine, the use of energy increased rapidly. Since 1900, the use of energy has increased much faster than the population growth.

## Our dependence on energy

How do you use energy? List all of the things you have done since you got up this morning. Which of these activities used energy? Was the source of energy electricity, natural gas, food, or some other fuel? What activites did not use energy?

People seldom think about the many ways in which they use energy. They take it for granted that it will be there when they need it. It was therefore a shock when on November 17, 1965, the lights went out in most of the New England states and all of New York City. The people of many towns and cities found themselves in total darkness. Thousands were stranded in subways and elevators. In some places power was not restored for several days. Fortunately, most of the people survived with only minor inconvenience. But a point was made. Our complex society is dependent upon energy. And the supply of energy can be cut off!

At present, oil is the most commonly used energy resource in the industrialized nations. The demand for oil in most of these countries is much larger than the supply. As a result, they have had to import much of the oil they use from countries in the Middle East.

Several times within the past decade, there have been shortages of gasoline and heating oil. You and your parents may remember waiting in long gasoline lines. These shortages served as another reminder that our energy supply is not unlimited.

Figure 11-2. A ringing alarm, a toaster, and bicycling all use energy.

## Main Idea

What are some ways in which the cost of energy has affected the lifestyle of people?

When there are fuel shortages, energy prices rise. An increase in the cost of energy has an effect on lifestyle. People buy small cars that get high mileage. They insulate their homes. They start to think about using other methods to heat their homes, such as solar heat. Even when fuel prices come down, people should not be fooled into thinking that there will always be plenty of fuel for everyone.

### Check yourself

1. What is the most commonly used source of energy in industrialized nations?

2. In what ways have people been reminded in recent times that the energy supply is limited?

### Energy in the universe

The energy supply in the universe seems endless. Huge stars and galaxies give off enormous amounts of energy each second. The energy of the universe seems to be concentrated in

Figure 11-3. Is the energy in the universe disappearing?

certain places, such as in hot stars. Other parts of the universe have little energy and are extremely cold and dark. Energy is constantly flowing from places of higher energy concentration to places of lower concentration. For example, energy flows from our sun to all the objects in the solar system and beyond. Or, even when we light a campfire on a cold night, energy flows out and warms all the people sitting around the fire.

We can trace this great flow of energy from the sun along many pathways. We use this energy to grow our food, heat our homes, and run our machines. Our very survival depends on this flow of energy.

Scientists have theorized that the energy of the universe is gradually becoming more evenly distributed. It is gradually flowing away from places of high concentration and spreading throughout the entire universe. They call this evening-off process an increase in **entropy** (EN′-truh-pee).

Entropy is a measure of the distribution of energy in a system. When the energy is evenly distributed, the entropy is at its highest, but the energy is no longer available. There are no hot and cold places for it to flow between. Look at the two model universes in Figure 11-4.

Does this mean that the universe will eventually become "wound down" once all of the energy is evenly distributed? No one is really sure, but such an event would be so far in the future that it is not worthy of our concern. The amount of energy stored in stars such as our sun is enormous. These stars are expected to be giving off energy for billions of years to come.

The fact that energy is constantly flowing to us from the sun *is* important to us. For all practical purposes, we have an unlimited source of energy in the sun. Why, then, are some people worried about an energy crisis? To find out, we need to study some of the pathways of energy from the sun.

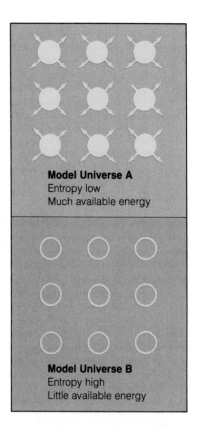

**Model Universe A**
Entropy low
Much available energy

**Model Universe B**
Entropy high
Little available energy

Figure 11-4. Model universe A has many hot stars surrounded by cold regions. Much available energy is flowing from the hot stars. Entropy is low.

In model universe B, the stars have all cooled off. They are the same temperature as the surrounding regions. Entropy is high. Why is there no available energy in universe B?

### Check yourself

1. How does energy seem to be flowing in the universe?
2. Explain what happens to the availability of energy as entropy increases.

## Energy pathways

Energy can change from one form to another. Yet energy changes are not reversible. That is, energy cannot be completely changed back into its original form. With each conversion the amount of usable energy gets smaller and smaller.

The bouncing ball shown in Figure 11-5 is an example of all energy pathways. At the height from which it is dropped, the ball has a certain amount of potential energy. As the ball falls, this energy changes into kinetic energy. When the ball strikes the ground, the energy again changes to potential energy. Since the ball is elastic, it rebounds. On the rebound the energy is again changed to kinetic energy. But the ball does not return to its original bounce-height. Some of the energy is changed, due to friction, into unusable heat energy. Each time the ball bounces, it does not go quite as high as the time before.

Energy keeps coming to us from the sun, but each time it changes form, some is lost. It is not destroyed, but it becomes unusable. However, we are finding ways of making more and more use of the sun's energy.

Heat from the sun causes water to evaporate and rise in the air. It later condenses and comes down as rain or snow.

Figure 11-5. What prevents the ball from bouncing to its original height?

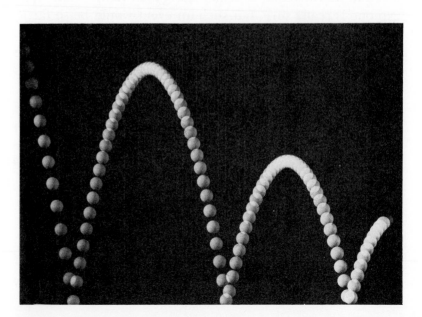

Run-off rainwater turns turbines which generate electricity. The heat energy of the sun is converted into kinetic energy in moving water. The energy in the moving water moves the turbines. The energy of motion of the turbine becomes electric energy in the generator.

Suppose that you were able to measure the energy at each step of this energy pathway. You would find that you had much less electric energy than the amount of energy from the sun at the start. Some energy was wasted with each change along the way.

Winds are caused by the heating of air by the sun. A windmill may change the energy in wind motion to energy of motion in a water pump. Or it may operate a generator to produce electricity. At what steps is energy wasted in this energy pathway?

A chemical called chlorophyll in green plants traps solar energy. Green plants change light energy into chemical energy in food. Food produced by green plants supplies the energy needs for all living things. Some of the sun's energy becomes stored in wood in trees. When the wood burns, the energy is released again as heat. Some of this heat may be used by people to keep warm and cook their food.

In some pathways, the sun's energy can be stored for a very long time, then later released and used. Coal, oil, and natural

Figure 11-6. What happens to the sun's energy as it travels through these pathways?

**Main Idea**

What role do green plants play in converting solar energy into another form of energy?

gas are the remains of organisms that lived hundreds of millions of years ago. The chemical energy stored in these **fossil fuels** originally came from the sun.

### Check yourself

1. Describe the energy changes that take place when a ball bounces.
2. Describe two energy pathways that include green plants.

### Fossil fuel pathways

Coal is the remains of plants that lived hundreds of millions of years ago. Scientists believe that tropical swamps once covered much of the earth's surface. The warm, wet climate was suitable for the growth of fern trees and huge mosses.

When the plants died, they fell into the swamp. Layer upon layer of dead plants built up in the swamp. The shallow water of the swamp prevented oxygen from reaching the dead plants. As a result, the plants were slow to decay.

These plants gradually turned into a spongy material called peat. In time, the peat beds became buried under layers of sediments. Pressure and heat caused by the layers of sediment compacted the peat. Hydrogen and oxygen were driven off. Nearly pure carbon, or coal, was left. About 350 million years were needed for this plant matter to change to coal.

Coal is not all alike. Some types give off more heat when burned than others. Some contain sulfur or other substances which pollute the air when the coal is burned.

**Anthracite** (AN′-thruh-sīt) coal is a top-grade fuel. It has a high energy content. It contains little sulfur and is considered a clean fuel. **Bituminous** (bī-TEW′-mih-nus) coal has a somewhat lower energy content and contains much sulfur. **Lignite** (LIG′-nīt) has a low energy content but contains little sulfur. Lignite does contain other air pollutants.

Crude oil, or **petroleum** (puh-TRŌ′-lee-um), and natural gas are usually found together. They likely had a similar origin. Scientists believe that they were formed from the remains of sea organisms. Covered by layers of sand and mud, the

**Library research**

Find out what is meant by the O.P.E.C. countries. What effect have they had on the world supply of petroleum?

**Data Search**

What percentage of the energy consumed in the United States in 1980 came from fossil fuels? Search page 558.

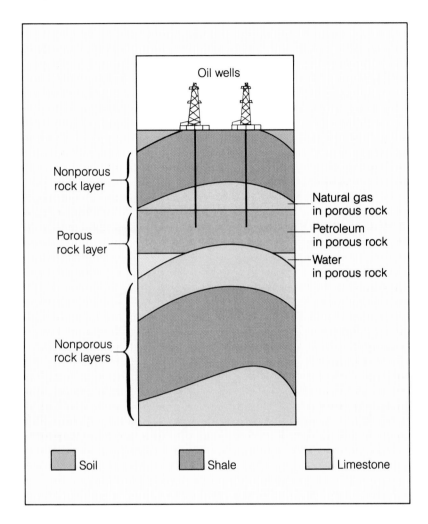

Figure 11-7. Crude oil and natural gas may be trapped in a layer of porous rock that curves up between layers of nonporous rock.

The natural gas fills the highest pores of the porous rock. Crude oil fills the next highest pores, while water fills the lowest pores.

remains gradually decayed. Heat, pressure, and the action of bacteria changed the remains into oil and natural gas.

Oil and natural gas seep through porous rock layers and sometimes become trapped under domes of nonporous rock. It is from these traps that oil and natural gas are pumped to the surface.

Fossil fuels are **nonrenewable** (non'-ree-NEW'-uh-bul) energy resources. That is, they are being used at much faster rates than they are formed. Most of the energy we use everyday travels through a fossil fuel energy pathway.

The energy pathway for each of the fossil fuels is similar but not identical. The energy in natural gas is most often

**Main Idea**

What are nonrenewable energy resources?

Figure 11-8. The "family tree" of the products made from crude oil. The main branches on the tree are the fuels and the petrochemicals.

burned to heat space inside buildings. Oil and oil products are burned in heat engines to produce energy of motion.

Coal, oil, and natural gas are also burned to heat water. Steam from the boiling water turns a turbine. The turbine powers a generator which produces electricity. The energy in petroleum can be found in many fuels and other products we use everyday.

### Check yourself

1. Name three different kinds of coal, and explain how they differ.

2. What two kinds of fossil fuel are often found together?

## The fossil fuel dilemma

It is possible to read in magazines and newspapers differing views on the energy problem. Some people say there is no shortage and that we will never run out of fossil fuels. Others say that our fossil fuel reserves will be used up within the next century.

In thinking about this conflict, keep in mind these questions:

☐ Are we likely to use more fossil fuels next year than this year?

☐ Is this rate of increase likely to stay the same in the future?

☐ How might continued use of fossil fuels affect the environment?

Coal represents a large percentage of the fossil fuel reserves in North America. Unfortunately, only a very small fraction

Figure 11-9. Principal coal reserves in North America.

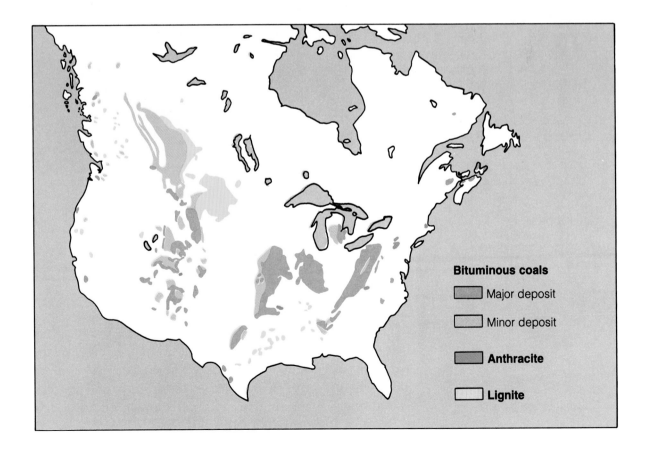

## Activity 11–1A        Oil Recovery

### Materials

| | |
|---|---|
| hot water | graduated cylinder |
| 3 100-mL beakers | cold water |

plastic bottle with spray pump
pebbles (enough to half fill the plastic bottle)
100 mL of motor oil
30 cm plastic tubing to fit the pump nozzle

### Purpose

To determine the difficulty of removing oil from a well.

### Procedure

1. Half fill the plastic bottle with pebbles. Pour 100 mL of motor oil over the pebbles. Make a table like the one shown.
2. Fasten the spray pump to the bottle. Attach a 30-cm length of plastic tubing to the nozzle of the spray pump. Insert the other end of the tubing into one of the beakers.
3. Using the spray pump, remove as much oil from the bottle as you can. Record how much oil you recovered in the beaker.
4. Add 70 mL of cold water to the spray bottle. Pump as much liquid as you can into a clean beaker. Record how much oil is floating on top of the water in the beaker.
5. Repeat the procedure using 70 mL of hot water. Record the recovered oil.

### Questions

1. What percentage of the oil did you recover when you pumped the first time?

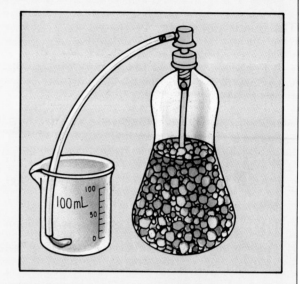

2. How much oil was left in the bottle after you pumped out the hot water?
3. What is the total percentage of the oil recovered from the bottle?

### Conclusion

Explain why it is difficult to remove all the oil from an oil well.

| | Oil beaker | Total recovered |
|---|---|---|
| After first pumping | | |
| After adding cold water | | |
| After adding hot water | | |

is clean, high-energy anthracite coal. Seventy percent of the coal reserves is in the Great Plains. The coal of this region is mainly lignite. Most of the coal in the Middle and Eastern United States is bituminous. Lignite is low in energy, while bituminous coal is high in sulfur.

It is more difficult to estimate the size of the oil and natural gas reserves. Since oil and gas are fluids, they often move from the sites where they were formed, and are more difficult to locate than coal. It is likely that new gas and oil fields will be discovered. Much of the oil discovered will be difficult to remove from the earth. At present, for each barrel removed, two are left in the ground.

The demand on our fossil fuel reserves has increased steadily in this century. In part this is due to the increase in the size of the human population. But in the industrialized nations of the world, the demand for energy is increasing even faster than the population.

Energy use is divided among four sectors: residential, commercial, transportation, and industrial. The demand for energy is increasing in each of these sectors.

Air conditioning, central heating, and many new appliances ranging from color TV to electric can openers have increased the demand for energy in the residential sector. The commercial sector is using more energy for lighting, heating, cooking, and the operation of electric office machines.

The automobile has contributed most heavily to the increased demand for energy in the transportation sector. Also, the transportation of freight is done more and more by truck or plane rather than by the more energy-efficient railroads.

The industrial sector is the largest user of energy. Part of the increase in this sector is due to the shift to plastics, aluminum, and other manufactured goods which take large amounts of energy to produce.

The largest industrial use of energy is in agriculture. Fifteen percent of the total energy used in North America goes into agriculture. Energy use on the farm is increasing at a rate faster than any other use. It takes an equivalent of 350 L of gasoline to run the tractors and other equipment needed to raise an acre of corn.

Methods using high energy have made farms in North America the most productive in the world. But to maintain production, farmers are dependent upon fossil fuels.

The demand for energy increases as the human population increases. In 1850 the human population on earth was one billion. Eighty years later, in 1930, the human population had doubled. By 1975 the human population was four billion. It had doubled again in a period of 45 years. Scientists estimate that the human population will reach 8 billion by the year 2010—a doubling time of 35 years.

**Main Idea**

What are the four sectors among which energy use is divided?

**Library research**

Use an almanac to find estimates of the world population for the latest five years for which data are available. What was the average growth rate per year between each pair of dates? Has the growth rate been increasing?

To find how many years it will take at the present rate for the population to double, divide the latest growth rate into 72.

Figure 11-10. According to this graph, which is increasing faster—the world population or fossil fuel usage? What do you predict fossil fuel usage will be by the year 2010?

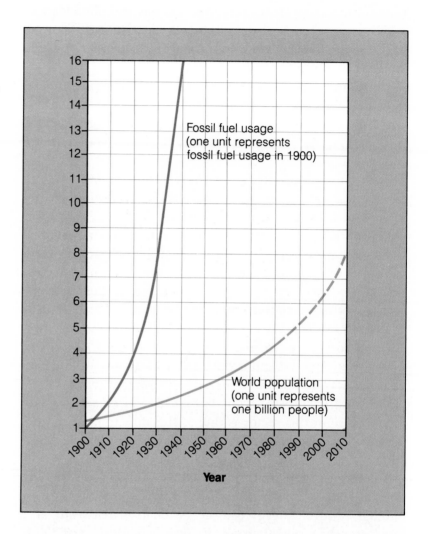

**Main Idea**

What is true for the length of time needed for the human population to double?

Look at the graph of the population growth shown in Figure 11-10. The graph line is not a straight line. It curves upward sharply. The growth rate in the human population is said to be **exponential** (eks-pō-NEN'-shul). The length of time needed for the population to double in size is becoming shorter. In just a few doublings, enormous numbers can be reached.

Our use of fossil fuels has grown exponentially. Fossil fuel usage has grown at a rate of about 7% each year. The amount of energy we use has doubled every 10 years. With a 7% per year increase in fossil fuel use, the amount used each decade is greater than the total previously used.

## Activity 11–1B        Exponential Growth

### Materials

260 pennies or other small objects
row of 10 squares on tile floor or table top

### Purpose

To determine how things increase exponentially.

### Procedure

1. Find a row of 10 squares on a floor or a table top. Label the squares 1 through 10. Place one penny on the first square. Place two of them on the second square. On each square put double the number of pennies you put on the preceding square.
2. Use a sheet of graph paper to show how the number of pennies increases on each square. On the horizontal axis of the graph, have each section represent the number of a square. Have each section along the vertical axis represent 50 pennies.

### Questions

1. What is the total number of pennies on Squares 1 through 3?
2. Compare the number of pennies on Square 4 to the total number on Squares 1–3.
3. How many pennies are there on Square 7?
4. Compare the number of pennies on Square 7 to the total number on Squares 1–6?
5. How many pennies would there be on Square 10?

### Conclusion

Describe the change in the number of objects that occurs with exponential growth.

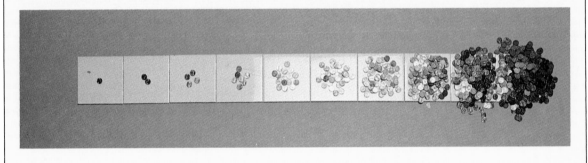

The exponential growth of population and the energy we use per person is at the heart of the fossil fuel problem. World fuel reserves may be large, but in the next 10 years we will need more energy than all we have used in the past.

### Check yourself

1. Describe how the human population has grown.
2. How does the need for fossil fuels compare with the human population growth?

## Environmental problems

Recovering, processing, and burning fossil fuels have produced many environmental problems. Our ground water and atmosphere have been seriously affected. Yet, even more important, living things have been affected. People and governments are more aware of these problems now than they were years ago. Even though problems have been increasing, people have been doing more to solve them.

Recovering coal from strip mines can cause severe damage problems. Poisonous chemicals seep out of the piles of earth that are dug from the mine. Miners have built drainage beds to help solve this problem. Work of this kind is necessary but costly. It has caused an increase in the price of coal.

Drilling for oil in the ocean has resulted in pollution of the water. On several occasions serious underwater oil leaks have occurred, causing contamination of beaches and death to much wildlife. Governments and oil companies have been working on developing methods of preventing and stopping these leaks. Laws have been passed that restrict off-shore drilling in certain areas.

Oil refineries occasionally catch fire, releasing many contaminating materials into the atmosphere. Sometimes toxic wastes get into the ground from plants where chemicals are

**Main Idea**

What problems can result when coal is removed from strip mines?

**Safety**

Many rivers, streams, lakes, and ponds are polluted by invisible toxic wastes. Therefore, never drink untreated water from any of these sources.

Figure 11-11. Auto exhaust is still our most serious source of air pollution. Explain why air pollution is most severe in urban areas.

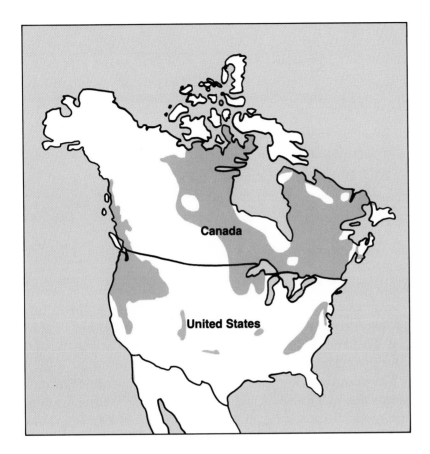

Figure 11-12. The areas marked on this map are endangered by acid rain. What causes this problem?

made from petroleum. These cause health problems for people who live nearby, and are often carried for long distances in the ground water.

The use of fossil fuels has caused air and water pollution. The greatest problem of this kind has been auto exhaust. Autos are now equipped with smog-reducing devices that have helped to cut down on air pollution. However, in areas where there are many cars, air pollution from auto exhaust is still a problem.

Another serious problem that seems to be caused by the use of high-sulfur coal is **acid rain**. Rainwater is normally neutral or very slightly acidic. It has been discovered that the rain over the eastern United States and Canada is much more acidic than normal. Many lakes have become so acidic from the acid rain that they have "died." That is, fish and other animal life cannot live in these lakes. Apparently, fumes from

**Library research**

Investigate the problem of air pollution from auto exhaust. What are the most toxic substances released? What has been done to reduce these substances? How effective have our efforts at cleaning up auto pollution been up to now?

the burning of high-sulfur coal react with water vapor in the air. An acid is formed. Winds carry the acid from industrialized areas to the lakes. Rain brings the acid to the ground.

### Check yourself

1. Describe an environmental problem that has been caused by petroleum.

2. What is the apparent cause of acid rain? What effect does acid rain have on the environment?

### Nuclear pathways

Some of our electricity is produced by nuclear fission, which was discussed in Chapter 10, Section 2. Does the pathway for nuclear energy also start with the sun? Scientists are uncertain. This energy has been locked up in matter on earth ever since the earth began.

The known nuclear pathway starts when an atomic nucleus breaks down. The energy given off produces a super-heated water, which causes steam to be produced in a boiler. This steam turns electric generators which produce electricity.

Nuclear power plants give off less chemical pollution than fossil fuel plants. Since only small amounts of fuel are used, there is less of a problem than with strip mining. Yet, nuclear

Figure 11-13. A fossil-fuel power plant (left) and a nuclear power plant (right). What is the obvious advantage of a nuclear power plant? What are the dangers?

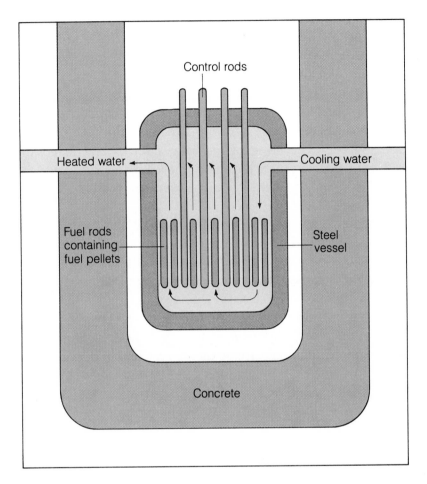

Figure 11-14. Protection around the nuclear fuel bundles in the core of a reactor.

fuel is highly dangerous. Therefore, costly and complex safety systems must be installed and constantly inspected to keep the plant safe.

Many safeguards are built into the system to control nuclear fission within the reactor. Several hundred fuel bundles make up the core of the reactor. Each bundle is made up of uranium oxide ceramic pellets. The arrangement of the bundles and the dilution of the fuel are done to prevent the possibility of a nuclear explosion.

Most of the radioactive byproducts of fission remain in the fuel pellets. The pellets are enclosed in sealed metal tubes. All of the fuel bundles are placed inside a vessel with steel walls 15 to 20 cm thick. Around this is a steel shell and a concrete structure over 1 m thick. Each of these coverings is

**Main Idea**

In a nuclear reactor, what happens to the radioactive byproducts of fission?

a barrier to prevent the escape of radioactive materials from the plant.

Water or another cooling material constantly flows through the core. If this coolant stops flowing, fission must stop immediately. The core, however, would still be very hot. To prevent meltdown and radioactive release, every reactor has safety systems to reflood the vessel and cool the core.

All electric generating plants have a waste heat disposal problem. Nuclear plants have even more waste heat then fossil fuel plants. At present, cooling towers are used to dispose of the heat.

Radioactive wastes are an environmental and health concern. About one third of the fuel rods in a nuclear reactor are replaced each year. Even though the fuel in these rods has been consumed, the removed rods are still radioactive and will remain radioactive for many years.

At present, spent fuel rods are stored at the reactor site in cooling tanks. Investigations on storing radioactive wastes in underground chambers are being made. Chambers would be mined in stable rock formations almost 1 km below the surface. Another solution is to reprocess spent fuel rods. A fully satisfactory method of waste disposal has not yet been agreed upon.

Uranium–236 is a limited natural resource. The **breeder reactor** could solve this supply problem. The breeder reactor uses uranium–238 and plutonium for fuel. In the fission of plutonium, neutrons strike the nuclei of the uranium. This produces more fuel, including plutonium. Nuclear fission was once thought to be the ideal solution to the energy problem. Since there have been several near accidents, many people feel that it will always be unsafe. In Section 2 you will investigate other alternative sources of energy.

## Main Idea

What advantage does a breeder reactor have over other fission reactors?

### Check yourself

1. How do nuclear pathways differ from most other energy pathways on earth?

2. What safeguards are used in nuclear power plants?

3. What methods of nuclear waste disposal are being considered?

# Practical Science

## Energy Use at Home

You use several sources of energy at your house including natural gas, electricity, and sometimes wood. For example, you use energy every time you turn on a water tap. Energy from electricity purifies that water and pumps it into pipes. Below is a record of some other ways you may use energy during a day at home.

**Morning** Your energy day starts when electricity switches on a clock radio. Soon after that, you get up and turn on the lights in the bathroom. On a cold morning, you may set the furnace thermostat higher. Central heating (or cooling) systems use the largest amount of home energy.

Your morning shower requires the hot water heater to work harder. Some hot water heaters use natural gas, while others use electricity. The hot water heater uses the second largest amount of home energy. After your shower, lights begin going on in other parts of the house..

Making breakfast may require electricity for a coffee maker, toaster, and an electric burner on the stove. You may take eggs, milk, and butter out of the refrigerator. The refrigerator-freezer uses the third largest amount of electricity in your home. You may run the garbage disposal which also uses electricity.

On the weekend, you may do a load of laundry after breakfast. The washer uses both hot water and electricity. The dryer may use either gas or electricity. An electric dryer uses the fourth largest amount of electricity at home, even more than the kitchen stove. Gas dryers use less energy and are cheaper to run.

**Afternoon** If you are at school, you will not be using any energy at home after breakfast. Other people at home may use the stove, open the refrigerator, and turn on lights, water taps, and the garbage disposal.

**Evening** This is the busiest time of your at-home energy use. You turn lights on and off as you move from one room to another. The thermostat of the furnace is set higher as the outdoor temperature drops.

You and your family will probably use several electric appliances to make dinner. These may include the oven or microwave (sometimes both), coffee maker, and garbage disposal. You also open and close the refrigerator and freezer doors several times.

The dinner dishes join those from breakfast and lunch in the dishwasher. If there is a full load, you start the dishwasher. It uses electricity to pump and heat water.

You use more electricity during the evening for the television or stereo and for lights to read by. Of course, the furnace continues to use gas and electricity. You or another family member may also burn some logs in a fireplace.

You also use energy as you get ready for bed. You use hot water for washing your face and cold water for brushing your teeth. You also use energy for electric lights.

**Night** Even though you are sleeping, energy is being consumed in your house. A few night lights, a clock radio, an electric blanket, electric clocks in the kitchen and other rooms, and the refrigerator-freezer continue to use energy.

**Something to try** Keep a record of how you actually use energy during one day at your home. Include activities requiring turning on water taps as well as electric switches.

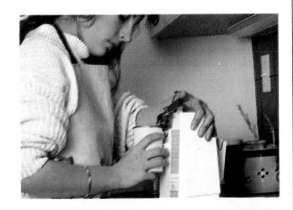

## Section 1 Review   Chapter 11

### Check Your Vocabulary

| | |
|---|---|
| acid rain | exponential |
| anthracite | fossil fuel |
| bituminous | lignite |
| breeder reactor | nonrenewable |
| entropy | petroleum |

*Match each term above with the numbered phrase that best describes it.*

1. Coal, oil, and natural gas
2. Seems to be caused by burning high-sulfur coal
3. Oil produced from the remains of sea organisms
4. Refers to anything that is used much faster than it is produced
5. Measure of energy distribution
6. High-energy, low-sulfur coal
7. Medium-energy, high-sulfur coal
8. Low-energy, low-sulfur coal
9. Increases fuel supply
10. Type of growth shown by human population

### Check Your Knowledge

*Multiple Choice: Choose the answer that best completes each of the following sentences.*

1. Energy flows from _?_.
   a) heavier objects to lighter objects
   b) places of higher concentration to places of lower concentration
   c) places of lower concentration to places of higher concentration
   d) colder objects to hotter objects
2. When energy is evenly distributed, _?_.
   a) the entropy is low
   b) the entropy is high

c) much is available
d) the temperature is high

3. Fossil fuels are _?_ energy resources.
   a) nonrenewable      c) recycled
   b) renewable         d) exponential
4. Acid rain is believed to have caused _?_.
   a) snowstorms
   b) growth of trees
   c) disappearance of fish
   d) eye infections
5. Nuclear power plants are an environmental problem because they _?_.
   a) pollute the air
   b) release toxic chemicals
   c) pollute the water
   d) produce dangerous wastes

### Check Your Understanding

1. Describe the energy pathways that would include laundering your clothes.
2. Explain what is happening to the usable energy in the universe.
3. What sort of environmental problems are caused by fossil fuels?

### Practical Science

1. Which is more expensive to operate, a gas clothes dryer or an electric clothes dryer? Why?
2. Name some ways you use energy at home in the evening.

# Alternative Energy Resources    Section 2

**Section 2 of Chapter 11 is divided into four parts:**

Alternative fuel sources

Energy directly from the sun

Energy from sun-powered systems

Energy from other natural sources

*Practical Energy: Pure Water from the Sun*

## Learning Objectives

1. To distinguish between renewable and nonrenewable energy resources.

2. To identify some alternative energy sources that may find use in the immediate future.

3. To describe different ways in which the sun's energy can be put to use.

4. To identify sources of energy that are the result of other natural causes.

Figure 11-15. This photo shows a solar-powered car. Energy from the sun is absorbed by the panels on top of the car. This energy is stored in the car battery which powers the car.

There are different opinions on how long our fossil fuel supply will last. However, all experts must admit that sooner or later it will be gone. What will happen then? We cannot really go back to living the way we did in earlier times. The present and estimated future world populations are much greater than they were in the days of horses and sailing ships. People need more energy for transportation, food supplies, sanitation, and other needs.

Unfortunately, the world cannot afford to wait to run out of fossil fuels before finding other energy resources. What will those resources be? Two alternative solutions are being studied: 1) finding new, untapped nonrenewable resources; 2) developing new ways to use **renewable** energy resources—those that can be replaced as rapidly as they are used up.

Since all nonrenewable resources will eventually run out, it is probably best to look toward developing renewable resources. However, many of the untapped nonrenewable resources could carry us a long way into the future.

## Our Science Heritage

### Changes in the Wood Stove

Fireplaces must have large open chimneys. Otherwise smoke would fill the house. This would be both unpleasant and unhealthy. The chimney carries out the smoke. Unfortunately, it also carries out a lot of the heat from the fire. Most fireplaces allow about 90% of the heat they produce to go up the chimney. Only 10% of the heat is used to warm the house.

Benjamin Franklin became aware of this problem. He set about to find a way to save more of the heat from the fireplace. He decided to put

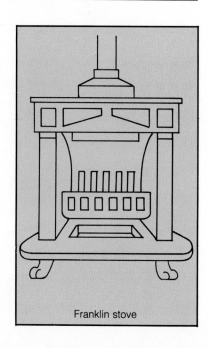

Franklin stove

## Alternative fuel sources

The fuels discussed here probably offer the greatest possibilities for the immediate future. However, other energy sources mentioned later in this section may seem more promising over the long term.

*Wood.*   Some people have changed to a "new" fuel to heat their homes. This "new" fuel is perhaps the oldest fuel in the world, wood.

In colonial times, people heated their homes, cooked their food, and heated their bath water with wood-burning fireplaces. In pictures, those early homes looked cozy and snug. Actually, many accounts of colonial life describe the homes as being quite uncomfortable. It was too hot near the fireplace, and too chilly and drafty away from it.

Today we have wood-burning stoves that are very efficient. Through modern methods, the heated air is circulated

more of the fire in the room with the people. How could this be done without bringing in the smoke, too, and possibly setting the house on fire?

He built a large iron stove in front of the fireplace and ran the flue of the stove back into the chimney. The iron became hot and radiated the heat of the fire into the room. The flue carried the smoke back into the chimney. The Franklin stove increased the fire's efficiency to about 40%. Some years later a "pot-bellied" stove was developed that had a round shape and could sit in the middle of a room. This spread the heat much more evenly around the room.

Today, there are modern wood stoves that are much smaller than the "pot-bellied" stove, but they radiate as much heat. Ceiling and floor fans can be made to circulate the heat throughout the house.

Some fireplaces have iron ducts running from top to bottom. The fire heats the air in the ducts. The hot air comes out a vent at the top of the fireplace. Cool air comes in the bottom of the duct and is heated by the fire.

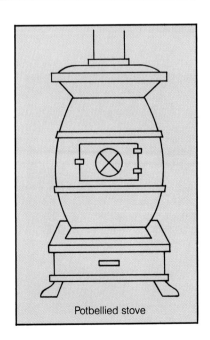

Potbellied stove

throughout a large area. Many people who live where wood is plentiful have switched to this "new" form of heat. People who live near national, state, and provincial forests can often get permission to remove fallen trees free of charge. The improvement of the wood stove is described in *Our Science Heritage*. Is wood a renewable or nonrenewable resource?

*Synfuels.*    Liquid and gaseous fuels made from other sources are called synthetic fuels, or **synfuels** (SIN'-fyoo-ulz). Two major synfuels are ethanol and methanol. Ethanol and methanol are kinds of alcohol. They are produced from wood and other kinds of vegetation such as corn, grain, sunflowers, and almost any crop that is plentiful. The material is mashed and then fermented by microscopic organisms. It is then purified by **distilling** (dih-STIL'-ing), that is, boiling and condensing the vapors.

One part ethanol and nine parts gasoline have been used to make gasohol. Gasohol can be used as a motor fuel in place of gasoline. Methanol can be used alone as a motor fuel.

Methane is a major part of natural gas. It can be produced synthetically and used like natural gas. Several synfuels, including methane, can be made from coal. Synfuels can also be made from oil shale, tar sands, and biomass. Many synfuel sources are nonrenewable, but methanol and ethanol can be produced from rapidly grown crops. They are fairly easily renewed.

*Oil shale.*    Ancient Indian legends tell about the rock that burns. When set on fire, the rock would smolder for several days. This rock is known as **oil shale**. Huge deposits are found in Colorado, Wyoming, and Utah.

Oil shales were likely formed from sediments in ancient inland lakes. The remains of many organisms were found in these sediments. Over time these remains formed a solid, waxy substance called **kerogen** (KEH'-ruh-jun).

Oil shale often has a banded appearance. The dark bands contain more organic matter. The bands were likely deposited in winter, the light bands in summer. Examine the photo of oil shale in Figure 11-16.

An oil that can be used like crude oil can be obtained from kerogen. But it is still cheaper to pump crude oil than to get

## Library research

Find out about the use of synfuels in Brazil. Most autos in that country run on alcohol. Find out how the alcohol is produced. In what other parts of the world are synfuels produced and used?

Figure 11-16. What causes banding in oil shale?

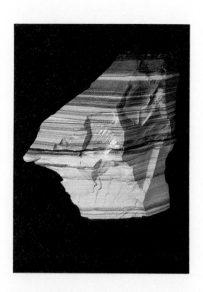

oil from shale. Only recently have scientists studied ways to get oil from shale in large quantities.

Two methods to process oil shale are being studied. In both methods, the shale is heated to 420°C. At this temperature the kerogen becomes a gas. The gas condenses as a thick black oil.

In one method, the shale is heated above ground in a large vessel called a retort. In the second method, the shale is heated below ground. Miners make vertical and horizontal tunnels which divide the underground shale into huge columns. Explosives are used to break up the rock in the underground columns. The shale oil at the top of the column is set on fire. As the surrounding rock is heated, oil is driven from the shale. The oil collects at the bottom of the column and is pumped to the surface.

Large-scale development of oil-shale plants is slow. Keep in mind that oil shale is a nonrenewable resource.

*Tar sands.*    An oil synfuel can be obtained from tar sands. Like oil shale, tar sands also formed from the remains of organisms in the sediments of ancient inland lakes. Scattered deposits of tar sands are found in many places in Canada and the United States.

To recover the oil, tar sands must be heated in a process similar to the one for oil shale. In order to get a sizable amount

**Main Idea**

What happens to oil shale when it is heated to 420°C?

Figure 11-17. What factors would add to the cost of oil coming from tar sands?

of oil from tar sands, huge amounts of tar sands must be processed. A large part of the energy obtained is used in getting the oil. This makes oil from tar sands very expensive. Tar sands are also a nonrenewable natural resource.

*Biomass.*     **Biomass** (BĪ'-ō-mas) is the remains, waste, or byproducts of living things. Biomass can be changed chemically to produce a liquid or gaseous fuel. Biomass can consist of any kind of vegetation, food-processing wastes, manure, garbage, and certain kinds of trash.

Each year we throw away enormous amounts of biomass. If this biomass could be processed, it would produce fuel and help the solid waste disposal problem at the same time. Unlike oil shale and tar sands, biomass is a renewable energy source.

In a special furnace, trash can be heated at high pressure and temperature to produce fuel oil. But perhaps the easiest way to change biomass to fuel is by fermentation. The biomass is placed in closed containers. Bacteria that can live with-

Figure 11-18. Much of the trash we throw away can be changed into fuel oil or methane.

Figure 11-19. Some scientists think that fuel could be made from ocean kelps.

out oxygen digest the biomass. In the digestion process, the gas methane is given off.

Crops such as sorghum and sugar cane produce a lot of vegetation quickly. These plants convert more solar energy into food than any other plant. Sorghum and sugar cane make a high-energy biomass. Some tropical countries are growing these crops just for their conversion into fuel. Making fuels from farm crops may bring much needed wealth to tropical areas of the world. Another form of biomass that is very plentiful in some places is ocean kelp.

*Electrochemical energy.*    Electric energy can be produced directly from chemical energy. This happens in a battery, but a battery can store only small amounts of energy. Some autos have been made that run on large rows of batteries.

A fuel cell can produce a more constant supply of energy. Recall from Chapter 10, Section 1, that a fuel cell uses hydrogen and oxygen to produce an electric current. At the same time, water is produced from the hydrogen and oxygen.

Fuel cells have several advantages. They are quiet. They are nonpolluting. Tanks of hydrogen and oxygen can be transported easily. The hydrogen and oxygen fuel can be used to produce electricity at the site where it is needed. Fuel cells have been used on space missions, where the water was consumed by the astronauts.

**Main Idea**

How can sorghum and sugar cane be used as a source of fuel?

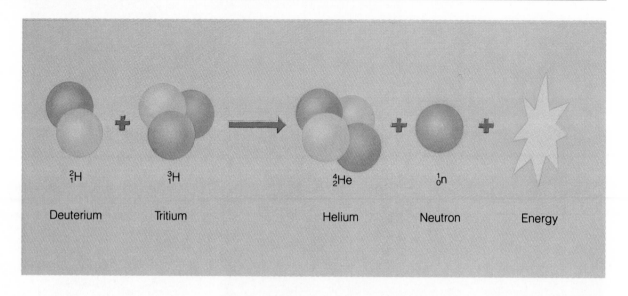

Figure 11-20. In nuclear fusion, hydrogen atoms become fused together, forming a helium atom.

*Nuclear fusion.*     You may recall from the discussion in Chapter 10, Section 2, that nuclear fusion might be an important source of energy in the future.

Successful experiments have been done with controlled nuclear fusion. By the end of this century, fusion reactors may be a reality.

## Check yourself

1. Name two fuels discussed here that are renewable. Tell how they can be renewed.

2. What is biomass? What kinds of fuel can be produced from biomass?

3. What kind of fuel is used in a fuel cell? What are the advantages of a fuel cell?

## Energy directly from the sun

Every day huge quantities of free energy reach the earth from the sun. The amount of solar energy striking the earth's upper atmosphere is thousands of times greater than the world's total energy needs. Year after year the supply remains constant.

Solar energy is a clean energy source. No harmful wastes are produced with its use. Is solar the energy of the future?

There are some problems with the use of solar energy. On a cloudy day as much as 80 percent of the solar energy striking the upper atmosphere never reaches the earth's surface. And, of course, at night almost no solar energy reaches even the upper atmosphere.

Sunlight striking the earth is a very dilute energy source. That is, it is spread out very thin. To meet our energy needs it must be collected and stored in some way.

*Passive solar energy.*    **Passive solar** energy is used primarily to heat the space inside of buildings. No pumps or motors aid the flow of the heat. Buildings may be designed to use passive solar energy directly, indirectly, or through a convection loop.

To use solar energy directly, buildings are constructed to either let in or keep out sunlight. Large windows on the south side of the building are good solar collectors. A roof overhang will screen sunlight in the summer and let sunlight in during the winter.

In a **direct-gain** solar building, the energy is stored in building materials which make up the floor, walls, and ceiling. Concrete, brick, or stone make good storage materials. Insulated window coverings slow down energy loss at night.

In the **indirect solar** building, massive heat-storage materials are placed behind south-facing windows. Storage materials might be a brick, stone, or concrete wall, or drums of water. The solar energy absorbed by the storage wall is radiated into the living space. Vents in the wall at floor and ceiling level provide natural convection currents.

**Main Idea**

What do buildings that use passive solar energy have in common?

Figure 11-21. (Left) Drums of water are heated by sunlight. (Right) A greenhouse attached to the south side of a home.

How do design features like these make use of solar energy to heat homes?

## Library research

Investigate some of the latest advancements in home solar heating. Find out what kinds of units are being installed in existing homes. What is being done in new homes?

**Data Search**

Solar heating systems depend on infrared light as well as visible light. What color of visible light has close to the same frequency as infrared light? Search page 357.

The passive collection and storage of solar energy may occur outside of the building to be heated. For example, a large collecting surface such as a greenhouse can be attached to the living space. Heat-storage material is built into the floor of the greenhouse. Vents from the greenhouse into the living space control the flow of energy. A reflector on the ground outside of the greenhouse will increase the amount of solar energy collected.

In the **convection loop** building, the living space is enclosed like an envelope by a second building. It is a building within a building. The outer building has a large glass wall facing south. The air behind the glass is heated by solar energy. The warm air circulates in the space between the two buildings. Vents control the direction of the flow. By changing the vents, a person can make the moving air either give off or take on heat from the living space.

*Active solar energy.*    Like a passive solar system, an **active solar** system requires collection and storage. But it also uses a fan or a pump to circulate the heated air or water.

Most active solar systems use a flat-plate collector, which is placed on the roof or on a slanted platform on the ground. The degree of slant depends on the latitude. The collector is tilted to collect the maximum energy from the sun. Because Miami is much farther south than Chicago, the sun's position in the sky is higher. The solar panel is slanted only a little

Figure 11-22. Solar panels should be placed at a higher angle in more northern areas because the sun is lower in the sky there.

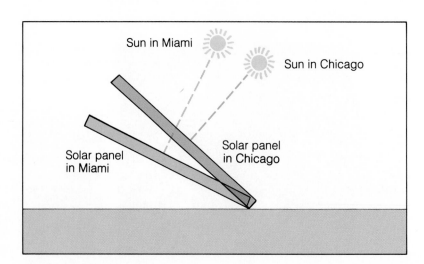

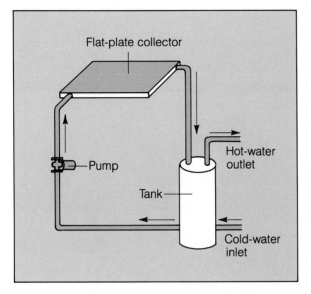

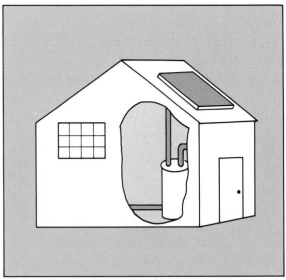

Figure 11-23. What factors should be considered before installing a solar-heated hot-water tank?

from the horizon in Miami. In Chicago, where the sun is always lower, the solar panel would have to be at a higher angle.

The hot air or water which has been heated inside the flat-plate collector is pumped into a large insulated storage tank. When needed, it is pumped through a centralized space-heating system. Many family homes and apartment buildings have systems for heating the hot water with solar energy. It is also used to heat swimming pools.

In order for a solar heating system to be efficient, the climate must be sunny. Even in regions where it is efficient, the equipment needed to operate the system is expensive. Storage of heat energy is still a problem.

*Solar conversion.*   Solar energy can be changed either directly or indirectly into electric energy. When the sun's rays are concentrated on a single point, intense heat can be produced. This is the principle used in indirect solar conversion.

Experimental stations have been built which heat water in a boiler with solar energy. Mirrors reflect and concentrate the sun's rays onto the boiler, which is located at the top of a tower. Curved or flat mirrors which surround the boiler tower may be used to reflect and concentrate the sun's rays. Computers keep the mirrors properly positioned at all times to reflect the sunlight.

**Main Idea**

What is the principle used in indirect solar conversion?

## Activity 11–2        A Solar Cooker

### Materials

old umbrella
aluminum foil
masking tape
slice of luncheon meat or marshmallow
pointed stick

### Purpose

To show how solar energy can be used to cook food.

### Procedure

1. Completely line the inside of an old umbrella with pieces of aluminum foil. Try to keep the foil as free of wrinkles as possible. Fasten the pieces of foil to the umbrella with masking tape.
2. Tape small pieces of foil under the support struts around the center pole.
3. On a sunny day, place the umbrella outdoors in a location where there is no wind. Put the top point of the umbrella into the ground so that the open part faces the sun. When aimed properly, the umbrella pole will cast almost no shadow. This experimental model of a curved foil mirror will focus the sun's rays at a point somewhere along the center pole.
4. Place the slice of meat on the pointed stick. Hold it close to the umbrella pole about midway. Slowly move it up and down until you find the spot where the food begins to cook.

### Questions

1. At what location along the center pole did the slice of meat begin to cook?
2. Why did the meat cook at that location?
3. About how long did it take for the meat to begin to cook?
4. What improvements would you make to construct a permanent solar cooker?

### Conclusion

Explain how solar energy can be used to cook food.

Liquids in the boiler can be heated to over 500°C. The heated liquid is pumped to a steam-powered electric generator. The heated liquid may be stored in specially insulated tanks for about 20 hours. Heated liquid from the storage tank permits the generation of electricity at night and on cloudy days.

Figure 11-24. In this experimental solar generating plant, solar energy is converted to electric energy. The mirrors reflect the solar energy toward the top of a boiler tower.

Long-term heat storage is a major problem in indirect solar conversion. Also, the method requires large amounts of land. Nevertheless, some scientists predict that by the year 2000 solar energy will be supplying 20 percent of our electricity.

Solar cells are discussed in Chapter 9, Section 2. With the use of solar cells, solar energy can be converted directly into electric energy. The solar cell is made of materials that release electrons when light strikes them. The flow of electrons into connecting wires sets up a current.

Large quantities of solar cells are needed to produce significant amounts of electricity. At present, electricity produced with solar cells costs 3 to 5 times more than other electricity. Perhaps with new research this cost will drop.

Solar cells are used to make electricity in space vehicles. Out at sea, fog horns and buoy lights are powered with solar cells. In remote areas, solar cells provide electricity for runway lights and communication stations.

Figure 11-25. The wings and top of this aircraft are covered with 16 000 solar cells. What are the limitations of solar-powered aircraft?

### Check yourself

1. How do active and passive solar heating compare?

2. How could the angle at which a flat solar collector is placed differ in New Orleans and Toronto?

3. Name two successful uses of solar cells.

### Energy from sun-powered systems

**Main Idea**

What do streams, wind, and sun-warmed water have in common?

We can tap the energy of streams, the wind, and sun-warmed water. All these systems receive their energy from the sun. The energy is completely renewable.

*Hydroelectric power.*     The sun provides the energy for water to evaporate. The water returns to the ground as rain or snow. As it flows downhill, the moving water can be used to turn turbines and generate electricity.

About 14 percent of the electric power in North America is hydroelectric, or produced with water. Most of this is produced at dams with large reservoirs.

Generating electricity with water power is efficient. Little heat is lost. No pollutants are produced. On the other hand, most of the desirable dam and reservoir sites have already been developed. Others are too far from regions where the power would be used.

Also, when an entire valley or canyon is flooded, the environment is changed drastically. Some people feel that too

Figure 11-26. Where does the energy come from to operate the generator in this hydroelectric generating plant?

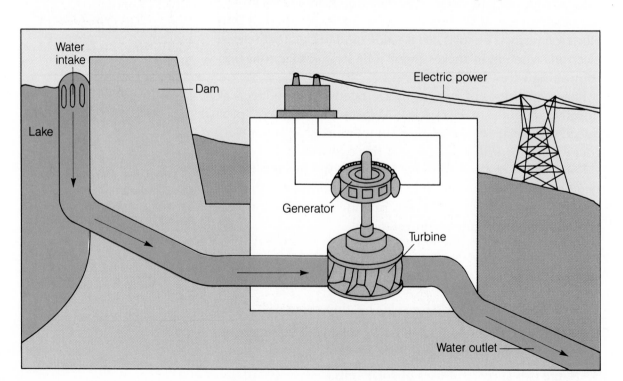

many of our wild rivers have been destroyed by hydroelectric projects.

Natural waterfalls such as Niagara have been used as sources of electric power. A column of water flows from the top of the falls. It passes through a hydroelectric plant, where it turns turbines which are connected to electric generators. The water flows back into the river at the bottom of the falls.

*Energy from wind.*    The unequal heating of the earth's surface by the sun causes winds to flow. Since early times, people have used energy from the wind. Sailboats were used very early in history. Dutch windmills were used for grinding grain and pumping water. Windmills have also been used on farms and ranches for bringing up underground water.

Today more and more windmills are being used to generate electricity. Some of these windmills are very large. Other smaller ones are placed in large groups known as **wind farms**. Some power companies have set up wind farms. They are likely to become much more widely used in the future.

In windy areas, some people have set up windmills in their own yards or farms. They generate their own electricity. Sometimes they generate more electricity than they need. A system has been developed that allows these people to send their surplus electric power back through the electric meter into the power company's lines. The meter moves in the opposite direction and records the amount of power they send into the lines. The power company then pays these people for the amount of electricity they supply.

*Saltwater systems.*    In many parts of the world, the sun shines most of the year, producing great heat. The problem in most of these places has been to find ways of collecting this heat. In areas where there are large deposits of natural salt, there may be an easy answer to this problem.

In most ponds and lakes, energy from the sun is absorbed by the water. But this energy is soon lost by radiation. The heat escapes into the air above. The cooled water at the surface sinks and pushes warmer water up from below.

The **solar pond** uses heavily salted water to prevent the escape of heat. The water at the bottom is kept much saltier than the water at the top. The saltier water is heavier. It will

Figure 11-27. Wind generators may help people in some areas to become energy self-sufficient.

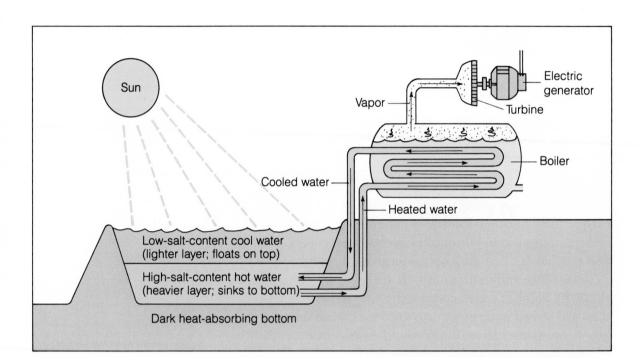

Figure 11-28. In a solar pond, the water with the highest salt content settles to the bottom. There it is heated by energy from the sun. The heated water may flow through a boiler and cause a liquid to become vaporized. The vapors turn a turbine, which turns an electric generator.

not rise even when it becomes very hot. The heated water is removed from the bottom. It may be allowed to heat a fluid that turns a turbine for an electric generator. Solar ponds were first used to generate electricity in Israel. One in Ohio is being used to heat a swimming pool.

Much of the solar energy which strikes the earth heats the surface water of the oceans. In deep tropical oceans, the difference in temperature between the bottom and surface water can be used to generate electricity.

Ocean heat conversion is a very expensive and inefficient way to generate electricity. However, for tropical islands and mid-ocean factories, it may be an answer to their future energy needs.

**Check yourself**

1. Explain how energy from Niagara Falls could have originally come from the sun.

2. What is meant by a wind farm?

3. In what kind of area would a solar pond be most practical?

## Energy from other natural sources

One source of energy we use that does not come directly from the sun is nuclear energy. There are two other sources being tried today that are also not directly traceable to the sun's energy. One is an offshoot of nuclear energy; the other is due to gravitation and the movement of the earth and moon.

*Geothermal energy.*    It is thought that natural nuclear decay and certain movements of the earth's crust have caused great amounts of heat to be trapped underground. This heat is known as **geothermal** (jee-ō-THER'-mul) **energy**. Sometimes geothermal energy bursts forth as a volcanic eruption or a geyser.

In some places, wells have been drilled into known geothermal energy areas in order to tap the energy. Boiling water and steam come to the surface and turn turbines for electric generators.

A large geothermal power plant is located in California, north of San Francisco. Several are operating in Iceland, where there is much geothermal activity.

**Main Idea**

What is geothermal energy?

Figure 11-29. A geothermal power plant.

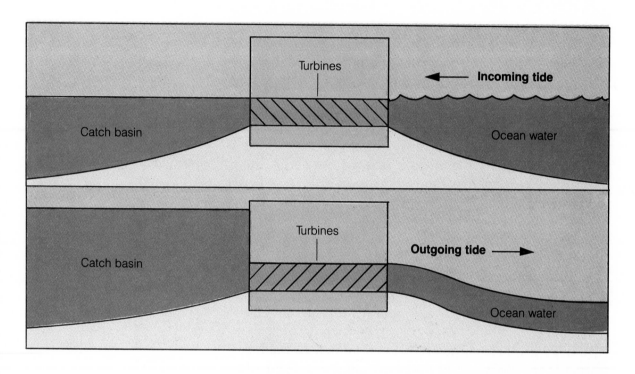

Figure 11-30. A tidal power plant. Water continually turns the turbine blades, whether the tide is coming in or going out.

**Library research**

Where are tidal power plants now in use? How do they operate? What differences are there between newer and older tidal plants? What conditions are needed in order to construct a tidal plant?

*Tidal energy.*    The water in the earth's oceans becomes higher in certain places than in others. This difference is caused by the gravitational attraction between the earth, moon, and to a lesser extent, the sun. The oceans bulge away from the earth on the side closest to the moon and on the side farthest from the moon. As the earth rotates, the high tides move around the world. In each coastal area, the tides move back and forth twice a day. The energy of the moving tides is called **tidal energy**.

As the tidal water moves up and down, the tidal energy can be tapped. This is usually done in a river or canal close to the ocean. As the tide comes in, the water becomes trapped behind a dam. It is allowed to flow out gradually, turning turbines for electric generators as it goes.

**Check yourself**

1. Describe a possible energy pathway that includes geo-thermal energy.

2. What natural event causes the tides to come in and out?

# Practical Science

## Pure Water from the Sun

Many areas of the earth's surface are arid. This means they are dry and have very little fresh-water. Others have large sources of *brackish*, or somewhat salty, water. There may be a plentiful supply of such water but it is too salty to use. The water can be made fresh for people, animals, and agriculture if the salts are removed. Removing salt from water is called *desalination*.

**Saltwater versus freshwater** The salty taste of sea and brackish water is caused by many different salts and minerals. One of the most common is sodium chloride ($NaCl$).

Too much salt will kill most forms of life. The creatures and plants of the sea as well as a few birds and land plants do survive on salty water. They are able to remove the salt from the water and use the remaining freshwater.

In this country, water containing 0.05% or less salt is fit to drink. Brackish water contains about 0.5% salt. This salt concentration is too high for most forms of life on the land. Sea water contains about 3.5% salt.

**Methods of desalination** The sun makes fresh water from saltwater all the time. It evaporates, or *distills*, pure water from the ocean and brackish ponds and lakes. The water vapor returns to the earth as rain and snow. *Distillation* is the name for commercial methods of desalinating water.

Several methods are used to distill salt water. All of them heat the water to drive off fresh water as steam. The steam is condensed on cool surfaces and collected. The simplest method uses the sun for a heat source. A *solar distillation still* uses the sun to heat water held in a tank covered by clear glass or plastic. As the heated water evaporates, the vapor rises and condenses on the cooler glass or plastic surface. The resulting freshwater is collected in a holding tank. Solar distillation stills are used in homes and sunny in farming regions.

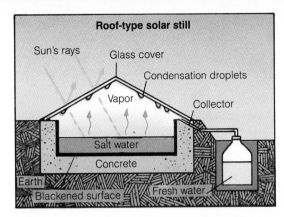

**Roof-type solar still** — Sun's rays, Glass cover, Condensation droplets, Vapor, Collector, Salt water, Concrete, Earth, Blackened surface, Fresh water

Other distilling methods use gas, oil, electricity, or steam from nuclear power plants to provide heat. One of these methods is called *flash distillation*. In this method, water is heated to a high temperature. It is then sprayed into a chamber where the air pressure is lower than normal. The hot water immediately flashes into steam at this lower pressure. The steam condenses on pipes carrying cool saltwater.

**The problems with desalination** Desalination plants are expensive to build. Most types use large amounts of natural gas, oil or electricity to heat the water. This makes them expensive to run. Only solar evaporation plants are cheaper to run. They are inefficient, however. Because a solar plant must cover a much larger area, it costs more to build. As a result, solar distilled water costs about the same as other types of desalinated water.

Desalinated water is expensive to make. The costs of building and running the plant, the cost of local water, and the location where the desalinated water will be used determine its affordability. Current distillation methods still cannot make large quantities of affordable water.

**Something to try** Make a solution of concentrated saltwater. Fill a can or cup with the solution and cover it tightly with clear plastic. Place it outside in direct sunlight for several hours. What do you see on the plastic? How does it taste? Why?

## Section 2 Review   Chapter 11

### Check Your Vocabulary

| | |
|---|---|
| active solar | passive solar |
| biomass | renewable |
| convection loop | solar pond |
| direct-gain | synfuel |
| geothermal energy | tidal energy |
| indirect solar | wind farm |
| oil shale | |

*Match each term above with the numbered phrase that best describes it.*

1. Rock containing fuel
2. Liquid or gaseous fuel made from another source
3. Renewable source of methane
4. House in an "envelope"
5. Solar energy that is collected and used with pumps or motors
6. Solar energy that is collected and used without pumps or motors
7. Group of wind generators
8. Contains salt water that becomes very hot
9. Can be replaced reasonably quickly
10. Caused by the earth's rotation and the moon's gravity
11. Found in heated regions underground
12. Energy stored in floors, walls, and ceilings
13. Energy stored behind south-facing windows

### Check Your Knowledge

*Multiple choice: Choose the answer that best completes each of the following sentences.*

1. A nonrenewable resource that may be used even more in the future is ?.
   a) ethanol    c) oil shale
   b) wood    d) methanol

2. One good source of biomass would be ?.
   a) gasohol    c) garbage
   b) sand    d) oil shale
3. Heated water is pumped from roof collectors in ?.
   a) an active solar home
   b) a passive solar home
   c) a convection loop
   d) a direct-gain solar home
4. Energy from evaporated water is caught in a ?.
   a) fuel cell    c) tidal plant
   b) hydroelectric plant  d) solar pond
5. Geothermal energy is produced from ?.
   a) synfuels    c) nuclear decay
   b) solar energy    d) tar sands

### Check Your Understanding

1. Explain what the difference is between a renewable and a nonrenewable energy resource.
2. Describe three different kinds of passive solar homes. How do they differ from active solar homes?
3. Tell what alternative energy resource you would recommend for each of the following places.
   a. The coast of Maine
   b. Southern California
   Give your reasons for each recommendation.

### Practical Science

1. What is desalination?
2. Why is desalination not used more extensively?

# Energy Conservation    Section 3

---

**Section 3 of Chapter 11 is divided into four parts:**

Transportation and energy conservation

Energy conservation in the home

Energy conservation in industry

Future energy usage and conservation

*Practical Science: Energy Conservation at Home*

---

## Learning Objectives

1. To recognize that energy conservation is needed to provide time to develop alternative energy sources.

2. To identify ways in which energy can be conserved.

3. To describe needs and practices for the future that would assist in conserving energy.

Figure 11-31. Carpooling helps conserve fossil fuel energy. Carpools mean fewer cars are on the roads. Fewer cars means less gasoline is being consumed. In what other ways can people conserve fossil fuel when they travel?

**Data Search**

How did U.S. consumption of petroleum fuels change between 1978 and 1983? Search page 558.

**Library research**

Search through back copies of consumer magazines. Make a comparison of different kinds of cars and how efficiently they use energy.

Figure 11-32. The pressure on the gas pedal should never be enough to break an egg between your foot and the pedal.

Most scientists agree that if we use fossil fuels at the projected rate, we will eventually run out. Alternative fuel sources need to be developed. This will take a lot of time.

In the meantime we should conserve the fuels we are now using. Using less energy and building more energy-efficient machines could greatly reduce the quantity of fuels consumed each year. The more energy we save now, the longer our present energy supply will last.

What is your energy conservation I.Q.? Which of the following save energy?

☐ Driving at a speed of 55 mi/h (88 km/h) instead of 65 mi/h (105 km/h)

☐ Removal of snow tires during summer months

☐ Keeping tires underinflated

☐ Taking a tub-bath instead of a shower

☐ Filling the washing machine half full when a half load is being washed

☐ Painting walls and ceilings a dark color

☐ Dusting bulbs and light fixtures regularly

☐ Lighting with one ceiling light rather than several lamps

☐ Covering pans when cooking

In this section you will find out if your answers are correct. You will also discover many other ways to save energy.

**Transportation and energy conservation**

Over one fourth of all the energy consumed in North America is used in transportation. Over one half of the energy used for transportation is consumed by the private automobile. By driving less and practicing fuel-efficient driving, people can save large amounts of energy.

As the speed of a car increases, friction between the tires and the road increases. To overcome friction, energy is needed. The higher the speed, the more fuel is used. Driving at 88 km/h (55 mi/h) instead of 112 km/h (70 mi/h) will increase mileage by more than 20 percent. Gasoline is used most efficiently at speeds between 56 and 64 km/h (35 and 40 mi/h).

The heavier the car, the more fuel it consumes. For better mileage, remove baggage that is not needed. Anything that increases friction or air resistance wastes fuel.

## Activity 11–3A   Surveying Your Car Usage

### Materials

family car
note book

### Purpose

To find out if your family's driving habits are wasteful.

### Procedure

1. In a note book, make a table like the one shown. Record the date. Give the size and the weight (if available) of the family car. Do this for each car you study.
2. Each day for two weeks, record on the chart the kinds of trips that were taken and if the car was used for city or freeway driving. Each time fuel is put into the car, record the odometer reading and the amount and cost of the fuel.
3. Each time fuel is put in, calculate the fuel cost per kilometer or mile driven. To do this, divide the total cost of the fuel used by the total number of kilometers or miles driven.
4. Each time fuel is put in, calculate the fuel-efficiency of each car. To do this, divide the total number of kilometers or miles driven by the total number of liters or gallons of fuel consumed.

### Questions

1. Which car surveyed by the class uses the least amount of fuel for the miles driven?
2. Is the most fuel-efficient car large or small?
3. What is the difference in fuel-efficiency between the cars that did mostly freeway driving and those cars that did mostly city driving? Be sure to take into consideration the weight and the size of the cars you compared.
4. Which trips made by your family were not essential? Which trips could be combined?
5. List some incentives that might be used to encourage your family to reduce car usage.

### Conclusion

How can you determine if your family's driving habits are wasteful?

Car size _____   Car weight _____

| Date | Fuel amount | Fuel cost | Odometer reading | Type of driving | Type of trip |
|------|------|------|------|------|------|
|  |  |  |  |  |  |
|  |  |  |  |  |  |

Air conditioners reduce gasoline mileage. Use them only when it is absolutely necessary. Reduce the need by parking the car in the shade. Air conditioners are most wasteful when the car is driving on local streets. On the highway, an air conditioner does not use more fuel than driving with the car windows open. Why do you suppose this is true?

Carburetors, spark plugs, and air filters should be checked regularly. Properly tuned engines save fuel. So do tires that are properly balanced, aligned, and inflated.

## Activity 11–3B    Tire Inflation and Coasting Distance

### Materials

2 bicycles of similar type
tire pressure gauge
bicycle tire pump

### Purpose

To show how the distance a bicycle will coast is affected by differences in tire inflation.

### Procedure

1. Mark two lines 30 m apart on a flat, paved surface, such as the school parking lot. Use one line as a starting line and the second as a coasting line. Use a table like the one below to record all your data.
2. Find the recommended air pressure printed on the side wall of each bicycle tire. Fill each of the tires to the air pressure recommended for that tire. Do this for Trial 1.
3. Beginning at the starting line, have one student pedal a bike until he reaches the coasting line. The student should then stop pedaling and coast until the bike stops completely. Measure and record the distance from the coasting line to the point at which the bike stopped.
4. For Trial 2, release enough air in each tire to bring the air pressure to one-half the amount recommended for that tire.
5. Using the same student rider, repeat Step 3. Make sure the student rides the bike at

the same speed from the starting line to the coasting line.
6. To test the second bicycle, repeat Steps 2 through five. Select a student of approximately the same mass and strength, or use the same student. Compare the data you collected.

### Questions

1. How far did each bike coast during each trial?
2. What single factor was different during the two trials?
3. During which trial were the bicycles slowed down? Why?
4. How would underinflated tires most likely affect the gas mileage of an automobile?

### Conclusion

How do differences in tire inflation affect the distance a bicycle will coast?

|  | Bike 1 trial 1 | Bike 1 trial 2 | Bike 2 trial 1 | Bike 2 trial 2 |
|---|---|---|---|---|
| Air pressure of front tire | psi | psi | psi | psi |
| Air pressure of back tire | psi | psi | psi | psi |
| Coasting distance | m | m | m | m |

The best way to conserve auto fuel is to use a car less often. This need not cause you inconvenience if you plan your travel. For example, you can walk or take public transportation whenever possible. Buses, subways, and streetcars are heavy and use much energy. But they are worthwhile because they carry so many people. How many private cars would be needed to carry the same number of people as one bus? If you need to commute to school by car, join a carpool.

Try to do several things on each shopping trip you take. Organize trips to avoid rush-hour traffic. Stops and starts waste fuel. Shop at centers where several of your errands can be done in the same area. Invite friends to do their errands with you.

The telephone can eliminate unnecessary travel. Call to make sure a store has the special item you want in stock. When taking a vacation, it helps to make motel or campsite reservations by phone. This will save hunting for a place to stay. If you are visiting a place for the first time, call to find out its location or use a map.

Figure 11-33. In what ways could you use carpools to save energy?

### Check yourself

1. At what speed do we get the most efficient use of auto fuel?

2. What is the single, largest consumer of energy in most families?

Figure 11-34. Which kind of clothing allows you to save more energy at home during winter?

### Energy conservation in the home

Space heating and cooling account for 60% of the energy use in the home. Another 13% is used in heating water. Over 20% is used in cooking and preserving food. The remainder is used for lighting and small appliances.

The most obvious way to save energy is to turn the thermostat down in the winter and up in the summer, if you use air conditioning. Don't heat or cool the entire house. Close off unoccupied rooms. Insulate ducts into these rooms. Make sure all vents in the foundation and attic are properly sealed during the cold season.

You can make a house more comfortable at a lower temperature by increasing the **humidity** (hyoo-MID′-ih-tee), or amount of water vapor in the air. To do this, use a humidifier or pans of water in front of hot air ducts. A properly humidified room at 18°C is as comfortable as a dry one at 20°C. You can make yourself more comfortable at a lower temperature by wearing warmer clothes. Sweaters over several layers of clothing help to hold in your body heat.

Properly insulating a home results in a great energy savings. All outside doors should have weather stripping. If a quarter slips easily under a door, so will a lot of warm air. Storm windows prevent heat loss by making an air space between the windows. Air spaces are good insulators.

Walls, attic floors, and basement ceilings should be properly insulated. Insulation comes in rolls, sheets, loose pellets, and foam. All of these work because they contain many trapped air spaces. The amount of insulation needed depends on climate. Insulation is measured in units called **R values**. The higher the R value is, the greater the insulation.

Insulating a hot-water heater and hot-water pipes saves energy. The oven and refrigerator doors should seal tightly.

Proper care of a home heating or cooling unit can save energy. Filters in forced-air furnaces should be replaced often. Vents should not be covered by furniture.

Proper use of windows and drapes can save energy. In the winter, keep drapes open on sunny days and closed at night. In the summer, draw drapes on sunny windows. Keep windows and doors closed during the hottest parts of the day.

## Main Idea

What can be done to a home heating or cooling unit to save energy?

Figure 11-35. What is the suggested insulation R value for the region where you live?

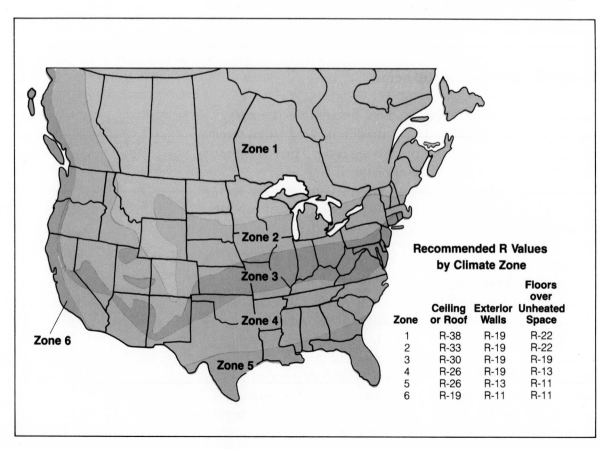

**Recommended R Values by Climate Zone**

| Zone | Ceiling or Roof | Exterior Walls | Floors over Unheated Space |
|---|---|---|---|
| 1 | R-38 | R-19 | R-22 |
| 2 | R-33 | R-19 | R-22 |
| 3 | R-30 | R-19 | R-19 |
| 4 | R-26 | R-19 | R-13 |
| 5 | R-26 | R-13 | R-11 |
| 6 | R-19 | R-11 | R-11 |

## Activity 11–3C        Your Shower Usage

### Materials

metric ruler            masking tape
plastic foam cup        home shower with a tub
thermometer

### Purpose

To determine if a shower uses less hot water than a tub bath.

### Procedure

1. On the first day, take a tub bath. Let the cold tap water run for a few minutes. Catch some of the cold tap water in a plastic cup. Immediately measure the temperature of the cold water. SAFETY NOTE: *Use care when handling a thermometer to avoid breaking it.* Fill the tub with as much warm water as you use to take a bath. Measure the water level in the center of the tub with a metric ruler. Measure the temperature of the warm water. Use a table like the one shown to record all your data.
2. The next day, take a shower with the tub drain closed. Catch some of the warm water in a plastic foam cup. Measure the water temperature. After you finish showering measure the depth of the water in the center of the tub. Record the data.

### Questions

1. What is the difference in the temperature of the water you use for a tub bath and the water you use for a shower?
2. What is the difference between the temperature of the cold tap water and the temperature of the water you use for a tub bath?
3. What is the difference, in cm, in the water depths at the center of the tub?
4. Which method of bathing uses the most hot water?
5. Name some things you can do to conserve some of the hot water used for bathing?

### Conclusion

Does a shower use less hot water than a tub bath?

|  | Tub bath | Shower |
|---|---|---|
| Warm water temperature | °C | °C |
| Cold tap water temperature | °C | °C |
| Depth of water at tub center | cm | cm |

In what other ways could you help conserve energy and help reduce your family's heating or cooling bill?

Could you heat less water in your home? Many household tasks can be done with cold water instead of hot. Faucet **aerators** (AYR′-ray-terz) mix water with air. The amount of water used is reduced. Yet the pressure is strong enough for washing. Special shower heads that cut down on water usage can be bought. **Flow regulators**, which limit the amount of water that comes out, can be installed in existing shower heads.

Any time less hot water is used, energy is conserved. Energy can also be conserved by adjusting the thermostat of the hot

Figure 11-36. When you use the oven, plan to cook everything in the oven at the same time. What other energy-saving methods can you use in cooking?

**Library research**

Find out how people in China have adapted their cooking techniques to the fact that cooking fuel is very expensive. What techniques do they use to reduce the amount of cooking fuel needed?

water heater. Reducing the temperature 15°C will result in a saving of 20% on the hot water heating bill.

Energy conservation means planning ahead. This is true for food preparation also. Whenever possible, thaw frozen food in the refrigerator before cooking. If the oven is used, it is a good idea to plan to bake several things at the same time. Try to plan foods that will bake in about the same amount of time. Opening the oven door allows much heat to escape. Also, studies have shown that energy is wasted when the oven is preheated.

One-pot meals cooked on top of the stove save energy. All the food is cooked at one time, and only one burner is used. If using an electric range, turn off the burner several minutes before the stated time. The food will continue to cook from the energy stored in the burner. Match the size of your pan to the size of the burner.

When boiling water, cover the pan. The water will come to a boil faster and save energy. Once the water boils, lower the burner so that the water is just barely boiling. A hotter burner cannot make the water any hotter than boiling temperature. The water will simply evaporate faster.

Energy is used in preserving as well as cooking. For preserving food we depend upon refrigerators and freezers. Both use much energy. They cool food by removing the heat from the air around it. Each time the refrigerator or freezer door is opened, heated air gets inside. More energy must be used to remove the heat. Conserve energy by opening the door as few times as possible. Leave the door open only as long as necessary.

Perhaps the easiest way to save energy is to turn off lights. When you leave a room unoccupied, turn off the lights. You save energy even if you return to the room in just a few minutes.

In areas that need to be brightly lit, use one bright light instead of several small ones. A 150-watt bulb produces more light than two 75-watt bulbs. The long or circular tubes known as **fluorescent** (flor-ES'-unt) lights are more energy-efficient than incandescent bulbs. Dimmers and 3-way switches can save electricity. More light is given off when bulbs, globes, and lamp shades are clean. Walls and ceilings painted white reflect light. Reflected light may reduce the need for additional lamps.

Figure 11-37. A new fluorescent tube for table lamps.

### Check yourself

1. In what ways should a home heating system be cared for?
2. What are three ways of saving energy while cooking?
3. What are three ways of saving energy in lighting the home?

### Energy conservation in industry

It takes an enormous amount of energy to manufacture some products. Much energy is used in transporting products. Of course, manufacturers want to save as much energy as possible. Doing so cuts their expenses and allows them to make bigger profits. Cutting energy costs can also mean lower prices on the products you buy.

There is also a way that you can have an effect on the energy used by industry. This can be done by careful consumption. Energy-concerned people will not buy things that are not

## Library research

Find out how iron is separated from its ore, and how it is made into steel. Which parts of the process require high energy? What energy sources are used in the iron and steel industry?

needed. When they do buy something, they make sure it is durable and will last a long time. Also, taking good care of things will increase the time they last.

You can also have an effect by saving and returning materials that can be **recycled**—that is, used again. Energy is saved when things are made from recycled materials.

It takes 70% less energy to make steel from scrap steel than from iron ore. To make an aluminum can from recycled cans takes only 5% of the energy needed to make it from raw ore. There is a 40% savings in energy when paper is made from recycled paper. Recycling glass bottles uses only 25% of the energy needed to make new ones. Find out where the nearest recycling center is. You might volunteer to help out there.

Buying habits can save energy. Buy clothes that can be washed in cold water and need little ironing. Compare similar items before buying. In clothing, look for quality of construction and strength of fabric.

A good shopper can save money and energy by reading labels. Laws now require manufacturers to put energy labels on each of their appliances. The federal government has established standard tests to measure the energy used by each

Figure 11-38. How does the recycling of materials help to conserve energy?

type of appliance. The label found on each appliance shows its estimated energy use.

The label can be used to compare the product to others of the same type. The label also gives an estimate of how much it would cost yearly to operate the appliance. Both the selling price and the operating cost must be considered in buying a product.

Products that do not get made will not use energy. This does not mean we should buy no products at all. What would that mean in terms of people's jobs and your comfort? It is wise, however, to plan what you purchase. Look for good-quality, long-lasting things that will save energy both when they are used and when they are made.

**Check yourself**

1. Name three materials that should be recycled.

2. Why is recycling important?

3. What kind of products do energy-conserving people look for?

**Future energy usage and conservation**

In the future, we are likely to see a trend toward many different sources of energy in different regions. In New Mexico, homes are now being built with enough solar cells on their roofs to provide more electricity than the residents need. The surplus will be sold to the electric company. Suppose all the houses in a city produced electricity in this manner. The need for centralized power plants would be greatly reduced.

Along the windy North-Atlantic coast and on the Hawaiian Islands, people have put up their own wind-driven generators. In the future, there will be many more. Surplus power from wind-driven generators can also be sold to power companies. In many other regions, electricity will be produced by whatever resource is present.

These new regional sources of energy will help us to conserve petroleum. Petroleum is still needed for transportation.

**Main Idea**

How could the need for centralized power plants be reduced in sunny areas?

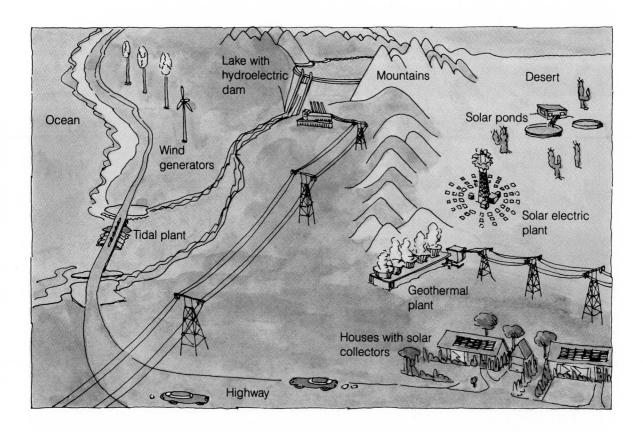

Figure 11-39. What sources of energy will you be using in the future?

Cars, buses, and planes still depend on petroleum products. In the short run, they may be replaced by synfuels, coal products, etc. Work is also being done on electric cars and steam cars.

However, none of these alternatives is really adequate. We eventually need a new form of transportation that runs on renewable fuel. Until such a fuel is perfected, it is wise for people to conserve the fuels we have. We will still be needing them for many years to come.

### Check yourself

1. What alternative energy resource is being used in New Mexico?

2. Where are wind generators being used?

3. What new sources of energy for transportation are being developed?

## Careers   Environmental Architect / Insulation Worker

### Environmental Architect

Architects design buildings, homes, and subdivisions. Environmental architects specialize in buildings and community projects that provide a healthy, compatible environment for people. They often use various passive solar features in designing energy-efficient buildings. They consider the existing environment in an area and provide a means by which the people of the community can become a part of this environment rather than make drastic changes in it.

This career requires a college degree. To prepare for a college program in architecture and environmental design you should take high school courses in mathematics, science, art, and mechanical drawing.

Environmental architects focus on the energy usage and environments of buildings.

### Insulation Worker

The insulation industry has been very busy trying to satisfy the increased need for insulation in homes and buildings. Workers in this industry are involved in the manufacture, sales, and installation of insulating materials.

Modern building codes require that new homes and buildings have much more insulation than in the past. Many existing buildings are being insulated for the first time or are having their insulation increased. It is usually more difficult and more expensive to install insulation in an existing building than in a new building. However, from the standpoint of saving energy, installing insulation is worthwhile.

Many insulation jobs can be learned while working at them. High school courses in industrial arts, general mathematics, and science provide a good background.

Insulation workers wear masks to avoid inhaling small fibers as they install insulation.

# Practical Science

## Energy Conservation at Home

There are many things you can do to conserve energy and reduce energy costs in your home. Some tips are given below for saving energy in different areas of your house. Encourage your family to also conserve energy in these ways.

**Heating and cooling**  The furnace and air conditioner in your home are the biggest energy consumers. However, there are ways to reduce their consumption of energy. For example, air conditioners and furnaces with dirty air filters use more energy than those with clean filters. Cleaning the filters once a month will help reduce energy consumption.

Other ways to reduce heating and cooling energy consumption include dressing appropriately instead of turning up the furnace or air conditioner. Keeping drapes and blinds closed in cold weather conserves warm air, while keeping them closed during the hottest part of the day conserves cool air. Also, if there is a fireplace in your house, make sure that the fireplace damper is closed when the fireplace is not being used.

**Laundry**  Washers and dryers are also big energy users. To conserve energy, wash only full loads unless the washer has a small load attachment or variable water levels. Set the water level according to the size of the load, and do not overload the washer. Use cold water for the wash and rinse cycles. Lightweight clothes dry faster, so a shorter dryer cycle can be used for them.

**Lighting**  Lighting is the smallest user of energy in your home. Even so, reducing its usage will result in worthwhile savings. For example, replacing two or more low-wattage bulbs with one having the equivalent wattage saves energy. A 100-watt bulb produces as much light as two 60-watt bulbs, yet uses less energy. Use high-wattage bulbs only where concentrated light is needed.

**Bathroom**  Energy is needed to bring water to your house and to heat your hot water. You can save energy by taking shorter showers or using less water in the bathtub. You can save even more energy while you shower if you first wet yourself and then shut off the water while you soap yourself. Turn on the shower again only when you are ready to rinse off the soap.

Another way to save energy in the bathroom is by not leaving the tap on while you wash. Instead, put a stopper in the sink and add a small amount of soap and warm water to it.

**Kitchen**  Use a microwave or toaster oven whenever possible. They use much less energy than a conventional oven. Also, use the lowest possible gas flame or electric burner setting, and do not preheat an oven for more than ten minutes.

Try to make as few trips to the refrigerator as possible. Opening and closing the refrigerator door cause the motor to work harder and use more energy.

Another way to save energy is by turning on the dishwasher only when there is a full load. Use the shortest cycle that does the job, and air-dry the dishes.

**Additional ways to save energy at home**  Keep your eyes open when you are at home for additional ways to save energy. These ways include repairing leaky faucets and turning off lights, radios, televisions and other appliances when you leave a room.

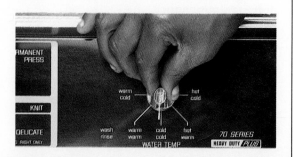

## Section 3 Review   Chapter 11

### Check Your Vocabulary

| | |
|---|---|
| aerator | humidity |
| flow regulator | recycle |
| fluorescent | R value |

*Match each term above with the numbered phrase that best describes it.*

1. Measure of effectiveness of insulation used in the walls and ceilings of buildings
2. Reduces amount of water that can come out of a faucet
3. Use over again
4. Amount of water vapor in the air
5. Mixes water and air
6. Type of light source found in long or circular tubes

### Check Your Knowledge

*Multiple Choice: Choose the answer that best completes each of the following sentences.*

1. The best way to conserve auto fuel is to _?_.
   a) keep tires soft
   b) warm the engine before starting
   c) use a car less
   d) use snow tires
2. Air conditioners in a car are most efficient when the car is _?_.
   a) traveling on a highway
   b) traveling on local streets
   c) stopped in traffic
   d) driven with the windows open
3. In most homes the biggest use of energy is for _?_.
   a) heating water
   b) heating and cooling the space
   c) cooking and preserving food
   d) lighting the rooms

4. Energy can be saved in lighting a large room by using _?_.
   a) many small bulbs together
   b) incandescent bulbs
   c) fluorescent lights
   d) dark paint on the walls

### Check Your Understanding

1. Frozen foods require a greater use of energy from the time they are processed until they are eaten than fresh foods do. Explain why.
2. A 3-way bulb has three different brightnesses. How can lamps that use 3-way bulbs help a person save energy?
3. What alternative energy source might be best for the region where you live?

### Practical Science

1. Which appliances are the biggest energy consumers in your home?
2. How can you reduce the amount and cost of the energy they consume?

# Chapter 11 Review

## Concept Summary

**Entropy** is a measure of the distribution of energy in a system.
- Energy flows from places of high concentration to places of low concentration.
- Entropy increases as energy becomes more evenly distributed.
- When entropy increases, the total amount of energy remains the same, but the energy becomes less available to use.

An **energy pathway** describes the set of changes energy goes through from its source, such as the sun, to its use by humans.
- Each time energy changes form, some of it becomes unusable.
- In a fossil fuel energy pathway, energy from the sun is stored for a very long time in the remains of organisms that slowly turn into coal, oil, and natural gas, the fossil fuels.

A **nonrenewable energy resource** is a source of usable energy that is used much faster than it can be replaced.
- Examples of nonrenewable energy resources are coal, oil, natural gas, oil shale, and tar sands.
- The demand for fossil fuels is increasing at a much higher rate than that at which the world population is growing.
- The supply of fossil fuels will run out sooner or later.

A **renewable energy resource** is a source of usable energy that can be replaced almost as fast as it is used.
- Examples of renewable energy resources are breeder reactors for nuclear fission, wood, synfuels made from biomass, hydrogen (used in fuel cells as well as in nuclear fusion), solar radiation, flowing and falling water, wind, geothermal energy, and tidal currents.
- Renewable energy resources will have to be used more and more to keep up with the world demand for energy.

**Conservation of energy** is the saving of energy by eliminating unnecessary uses and preventing waste of energy.
- Conservation of fossil fuels will make them available for a longer time.
- Large amounts of energy can be saved through wiser use of the automobile.
- In the home, energy can be saved by making the heating and cooling of space more efficient.
- Recycling of materials can reduce the energy used in manufacturing.

## Putting It All Together

1. What do scientists mean when they say that the entropy of the universe is increasing?
2. Why are fossil fuels considered nonrenewable resources?
3. At the present rate of increase, how long will it take before people are using twice the energy being used today?
4. Name two environmental problems that can arise from the recovery of fossil fuels from the ground.
5. How is the waste heat in nuclear power plants disposed of?
6. How is it that methane can be called a synfuel?
7. What processes can be used to produce a fuel from biomass?
8. What is the major task in attempting to make use of solar energy?
9. Even though solar cells are very expensive, under what conditions does it make sense to use them?
10. What factors limit the use of hydroelectric plants to generate electric power?
11. How is tidal energy being used as an energy resource?
12. Identify three practices that can save automobile fuel.
13. What conservation practices help reduce the amount of fuel used in heating a home?

14. Why is the recycling of aluminum, paper, and glass such a good idea?
15. What two alternative sources of energy are now being used by homeowners to generate electricity for themselves and as a surplus they can sell to the power companies?

## Apply Your Knowledge

1. Energy cannot be created or destroyed. What is meant when it is said that some energy is lost when it changes form?
2. Why is it that coal is considered a nonrenewable resource while wood is considered a renewable resource?
3. The use of energy in agriculture is increasing at a faster rate than the use of energy for any other purpose. Suggest two or three reasons for this rapid increase.
4. Suppose methane produced from biomass is used to generate electricity. Trace the energy pathway from the sun to the electricity that is produced.
5. How does a roof overhang on the south side of a building with many large windows reduce the amount of energy used?
6. How is conservation of energy almost like finding a new source of energy?

## Find Out on Your Own

1. Use pH paper to measure the acidity of a local pond or lake. Find out whether the acidity of this pond or lake has been changing and whether the types of plants and animals that live in it have been changing.
2. Focus sunlight on a white piece of paper with a small hand lens that is in a fixed position. Outline the lighted area on the paper. During the next half hour, observe the change in position of the lighted area on the paper. Find out how this movement relates to problems associated with the generation of electricity using solar energy.
3. The amount of light given off by a light bulb is measured in lumens. Look at the packages of several different light bulbs in a store. For the same wattage rating, what kinds of bulbs give off the most light? Why might a person choose to buy a bulb that uses the same amount of energy but gives off less light?
4. Find out approximately how much energy is used each day throughout the entire country. Compare this usage with that of five years ago or even ten years ago. What changes are taking place?

## Reading Further

Asimov, Isaac. *How Did We Find Out About Solar Power?* New York: Walker, 1981
   Uses of solar power from ancient times to the present is discussed.

Deudney, Daniel, and Christopher Flavin. *Renewable Energy: The Power to Choose.* New York: Norton, 1983
   This book surveys renewable energy technology, including solar, geothermal, wind, and water power.

Douglas, John H. *The Future World of Energy.* Grolier, ed. New York: Franklin Watts, 1984
   This book describes what energy is, a history of its uses, and the importance of finding future energy sources.

Goldin, Augusta. *Geothermal Energy; a Hot Prospect.* New York: Harcourt, 1981
   This book describes how geothermal energy has been used and possible future uses.

Goldin, Augusta. *Oceans of Energy; Reservoirs of Power for the Future.* New York: Harcourt, 1980.
   A nontechnical report on the variety of ways energy can be obtained from the ocean is given.

# Data Bank

| Selected Nobel Prizes Awarded for Physics and Chemistry | | |
|---|---|---|
| Year | Accomplishment | Winner (country) |
| 1903 | Discovering radioactivity and for studying uranium | A. Henri Bacquerel (France) Pierre and Marie Curie (France) |
| 1911 | Discovering and working with the elements radium and polonium | Marie Curie (France) |
| 1922 | Furthering knowledge of atomic and sub-atomic structure and movements | Niels Bohr (Denmark) |
| 1925 | Research on the movement of electrons within the atom | James Franck and Gustav Hertz (Germany) |
| 1947 | Discovering the layer of atmosphere that reflects radio short waves | Sir Edward Appleton (England) |
| 1960 | Developing a method of age-dating materials using the carbon-14 isotope | Willard F. Libby (U.S.A.) |
| 1960 | Inventing the bubble chamber to study sub-atomic particles | Donald A. Glaser (U.S.A.) |
| 1961 | Studying the shape and size of the nucleus | Robert Hofstadter (U.S.A.) |
| 1974 | Using small radiotelescopes to probe outer space with great accuracy | Martin Ryle (England) |
| 1977 | Helping to develop solid-state electronic devices | Philip W. Anderson and John Van Vleck (U.S.A.) Sir Nevill F. Scott (U.K.) |

| Mercalli Earthquake Scale | Richter Scale | Joules | TNT Equivalent |
|---|---|---|---|
| II. Detected indoors by a few people | 3.5 | $1.6 \times 10^7$ | 3.45 kg |
| IV. Moderate rattling of dishes and windows | 4.5 | $4.0 \times 10^9$ | 846 kg |
| VI. Strong vibrations; damage to poorly constructed buildings | 5.4 | $5.7 \times 10^{11}$ | 123 t |
| VIII. Trees shake vigorously; flow of springs and wells disrupted | 6.5 | $2.5 \times 10^{14}$ | 54.4 kt |
| X. Considerable landsliding; dams and houses are damaged | 7.3 | $2.1 \times 10^{16}$ | 4.54 Mt |
| XII. Total damage to most buildings; disturbs water channels; rock slides occur | 8.1 | $1.7 \times 10^{18}$ | 376.4 Mt |

| Consumption of Major Fuels in the U.S. ($\times$ 1 000 000 000 000 J) | | | | | | |
|---|---|---|---|---|---|---|
| Year | Coal | Natural gas | Petroleum | Water Power | Nuclear | Total |
| 1947 | 16 686 | 4 764 | 11 987 | 1 398 | 0 | 34 835 |
| 1960 | 10 661 | 13 065 | 21 006 | 1 740 | 11 | 46 483 |
| 1970 | 13 287 | 22 978 | 31 129 | 2 794 | 253 | 70 441 |
| 1975 | 13 303 | 21 035 | 34 515 | 3 394 | 2 004 | 74 251 |
| 1978 | 14 595 | 21 090 | 40 034 | 3 312 | 3 189 | 82 220 |
| 1980 | 16 172 | 21 502 | 36 066 | 3 288 | 2 888 | 79 916 |
| 1982 | 16 100 | 19 516 | 31 880 | 3 772 | 3 285 | 74 553 |
| 1983 | 16 725 | 18 491 | 31 715 | 4 092 | 3 411 | 74 434 |

## Properties of Common Elements

| Element | Symbol | Atomic number | Atomic mass | Melting point (°C) | Boiling point (°C) | Density (g/cm$^3$) | Specific heat capacity |
|---------|--------|---------------|-------------|--------------------|--------------------|--------------------|------------------------|
| Aluminum | Al | 13 | 26.982 | 660 | 2467 | 2.7 | 0.215 |
| Arsenic | As | 33 | 74.922 | 817 | 613 | 5.7 | 0.079 |
| Bromine | Br | 35 | 79.904 | −7 | 59 | 3.1 | 0.113 |
| Calcium | Ca | 20 | 40.08 | 839 | 1484 | 1.6 | 0.156 |
| Carbon | C | 6 | 12.011 | 3550 | 4827 | 2.3 | 0.170 |
| Chlorine | Cl | 17 | 35.453 | −101 | −35 | .0032 | 0.114 |
| Chromium | Cr | 24 | 51.996 | 1857 | 2672 | 7.2 | 0.107 |
| Copper | Cu | 29 | 63.546 | 1083 | 2567 | 8.96 | 0.092 |
| Fluorine | F | 9 | 18.998 | −220 | −189 | .00179 | 0.197 |
| Gold | Au | 79 | 196.966 | 1064 | 3080 | 19.3 | 0.031 |
| Helium | He | 2 | 4.003 | −272 | −269 | .00018 | 1.24 |
| Hydrogen | H | 1 | 1.008 | −259 | −253 | .00009 | 3.41 |
| Iodine | I | 53 | 126.904 | 114 | 184 | 4.93 | 0.102 |
| Iron | Fe | 26 | 55.847 | 1535 | 2750 | 7.87 | 0.106 |
| Lead | Pb | 82 | 207.2 | 328 | 1740 | 11.35 | 0.038 |
| Lithium | Li | 3 | 6.941 | 181 | 1342 | 0.53 | 0.85 |
| Magnesium | Mg | 12 | 24.305 | 649 | 1090 | 1.74 | 0.243 |
| Mercury | Hg | 80 | 200.59 | −39 | 357 | 13.55 | 0.033 |
| Neon | Ne | 10 | 20.179 | −249 | −246 | 0.0009 | 0.246 |
| Nickel | Ni | 28 | 58.71 | 1453 | 2732 | 8.9 | 0.106 |
| Nitrogen | N | 7 | 14.007 | −210 | −196 | 0.0013 | 0.249 |
| Oxygen | O | 8 | 15.999 | −218 | −183 | 0.00143 | 0.219 |
| Phosphorus | P | 15 | 30.974 | 44 | 280 | 1.82 | 0.181 |
| Platinum | Pt | 78 | 195.09 | 1772 | 3827 | 21.45 | 0.0317 |
| Potassium | K | 19 | 39.098 | 63 | 760 | .862 | 0.180 |
| Radium | Ra | 88 | 226.025 | 700 | 1140 | 5.5 | 0.029 |
| Silicon | Si | 14 | 28.086 | 1410 | 2355 | 2.3 | 0.168 |
| Sodium | Na | 11 | 22.990 | 98 | 883 | 0.97 | 0.293 |
| Sulfur | S | 16 | 32.06 | 113 | 445 | 2.07 | 0.175 |
| Tin | Sn | 50 | 118.69 | 232 | 2270 | 7.31 | 0.051 |
| Tungsten | W | 74 | 183.85 | 3410 | 5660 | 19.3 | 0.032 |
| Uranium | U | 92 | 238.029 | 1132 | 3818 | 19 | 0.028 |
| Zinc | Zn | 30 | 65.38 | 420 | 907 | 7.133 | 0.093 |

| Boiling Point of Water at Different Altitudes | | |
|---|---|---|
| City | Altitude (meters) | Boiling point (°C) |
| Vancouver, B.C. | sea level | 100 |
| Dead Sea | −389 | 101 |
| Denver, Colorado | 1584 | 95 |
| Mount St. Helens | 2805 | 91 |
| Mount Everest | 8700 | 71 |

| Speed of Sound | |
|---|---|
| Material (temperature) | Speed of sound (m/s) |
| air (0°C) | 331 |
| helium (0°C) | 965 |
| ethyl alcohol (25°C) | 1207 |
| water (25°C) | 1498 |
| copper | 3800 |
| glass, pyrex | 5170 |

| Electrical Conductivity of Metals at 20°C | |
|---|---|
| Material | % IACS* |
| aluminum | 65 |
| arsenic | 5 |
| copper | 100 |
| gold | 77 |
| iron | 18 |
| lead | 8 |
| magnesium | 39 |
| nickel | 25 |
| platinum | 16 |
| silver | 108 |
| zinc | 29 |

*International Annealed Copper Standard—a value of 100% is given to copper when it is at a specific conductive state.

| Pitch Frequency Ranges of Musical Instruments | |
|---|---|
| Instrument | Pitch (in Hertz) |
| Piano | 30-4186 |
| Harp | 30-3136 |
| Bass tuba | 55-311 |
| French horn | 60-698 |
| Guitar | 80-698 |
| Clarinet | 150-1568 |
| Trumpet | 170-932 |
| Violin | 200-2093 |
| Piccolo | 600-3729 |

| Solar Radiation Reflected from the Earth (Albedo) | |
|---|---|
| Surface | Percent of radiation reflected |
| Concrete | 17-27 |
| Crops, green | 5-25 |
| Forest, green | 5-10 |
| Ploughed field, moist | 14-17 |
| Road, blacktop | 5-10 |
| Sand, white | 30-60 |
| Snow, fresh fallen | 80-90 |
| Snow, old | 45-70 |
| Soil, dark | 5-15 |
| Soil, light | 25-30 |

| Surface Gravity of Bodies in Solar System | |
|---|---|
| Body | Surface Gravity |
| Sun | 27.9 |
| Jupiter | 2.91 |
| Saturn | 1.32 |
| Neptune | 1.32 |
| Uranus | 1.18 |
| Earth | 1.00 |
| Venus | 0.90 |
| Mars | 0.38 |
| Pluto | 0.23 |
| Moon | 0.16 |

The surface gravity of each body is based on the surface gravity of the earth, which is expressed as 1.00.

| World Record Airspeeds | | |
|---|---|---|
| **Record holder (year of record)** | **Aircraft flown** | **Speed flown (km/h)** |
| P. Tissandier (1909) | Wright biplane | 55 |
| J. Védrines (1912) | Deperdussin monoplane | 161 |
| S. Lecointe (1922) | Nieuport-Delage 29 | 330 |
| H. Stainforth (1931) | Supermarine S6B | 655 |
| J. Wilson (1945) | Gloster Meteor F4 | 976 |
| A. Hanes (1955) | F-100C Super Sabre | 1323 |
| P. Twiss (1956) | Fairey Delta 2 | 1820 |
| B. Robinson (1956) | McDonnell F4H-1F Phantom II | 2585 |
| W. Joersz and G. T. Morgan (1976) | Lockheed SR-71A | 3529 |

| U.S. Environmental Air Pollutant Concentrations | | | | | |
|---|---|---|---|---|---|
| **Pollutant** | **Unit** | **Standard** | **1975** | **1979** | **1983** |
| Carbon monoxide | ppm | 9.0 | 11.9 | 9.6 | 7.9 |
| Ozone | ppm | 0.12 | 0.15 | 0.14 | 0.14 |
| Sulfur dioxide | ppm | 0.13 | 0.015 | 0.012 | 0.01 |
| Nitrogen dioxide | ppm | 0.053 | 0.03 | 0.03 | 0.026 |
| Lead | $\mu$g/m$^3$ | 1.5 | 0.69 | 0.69 | 0.34 |
| Total suspended particles | $\mu$g/m$^3$ | 75.0 | 60.8 | 61.1 | 48.7 |

ppm—parts per milligram
$\mu$g/m$^3$—micrograms per cubic meter

The U.S. Environmental Protection Agency sets air pollutant standards to protect the health of people. Pollutant levels above the standard may endanger people's health.

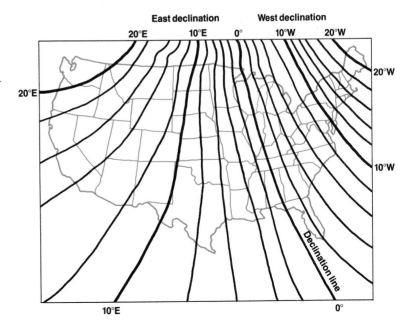

Each of the lines on this magnetic map shows the number of degrees a magnetic compass varies from true or geographic north. East declination means the compass needle is pulled to the east of true north. West declination means the compass needle is pulled to the west of true north.

# Glossary

A simple, phonetic spelling is given for the words in this book that may be unfamiliar or hard to pronounce.

CAPITAL LETTERS followed by an accent mark (') indicate the syllable that receives the heaviest stress. An accent mark following a lowercase syllable indicates a syllable that receives secondary stress.

Example: *Acceleration* is phonetically spelled ak-sel'-er-RAY'-shun.

The phonetic spellings are simple enough so that most can be interrupted without referring to the following key, which gives the sound of letters that are commonly used for more than one sound.

## Pronunciation Key

| | | | | | | | |
|---|---|---|---|---|---|---|---|
| a | c**a**t | ew | **new** | or | **for** |
| ah | f**a**ther | g | **g**rass | ow | n**ow** |
| ar | c**ar** | i, ih | h**im** | oy | b**oy** |
| ay | s**ay** | ī | k**i**te | s | **s**o |
| ayr | **air** | j | **j**am | sh | **sh**ine |
| e, eh | h**e**n | ng | si**ng** | th | **th**ick |
| ee | m**ee**t | o | fr**o**g | u, uh | s**u**n |
| eer | d**eer** | ō | h**o**le | z | **z**ebra |
| er | h**er** | oo | m**oo**n | zh | plea**s**ure |

**A** The symbol for *ampere*. (p. 392)

**accelerating** (ak-SEL'-er-rayt'-ing) Changing speed and/or direction. (p. 125)

**acceleration** (ak-sel'-er-RAY'-shun) The changing of the speed and/or direction of an object. (p. 125)

**acid** (AS'-id) A substance that makes litmus dye turn from blue to red and makes bromthymol blue turn from blue to yellow. (p. 101)

**acid indicator** A substance that is changed in color by an acid. (p. 102)

**acid rain** Rain which is much more acidic than normal rain and which has made many lakes so acidic that the fish and other animal life in them have died. (p. 515)

**active solar energy system** A system that collects and stores energy from the sun and uses a fan or a pump to circulate heated air or water. (p. 530)

**activity** The tendency of a metal to give up electrons. (p. 462)

**aerator** (AYR'-ray-ter) A device that mixes water with air and thus reduces the amount of water coming out of a faucet. (p. 547)

**alkali metal** (AL'-kuh-lī MET'-ul) Any of the elements in the left-hand column of the periodic table. Examples include lithium and sodium. (p. 84)

**alkaline cell** (AL'-kuh-lin SEL) A type of dry cell in which the electrolyte is potassium hydroxide. (pp. 464, 473)

**alloy** (AL´-oy) A uniform, molecular mixture of two or more metals. (pp. 74, 255)

**alpha radiation** (AL'-fuh ray'-dee-AY'-shun) Positively charged helium nuclei (alpha particles) given off by the nuclei of certain radioactive atoms. (p. 478)

**alternating current** An electric current in which electrons move back and forth in a regular repeating cycle. (p. 391)

**ammeter** (AM'-mee-ter) A device that measures electric current. (p. 393)

**ampere** (AM'-pihr) The SI unit of electric current. (p. 392)

**amplify** (AMP'-lif-fī) To make sounds louder. (p. 282, 301)

**amplitude** (AMP'-lih-tewd) The distance a particle moves from its original position as a compressional wave passes through a substance. (p. 297) Also, the height of a wave's crest above the normal surface. (p. 357)

**anode** (AN'-ōd) The positive electrode in a cell. (p. 470)

**anthracite** (AN'-thruh-sīt) A kind of coal that has a high energy content and little sulfur. (p. 506)

**area** The amount of space on a surface. (p. 25)

**atmosphere** (AT'-mus-feer) The layer of air that surrounds the earth. (p. 201)

**atom** (AT´-um) The smallest particle of an element; derived from the Greek word for *indivisible*. At one time an atom was believed the smallest particle of matter possible and could not be broken up. (p. 65)

**atomic mass** The mass of one atom of an element. (p. 79)

**atomic mass unit** A unit used to measure the atomic mass of each element. (p. 81)

**atomic number** The number of protons in one atom of a particular element. In the modern periodic table, elements are arranged in order of atomic number. (p. 86)

**average speed** The overall speed by which something or someone moves for a given period of time. Dividing total distance traveled by total time gives average speed. (p. 120)

**balanced** A word used in discussing chemical equations and referring to the need for the number of atoms of each element to be the same on the left and right sides of the equation. (p. 93)

**balanced forces** Forces that oppose each other with equal strength. (p. 131)

**bar magnet** A straight, flat magnet with a south pole at one end and a north pole at the other end. (p. 421)

**base** A substance that can neutralize an acid. (p. 102)

**basic oxygen process** A process commonly used to make steel. (p. 255)

**battery** A series of dry cells. (p. 388)

**beta radiation** (BAY'-tuh ray'-dee-AY'-shun) Negatively charged electrons (beta particles) given off by the nuclei of certain radioactive atoms. (p. 478)

**biomass** (BI'-ō-mas) The remains, waste, or byproducts of living things. (p. 526)

**bituminous coal** (bī-TEW'-mih-nus KŌL) A fuel containing much sulfur and having a lower energy content than anthracite coal. (p. 506)

**blast furnace** A structure used to heat iron ore. (p. 254)

**block and tackle** A combination of pulleys used to provide a large mechanical advantage. (p. 182)

**boiling** The process in which bubbles of gas form within a liquid that has been heated to a high enough temperature. (p. 45)

**boiling point** The temperature at which boiling begins. (p. 45)

**breeder reactor** A type of nuclear reactor that uses the fission of plutonium to produce more fuel. (p. 518)

**caloric** (kuh-LOR'-ik) An invisible fluid that was thought to be the true nature of heat. This early model of heat is no longer accepted. (p. 197)

**calorie** (KAL'-uh-ree) A unit used to measure the amount of heat gained or lost by a substance. One calorie is the amount of heat needed to raise the temperature of 1 g of water by 1°C. (pp. 194–195)

**catalyst** (KAT'-uh-list) A substance that can speed up a chemical reaction without being changed itself. (p. 236)

**cathode** (KATH'-ōd) The negative electrode in a cell. (p. 469)

**cell** (SEL) A device that either uses a chemical change to produce electric energy (p. 460) or uses electric energy to produce a chemical change. (pp. 468, 473)

**Celsius** The everyday temperature scale used with SI units. (p. 31)

**centimeter** One hundredth of a meter. (p. 24)

**chain reaction** A series of repeated nuclear changes that occur very rapidly. (p. 488)

**charged** A word used to describe an object with more of one kind of electric charge than another. (p. 95)

**chemical bond** An invisible attraction between two atoms that have transferred or shared electrons. (p. 99)

**chemical change** A change that produces a new substance. (p. 49)

**chemical equation** A summary of a chemical change. Written in terms of formulas, plus signs, and an arrow. In the change, the substances to the left of the arrow react and produce the substances to the right. (p. 93)

**chemical formula** The chemical recipe that specifies the relative number of atoms of each element in a particular substance. (p. 18)

**chemical reaction** (KEM'-ih-kul ree-AK'-shun) A chemical change. (p. 233)

**circuit** (SER'-kit) A path of conductors through which electric charges move. (p. 389)

**circuit breaker** An electrical safety device that opens a circuit when an electric current becomes too large for safety. (p. 412)

**circumference** (ser-KUM'-fer-ens) The distance around a circle. (p. 33)

**classification** (klas-ih-fuh-KAY'-shun) The process of organizing information, often by putting things into groups based on shared properties. (p. 11)

**closed circuit** An unbroken circuit. (p. 390)

**cm** The symbol for *centimeter.* (p. 24)

**cochlea** (KOK'-lee-uh) The part of the inner ear affected by sound waves. (p. 304)

**color-blind** Unable to distinguish one color from another. (p. 346)

**color spectrum** (KUH'-ler SPEK'-trum) A band of colors—starting with red and including orange, yellow, green, blue, and violet—into which white light can be split. (p. 342)

**combustible** (kum-BUS'-tih-bul) Able to burn. (p. 52)

**combustion** (kum-BUS'-tyun) Burning; a chemical change in which a substance combines with oxygen. (p. 52)

**complete burning** A burning of a hydrocarbon fuel in which the only products are carbon dioxide and water vapor. (pp. 239)

**composite** A material made of two or more distinct substances having structural or functional properties not present in any individual substance. (p. 263)

**compound** (KOM'-pownd) A combination of two or more elements. A compound has very different properties from those of the elements that make it up and is normally difficult to break down into elements. (p. 18)

**compressibility** A property of gases that allows large amounts of them to be forced into a small space. (p. 63)

**compression** A squeezing together. (p. 287)

**compressional wave** A series of compressions and rarefactions that carry energy through a substance. The wave makes particles of the substance move back and forth as it passes through. (p. 291)

**concave** A term applied to surfaces that curve inward in the center. (p. 325)

**concave lens** A lens thinner in the middle than at the edge. (p. 329)

**condensation** (kon'-den-SAY'-shun) The change in phase from gas to liquid; the reverse of evaporation or boiling. (p. 45)

**conduction** (kun-DUK'-shun) The type of heat transfer in which heat moves through a material without the material itself moving. (p. 200)

**conductor** A material through which heat can move in conduction. (p. 14) Also, a material through which electrons can move easily. (p. 379)

**cone** One of the cells in the eye's retina that are sensitive to color. (p. 344)

**constant speed** Unchanging speed. An object traveling equal distances in equal times is traveling at constant speed. (p. 121)

**control rod** Rod made of materials such as cadmium or boron and used to slow down a chain reaction. (p. 488)

**convection** (kun-VEK'-shun) The type of heat transfer in which heat moves through a material by actual movement of the material. (p. 201)

**convection current** Movement within a liquid or gas due to temperature differences. (p. 201)

**convection-loop building** A building in which the living space is enclosed by a second building with a large glass wall facing south. The warm air behind the glass is heated by solar energy, and its circulation in the space between the inner and outer buildings is controlled by vents. (p. 530)

**convex** A term applied to surfaces that curve outward in the center. (p. 324)

**convex lens** A lens thicker in the middle than at the edge. (p. 328)

**cornea** (KOR'-nee-uh) A tough, transparent tissue at the front of the eye that refracts light. (p. 330)

**corrosion** (kuh-RŌ'-zhun) The combining of a metal with water, air, or other materials in the atmosphere. (p. 457)

**coulomb** (KOO'-lōm) The SI unit of electric charge. (p. 380)

**covalent bond** (kō-VAYL'-unt BOND) A bond between atoms due to shared electrons; usually formed between atoms of nonmetals. (p. 100)

**crest** One of the places in a transverse wave where the surface is highest. (p. 356)

**critical mass** The amount of atomic fuel needed to sustain a chain reaction. (p. 488)

**crystal** A solid piece with many small, flat sides. (p. 20)

**cubic centimeter** The volume of a cube that is one centimeter on each side. (p. 26)

**cubic meter** The volume of a cube that is one meter on each side; the basic SI unit of volume; symbol is m³. (p. 26)

**current** See *electric current.*

**decibel** (DES′-uh-bel) A unit by which noise level is measured. (p. 281)

**density** The mass of a substance per unit volume. (p. 29)

**desalination** The process of removing salt from water. (p. 539)

**diameter** (dī-AM′-uh-ter) The straight-line distance through the center of a circle. (p. 33)

**diatomic** (dī′-uh-TOM′-ik) A word used to describe a molecule with two atoms. (p. 71)

**diffusion** (dih-FYOO′-zhun) The natural movement within gases and liquids that spreads out odors and colors. (p. 208)

**direct current** An electric current in which the electrons move in only one direction. (p. 390)

**direct-gain solar building** A building that uses materials such as concrete, brick, or stone to store solar energy. (p. 529)

**dissolve** (duh-ZOLV′) To form a solution. (p. 16)

**distance-time graph** A graph showing the distances traveled in particular amounts of time. (pp. 126–127)

**distill** (dih-STIL′) To purify a liquid by boiling and condensing. (p. 524)

**Doppler effect** The sudden drop in pitch when the source of a sound and the listener pass each other. (p. 299)

**Doppler shift** The apparent change, due to motion of the source or observer, of a wave's frequency. (p. 299)

**dry cell** An electrochemical cell in which the electrolyte is a paste. (pp. 461, 473)

**ear canal** The part of the ear that receives sound waves and directs them through an opening in the skull. (p. 304)

**eardrum** A membrane at the end of the ear canal that vibrates when sound waves reach it. (p. 304)

**efficiency** The work output of a machine divided by the work input, usually described as a percentage. (p. 184)

**electric charge** What makes some materials stick together or crackle when pulled apart. Electric charges can be traced to the particles that make up matter: the proton with its positive charge and the electron with its negative charge. (pp. 94–95)

**electric current** A movement of electric charges, usually due to moving electrons. (p. 438)

**electric energy** The energy carried by electric currents. (p. 438)

**electric generator** (ih-LEK′-trik JEN′-er-rayt-er) A device that produces electric current by turning a coil through a magnetic field. (p. 432)

**electric motor** A device that converts electric energy to energy of motion. (p. 446)

**electrochemical cell** (ih-lek-trō-KEM′-ih-kul SEL) A device that uses a chemical change to produce electric energy. (p. 461)

**electrode** (ih-LEK′-trōd) A conductor that carries electrons in or out of a cell. (p. 464)

**electrolysis** (ih-lek-TROL′-uh-sis) The breakdown of a compound by use of an electric current. (p. 468)

**electrolyte** (ih-LEK′-truh-līt) The liquid or paste in a cell that is made of ions and that conducts electric charges between the two electrodes in the cell. (p. 461)

**electromagnet** (ih-lek′-trō-MAG′-net) An iron bar inside a wire coil that carries a current and thus sets up a magnetic field. (p. 429)

**electromagnetic induction** (ih-lek′-tro-mag-NET′-ik in-DUK′-shun) The production of an electric current by using a magnet. (p. 432)

**electromagnetic radiation** (ih-lek′-trō-mag-NET′-ik ray′-dee-AY′-shun) Energy similar to light that moves as transverse waves at the same speed as light and can move through empty space. (p. 366)

**electromagnetic spectrum** The whole range of electromagnetic radiation from highest to lowest frequency. (p. 366)

**electromagnetism** (ih-lek′-trō-MAG′-neh-tizm) The branch of physics dealing with electric and magnetic effects. (p. 433)

**electron** (uh-LEK′-tron) A basic particle of an atom. An electron has a negative charge and is in the space outside the nucleus. (p. 85)

**electron cloud model** A model used to explain how the number of electrons in an atom determines the properties of an element. (p. 87)

**electron dot structure** An illustration of how electrons are shared between atoms. The valence electrons are represented as dots. (p. 98)

**electroplating** (ih-LEK′-trō-play′-ting) A process in which electric energy is used to deposit a metal on a conducting material. For example, a thin layer of chromium is plated on a steel surface. (p. 471)

**element** (EL′-uh-ment) A substance that cannot be broken down into other substances. Hydrogen, oxygen, sodium, and chlorine are elements. (p. 19)

**energy** The ability of an object to cause change. (p. 154)

**energy conversion** (EN′-er-jee kun-VER′-zhun) The change of energy from one form to another; for example, the change from potential energy to kinetic energy. (p. 158)

**entropy** (EN′-truh-pee) A measure of the distribution of energy within a system. Entropy increases when energy becomes more evenly distributed. (p. 503)

**escape speed** The speed at which an object can escape from the earth's gravity. (p. 148)

**estimate** (ES′-tuh-mayt) To make a rough measurement by guesswork. (p. 36)

**evaporation** (ih-vap′-uh-RAY′-shun) The change in phase from liquid to gas at a temperature below the boiling temperature. (p. 45)

**exponential** (eks-pō-NEN′-shul) A term that describes a change that occurs at a rapidly increasing rate. The growth of the usage of fossil fuels has been exponential. (p. 512)

**external combustion engine** An engine that does work as a result of the burning of fuel outside the engine itself. (p. 241)

**fact** An observation that has been repeated by many observers under different conditions and in many situations and has thus been confirmed. (p. 61)

**family** A group of elements with similar properties. (p. 80)

**farsighted** A term applied to people whose eyeballs are too short for images of distant objects to be focused on the retina. (p. 331)

**firing** The process of heating clay at high temperatures to produce hard and durable objects. (p. 259)

**first-class lever** A lever in which the fulcrum is between the applied force and the force the lever applies. (p. 178)

**flow regulator** A device which can be installed in a shower head and which limits the amount of water coming out. (p. 547)

**fluorescent light** (flor-ES′-unt LĪT) Long or circular light tube that is more energy-efficient than incandescent bulbs. (p. 549)

**focal length** (FŌ′-kul LAYNGTH) The distance between the center of a lens and the point where parallel rays of light actually or appear to come together. (p. 328)

**force** A push or pull. (p. 131)

**fossil fuel** The remains of organisms which lived hundreds of millions of years ago. These remains—such as coal, oil, and natural gas—release energy when they are burned. (p. 506)

**freezing** The change in phase from liquid to solid. (p. 45)

**frequency** (FREE′-kwen-see) The number of compressions arriving per second as a compressional wave travels. (p. 291) Also, the number of crests that pass a point per second as a transverse wave travels. (p. 357)

**friction** (FRIK′-shun) A force that acts to slow down a moving object that is passing through or against a material. Also, a force that prevents an object from moving when it is pushed gently. (pp. 133–134)

**fuel** A substance burned to supply energy. (p. 237)

**fuel cell** An electrochemical cell for which some of the materials that react are supplied from outside the cell. (p. 467)

**fulcrum** (FUL′-krum) The point on a lever that does not turn. (p. 178)

**fuse** A safety device designed to prevent short circuits. A bar in the fuse melts and breaks a circuit when the current is too large. (p. 411)

**g** The symbol for *gram*. (p. 29)

**galvanometer** (gal-vuh-NOM′-uh-ter) An instrument that can detect small electric currents. (p. 429)

**gamma radiation** A kind of electromagnetic radiation, at the high-frequency end of the electromagnetic spectrum. (pp. 366–367)

**gas** A kind of matter that has no definite shape or volume and tends to fill whatever space is available to it. (p. 13)

**gasohol** A motor fuel that consists of one part ethanol and nine parts gasoline. (p. 524)

**Geiger tube** (GĪ′-ger TWEB) A device for detecting nuclear radiation. (p. 481)

**generator** See *electric generator*.

**geothermal energy** (jee-ō-THER′-mul EN′-er-jee) Heat trapped underground which can be tapped to obtain energy. (p. 537)

**gram** A thousandth of a kilogram. (p. 29)

**graph** A diagram that pictures relationships between two or more measurements. (p. 33)

**gravity** (GRAV′-ih-tee) The force between any two objects because of their mass. In particular, the force that pulls objects toward the surface of the earth. (p. 131)

**ground** A conductor that prevents a buildup of charge by allowing excess electrons to leave an object. (p. 384)

**ground-fault interrupter** An electric safety device designed for bathrooms or other places where there is water. (p. 412)

**half-life** The time required for half of the nuclei in a sample of a radioactive isotope to decay. (p. 485)

**halogen** (HAL′-uh-jen) Any of the elements in Group 7A found just to the left of the noble gases on the periodic table. When a halogen combines with an element from the left side of the table, it forms a compound known as a salt. (p. 81)

**heat** Energy that is transferred as a result of differences in temperature. (pp. 191–192, 199)

**heat of fusion** (HEET uv FYOO′-zhun) The amount of heat required to melt each gram of a pure solid substance. (p. 196)

**heat of vaporization** (HEET uv vay-per-uh-ZAY′-shun) The amount of heat required to turn each gram of a pure substance from a liquid into a gas. (p. 197)

**hertz** (HERTS) The SI unit for frequency. (p. 291)

**horizontal axis** In a graph, the horizontal line labeled with one of the measured quantities. (pp. 33–34)

**humidity** (hyoo-MID′-ih-tee) The amount of water vapor in the air. (p. 545)

**hydrocarbon** (HĪ′-drō-kar-bun) A compound of two elements, carbon and hydrogen. (p. 237)

**hydroelectric** (hī′-drō-ih-LEK′-trik) A term that refers to the generation of electric energy by using falling water. (p. 439)

**hydroxide ion** (hī-DROK′-sīd ī′-un) The negative ion, $OH^-$, formed when a base is broken up by water into positive and negative ions. (p. 103)

**hypothesis** (hī-POTH′-uh-sis) An explanation based on a group of facts or observations. (pp. 62–63)

**Hz** The symbol for *hertz*. (p. 292)

**image** A likeness, such as a reflection in a mirror. (p. 320)

**incandescent** (in-kun-DES′-ent) Glowing with intense heat. (p. 448)

**incident ray** (IN′-sid-ent RAY) A path of light moving toward something. (p. 322)

**inclined plane** A flat surface (plane) that slants; one kind of machine. (p. 174)

**incomplete burning** A burning in which carbon monoxide and soot, in addition to carbon dioxide and water vapor, are formed. (p. 239)

**indirect measurement** A quick way of measuring a distance, amount, or time by measuring a larger or smaller unit or amount and dividing or multiplying. (pp. 36–37)

**induce** (in-DEWS′) To produce an electric current by using a magnet. (p. 432)

**induction** (in-DUK′-shun) The process of charging an object by bringing it near a charged object. (p. 382)

**inert gas** (in-NERT′ GAS)  Any of the elements in the far right column of the periodic table. An inert gas is not likely to react with other elements. (p. 81)

**inertia**  The tendency of an object to resist change in its motion or resting state. (p. 133)

**infer** (in-FER′)  To arrive at a possible relationship or cause between observations. (p. 61)

**inference** (IN′-fer-uns)  A possible relationship or cause between observations. (p. 61)

**infrared** (in-fruh-RED′)  Heat radiation. (p. 202)

**injection molding**  The process of liquifying plastic pellets and injecting the liquid under pressure into a mold. (p. 262)

**inner ear**  A part of the ear beyond the middle ear and separated from it by a membrane. (p. 304)

**in parallel**  A term that describes the connections of branches of an electric circuit so that the current divides up among the branches. (p. 408)

**in series**  A term that describes the connection of parts of an electric circuit so that the same current goes through all the parts. (p. 404)

**insulator** (IN′-suh-lay-ter)  A substance that is a poor conductor of heat. (p. 200) A material through which electrons cannot move. (p. 379)

**intensity**  The amount of sound energy received per second. (p. 281)

**interference**  The reinforcement or cancellation of two waves as they pass through each other. (p. 360)

**internal combustion engine**  An engine in which fuel is burned inside the engine. (p. 241)

**internal energy**  The energy inside a substance. (p. 199)

**ionic bond** (i-ON′-ik BOND)  A sort of invisible tie between oppositely charged atoms (ions), created by the pull between opposite charges. (p. 99)

**ionic compound** (ī-ON′-ik KOM′-pownd)  A compound held together by bonds between oppositely charged atoms (ions). (p. 99)

**iris** (Ī′-ris)  The colored part of the eye. (p. 330)

**isotope** (Ī′-suh-tōp)  Any of the atoms of the same element with different numbers of neutrons. (p. 86)

**J**  The symbol for *joule*. (p. 173)

**joule** (JOOL)  The unit by which force is measured; named after James Joule, a nineteenth-century English scientist. (p. 172)

**kerogen** (KEH′-ruh-jun)  A solid waxy substance, found in oil shale, from which oil can be obtained. (p. 524)

**kg**  The symbol for *kilogram*. (p. 29)

**kilogram**  The basic SI unit for mass. A liter of water has a mass of one kilogram. (p. 29)

**kilometer** (KIL′-uh-meet′-er)  One thousand meters. (p. 24)

**kinetic energy** (kih-NET′-ik EN′-er-jee)  The energy of an object in motion. (p. 154)

**kinetic theory of matter**  A theory that relates the motion of particles of matter to the temperature of a substance. (p. 211)

**km**  The symbol for *kilometer*. p. 24)

**L**  The symbol for *liter*. (p. 27)

**length**  The measure of how long a thing is. (p. 24)

**lens** (LENZ)  A curved, transparent object that forms images through refraction of light. (p. 328) Also, a sac of jelly at the center of the eye. (p. 330)

**lever** (LEE′-ver)  A machine that does work by turning around a fulcrum. (p. 178)

**light**  Energy that moves through empty space at very high speed and can be detected by the eye. (p. 319)

**lightning rod**  A device that protects a building from lightning. (p. 383)

**lignite** (LIG′-nīt)  A kind of coal that has a low energy content and little sulfur. (p. 506)

**liquid**  A kind of matter that has a definite volume but takes the shape of the container that holds it. (p. 13)

**liter**  The volume of a cube that is ten centimeters on each side. (p. 26)

**m**  The symbol for *meter*. (p. 24)

**machine**  Anything that changes the size or direction of a force used in doing work. (p. 174)

**magnet**  A piece of iron, steel, nickel, or certain other materials, that attracts those same materials.

(p. 422) Also, an iron bar with a coil around it that attracts those materials when a current passes through the coil. (p. 430)

**magnetic field** Something that fills a region where magnetic forces can act. (p. 423)

**magnetic field lines** Curving lines that represent the direction and strength of a magnetic field. (p. 423)

**magnetic force** A push or pull between a magnet and a magnetic material or another magnet, or a push or pull due to a current that acts like one due to a magnet. (pp. 422, 426)

**magnetic material** Any material that is attracted to a magnet. (p. 422)

**magnetic pole** One of the places on a magnet where the magnetic force is strongest. (p. 421)

**mass** A property of matter that makes the earth pull downward on it. (p. 6) Also, a property of matter that affects how much its speed or direction changes when an unbalanced force acts on it. (p. 136)

**mass number** The sum of the numbers of protons and neutrons in one atom. The mass number of an isotope is written after the name of the element, as in carbon-12. (p. 481)

**matrix** The material in which the fibers of another material are embedded to form a composite. (p. 263)

**matter** Anything that takes up space and has mass. (p. 3)

**measurement** A description of a property in terms of numbers and units. (p. 23)

**mechanical advantage** A comparison of the force needed to do work directly with the force applied to a machine. A machine with a mechanical advantage (M.A.) greater than 1 increases the force applied to the machine. (p. 174)

**mechanical energy** Energy due to motion. Kinetic and potential energy are two forms of mechanical energy. (p. 161)

**melting** The change in phase from solid to liquid. (p. 45)

**melting point** The temperature at which a substance will change from solid to liquid. (p. 45)

**metallurgy** The process of purifying metals and creating useful products with them. (p. 254)

**metal** A material that is shiny, can be formed into

thin wire, and is a good conductor of heat and electricity. (p. 14)

**meter** The basic SI unit of length. One meter is about the distance from the floor to the knob of a door. (p. 24)

**mg** The symbol for *milligram*. (p. 29)

**microwave** A kind of electromagnetic wave with a frequency lower than that of infrared. (p. 367)

**middle ear** An air-filled space beyond the eardrum. (p. 304)

**milliammeter** A device that measures thousands of an ampere. (p. 460)

**milligram** One thousandth of a gram. (p. 29)

**milliliter** One thousandth of a liter. (p. 26)

**millimeter** One thousandth of a meter. (p. 24)

**millisecond** One thousandth of a second. (p. 31)

**mixture** A substance made of two or more substances that could vary in amount and often are easily separated. For example, sand and water can form a mixture. (p. 15)

**mL** The symbol for *milliliter*. (p. 27)

**mm** The symbol for *millimeter*. (p. 24)

**model** A description of something unfamiliar in terms of something familiar. A model is used to explain observations and predict behaviors. (p. 69)

**moderator** (MOD'-er-ray-ter) A material used to slow down the neutrons released during the process of nuclear fission. (p. 488)

**molecule** (MOL'-uh-kyool) A particle of matter with more than one atom. The smallest particle of a compound that has the same formula as the compound. (p. 71)

**motor** See *electric motor*.

**ms** The symbol for *millisecond*. (p. 30)


**N** The symbol for *newton*. (p. 137)

**nearsighted** A term applied to people whose eyeballs are too long for images of distant objects to be focused on the retina. (p. 331)

**negative ion** (NEG'-ah-tiv Ī'-un) An atom (or group of atoms) that has accepted one or more extra electrons and thus has a negative electric charge. (p. 97)

**negative terminal** The part of a dry cell or battery (cathode) from which electrons leave. (p. 338)

**neutral** (NEW'-trul) A word used to describe an object which seems to have no electric charge. (p. 96) Also, a word that describes a substance which is neither acid nor basic. (p. 102)

**neutralize** (NEW-truh-līze) To cancel the acidic or basic properties of a substance. (p. 102)

**neutron** (NEW'-tron) The neutral particle that is one of the two kinds of particles that make up the nucleus of an atom. (p. 86)

**newton** The SI unit of force, named after Isaac Newton (1642–1727). One newton is the amount of force required to speed up a 1-kg mass an additional 1 m/s every second. (p. 137)

**noise level** The intensity of a sound compared with the intensity of the quietest sound the ear can hear. (p. 281)

**nonmetal** A material that does not have all the properties of a metal. (p. 15)

**nonrenewable** (non'-ree-NEW'-uh-bul A term applied to energy sources that are used up at a much faster rate than that at which they are formed. (p. 507)

**north pole** The part of a magnet that tends to line up toward the earth's magnetic north pole. (p. 421)

**nuclear decay** The breakdown of the nucleus of an atom. (p. 484)

**nuclear fission** (NEW'-klee-er FISH'-un) The process in which the nucleus of an atom breaks up into two or more smaller nuclei. (p. 487)

**nuclear fusion** (NEW'-klee-er FYOO'-zhun) The joining together of two or more atomic nuclei. (p. 491)

**nuclei** (NEW'-klee-ī) Plural of *nucleus*. (p. 478)

**nucleus** (NEW'-klee-us) The center of an atom, having almost all the mass of an atom. A nucleus is made up of two kinds of particles: protons and neutrons. (p. 86)

**observation** What is noticed when one of the five senses is used, perhaps with the aid of instruments. (p. 61)

**octave** (OK'-tiv) A group of eight musical notes in which the highest note has double the frequency of the lowest note. (p. 308)

**OH⁻** The symbol for *hydroxide ion.* (p. 103)

**ohm** (ŌM) The SI unit of resistance. (p. 395)

**oil shale** Rock that can be set on fire and that contains kerogen, a substance from which oil can be obtained. (p. 524)

**opaque** (ō-PAYK') Not capable of being seen through because light is reflected and/or absorbed. (p. 320)

**open circuit** An electric circuit in which there is an opening in the path. (p. 390)

**ore** Rock-like substance from which metals and other useful substances can be extracted. (p. 254)

**origin** In a graph, the point where the two axes cross and where both measurements have a value of zero. (pp. 33–34)

**outer ear** The visible part of the ear plus the ear canal. (p. 304)

**overtone** One of the higher frequencies of a musical sound. (p. 301, 309)

**oxidation** (oks'-ih-DAY'-shun) The loss of electrons. (pp. 457–458)

**oxidize** (OKS'-ih-dīz) To cause atoms to lose electrons. (p. 457)

**ozone** (Ō'-zōn) A form of oxygen made up of molecules having three oxygen atoms each. (p. 72)

**parallel circuit** An electric circuit that contains branches that cause the current to divide up among them. (p. 408)

**passive solar energy** Energy obtained from sunlight without the use of pumps or motors to aid the flow of heat. (p. 529)

**periodic table** A table in which the elements are arranged in order of increasing atomic number and in which elements with similar properties are in the same vertical column called a group. (pp. 80–81)

**petroleum** (puh-TRŌ'-lee-um) Crude oil. (p. 506)

**pH** A measure of the acidity of a substance. (p. 102)

**phase** (FAYZ) The property of matter that has three common forms—solid, liquid, and gas—and one rare form—plasma, which exists at high temperatures. (pp. 12–13)

**photoelectric effect** The release of electrons due to light. (p. 368)

**photon** (FŌ′-ton) An energy particle that moves at the speed of light and whose energy is related to the frequency of light in the wave model of light. (pp. 368–369)

**physical change** A change in the properties of a substance without a change in the substance itself. For example, ice that melts to become water undergoes a physical change. (p. 42)

**pitch** A term that refers to how high or low a sound is; depends upon frequency. (p. 281)

**planetary model** A model of the atom in which the electrons revolve around the nucleus at different distances much as the planets revolve around the sun. (p. 87)

**plasma** (PLAZ′-muh) Matter, existing at very high temperatures, that consists of bare nuclei and free electrons. (pp. 13, 491)

**polarize** PŌ′-ler-īz) To permit light wave vibrations to pass through a polarizing filter in only one direction. (p. 365)

**polarizing filter** (PŌ′-ler-ī-zing FIL′-ter) A material that reduces glare from shiny surfaces. (p. 362)

**pole** See *magnetic pole.*

**positive ion** (POZ′-uh-tiv ī′-un) An atom (or group of atoms) that has given up one or more electrons and thus has a positive electric charge. (p. 96)

**positive terminal** The part of a dry cell or battery (anode) toward which electrons move. (p. 388)

**potential energy** (pu-TEN′-shul EN′-er-jee) The ability of an object to cause change due to its position. (p. 156)

**power** The rate of using energy and the rate of doing work. (p. 186)

**prism** (PRIZ′-um) A device that splits white light into a color spectrum. (p. 343)

**product** A substance that is formed during a chemical change. (p. 93)

**property** A quality that can be used to describe something so that it can be distinguished from something else. (p. 5)

**proton** (PRŌ′-ton) The positive charged particle that is one of the two kinds of particles that make up the nucleus of an atom. (p. 86)

**pulley** A simple machine; a type of lever that is a wheel with a groove in its rim. It is turned by a rope or chain that lies against the groove. (p. 182)

**pupil** An opening in the eye that can change size and affect how much light enters the eye. (p. 330)

**quality** The property, other than loudness and pitch, that makes one sound different from another. For example, a note played on a piano has a different quality from the same note played on a violin. (p. 283)

**R value** The unit used in measuring the effectiveness of insulation in a building. (p. 546)

**radiant energy** (RAY′-dee-unt EN′-er-jee) Another name for *radiation.* (p. 202)

**radiation** (ray-dee-AY′-shun) Pure energy that moves through space. (p. 202) Also, the particles and/or energy given off by radioactive nuclei. (p. 477)

**radioactive** (ray-dee-ō-AK′-tiv) A term applied to atoms that release particles and/or energy from their nuclei. (pp. 476)

**radioactivity** (ray′-dee-ō-ak-TIV′-uh-tee) The release of particles and/or energy from the nucleus of an atom. (p. 476)

**radioisotope** (ray′-dee-ō-ī′-suh-tōp) A radioactive isotope. (p. 483)

**radio waves** The lowest-frequency electromagnetic waves. (p. 367)

**random** Without pattern. (p. 209)

**rarefaction** (rayr-uh-FAK′-shun) A thinning out. Sound waves consist of compressions and rarefactions in various materials. (p. 290)

**ray** A line that represents the path of a very narrow beam of light. (p. 322)

**reactant** In a chemical change, one of the substances that exist before the change. For example, carbon and oxygen are the reactants that react to form carbon dioxide. (p. 93)

**reaction** According to Newton's third law of motion, the effect of an equal and opposite force that acts on whatever is exerting a force. (p. 138) Also, a chemical change. (p. 233)

**real image** An image caused by light rays that actually meet. A real image can be focused on a white surface. (p. 326)

**recycle** To save and return materials so that they can be used again. (p. 550)

**reduce** To cause atoms or positive ions to gain electrons. (p. 458)

**reduction** (ree-DUK'-shun) The gain of electrons. (p. 458)

**reference object** An apparently stationary object by which motion is judged. (p. 115)

**reflected ray** A path of light after it has been reflected from a surface. (p. 322)

**refraction** (ree-FRAK'-shun) The bending of light as it moves from one substance to another. (p. 326)

**reinforce** (ree-in-FORS') To increase the effect of a wave because the crests (or troughs) from two different waves are reaching the same point so that the wave is twice as high or low as it would otherwise be. (p. 360)

**renewable** A term applied to energy sources that can be replaced as rapidly as they are used up. (p. 522)

**repel** (ree-PEL') To push away. (p. 378)

**resistance** The measure of how hard it is for an electric charge to move through a conductor. (p. 395)

**retina** (RET'-ih-nuh) A part of the eye containing nerve cells sensitive to light. (p. 330)

**ripple tank** A device for studying water waves. (p. 355)

**rod** One of the cells of the eye's retina that are sensitive to low levels of light but not to color. (p. 346)

**s** The symbol for *second*. (p. 30)

**salt** A compound formed from the positive ion of a base and the negative ion of an acid. Sodium chloride (table salt) is one of many salts. (p. 105)

**scatter** To redirect light in all directions. Air and water molecules and tiny dust particles scatter sunlight as it passes through the atmosphere. (p. 348)

**scientific method** A way of solving problems by developing and testing hypotheses. (pp. 62–63)

**screw** A form of inclined plane that, as it moves forward, presses against the material around it. (p. 178)

**second** The basic SI unit of time. (p. 31)

**second-class lever** A lever in which the fulcrum is always at one end, the force is applied to the lever at the other end, and the lever applies a force to something between the two ends. A wheelbarrow is a second-class lever. (p. 179)

**series circuit** An electric circuit that contains a single path with no branches, so that the same current passes through all the conductors in the circuit. (p. 404)

**short circuit** A dangerous condition that results when the part of an electric circuit with the most resistance is bypassed. A short circuit can cause a fire. (p. 410)

**SI** The modern metric system of measurement. The letters *SI* come from the French name for *international system*. (p. 23)

**solar cell** A device that releases electrons, thus creating a current and producing electric energy, when sunlight strikes it. (p. 441–442)

**solar pond** A pond containing heavily salted water from which heat does not escape. The heat can be used to generate electricity or to heat water. (pp. 536–537)

**solid** A kind of matter that has a definite volume and that keeps its shape when put in a container of another shape. (p. 12)

**solubility** (sol-yoo-BIH'-lih-tee) The ability of a substance to dissolve in a particular substance. (p. 48)

**soluble** (SOL'-yoo-bul) A term applied to a substance that is able to dissolve in a particular substance. For example, table salt is soluble in water but pepper is not. (p. 46)

**solute** (SOL'-yoot) The substance that dissolves in another substance. For example, when sugar dissolves in water, sugar is the solute. (p. 16)

**solution** (suh-LOO'-shun) A molecular mixture in which the substances are spread evenly throughout each other. (p. 16)

**solvent** (SOL'-vent) The substance in which another substance dissolves. For example, when sugar dissolves in water, water is the solvent. (p. 16)

**sound** Energy that travels with a compressional wave that can move through matter but not through empty space. (p. 293)

**sound insulator** A material that carries sound poorly. All sound insulators are made of materials that trap air. (p. 276)

**south pole** The part of a magnet that tends to line up toward the earth's magnetic south pole. (p. 421)

**specific heat** The property of a substance that describes the amount of heat that substance will absorb or give up per gram of the substance and per degree Celsius temperature change. (p. 195)

**spectrum** The unique pattern of colors produced by a gas when it is heated. (p. 90)

**speed** How fast an object is moving in relation to a reference object. (p. 118)

**spontaneous** (spon-TAYN'-ee-us) A term applied to chemical changes that do not need any energy to get started. (p. 468)

**square centimeter** The area of a square that is one centimeter on each side. (p. 25)

**square meter** The area of a square that is one meter on each side; the basic SI unit of area. (p. 25)

**square millimeter** The area of a square that is one millimeter one each side. (p. 25)

**static charge** A positive or negative charge that is not moving. (p. 377)

**static friction** Friction that tends to keep an object at rest. (p. 134)

**steam turbine** (STEEM TER'-bin) A type of steam engine in which entering steam pushes against the engine's blades and causes them and the shaft to rotate. (p. 243)

**step-down transformer** A device that lowers voltage. (p. 444)

**step-up transformer** A device that increases voltage. (p. 444)

**storage battery** A group of electrochemical cells in which the reaction producing electricity can be reversed and the battery recharged. (p. 465)

**sublimation** (sub'-lih-MAY'-shun) The change from solid to gas or gas to solid without going through the liquid phase. (p. 46)

**substance** (SUB'-stuns) A particular kind of matter. Water and glass are different substances. (p. 5)

**synfuels** (SIN'-fyoo-ulz) Synthetic fuels; liquid and gaseous fuels made from other sources, such as oil shale, tar sands, and biomass. (p. 524)

**temperature** A measure of how hot or cold something is. (p. 190)

**theory** A way of explaining a certain set of observations, based on considerable testing. (p. 62)

**thermocouple** (THER'-mō-kuh-pul) A device that produces electric current by a contact between two different metals that are at different temperatures. Thermocouples are used to measure very high temperatures. (p. 440)

**thermostat** A device to control heating and cooling. (p. 44)

**third-class lever** A lever in which the fulcrum is always at one end, the lever applies a force to something at the other end, and a force is applied to the lever between the two ends. A rake is a third-class lever. (p. 180)

**tidal energy** The energy of moving water tides. (p. 538)

**transformer** A device that raises or lowers voltage. (p. 444)

**translucent** (trans-LOO'-sent) Partly capable of being seen through because some light is transmitted but some light is reflected and absorbed. (p. 320)

**transmit** (trans-MIT') To send through an intervening distance. (p. 319)

**transparent** (trans-PA'-rent) Capable of being seen through. (p. 119)

**transverse wave** (trans-VERS' WAYV) A wave, such as a water wave, in which particles move crosswise to the direction of the wave motion. (pp. 355–356)

**trough** (TROF) One of the places in a transverse wave where the surface is lowest. (p. 356)

**turbine** (TER'-bin) A type of engine in which a gas pushes against the engine blades and causes them and the shaft to rotate. (p. 241)

**u** The symbol for *atomic mass unit*. (p. 81)

**ultrasound** High-frequency sound beyond the range of human hearing. (p. 306)

**ultraviolet** A kind of light beyond violet that the human eye cannot detect but the bee eye can. (p. 347)

**V** The symbol for *volt*. (p. 388)

**valence electron** An electron that belongs to the highest energy level in an atom. (p. 96)

**variable** The conditions in a controlled experiment which may be changed. (p. 62)

**vertical axis** In a graph, the vertical line labeled with one of the measured quantities. (pp. 33–34)

**vibrate** To move back and forth. (p. 212)

**virtual image** (VERCH'-uh-wul IH'-muj) An image caused by light rays that appear to meet but do not actually do so. A virtual image cannot be projected on a screen. (p. 323)

**vocal cords** Organs which vibrate in your throat to produce sound. (p. 275)

**volt** The SI unit of voltage. (p. 388)

**voltage** (VŌL'-tuj) The amount of energy supplied per unit of electric charge by a cell or battery. (p. 388)

**voltage drop** The energy removed per unit of electric charge passing through a conductor. (p. 396)

**voltmeter** A device that measures voltage drop. (p. 396)

**volume** (VOL'-yoom) The amount of space taken up by something. (p. 7)

**W** The symbol for *watt*. (p. 185)

**water vapor** (WOT'-ter VAY'-per) Water in the gas phase. (p. 45)

**watt** The SI unit of power. When one joule of work is done or one joule of energy is used per second, the power is one watt. (p. 185)

**wave** A repeating pattern that moves without the movement of matter along with it. (p. 291)

**wavelength** The distance between two neighboring crests in a waive. (p. 356)

**wave model of sound** The theory that sound is energy that travels in a compressional wave. (p. 293)

**wedge** A form of inclined plane that tapers from a very thick end to a very thin end. (p. 176)

**weight** The pull of gravity on an object. Weight is measured in newtons. (p. 142)

**wet cell** An electrochemical cell in which the electrolyte is liquid. (p. 461)

**wheel and axle** A simple machine that is a type of lever. A steering wheel is an example of a wheel and axle. (p. 182)

**white light** Light that allows all the different colors to be seen because it contains light of all colors. Sunlight is an example. (p. 340)

**wind farm** A large group of windmills used to generate electricity. (p. 535)

**work** What is done on an object when two conditions are met: the object must move; a force must be acting on the object partly or entirely in the direction of motion. (p. 171)

**X-rays** A kind of electromagnetic radiation just lower in frequency than gamma radiation. (p. 367)

# Index

Note: **Boldface** denotes definitions

# Acknowledgments

## Photographs

**003 R** Michael Markiw/Bruce Coleman Inc. **014** Stephen Lambert/Tom Stack & Associates **028** Leif Skoogfors © 1985/Woodfin Camp & Associates **029** Wayland Lee*/ Addison-Wesley Publishing Company **041** Michael Markiw/ Bruce Coleman Inc. **046** Gary Milburn/Tom Stack & Associates **059** Wayland Lee*/Addison-Wesley Publishing Company **090** F. Stuart Westmorland/Tom Stack & Associates **106** Grant Heilman Photography **112** © Greg Vaughn/ Black Star **113 C** Life Science Library/THE GIANT MOLECULES Photograph by Donald Miller © 1966 Time-Life Books Inc. **116** Tom Stack/Tom Stack & Associates **130** Life Science Library/THE GIANT MOLECULES Photograph by Donald Miller © 1966 Time-Life Books Inc. **143** Culver Pictures **158** Frank S. Balthis **163** © Arnold/Magnum Photos **168** © Bill Pierce/Rainbow **169 c** E. Hartmann/Magnum Photos **169 R** Wayland Lee*/Addison-Wesley Publishing Company **189** E. Hartmann/Magnum Photos **207** Wayland Lee*/Addison-Wesley Publishing Company **214** Culver Pictures **215** Culver Pictures **225** Richard Pasley/ Stock, Boston **230** © S. L. Craig Jr./Bruce Coleman Inc. **231** © Richard Pasley/Stock, Boston **244** Nicholas deVore III/Bruce Coleman Inc. **252** © Richard Pasley/Stock, Boston **255** © Larry Lee/West Light **258 T** Wayland Lee*/ Addison-Wesley Publishing Company **265** © 1978 Fred Ward/Black Star **266** Gary Wilburn/Tom Stack & Associates **267 B** © Annie Griffiths/West Light **267 T** © George Hall 1982/Woodfin Camp & Associates **272** Dale Rosene/ Bruce Coleman Inc. **280** Andree Abecassis* **304** Jet Propulsion Lab **311** © Jane Lidz 1981 **317 C** D. Wilder/Tom Stack & Associates **317 L** W. E. Ruth/Bruce Coleman Inc. **317 R** Keith Gunnar/Bruce Coleman Inc. **318** W. E. Ruth/Bruce Coleman Inc. **326** Bill Ross/West Light **327** Keith Gunnar/Bruce Coleman Inc. **339** D. Wilder/Tom Stack & Associates **342** Runk-Schoenberger/Grant Heilman Photography **349** Bob McKeever/Tom Stack & Associates **375 L** © William James Warren/West Light **376** © William James Warren/West Light **398** U. S. Dept. of Interior, National Park Service, Edison National Historic Site **408** Wayland Lee*/Addison-Wesley Publishing Company **413** Jim Balog/Black Star **419 R** © M. Warren Williams/Taurus Photos **428** The Bettmann Archive, Inc. **431** © M. Warren Williams/Taurus Photos **439** Brian Parker/Tom Stack & Associates **443** Dave Spier/Tom Stack & Associates **445** Brian Parker/Tom Stack & Associates **455 R** © John Coletti/Stock, Boston **457** George Hall/Woodfin Camp & Associates **469** Alcoa Aluminum **475** © John Coletti/ Stock, Boston **477** Culver Pictures **493** © Story Litchfield/ Stock, Boston **494** © 1981 James Mason/Black Star **498** © Kevin Schafer 1984/Tom Stack & Associates **499 C** David Austen/Black Star **499 L** © 1982 Wendell Metzen/ Bruce Coleman Inc. **500** © 1982 Wendell Metzen/Bruce Coleman Inc. **504** Dr. Harold Edgerton, MIT, Cambridge, Mass. **516 L** Gary Milburn/Tom Stack & Associates **516 R** Douglas Kirkland/Contact Photos **521** David Austen/Black Star **524** Dennis Hogan/Tom Stack & Associates **533** Peter Arnold/Peter Arnold Inc.

All other photographs by Stephen Frisch*.

*Photographs provided expressly for the publisher.

## Illustrations

Barbara Hack Barnett
253, 305, 330

Shirley Bortoli
T47, T56, T96, T97, T116, 4, 10, 11, 62, 96, 97, 98, 100, 350

Marlene May
306

Yoshi Miyake
134, 139 (bottom), 146, 173, 287, 328

Masami Miyamoto
T10, T11, T56, T65, T116, 9, 11, 15, 17, 24, 27, 39, 43, 50, 54, 62, 63, 75, 96 (top), 103, 104, 117, 127, 128, 132, 139 (top), 141, 148, 150, 151, 156, 159, 164, 171, 173, 175, 177, 179 (bottom), 180, 196, 198, 205, 221, 224, 226, 234, 236, 250, 259, 261, 279, 284, 288, 289, 295, 307, 308, 326, 327, 333, 334, 337, 349, 354, 356, 361, 364, 378, 380, 381, 382, 383, 389, 390, 391, 401, 403, 415, 423, 426, 430, 431, 433, 435, 439, 441, 444, 447, 461, 463, 468, 472, 489, 490, 494, 508, 510, 522, 523, 532, 538, 561

Deborah Morse
13, 73, 154, 297

Judy Sakaguchi
290 (bottom), 291, 298, 299

Lois Stanfield
19, 25, 26, 27, 33, 35, 48, 62 (bottom), 68, 78, 80, 82–83, 87, 88, 96 (bottom), 97, 98, 99, 123, 124 (right), 127, 129, 177, 181, 211, 217, 218, 240, 247, 249, 258, 266, 292, 294, 323, 324, 325, 326, 329, 331, 346, 347, 350, 357, 358, 359, 360, 366, 406, 407, 421, 422, 425, 459, 466, 467, 470, 478, 480, 481, 485, 487, 503, 507, 509, 512, 515, 517, 521, 530, 531, 534, 536, 546

Ed Taber
30, 36, 52, 72, 105, 124 (left), 133, 137, 144, 157, 178, 179 (top), 185, 186, 192, 223, 254, 290 (top), 321, 377, 398, 501, 505, 543, 545, 552

Tom Wilson
67, 70, 71, 74, 79, 86, 94, 100, 160, 201, 212, 213, 242, 335, 368, 393, 464, 479, 528

Special thanks to Davidson Middle School, San Rafael, California; 464 Magnolia Restaurant, Larkspur, California; Lawrence Berkeley Laboratory, Berkeley, California.